Time Out

Edinburgh

timeout.com/edinburgh

Penguin Books

PENGUIN BOOKS

Published by the Penguin Group
Penguin Books Ltd, 80 Strand, London WC2R ORL, England
Penguin Books USA Inc., 375 Hudson Street, New York, New York 10014, USA
Penguin Books Australia Ltd, 250 Camberwell Road, Camberwell, Victoria 3124, Australia
Penguin Books Canada Ltd, 10 Alcorn Avenue, Toronto, Ontario, Canada M4V 3B2
Penguin Books (NZ) Ltd, cnr Rosedale and Airborne Roads, Albany, Auckland, New Zealand

Penguin Books Ltd, Registered Offices: Harmondsworth, Middlesex, England

First published 1998
Second edition 2000
Third edition 2002
10 9 8 7 6 5 4 3 2 1

Colour reprographics by Icon, Crowne House, 56-58 Southwark Street, London SE1 1UN
Printed and bound by Cayfosa-Quebecor, Ctra. de Caldes, Km 3 08 130 Sta, Perpètua de Mogoda, Barcelona, Spain

Edited and designed by
Time Out Guides Limited
Universal House
251 Tottenham Court Road
London W1T 7AB
Tel + 44 (0)20 7813 3000
Fax + 44 (0)20 7813 6001
Email guides@timeout.com
www.timeout.com

Editorial
Editor Ros Sales
Deputy Editor Sophie Blacksell
Consultant Editor Thom Dibdin
Listings Editors Emily Simpson, Val Reid
Proofreader Phil Harriss
Indexer Marion Moisy

Editorial Director Peter Fiennes
Series Editor Ruth Jarvis
Deputy Series Editor Jonathan Cox
Guides Co-ordinator Anna Norman

Design
Group Art Director John Oakey
Art Director Mandy Martin
Art Editor Scott Moore
Designers Peter Charles, Benjamin de Lotz, Sarah Edwards, Lucy Grant
Picture Editor Kerri Miles
Deputy Picture Editor Kit Burnet
Picture Librarian Sarah Roberts
Scanning & Imaging Dan Conway
Ad make-up Glen Impey

Advertising
Group Commercial Director Lesley Gill
Sales Director Mark Phillips
Advertisement Sales (Edinburgh) Christie Dessy
International Sales Co-ordinator Ross Canadé

Administration
Chairman Tony Elliott
Managing Director Mike Hardwick
Group Financial Director Kevin Ellis
Marketing Director Christine Cort
Marketing Manager Mandy Martinez
US Publicity & Marketing Associate Rosella Albanese
Production Manager Mark Lamond
Production Controller Samantha Furniss
Accountant Sarah Bostock

Features in this guide were written and researched by:
Introduction Thom Dibdin. **History** Barry Didcock (*The tartaniser* Keith Davidson; *Body matters* Ros Sales). **Edinburgh Today** Thom Dibdin. **Architecture** Keith Davidson, Susanna Beaumont (*Freedom at a price* Keith Davidson). **Edinburgh in Fiction** Thom Dibdin. **Accommodation** Jason Hall (*Modern times* Ros Sales). **Sightseeing Introduction** Thom Dibdin. **Old Town** Thom Dibdin, Alastair Mabbott (*Witches and wynds, Feeding love* Thom Dibdin). **New Town** Thom Dibdin, Susanna Beaumont (*The making of the New Town* Thom Dibdin). **Stockbridge** Thom Dibdin, Susanna Beaumont (*Galleries and graveyards* Thom Dibdin). **Calton Hill & Broughton** Thom Dibdin. **Arthur's Seat & Duddingston** Thom Dibdin, Alastair Mabbott (*Climbing the seat* Thom Dibdin). **South Edinburgh** Thom Dibdin, Keith Davidson. **West Edinburgh** Thom Dibdin, Keith Davidson (*Canal dreams* Thom Dibdin). **Leith** Thom Dibdin, Alastair Mabbott. **Restaurants** Keith Davidson, Jonathan Trew (*Fish food* Keith Davidson, Jonathan Trew; *Scottish icons: Haggis* Keith Davidson). **Cafés** Keith Davidson, Jonathan Trew. **Pubs & Bars** Emily Simpson, Jonathan Trew (*Scottish icons: Whisky, Pub etiquette, Only here for the beer* Emily Simpson. **Shops & Services** Katrina Dixon (*Scottish icons: The kilt* Katrina Dixon, Keith Davidson). **By Season** Maureen Ellis, Thom Dibdin. **Children** Jane Ellis. **Film** Miles Fielder, Thom Dibdin. **Galleries** Moira Jeffrey, Susanna Beaumont (*Talent spotting* Moira Jeffrey). **Gay & Lesbian** John Binnie, Jane Hamilton, Nancy Riach, Bob Orr. **Music** Kelly Apter, Catherine Bromley, Alistair Mabbott, Sue Wilson (*Breaking the sound barrier* Val Reid). **Nightlife** Catherine Bromley, Thom Dibdin, Alistair Mabbott. **Sport & Fitness** Maureen Ellis, Mike Wilson (*A taste for adventure* Jane Ellis). **Theatre & Dance** Kelly Apter, Thom Dibdin. **Getting Started** Thom Dibdin. **Glasgow** Caroline Ednie (*Gay Glasgow* John Binnie, Jane Hamilton; *Mackintosh* Caroline Ednie). **Around Edinburgh** Jane Ellis, Susanna Beaumont (*The mysteries of Rosslyn Chapel* Susanna Beaumont; *Going further, Trips and tours* Jane Ellis). **Directory** Clare Simpson (*Speak Scots* Thom Dibdin).

The Editor would like to thank:
Susanna Beaumont, Will Fulford-Jones, Lesley McCave, Ronnie Haydon, Caro Taverne, Inger Davidson at the Point Hotel, Robin Hodge and the staff at the *List*.

Maps by JS Graphics (john@jsgraphics.co.uk).
Edinburgh street map based on material supplied by Alan Collinson through Copyright exchange.
West End map material supplied by the XYZ Digital Map Company.

Photography by Alys Tomlinson except: pages 5 and 10 AKG London; pages 7, 8 and 34 Hulton Archive; pages 12 and 16 National Museums of Scotland; page 14 the Scottish National Portrait Gallery; pages 28, 36, 40, 44, 47, 80, 87, 88, 94, 139, 144, 149, 166, 172, 175, 176, 179, 182, 183, 266, 205, 211, 217, 218, 236, 239, 240 and 255 Kathryn Mussallem; pages 59, 259, 262-263, 267 and 268 Historic Scotland; pages 60, 70, 92, 113, 257, 188, 244 and 266 Marius Alexander; page 223 Stu Forster/Allsport.
The following images were supplied by the featured establishments: pages 9, 21, 23, 32, 52, 95, 156, 184, 187, 190, 193, 198, 200, 201, 202, 203, 221 and 248-249.

Contents

Introduction

Edinburgh is not a large city. You can see all of it in one go if you stand on top of Arthur's Seat, on the rocky outcrop smoothed by the tread of millions of curious visitors. In the east towards the rising sun is Portobello, Edinburgh's one-time seaside holiday resort, and the east-coast mainline railway to London. Look south, and the city rises through villa and dormitory enclaves to the Pentland Hills. In the far west are Corstorphine Hill and the zoo, with the airport beyond. North lies the Firth of Forth, with the elegant bridges at one end of the view and, straight ahead at Leith, a tangle of port area in the process of being reclaimed from industrial use.

For all this delicious spread, it is the area just beneath your feet that attracts most attention. The part of Edinburgh that, on a clear morning with the sun rising, you could almost pick up and eat. The Old Town, where castle and palace are joined by a crinkling path of folded and sparkling rooftops. The carefully calculated curves and angles of the New Town – displayed like a tray of formal party nibbles. Even on a cold day, when the open sky closes in and the clouds come down low, Edinburgh refuses to be enfolded by the weather. Spires and battlements are outcrops of resistance.

The city's residents have a reputation for tight-lipped indifference – just as Glasgow's have a reputation for vivacious chat and comment. Edinburgh may open up in August to welcome visitors to the Festival, but behind the flamboyance of the cultural extravaganza, the city's austere façade remains. In the New Town the grey, grand exteriors of the townhouses are still said to hide all manner of sins. The people are withdrawn, douce even, hiding behind a formality in their social and business lives as well as in their homes. But lift a bit of that old drab surface and all manner of colourful lives are revealed. By contrast, out in the modern suburbs, where the housing is of a rather less solid design, and in the tenements, where everyone lives cheek-by-jowl, people are a lot more open. Not up to Glasgow's standards, perhaps, but it is in these places that Edinburgh's heart beats rather closer to the surface. It may not always be a pretty sight, but what you get is a reality, not some stiff projection.

The point is that Edinburgh's architecture and design, justifiably judged to be of World Heritage Site standard, are not the whole story. This guide aims to provide a route into another Edinburgh, the one that is never going to become a museum. We hope you enjoy it as much as we do.

ABOUT THE TIME OUT CITY GUIDES

The *Time Out Edinburgh Guide* is one of an expanding series of *Time Out* City Guides, now numbering over 35, produced by the people behind London and New York's successful listings magazines. Our guides are all written and updated by resident experts who have striven to provide you with all the most up-to-date information you'll need to explore the city or read up on its background, whether you're a local or a first-time visitor.

THE LOWDOWN ON THE LISTINGS

Above all, we've tried to make this book as useful as possible. Addresses, telephone numbers, websites, transport information, opening times, admission prices and credit card details have all been included in the listings. And, as far as possible, we've given details of facilities, services and events, all checked and correct as we went to press.

However, owners and managers can change their arrangements at any time, and they often do. Before you go out of your way, we'd advise you to telephone and check opening times, ticket prices and other particulars. While every effort has been made to ensure the accuracy of the information contained in this guide, the publishers cannot accept responsibility for any errors it may contain.

PRICES AND PAYMENT

We have noted where venues such as shops, hotels, restaurants, museums and the like accept the following credit cards: American Express (AmEx), Diners Club (DC), MasterCard (MC) and Visa (V). Many will also accept other credit cards (including JCB, Discover or Carte Blanche), travellers' cheques issued by a major financial institution and debit cards such as Switch and Delta.

The prices we've supplied should be treated as guidelines, not gospel. If prices vary wildly from those we've quoted, please write and let

us know. We aim to give the best and most up-to-date advice, so we always want to know if you've been badly treated or overcharged.

THE LIE OF THE LAND

In order to make the book (and the city) as easy to navigate as possible, we have divided Edinburgh into areas that are convenient to walk around, and assigned each one its own chapter in our Sightseeing section starting on page 55. Although these area designations are a simplification of Edinburgh's geography, we hope they will help you to understand the city's layout and to find its most interesting sights. For consistency, the same areas are used in addresses throughout the guide.

We've included bus services in our listings. Edinburgh's bus system is extensive and surprisingly efficient, with some central destinations served by as many as 20 different routes. For convenience, we've grouped buses for some of these busy destinations together; for details, see page 273.

We've given postcodes for those venues you might want to write to and website addresses wherever possible. Finally, there is a series of fully indexed colour maps of both Edinburgh and Glasgow at the back of the guide, starting on page 299.

TELEPHONE NUMBERS

The area code for Edinburgh is 0131. All telephone numbers printed in this guide take this code unless otherwise stated. Glasgow telephone numbers are listed in full with their 0141 prefix; other destinations in our Trips Out of Town section are also listed with their full code. Numbers preceded by 0800 in the listings can be called free of charge from within the UK; some of them are obtainable from outside the UK, but are unlikely to be free of charge.

There is an online version of this guide, as well as weekly events listings for over 30 international cities, at www.timeout.com.

ESSENTIAL INFORMATION

For all the practical information you might need for visiting the city – including visa and customs information, advice on facilities and access for the disabled, emergency telephone numbers, health services, the local and national media, a lowdown on the local transport network, information on studying and working in the city, as well as tips on books, films and websites for further reference – turn to the **Directory** chapter at the back of the guide. It starts on page 271.

MAPS

Wherever possible, map references have been provided for all the places listed in the guide, indicating the page and grid reference at which it can be found on our maps. These fully indexed colour maps are located at the back of the book (starting on page 299), and include an overview of the areas we have used in the guide, a detailed map of Princes Street, street maps of Edinburgh and Leith, overview maps of Edinburgh and Glasgow, street maps of central Glasgow and a map of Scotland.

LET US KNOW WHAT YOU THINK

We that you enjoy the *Time Out Edinburgh Guide*, and we'd like to know what you think of it. We welcome tips for places that you consider we should include in future editions of the guide and take note of your criticism of our choices. There's a reader's reply card at the back of this book for your feedback, or you can email us at edinburghguide@timeout.com.

Advertisers

We would like to stress that no establishment has been included in this guide because it has advertised in any of our publications and no payment of any kind has influenced any review. The opinions given in this book are those of *Time Out* writers and entirely independent.

Time Out Edinburgh Guide **3**

In Context

Oloroso Spices Up Entertaining in Edinburgh

Oloroso has been spicing up the social scene in Edinburgh since its launch in December 2001.

Consisting of a lounge bar, restaurant, private dining room and roof terrace, Oloroso presents its guests with exemplary service and imaginative contemporary cooking in what has quickly become one of Scotland's key places to be and be seen.

Oloroso, which is Spanish for aromatic and is also a style of sherry, occupies a key top floor corner site on Edinburgh's bustling George Street. Due to its unique position, the large roof terrace provides stunning views across both the Firth of Forth and Edinburgh Castle.

The constantly changing menus are devised and prepared by Head Chef Tony Singh who is a former ITV Chef of the Year and was previously Head Chef on the Royal Yacht Britannia.

For bookings or further information
please call 0131 226 7614

33 Castle St.   oloroso.co.uk

ROOF TERRACE
RESTAURANT
LOUNGE BAR
PRIVATE DINING

O
L
O
R
O
S
O

History

From castle on a rock to capital city.

With its sprawling fortress perched high on a rocky outcrop, there can be few cities in the world that have as dominant or as historically important a focus as Edinburgh. That this castle in the air is joined to a palace on the ground by an ancient road, along whose route history has been made a hundred times over, only adds drama to the story.

But strip away the clutter of the Old Town in your mind's eye, ignore the grandeur of the Georgian New Town, the rigid Victorian tenements and the bleak 20th-century architecture; put back the man-made loch that skirted the Castle Rock's northern edge for centuries and the open moorland which stretched both north and south from this ancient volcanic plug since before history was even written, and you have a sense of the breathtaking physical geography that has drawn people to this place for thousands of years.

EARLY HISTORY

There is no evidence that the Romans occupied the Castle Rock, although from their fort at Inveresk, five miles (eight kilometres) away,

they would have had a fine view of its imposing bulk. But it is known to have been a stronghold for Celtic tribes such as the Gododdin. King Mynyddog ruled from the Castle Rock around the start of the seventh century, and it was the Gododdin tribe who named it Dunedin, meaning 'hill fort'.

In AD 638, southern Scotland was conquered by the Northumbrians, who built on the rock and Anglicised its name to Edinburgh. Popular belief has it that the etymology of the name is 'Edwin's burgh', though this is incorrect. Later the Castle became known as Castrum Puellarum, or Maidens' Castle. In the mid-tenth century, the MacAlpin kings repelled the Northumbrians southwards again and, in 1018, Malcolm II (1005-34) defeated them at Carham. The Castle Rock and the surrounding area became Scottish.

Malcolm III (1058-93) built a hunting lodge on the Rock. It is Malcolm, also known as Malcolm Canmore ('big head'), who is commemorated in Shakespeare's *Macbeth*. But in Edinburgh, he is best remembered as the husband of Margaret, the Saxon princess he

Malcolm III: the one from *Macbeth. See p7*.

married in about 1070. The union produced three daughters and six sons, three of whom ruled as King of Scotland.

Margaret built a chapel on the Rock, St Margaret's Chapel, now the oldest building in Edinburgh (*see p64*). She died there after her husband was killed in an ambush near Alnwick in 1093. A power struggle ensued and Malcolm's brother Donald Bane (also featured in *Macbeth*) laid siege to the Castle. According to the historian John of Fordun, writing in the late 14th century, Margaret's sons took her body and escaped down the western side of the Rock, enveloped in a cloaking fog.

David I (1124-53) was the last of Margaret's sons to assume the throne of Scotland. He ruled for nearly 30 years and was the first Scottish king to strike his own coinage. In 1128 he founded the Augustinian abbey at Holyrood (now a ruin). Edinburgh folklore has it that he was hunting one day when he was knocked from his horse and attacked by a stag, only to be saved when a cross (or 'rood') appeared in his hand. To show his thanks to God he founded the abbey.

In truth, Holyrood Abbey was only one of several founded by David I at established royal centres throughout his reign, part of the 'Davidian Revolution'. This also saw 15 or so Scottish towns granted the status of royal burgh. Edinburgh was not the most important of these – Berwick, Scotland's largest town, and Roxburgh were described as burghs even before 1124, and Perth had long-standing importance. But by 1153 Edinburgh had its own mint and could be said to be one of Scotland's major towns.

GETTING RELIGION
Holyrood Abbey was completed in 1141 and Augustinian monks were brought from St Andrews to fill it. The lower half of what is now the Royal Mile became known as the Canongate after the canons at Holyrood, who used it to reach the gates of Edinburgh. Canongate was cut off from the fortified settlement by the defensive gate at the Netherbow and remained a separate burgh until 1856. The monks were also responsible for bringing beer and brewing to Edinburgh, and others in the area followed suit.

The Palace of Holyroodhouse (*see p74*) wasn't built until 1498, but with the Abbey in place, Edinburgh began to creep down the spine of the volcanic ridge from the Castle Rock. The Cowgate, running parallel to the Canongate, developed as the entrance through which cattle were herded to market, and in 1230 the newly arrived Black Friars (Dominicans) established a friary at its eastern end. With the Abbey already a major feature and a succession of religious orders arriving in the town (the Dominicans were followed by the Franciscans, or Grey Friars, in 1429), Edinburgh became an ecclesiastical centre of some importance.

The other main religious building in the settlement was the Church of St Giles (today's High Kirk of St Giles; *see p69*). Historians have found mention of a church in Edinburgh as early as 845, but whatever was on the site of St Giles' was replaced by Alexander I in 1120 and the church was formally dedicated by Bishop David de Bernham of St Andrews in 1243.

THE MIDDLE AGES
In 1328 the Treaty of Edinburgh was signed, ending the wars of independence that had taken place with England (in Scotland's favour). The following year Robert the Bruce granted Edinburgh the status of royal burgh, thus giving it an important degree of fiscal independence. Bruce died the same year. His heir, David II, was only five in 1329, so Edward III once again tried to conquer Scotland. In 1337, the Countess of March – known as Black Agnes – led the defence of the Castle for five months before Edward took it. The English king rebuilt it in parts, but a mere four years later Sir William Douglas

recaptured it for the Scots. The Canongate was less lucky in this period: it was burned by Richard II's troops in 1380.

David II died in 1371 with no heir and Robert the Steward, who had already been Guardian of Scotland twice, became Robert II. The Stewart succession had begun. This was a period of lawlessness that saw successive kings murdered or killed in battle, to be succeeded by children who were too young to rule in their own right. It was also the period in which Edinburgh came to be recognised as a royal city.

The need for strong regents was vital and the people of Edinburgh witnessed some bloody power plays as the various court factions slugged it out. James I (1406-37) tried to curb the power of the nobles, but was murdered in Perth in 1437 for his troubles. His son, James II (1437-60), was only six at the time and he was crowned hastily in Holyrood Abbey by his mother. Three years later, in 1440, James himself witnessed a political assassination in Edinburgh Castle when the young Earl of Douglas was murdered by Sir William Crichton and Sir Alexander Livingstone, the acting regents.

The Old Town began to take shape during this period; the Grassmarket and the Cowgate started to form more fully, though development to the south and north was made difficult by physical features such as the Craig Burn, which was dammed in the mid-15th century for defensive purposes and became the Nor' Loch. At the same time the town's first defensive wall

was built: called the King's Wall, it ran eastwards from half way down the south side of the Castle Rock, above the Grassmarket and the Cowgate, to the Netherbow, and then dipped down to the Nor' Loch. As the town crept along the spine of the ridge, the familiar herringbone pattern of closes and wynds began to emerge. This is still visible today in parts, but in medieval times the closes and wynds would have been muddy, steep, slippery and, as like as not, covered in ordure from humans as well as animals. Soap was not manufactured in Edinburgh until 1554.

The principal landmarks in the medieval city were the Castle, the Lawnmarket immediately east of it, the High Kirk (church) of St Giles, the Mercat Cross and the Tolbooth (*see p63*), on the south side of the High Street. The Tolbooth was, literally, the booth where tolls were paid and the buildings on the site were regularly destroyed, rebuilt and upgraded. A bell in the Tolbooth sounded when goods were to be sold and to mark the start of the curfew; later a prison was added and by the 15th century both the Scottish Parliament and the Court of Session would meet there.

The reign of James III (1460-88), like that of his father, was turbulent. He was nine when he came to the throne and struggles over the regency soon broke out. His mother, Mary of Gueldres, demanded that Parliament (sitting in the Castle) name her regent. Meanwhile, the young king was at the bottom of the hill in

Palace of Holyroodhouse: Scene of the murder of David Rizzio. *See p11.*

Holyrood Abbey, with the Bishop of St Andrews. The precarious situation caused the Edinburgh mob to riot. It was the first recorded glimpse of the volatile and well-organised body that would regularly cause havoc over the next few hundred years.

Despite the turbulence, it was during James III's reign that the Cowgate began to be seen as the fashionable place to live, and from 1485, dwellings were also built in the Canongate. The walled city was hemmed in and was becoming overcrowded, while the Canongate houses were notable for their spacious rooms and back gardens. But the lack of a defensive wall left this area open to attack: the Abbey itself was sacked and looted by a host of interlopers over the centuries.

The area around the town was sprinkled with small villages that were later subsumed by the city. Restalrig, for instance, whose church dates back to the 12th century, is now part of Edinburgh. Fortified tower houses were built at Liberton, Cramond, Craiglockhart and Merchiston – where the inventor of logarithms, John Napier, was born in 1550.

COMMERCIAL BREAKS
Commerce flourished under James III. Between 1320 and 1450 Edinburgh's share of wool exports rose from 21 per cent to 71 per cent – as the only major town with a port between the Tweed and the Forth, it was ideally placed to capitalise on foreign trade opportunities. In 1469 the town ceased to be ruled by the merchant burgesses and became a self-electing corporation. Cloth sellers, beggars and fishwives plied their trade from stalls and booths around St Giles' on the High Street. Once these stalls became permanent fixtures that could be properly locked up, they were known as 'luckenbooths'. In 1477 James III chartered markets to be held in the Grassmarket, partly because of the congestion of traders on the High Street.

In 1482, James granted the Blue Blanket to the citizens of Edinburgh. This was a symbol of the independence of the municipality, of its right to levy customs at the port of Leith and of the exclusive rights of the town's craftsmen. These included the candlemakers, who are known to have been organised into a guild by 1488 and who worked in the area around Candlemaker Row.

There was a reason for James's kindness to Edinburgh. Three years earlier, in 1479, he had imprisoned his two brothers at the behest of his Flemish astrologer. One, the Earl of Mar, had died in the Canongate Tolbooth; the other, the Duke of Albany, had escaped from the Castle by drugging his jailers and fled to France. The

Mary Queen of Scots. *See p11.*

English then attempted to put Albany on the throne. James mustered an army to face them, but a group of disgruntled Scottish nobles took the opportunity to hang James's favourites and imprison him in the Castle. The English, under the command of the future Richard III, entered the Tolbooth and demanded that James be released into Richard's hands. Once more the Edinburgh mob rioted, causing Albany to realise that his brother still had popular support; James kept the throne.

His son, James IV (1480-1513), repaid their support in bricks and mortar when he founded the Palace of Holyroodhouse in 1498, though the monks of the Abbey were less pleased at being displaced by the building work.

CAPITAL IN WAITING
With the Scottish kings increasingly treating the town as their royal residence, the idea that Edinburgh should become Scotland's capital began to gain currency.

James IV's reign coincided with the end of the medieval age and he was eager to seem modern and forward-looking. In keeping with this spirit of the new age, the king allowed the barbers and surgeons of Edinburgh – both already allowed to practise medicine – to form the guild of barber surgeons. He gave them the sole right to sell whisky (which was regarded as a medicine) and decreed that once a year they should be given the body of a hanged criminal from which to learn more about human anatomy. James also founded the Scottish navy.

The arts benefited as well. The first Scottish printing press opened in 1507, at the foot of Blackfriars Wynd, the narrow street that led from the High Street to the Dominican Friary. Founded by Walter Chapman and Andro Myllar, it published books on government and law, and works by two of Scotland's greatest poets, William Dunbar and Robert Henryson.

The first of Dunbar's work to be published was in 1508 and his words offer a snapshot of life in the town. In one vitriolic passage he attacks the city fathers for their tight-fisted attitudes and in another voices a concept that has currency to this day: Edinburgh is a city of two contrasting faces, one rich and one poor. Among Edinburghers the distillation of that idea can still be found in the phrase 'fur coat and nae knickers'. Writers from James Hogg to Robert Louis Stevenson have found mileage in the idea that behind Edinburgh's elegant façade lurks something demonic.

THE BATTLE OF FLODDEN

Holyrood witnessed an event of some splendour on 8 August 1503, when James married Henry VII's 12-year-old daughter, Margaret Tudor. Less splendid were the events that followed. As part of the marriage settlement, James had signed the Treaty of Perpetual Peace with England. The grand title failed to live up to political reality, and only a decade later the countries went to war when the French persuaded James to attack England. In early autumn 1513, the citizens of Edinburgh mustered at the Mercat Cross on the High Street to join an army that, when it took its fateful position on Branxton Hill in Northumberland, was 20,000 strong. The Battle of Flodden was a disaster for the Scots. The army was routed and 10,000 Scots were killed, James among them.

In Edinburgh, the shock of the defeat was palpable. Disbelief turned to panic when the townspeople realised the English might press north and attack Edinburgh. Work on the Flodden Wall began, though the attack never materialised. Still visible in parts today (*see p59*), it had six entry points and, once completed in 1560, formed the town's boundary for a further two centuries.

RELIGIOUS RIVALRIES

The death of James V, in 1542, continued the dynastic turmoil and added a religious element. It was thought that stability could be ensured by marrying off his infant daughter, the future

Mary, Queen of Scots. But to whom? The Scots were split between those who wanted a French alliance (Cardinal Beaton and Mary's mother, Mary of Guise) and those who wanted an English one. Henry VIII of England sent the Earl of Hertford's army to Scotland to 'persuade' the Scots that a marriage to his son, Edward, was preferable. Hertford landed at Leith in the early summer of 1544 and looted both Holyrood Abbey and Palace in an episode that has come to be known as the 'rough wooing'. Hertford's force of 10,000 men then stormed the Netherbow but were repulsed; instead they seized £50,000-worth of grain and two ships.

> ### 'One aspect of this "crisis of the intellect" was the witch hunts, which took place regularly until 1670.'

Three years later, the English returned with an army commanded by the Duke of Somerset. They set up a base at Haddington, 18 miles East of Edinburgh, and, in September 1547, the Battle of Pinkie Cleuch was fought at Musselburgh, just outside the town. The Scots lost and were chased back to the gates, but the Castle was held. The harassment only stopped in 1548, when a force of French and Dutch troops landed at Leith. Mary was sent to live in France and, in 1549, the port was fortified against further attack. She eventually married her cousin, Lord Darnley, in 1565. By that time Scottish politics was dominated by religious unrest, with churchman John Knox at the head of the movement for Reformation in Scotland.

REFORMING ZEAL

In 1560, the Reformation Parliament declared Protestantism Scotland's official religion and John Knox became the leader of the Reformed Church. The faction that had previously been pro-French and pro-Mary now also became pro-Catholic, while the Protestant forces rallied against them. Knox hated Mary, and the period between her arrival at Leith from France in August 1561 and her abdication in 1567 saw much friction between the Catholic monarchy and the Protestant Church.

Mary remains one of Scotland's most romantic figures. Much of the myth-making turns on the events of 1566, when her favourite, the Savoyard David Rizzio, was murdered by a group of noblemen in Holyroodhouse led by her husband, Lord Darnley. Not long afterwards, Darnley himself was killed in an explosion at his house and Mary married Lord Bothwell. The marriage was opposed and a rising of the nobles caused Mary to flee to England after relinquishing the throne to the son she had borne Darnley, the future James VI (1567-1625).

James was born in a tiny room in the Castle, which can still be seen today. He proved to be a man of great learning and wrote the first anti-tobacco tract, *Counterblast Against Tobacco*, in 1604. But if he was forward-looking in that respect, he was less so in others: Knox believed James ruled Scotland for God, whereas James believed in the divine right of kings. James later forced through the Five Articles of Perth, which tempered the power of the Kirk as a Protestant vehicle.

James also hankered after the throne of England. On 26 March 1603 the King was woken by Sir Robert Carey, who had ridden for 36 hours with news from London: Queen Elizabeth was dead. James was to be crowned king of England.

ABSENTEE RULE, SOCIAL TURMOIL

Scotland lost its king to London when James VI (or 'Jamie Saxt' as he was known) succeeded to the English throne. History remembers him as James VI (of Scotland) and I (of England). A century later Scotland was to lose its Parliament, too, when the Act of Union was signed and the Scottish Parliament dissolved.

The years between 1603 and 1707 were ones of social unrest and religious turmoil as Scotland came to terms with absentee rule. James said he would return every three years, but it was 14 years before he set foot on Scottish soil again. The country suffered a loss of national identity and a feeling of uncertainty. One aspect of this 'crisis of the intellect' was the witch hunts, which were initiated in James VI's reign but took place regularly until 1670. They resulted in hundreds of (mainly) women being burned at the stake in Edinburgh, after first being half-drowned in the Nor' Loch.

But the first years of the 17th century were not unprofitable for Edinburgh. Merchants were thriving, as was the University of Edinburgh, founded in 1582 as the Townis College. Other building work in the early 17th century bears testament to the town's prosperity: the east wing of the Castle was rebuilt by Sir James Mason, Parliament House (*see p68*) was begun in 1632 (the Scottish Parliament was by then resident in the city) and a year later Holyroodhouse was extended. Gladstone's Land (*see p67*), one of many merchant houses erected in this period, was built in the early decades of the century.

Goldsmiths, watchmakers and bookbinders flourished in Parliament Square and with Edinburgh now the legal centre of Scotland,

A witches brank, or collar.

the town's lawyers amassed great wealth. In 1609, James ordered that the magistrates should wear robes like those of the aldermen of London and gave royal assent for a sword to be carried in front of the provost on official occasions.

THE NATIONAL COVENANT

But in 1637 something happened to reignite a religious passion not seen in Scotland since the days of the Reformation, 90 years earlier. And the Edinburgh mob played a significant role.

James died in 1625 and was succeeded by his son, Charles I, who was crowned King of Scotland in 1633 at Holyroodhouse. In an effort to impose religious uniformity on both countries of his domain, Charles introduced a new prayer book to Scotland. Called the *Book of Common Prayer*, it followed the pattern of the Episcopalian church service, and was highly unpopular with the Presbyterians.

The new prayer book proved so unpopular in fact that on the occasion of its first use in St Giles, on 23 July 1637, an old cabbage seller by the name of Jenny Geddes threw her stool at Dean Hanna shouting: 'Dost thou say Mass at my lug?' The Bishop of Edinburgh mounted the pulpit to calm the crowd but was mobbed. The riot spread outside and into the streets. This 'spontaneous' uprising is another great

Edinburgh folk story – but in truth, trouble had been brewing for some time and it is likely that the riot was carefully planned beforehand.

Either way, the *Book of Common Prayer* and the heavy taxes the King had levied on Edinburgh were thoroughly hated by the Scots. A document called the National Covenant was drawn up, and signed in blood by some, asserting the Scots' rights to both spiritual and civil liberty. On the last day of February 1638, the National Covenant was read from the pulpit of Greyfriars Kirk (*see p78*), and over the next two days a host of lairds and burgesses came to sign it.

Charles was distracted from events in Edinburgh by the outbreak of civil war in England, and though Edinburgh Castle was held by forces loyal to the King, in the town the rule of the Covenant held sway. By 1649, Oliver Cromwell had assumed power in England and on 30 January, Charles I was executed in London. The Scots were outraged that their Parliament had not been consulted – Charles had been their king too – and six days later proclaimed Charles II king of Scotland on condition he accepted the Covenanters' demands.

> **'The old walls still formed the town boundaries, so as the population grew the only way to build was up.'**

Instead, Charles asked the Marquis of Montrose, who had been loyal to his father, to conquer Scotland for him. Montrose was defeated by the Covenanters, captured and brought to Edinburgh where he was paraded up the High Street. On 21 May 1650 he was executed in front of a crowd that was not entirely unsympathetic towards him. Despite the violent demise of his deputy, Charles came to Scotland, landing at Leith later that year. No other monarch would visit Edinburgh until George IV in 1822.

Cromwell's response was to invade. He defeated the Scots under General Leslie at the Battle of Dunbar on 3 September 1650, and while Charles escaped to be crowned King of Scotland, in January 1651 Cromwell burned Holyroodhouse and imposed crippling taxes for the maintenance of his army.

PESTILENCE AND PLAGUE

Those 13 years of rebellion and religious turmoil hit Edinburgh hard: trade dropped off dramatically and plague ravaged the city in 1644, killing 20 per cent of the population. Nevertheless, it remained a lively place throughout the 17th century. Golf was played in

virtually any open space, archery was practised and the young men of the town were apt to use their pistols to shoot fowl from their windows. The Kirk, meanwhile, was forever berating the townspeople for spending Sundays in ale houses.

Sanitation got no better, though: plague visited the city again in 1645 and it wasn't until 1687 that Parliament decreed that the council should provide 20 carts to remove refuse. Water was still being taken around town in barrels by the water caddies, or drawn from private wells.

Tea was tasted for the first time in the city in 1681, the same year James Dalrymple published his *Institutions of the Law of Scotland*. He is remembered as the 'Father of Scottish Law', an important sobriquet as it was Scotland's independent legal system (along with its separate religious and educational set-ups) that came to be seen as proof of nationhood after 1707.

A map drawn in 1647 shows a bewildering number of closes running off the High Street and down through the Cowgate, with St Giles and the old burying ground behind. Edinburgh spread a little beyond the Flodden Wall in 1617 when High Riggs was bought by the town; further areas were added in 1639, notably Calton Hill and the Pleasance to the north and south of the Canongate.

THERE MAY BE TROUBLE AHEAD

When Charles II was returned to the throne in 1660 after Cromwell's death – the period known as the Restoration – he reneged on acts made in favour of Covenanters and discontent simmered once again. Revolt broke out in Galloway in 1666 and, in 1679, the Covenanters won a victory at the Battle of Drumclog. Charles sent the Duke of Monmouth to crush the Covenanters, which he did at the Battle of Bothwell Brig later that year. In a period of history that has become known as 'the killing time', the survivors were marched to Greyfriars Kirkyard in Edinburgh and imprisoned there for five months. They had little food, shelter or water and many died or were executed. Several hundred others were sent as slaves to Barbados.

James VII (II) ascended the thrones of England and Scotland in 1685 on the death of his brother Charles, but his Catholicism made him unpopular. The Dukes of Argyll and Monmouth tried to unseat him but failed, and James's reign stuttered on. In 1688, when he fathered a male heir, a group of English noblemen sought to replace him with the Protestant, William of Orange, and his wife Mary (James's daughter). James fled to France and the protection of Louis XIV.

The tartaniser

Up until the late 18th century, Scotland was split in two. Lowlanders saw themselves as cultured, forward-looking and fond of trousers, while they regarded the Highlanders as Gaelic-speaking hoodlums in barbaric attire. Highland costume included a great length of material wrapped around the upper body and thighs, fastened at the waist so the lower part formed a skirt – the belted plaid. Those who had money wore a plaid of ostentatious design; those who did not wore brown. Tartan-style designs, even for the rich, didn't reach Scotland until the 16th century and probably came from Flanders.

It wasn't until the 1720s that the kilt as we know it today was invented. An English businessman struck a deal with a clan chief near Inverness to smelt iron ore on his land.

Local men were employed and their belted plaid proved such a hindrance when it came to felling trees or working a furnace that the inventive Englishman came up with a sawn-off plaid that dispensed with the upper portion and left just the skirt. The kilt was born – but still there was no relation between tartan and clan identity.

Use of the kilt spread and, by the time of the Battle of Culloden in 1746 (when Bonnie Prince Charlie was defeated), it was seen as part of traditional Highland dress. It was subsequently banned by a London-based government intent on wiping out all traces of a culture that could lend armed support to Catholic rebellion against the British crown. In a generation, the Highland way of life – not to mention its fashion sense – was destroyed.

William and Mary came to the throne in 1688. Many in Edinburgh and in the Scottish Parliament favoured William – they burned effigies of the Pope on hearing the news of his landing – but Scotland as a whole was largely pro-James, especially in the Highlands. This lobby became known as the Jacobites, after 'Jacobus', the Latin word for James. The Duke of Gordon held Edinburgh Castle for James, but only until 1689.

The 1690s were bad for Edinburgh: a series of terrible harvests affected food supplies; an English war with France had a negative impact on for trade; Catholic and Protestant factions were once more circling each other warily; and,

in 1698, the failure of the Darien Scheme virtually bankrupted the nation.

Funded partly by the Edinburgh financiers and merchants who had helped set up the Bank of Scotland in 1695, the Darien Scheme involved sending an expedition out from Leith to the Caribbean in order to establish a trading link between east and west. Through a combination of misfortune and English hostility, the scheme was a disaster. When news of the its failure reached Edinburgh rioting broke out on a massive scale: the Tolbooth was stormed and all the prisoners released, while much of the Cowgate and the Royal Exchange were torched.

reported to have touched it with his sceptre and said: 'There's an end of an auld sang'. It would be nearly 300 years before the Scottish Parliament sat again.

But once the clan structure had been broken, the people 'pacified', and the men directed into Highland regiments of the British Army, public opinion in the Lowlands and England started to feel more comfortable with the now harmless 'noble savage' from the north. The Highlands became hip...

The crucial turning point, the time when Highland imagery became the basis of a national identity for all Scots, came in 1822 with George IV's visit to Edinburgh. No reigning British monarch had set foot over the border in two centuries, so a visit of some note was required, in an Edinburgh that was in the midst of re-inventing itself with the building of the monumental public works of the New Town. Novelist and arch-romantic Sir Walter Scott was entrusted with the organisation of the visit.

The result was a sick joke. The king, an ailing blimp with a taste for cherry brandy and opium, arrived in Edinburgh to take part in a caricature of a Highland pageant entirely invented by the novelist. The Scottish aristocracy and bourgeoisie, clad in a comical pastiche of Highland costume (as directed by Scott, with an arbitrary choice of garish tartans), fell over themselves to fawn before the king, quite happy to forget that his great uncle (Butcher Cumberland) had bloodied the glens 76 years before.

From George IV's visit on, manufacturers created and provided tartans for all. Any linkage to clan names was, in effect, one giant 19th-century marketing scam.

The collapse of the Darien Scheme served to strengthen the hand of those south of the border who sought to bully Scotland into a union with England.

END OF AN AULD SANG

On 3 October 1706 a crowd gathered along the High Street to watch, for the last time, the 'Riding' – the ceremony that preceded the opening of the Scottish Parliament. The Act of Union became law in January 1707, and the dissolution of Parliament took place the following April. When the Lord High Chancellor of Scotland, Lord Seafield, was presented with the act for royal assent, he is

THE AGE OF IMPROVEMENT

The 18th century is known in Edinburgh as the 'Age of Improvement'. The phrase refers both to the massive building programme that was implemented in the 1760s, and to the influence of the Enlightenment – the spirit of intellectual inquiry that flourished in the 18th century – among the lawyers, academics and churchmen off the city. Edinburgh was buzzing with the words of men like philosopher David Hume and Adam Smith, author of *The Wealth of Nations*.

By 1720 the city had two newspapers; the Honourable Company of Edinburgh Golfers was founded in 1744; the formation of a school of design, in 1760, pre-dated London's Royal Academy by eight years, and in 1777, the Royal High School moved to grand new premises in High School Yards, at the foot of Infirmary Street. The number of students at the university doubled between 1763 and 1783 (the year the Royal Society of Edinburgh was founded); it had quadrupled by 1821. Lawyers were everywhere – there were 65 wig-makers in the city by 1700 – and the Faculty of Advocates became pivotal in the city's social and intellectual life.

In 1725 the Lord Provost, George Drummond, drew up plans for a new medical school and, in 1729, the first infirmary opened at Robertson's Close. In 1731 the Medical Society was founded and, in 1736, the infirmary was granted a Royal Charter. A second hospital opened in College Wynd in the same year.

But despite these improvements, at the start of the century, the city was still medieval in its geography. It gave the appearance of being one cramped, towering, organic whole, clinging grimly on to the hillside with an enormous channel – the High Street – running down the middle. The old city walls still formed the town boundaries, by and large, so as the population grew to well over 50,000 during the 18th century, the only way to build was up. This resulted in the 'lands'; six, seven, eight storey buildings that were prone to collapse with great loss of life.

Nobles and lairds lived almost side by side with the common people, and visitors regularly commented on the well-established Edinburgh tradition of emptying chamber pots out of the top windows. 'Gardey loo', was the famous warning shout, often matched by a hasty 'Haud yer haun!' (Hold your hand!) from the pedestrians getting showered beneath.

Defeat for the Jacobites and bloody carnage at the **Battle of Culloden**. *See p17.*

BIRTH OF THE NEW TOWN

So it was with a lungful of fresh air that
Edinburgh finally burst out across the
valley to the north, creating one of the finest
architectural enclaves in the world – the New
Town. Progress, harmony, rationalisation –
and claret – were the order of the day as far as
the Enlightenment was concerned. And three
of those four principles were brought to bear
on the competition, announced in 1766, for the
best plan to extend Edinburgh to the north.

The competition was won by a 21-year-old
architect called James Craig. The prize-
winning plan has not been saved, but a later
plan, from 1767, shows three main streets –
South, North and Principal – crossed by
smaller streets and positioned between two
Grand Squares. These streets eventually
became Princes Street, George Street and
Queen Street in the New Town.

As part of the overall scheme, the Nor' Loch
was drained and the North Bridge, which
spanned the valley, was started in 1763. In
1781, the Mound (*see p67*) was begun, using the
earth from the work going on to the north. By
the time the Mound was completed, in 1830, an
estimated two million cartloads of earth had
been dumped on it. In 1768, the Theatre Royal

had gone up in what was known as
Shakespeare Square. It was the first licensed
stage in Scotland and stood on the site of the
old post office at the east end of Princes Street.

Overspill from the Old Town to the New
Town was considerable and by 1791 there were
7,200 people living there. The city had also
pushed southwards: George Square was laid out
in 1766 and a new college for the university was
built in 1789 at the old Kirk O'Fields. But, with
its panoramic views over the Forth, it was the
New Town that became a haven for lawyers
and merchants. David Hume was one of the first
people to move to the New Town: he built a
house at the corner of St Andrew Square. The
result of this movement of the wealthier classes
northwards was that a type of social apartheid
formed and the notion of the city with two faces
surfaced once more.

The late 18th century also provided Edinburgh
with one of its most fascinating characters:
Deacon William Brodie, town councillor by day,
burglar by night. He was hanged in 1788, and it
is his double life that Stevenson is said to have
used as the model for his novel *The Strange
Case of Dr Jekyll and Mr Hyde*.

With the easing of congestion in the Old
Town, tempers seemed to cool a little – the mob

saw relatively little action in the 18th century. The Porteous Riots of 1736, however, were a notable and violent exception. Irritated by the decision to hang two smugglers and incensed by the shooting of several townspeople by soldiers at the hanging, the mob stormed the Tolbooth and 'arrested' the unpopular captain of the guard, Captain Porteous. He was marched down to the Grassmarket, lynched and left dangling from a dyer's pole.

Neither was Edinburgh much affected by the two significant Jacobite rebellions of 1715 and 1745, though Prince Charles Edward Stuart – aka Bonnie Prince Charlie – did spend six weeks in Edinburgh in 1745 after his victory over Sir John Cope at Prestonpans. Charlie's dream of reclaiming Scotland for the Stuarts died at Culloden a year later. After the defeat, 14 of the standards carried by the clan chiefs at Culloden were taken into the town by chimney sweeps and burned.

But violence came knocking again at the end of the century, when revolution broke out in France and many in Great Britain feared an invasion. The Edinburgh Volunteers were formed to defend the city. With the violence came political discourse, and parliamentary reform was discussed. In 1802, the *Edinburgh Review* was founded and it became a forum for anti-government opinions; other publications followed as Edinburgh became pre-eminent in the world of publishing and bookselling.

GREAT SCOTT
Edinburgh-born Sir Walter Scott was a titan of the later years of this era. He was internationally respected and, in early-19th-century terms, a blockbuster novelist. It was pressure from him that led to the 'Honours of Scotland' – the crown, sceptre and sword of state, which had been lost since 1603 – being searched for and uncovered in the Castle in 1818. Scott was able to entice George IV to Edinburgh, in 1822, for what was the first official visit of a monarch to Scotland since Charles I in 1641. *See p14* **The tartaniser**. If he could have seen beyond the pomp of this curious occasion, George would have discovered a city on the slide. In 1818, work began on the Union Canal to join Edinburgh with the Forth and Clyde Canal, but the National Monument to the dead of the Napoleonic Wars, which was begun in 1822 on Calton Hill, was never finished. The Parthenon-like structure stands there still (*see p98*), long ago dubbed 'Scotland's Disgrace', and at the time also a reminder that Scotland was once again losing its way. Power was in held in London and the intellectual activity of the Enlightenment was declining – Edinburgh's glory days were behind it.

THE VICTORIAN ERA
Edinburgh underwent a third period of expansion during the Victorian era, when suburbs such as Marchmont, Morningside and Bruntsfield were built. The city that had become two when the New Town was built found itself with more faces. Each 'city' had its own character and type of inhabitants: the solid Victorian suburbs were peopled by the growing middle class, the grand New Town remained the area of choice for lawyers and judges, while the teeming Old Town became a slum.

At the start of the 19th century, the population of Edinburgh and Leith was 102,987. By 1881, the population of Greater Edinburgh was 320,549. One of the reasons for the dramatic increase was the influx of people from other parts of Scotland and from Ireland. Indeed, Burke and Hare, two of Edinburgh's most infamous criminals, were both Irish immigrants. *See p18* **Body matters**.

With the increase in population came unemployment. The riots of 1812 and 1818 both had economic causes, and by the 1830s outbreaks of cholera and typhoid had decimated the Old Town. This devastation was compounded, in 1824, by a fire that destroyed much of the High Street with great loss of life; it resulted in the formation of the world's first municipal fire service.

> **'An 1842 study found that most of the city's 200 brothels were located in the Old Town.'**

Cholera returned to the city in 1848. Meanwhile, a study conducted by Dr George Bell in the 1850s found that 159 of the Old Town's closes lacked drainage and fresh water and concluded that Blackfriars Wynd was home to 1,000 people, sharing just 142 houses. Bell also bemoaned the alcoholism endemic among the Old Town's inhabitants. A separate study undertaken in 1842 by a young Edinburgh doctor, William Tait, found that most of the city's 200 brothels were located in the Old Town. Attempts were made to restore the Old Town, particularly by William Chambers (Lord Provost 1865-69), but the area was on a downward spiral that was to continue into the 20th century.

In contrast to the decrepitude of housing in the Old Town were the public buildings thrown up during the 19th century: schools, churches, galleries, railway stations, hospitals, banks and bridges – the optimistic Victorians had a zeal for them all.

Body matters

Lack of bodies was a persistent problem in the anatomy theatres of early 19th-century Britain. One Edinburgh medical student wrote in 1810: 'Unless there be a fortunate succession of bloody murders, not three subjects are dissected in the year. On the remains of a subject fished up from the bottom of a tub of spirits are demonstrated those delicate nerves which are to be avoided or divided in our operations.'

The fact that the few legally obtained corpses dissected at Edinburgh's medical school were those of murderers sentenced to the extra-severe punishment of 'hanging with dissection' reflected society's deeply held cultural and religious view that to have one's body cut up after death was a dreadful fate. This belief found itself in diametric opposition to the anatomists' quest for scientific knowledge, which required corpses for dissection. Progress was paramount: science must triumph over superstition.

By the beginning of the 19th century, medical advances were increasing rapidly; surgery had become a respectable and lucrative profession, and Edinburgh – with its prestigious medical school – was the place to train. The large number of medical students in the city, combined with poor university teaching and a scarcity of corpses,

led students to private lecturers. The most popular of these was Dr Robert Knox. Charisma and intellectual rigour aside, students were attracted by Knox's promise – in an advertising pamphlet – of a good supply of fresh corpses for dissection.

The method by which anatomists obtained most of their corpses was an open secret: the market was supplied by 'resurrectionists' or graverobbers. Buying corpses on a 'don't ask, don't tell' basis, anatomists and their students led double lives, forced to mingle with society's criminal underclass. It made their public image an ambiguous one: on the one hand the surgeon was a potential lifesaver; on the other he was a dark and threatening figure.

William Burke and William Hare got into the body business by chance – but opportunism was soon to turn to murder. The pair were Irish immigrants, ekeing out a living in Edinburgh's cramped and filthy tenements. Hare and his wife owned a lodging house for the many poor and transient people passing through the city; Burke and his mistress moved in as lodgers.

When an elderly man died at the lodging house owing Hare £4, Burke and Hare took him to Dr Knox to recoup the debt; they were paid £7 10s. It was all so simple, and it gave

The building frenzy was matched, after the 'Disruption' of 1843, by the missionary zeal of the Free Kirk, which came into being in May 1843 when 474 ministers seceded from the Church to form a breakaway organisation. The occasion was the General Assembly, the grievance was the right of congregations to choose their own minister, and the scene of the split was the Church of St Andrew and St George on George Street (see p87). The dissenting churchmen marched down Hanover Street to Tanfield Hall in Canonmills. 'No spectacle since the Revolution,' noted Lord Cockburn in his journal, 'reminded one so forcibly of the Covenanters.' The split wasn't resolved until 1929.

MAKING PROGRESS

In 1847 one of the dissenting churchmen, Thomas Guthrie, helped set up three charity schools after meeting some boys in Holyrood Park who said they had never been to school. Guthrie also became active in the temperance movement, which sought to curb the kind of

drinking that Dr George Bell had identified as a social ill some years earlier. This movement had some success, in 1853, when a bill was passed that shut the inns on Sundays. Meanwhile, public hangings were stopped, in 1864, and moved to within the walls of Calton jail. George Bryce was the last criminal to suffer the indignity of a public execution and it is said that 20,000 people turned up to watch him die.

Fewer turned up to the early meetings of those engaged in the struggle for women's suffrage. Nevertheless, one of the first three women's suffrage societies was formed in Edinburgh, in 1867. The same year saw the Improvement Act, which stripped the old wooden fronts from the lands (a terrible fire hazard) and opened up some of the most crowded areas.

This moral and ideological progress was matched by technological advances, particularly in the fields of transport and medicine. In the early 17th century London was 13 days away by coach; towards the end of the century the journey could be done in four. But, them an idea: perhaps they could hasten death a little and earn themselves a small fortune in the process. They went on to commit 16 murders – luring victims to the lodgings with promises of hospitality, plying them with drink and then smothering them in such a way that their bodies could be presented in perfect condition.

This money-spinning murder spree came to an end in 1828, when a couple who also lodged with Hare spotted the body of an elderly woman hidden under a bed. By the time the couple had alerted a policeman, the body had disappeared, but a tip-off led investigators to Dr Knox's rooms.

The story caused a storm. Hare gave King's evidence against Burke to escape trial himself. Meanwhile, medical and legal establishments closed ranks around Knox; he was not required to give evidence, but his presumed complicity fuelled the anger of the Edinburgh mob.

Burke was hanged in front of nearly 25,000 people, Sir Walter Scott among them. He wrote: 'The mob… demanded Knox and Hare, but, though greedy for more victims, received with shouts the solitary wretch who found his way to the gallows.' The mob's worst fears about surgeons had been confirmed. They made an effigy of Knox, marched with it to the doctor's home and later tore it limb from limb.

Many fought to gain entry to the university lecture theatre where Burke's corpse was publicly dissected, as directed by the judge.

Protected by loyal students, Knox evaded both the masses and the courts. At first it seemed his career was unaffected by the scandal, but he failed to capitalise on the brilliance of his earlier years and ended his life as a pathologist in London. Knox always protested his innocence, but how much did he really know? It would have been clear that the bodies had been nowhere near the graveyard, but could Knox really have believed they were the unclaimed corpses of unknown transients, as Burke and Hare claimed? The case of Mary Patterson does little to convince.

Mary may have been poor but, unlike the other victims, she was not anonymous; several of Knox's students recognised the young prostitute. However, Knox chose to accept Burke and Hare's explanation that Mary had choked on her own vomit and that her body had been handed over to them.

Knox preserved Mary for some time as an example of the perfect female form before undertaking an intricate dissection. Was this naivete on his part, or professional arrogance, combined with a subconscious conviction that certain lives were worth sacrificing for the sake of medical knowledge?

with the age of steam, travel became far easier – 1850 saw the first public train from London to Edinburgh and, in 1862, the famous *Flying Scotsman* did the run in just ten-and-a-half hours. In 1890, the Forth Railway Bridge, an imposing structure spanning the Forth at South Queensferry, was built, and hailed as the 'Eighth Wonder of the World'.

Between 1845 and 1846, rail tunnels were built between Haymarket and Waverley Stations, through the south flank of Calton Hill and under the Mound. These brought tourists and travellers straight into the heart of the city, where they would emerge to face the Castle, the Gothic bulk of the Scott Monument (begun in 1840, *see p86*), the galleries at the foot of the Mound and the splendour of Princes Street Gardens. A century and a half later, this is still the best way to arrive in the city. Meanwhile, in the world of medicine, men such as James Young Simpson and Joseph Lister were gaining international renown for their work in the fields of anaesthetics and antiseptics.

Towards the end of the Victorian era, Glasgow had begun to assume increasing importance in Scotland to the detriment of Edinburgh. The two international festivals that Glasgow held – in 1888 and 1901 – far outshone the one that took place on the Meadows in Edinburgh in 1886, and men such as the designer Charles Rennie Mackintosh were creating an artistic and architectural legacy that is still revered today. As the historian and journalist Allan Massie has pointed out, Edinburgh at the end of the 19th century was just the biggest small town in Scotland.

THE 20TH CENTURY

Look around Edinburgh today and the most obvious legacy of the 20th century is the dappling of hideous, grey edifices thrown up in the 1960s and '70s. The St James Centre and New St Andrew's House, built at the east end of Princes Street in 1971, are some of the most striking examples. Leith Street was flattened to make way for these buildings. In the process,

The **Flying Scotsman** made the journey from London to Edinburgh in record time. *See p19.*

Edinburgh lost the house in Picardy Place in which Sherlock Holmes' creator, Arthur Conan Doyle, was born in 1859.

The shape of the city had continued to change throughout the 20th century, although little of any note was added architecturally. The suburbs continued to creep outwards, but buildings were more likely to be pulled down than put up, as the city fathers (and private contractors) finally got to grips with the decaying Old Town and moved the population outwards to areas such as Niddrie and Craigmillar. Meanwhile, Edinburgh's infrastructure was being upgraded. New reservoirs were built to bring more water into the city, the telephone service was expanded and, in 1924, a radio station opened.

The civil unrest that broke out in Ireland in the first decade of the 20th century caused a rise in religious intolerance in the city – although it has never suffered the sectarian divisions of Glasgow. Edinburgh also felt the effects of the women's suffrage movement. Between 1912 and 1914 supporters regularly damaged post boxes, though their more adventurous exploits included attempts to blow up the Royal Observatory and Rosslyn Chapel, and the setting of a fire at Fettes College. Post boxes came under attack again in Edinburgh in the 1950s, when they were defaced by Scottish Nationalists after the coronation of Queen Elizabeth II.

Edinburgh's lack of heavy industry was to save the city twice during the middle years of the 20th century. It allowed it to avoid the worst ravages of the Depression during the 1930s and, a decade or so later, the bombs of the Luftwaffe. Leith was one of the few areas that was badly affected.

LEISURE PURSUITS
Sport became woven into the fabric of Edinburgh life in the 1900s, although most of the city's sporting institutions were born in the previous century. The city's two football teams were founded within a year of each other – Heart of Midlothian in 1874 and Hibernian in 1875. Both have enjoyed (occasional) periods of success over the years. *See also p220.*

Rugby union has been played in the city since the 19th century. In 1922 the Scottish Football Union (as it was then called) bought a plot of land at Murrayfield and built a stadium (*see p222*). It was inaugurated on 21 March 1925, when Scotland played England for the Grand Slam.

The oldest of all these sports, however, is curling. Its origins are lost in time, but the Royal Caledonian Curling Club was formed in Edinburgh in 1838 and is now regarded as the sport's 'mother club'. The World Curling Federation is also based in Edinburgh.

But if sport didn't appeal there were other leisure pursuits to follow. In 1913 the Zoological Gardens were established and, 20 years later, a huge Olympic-size open-air swimming pool opened on the coast at Portobello. City folk could now catch a tram to the seaside (the system was city-wide by 1922), spend their days in the sun and enjoy a view over the Forth.

Perhaps the most notable achievement of 20th-century Edinburgh was the Festival. The event began in 1947, and featured the Vienna Philharmonic Orchestra, Sadlers Wells Ballet and the Old Vic Theatre Company. That year, eight theatre companies not included in the official programme put on shows in smaller venues. In subsequent years others followed, and the Fringe was established. Many famous careers have begun here: Dudley Moore, Peter Cook, Alan Bennett and Jonathan Miller made their names with satirical revue *Beyond the Fringe* in 1960, and Tom Stoppard's breakthrough play *Rosencrantz and Guildenstern are Dead* was first performed at the Festival in 1966.

END OF THE MILLENNIUM

Many of Edinburgh's traditional industries, such as publishing, declined during the 20th century. The addition of two new universities (Heriot-Watt and Napier) helped build the city's already-strong academic reputation, however. Edinburgh has also become one of Europe's top financial centres, specialising in fund management and insurance. And, as in the rest of Scotland, the tourist industry continues to be vital to the city's economy.

The International Festival has kept the city on the artistic map since 1947, while in the inter-war years, the 'Scottish Renaissance' saw a flowering of literary and artistic talent. It centred around writers and artists such as Hugh MacDiarmid, James Bridie, Edwin Muir, Naomi Mitchison, Lewis Grassic Gibbon and Neil Gunn. Milnes Bar on Hanover Street was a regular meeting place and many of the writers are pictured around the walls.

Something of that feel returned during the 1990s, thanks to the success of a few vibrant publishing houses and the international success of Irvine Welsh's novel *Trainspotting* (*see also p33*). The novel also brought some realism to the image of Edinburgh by throwing the spotlight on the city's ills – such as the heroin epidemic that swept through the place in the 1980s.

But the event that history may come to regard as the century's most significant came right at its close, with the partial devolution of Scotland and the establishment of a Scottish Parliament in the capital once again. This adventure in parliamentary activity seems to be leading to the emergence of a new style in UK politics: less adversarial, more consensual and more representative. With the forging of a new identity through political life, Edinburgh today is looking to its capital-city status – rather than its striking physical landscape – to define itself.

An early **Heart of Midlothian** (Hearts) line-up. The team was founded in 1874. *See p20.*

Key events

c638 Southern Scotland under the control of Northumbria.
c950 The MacAlpin kings repel Northumbrians.
1018 Malcolm II defeats the Northumbrians and Edinburgh Castle becomes Scottish.
1093 Malcolm III killed. Civil war follows.
1128 Augustinian Abbey of Holyrood founded by David I.
1314 Robert the Bruce's nephew, Thomas Randolph, retakes the castle from the English.
1329 Edinburgh receives royal charter from Robert the Bruce.
1333 Berwick lost to the English.
1349 The Black Death arrives, returning in **1362** and **1379**: a third of Scottish population estimated to have died from the plague.
1477 James III charters markets to be held in the Grassmarket.
1482 James III grants town the Blue Blanket.
1498 Holyroodhouse built by James IV.
1513 Citizens muster under the Blue Blanket at the Mercat Cross to march to Flodden. James IV is killed in the battle. Following the defeat, the Flodden Wall is built to defend the city.
1544 English army attacks from the sea, sacks Holyroodhouse and its Abbey, but fails to gain entrance to the city.
1566 David Rizzio murdered in Holyroodhouse.
1582 James VI issues a charter for the Townis College, later Edinburgh University.
1603 James VI accedes to the English throne and removes the Court to London.
1633 Edinburgh becomes capital of Scotland.
1639 Parliament House finished. Used by Scottish Parliament until 1707.
1673 The city's first coffeehouse opens, in Parliament Close.
1675 Physic Garden founded by the Nor' Loch.
1681 Tea tasted in the city for the first time; James Dalrymple publishes his *Institutions of the Law of Scotland*.
1695 Bank of Scotland chartered.
1698 A run of seven disastrous harvests begins, increasing discontent and rioting.
1702-7 Scottish Parliament sits in Edinburgh discussing the Act of Union. It is eventually ratified in 1707.
1726 Last burning of a witch in Edinburgh.
1727 Royal Bank of Scotland founded.
1736 Porteous Riots.
1749 William Younger founds his brewery.

1767 James Craig's plans for the New Town adopted. Theatre Royal, Edinburgh's first licensed theatre, opens.
1771 *Encyclopedia Britannica* published by William Smellie in Anchor Close; Sir Walter Scott born in College Wynd.
1784 Last execution in the Grassmarket.
1787 Edinburgh edition of Robert Burns' poems published. The opening lines of his *Address to Edinburgh* are: 'Edina, Scotia's darling seat'.
1788 Deacon Brodie hanged at the Tolbooth.
1792 Riots in George Square.
1802 *Edinburgh Review* founded.
1817 *Blackwood's Magazine* and *Scotsman* are founded.
1821 Edinburgh School of Arts formed.
1822 Work is begun on National Monument.
1824 The Great Fire destroys much of the High Street. It lasts three days and results in the formation of the world's first municipal fire service. The Botanic Garden moves to Inverleith.
1832 Dean Bridge built; New Town extended across it in 1850.
1836 Waverley Station begun.
1843 The Disruption splits the Church.
1847 Alexander Graham Bell, the inventor of the telephone, born in South Charlotte Street.
1864 Last public hanging in Edinburgh.
1886 Edinburgh International Exhibition held on the Meadows.
1890 Forth Rail Bridge opened.
1895 Electric street lighting introduced.
1908 Scottish National Exhibition held in Saughton Park.
1912-14 Suffragette attacks in the city.
1916 A German zeppelin bombs Edinburgh.
1947 The first Edinburgh International Festival takes place.
1956 Last tram runs. National Library opened by Elizabeth II.
1964 Heriot-Watt University founded.
1970 Commonwealth Games held in the city; Meadowbank Stadium opened.
1993 Irvine Welsh's novel *Trainspotting* is published.
1997 Scotland votes 'Yes' for the return of a Scottish parliament with tax-varying powers.
1998 Holyrood announced as the site of the Scottish Parliament.
1999 The Queen opens Scottish Parliament.
2000 Death of Scottish First Minister Donald Dewar.

Computer-generated image of Miralles'
Scottish Parliament building.

Edinburgh Today

The political process has been a long time coming –
and seems to be taking a long time to deliver.

On 1 July 1999, Scotland held its breath as the Queen processed up the Royal Mile with the Duke of Edinburgh and the Prince of Wales to open the first Scottish Parliament for 300 years. The country stopped and watched, in person and on television.

It was a momentous occasion, a day on which to celebrate. And in Edinburgh it was especially sunny, both literally and metaphorically. While Scotland had got its own parliament, Edinburgh had once again come into its own as a capital city. The monarch already kept a home at Holyrood, and the arrival of a parliament – even one whose brand new home had not yet been built – was the final piece in the jigsaw of State. Monarch, parliament and civil service all now resided (or could reside) within the city.

It didn't matter that Edinburgh was not the capital of an independent Scotland. Having a parliament was enough: surely everything else would now fall into place? On that afternoon and evening, with First Minister Donald Dewar

introducing free public concerts in Princes Street Gardens in a golden glow of achievement, it seemed that any political obstacles could be overcome. If Scotland wanted it, the parliament could do it – whatever 'it' might be.

Three years later, and the reality is beginning to bite. Problems of health, education, roads, crime and the environment have yet to find their perfect Scottish solutions, and the Members of the Scottish Parliament (MSPs), have been found to be far from perfect too. An attempt by Westminster to reduce the number of MSPs in 2002 provoked not horror but public ambivalence – the inflation-busting pay rise that MSPs had recently voted for themselves obscured hard-won principles. And so the high ideals of democracy have become lost in the low realities of life: that solutions are not instantaneous, and that people are not infallible.

The first notion that the brave new Scotland may be mortal after all came with the tragic and untimely death of First Minister Donald Dewar on 11 October 2000. An architect of Scottish devolution, he was not merely a politician with vision: he was one with integrity. He was a man whom the Scottish people trusted to take the country and its institutions forward.

The second blow came with the resignation of Dewar's successor just over a year later. Embroiled in a petty scandal involving the misallocation of expenses, First Minister Henry McLeish made a short, perfunctory speech to his fellow MSPs on 8 November 2001 and then left the position to his political rival, Jack McConnell.

With the honeymoon now demonstrably over, the citizens of Scotland became restless that more had not been achieved in a shorter time. The problem was that Dewar's vision was a political structure fit for the 21st century, a structure in which every person could have their say. Log on to the Scottish Parliament website (www.scottish.parliament.uk) and the whole process of government is being carried on quite transparently and in such a way that the public can get actively involved. But on the parliament's doorstep, things don't look quite so simple. Having won the right to vote for their own representatives, Edinburgh's citizens have forgotten that for the democratic process to work efficiently and fairly, it needs them actively to take part.

The problem in Edinburgh is that its people have never really been at home with ephemeral symbols. So until the actual Scottish Parliament building is finally complete, down in Holyrood, they will not have anything concrete to hold on to. Edinburgh likes to be able to see what it's supporting.

THE OLD SONG

An understanding of both the parliament and its political history helps in understanding Edinburgh today. Scotland's parliamentary origins can be traced back to the 12th century, but parliament was entirely subordinate to the monarch until 1560, when the exiled Mary, Queen of Scots allowed it to meet in her absence. Her son, James VI, however, reasserted the royal authority and neither he nor his successor, Charles I, felt any need for a Parliament to help rule. In 1638, the National Covenant called for free assemblies that were independent of the monarch and there followed 12 years of unprecedented freedom of speech until Cromwell banned any parliaments other than the Palace of Westminster (although the Scots were allowed to send 30 MPs there). In 1661, the Parliament was revived again, but worsening economic conditions brought about the 1707 Act of Union with England and it was disbanded.

Temporary **debating chamber**.

Modern Scotland is still not an independent nation, merely one that has had certain powers devolved to it in matters such as housing, law and order, social work services, health services and the arts. The Scottish Parliament also has the right to vary income tax by up to three pence in the pound. But Westminster is still the sovereign power in the United Kingdom, retaining control over such matters as defence, foreign policy, the civil service, social security, broadcasting and immigration. Seventy-two Scottish seats remain there, with some MSPs doubling as MPs in the House of Commons.

It was no surprise to anyone but the most optimistic Scottish National Party activist that the Labour Party should dominate the first Parliament. The Scottish Labour Party, founded by Keir Hardie in 1888, has the firmest hold on both the Scottish psyche and Scotland's political institutions, particularly in the urban and industrial areas of the central belt. Indeed, its unchallenged strength in some areas has rebounded on the party in recent years, with accusations of cronyism and 'jobs for the boys' carrying over into the first Parliament.

With considerations such as these in mind, the Conservatives are starting to claw back some of the ground lost in the 1997 general election. At the peak of their popularity here in 1955, the Tories scored 50.1 per cent of the

Scottish vote. This figure was gradually eaten away, until in 1997 they were left with no Scottish MPs at Westminster at all. The party's traditional heartlands are the well-heeled farming areas of the Lowlands and Perthshire and the more affluent districts of the major cities. Unable to mimic their southern colleagues' increasingly 'little Englander' stance without looking ridiculous to the Scottish electorate, they are having to forge a new and distinctly Scottish identity and may, in fact, recover faster than their English counterparts.

The north and the Highlands and Islands tend to vote SNP or Liberal Democrat, though rogue patches of this or that political hue crop up all over the country. In 1908, 58 per cent of the Scottish electorate voted for the Liberals, their predecessors. Now they are only the fourth largest party and rely on their coalition with Labour for what influence they have.

'Where to site the new Parliament was one of the hardest fought debates in Scottish political history.'

The Scottish Nationalist Party (SNP) is currently the second most powerful force in Scotland. It was founded in 1928 as a response to the failure of both Labour and the Liberals to support home rule bills and won its first seat at Motherwell in 1945, only to lose soon afterwards in the general election. From then until the 1970s, when the discovery of North Sea oil pushed the independence question further up the political agenda, the party fell into a pattern of winning seats in spectacular victories only to have them snatched back a few years later.

A referendum was finally held in 1979, with 52 per cent of those who voted favouring devolution. Unfortunately, Labour Prime Minister James Callaghan decided that a mandate could only be achieved if the majority of the entire Scottish electorate voted in favour, so the referendum failed. Such shifting of the democratic goalposts earned Callaghan little but scorn. His government was swept aside by a vote of no confidence and a Conservative landslide.

Despite being passionately opposed to devolution, Callaghan's successor, Margaret Thatcher, probably did more than any other individual to bring it about. Through policies that were felt to be anti-Scottish – foremost among them the hated Community Charge (Poll Tax) – she created a climate hostile to rule from London. Even after she had been deposed, the bond of trust between Scotland and

Westminster remained broken. Conservative presence in Scotland was annihilated in the 1997 general election; on 11 September that year, Scots voted in a referendum in favour of a Scottish Parliament. The knotty decision of where to put it was not yet on the agenda.

A NEW HOUSE

Things did not stay this way for long; soon the issue of where to site the Parliament had become one of the hardest fought debates in Scottish political history. The site that was finally chosen, down by the Queen's Edinburgh pad, is certainly appropriate in symbolic terms. It is here that John Knox went to have a few words with his queen, and is where the ultimate authority in Scotland resides. Besides, it fills in a gap that even in Robert Louis Stevenson's day was a mess of breweries and gas works.

However, two other sites vied for supremacy. The Royal High School on Calton Hill had been earmarked since the 1970s, but as symbol of SNP nationalism, it was conveniently found to be too hard to upgrade. A new-build site in Leith did not have such difficulties, but was too far away from the centre of the city. The final decision was not arrived at by simply choosing the best site – far too easy an option for this city where Machiavellian intrigue fits as easily as a Masonic emblem. Nor, indeed, was the best site necessarily chosen. It was a decision arrived at through an impressively overt bout of political manoeuvring and horse-trading.

A more positive decision was the appointment of the Catalan architect Enric Miralles as the head of the project. Although it may be insular and guarded towards its neighbours, Scotland has a far better record when it comes to foreign liaisons. An English architect would have been anathema to most Scots, but where continental Europe is concerned, the Scots tend to be far more open than their southern counterparts; Edinburgh, in particular, is proud of its internationalism. Miralles' death in July 2000 was a bitter blow, although the project and his design live on.

While Edinburgh waits for its shiny new fur coat, life continues as it always did. For the moment, there is not much in politics that will bring the city or the country to a halt. Until the Parliament building is completed and the Scottish Executive can get some satisfactory results under its belt, the only concern that is likely to unite all Edinburgh in debate is the great political issue of Scottish football: whether the ten minnow sides in the Scottish Premier League can successfully leave the two giants of Rangers and Celtic to their own devices, and strike out on their own.

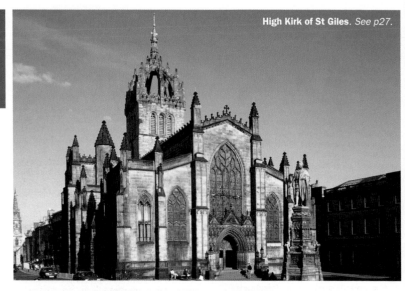

High Kirk of St Giles. *See p27.*

Architecture

When haphazard expansion met rigid urban planning.

Edinburgh is justifiably classed as one of Europe's finest cities, so it's not surprising that it has a knowingly handsome air. A 'dream of a great genius', wrote one 1820s visitor, while Mary Shelley had the narrator of her Gothic classic *Frankenstein* comment on 'the beauty and regularity of the New Town of Edinburgh, its romantic castle and its environs, the most delightful in the world…'.

Topographically, Edinburgh has been dealt a spectacular hand. The Pentland Hills lie to the south and a coastal plain stretches north and east to the Firth of Forth, while Arthur's Seat and Castle Rock – impressive remnants of volcanic action – along with Calton Hill and the Salisbury Crags, lend geographical drama to the city. This setting has helped shape a city of two distinct characters. Crowned by Edinburgh Castle, hugging tightly to Castle Rock, the Old Town looks across to the New Town, a triumph of classical formality played out in a gridiron of well-disciplined streets. In 1995 UNESCO designated the Old Town and New Town a World Heritage Site, an honour that recognised this city's knack for seducing the visitor.

PREHISTORIC TO MEDIEVAL

Bronze Age settlers first colonised the natural citadel of the Castle Rock in around 900 BC. In the first century AD, after centuries of relative inactivity, the rocky outcrop became home to a succession of settlements.

Under the ambitious rule of the House of Canmore, the Castle Rock emerged as a fortified stronghold (today's **Edinburgh Castle**; *see p63*). The small but squatly Romanesque **St Margaret's Chapel** (c1110), with its characteristic rounded, chevron-decorated chancel arch, is the earliest architectural survivor.

In 1125, the expanding settlement was declared a royal burgh and in 1128 **Holyrood Abbey** (*see p74*) was founded. Linear development gradually linked Holyrood to the Castle Rock along the rocky spine of the Old Town, defining the route of today's Royal Mile.

Architecturally, little remains from Edinburgh's infant years. Instability and limited funds meant that few structures were built of stone. Most of the houses were crudely constructed from wattle and post, covered in clay for insulation and thatched with straw, rushes or heather. Their lifespan was no more than a couple of decades, even assuming they escaped the fires that were a common occurrence during the frequent raids by the English.

Of the handful of stone structures, St Giles (today's **High Kirk of St Giles** on the Royal Mile; *see p69*) dates from 1120, but little remains of the original building. It was extensively remodelled in the late 14th century, when Gothic transepts and a series of chapels were added. Holyrood Abbey was also virtually rebuilt, between 1195 and 1230, with the addition of arcades of pointed arches to emphasise the vertical.

The Castle fell twice to the English during this period, prompting a huge rebuilding programme in 1356.

SCOTTISH RENAISSANCE

As its national stature grew during the reign of James III (1460-88), Edinburgh witnessed a surge in confidence and building activity. Holyrood Abbey became a royal residence and was expanded, leading to the 1498 addition of the **Palace of Holyroodhouse** (*see p74*), and Edinburgh Castle was augmented by Crown Square and its baronial Great Hall, topped with a hammerbeam roof.

Money was pumped into churches, most notably the now-demolished Trinity College Church and, in around 1500, a crown spire was added to the central tower of St Giles. An array of flying buttresses bedecked with gilded pinnacles, it became a template for the numerous crown spires to be found across Scotland.

Further invasion attempts by the English in the 1540s prompted Scotland to improve relations with France and open up trade with Europe, heralding the Old Town's mercantile boom years. Edinburgh's growing internationalism was mirrored in a fusion of local and continental building patterns.

THE RISE OF THE TENEMENT

As the population of the city increased, more housing was required, but the rocky and uneven terrain of the Old Town, combined with the ancient 'feu' system of land tenure (which granted leases in perpetuity) made horizontal development problematic. Thus expansion was forced upwards, leading to the birth of the tenement. Originally denoting a holding of land, the word 'lands' came to mean separate dwellings stacked in storeys, linked by a common stairwell.

Lanes, known locally as wynds and closes developed rib-like from the Royal Mile. Existing houses had extra storeys tacked on to them, often haphazardly, in addition to jutting

windows and a confusion of roof levels.

John Knox's House (c1490; *see p72*), with its protruding upper windows and storeys, is one of the few remaining examples, but it's a relatively restrained one – some timber-framed structures protruded as far as two metres (seven feet) into the street.

Building regulations, however, reined in the quick-buck property speculators, stipulating, from the 1620s, tile or slate roofs and, in 1674, stone façades as fire precautions.

'Edinburgh soon came to see architecture as an essential way of asserting the city's character.'

Daringly exploiting the ridge of the Old Town, tenements frequently bridged different levels down the side of the ridge, making them some of the tallest domestic buildings in Europe, on one side at least. Those that stood cheek-by-jowl along the Royal Mile had more in common with the architecture of northern continental Europe than that of England.

By the late 17th century tenements built in sandstone or harling (a mix of rubble and plaster) soared up along the Royal Mile. These were characterised by flat frontages and a vertical form accentuated by gables and dormer windows. The Lawnmarket, below the Castle, was home to grander examples. The five-storey **Gladstone's Land** (c1620-30, *see p67*) retains the once-commonplace street arcade and an oak-panelled interior. With the upper Royal Mile awash with merchants, its lower reaches had become the choice location of the nobility, with mansions flanking the approach to the Palace of Holyroodhouse. **Moray House** (c1628), with its pyramid-topped gate-piers, and the vast **Queensberry House** (c1634), currently redundant but to be converted into offices for the new Scottish Parliament, are the grandest survivors. The Palace itself was rebuilt in the 1670s in a triumphant blend of Scottish and European influences, to create a thick-set façade with turreted towers fronting an inner courtyard with classical arcades.

With the city becoming increasingly wealthy, a new **Parliament House** was built next to St Giles in 1637, adding weight to Edinburgh's role as Scotland's capital. The building was given a classical overhaul in the early 19th century.

Elsewhere the city flaunted its internationalism, exemplified by its easy handling of Renaissance style in the grandly ornamented **George Heriot's School** (1628; *see p81*), south of the Royal Mile. Along the

In Context

Charlotte Square: well-mannered classicism.

Royal Mile, churches were built, namely John
Mylne's handsome **Tron Kirk** (1663, today
the Old Town Information Centre; *see p71*)
and the aristocratic and slightly Dutch-looking
Canongate Kirk (1688; *see p73*), with its
delicate, curving gables.

GETTING DOLLED UP

The 1707 Act of Union with England provoked
an identity crisis for Edinburgh, and some
dubbed the city 'a widowed metropolis'. But
Edinburgh, not given to extended periods of
mourning, soon came to see architecture as an
essential way of asserting the city's character.

The collapse in 1751 of a Royal Mile
tenement highlighted the old-fashioned and
run-down state of the Old Town and the need

for 'modern' living quarters. In 1752 the city's
Lord Provost, George Drummond, drew up
proposals to expand Edinburgh, creating the
grandiose **Exchange** (now the City Chambers)
on the Royal Mile and, in 1765, the **North
Bridge**. The Bridge, which was the first to
cross Nor' Loch, gave easy access to Leith and,
importantly, to a swathe of redundant land to
the north of the Old Town. This was to become
the site of the 'new towns', collectively known
as today's New Town.

Conceived as Edinburgh's 'civilised' face,
the first new town, designed in 1766 by James
Craig, was built to a regimented layout (*see p86*
The making of the New Town). Influenced
by the growing Europe-wide fascination with
the ancient Greek and Roman civilisations
and the increasingly popular fashion for
neoclassicism, Edinburgh's new architecture
adopted proportion, grandeur and classical
trimmings as its hallmarks.

A leading practitioner, Robert Adam, designed
Charlotte Square (from 1792; *see p88*), a
residential enclave acting as a grand full stop
to the west end of George Street. Its buildings
boasted rooftop sphinxes, balustrades and
fanlights (semicircular windows above the front
door) and, importantly after the cramped
conditions of the Old Town, the space of the
square itself. **Register House** (c1788, *see p85*),
on the axis of North Bridge, is another example
of Adam's well-mannered classicism. Its cupolas
and pedimented portico are a gracious retort to
the haphazard gables of the Old Town.

CLASSICAL REINVENTION

By the early 1800s, architecture had taken on an
increasingly crucial role in expressing the city's
newly cultivated identity. As early as 1762, it
was dubbed the 'Athens of the North'. The
city's topography made the analogy plausible
and, besides, Edinburgh liked the idea of being
an intellectual 'Athenian' metropolis compared
to the imperial 'Roman' capital, London.

As the Scottish Enlightenment (*see p15*) held
sway, the architect William Playfair provided a
stone and mortar representation of Calton Hill's
status as Edinburgh's 'Acropolis'. His **City
Observatory** (1818; *see p98*), a mini-cruciform
temple capped by a dome, stands next to his
Parthenon-esque **National Monument** (*see
p99*). Begun in 1826 to commemorate the
Napoleonic Wars, its 12 huge columns, set
on a vast stepped plinth, were an attempt to
provide the classical illusion to end all classical
illusions. But it remained unfinished due to
a funding crisis – earning it the nickname
'Edinburgh's Disgrace'. Later it formed a visual
link to Thomas Hamilton's **Royal High
School** (1829), on the lower slopes of Calton

Hill. Described as the 'noblest monument of the Scottish Greek revival', the structure was neoclassicism at its most authoritarian, with a central 'temple' flanked by grand antechambers.

On the Mound, meanwhile, the prolific Playfair produced further classical rhetoric in the form of the **Royal Scottish Academy** (1823; *see p84*) and the **National Gallery of Scotland** (1850; *see p83*), a monumental, temple-inspired duo parading an army of columns and classical trimmings.

On the residential front, a succession of upmarket new towns clustered around Craig's original. The ostentatiously wide **Great King Street** and the columned residences of **Moray Place** contributed to what was, by the 1840s, one of the most extensive and well-ordered neoclassical suburbs in Europe.

Punctuated by private 'pleasure gardens', the New Town gave urban living a picturesque rural charm and trumpeted Edinburgh as an ambitious and architecturally inspired city.

SCOTTISH BARONIAL STYLE AND ECLECTICISM

In 1822 George IV visited Edinburgh dressed in pink stockings and a kilt. His sartorial advisor was Sir Walter Scott, author and campaigner for the 'tartanisation' of Scotland.

With its internationalism established in the determinedly classical New Town, Edinburgh turned its attention to the home-grown architecture of the Old Town. The city's commercial, political and legal centre needed upgrading. The 1827 Improvement Act advised that new buildings and those in need of a facelift should adopt the 'Old Scot' style. Turrets, crenellations and crows' feet, à la Scots baronial, elbowed their way into the city's architecture; **Cockburn Street**, the first vehicular link between the Royal Mile and what is today Waverley Station, is a determined example.

Elsewhere, new public buildings masqueraded as rural piles airlifted from the Scottish Highlands. The **Royal Infirmary** (1870), to the south of the Royal Mile, sported a central clocktower and an array of turrets. **Fettes College** (1865-70; *see p94*), north of the New Town, was an exuberant intermarriage of local baronial seat and French chateau. The 'tartan touch' also hit the expanding tenement suburbs – **Marchmont**, to the south of the city, sports numerous turrets and gables.

This growing adventurousness gave way to architectural promiscuity. The city's well-off institutions showed confident but sometimes florid excess, with a pick and mix approach to building style. The headquarters of the **Bank of Scotland** (*see p87*), grandly posed on the precipice of the Mound, adopted full-on baroque;

the **British Linen Bank** (now a Bank of Scotland branch) on St Andrew's Square opted for the Renaissance palazzo look, its Corinthian columns topped by six colossal statues.

The Gothic revival also made its mark, courtesy of Augustus Pugin. The master of the decorated pinnacle and soaring spire designed the **Tolbooth Church** (1844) below Castle Esplanade. Today it is the Hub (*see p64*), a café and ticket centre run by the Edinburgh International Festival. But the finest line in romantic Gothic came in George Meikle Kemp's **Scott Monument** (1840; *see p86*) on Princes Street – an elaborate, filigreed, spire-like affair enshrining a statue of Sir Walter Scott.

MUSCULAR POST-MODERNISM

Little disturbed by industrialisation, late 19th-century Edinburgh saw no huge bursts of construction, and in the 20th century the impetus to build was further anaesthetised by two world wars. Europe-wide, clean-cut, 1930s modernism made little impression, save in the robustly authoritarian government edifice **St Andrew's House** (1937-39; *see p97*), on the lower reaches of Calton Hill. Designed by Thomas Tait, it is a true architectural heavyweight, with an imposing, symmetrical façade.

In the suburbs a few avant-garde adventurers experimented. The architect **William Kininmonth's house** in Dick Place (1933), with its cool play of curves and verticals, is one of the finest examples of the international style in Scotland.

> **'In 1949, the Abercrombie Plan saw slum tenements demolished, along with the grander George Square.'**

The redevelopment of the Old Town was the major planning and social issue during the first half of the 20th century. With the upwardly mobile residents siphoned off to the New Town, a large part of the Old Town had, by the Victorian era, developed into an overcrowded slum. As early as 1892 the influential urban planner Sir Patrick Geddes (who inspired the revamp of Ramsey Gardens, just below Castle Esplanade) had proposed seeding the area with members of the university as a means of adding to its intellectual weight. But his plan was not adopted.

Instead, by the inter-war years, residents were being encouraged to decamp to a series of council-built satellite townships on the periphery of the city, first among them the Craigmillar Estate. This social engineering, achieved through town planning, was a crude mirror of the earlier and socially exclusive

Freedom, at a price

From the 1970s there was a growing sense of disenfranchisement in Scotland. While the UK as a whole voted for four successive Tory governments, Scotland tended to vote Labour. The UK parliament in London was seen as distant and unrepresentative, and by the time the Labour Party finally won a general election, in 1997, change was in the air.

Within months there was a referendum in Scotland that gave overwhelming support to devolution, a process which would decentralise some of the powers exercised 'down south' and set up a parliament in Edinburgh. It was at this point that the fun started – architecturally speaking.

If you're going to have a parliament, you need a building to house it. In 1997 Government advisors estimating the cost of creating such a structure managed to pluck a figure of £40 million out of the air – a bizarrely low figure as things turned out. The first real controversy, however, was the refusal to consider the old Royal High School on Calton Hill as a potential home. The school had been the site of a spontaneous vigil for Scottish democracy that started after the 1992 UK general election and went on throughout the decade – perhaps making it something of a nationalist and separatist hot potato. Instead, it was decided, there would be a new building on Holyrood Road.

In 1998 prize-winning Catalan architect Enric Miralles was chosen to head up the project, in partnership with the Edinburgh-based firm RMJM. Miralles was much influenced by the natural forms in the work of Charles Rennie Mackintosh and, after a good look around Edinburgh, had decided the city had quite enough classical columns. When the designs for the parliament were published (leaf shapes, upturned boat shapes) the reaction was as petty-minded as it was

predictable. A fair proportion of the Scottish media and the public decided the whole business was fanciful, and the building costs only added fuel to their fire. The first wild guesstimate of £40 million paled into insignificance besides the reality of actually getting a modern design constructed on site. In summer 1999 a supposedly realistic budget was set at £109 million.

Meanwhile, the new Scottish parliament conducted its business at a temporary home in the Assembly Hall on the Mound. During the day-to-day running of the parliament it became clear that more support staff and more space would be needed once it moved to Holyrood. That meant revisions to Miralles's design – or a fudge – depending on your point of view. Add in building industry inflation and the odd contractor going bust, and costs rose quite spectacularly: by 2000 £200 million was being mentioned.

The project suffered two major setbacks later that year when first Miralles and then First Minister Donald Dewar died within a few months of each other. Dewar had been the central political figure in the whole project, Miralles was the artist. The costs kept rising regardless. By the end of 2001 estimates stood at £275 million and in spring 2002 they punched through the £300 million mark, with completion not planned until 2003 – well behind schedule.

Will it be worth it? Dewar certainly thought so. Miralles was an accomplished architect and the finished building should work well in its landscape, but public opinion remains divided. At the Scottish Parliament Visitor Centre on Holyrood Road (see p70), the visitors' book has scribbled comments such as 'a monumental waste of taxpayers' money'. But it also has 'absolutely fabulous'. Watch this space.

New Town. The fate of the increasingly depopulated Old Town however, remained in the balance.

In 1949, the Abercrombie Plan saw slum tenements demolished, along with the grander George Square, to create space for a new university campus. The sacrifice of George Square, in particular, its buildings replaced by unpopular 1960s-style architecture, sent a rallying call to the preservation troops. Much of the Old Town was saved as a result – thereafter resolutely contemporary architecture has dared

make only rare appearances in the Old Town. Even outside the Old Town there are few notable exceptions save the low-slung, glass-panelled **Royal Commonwealth Pool** (1967; see p225) and Basil Spence's **University Library** (1965) to the south. The city instead suffered explosions of 1960s brutalism, as seen in the ugly, blockish **St James Centre** just off Princes Street. The subsequent backlash sent the city planners into cautious mode, inviting accusations of architectural timidity. These reached their height in 1989 when a redundant site on the Royal Mile was filled by the Scandic Crown Hotel (now the **Crowne Plaza**), built in Old Town-imitation style.

A flirtation with late 20th-century architecture is shown in the Exchange, the city's new financial quarter to the west side of Lothian Road. Terry Farrell's **Edinburgh International Conference Centre** (1995) on Morrison Street forms the nucleus, with big-name companies inhabiting the surrounding office blocks. Edinburgh is the fourth largest financial centre in Europe, thanks to the efforts of actuaries and fund managers among others – not a species known for its adventurous artistic spirit. The frontage of **Festival Square** and **Standard Life House** (1997) are one-liners in an overly muscular commercial architecture; sad examples of modernism at its most mediocre. The **Standard Life Bank** building (2001), meanwhile, runs in an even more tedious sweep all the way from Clydesdale Bank Plaza to the conference centre. It is a little healthier at the Morrison Street side of Festival Square, though, which is dominated by the funky colours and glass of **One** (2001), the fitness centre extension at the rear of the Sheraton, designed by Sir Terry Farrell. However, the central parabolic sweep of the **Scottish Widows** building (1998) on Morrison Street itself still offers the only real gee-whizz design gesture in the whole Exchange precinct.

CATCHING UP

Despite the overall lack of imagination around the Exchange, contemporary Edinburgh does have some interesting buildings – the focus for many of these being the new Scottish

parliament on Holyrood Road (*see p30* **Freedom, at a price**); opposite the parliament sits Michael Hopkins' **Our Dynamic Earth** (*see p74*), a vast tent-like structure that opened in 1999. And in the closes and hidden streets between Holyrood Road and the Royal Mile there are a couple of real gems. The **Scottish Poetry Library** (*see p76*) in Crichton's Close was designed by Malcolm Fraser Architects and shortlisted for the Channel 4 Building of the Year Award in 2000. But the boldest flourish so far is the **Tun** in Holyrood Road (2002), a mix of offices and a café-bar in another former brewery building. It stands out as a prognathous glass challenge to the blandness of the new *Scotsman* newspaper offices over the way.

Leith has also seen major changes, with the arrival of the **Ocean Terminal** shopping centre (2001; *see p161*) near the Scottish Executive. Perhaps the biggest architectural hit of the last few years is the **Museum of Scotland** (*see p79*). Situated next to the Royal Museum of Scotland on the fringes of the Old Town, it was designed by architects Benson and Forsyth and opened in 1998. Built in sandstone, it is warmly monumental and topped by a vast turret. And, importantly, it is seen as successfully combining the resolutely contemporary with a sensitivity to Edinburgh's architectural past.

Having been accused of suffering from 'post-New Town siesta' syndrome by some critics, Edinburgh now seems more conscious of the need to protect its architectural heritage, wake up to the future, and ensure that the 'dream of a great genius' is an architectural reality.

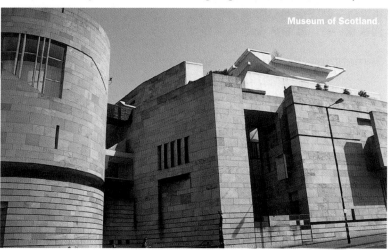
Museum of Scotland.

Maggie Smith in the film version of **The Prime of Miss Jean Brodie:** for many the ultimate Edinburgh novel.

Edinburgh in Fiction

Sometimes the city is the story.

From the dark wynds of the Old Town, with their dank ghosts and ancient corners, to the solid grey edifices and twitching curtains of the New Town; from the wide space of Princes Street, overlooked by the castle, to the claustrophobic thoroughfares of Leith, overlooked by high-rise blocks, Edinburgh is a city that could have been built to appear in fiction. It is small wonder that the City Library is able to devote a full card index to novels set, either wholly or partly, in the Scottish capital. If you had time to read them all – there were more than 400 at the last count – there are few parts of the city you would not encounter.

SETTING THE SCENE

Some writers use Edinburgh as a backdrop, a piece of scenery against which to set their fiction. In Iain Banks' novel *Complicity* (1993), the writer's trademark casual violence spills out into nightclubs and pubs across the city. Set in 1993, when the *Scotsman* newspaper was still based on North Bridge (now the Scotsman Hotel), it caused a stir when it was published, with every reviewer claiming to recognise the dope-smoking, fast-track hack hero, Cameron Colley. Isla Dewar makes stronger use of Edinburgh as a backdrop in *Women Talking Dirty* (1996), particularly in her portrayal of the suffocating middle-class suburb where co-heroine Ellen Quinn spends her childhood. James Meek, meanwhile, is almost merciless in steeping his heroine in a wintry 1980s Edinburgh in *McFarlane Boils the Sea* (1989). His poetic vision of the city is instantly recognisable to anyone who has been there.

Others weave the city rather more deeply into their stories. They use its different neighbourhoods – with their very distinct characters and atmospheres – to evoke and balance the tensions and complexities of the narrative. First among these, and the ultimate Edinburgh novel to many people, is Muriel Spark's *The Prime of Miss Jean Brodie* (1961). It could, possibly, have been set elsewhere, but schoolteacher Jean Brodie's character seems to get right into the very bones of the city's being; the passage where she takes her middle-class pupils into the Old Town slums is particularly evocative.

'Other writers use the narrative to explore the city and its complexities.'

William Boyd begins *The New Confessions* (1987) in Edinburgh. The city does not get a huge billing, but the perceptive portrait of the hero growing up in an austere 19th-century Edinburgh household forms an integral part of his characterisation. Few writers make better use of the city to evoke a particular atmosphere than Christina Koning in her brilliant *A Mild Suicide* (1992). Set in 1977, the year of the Queen's Silver Jubilee, it describes a tragic and adulterous love affair that takes place across the city. Wherever her characters go, from their first chat alone in a cramped Old Town pub to the blooming of their affair in a sprawling New Town flat, the state of their relationship is perfectly echoed by their location.

STARRING THE CITY AS ITSELF
For other writers, rarer these, Edinburgh is a character in itself: rather than being used to help the narrative along, the narrative is there to explore the city and its complexities. The most famous of these works is not, technically, an Edinburgh novel at all. Robert Louis Stevenson's *The Strange Case of Dr Jekyll and Mr Hyde* (1886) may be set in London, but it is nevertheless such a brilliant metaphor for Edinburgh's split personality – which Stevenson himself famously enjoyed when escaping his stultifying New Town home for the bought pleasures of Leith Walk – that it is hard to imagine that he would not rather have set it in Edinburgh.

Ian Rankin is Edinburgh's second most famous contemporary author (after JK Rowling, who hasn't actually written about the city). Rankin, whose astute and fast-paced detective fiction has won him prizes, is creator of policeman John Rebus, a fallible, not always likeable, but always convincing character. In the course of the 14 books in the Rebus series, all of which are set contemporaneously with their publication date, Edinburgh has become a character in its own right, which the novels set out to observe and explore. *Dead Souls* (1999), *Set in Darkness* (2000) and *The Falls* (2001) are particularly convincing examinations of turn-of-the-millennium Edinburgh.

In *The Fanatic* (2000), James Robertson combines modern and historical Edinburgh with the story of the strange Hugh Carlin, who is employed to portray the ghost of Major Weir, the 17th-century preacher who was strangled and burned as a witch, for one of the Royal Mile ghost tours. Carlin unearths more and more detailed information about the tyrannical puritanism and fanaticism of 1670s Scotland. The corruption of that era has a rather more gentle echo in the events of the 1997 election, which is the background to Carlin's search, when a Labour government came to power after 18 years of Conservative rule from London.

BEHIND THE GENTEEL FAÇADE
Edinburgh might make a pretty backdrop, but few writers get to grips with the reality of the modern city. Irvine Welsh was the first and most vocal of the new 'radge' generation of writers who were unafraid to talk about the drugs, clubs, drinking and violence that Edinburgh's more genteel residents would much rather ignore. *Trainspotting* (1993) was his first, most famous and certainly the best of his novels. Some of his later work was self-indulgent, but *Glue* (2001) is a much more mature, but no less visceral portrayal of the city seen through the eyes of four friends growing up there. For a less macho, but equally realistic vision of Edinburgh's underbelly, Laura Hird's *Born Free* (1999) can't be beaten. It's a brutal look at a hellish family life that is as hilarious as it is acerbic and well observed.

The antithesis of such gritty urban realism are the Festival novels. Although they may not tackle difficult contemporary issues, books like *Murder at the Fringe* (1987) by Gordon Demarco or *Festival* (1977) by Robert Blyth do succeed in capturing a summer snapshot of life in the city. The former serves as a sort of map of Edinburgh in 1987, while Blyth gives readers a taste of the International Festival as it was in the 1960s and '70s.

KIDS' STUFF

Edinburgh is also a popular setting for children's fiction. JK Rowling wrote the first Harry Potter books while living here, and although the city is not featured directly, Hogwarts School of Witchcraft and Wizardry is said to be based on Fettes College. *Maisie Comes to Morningside* (1984) and the many other 'Maisie' books by Aileen Paterson provide an exciting taste of the city for the very young. They're fun for adults too: Paterson's portrait of Morningside is brutally witty, featuring characters such as Mrs McKitty, Maisie's upstairs neighbour, who has a fastidious penchant for sweeping the stairs.

For teenagers, Honor Arundel's *The High House* (1967) is about a 13-year-old girl who goes to live with a dotty aunt in the tenements at the top of the Royal Mile when her parents are killed in a car crash. Arundel's casual use of the city as a backdrop is appealing and the book provides a well-drawn glimpse of the area in the 1960s. Molly Hunter is another Edinburgh writer of note. Several of her stories for older teenagers are set in the city; of these, *The Spanish Letters* (1964), set in 1589, and *The Lothian Run* (1971), set in 1736, are exciting historical yarns.

HISTORY, HORROR AND BODY BAGS

With the likes of Mary Queen of Scots having held their court in Edinburgh, it is unsurprising that a disproportionately large number of historical novels are set in the city or pass through it. However, the preeminent writer

Sir Walter Scott (1771-1832).

of historical Edinburgh novels has to be Walter Scott, who was so revered that Waverley Station was named after his novel *Waverley* (1814). *The Heart of Midlothian* (1818), *Red Gauntlet* (1824), *The Abbot* (1820) and *Guy Mannering* (1815) also draw on Edinburgh and its history for their narrative. James Hogg is another historical writer who used his own history to good effect. *The Private Memoirs & Confessions of a Justified Sinner*, first published in 1824, is an ironic jibe against the religious bigotry of the 17th and 18th centuries; it also contains a ghostly walk across Arthur's Seat that could be recreated to this day.

Edinburgh has its fair share of genre fiction as well. Surprisingly, horror is the least well served; perhaps writers are scared off by the success of *Dr Jekyll and Mr Hyde*. However, Jonathan Aycliffe uses the city well in *The Matrix* (1994), creating an air of Gothic claustrophobia into which the elements of magic and horror are easily dropped.

Detectives, however, are rife in Edinburgh's literary streets. So prevalent are they – and the crimes they investigate – that the annual fictional body count is at least ten times the real-life figure. To Ian Rankin and his creation John Rebus must be added the names of Alanna Knight and her Victorian detective Jeremy Faro, and Quintin Jardine, who writes about modern-day Edinburgh cop Inspector Skinner. Skinner is rather too perfect for comfort and reflects the morally aloof side of the city's psyche. *Skinner's Festival* (1994) is perhaps the best of this series.

TO INFINITY AND BEYOND

But what of the future? Well that's covered too. According to Paul Johnston's sci-fi series, in 2020 the city will become a city state on the Ancient Greek model, and Edinburgh will truly become the Athens of the North. In this city of the future, pop music, TV and private cars are banned, Edinburgh is dependent on its tourist income, and citizen Quintin Dalrymple is the only man left with the ability to solve crimes. *Water of Death* (1999) is the best of this series. And Ken MacLeod has great fun in generating a vision of a post-apocalyptic technological future for the opening book in his science fiction 'Engines of Light' series: *Cosmonaut Keep* (2000). This is 2049 Edinburgh with an ironic twist – or, perhaps, a reflection of the city as it is now.

▶ For further information on these and other Edinburgh books, *see chapter* **Further Reference**.

Accommodation

Accommodation   **36**

Features

The best hotel services   37
Modern times   45

Accommodation

A spate of major refurbishments has brought Edinburgh's hotels up to scratch.

Edinburgh hoteliers have always been able to attract top dollar for their rooms but, until very recently, this has not necessarily been reflected in the quality of accommodation. That situation has now changed, thanks largely to the success of the Edinburgh International Conference Centre in bringing high-spending – and very demanding – corporate clients into the city. With newer establishments raising the stakes in terms of overall standards and services, some of Edinburgh's more established hotels have had to dig deep and gamble on major refurbs just so they can stay in the game. Consequently, if you're planning a luxurious stay you can expect a high degree of comfort and plenty of choice.

Many hotels, particularly the biggest, are owned by large hotel groups. **Chain** hotels offer standard amenities and decor wherever they are in the world, which means that you know exactly what you're getting. This, however, is also their biggest drawback: if

A charmed hotel? **The Witchery**. *See p37*.

you want to capture something of the spirit of Edinburgh, look elsewhere. Luckily this is a city where intimate, traditional townhouse hotels such as **17 Abercromby Place** (*see p47*) or the **Albany Hotel** (*see p44*) are very much the norm. Even if you're paying budget prices, you still have the opportunity to stay in a converted Georgian house – try **Ailsa Craig Hotel** (*see p48*), the **Balfour Guest House** (*see p49*) or the **Claremont** (*see p49*).

Edinburgh is a compact city; if you stay near the centre, you'll find that many places are accessible on foot. But if being in the heart of town isn't crucial, you may prefer to opt for the coast – the regenerated Leith Docks, home to the landmark **Malmaison** (*see p53*) is only a 10-minute drive from the town centre.

RATES AND RESERVATIONS

At certain times of the year, significant savings can be made if you're prepared to wait until the last minute before booking. Most clued-up hoteliers would rather sell their beds at a discount than leave them empty, so always ask if stand-by rates are available. Some hotels offer this as standard, others will recognise it as a coded way of saying 'do me a deal'. This applies equally to the more expensive hotels – they may command top rates from business clients from Monday to Thursday, but at the weekends they rely on budget-conscious leisure travellers, same as everyone else. Bargain deals are increasingly commonplace – particularly from October to April when rates can drop by more than 50 per cent – but watch out for those major events that book out the whole city. If you're planning your visit during a major rugby international, Hogmanay, an international conference or weekends during August, our advice is simple: book early or pay dearly.

Hotels in this chapter have been arranged by area and placed into different categories according to the price of the cheapest double room with breakfast – usually continental. We've noted where breakfast costs extra. Room prices include VAT and are the standard, year-round rate.

Rates for **hostel** accommodation are given per person per night unless stated otherwise. The independent hostels get very busy, so try to book ahead if possible. If you intend staying out late, remember to check about curfews when booking.

The best Hotel services

Apex Hotels
If you're paying for a room for the night, why should you have to pay extra for overpriced soft drinks from the minibar? At Apex hotels, you don't have to – and there are free DVDs, CDs and PS2 games too. *See p39 and p52.*

Express by Holiday Inn
Home delivery menus from every local takeaway form an unofficial 'room service' menu at the Holiday Inn in Leith. Simple, but delicious. *See p53.*

Holyrood Hotel
For a small extra supplement, you can have the services of your very own butler to cater to your every whim. *See p39.*

Minto Hotel
If the unmistakeable strains of the bagpipes are music to your ears, you may appreciate the service at the budget Minto Hotel, where a piper calls in to serenade the guests every Saturday during the summer months. *See p51.*

The Scotsman
In addition to high-tech facilities and original artworks, rooms here boast a hole-in-the-wall feature – a serving hatch between the corridor and your hotel room that allows you to collect your club sandwich whenever it suits you. A brilliant idea for anyone who has ever had to step out of the bath to open the door for room service. *See p43.*

OTHER INFORMATION
Parking in Edinburgh can be very difficult, particularly in the centre of town and in residential areas. If you're travelling by car, you should check out the parking situation with the hotel before you arrive, especially if the parking is listed below as 'on street'.

Many hotels have disabled access and specially adapted rooms; the **Edinburgh & Lothians Tourist Board** (*see below*) will send you a list. Other advice is available from **Disability Scotland** and the **Lothian Coalition of Disabled People** (for both, *see chapter* **Resources A-Z**). Holiday accommodation solely for the disabled, their carers and guide dogs is provided by **Trefoil House** (*see p54*) to the west of the city.

Edinburgh & Lothians Tourist Board
Top floor of Waverley Shopping Centre, 3 Princes Street, New Town, EH2 2QP (473 3800/fax 473 3881/www.edinburgh.org). Princes Street buses. **Open** *Oct-Mar* 9am-5pm Mon-Wed; 9am-6pm Thur-Sat; 10am-5pm Sun. *Apr* 9am-6pm Mon-Sat; 10am-6pm Sun. *May, June, Sept* 9am-7pm Mon-Sat; 10am-7pm Sun. *July, Aug* 9am-8pm Mon-Sat; 10am-8pm Sun. **Booking fee** £3 plus 10% deposit (£1 per head for 4 or more). **Credit** MC, V. **Map** p309 F5.
The Tourist Board is a useful resource for the bed-seeking visitor: it can make reservations across the city from its office and grades accommodation using a star rating system based on the standard of furnishings and overall welcome.

Scottish Youth Hostel Association
7 Glebe Crescent, Stirling, FK7 2JA (01786 891 400/fax 01786 891 333/central reservations 08701 553 255/www.syha.org.uk). **Open** 9am-5pm Mon-Fri. **Membership** £6 per year.

The SYHA will provide information on accommodation in its hostels around Scotland. You have to be a member to stay in them, but you can join when you arrive for £6. In addition to the Bruntsfield (*see p51*) and the Eglinton (*see p52*), the SYHA operates the seasonal Pleasance Youth Hostel on New Arthur Place, South Edinburgh (open Aug only) and the new Edinburgh International Youth Hostel on Kincaids Court in the city centre (open July, Aug only). Phone for further information.

Hotels & Hostels

Old Town

Deluxe (over £175)

The Witchery by the Castle
Castlehill, EH1 2NF (225 5613/fax 220 4392/ www.thewitchery.com). Bus 23, 27, 35, 41, 42. **Rates** £195 suite. **Credit** AmEx, DC, MC, V. **Map** p309 E6.
Warm, incredibly romantic, charismatic and filled with history, the Witchery is not so much a hotel as a restaurant with six suites attached. The six suites are lavished with original antiques and ooze an air of self-indulgent decadence that simply cannot be manufactured. Many hotels – particularly in Edinburgh – try to replicate this level of traditional, opulent elegance, but this is the real deal.

Chairs made for Queen Victoria herself, furnishings from the House of Lords and the type of wallpaper that got Lord Irvine into trouble all clutter up the suites in beautifully chaotic style. For further proof that this place really is something special, check out the online guest book. If Andrew

Lloyd Webber was attracted by the Bose sound system in every room, you can imagine that Jack Nicholson and *The Simpsons*' creator Matt Groening might have appreciated the quirky touches: a kid's rubber duck nestling alongside a stuffed mallard in the bathroom; a fake plastic crown hanging over the throne-like lavatory. If you have the means – and if you can get a room – The Witchery is the place to indulge yourself.
Hotel services *Restaurant.* **Room services** *Complimentary champagne. TV: cable, VCR.*

Expensive (£110-£175)

Crowne Plaza

80 High Street, EH1 1TH (557 9797/fax 557 9789/ www.crowneplazaed.co.uk). Bus 35/Nicolson Street– North Bridge buses. **Rates** £110-£250 single/double; £250-£300 suites. **Credit** AmEx, DC, MC, V. **Map** p310 G5.

This turreted hotel may look like one of the original stone buildings on the Royal Mile but it was only actually constructed at the beginning of the 1990s. Bustling and modern within, it provides all of the benefits associated with an American chain. The Great Scottish Hall occasionally hosts ceilidhs and there's regular live music in the Piano Bar downstairs. The newly refurbished restaurant overlooks the cobbled High Street, and Carrubers bistro serves light lunches. Equidistant from the Castle and Holyrood Palace, it's a great spot for any Scottish-royalty-obsessed tourists. The Crowne also boasts that most elusive of features among Edinburgh hotels – ample car parking space.
Hotel services *Bar. Business services. Concierge. Disabled: access, adapted rooms (3). Gym. Limousine service. No-smoking rooms & floors. Parking. Restaurant. Swimming pool.* **Room services** *Dataport. Minibar. Refrigerator. Room service (24hr). TV: satellite.*

Holyrood Hotel

81 Holyrood Road, EH8 6AE (550 4500/fax 550 4545/www.macdonaldhotels.com). Bus 30, 35. **Rates** £90-£180 single; £110-£250 double; £165-£325 suite. **Credit** AmEx, DC, MC, V. **Map** p310 H5.

This brand-new hotel is located close to the offices of Scotsman Publications and the building site that is the new Scottish Parliament, so it comes as no surprise to find it has been built with business travellers in mind. That said, tourists will find it convenient too as it's close to the attractions of the Royal Mile, Dynamic Earth and Holyrood Palace. The brochure describes its look as 'bold contemporary style harmonising with the historic area'; we say it's a big yellow block. There's no denying the level of opulence and sophistication to which the Holyrood aspires, however; the marbled lobby sets the tone. There's an impressive gym, a swimming pool and, on the Club Floor, the services of a private butler to attend to your every whim.

Hotel services *Air-conditioning. Bars (2). Beauty salon. Business services. Concierge. Disabled: access, adapted rooms (16). Gym. No-smoking rooms. Parking. Restaurant. Swimming pool.*
Room services *Dataport. Minibar. Refrigerator. Room service (24hr). TV.*

Moderate (£70-£110)

Apex International Hotel

31-35 Grassmarket, Old Town, EH1 2HS (300 3456/fax 220 5345/www.apexhotels.co.uk). Bus 23, 27, 35, 41, 42. **Rates** from £80 single/double. **Credit** AmEx, DC, MC, V. **Map** p309 E6.

Refurbished, re-styled and re-launched in spring 2002, the Edinburgh-based Apex hotel group has undergone a transformation from comfortable but bland, mid-budget properties to sleek, stylish, designer luxury. With black rubberised floors, brown leather furnishings, American cherrywood panelling and shiny chrome fittings, the Apex International is the epitome of contemporary style with a retro twist. In the rooms, wardrobes hide minibars filled with soft drinks, while gadgetry includes Playstation 2, DVDs, CDs and interactive TVs. The Heights restaurant has what could be the city's finest views of Edinburgh Castle. The Apex European (*see p52*) is the International's sister hotel. At the time of writing, the new flagship property, Apex City in the Grassmarket, was still under construction. Early signs are promising, but if it is to achieve the superior four-star grading it's aiming for, it will have to make the rooms a little more spacious than those in the existing hotels.
Hotel services *Bar. Business services. Disabled: access, adapted rooms. No-smoking rooms. Parking. Restaurants.* **Room services** *Minibar. Refrigerator. Room service (24hr). TV: satellite.*

Bank Hotel

1 South Bridge, EH1 1LL (556 9940/fax 622 6822/ www.festival-inns.co.uk). Nicolson Street–North Bridge buses. **Rates** £65-£80 single; £75-£120 double/twin; £140 family. **Credit** AmEx, MC, V. **Map** p310 G5.

The Bank Hotel consists of nine rooms above Logie Baird's Bar (*see p149*) at the noisy intersection of the Royal Mile and the Bridges. The mood is determinedly Gaelic, with wood panelling and dark tartan. Each bedroom is individually themed around a famous Scot: the James Young Simpson room, for example, plays on the anaesthetic motif with anatomical sketches, bookcases and old potion bottles. Cheesy? Perhaps. But it all works surprisingly well, and it's good to see a hotel displaying a more original approach to its Scottish heritage than an excess of tartan and Ceud Mille Failte signs at every turn. The bar is open round the clock and executive rooms now feature added extras including a fridge, CD player and safe.
Hotel services *Bar. Parking. Restaurant.*
Room services *Dataport. Room service (24hr). TV: satellite.*

From newspaper empire to luxury hotel: **The Scotsman**. *See p43.*

Tailors Hall Hotel

139 Cowgate, EH1 1JS (622 6801/fax 622 6818/ www.festival-inns.co.uk). Nicolson Street–North Bridge buses. **Rates** £90 single; £110 double; £125 suite. **Credit** AmEx, DC, MC, V. **Map** p304 D3.

Anyone wishing to turn up the volume on their Festival experience should make this their base. With its Cowgate location, Tailors Hall is only five minutes from two of the Fringe super-venues, the Pleasance and the Gilded Balloon, and has the Three Sisters (*see p150*) – if not the most popular bar in town, then certainly the busiest – right under its feet. Built around a courtyard which acts as overspill for the bars, the 17th-century building houses a thoroughly modern interior. Rooms vary greatly in size and shape, but all are comfortable and clean. If you value your sleep, ask for the new wing, which is less noisy. Whichever room you plump for, take solace in the fact that earplugs are provided free of charge. **Hotel services** *Bars (3). Business services. Disabled: access, adapted rooms (4).* **Room services** *Room service (9am-9pm daily). TV.*

Travelodge

33 St Mary's Street, EH1 1TA (08701 911 637/ fax 557 3681/www.travelodge.co.uk). Nicolson Street–North Bridge buses. **Rates** (breakfast not incl) £69.95 double/family. **Credit** AmEx, DC, MC, V. **Map** 310 G5.

If you want a fair-sized room that's comfortable, clean and moments from the Royal Mile, then this is a good, moderately priced option.
Hotel services *Bar. Business services. Disabled: access, adapted rooms (11). No-smoking rooms. Parking (limited). Restaurant.* **Room services** *TV.*

Budget (under £60)

Hotel Ibis

6 Hunter Square, EH1 1QW (240 7000/fax 240 7007/www.ibishotel.com). Nicolson Street–North Bridge buses. **Rates** £45-£70 single; £55-£70 double. **Credit** AmEx, DC, MC, V. **Map** p304 D3.

This international chain has a reputation for efficiency and good value, but the downside is a certain bland anonymity. Because of its bright, modern style, designed to appeal to all, you're unlikely to appreciate the fact that you're right in the heart of the Old Town. Still, the rooms are comfortable and clean, rates are reasonable and the location is great for business or pleasure.
Hotel services *Air-conditioning. Bar. Disabled: access, adapted rooms (6). No-smoking rooms. Parking.* **Room services** *Dataport. TV: cable.*

Jurys Inn

43 Jeffrey Street, EH1 1DG (200 3300/fax 200 0400/www.jurys.com). Nicolson Street–North Bridge buses. **Rates** £47-£130 single/double. **Credit** AmEx, DC, MC, V. **Map** p310 G5.

This converted office block may not be the most attractive hotel in town, but few can match its ideal location. To the front lies Waverley Station, Princes

Street and the New Town, while the wynd to the rear leads up into the heart of the Royal Mile. The rooms are all identical, with double beds as standard and inoffensive, soft-coloured furnishings. With sparse public facilities, the Jurys encourages its guests to go out rather than stay in, although the less adventurous might appreciate the bar. Some rooms are partially adapted for the disabled.
Hotel services *Bar. Business services. Disabled: access, adapted rooms (2). No-smoking rooms. Parking (on street). Restaurant.* **Room services** *Dataport. TV: satellite.*

Hostels

Castle Rock Hostel

15 Johnston Terrace, EH1 2PW (225 9666/fax 226 5078/www.scotlands-top-hostels.com). Bus 23, 27, 35, 41, 42. **Beds** 250. **Open** *Reception* 24hrs daily. No curfew. **Rates** £11-£12. **Credit** AmEx, MC, V. **Map** p304 B3.

Edinburgh Backpackers Hostel

65 Cockburn Street, EH1 1BU (reception 220 1717/ fax 220 5143/reservations 220 2200/reservations fax 539 8695/www.hoppo.com). Nicolson Street–North Bridge buses. **Beds** 97 dorm; 3 double; 2 twin; 1 triple. **Open** *Reception* 24hrs daily. *Reservations* 9am-5.30pm Mon-Fri. No curfew. **Rates** *Dorm* Sept-Mar £12.50; Apr, May £13; June £13.50; July £14; Aug £15. *Double/twin* (price per room) Sept-Mar £42.50; Apr-June £44.50; July £46.50; Aug £49. *Triple* (price per room) Sept-Mar £55; Apr, May £57.50; June £58; July £60.50; Aug £64. **Credit** MC, V. **Map** p304 D3.

Edinburgh Central Youth Hostel

Robertson's Close, Cowgate, EH1 1LY (556 5566/central reservations 08701 553 255/www.syha.org.uk). Nicolson Street–North Bridge buses. **Beds** 200. **Open** (28 June-29 Aug) *Reception* 7am-11.30pm daily. No curfew. Closed 30 Aug-27 June. **Rates** £16-£18.50. **Credit** MC, V. **Map** p310 G6.

Royal Mile Backpackers

105 High Street, EH1 1SG (557 6120/fax 556 3999/ www.scotlands-top-hostels.com). Bus 35/Nicolson Street–North Bridge buses. **Beds** 38. **Open** *Reception* 7am-2.30am daily. No curfew. **Rates** £11-£12. **Credit** AmEx, MC, V. **Map** p304 D3.

New Town

Deluxe

The Balmoral

1 Princes Street, EH2 2EQ (556 2414/fax 557 3747/ www.thebalmoralhotel.com). Princes Street buses/ Nicolson Street–North Bridge buses. **Rates** £184-£260 single; £210-£315 double; £440-£1,100 suite. **Credit** AmEx, DC, MC, V. **Map** p304 D2.

The Balmoral has all the trappings you would expect from a top-drawer, classic hotel: marble floors, fine art, crystal chandeliers and service that

is always attentive but rarely intrusive. Sumptuous and stylish, the Balmoral is undoubtedly the most prestigious address for those keen to impress. However, some of the standard rooms do not justify the overblown prices – you may find yourself paying for the name and not for the product. If you have the means, fork out the extra for a castle-view room or splash out on one of the huge suites.
Hotel services *Air-conditioning. Babysitting. Bars (3). Beauty salon. Business services. Concierge. Disabled: access, adapted rooms (4). Gym. No-smoking rooms. Parking (valet). Restaurants (3). Swimming pool.* **Room services** *Dataport. Fax. Minibar. Refrigerator. Room service (24hr). TV: satellite.*

George Intercontinental

19-21 George Street, EH2 2PB (225 1251/fax 226 5644/www.edinburgh.interconti.com). Princes Street buses. **Rates** £185-£195 single; £205-£240 double; £520 suite. **Credit** AmEx, DC, MC, V. **Map** p304 C1.
The George is conveniently located on Edinburgh's smartest street in the town centre. The building was designed by George Adam in 1775, and its best feature is his trademark domed cupola in the roof of the opulent Carvers restaurant (renowned for its Sunday roasts). The east-wing bedrooms are aimed at the corporate guest – ten of the rooms have fully equipped office facilities – while the west wing has a softer 'classic country' style. Le Chambertin restaurant has two AA stars and is a favourite for business lunches. The place is mobbed by the media set during the television festival in August.
Hotel services *Babysitting. Bar. Business services. Concierge. Disabled: access, adapted rooms. Gym (not on site). Limousine service. No-smoking rooms. Parking. Restaurants (2).* **Room services** *Dataport. Minibar. Refrigerator. Room service (24hr). TV: satellite.*

The Hilton Caledonian

4 Princes Street, EH1 2AB (222 8888/fax 222 8889/www.hilton.com). Princes Street buses. **Rates** £155-£180 single; £215-£245 double; £280-£875 suite. **Credit** AmEx, DC, MC, V. **Map** p304 A2.
Recently acquired as the Scottish flagship of the Hilton chain, the grand old dame of Princes Street was once in danger of becoming as pathetic a figure as Norma Desmond in *Sunset Boulevard.* Trading primarily on reputation, the hotel had a hard time convincing the public that she had more to offer than a grandiose Edwardian façade. Following extensive refurbishment, however, the huge Caledonian has been brought back to its former glory. It steadfastly refuses to follow any current design trends, retaining instead a sense of a bygone Edwardian era throughout: huge arched corridors lead past grand staircases with stained-glass windows. Elegant, opulent and more than a little ostentatious, the Caledonian has a warm, luxurious feel. A high standard of service has made it a favourite of auspicious guests over the years, including Sean Connery and Nelson Mandela. After an investment of £8 million, the old dame is back to her best.

Hotel services *Babysitting. Bar (3). Beauty salon. Business services. Concierge. Disabled: access, adapted rooms (4). Garden. Gym. Limousine service. No-smoking rooms. Parking. Restaurants (3). Swimming pool.* **Room services** *Dataport. Minibar. Room service (24hr). TV: satellite.*

The Howard

34 Great King Street, EH3 6QH (557 3500/ reservations 315 2220/fax 557 6515/www.the howard.com). Bus 19A, 23, 27, 28. **Rates** £140 single; £245-£275 double; £325-£475 suite. **Credit** AmEx, DC, MC, V. **Map** p306 E3.
This discreet terraced residence only reveals its identity through the brass plaque on the front door. The hotel is a perfect example of how successfully to combine Georgian style and architecture with contemporary comfort and luxury. The breakfast room overlooks Great King Street, a cobbled thoroughfare that was built as Edinburgh's 'second New Town' *(see p90).* Inside, there are original 19th-century murals, some of which are so fragile they have had to be papered over to preserve them. Each of the 15 rooms at the Howard is decorated individually – the Abercrombie Suite, for example, has a four-poster bed. Large bathrooms, state-of-the-art showers with steam jets and rolltop baths are luxurious bonuses.
Hotel services *Business services. No-smoking rooms. Parking.* **Room services** *Dataport. Room service (24hr). TV: cable.*

The Scotsman

20 North Bridge, EH1 1YT (556 5565/fax 652 3652/www.thescotsmanhotel.co.uk). Nicolson Street-North Bridge buses. **Rates** (breakfast not incl) £175 single/double; £350-£950 suite. **Credit** AmEx, DC, MC, V. **Map** p304 D2.
Opened in April 2001 in the former home of the Scotsman newspaper group, this hotel has become the benchmark in the five-star bracket. With far fewer rooms than other de luxe hotels, the Scotsman was always going to have a more exclusive appeal, but this is not solely a result of its limited room numbers. The designers have preserved and restored the historic building's original features – elegant cornicing, marble floors, walnut panelling and stained-glass windows – while packing the hotel with a whole host of innovations. Interactive TVs, DVD players and Molton Brown toiletries may be de rigueur for luxury hotels these days, but the Scotsman takes the concept of added extras to a whole new level. Each room is individually styled with original art and exclusive estate tweeds, in place of bulk-bought fabrics; each has a well-stocked and competitively priced private wine bar (full bottles – not halves) and Edinburgh Monopoly tables. In fact, it's worth the premium prices for the breakfast alone – a riot of colour with fresh fruits, cold meats and cheeses and ten types of sausage. Add a state-of-the-art gym, 60m pool and a classy, informal grill room and the result is a broadsheet property in a tabloid world.

Expensive

Albany Hotel

39-43 Albany Street, EH1 3QY (556 0397/fax 557 6633/www.albanyhoteledinburgh.co.uk). Bus 8/ Playhouse buses. **Rates** *(breakfast not incl) £85-£115 single; £120-£185 double; £185-£225 suite.* **Credit** *AmEx, MC, V.* **Map** *p306 F4.*

Tucked away in a corner of the New Town, yet only minutes from Princes Street and Broughton, the Albany is a discreet and charming gem of a hotel. Despite a touch of over-kill with some of the period features, the Georgian-style rooms – all rich red fabrics and warm mahogany tones – are inviting and homely. Quiet, intimate and with a high standard of personal service, this would be a good hotel for a romantic weekend.

Hotel services *Babysitting. Bar. Business services. No-smoking rooms. Parking (on street). Restaurant.* **Room services** *Dataport. Minibar. Room service (7-10am, 6-9pm daily). TV: satellite.*

The Bonham

35 Drumsheugh Gardens, EH3 7RN (226 6050/ reservations 623 6060/fax 226 6080/www. thebonham.com). Bus 19, 29, 29A, 37, 37A, 41, 42. **Rates** *£135 single; £165-£225 double/twin; £295 suite.* **Credit** *AmEx, DC, MC, V.* **Map** *p308 C5.*

Ever-popular with style-conscious visitors, the townhouse exterior of the Bonham houses a contemporary blend of comfortable, light minimalism that avoids becoming too Starck. Neutral colours with some bright splashes and art deco furniture complement the high ceilings and cornices of the original Victorian building. Several Edinburgh hotels have attempted this fusion of modern style with traditional features, but few have achieved it as successfully. All this and a great location on a quiet, residential street in the West End: no wonder it is a former recipient of the AA Hotel of the Year award in Scotland.

Hotel services *Babysitting. Business services. Concierge. Disabled: access, adapted room. Limousine service. No-smoking rooms. Parking (on street). Restaurant.* **Room services** *Dataport. Minibar. Room service (24hr). TV: cable, DVD.*

Melvin House Hotel

3 Rothesay Terrace, EH3 7RY (225 5084/fax 226 5085/www.melvinhouse.co.uk). Bus 19, 29, 29A, 37, 37A, 41, 42. **Rates** *£75-£100 single; £120-£160 double.* **Credit** *AmEx, DC, MC, V.* **Map** *p308 B5.*

Former home of the founder of *The Scotsman* newspaper, Melvin House combines startling original features with modern home comforts. With its fine oak panelling, wonderful gallery library and beautifully carved staircase, this is the kind of house where you expect to find that Colonel Mustard did it in the study with the candlestick.

Privately owned, the hotel offers friendly, personal service more in keeping with a B&B than an upmarket hotel. The location is perfect – a quiet

The Bonham: a fusion of old and new.

Hotel services *Air-conditioning. Babysitting. Bars (2). Beauty salon. Business services. Concierge. Disabled: access, adapted rooms (3). Gym. No-smoking rooms. Parking. Restaurant. Swimming pool.* **Room services** *Dataport. Minibar. Room service (24hr). TV: cable, DVD.*

residential street, minutes from the West End and with fine views over the greenery of the Dean Village. After the splendour of the public areas, the rooms are disappointingly modern, but this is a minor gripe. A real find.
Hotel services Bar. No-smoking rooms. Parking (on street). **Room services** TV.

Roxburghe Hotel
38 Charlotte Square, EH2 4HG (240 5500/fax 240 5555/www.macdonaldhotels.co.uk). Princes Street buses. **Rates** (breakfast not incl) £60-£130 single; £110-£180 double; £210-£300 suite. **Credit** AmEx, DC, MC, V. **Map** p304 A1.
Despite costing more than building a new hotel from scratch, the major refurbishment of the 197-room Roxburghe has paid off. The façade of this cornerstone of Charlotte Square is still faithful to Robert Adam's Georgian design, but the interior has been totally transformed into an (almost seamless) blend of 19th-century elegance and 21st-century style. The huge leather armchairs sit comfortably on the stylish beechwood floors in the lobby, while the contemporary furnishings feel at home amid the high ceilings and delicate cornices of the sizeable bedrooms. Some of the rooms in the extension at the back are a little featureless, but are nevertheless comfortable. Nostalgic locals may mourn the loss of some of the Roxburghe's original character and natural charm, but perhaps that's the price you pay for a facelift.
Hotel services Bars (2). Beauty salon. Business services. Concierge. Disabled: access, adapted rooms (6). Gym. No-smoking rooms. Parking (on street). Restaurant. Swimming pool. **Room services** Dataport. Room service (24hr). TV: satellite.

Royal Scots Club
30 Abercromby Place, EH3 6QE (556 4270/fax 558 3769/www.scotsclub.co.uk). Bus 23, 27, 28. **Rates** £110 single; £140-£160 double; £200 suite. **Credit** AmEx, DC, MC, V. **Map** p306 E4.
The gentleman's club vibe is very much in evidence on entering this classic Georgian townhouse. The Royal Scots Club was founded in 1919 as a tribute to those who fell in the Great War, and today the air of tranquillity and strong sense of history is palpable and genuine. The rooms, originally built for members wishing to stay overnight, have undergone extensive refurbishment in recent years. All are tastefully furnished in a traditional style, some with four-poster beds and fine views towards the Firth of Forth. The cosy atmosphere and classic features extend into every room, from the lounge with the real fire to the elegant restaurant. Here you'll find some fine Scottish fare and old-fashioned puddings (as opposed to 'desserts'). The Scots Club is minutes away from Princes Street yet a million miles from the commercial modernity of that thoroughfare.
Hotel services Bar. Business services. Concierge. Garden. Gym. Parking (on street). Restaurant. **Room services** Room service (24hr). TV: cable.

Modern times

The Georgian townhouse hotel, complete with antique furnishings and atmosphere of timeless graciousness, is very much an Edinburgh classic (the **Royal Scots Club**, see below, is a typical example).
But if you like your style modern and lines minimal, don't despair. You won't have to jettison your aesthetics when you visit the city. The **Bonham** (see p44), for example, successfully fuses Victorian high ceilings and cornices with contemporary furniture and neutral colours (with the odd bright splash). Meanwhile, over at **Channings** (see p48), the chintz has been ripped out of the Edwardian premises in favour of beech floors and colours from the cream-to-chocolate palette.
Architects and designers have also been at work on Edinburgh's disused buildings. The old seamen's mission at Leith docks is now one of the city's most stylish hotels, the sleek and chic **Malmaison** (see p53). And on the other side of town, another conversion – the work of architect Andrew Doolan – has transformed an old factory into the **Point Hotel** (see p49), where space, light and rounded lines make for a relaxing kind of minimalism.

Moderate

Carlton
North Bridge, Edinburgh, EH1 1SD (472 3000/fax 556 2691/www.paramount-hotels.co.uk). Nicolson Street–North Bridge buses. **Rates** £70 single; £110 double. **Credit** AmEx, DC, MC, V. **Map** p304 D2.
Straddling North Bridge, the Carlton offers fine views of the city from each and every room – something which even its five-star competitors cannot match. It has also undergone a dramatic transformation in the past 12 months – and not before time. Every room has been gutted and revamped, every fabric changed and some of the smallest rooms have been sacrificed to make space for enlargements elsewhere. However, despite a multi-million pound investment, this is a fairly conservative renovation that may not suit those seeking cutting-edge style or all mod cons. It's also worth noting that, so far, the extensive leisure facilities and swimming pool have not benefitted from the much-needed refurbishment.
Hotel services Air-conditioning. Babysitting. Bar. Beauty salon. Business services. Concierge. Disabled: access, adapted rooms. Gym. No-smoking floors. Restaurants. Swimming pool. Valet parking. **Room services** Dataport. Minibar. Room service (24hr). TV.

The original grand staircase at the **Melvin House Hotel**. *See p44.*

Greens Hotel

24 Eglinton Crescent, EH12 5BY (337 1565/
fax 346 2990/www.british-trust-hotels.co.uk).
Bus 12, 21, 25, 26, 31, 33, 44. **Rates** £55-£85
single; £80 £120 double. **Credit** AmEx, DC, MC, V.
Map p308 B6.
Just north of Haymarket Station, this Georgian
townhouse houses a warm, traditional hotel located
in a secluded residential street. Like Carlton Greens
(*see p48*), it is owned and managed by a charitable
trust. The guest rooms offer good quality consider-
ing the price and the best have lovely views of
Edinburgh Castle.
Hotel services *Bar. Business services. Concierge.*
Disabled: access. Garden. No-smoking rooms.
Parking (on street). Restaurant. **Room services**
Room service (24hr). TV.

17 Abercromby Place

Abercromby House, 17 Abercromby Place, EH3
6LB (557 8036/fax 558 3453/www.abercromby
house.com). Bus 23, 27, 28. **Rates** £45-£60 single;
£90-£120 double. **Credit** MC, V. **Map** p306 E4.
The apotheosis of the townhouse hotel can be found
in Edinburgh, particularly in the Georgian New
Town, where the architecture, atmosphere and aloof
gentility rub off on the area's numerous hotels.
The Lloyd family's townhouse is one of the best.
Formerly the home of the distinguished architect
William Playfair, it is located on one of the New
Town's most sought-after cobbled streets, opposite
Queen Street gardens. Five stunning floors retain
their original features and display the family's col-
lection of antiques, paintings and tapestries. The

nine rooms are large, with bay windows looking on
to the Forth estuary and Fife hills. Evening meals
are available by arrangement and pets are allowed
with advance notice.
Hotel services *Business services. Garden.*
No smoking. Parking. **Room services** *Dataport.*
Refrigerators (3 rooms). TV: cable.

Budget

Frederick House Hotel

42 Frederick Street, New Town, EH2 1EX (226
1999/fax 624 7064/www.townhousehotels.co.uk).
Bus 28, 29, 37/Princes Street buses. **Rates** £40-£90
single; £50-£120 double; £130-£220 suite. **Credit**
AmEx, DC, MC, V. **Map** p304 B1.
The Frederick House Hotel is bang in the centre of
town, near St Andrew Square bus station and
Waverley train station. The listed building has been
transformed from offices into five floors of bedrooms
in patterned greens, golds and reds; the best rooms
are at the front of the hotel, while the Skyline suite
has views across to the Forth. Breakfast is taken in
Rick's bar opposite the hotel (and is included in the
tariff; *see p153*).
Hotel services *Parking (on street).* **Room**
services *Dataport. Refrigerator. TV: satellite.*

Grosvenor Gardens Hotel

1 Grosvenor Gardens, EH12 5JU (313 3415/fax
346 8732/www.stayinedinburgh.com). Bus 12, 21,
25, 26, 31, 33, 44. **Rates** £45-£65 single; £50-£135
double; £75-£200 family room. **Credit** MC, V.
Map p308 B6.

Tucked away in a quiet cul-de-sac, this hotel is sumptuously swathed in cream, gold and pink. The eight large bedrooms have high ceilings and bay windows, but the en suite bathrooms are small. It's immaculately kept and exudes tranquillity and style. **Hotel services** *Bar. Garden. Parking (on street).* **Room services** *TV.*

Hostels

Princes Street East Backpackers

5 West Register Street, EH2 2AA (556 6894/fax 557 3236/www.princesstbackpackers.com). Princes Street buses/Nicolson Street–North Bridge buses. **Beds** 120. **Open** *Reception* 24hrs daily. No curfew. **Rates** £10 per person dorm; £28 per room double/twin. **Credit** MC, V. **Map** p304 D1.

Stockbridge

Deluxe

Channings

15 South Learmonth Gardens, EH4 1EZ (315 2226/reservations 332 3232/fax 332 9631/www.channings.co.uk). Bus 19, 29, 37, 41, 42. **Rates** £140-£160 single; £185-£210 double/twin; £250 suite. **Credit** AmEx, DC, MC, V. **Map** p305 B4.
This popular hotel in an Edwardian terrace has recently finished a major revamp to bring it more in line with its sister hotels, the Bonham (*see p44*) and the Howard (*see p43*). Gone is the flowery chintz and the country cottage feel, although the hotel has retained its homely character and air of hushed intimacy. Starting with the lower ground floor (which the owners refuse to call the basement), the rooms have been brought bang up to date with stylish chequer-board carpets and single-colour fabrics in mushrooms and creams. The upper floors have been updated rather than redesigned, but have the advantage of terrific views of Fettes School – Tony Blair's alma mater and, according to popular wisdom, inspiration for Harry Potter's Hogwarts. Most striking of all is the new bar and restaurant, decked out with beech floors, rich red walls and brass fittings. The Channings has always had a good reputation for food, but now it has the stylish surroundings to match.
Hotel services *Babysitting. Bar. Business services. Garden. No-smoking rooms. Parking (on street). Restaurant.* **Room services** *Dataport. Room service (24hr). TV: satellite.*

Calton Hill & Broughton

Expensive

Parliament House Hotel

15 Calton Hill, EH1 3BJ (478 4000/fax 478 4001/www.scotland-hotels.co.uk). Playhouse buses. **Rates** (breakfast not incl) £100 single; £150 double; £190 suite. **Credit** AmEx, DC, MC, V. **Map** p307 G4.

Located next to Calton Hill, this hotel was named before the decision to locate the Scottish Parliament at Holyrood rather than at the nearby Royal High School. The rooms are medium sized and have comfortable furnishings. If the busy, navy-patterned wallpaper is too straining on the eye, the views across to Leith and the Forth are far more pleasant. Full Scottish breakfasts are served in the MPs' Bistro. **Hotel services** *Bar. Business services. Disabled: access, adapted rooms (3). Parking (on street). Restaurant.* **Room services** *Dataport. Minibar. Refrigerator. Room service (7-10am, 6-9.30pm). TV.*

Moderate

Carlton Greens Hotel

2 Carlton Terrace, EH7 5DD (556 6570/fax 557 6680/www.british-trust-hotels.com). Bus 5, 15, 19, 26. **Rates** £45-£65 single; £85-£110 double. **Credit** MC, V. **Map** p307 J4.
This Georgian townhouse property is hidden down a quiet residential street under Calton Hill, only ten minutes' walk from Princes Street. A recent refurbishment has modernised the public areas but, like its sister establishment, Greens (*see p47*), this hotel still offers good-quality rooms at a realistic price. **Hotel services** *Bar. Disabled: adapted rooms (2). Garden. No-smoking rooms. Parking (on street). Restaurant.* **Room services** *Room service (8am-11pm). TV.*

Le Meridien Hotel

18 Royal Terrace, EH7 5AQ (557 3222/fax 557 5334/www.lemeridien.com). Playhouse buses. **Rates** £135 single; £175-£205 twin/double; £255 suite. **Credit** AmEx, DC, MC, V. **Map** p307 H4.
Recent developments elsewhere in the city left the former Royal Terrace Hotel lagging behind, but a buyout by Le Meridien group could mean a much-needed injection of cash is in the offing. Designed by William Playfair in 1822, this quiet terrace sits beneath Calton Hill with views towards Leith. The Georgian opulence (now a little faded) is echoed in the swags and flounces of the soft furnishings and chandeliers, but contemporary touches include a small gym and pool in the basement. The courtyard garden, with its life-size chess board and fountain is popular in the summer months. Rooms on the top floor are small due to the sloped attic ceilings. **Hotel services** *Babysitting. Bar. Business services. Concierge. Garden. Gym. Limousine service. No-smoking rooms. Parking (on street). Restaurant. Swimming pool.* **Room services** *Dataport. Minibar (on request). Room service (24hr). TV: satellite.*

Budget

Ailsa Craig Hotel

24 Royal Terrace, EH7 5AH (556 1022/fax 556 6055/www.townhousehotels.co.uk). Playhouse buses. **Rates** £25-£55 single; £45-£90 double; family rooms negotiable. **Credit** AmEx, DC, MC, V. **Map** p307 H4.

Like its sister hotel, Greenside, just a few doors down (9 Royal Terrace; 557 0022), Ailsa Craig boasts big, clean rooms that have retained their original Georgian features. Though they're a bit on the basic side, some have views towards the Forth and all enjoy the quiet of this residential crescent. The rooms at Ailsa Craig tend to be bigger than those at Greenside, and some are kitted out with five beds. Both hotels are popular with local people in town to see a show at the nearby Playhouse Theatre, and also with low-budget and student groups. Evening meals are available on request.

Hotel services *Bar. Garden. Parking (on street).* **Room services** *TV.*

Balfour Guest House

90-92 Pilrig Street, EH6 5AY (554 2106/fax 554 3887). Bus 7, 10, 11, 12, 14, 16, 22. **Rates** *£20-£35 single; £30-£60 double.* **Credit** *AmEx, DC, MC, V.* **Map** p307 H1.

Isabel and Richard Cowe's large Georgian house is often full of visiting school parties enjoying some friendly hospitality. The central location, with free parking and a mini-bus to ferry visitors around makes this a popular choice for groups, who can take advantage of dinner in the basement dining room and packed lunches on request. The rooms are all reasonably furnished but do not have telephones. Limited business services are available from reception and there's cable TV in the lounge.

Hotel services *Bar. Garden. Mini-bus taxi service. Packed lunches. Parking (on street). Restaurant.* **Room services** *Room service (8am-9pm).*

Claremont

14-15 Claremont Crescent, EH7 4HX (556 1487/fax 556 7077). Bus 8. **Rates** *£25-£35 single; £50-£70 double.* **Credit** *AmEx, DC, MC, V.* **Map** p306 F2.

This hotel comprises two huge Georgian houses knocked into one. The reception area is sparse and the rooms are clean, comfortable and very large, with views of Arthur's Seat and the Forth. The place is a hive of activity, with quiz nights in the public bar and a disco downstairs. Full Scottish breakfast and evening meals are available, too. Parking is at the rear of the hotel.

Hotel services *Bar. Parking.* **Room services** *TV.*

South Edinburgh

Expensive

Point Hotel

34 Bread Street, EH3 9AF (221 5555/fax 221 9929/ www.point-hotel.co.uk). Bus 1, 10, 11, 16, 17, 28, 34, 35. **Rates** *£95-£110 single; £120-£140 double/ twin; £200 suite.* **Credit** *AmEx, DC, MC, V.* **Map** p309 D6.

Owned and designed by architect Andrew Doolan, this 140-room hotel epitomises state-of-the-art metropolitan minimalism. Clean lines, sweeping curved walls and blocks of soft colour (a painter is in residence for touch-ups) give a feeling of

fluidity and space. The white bedrooms – some with wide stripes of colour – plus black leather furniture and low-level beds swathed in white linen, have an understated simplicity, but there's no compromise on comfort. The executive suites are huge, as are the bathrooms; some have square jacuzzis, which are lit internally. Environmentally friendly sensor heating clicks on as you enter the rooms, some of which have Castle views. The ground-floor restaurant serves mainly modish European dishes with a local flavour, with some classics and the occasional eastern fusion dish thrown in – three courses are a mere £14.90. The glass-fronted Monboddo bar is popular (*see p156*). We've found staff friendly and helpful.

Hotel services *Bar. Disabled: access, adapted rooms. No-smoking rooms. Parking (on street). Restaurant.* **Room services** *Room service (11am-11pm). TV.*

Prestonfield House Hotel

Priestfield Road, Prestonfield, EH16 5UT (668 3346/fax 668 3976/www.prestonfieldhouse.com). Bus 2, 14, 21, 33. **Rates** *£145-£185 single; £145-£245 double; £325-£490 suite.* **Credit** *AmEx, DC, MC, V.*

Built in 1687 and former home to the Lord Provost, this country house nestling below Arthur's Seat is surrounded by parkland. The heavy cornicing and plasterwork on the ceilings (allegedly by the craftsmen who worked on the Palace of Holyroodhouse) give the house its Jacobean character. The hotel was recently extended, but, fortunately, the contemporary comfort of the new wing is very much in keeping with the atmosphere of the house. Access to the adjacent 18-hole golf course adds to the unique appeal of this spacious, peaceful manor house with the city right on its doorstep.

Hotel services *Babysitting. Bar. Business services. Disabled: access, adapted rooms (2). Garden. No-smoking rooms. Parking. Restaurant.* **Room services** *Dataport. Room service (24hr). TV: satellite.*

Moderate

Simpsons Hotel

79 Lauriston Place, EH3 9HZ (622 7979/fax 622 7900/www.simpsons-hotel.com). Bus 23, 27. **Rates** *£70-£95 single; £85-£130 double; £140 suite.* **Credit** *AmEx, DC, MC, V.* **Map** p309 E7.

Unfussy and unpretentious, this is a smart, no-frills establishment. Formerly a maternity hospital, Simpsons has been reborn as a hotel that uses the building's characteristics to positive effect. Natural daylight in the window-lined corridors gives it a comfortable, airy feel rarely found in other hotels. Rooms are all of a fair size, with contemporary fabrics in pastels and greys – nothing spectacular, but comfortable, with all mod cons.

Hotel services *Babysitting. Bar. Business services. Concierge. Disabled: access, adapted rooms (3). Parking (on street). Restaurant.* **Room services** *Dataport. Room service (7am-10pm daily). TV: satellite.*

Budget

Minto Hotel

16-18 Minto Street, EH9 9RQ (668 1234/fax 662 4870/www.edinburghmintohotel.co.uk). Bus 7, 8, 31, 80. **Rates** £45-£60 single; £50-£95 double; £95-£120 family room. **Credit** AmEx, DC, MC, V.

The Minto Hotel provides a cheap stopover for groups. There's invariably a wedding or party taking place in the hotel's function suite and a piper calls every Saturday to pipe in the happy couple during the summer months. Sporting heavily patterned decor in pinks and blues, the Minto is fairly basic but comfortable. It's the warmth of the welcome that keeps the regulars flocking back.

Hotel services *Bar. Business services. Concierge. Disabled: access, adapted rooms (2). Garden. No-smoking rooms. Parking (limited). Restaurant.* **Room services** *Dataport. Room service (7am-9.15pm daily). TV.*

Nova Hotel

5 Bruntsfield Crescent, EH10 4EZ (447 6437/fax 452 8126/www.infotel.co.uk). Bus 11, 15, 16, 17, 23. **Rates** £35-£55 single; £60-£90 double; £80-£150 family room; £350-£1,000 apartment (up to 8 people). **Credit** AmEx, DC, MC, V.

This Victorian building to the south of the city is just off Bruntsfield Links. Rooms vary in size; all are spacious, some are huge, with more than enough room for five single beds, and there are also two recently added luxury apartments catering for up to eight people. The Nova has a pleasant and relaxing bar with the atmosphere and decor of a traditional pub – and there are plenty more pubs to choose from in the local area. What's more, it's only ten minutes from the heart of town, so guests will never feel too far from the action.

Hotel services *Babysitting. Bar. Business services. Garden. No-smoking rooms. Parking. Restaurant.* **Room services** *Room service (24hr). TV: satellite.*

Sutherland House

16 Esslemont Road, EH16 5PX (tel/fax 667 6626). Bus 3, 7, 8, 24, 31, 32, 33, 37, 38, 42, 49, 52. **Rates** £25-£50 single/double; long term lets available from £70 per week. **No credit cards**.

Mayfield Road to the south of the city is where you will find countless B&Bs of varying quality and price. For the best of both worlds, however, keep travelling south until you reach this wonderful three-bedroom property near the Cameron Toll shopping centre. With the style and comfort of a three-star hotel but the warmth and welcome of a guesthouse, the quiet sophistication of Sutherland House is disturbed only by the occasional bark from the owner's friendly dalmatian. It's not often that you can describe bed and breakfast accommodation as 'elegant'; this place is a notable and welcome exception.

Hotel services *Garden. No-smoking. Parking.* **Room services** *TV.*

Town House Guesthouse

65 Gilmore Place, Tollcross, EH3 9NU (229 1985/ www.thetownhouse.com). Bus 1, 10, 11, 15, 16, 17, 23, 27. **Rates** £30-£38 single; £60-£76 double. **No credit cards. Map** p309 D7.

This detached Victorian house sits next to a church on a busy route into town. It's close to the major theatres and, therefore, a popular Festival stopover. Spread over three floors, the house is very comfortable and is run with pride by its amiable hostess, Susan Virtue. Everywhere is clean and well maintained, although the bathrooms tend to be on the small side and there are no phones in the rooms. The owners also have a self-catering apartment in Newington, which can be rented for several nights or by the week.

Hotel services *No smoking. Parking.* **Room services** *TV.*

Hostels

Edinburgh Bruntsfield Youth Hostel (SYHA)

7 Bruntsfield Crescent, EH10 4EZ (447 2994/ central reservations 08701 553 255/fax 452 8588/ www.syha.org.uk). Bus 11, 15, 16, 17, 23. **Beds** 132. **Open** *Reception 7am-11pm daily. No curfew.* **Rates** (membership not incl) Sept-May £11.50; June, July £12.50; Aug £14.50. **Credit** MC, V.

West Edinburgh

Deluxe

Sheraton Grand Hotel

1 Festival Square, Lothian Road, EH3 9SR (229 9131/fax 229 6254/www.sheraton.com/grand edinburgh). Bus 10, 11, 16, 17. **Rates** (breakfast not incl) £174-£230 single; £214-£270 double; £300-£395 suite. **Credit** AmEx, DC, MC, V. **Map** p309 D6.

This imposing concrete hotel block next to the Edinburgh International Conference Centre is always swarming with business delegates. Recent modifications to create a more Scottish ambience mean the staff now wear tartan uniforms, but the feeling that you could be anywhere in the world remains. The mood at the Sheraton is brisk; marble, chandeliers and American cherrywood panelling abound in the large reception, where coolly efficient international staff bustle officiously. Each of the 260 rooms has the same decor, double glazing and air-conditioning. Additions in 2001 included a state-of-the-art spa health centre and Santini's restaurant, promising Italian cuisine that is hopefully more authentic than the hotel's pseudo-Scottishness.

Hotel services *Air-conditioning. Bar. Beauty salon. Business services. Concierge. Disabled: access, adapted rooms (2). Gym. Limousine service. No-smoking rooms. Parking. Restaurants (3). Swimming pool.* **Room services** *Dataport. Minibar. Refrigerator. Room service (24hr). TV: satellite.*

Expensive

Apex European

90 Haymarket Terrace, EH12 5LQ (474 3456/fax 474 3400/www.apexhotels.co.uk). Bus 12, 21, 25, 26, 31, 33, 44. **Rates** £60-£95 single; £70-£180 double. **Credit** AmEx, DC, MC, V. **Map** p308 B6.
The sister hotel to the Apex International (*see p39*) shares a similar modern design. At the time of writing the European was upgrading and refurbishing some rooms, so facilities and rates may change. **Hotel services** *Bar. Business services. Disabled: access, adapted rooms. No-smoking rooms. Parking. Restaurants.* **Room services** *Minibar. Refrigerator. Room service (24hr). TV: satellite.*

Moderate

Ramada Jarvis Edinburgh Murrayfield Hotel

Ellersly Road, EH12 6HZ (337 6888/fax 313 2543/ www.ramadajarvis.co.uk). Bus 12, 26, 31, 38. **Rates** (breakfast not incl) £39.50-£120 single; £79-£140 double; £134-£155 executive rooms. **Credit** AmEx, DC, MC, V.
Due to Jarvis Hotels' recent merger with Ramada, the former Ellersly House Hotel now has the most convoluted name in the city. Thankfully, little has changed in the property itself, so it's easy to forget that you're just moments from Murrayfield Stadium. Park the car on the gravel drive in front of the hotel's moss-covered exterior, and then stroll inside to relax in front of the open fire in the bar. The patio doors at the back of the building lead onto a croquet lawn, which adds to the overall impression that you've stumbled into a Merchant Ivory production. It's all very charming and – dare we say it? – English. The small and rather ordinary rooms are somewhat out of kilter with the rest of the hotel, but for a quiet retreat this is a popular business and tourist choice. **Hotel services** *Bar. Business services. Garden. No-smoking rooms. Parking. Restaurant.* **Room services** *Room service (24hr). TV: satellite.*

Budget

Original Raj

6 West Coates, EH12 5JG (346 1333/fax 337 6688/ www.aboutscotland.com/edin/raj). Bus 12, 26, 31, 38. **Rates** £30-£60 single; £50-£90 double. **Credit** AmEx, MC, V.
A short drive from the centre and just a drop kick away from Murrayfield Stadium, this small, well-run India-themed hotel is probably the most exotic place to stay in the city. With hand-crafted furniture imported from Jaipur, colourful silk fabrics and generously sized bedrooms, standards are high. The trade-off is a lack of public areas and limited facilities, but for those wishing to explore town on a budget, this is an excellent and unusual option. **Hotel services** *Business services. Garden. No-smoking rooms.* **Room services** *TV.*

The sleek and chic **Point Hotel**. *See p49.*

Travel Inn

1 Morrison Link, EH3 8DN (228 9819/fax 228 9836/www.travelinn.co.uk). Bus 12, 21, 22, 25, 26. **Rates** £54.95. **Credit** AmEx, DC, MC, V. **Map** p308 C6.
This colossal branch of Britain's largest budget hotel chain boasts one of the cheapest room rates in town. The Travel Inn has 282 rooms; all are priced at £54.95 and each can squeeze in two adults and two kids. Decor-wise they're all exactly the same, of course – right down to the light switches. The financial incentive has obviously worked because, despite being little more than a faceless, classless and bland slumber land, the hotel boasts a year-round occupancy rate of 97%. The informal ground-floor restaurant is open all day. There's no room service or phones. **Hotel services** *Bar. Disabled: access, adapted rooms (15). No-smoking rooms. Parking. Restaurant.* **Room services** *Dataport. No phone. TV.*

Hostels

Edinburgh Eglinton Youth Hostel (SYHA)

18 Eglinton Crescent, West End, EH12 5DD (337 1120/central reservations 08701 553 255/fax 313 2053/www.syha.org.uk). Bus 12, 21, 25, 26, 31, 33. **Beds** 150. **Open** *Reception 7am-11pm daily. No curfew.* **Rates** (membership not incl) Sept-June £11.50; July, Aug £12.50. **Credit** MC, V. **Map** p308 B6.

Leith & the coast

Expensive

Malmaison

*1 Tower Place, EH6 7DB (555 6868/fax 468 5002/
www.malmaison.com). Bus 10A, 16, 22, 35.* **Rates**
£120 single/double; £130-£170 suite. **Credit** AmEx,
DC, MC, V. **Map** p311 Jx.

This ex-seamen's mission on the Leith dockside, dating from 1881, has been transformed by designer
Amanda Rosa. The subtle style and sexy sophistication of this award-winning hotel have helped to
breathe new life into Edinburgh's hotel trade by
setting a new standard in chic, sleek decor at affordable prices. All bedrooms are decorated in either
checks or wide stripes, using a muted but effective
palette of coffee and cream through to navy and
olive. The best rooms are the suites at the front and
the four-poster rooms. Attention to detail is clearly
a priority, as evidenced by the custom-made aromatherapy toiletries in the bathrooms and the CD
choice in reception. The brasserie's chef, Lawrence
Robertson, has won a loyal following for his uncomplicated French-style food and the adjacent café
serves wholesome vegetarian fare. Thoroughly recommended for its winning combination of comfortable style and value for money.
Hotel services *Babysitting. Bar. Business services.
Disabled: access, adapted rooms (2). Parking (on
street). Restaurant. Terrace.* **Room services**
*Dataport. Minibar. Refrigerator. Room service
(24hr). TV: satellite.*

Budget

Bar Java

*48-50 Constitution Street, EH6 6RS (553 2020/
www.javabedandbreakfast.co.uk). Bus 16, 22, 34.*
Rates £25 single; £50 double. **Credit** MC, V.
Map p311 Jz.

Near the rejuvenated Leith dock area and popular
with Festival and Hogmanay performers, Bar Java
has ten rooms, each named after a different island.
Below the accommodation is a funky bar with a beer
garden out the back that is enjoyed by some of the
area's 'colourful' locals. Snacks and a wide variety
of flavoured teas, coffees and smoothies are available all day, along with an excellent brunch on
Sundays. Guests can make full use of the bar, café
and satellite TV lounge.
Hotel services *Bar. Garden. Parking (on street).*
Room services *TV.*

Express by Holiday Inn

*Britannia Way, Ocean Drive, EH6 6LA (555 4422/
fax 555 4646/www.hiex-edinburgh.com). Bus 10, 16,
22, 34.* **Rates** £58-£85 twin/double/family room.
Credit AmEx, DC, MC, V. **Map** p311 Gx.

The owners of this particular franchise couldn't
believe their luck when the Royal Yacht *Britannia*
became the hotel's new neighbour. Now, rather than

looking out over a rather unsightly industrialised
port, guests enjoy views of one of the city's most
popular tourist attractions.

The accommodation itself has all the pros and
cons that go with a purpose-built hotel. It may be
blocky and featureless, but the owners have at least
tried to inject a little character: the furnishings are
contemporary, with Ikea-style fittings, while the
shower-only bathrooms are a masterpiece of space-saving design. This being a limited-service hotel, the
restaurant only serves breakfast, but this lack is
fully compensated by a great room delivery service
provided by a variety of local eateries.
Hotel services *Bar. Business services. Disabled:
access, adapted rooms (6). No-smoking rooms.
Parking.* **Room services** *Dataport. TV: satellite.*

Joppa Turrets Guest House

*1 Lower Joppa, Portobello, EH15 2ER
(tel/fax 669 5806/www.joppaturrets.demon.co.uk).
Bus 26, 26A.* **Rates** £20.50-£35 single/double.
Credit MC, V.

Not ideal if you want to be right at the heart of
things, but this well-run, friendly guesthouse is perfect if you're looking for a more peaceful location
within easy reach of the city. The Joppa Turrets is
a good example of the many guesthouses that have
survived from the time when Portobello was the seaside holiday spot of choice for many city-dwellers.
Situated right on the beach, three miles east of the
centre, it offers five guest rooms, all with views over
the Firth of Forth and across to the hills of Fife.
There's unrestricted hotel parking, and a tandem
bicycle for hire. All rooms are no-smoking. Public
phone available.
Hotel services *Garden. No-smoking. Parking (on
street).* **Room services** *TV.*

Alternative Accommodation

In addition to hotels and hostels, Edinburgh
offers a variety of other accommodation
options, including campsites and caravan
parks, private apartments and seasonal lets.

Camping & caravanning

Edinburgh Caravan Club Site

*Marine Drive, Silverknowes, EH4 5EN (312 6874/
fax 336 4269/www.caravanclub.co.uk). Bus 16, 27,
28, 29.* **Open** *Reception* 8am-8pm daily. **Rates**
£3.75-£4.75, £1.20 children; plus £3 tent, £7-£8
caravan, £1.50 car, 50p motorbike. **Credit** MC, V.

Mortonhall Caravan Park

*Frogston Road East, EH16 6TJ (664 1533/fax 664
5387/ www.meadowhead.co.uk/mortonhall). Bus 11,
32, 52.* **Open** *Reception* low season 8am-6pm daily.
High season 8am-10pm daily. **Rates** £9.50-£13.90
pitch & 2 adults; £1 extra adult. **Credit** MC, V.

Disabled accommodation

Trefoil House

Gogarbank, Ratho, EH12 9DA (339 3148/
fax 317 7271/www.trefoil.org.uk). SMT Bus 37.
Rates *Full weekly board* £275 guest; £258 carer.
Per night £50 guest; £45 carer. Other rates on
request. **No credit cards**.
Hotel services *Business services. Children's play*
area. Disabled: access, adapted rooms (11). Garden.
Lift. No-smoking rooms. Swimming pool.
Woodland walk.

Private apartments

Renting a private flat is a popular form of
accommodation during the Festival and
Hogmanay – so, as always, it's best to book
early. Alternatively, look in the Thursday
property section of *The Scotsman*. The **Town
House Guesthouse** (*see p51*) also has an
apartment for rent.

Canon Court Apartments

20 Canonmills, New Town, EH3 5LH (474 7000/fax
474 7001/www.canoncourt.co.uk). Bus 8, 23, 27.
Open *Reception* 8am-8pm Mon-Fri; 8.30am-2pm Sat,
Sun. **Rates** (per night) £87-£170. **Credit** AmEx, DC,
MC, V. **Map** p306 E2.

Glen House Apartments

101 Lauriston Place, South Edinburgh, EH3 9JB
(228 4043/ fax 229 8873/www.edinburgh-
apartments.co.uk). Bus 23, 28, 45. **Open** 9am-
5.30pm Mon-Fri. **Rates** £280-£1,500 per wk.
Credit AmEx, MC, V. **Map** p309 E7.

No.5 Self-catering Apartments

3 Abercorn Terrace, Portobello, EH15 2DD (tel/fax
669 1044/www.fiveholidays.co.uk). Bus 2, 15, 19, 26,
32. **Open** *Reception* 9am-10pm daily. **Rates** £70-
£360 per wk. **No credit cards**.

West End Apartments

2 Learmonth Terrace, Stockbridge, EH4 1PQ (332
0717/226 6512/fax 226 6513). Bus 19, 40, 41.
Open 9am-11pm daily. **Rates** £210-£800 per wk.
No credit cards. **Map** p305 B4.

Agencies

Factotum

40A Howe Street, New Town, EH3 6TH (220 1838/
fax 220 4342/www.factotum.co.uk). Bus 19A, 23,
27, 28. **Open** 9am-5.30pm Mon-Fri. **Credit** MC, V.
Map p306 D4.

Festival Beds

Information & reservations 225 1101/fax 225 2724/
www.festivalbeds.co.uk). **Open** 9am-5.30pm Mon-Fri.
Credit MC, V.
If you arrive when the Festival is in full swing and
have nowhere to stay, then this is the place to contact for bed and breakfast in a private house; around

60 properties contribute. In the past, the occupancy
rate has been as low as 50% during the Festival season, so you're more than likely to find a proper bed.
Less clued-up visitors have been spotted sleeping on
the streets – not recommended, even in the summer.

Festival Flats

3 Linkylea Cottages, Gifford, East Lothian, EH41
4PE (01620 810 620/fax 01620 810 619/festflats@
aol.com). **Open** 9am-5pm Mon-Fri. **No credit cards**.

Greyfriars Property Services

29-30 George IV Bridge, Old Town, EH1 1EN
(220 6009/fax 220 6008). Bus 23, 27, 41, 42.
Open 9.30am-5pm Mon-Fri. **No credit cards**.
Map p309 F6.

Mackay's Agency

30 Frederick Street, New Town, EH2 2JR (225
3539/fax 226 5284/www.mackays-scotland.co.uk).
Bus 19A, 23, 27, 28. **Open** *Office* 9am-5pm Mon-
Fri; 9am-4pm Sat; 10am-2pm Sun. *Phone enquiries*
9am-7pm Mon-Fri. **Credit** MC, V. **Map** p304 B1.

Seasonal lets

Universities let out their halls of residence
during student holidays. They can be out of
town, but are a useful form of basic
accommodation.

Carberry Tower Conference Centre

Musselburgh, EH21 8PY (665 3135/fax 653 2930/
www.carberry.org.uk). Bus 15, 26, 40, 44. **Rates**
(B&B) £25-£35. **Credit** MC, V.

Edinburgh University Accommodation Service

18 Holyrood Park Road, South Edinburgh, EH16
5AY (667 1971/fax 668 3217/www.accom.ed.ac.uk).
Bus 2, 14, 21, 23. **Rates** phone for details. **Credit**
MC, V. **Map** p310 J8.

Fet-Lor Youth Centre

122 Crewe Road South, EH4 2NY (332 4506).
Bus 19, 29, 37. **Rates** £8 per person per night.
No credit cards. Available during Festival only.

Heriot-Watt Conference Office

Heriot-Watt University, Riccarton Campus, EH14
4AS (451 3669/fax 451 3199/www.eccscotland.com).
Bus 25, 34, 35, 45. **Rates** (B&B) phone for details.
Credit MC, V.

Napier University Conference & Letting Services

219 Colinton Road, Craiglockhart, West Edinburgh,
EH14 4DJ (455 4331/fax 455 4411/www.napier.
ac.uk). Bus 4, 10, 18, 27, 45. **Rates** £340-£525 per
wk. **Credit** MC, V.

Queen Margaret University College

Hospitality Services Department, Clerwood Terrace,
EH12 8TS (317 3310/fax 317 3169/www.qmuc.
ac.uk). Bus 26, 103, 203. **Rates** (B&B) £24-£27
single; £36-£44 double. **Credit** MC, V.

(sidebar) **Accommodation**

Sightseeing

Introduction

So many sights, so little time.

Edinburgh, the elegant capital of a small, northern country, clings to the land on which it is built. Centred around the Castle Rock, sheltered by the monumental Arthur's Seat, the city's development may have been dictated by its geography, but it has also, over the years, come to impose its own characteristics on the landscape: house has been built on top of house; bog and heath have been drained, tamed and built over, so that the conurbation now flows down from the foothills of the Pentlands to the shores of the Firth of Forth.

Despite these changes, Edinburgh still lives in relative harmony with its surroundings: the houses do not cover all the hills, nor quite encroach on the valleys, and there are pockets of greenery to be found in all corners of the city, whether they be the vaguely wild banks and gorges along the **Water of Leith** or the fully tamed lawns and borders of the **Princes Street Gardens**.

ORIENTATION

The city is best described in terms of its historical development. First came the **Old Town** (*see pp59-81*), bound to the north by the valley of the Nor' Loch, now Princes Street

Gardens, and to the east and south by the Flodden Wall, which went up to the Pleasance and had its south boundary just past where the Museum of Scotland now stands. Originally, the town ended halfway down the Royal Mile, the road that stretches along the long, straight spine of a natural outcrop from the Castle to Holyrood House, but for convenience, we have also included the Palace of Holyroodhouse and the new developments of the Parliament and Our Dynamic Earth.

Looking north from the Castle, the **New Town** (*see pp82-90*) is the succession of planned developments that stretch from Princes Street down the hill towards the Forth, and end at the Water of Leith. They are bounded to the east by Calton Hill, and to the west by the triple towers of St Mary's Episcopal Cathedral.

Stockbridge (*see pp91-5*) is the village surrounding the Stock Bridge over the Water of Leith on the north-western edge of the New Town. Surrounding it are the rather less regimented developments of the Raeburn Estate, the Dean Village, with its two modern art galleries, and the Royal Botanic Garden.

Calton Hill (*see pp96-9*) and the small area of **Broughton**, just to the north, lie to the east of the New Town, while **Arthur's Seat** (*see pp100-103*), with **Duddingston** and the loch nestling in its lea to the south, is a complete rural enclave.

Rather less easy to group together are the suburbs of Edinburgh. **South Edinburgh** (*see pp104-107*) stretches inland from the Meadows up towards the Pentland Hills. It includes the so-called villages of Bruntsfield and Marchmont, as well as Craigmiller Castle in Little France, and the Royal Observatory on Blackford Hill. **West Edinburgh** (*see pp108-111*) goes from Lothian Road and the New Town out towards the airport, including the Union Canal, the Zoo and the old Roman port of Crammond on the Forth.

Finally, the port of **Leith** (*see pp112-116*) is a distinct district on its own, and though it is joined to Edinburgh by Leith Walk, it has retained a separate identity. Further west is the small fishing village of **Newhaven**.

MUSEUMS

Despite being well-preserved, Edinburgh is far from being a living museum. Although the tartan myth started by Sir Walter Scott

---

The best Views

Head to these five sights for the best views of the city.

Arthur's Seat
All of Edinburgh, the Forth and, on a sunny day, up to the Trossachs. *See p100.*

Edinburgh Castle
The full panorama, from hills to coast. *See p61.*

Nelson Monument
A small door, but a huge vista. *See p99.*

Royal Observatory
A different perspective, with telescopes for more intimate detail. *See p107.*

Scott Monument
Great for spying on Princes Street shoppers. *See p85.*

Your entrance to Edinburgh.

is perpetuated in various tourist 'experiences' by tartan-clad guides, there are plenty of museums that portray the city's past in a credible manner, and a visit to these will enhance the pleasures of a subsequent walk around the city.

A majority of visitors to the city will use **Edinburgh Castle** (*see p61*) and the **Palace of Holyroodhouse** (*see p76*) to provide a solid backbone to their sightseeing itinerary. (It is worth remembering that the Palace of Holyroodhouse is the Queen's residence in Edinburgh and is closed to the public when she is there.) The two big museums to see are the double whammy of the **Royal Museum** and the **Museum of Scotland** (*see p81*), situated together on Chambers Street. The latter has the most to offer the visitor to Scotland. Organised in a thematically arranged journey from pre-history in the basement to icons chosen by modern Scots on the top floor, it provides a strong basis for an understanding of the history of the city itself, which can be seen from the museum roof.

For an insight into the events and people who made Edinburgh the city it is today, the smaller museums and attractions create a complex and fascinating picture. The **Museum of Edinburgh** (*see p75*) on the Canongate might display the civic museum's worst tendencies to cram everything into glass cases, but its range of exhibits adds an extra level of understanding to the more modern, naturalistic displays at **The People's Story** (*see p76*), **Gladstone's Land** (*see p65*) or the **Georgian House** (*see p88*).

Then there are the tiny, specialist museums that add their own peculiar twist to the Scottish capital's story. Read between the lines at the **Sir Jules Thorn Exhibition of the**

History of Surgery (*see p105*) and you'll learn much about changing social attitudes in the city; or listen to recordings of local residents at the **Newhaven Heritage Museum** (*see p116*) to discover how working lives have altered in the last 100 years.

All museums are reviewed in the relevant sightseeing chapters that follow. Details of the City of Edinburgh-run museums are given on their website: www.cac.org.uk.

Sightseeing tours

If walking round Edinburgh gets too much – and there are enough hills for that to be likely sooner rather than later – three operators run open-top bus tours around the Old and New Towns. All start from Waverley Bridge and while each offers a slightly different route, there is not a lot to choose between them. All tours take about an hour, if traffic is not too heavy, and leave every ten to 20 minutes from about 9am to 7pm in the summer, 9am to 5pm in the spring and autumn, and 10am to 4pm in the winter. All go past most of the major sights and offer a one-day, 'hop on, hop off' ticket, which allows passengers to alight or rejoin the tour at any point along the way.

Edinburgh Classic Tour
Information 555 6363. **Tickets** £7.50; £2.50-£6 concessions. **Credit** MC, V.
These white and blue buses are run by local bus company LRT. The driver provides a commentary but all passengers also have their own headphones with a choice of pre-recorded commentaries in English, German, French, Spanish, Italian, Dutch or Japanese.

Guide Friday
Information 556 2244. **Tickets** £8.50; £2.50-£7 concessions. **Credit** MC, V.
A guide provides a running commentary on these green and cream buses, and can answer questions along the route.

Mac Vintage Tours
Information 220 0770. **Tickets** *Red route* £8; £2.50-£7 concessions. *Blue route* £7.50; £2-£6.50 concessions. *Grand Tour* phone for details. *Royal Edinburgh Ticket* phone for details. **Credit** MC, V.
The red and cream buses belonging to this locally run company are all over 30 years old and come with a conductor as well as a guide. The Red route aims to emphasise the contrast between the Old and New Towns, while the Blue route goes past the Botanics to Leith and Newhaven. There is a Grand Tour option of combined travel on both routes for one or two days, and it's also worth asking about the Royal Edinburgh Ticket, which includes entry to Holyroodhouse, the Castle and *Britannia* in the price of the tour.

Reform Restaurant

Intimate and
Individual

267 Canongate, The Royal Mile, Edinburgh
www.reformrestaurant.com
Telephone 0131 558 9992

Old Town

Every stone has a story to tell in the ancient buildings of Edinburgh's Old Town.

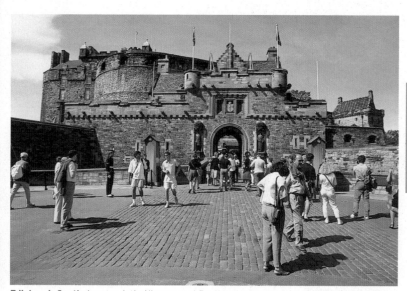

Edinburgh Castle is a tourist's Nirvana and Scotland's most visited attraction. *See p61.*

Edinburgh's natural fortifications of **Castle Rock** and the **Nor' Loch** helped define its parameters from the first pre-historical settlements until the creation of the New Town in the 18th century. Until the 16th century, the burgh of Edinburgh was defended only by minimal fortifications to the south and west. This changed with the military disaster at Flodden in 1513, which inspired the burghers to create what became, over the following 40 years, the **Flodden Wall**. It consolidated the parameters of the burgh to create the area known today as the Old Town. The wall ran east from the foot of the Nor' Loch, now Waverley Station, then south over the ridge of the Royal Mile, up the Pleasance and turned west along Drummond Street. It continued to the south of Greyfriars, turned down the Vennel across the West Port and back up the hill to Castle Rock. The final extension came a century later when the Telfer Wall was built to include Heriot's School to the south.

From the 16th century onwards, population growth in the walled city led to the construction of higher and higher buildings interspersed

with a warren-like network of wynds (alleys) and closes (entries closed at one end). Due to the precipitous drops on either side of the ridge of the **Royal Mile**, tenements that were a few floors high facing inwards to the street were often many storeys high on the other side. The tenements, known as 'lands', from the parcels of land on which they were built, became so densely populated that different parts of society often shared the same houses, usually with the prosperous and noble on the upper floors.

Primitive sewage arrangements gave rise to the famous Old Town cry of 'gardey loo' (a corruption, according to some, of the French *gardez l'eau*) when flinging household waste out of the window. In fact, Edinburgh was so dirty and unwholesome at the turn of the 16th century that a third of the population was wiped out by bubonic plague. The Old Town is still infused with the intrigue and drama that come from a long and often turbulent history, and the chaotic, crowded, smelly, noisy city of the 17th and 18th centuries still seems to lurk just under the surface – but luckily, sanitation facilites have improved since then.

Makars' Court.
See p67.

After the **North Bridge** was opened in 1772, the gentry moved away from the overcrowded Old Town to populate the spacious squares and crescents of the New Town. The tenements started to fall into disrepair during the 19th century, but their decay was checked and they still dominate the streetscape on the Royal Mile. Only 60 or so of the hundreds of closes and wynds remain.

To the east, old Edinburgh continues down to the Palace of Holyroodhouse through the **Canongate**, once a separate burgh, but now a distinctive part of the Old Town. A brewery and gas works once occupied the eastern end of the Royal Mile, but these have been replaced by the new Parliament building, offices for the *Scotsman* newspaper and the high-tech Our Dynamic Earth attraction.

The Royal Mile

The Royal Mile is the oldest part of Edinburgh and marks the road running directly from Edinburgh Castle down to the Palace of Holyroodhouse. If the atmosphere in the remaining closes makes them perfect for ghost tours (*see p74* **Witches and wynds**), then the Royal Mile's larger monuments are a reminder of Edinburgh's capital city status. The vast majority of shops along this stretch are aimed squarely at the tourist market: woollen mills, craft shops, tartan outfitters – they're all here.

Castlehill

Unlike so many castles that lie in ruins, the grey and imposing fortress that is **Edinburgh Castle** (*see p63*) has been in constant use for 1,000 years. It is extraordinarily well preserved and is kept scrupulously tidy. The continuing military presence gives it a brisk atmosphere (although that could just be the wind) and ensures that it is devoid of the tackiness found at other historic sites.

The Castle was a royal residence until the Lang Siege of 1571-3 when Mary, Queen of Scots' supporters in the Castle were bombarded by the Regent, governing on behalf of her son, the infant King James VI of Scotland (and I of England). The refurbishment that followed was intended to turn the Castle into an impregnable military fortress; the royal residence was moved to Holyroodhouse.

The Castle is entered from the Esplanade, where the world-famous and nearly always sold-out **Edinburgh Military Tattoo** has been held every Festival since 1950 (*see p185*). When the Esplanade is not covered by the seats set up for the Tattoo (from mid-July to mid-September), the Castle's most impressive visible feature is the curve of the massive artillery emplacement, the **Half Moon Battery**, built to protect the Castle's vulnerable eastern side after the Lang Siege. Behind it on the left is the Palace, now one of the Castle's museums. The Gatehouse – with the bronze statues of Robert the Bruce and William Wallace on either side – was added in 1886-8 as a conscious attempt to make the Castle look more picturesque. Behind the Half Moon Battery, the Palace buildings drop sheer down to Johnston Terrace. The Mills Mount Battery, from where the one o'clock gun is fired, is not visible from here – it's behind the trees to the right, facing out over Princes Street. Cliché though it is, you can always tell Edinburgh natives because, instead of flinching when the gun goes off, they automatically check their watches.

The view from the southern parapet of the Esplanade looks out over the suburbs of Edinburgh, which were once open heath, up to the Pentland Hills. The northern aspect is over the New Town, across the Firth of Forth to Fife. A small gate at the eastern end of the north side leads down winding paths to **Princes Street Gardens**. There are various military memorials on the Esplanade remembering Scottish soldiers killed in action overseas. Rather more poignant, however, is the small **Witches' Memorial** on the left of the gate leading to the Royal Mile. This bronze, wall-mounted well marks the place where over 300 women were burned as witches between 1479 and 1722.

Also visible from the Esplanade – on the extreme left as you face away from the Castle – is **Ramsay Gardens**, an irregular complex of romantic baronial buildings bristling with spiral staircases and overhangs. Constructed around the poet Alan Ramsay's octagonal 'goose-pie' house, the buildings were mostly erected in the late 19th century to lure the upper classes back into the Old Town. The low, flat building beside them was once the Castlehill reservoir, built in 1851, which supplied water to Princes Street. Nowadays, it houses the **Edinburgh Old Town Weaving Company** (*see p64*), an exhibition and working weaving mill for tartan cloth. The **Camera Obscura** (*see p63*) is in the black-and-white tower on the roof of the next building. It contains a system of lenses and mirrors that project images of the surrounding area onto a disc inside.

The building on the right of Castlehill is **Cannonball House**, so called because of the two cannon balls lodged in the west gable end wall, about halfway up. They are said to have been placed there to mark the level to which water piped from Comiston Springs in the Pentland Hills would rise, proving that it could be used to feed the Castlehill reservoir.

The Old Town at the mercy of the **Half Moon Battery** gun emplacement. *See p61.*

Opposite Ramsay Lane, the narrow cobbled road down to the Mound, is the **Scotch Whisky Heritage Centre** (*see p65*). There are guided tours through a three-floor exhibition, which culminates in the tasting bar.

The Hub (*see p64*), standing where Castlehill meets the top of Johnston Terrace, was designed by Augustus Pugin in 1844 and built as the Tolbooth St John's Kirk. Its 73-metre (240-foot) Gothic spire is the highest point in Edinburgh. The church was bought by the Edinburgh International Festival in 1998 and beautifully refurbished as its headquarters. It also houses a year-round café, shop and ticket centre, where tickets for all official Festival events (including the Science Festival and Edinburgh's Hogmanay) are sold.

Camera Obscura

Castlehill, EH1 (226 3709). Bus 23, 27, 28, 35, 41, 42, 45. **Open** *Nov-Mar* 10am-5pm daily. *Apr-Oct* 9.30am-6pm daily. **Admission** £4.95; £2.50-£3.95 concessions; £14.50 family. **Credit** MC, V. **Map** p64 A1.

It's all done with mirrors in this attraction at the top of the Royal Mile, which was created by optician Maria Short in the 1850s. The main event is a 20-minute show in the domed hut on the roof. Images of the surrounding area – and from this high up that's pretty extensive – are reflected and refracted on to a white disc in the middle of the small,

darkened room. As the lenses turn the circle, the guide will invite kids to 'pick up' people and buses on pieces of paper, which is quite amusing but ultimately a bit twee. The hologram exhibition on the way up is thorough and well presented. It's worth leaving time to go out on the roof afterwards as the binoculars there give excellent views over the New Town and Calton Hill. It is not, however, worth visiting on a cloudy day as the camera is dependent on natural light for the strength of the image.

Edinburgh Castle

Castlehill, EH1 (enquiries 668 8800/ticket office 225 9846/www.historic-scotland.gov.uk). Bus 23, 27, 28, 35, 41, 42, 45. **Open** *Apr-Sept* 9.30am-6pm daily. *Oct-Mar* 9.30am-5pm daily (last entry 45 mins before closing). **Admission** £8; £2-£6 concessions. *Guided tour or audio guide* £3 extra. **Credit** AmEx, DC, MC, V. **Map** p64 B2.

Edinburgh Castle is a fascinating hotchpotch of buildings built between the 12th century and the present day. Allow a good hour to see the main sights, and plenty of extra time for exploring. There's a lot of walking on uneven cobbled pathways, so sensible shoes are advisable. Tours are available, led by very friendly guides who are happy to answer questions or have their photo taken with visitors, and there's also a very good taped audio guide in six languages. Operating the audio guide can be a bit confusing but its soundtrack, including gunfire and spooky music, certainly helps the imagination along.

Close to the summit of the castle is **St Margaret's Chapel**, a tiny, simple and contemplative space that is the oldest building in Edinburgh. Further along, **Crown Square** was created in the reign of King James III (1460-88) as the focal point of the Castle and contains the main sights. On the immediate right of the square's entrance is the **Scottish National War Memorial**, a grandly sober building that was formerly a barracks; it was transformed into a shrine to the war dead in 1927. Stand well back to get the full impact. The **Great Hall**, opposite, is a breathtaking room, with an original (early 16th-century) timbered roof, Victorian wood-panelling and elaborate displays of medieval weaponry. On the left side of the Square as you face the Great Hall is the **Palace**, which was inhabited by the later Stuart monarchs and contains the apartment in which Mary, Queen of Scots gave birth to James VI in a tiny wood-lined room known as the Cabinet. On the Palace's first floor is an exhibition, built around the Honours of Scotland – the Scottish crown jewels with the addition of the Stone of Scone, or Stone of Destiny, which is the ancient coronation stone of Scotland, stolen by Edward 1 in 1296 and finally brought here from Westminster Abbey in 1996.

The Castle is a paradise for anyone interested in military history, with various regimental museums housing displays of weapons, uniforms and medals, not to mention Mons Meg – a giant 500-year-old cannon – and a dog cemetery. This is also the site of the **National Museum of Scotland's National War Museum**, which examines how war and military service have influenced Scotland's history over the last four centuries. Weather permitting, you can wander along the battlements and admire the views. To round everything off, you'll find a beautifully designed but overpriced café and lots of gift shops crammed with tartan kitsch.

Edinburgh Old Town Weaving Company

555 Castlehill, EH1 (226 1555/www.scotweb.co.uk/ edinburgh/weaving). Bus 23, 27, 28, 35, 41, 42, 45. **Open** *Exhibition* 9am-6.30pm Mon-Sat; 9am-5.30pm Sun. *Shop* 9am-6pm Mon-Sat; 10am-5.30pm Sun. **Admission** *Building* free. *Tour* £4.50; £2.50-£3.50 concessions; £9 family. **Credit** AmEx, MC, V. **Map** p64 A1.

Wander round the looms at this noisy working attraction and watch the skilled tartan weavers at work, before buying their output in the shop. There is also an exhibition and guided tour about the production of tartan – 'from sheep to shop', the chance to have a go at tartan-weaving yourself, and a display of tartan through the ages.

The Hub

348 Castlehill, EH1 (473 2000/www.eif.co.uk/ thehub). Bus 23, 27, 28, 35, 41, 42, 45. **Open** *Shop* 9.30am-5.30pm Mon-Sat; noon-4pm Sun. *Ticket office* 10am-5pm Mon-Fri. *Festival office* 9am-7.30pm Mon-Sat; 10am-7.30pm Sun. **Admission** free. **Credit** AmEx, DC, MC, V. **Map** p64 A1.

The Tolbooth St John's Church was built as the Victoria Hall for the Established Church General Assembly in 1844, in response to the religious 'Disruption' of the previous year (*see p18*). Having fallen out of use as a church during the 1960s, it was lovingly refurbished in 1999 – using the

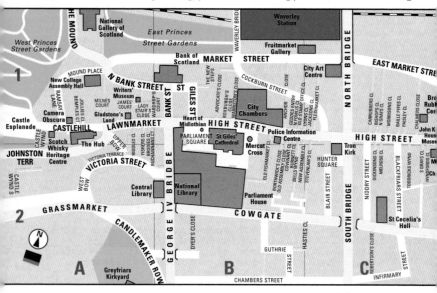

Old Town

Deacon Brodie's Tavern. *See p67.*

highest-quality craftsmanship – for the Edinburgh International Festival, which has its offices in the roof. The bold colour scheme of the Assembly Hall upstairs – said to adhere to Pugin's original palette but audacious nonetheless – is worth seeing all by itself. The rich, red stairwell is decorated with some 200 plaster statues by Jill Watson representing people who have performed in the International Festival over the years. The ground floor and terrace café serves excellent, if rather pricey, food (*see p138*).

Scotch Whisky Heritage Centre

354 Castlehill, EH1 (220 0441/www.whisky-heritage.co.uk). Bus *23, 27, 28, 35, 41, 42, 45.* **Open** *Apr-Sept* 9.30am-6.30pm daily. *Oct-Mar* 10am-6pm daily (last tour 4.45pm). **Admission** £6.95; £3.40-£4.75 concession; £15 family. **Credit** AmEx, DC, MC, V. **Map** p64 A1.

A blatantly tourist-oriented attraction. Visitors are led by a guide through rooms illustrating the production of the Scottish national drink, before embarking on a ghost-train-like tour through various tableaux on the history of distilling and finally receiving a free dram in the tasting bar. Overall, it's well thought-out, if a bit too long. The shop has some good blends but is distinctly lacking in single malts; it's best to buy them further down the High Street.

Lawnmarket

The Lawnmarket is the part of the Royal Mile between The Hub and the traffic lights on George IV Bridge. It is named after the fine cotton and linen cloth – known as 'lawn' – that was sold here, and boasts a fine example of a 17th-century Edinburgh townhouse. **Gladstone's Land** (*see p67*), a property dating from 1550, was extensively rebuilt 70 years later by an ancestor of Prime Minister William Gladstone and is now owned by the National Trust for Scotland. The original interior, with its oriel-shaped balcony and segmental arch, are all well preserved, but visitors should note that the house is only open between April and October.

Sightseeing

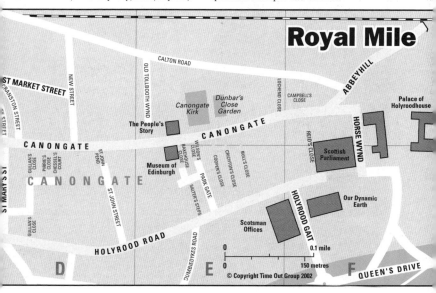

Royal Mile

© Copyright Time Out Group 2002

There are numerous closes and wynds to investigate on the Lawnmarket. On the north side they run through to the Mound and include Mylne's Court, which affords access to the **Scottish Parliament Debating Chamber** (*see p68*), and **James's Court**, where James Boswell lived and was visited by Dr Johnson. In the restored 18th-century courtyard at the bottom of James's Court is the Jolly Judge (*see p149*), a convenient and cosy pub with an open fire and a wooden ceiling painted with flowers and fruit. Robert Burns stayed in a house on **Lady Stair's Close** on his first visit to Edinburgh, so it is appropriate that Lady Stair's House, built in 1622, has been turned into the **Writers' Museum** (*see p68*), which displays memorabilia of Burns, Sir Walter Scott and Robert Louis Stevenson. The whole court is now known as **Makars' Court**, from 'makar', the archaic Scots word for poet; 17 Scottish writers of note are commemorated in paving stones approaching the Writer's Museum.

Johnston Terrace, at the head of the Lawnmarket, is worth wandering along for its classic view back up to the Castle. The **Upper Bow**, like the wynds to the south of the Lawnmarket, leads down to the raised pavement above Victoria Street. **Riddles Close** is the most interesting entry to explore, leading into two courtyards; it was from here that David Hume published his *Political Discourses*. **Brodie's Close** was the home of the notorious Deacon Brodie, a respected member of Edinburgh society who led a double life as a burglar. He was put to death outside St Giles' on a gibbet he had designed himself – an irony remembered in the plaque on the wall of **Deacon Brodie's Tavern** (225 6531).

The ugly block of the **Scottish Parliament** offices on the corner of George IV Bridge is the only modern architectural carbuncle on the Royal Mile. At this point the Royal Mile is intersected by George IV Bridge on the right and the Mound, winding down to Princes Street, on the left. The **Mound** was constructed at the end of the 18th century, using the excavated soil from the building of the New Town. It is dominated by the head office of the **Bank of Scotland**, designed on classical lines but embellished with baroque flourishes in the 1860s that make it look more like a palace as it gazes imperiously over the New Town. It is especially striking when floodlit at night. The Bank has a collection of maps, notes and banking paraphernalia, which is on view at the **Museum on the Mound** (*see below*) during banking hours in the summer. Past here and to the left is the Gatehouse of the **Church of Scotland New College & Assembly Hall**, which has been pressed into service as the

temporary premises of the Scottish Parliament until its custom-built home at Holyrood is completed in 2003. The view from the entrance back towards the Castle is a classic Edinburgh image, immortalised in countless photographs.

George IV Bridge leads south towards **Greyfriars Kirk** (*see p78*), resting place of Greyfriars Bobby, and the museums on **Chambers Street** (*see p79*). On the left is the **National Library of Scotland** (*see below*), facing the **Central Library** (*see below*).

Central Library

George IV Bridge, EH1 (242 8030/www.edinburgh. gov.uk/Libraries). Bus 23, 27, 28, 35, 41, 42, 45. **Open** 10am-8pm Mon-Thur; 10am-5pm Fri; 9am-1pm Sat. **Admission** free. **Map** p64 B2.
The headquarters of Edinburgh's library service was built in 1870 and houses the Edinburgh room, Scottish department, reference library and fiction and lending libraries. The children's and music libraries are housed in the building across the bridge over the Cowgate. The Edinburgh room is for reference only, but contains over 100,000 individual items pertaining to the city, from newspaper cuttings to historical records and prints. Some of these are available on loan from the Scottish department below.

Gladstone's Land

477B Lawnmarket, EH1 (226 5856). Bus 23, 27, 28, 35, 41, 42, 45. **Open** *Apr-Oct* 10am-5pm Mon-Sat; 2-5pm Sun. Guided tour 1-2pm Sun (no booking; max 10). Closed Nov-Mar. **Admission** £5; £3.75 concessions; £13.50 family. **No credit cards.** **Map** p64 A1.
This National Trust for Scotland property is kept in the 17th-century style of its former owner, Thomas Gledstanes. Gledstanes bought the six-storey house in 1617 and extended it into the street to create room for an arcade and booths at the front. The NTS displays are not really suited to such confined rooms, but the guides are helpful. This is an essential stop in any tour of the Royal Mile that hopes to get under the un-soaped skin of historic Edinburgh.

Museum on the Mound

Bank of Scotland Head Office, The Mound, EH1 (529 1288/www.bankofscotland.co.uk). Bus 23, 27, 28, 41, 42, 45. **Open** *June-Sept* 1-4.45pm Mon-Fri; by appointment at other times. **Admission** free. **Map** p64 B1.
This small museum displays some of the Bank of Scotland's old documents, artefacts, notes and coins. The bank was founded by the Parliament of Scotland in 1695 and is one of the few institutions created by that parliament to have survived.

National Library of Scotland

George VI Bridge, EH1 (226 4531/www.nls.uk). Bus 23, 27, 28, 41, 42, 45. **Open** *Exhibition hall* June-Oct 10am-5pm Mon-Sat; 2-5pm Sun. Closed Nov-May. *Reading rooms* 9.30am-8.30pm Mon, Tue, Thur, Fri; 10am-8.30pm Wed; 9.30am-1pm Sat. **Admission** free. **Map** p64 B2.

Surprisingly, Scotland did not have a national library until 1925, because this function was fulfilled by the Faculty of Advocates Library. The NLS is one of the UK's deposit libraries and contains seven million printed books, 1.6 million maps, 120,000 volumes of manuscripts, and over 20,000 newspaper and magazine titles. These are available to view for research purposes here and in the Causewayside Building to those 'requiring material not readily available elsewhere'. Admission to the reading rooms is by ticket only, for which identification is required. During the summer and autumn, the Exhibition Hall just inside the main door houses small exhibitions pertaining to Scottish books and writers; no ticket is required for this.

Scottish Parliament Debating Chamber

Milne's Court, Lawnmarket, EH1 (348 5411/ www.scottish.parliament.uk). Bus 23, 27, 28, 41, 42, 45. **Open** (last admission 15mins before close) 10am-12.30pm, 1.45-4.15pm Mon, Tue, Fri; 9.30am-12.30pm, 1.45pm-end of parliamentary session Wed, Thur. **Admission** free. **Map** p64 A1.

Until the opening of Holyrood in 2003, this is where the Members of the Scottish Parliament, MSPs, hold their debates. For debates, most public seats are available on a first come, first served basis, although some can be booked up to seven days in advance. The best time to see the parliament at work is on Wednesdays and during Question Time on Thursday afternoons. The debating chamber is also open to visitors at the above times when the parliament is not sitting.

Writers' Museum

Lady Stair's House, Makars' Court, Lawnmarket, EH1 (529 4901/www.cac.org.uk/). Bus 23, 27, 28, 35, 41, 42, 45. **Open** *Sept-July* 10am-5pm Mon-Sat. *Aug* 10am-5pm Mon-Sat; noon-5pm Sun. **Admission** free. **Map** p64 A1.

Lady Stair's House, built in 1622, provides a fitting Old Town environment in which to contemplate the combined literary might of Robert Burns, Sir Walter Scott and Robert Louis Stevenson. The exhibits are skewed towards memorabilia – Scott's chess set, Burns' snuff box and the like – but the museum's atmosphere is suitably reverent and evocative. Other Scottish writers, including contemporary authors, are featured in the museum's programme of temporary exhibitions.

High Street above the Bridges

Daniel Defoe called the High Street 'the largest, longest and finest street for buildings and number of inhabitants, not in Britain only, but in the world'. The section above the Bridges is undeniably impressive and was used in the film version of Thomas Hardy's *Jude the Obscure* as a stand-in for Oxford. The High Court of Justiciary, the supreme criminal court in Scotland, stands at the crossroads, in front

of which is a bronze statue of David Hume, absurdly (for a 1997 statue of an 18th-century philosopher) garbed in classical dress. Round the back of the Court, in Giles Street, Pâtisserie Florentin (*see p139*) is a fashionable place to down coffee and cake. It is worth remembering its extended opening hours if you're partial to a cup of joe in the late evening.

The three brass bricks laid into the pavement opposite Hume mark the place where the last public hanging in Edinburgh took place: of George Bruce on 21 June 1864; it was watched by 20,000 people. Next to these bricks is the building where Scottish Parliamentary committees meet, with the **Parliament Visitor Centre** (*see p70*) taking up the ground floor. Built in 1818 to a design based on the Acropolis in Athens, this block forms one wall of Parliament Square. **Parliament House**, which runs along the back of the square, has a great hall used by lawyers from the adjoining District Court, Court of Session and High Court.

The **Heart of Midlothian**, laid out in cobblestones by the roadside near the entrance of the **High Kirk of St Giles** (*see p69*), marks the spot of the old Tolbooth Prison, where executions took place; the victims' heads were frequently displayed afterwards. It is a local custom to spit on this spot. St Giles' is where John Knox preached the Reformation. For the pedantic, the fabric of the building itself is referred to as St Giles', while the church is known as the High Kirk of Edinburgh. The Lower Aisle Restaurant, entered round the corner of the church on the south side, is good for a reasonably priced lunchtime bite, and is popular with the city's lawyers.

Although it is an open space now, Parliament Square used to be crowded by many shops and 'lucken booths' – lockable shop stalls built in the 15th century to offset the cost of constructing St Giles'. In the shadow of the **Mercat Cross**, to the east of the cathedral, traders struck deals in a thriving commercial climate. Executions were carried out here too, and it is also the spot where royal proclamations were read out.

From the north side of the High Street, several closes and wynds descend to Cockburn Street. The first of these, **Advocates Close**, includes what is allegedly the oldest surviving house in Edinburgh at No.8, built in the 1480s and now open to the public thanks to the **DOM Arts Project** (*see p69*), which uses it as a gallery and shop. The house was built at a time when the sloping land below the building would still have been open fields and when most merchants in the city could only have afforded timber houses.

On the High Street, the **City Chambers** face St Giles' and the Mercat Cross from the other side of the road. Completed in 1761, and thus one of the first truly Georgian buildings in Edinburgh, it was originally the Royal Exchange but failed because traders still preferred to do their business in the open air at the Mercat Cross. The building was also an attempt to bury Mary King's Close – both literally and in people's memories. During the plague in 1645, Mary King's Close was subjected to a brutal form of quarantine that involved the whole close being blocked up and all its inhabitants left to die. Butchers were sent in later to dismember the corpses. Large sections of the close are still intact amid the City Chambers' foundations and it is reputed to be one of the most haunted places in Scotland; even sceptics find it eerie. In one room the ghost of a little girl has been placated with gifts – dolls, sweets and coins – left by visitors. *See also p74* **Witches and wynds**.

Further down the High Street, just past the **Police Information Centre** (*see below*), is the Fringe Office, the epicentre of Edinburgh Festival Fringe activity. During August the pavements are close to impassable due to the long, snaking queues of ticket-hungry visitors, actors in weird costumes pressing flyers on passers-by and the crowds who throng around the street performers.

DOM Arts Project

8 Advocate's Close, EH1 (225 9271/www.dom-arts.com). Bus 23, 27, 28, 35, 41, 42, 45/Nicolson Street–North Bridge buses. **Open** *11am-5pm daily.* **Admission** free. **Map** p64 B1.

Built in the 1840s for Henry Cant, a wealthy claret importer, this is reputed to be the oldest surviving house in Edinburgh, thanks to its stone walls. It survived at least one attempt to burn it down during Henry VIII's 'rough wooing' of 1544. Now it is home to the DOM Arts Project, named after the Russian for 'home'. The project sells arty gifts in its ground-floor shop and hosts regular art shows of a metaphysical nature in its tranquil upstairs gallery.

The High Kirk of St Giles

High Street, EH1 (225 4363/visitor services 225 9442). Bus 23, 27, 28, 35, 41, 42, 45/Nicolson Street–North Bridge buses. **Open** *Easter-mid Sept 9am-7pm Mon-Sat; 1-5pm Sun. Mid-Sept-Easter 9am-5pm Mon-Sat; 1-5pm Sun.* **Services** *8am, noon Mon-Fri; noon, 6pm Sat; 8am, 10am, 11.30am, 6pm, 8pm Sun.* **Admission** free; donations welcome. **Map** p64 B1.

There has been a church on the site of St Giles' since 854. The oldest remnants are the four pillars surrounding the Holy Table in the centre, which date from around 1120. The ornate crown spire they support was completed in 1495. St Giles' suffered the usual destruction wrought by the English armies and the Reformation, but after the dust had settled

John Knox (1505-72) spent 12 years as its parish minister and Charles I made it a cathedral in 1633. It was still referred to as a cathedral even after the bishops were banished in the Glorious Revolution of 1688 (*see p13*), although as a Presbyterian place of worship it cannot technically be considered a cathedral at all. Inside, a great vaulted ceiling shelters a medieval interior dominated by the banners and plaques of many Scottish regiments. The main entrance takes visitors past the West Porch screen, originally designed as a royal pew for Queen Victoria. The dazzling West Window is by Icelandic stained-glass artist Leifur Breidfjord and was dedicated to Robert Burns' memory in 1984. The organ is an even more recent addition, from 1992, with a glass back revealing the workings. The Knights of the Thistle – an order of chivalry founded in 1687 – has its own chapel, an intimate panelled room with intricate wooden carvings of thistles, roses and shamrocks, divided into knights' stalls.

Police Information Centre

188 High Street, EH1 (226 6966). Bus 23, 27, 28, 35, 41, 42, 45/Nicolson Street–North Bridge buses. **Open** *May-Aug 10am-10pm daily. Sept, Oct, Mar, Apr 10am-8pm daily. Nov-Feb 10am-6pm daily.* **Admission** free. **Map** p64 B1.

The Hub: Festival focus. *See p63.*

The towering **City Chambers** buried plague-ridden Mary King's Close. *See p69.*

Even the police in Edinburgh have a museum of sorts, housed in their fully functional information centre. There's not much to see: a bit of history of policing in Edinburgh and a couple of cabinets containing memorabilia – the choicest exhibit is an artefact covered in the cured skin of executed serial killer William Burke (*see p18* **Body matters**). Yummy.

Scottish Parliament Visitor Centre & Shop

George IV Bridge, EH1 (348 5411/www.scottish-parliament.uk). Bus 23, 27, 28, 35, 41, 42, 45. **Open** from 9am Tue-Thur when parliament is sitting; 10am-5pm Mon-Fri at other times. **Admission** free. **Map** p64 B1.

In the borrowed offices of the Regional Council are the Scottish Parliament's Committee Chambers with a visitor centre, shop and information desk. In addition to a few screens setting out, in simple terms, the Parliament's powers and objectives, there are detailed architects' models and plans of the permanent Parliament building being constructed at Holyrood, and facsimiles of a few interesting historical documents: the Roll of the first Parliament in 1293; an act from 1457 banning the playing of football and golf; and the record of proceedings on the final day of the last Parliament in 1707.

Cockburn Street & the Bridges

The atmosphere of Cockburn Street, to the north of the High Street, tends to fluctuate with the vitality of the city's youth culture; it has been looking rather tired for a few years now. A range of identikit clothing stores notwithstanding, it veers towards the biker end of hippie with a touch of goth and the scent of New Age nosing its way in. The arrival of upmarket craft shops and two modern art

spaces, the **Collective Gallery** (*see p71*) and the **Stills Gallery** (*see p72*), hasn't completely shaken off the whiff of patchouli oil. From Cockburn Street the Scotsman Steps are a convenient but steep route down to the **City Art Centre** (*see p71*) and the **Fruitmarket Gallery** (*see p71*) on Market Street. Opposite the bottom of Cockburn Street are the offices and ticket office for the Tattoo (*see p185*), and below them, the cellars of the **Edinburgh Dungeon** (*see p71*) a tourist experience that comes close to achieving its aim of scaring the living daylights out of visitors.

At the top of the street, meanwhile, on the corner with South Bridge, is the **Tron Kirk**. This area was the traditional gathering place for revellers seeing in the New Year until Edinburgh's official Hogmanay celebrations began in 1993 and the focus moved down to Princes Street. The Kirk is now used as the **Old Town Information Centre** (*see p71*). Hunter Square, beside it, was given an overhaul a few years ago and is now a pleasant place to sit and watch the world go by. The City Café (*see p148*) may have been superseded as one of the capital's hippest bar and café joints since it opened in the late 1980s, but it remains an attractive, cosmopolitan place to enjoy a drink or a meal.

At the traffic lights here, the High Street is cut in two by **North Bridge** and **South Bridge**, known together as 'the Bridges' and built to open up the New Town in the late 18th century. Although South Bridge looks like a continuous street, it is in fact supported by 19 massive arches, only one of which is visible. The last building on the left of North Bridge, looking towards the New Town, is the rugged, iconic building that housed **Scotsman Publications** (publishers of the *Scotsman, Scotland on Sunday* and the *Evening News*) throughout the 20th century. Purpose-built for the company, it was vacated in 1999 in favour of new premises at Holyrood and has since been transformed into a luxury hotel (*see p43*). At the front of the building is an enclosed spiral staircase that provides a short cut down to Market Street and Waverley Station; don't use it unless you enjoy the stench of stale urine. This dank stairway is the entirely believable setting for foul murders in several Edinburgh-set detective thrillers.

City Art Centre

2 Market Street, EH1 (529 3993/www.cac.org.uk). Princes Street buses. **Open** *Sept-June* 10am-6pm Mon-Sat. *July, Aug* 10am-6pm Mon-Sat; noon-5pm Sun. **Admission** free; charge for occasional exhibitions. **Credit** MC, V. **Map** p64 C1.

Built as offices for the *Scotsman* newspaper towards the end of the 19th century, this six-storey building was converted into the City Art Centre in 1979. It is funded by the City of Edinburgh Council and has been described as the 'Ford Cortina of art galleries', in as much as it puts on exhibitions for all the family – not that there's anything wrong with that. Past successes have included the blockbuster 'Star Trek' exhibition as well as shows of Chinese artefacts and contemporary photography. The Centre frequently hosts temporary exhibitions drawn from the city's collection of 19th- and 20th-century Scottish art, although sadly the bulk of this is in semi-permanent storage. Cultural consumerism is encouraged in the gallery's shop, and relaxation in the ground-floor licensed café.

Collective Gallery

22-28 Cockburn Street, EH1 (220 1260/collgall @aol.com). Bus 35/Nicolson Street–North Bridge buses or Princes Street buses. **Open** noon-5pm Wed-Sat; 3-5pm Sun. **Admission** free. **No credit cards**. **Map** p64 B1.

One of the city's more vibrant exhibition spaces, the Collective boasts a resource centre, the so-called 'Lounge', furnished with an appropriate line-up of comfy chairs for use both by the casual browser and the keen researcher. There is also the 'Mind Bar', with bar stools, an array of art mags to flick through and glasses of water – no liquor, sadly – for the thirsty. Established in 1984, the Collective is known for showcasing work by the most dynamic artists on Scotland's art scene. Besides trumpeting local talent, the artist-run gallery has a track record for guest-curated shows that bring together established artists from further afield. The shows in the three-roomed space are not consistently strong but can be relied on to be adventurous. The small Project Room has also carved itself a niche by hosting a programme of debut solo shows. It provides a glimpse of who might be who in contemporary Scottish art. *See also p201* **Talent spotting**.

Edinburgh Dungeon

31 Market Street, EH1 (240 1000/www.the dungeons.com). Princes Street buses. **Open** 10am-5pm daily. **Admission** £7.50; £5.50-£6.50 concessions. **Credit** AmEx, MC, V. **Map** p64 B1.

From the makers of the York and London Dungeons, this is a spooky and genuinely nasty experience that uses actors as guides to good effect. A conscious effort has been made to ensure various parts of the dungeon are relevant to Edinburgh and Scotland, particularly those relating to Burke and Hare (*see p18* **Body matters**), the anatomy theatre and 14th-century cannibal Sawney Bean. Unfortunately, in the overriding desire to be as gruesome and spooky as possible, many of the more subtle horrors of Edinburgh's worst excesses of religious brutality are skimmed over. All in all, a lot more historical fact could have been included without compromising theatrical effect.

Fruitmarket Gallery

45 Market Street, EH1 (225 2383/www.fruitmarket. co.uk). Princes Street buses. **Open** 11am-6pm Mon-Sat; noon-5pm Sun. **Admission** free. **Credit** AmEx, MC, V. **Map** p64 B1.

Next door to Waverley Station, this one-time fruit market was given a major overhaul in 1992 by the high-profile Edinburgh architect Richard Murphy. A two-level rectangular, glass-fronted space, it is billed as Scotland's top contemporary art gallery, and receives the highest gallery grant from the Scottish Arts Council. As well as regularly hosting touring shows – frequently from Oxford's Museum of Modern Art – including exhibitions by Marina Abramovic, Yoko Ono and Kiki Smith, the Fruitmarket curates its own exhibition programme. Scotland-based artists with international reputations, such as Martin Boyce and Ross Sinclair and the collaborating duo Stephanie Smith and Edward Stewart, have shown here, along with a diverse range of artists from further afield. Over the years the Fruitmarket has also established a tradition of bringing to Britain, often for the first time, work by non-Western artists, including a hugely popular show of paintings by Chinese artists. In addition to art shows, the gallery operates a strong programme of artist talks and events. The lower floor is partly given over to a stylish café and a well-stocked book-shop selling everything from exhibition catalogues to philosophical treatises.

Old Town Information Centre

Tron Kirk, High Street, EH1 (557 4700). Bus 35/Nicolson Street–North Bridge buses. **Open** noon-5pm daily. **Admission** free. **Map** p64 C2.

The Tron Kirk was completed in 1648 but was reduced in size to accommodate the South Bridge in 1785. The current steeple was built after the original was destroyed in the fire known as the 'Great Conflagration' of 1824. The building is now owned by the City Council and houses an informative exhibit about the development of the Old Town, including excavated remains of Marlin's Wynd – an early 1600s alley that was demolished in the 17th century to make way for the Kirk.

Stills Gallery

23 Cockburn Street, EH1 (622 6200/www.stills.org). Bus 35/Nicolson Street–North Bridge or Princes Street buses. **Open** phone for details. **Admission** free. **Credit** MC, V. **Map** p64 B1.

Since opening in the late 1970s, Stills has evolved from a primarily photographic space into one of the city's most dynamic contemporary art venues. Revamped and enlarged in 1997 by Edinburgh architects Reiach and Hall in collaboration with Glasgow artist Nathan Coley, the gallery is today a clean-cut, concrete-floored rectangular space. Within the Stills complex you'll find a mezzanine café, which frequently puts on small exhibitions, digital imagery labs, which can be booked in advance, and a small bookshop. The widening of the exhibitions policy has enabled Stills to bring some exciting artists – such as Tomoko Takehashi, Joel-Peter Witkin and Tracey Emin – to Scotland, as well as to show work by artists based here. Hence, it presents some of the sharpest contemporary art shows in Edinburgh.

High Street below the Bridges

Beyond the traffic lights, just behind the upmarket but welcoming Bank Hotel (*see p39*), **Niddry Street** dips steeply down towards the Cowgate. Its shabby walls have been done up to represent 19th-century Edinburgh in at least one BBC drama, and behind them is a rabbit warren of cellars built into the arches of South Bridge and long forgotten. These subterranean expanses are atmospheric places, recently opened to guided tours, and gradually becoming used by pubs like Nicol Edwards (*see p150*); not all of the cellars have been opened up, though. The Honeycomb, just up Niddry Street from the cellars, is a popular night spot (*see p216*). The **Medieval Torture Museum** is here too, displaying instruments of torture that were used on suspected witches in Germany during the Middle Ages. Its range of devices is steadily expanding, and it hopes soon to be the largest museum of its kind in the world; at the moment it is only accessible on the Mercat tour of the vaults (*see p74* **Witches & wynds**).

The Crowne Plaza Edinburgh (*see p39*; also still referred to by its former name, the Scandic Crown) has been much maligned for its individual interpretation of Scottish baronial style. Actually, it is a valiant and largely successful attempt by the hotel to blend into its Old Town surroundings. On the right is **Blackfriars Street**, a thoroughfare well known to backpackers and hostellers.

It also boasts Black Bo's (*see p147*), a pub that is well on its way to becoming a fully fledged Edinburgh institution.

A tasteful glass façade fronts the **Museum of Childhood** (*see p73*), opened in 1955 as the first museum in the world to examine the history of childhood. Its founder made sure that visitors understood the difference between a museum of childhood and a museum for children, but the multitude of toys, games and displays are good enough to fascinate both kids and adults. The **Brass Rubbing Centre** (*see below*), which is also popular with kids, is on Chalmers Close, just opposite the museum.

Reverence for its illustrious former occupant was all that saved the awkwardly positioned house that is now the **John Knox House Museum** (*see below*) from demolition in 1830. In fact, it is now widely believed that the leader of the Scottish Reformation never lived here at all, but the property's preservation is an asset as it retains many original features: timber galleries and gables, overhanging beams, and religious quotations and carvings around the outside walls. The house was built by goldsmith James Mossman, whose workbench is reconstructed inside. There are also exhibits associated with Knox. The house is connected to the **Netherbow Arts Centre**, which contains a 75-seat theatre, storytelling centre and café.

The east gate of the city, the **Netherbow**, used to stand at this point on the High Street. Along **Tweeddale Court**, is a surviving length of the city wall and sheds that were once used to store sedan chairs. Back on the High Street, there's a reference to the city boundary in the name of the pub on the corner: the World's End (*see p151*), which serves reasonable food and well-kept beer.

Brass Rubbing Centre

Trinity Apse, Chalmers Close, High Street, EH1 (556 4364/www.cac.org.uk). Bus 30, 35/Nicolson Street–North Bridge buses. **Open** Apr-July, Sept 10am-5pm Mon-Sat. *Aug* 10am-5pm Mon-Sat; noon-5pm Sun. Closed Oct-Mar. **Admission** free; rubbings cost from 90p. **Map** p64 C1.

Just up from John Knox House Museum, the Brass Rubbing Centre is housed in an airy church – the only surviving fragment of the Gothic Trinity College Church, which was founded in 1460. The centre demonstrates that, although brass-rubbing might be a good kid's activity, it has an artistic side, too, particularly when Celtic knots are involved. Cheery, friendly staff and good schematic guides show how it's done.

John Knox House Museum

43 High Street, EH1 (556 9579). Bus 30, 35/ Nicolson Street–North Bridge buses. **Open** 10am-4.30pm Mon-Sat. **Admission** £2.25; £1.75 concessions. **Credit** MC, V. **Map** p64 C1.

John Knox woz here... maybe. *See p72.*

Although it is only probable that the religious reformer John Knox died here in 1572, the belief that he did has been enough to stop one of Edinburgh's oldest residences, built in 1450, from being razed. The house now holds a detailed exhibition on the Scottish Reformation, complete with an audio re-enactment of Knox's debate with the Catholic Mary, Queen of Scots. Covering such a complex topic, the displays are by necessity very wordy and the house itself is not shown to its best advantage. But the trick of contrasting Knox with royalist James Mossman (who certainly did live here and who made the Scottish Crown on view in the Castle; *see p64*) works well.

Museum of Childhood

42 High Street, EH1 (529 4142/www.cac.org.uk). Bus 30, 35/Nicolson Street–North Bridge buses. **Open** *Sept-June* 10am-5pm Mon-Sat. *July, Aug* 10am-5pm Mon-Sat; noon-5pm Sun. **Admission** free. **Credit** MC, V. **Map** p64 C2.

Don't think yourself too old for this one. The museum, founded by local councillor Patrick Murray in 1955, is about childhood and not a venue for children. Its small rooms and winding staircases are packed with centuries of toys, schoolbooks and kids' paraphernalia. There's so much here that you need to take your visit slowly to appreciate the masses of tiny objects in dolls' houses, toy circuses and train sets. Some of it is quite recent and frequently evokes a heartfelt 'I had one of those!' from misty-eyed visitors. There are occasional temporary exhibitions and a good shop.

Canongate

The next section of the Royal Mile to the east, the Canongate, takes its name from the route used by Augustinian canons to reach the gates of Edinburgh after their arrival at Holyrood Abbey in 1141 (*see p8*). Located outside the city wall, Canongate remained an independent burgh, separate from Edinburgh, until as recently as 1856. Recognisable from its clock, bell tower and outside stairway, the **Canongate Tolbooth** was built in 1592 to

collect tolls from people entering the city, but it also served as council chamber, police court and prison for the burgh of Canongate. It now houses the **People's Story** (*see p76*), an absorbing museum of Edinburgh's social history. Next to it lies the Tolbooth Tavern, a classic Edinburgh watering hole (556 5348). **Huntly House**, opposite, is three timber-framed houses joined into one in 1570 and surmounted by three overhanging white-painted gables of a kind that were once common in the Old Town. It is also home to the **Museum of Edinburgh** (*see p75*), exhibiting artefacts from the earliest known inhabitation of the area right through to the Victorian age. Bakehouse Close, under Huntly House, leads through to the offices of the **Royal Fine Art Commission for Scotland** (*see p76*). This is not, as the name might suggest, a fine art exhibition space, but the national body for promoting the fine art of planning and architectural design.

Few know of **Dunbar's Close Garden**, a secret little park at the end of an unassuming close on the north side of the Canongate. It is laid out in the manner of a 17th-century garden, with ornamental flower beds and manicured hedges, and is a beautiful refuge from the summer crowds. There's a fine view of the old Royal High School from here, which for many years was intended as the site for the new Scottish Parliament.

The bell-shaped Dutch design of **Canongate Church** marks it out distinctly from the rest of the buildings on the Royal Mile as one of Edinburgh's most individual and attractive churches. It was built for the displaced congregation of Holyrood Abbey, which was destroyed in 1688. Canongate is Edinburgh's official military church, but is also worth visiting for the famous bodies buried in the churchyard. These include David Rizzio, murdered secretary of Mary, Queen of Scots; economist Adam Smith; and Robert Burns' beloved 'Clarinda' (Mrs Agnes McLehose), for whom he wrote 'Ae Fond Kiss'.

Burns' muse is also commemorated by a tea-room, **Clarinda's** (*see p138*), a little further down. Just on the right side of twee, with patterned plates on the wall and flowers on the tables, it provides the best chance of a light meal at this end of the Canongate. The work of rather more modern poets can be perused at the **Scottish Poetry Library** (*see p76*), which is down Crichton's Close, on the opposite side of the Canongate to Clarinda's.

There are some attractive houses near the gates of Holyrood, most obviously the two well-kept, gleaming white edifices of **Canongate Manse** and **Whiteford House**, now a

Sightseeing

Scottish war veterans' residence. **White Horse Close** is pretty too. The gabled building at the end was once a coaching inn and the departure point for the stage coach to London. In 1745 it was called into service as the officers' quarters of Prince Charles Edward Stuart's army.

At the bottom of the Royal Mile stands the **Palace of Holyroodhouse** (*see p75*). It was built by James IV to be near the now-ruined Abbey and was variously added to and refurbished by subsequent monarchs. Despite being burned and looted by Henry VIII's army in 1544, and further damaged in 1650 when Cromwell's army used it as a barracks and accidentally burned down the south wing, its finished form radiates a combination of solidity and elegance. The purpose of the strange, squat building just inside the fence by the main road is unknown. It might have been a bathhouse, or perhaps a doocot (where 'doos' or pigeons nest). **Holyrood Abbey**, an irreparable ruin, was founded by David I in 1128. It was sacked by Edward II in 1322, damaged in 1544 and 1570 with the loss of the choir and transepts and violated further by a Presbyterian mob in 1688.

Opposite the gates of Holyroodhouse is the site of the new **Scottish Parliament**, now scheduled for completion in autumn 2003 (*see also p30* **Freedom, at a price**). Designed by Spanish architect Enric Miralles, it was criticised from the start by a lobby which

sees it as an 'unedifying collection of upturned boats'. It is, however, the cornerstone of one of the most radically transformed areas of Edinburgh. The new **Parliament Building Visitor Centre** (*see p70*) gives an overview of the whole project.

At the time of writing, the bottom of Holyrood Road, which runs parallel to the Canongate, was blocked off by the parliamentary building site. The road should, however, be back in action – as pedestrian access only – by autumn 2002. In the meantime the whole lower half of Holyrood Road has been refurbished in anticipation of the forthcoming Parliament with fashionable new apartment blocks, hotels, upmarket shops and the businesslike but attractive new premises of Scotsman Publications.

The first element of the new development to be completed was the multimedia tourist attraction **Our Dynamic Earth** (*see p75*), which uses varied means to tell the story of the planet from the Big Bang to the present day. With the crags of Arthur's Seat (*see p100*) as its backdrop, it stands on the site where James Hutton, 'the father of geology', lived and worked. Doubling back up Holyrood Road towards the Old Town, you will pass the plain but striking Queensberry House Hospital and the Moray House Teacher Training College en route to the Cowgate.

Witches and wynds

Descending from either side of the Royal Mile are 61 closes and wynds: narrow, steeply sloping passageways with houses towering six or even ten storeys above. The word 'close' referred to an alley that is open only at one end and could be closed at night, although as the Old Town has been redeveloped, many 'closes' are now open at both ends. The word is also used in Scotland to refer to the central stairwell in tenements. A 'wynd' is an alley that is open at both ends. During the Middle Ages, Edinburgh was one of the most overcrowded cities in Europe and these alleys were the most densely populated and sordid areas of all. Walking tours through and under these medieval closes combine stories of historical brutality with tales of ghosts and the supernatural.

Not all guided tours are as fanciful as the ghosts and ghoulie tours, however. During the Fringe, there are free tours of the Royal Mile, led by the **Edinburgh Festival Voluntary**

Guides Association. The tours last about two hours and leave frequently. Year round, **Mercat Tours'** Grand Tour is the most intensive, and the most informative, visiting the New Town and the Old Town in three hours; Mercat's Royal Mile Walk lasts two hours. The **McEwan's 80/- Edinburgh Literary Pub Tour** makes the most of the fact that many of Edinburgh's more prominent writers were partial to a drop or two. Led by a pair of arguing Edinburgh residents – Clart and McBrain – the tour visits pubs from the Grassmarket to the New Town and concentrates on past, rather than contemporary, writers.

Mary King's Close, the historically most terrifying and supernaturally most potent of Edinburgh's closes, is now buried under the City Chambers, inaccessible except via the trip operated by Mercat Tours. The story of the close is horrific. All the street's residents were killed during an epidemic of the Black Death.

Museum of Edinburgh

*Huntly House, 142-146 Canongate, EH8 (529 4143/
www.cac.org.uk). Bus 30, 35/Nicolson Street–North
Bridge buses.* **Open** *Sept-July* 10am-5pm Mon-Sat.
Aug 10am-5pm Mon-Sat; 2-5pm Sun. **Admission**
free. **Map** p65 E2.

This is a packed, old-fashioned museum housed in
three original tenements opposite the Canongate
Tolbooth. There's too much to see, so many of the
displays appear as no more than crammed glass
cases, but there are some real oddities in this eclectic collection, including the National Covenant and
Greyfriars Bobby's collar and feeding bowl. With
the aid of the guidebook, the museum's artefacts
help form a rounded picture of Edinburgh as it
developed from Roman times, through the building
of the New Town, to the 19th century. However, it
is the tenements themselves, united into a single
block in 1570, that are the real treat here. The buildings' structure is fascinatingly visible, with corners
that would have been whole rooms furnished and
laid out in their original style.

Our Dynamic Earth

*Holyrood Road, EH8 (550 7800/www.dynamic
earth.co.uk). Bus 30, 35.* **Open** *Apr-Oct* 10am-6pm
daily. *Nov-Mar* 10am-5pm Wed-Sun. **Admission**
£7.95; £4.50-£5.50 concessions. **Credit** MC, V.
Map p65 F2.

The gleaming, tent-like entrance hall of this ultra-
modern attraction is just the tip of a subterranean
playground, with simulated earth tremors, a dizzying 'helicopter ride' across glaciers and well-planned

displays depicting the different zones of Earth, its
weather, flora and fauna. The experience is hugely
successful, and the acclaim it drew from the public
meant that comparisons with the underachieving
Millennium Dome in London were inevitable.
Unfortunately, passage through the experience is
one way, meaning that there is no coming back
to bits that you found particularly interesting.

Palace of Holyroodhouse

*Holyrood Road, EH8 (556 7371/www.royal
residences.com/Holyrood.htm). Bus 30, 35.*
Open *Apr-Oct* 9.30am-6pm daily (last entry 5.15pm).
Nov-Mar 9.30am-4.45pm daily (last entry 3.45pm).
Admission £6.50; £3.30-£5 concessions.
Credit AmEx, MC, V. **Map** p65 F1.

Originally built by James IV with refurbishments
made by subsequent monarchs, the Palace was
frequently used by Queen Victoria when travelling
to or from Balmoral, a tradition kept up by the present Queen, who frequently stays here. When she is
in residence, the Palace is closed to the public, but
when it is open, the furniture, tapestries, paintings
and objets d'art from several centuries are on
display, as are the private apartments and lavishly
decked-out bed of Mary, Queen of Scots.

The memory of Mary is indelibly associated with
the Palace. In 1576, six months pregnant, she
watched as four Scottish noblemen murdered her
secretary David Rizzio with the consent of her
husband, Lord Darnley, who wanted to kill the baby
she was carrying. She fled to Edinburgh Castle
where she gave birth to James VI.

Sightseeing

What is most shocking is that the City Fathers
walled off the close in a failed attempt to
quarantine the plague, denying everyone who
lived there both food and water. It is difficult
for the guide's stories to compete with the
unimaginable terror of the past.

Other tours highlight the routine tortures,
murders and witch hunts of the medieval city.
Mercat's various walks mix tales of the
supernatural with local history, and offer the
chance to descend into the buried vaults and
streets that run beneath the city. The guides
don't take themselves, or their subject matter,
too seriously. **Auld Reekie Tours**, on the other
hand, which are run from the Medieval Torture
Museum, do like to dwell on the gruesome,
though their Witchcraft & Persecution Tour is
apparently led by genuine white witches. **Black
Hart Storytellers** are the most frightening;
their City of the Dead walking tour ends up in
Greyfriars graveyard and has allegedly induced
genuine paranormal encounters.

Witches' Memorial on Castlehill. *See p61.* ▶

The Great Gallery alone would make a visit worthwhile. It is 45m (150ft) long and is decked out with over 100 bizarre portraits by Dutch artist Jacob de Wit, who was under contract to Charles II. The king wanted to be surrounded by representations of 2,000 years' worth of his ancestors and de Wit complied, creating a host of imaginary monarchs and giving every single one, real or fabled, Charles II's protuberant nose. The Great Gallery is also notable as the place where Prince Charles Edward Stuart held dances that captivated Edinburgh high society for a month in 1745.

The People's Story

Canongate Tolbooth, 163 Canongate, EH8 (529 4057). Bus 30, 35/Nicolson Street–North Bridge buses. **Open** *Sept-July* 10am-5pm Mon-Sat. *Aug* 10am-5pm Mon-Sat; 2-5pm Sun. **Admission** free. **Map** p65 E1.

This intelligently organised museum focuses on the lives of working-class people of Edinburgh from the late 18th century to the present day. Many of the artefacts and documents stem from the organisation of labour, with tableaux illustrating the common people's living and working conditions. Use of authentic smells and tape loops enhance the authenticity of the experience. The Tolbooth, which was built in 1591, was used as the Canongate's jail, so the museum's law and disorder section seems particularly appropriate. The video show in the top room puts the whole exhibition into perspective, while the accompanying guidebook contains some fascinating anecdotes.

Royal Fine Art Commission for Scotland

Bakerhouse Close, 146 Canongate, EH8 (556 6699/ www.royfinartcomforsco.gov.uk). Bus 30, 35/ Nicolson Street–North Bridge buses. **Open** noon-3pm Tue-Fri; extended opening hours during Festival. **Admission** free. **Map** p65 E2.

The Commission is housed in offices that were converted from a derelict brewing laboratory and warehouse in 1997. This is not a fine art institution, but rather an advisory body that consults with the government on good architectural design in Scotland. No painting displays here, then, although during the Festival in August the Commission's offices normally host an exhibition that attempts to cast some light on contemporary architectural and design practices.

Scottish Poetry Library

5 Crichton's Close, Canongate, EH8 (557 2876). Bus 30, 35/Nicolson Street–North Bridge buses. **Open** noon-6pm Mon-Fri; noon-4pm Sat. **Admission** free; donations welcome. *Annual membership* £15; £10 concessions. **No credit cards. Map** p65 E1.

The focus of this library's extensive collection is 20th-century poetry, written by Scottish poets in Scots, Gaelic or English. The library also has a good collection of older Scottish poetry as well as contemporary work from around the world. Everyone is welcome to peruse the books in the collection, and there is a computer for generating specialist lists and bibliographies.

▶ # Witches and wynds (continued)

The **Witchery Murder & Mystery Tour**, with your guide Adam Lyal (deceased), doesn't go underground and is more in the tradition of pantomime than history lecture. But the guide works the crowd effectively, drawing shrieks and giggles if not real fright. An overemployed extra ambushes the tour at various points, dressed as a mad monk or medieval harridan, which is a bit naff, although this trip down the Cowgate after dark does suggest that the shady world of Burke and Hare could still exist in contemporary Edinburgh.

Bus details and map references given below are for tour meeting points.

Auld Reekie Tours

Medieval Torture Museum, 45 Niddry Street, EH1 (557 4700). Nicolson Street–North Bridge buses. **Open** *Information* 10am-10pm daily. **Tours** *Underground City Tour* Sept-June 12.30-3.30pm daily on the hr. July, Aug 10.30am-5.30pm daily on the hr. *Ultimate Ghost & Torture Tour* Sept-June 7-10pm on the hr. July, Aug 6-10pm on the hr. **Meeting point** (all tours) Tron Kirk, High Street. **Tickets** *Underground City Tour* £5; *Ultimate Ghost & Torture Tour* £6; £5 concessions. **Credit** AmEx, MC, V. **Map** p64 C2.

Organises other tours by arrangement: phone for details.

Black Hart Storytellers

Meeting point: Mercat Cross, St Giles', High Street (225 9044). Bus 23, 27, 28, 28A, 35, 41, 42, 45. **Open** 10am-10pm daily. **Tours** 8.30pm, 10pm daily. **Tickets** £6; £5 concessions. **No credit cards. Map** p64 B2.

There are often extra tours in the summer.

Edinburgh Festival Voluntary Guides

Meeting point: Cannonball House, Castlehill, EH1 (no phone). Bus 23, 27, 28, 28A, 35, 41, 42, 45. **Tours** *Aug only* frequently between 10-11am, 2-3pm Mon-Sat; 2-3pm Sun. **Tickets** free. Map p64 A1.

Museum of Scotland. See p79.

The Cowgate & south

At the junction of the Cowgate and Holyrood Road, you can turn left, up the Pleasance towards the famous Fringe super-venue of the same name (see p213). Halfway up is the edge of the Old Town, marked by a remaining corner of the **Flodden Wall** (see p59). Turning from here along Drummond Street provides a neat shortcut to the Museum of Scotland and the Royal Museum on Chambers Street (see p79).

Turning right from the end of Holyrood Road up St Mary's Street leads back to the Netherbow. This crossroads was at one time an entrance to the Old Town: the Cowgate Port, through which cattle passed to and from the fields in the morning and at night. Continuing straight ahead along the Cowgate leads in to the most atmospheric street in the Old Town.

The Cowgate

Just before the darkness of the Bridges over the Cowgate, is the church of **St Patrick**, built in 1771. Its gardens, accessible from South Gray's Close, are a tranquil place to pause. Nearby, on the corner of Blackfriars Street, is St Cecilia's Hall, which houses the **Russell Collection of Early Keyboard Instruments** (see p80

McEwan's 80/- Edinburgh Literary Pub Tour

Suite 2, 97B West Bow, EH1 (226 6665/ recorded information 226 6665/www.scot-lit-tour.co.uk). Bus 2, 23, 27, 28, 28A, 41, 42, 45. **Open** 9am-6pm Mon-Fri. **Tours** Apr, May, Oct, Nov 7.30pm Thur-Sun. June-Sept 7.30pm daily. Dec-Mar 7.30pm Fri. **Meeting point** Beehive Inn, Grassmarket. **Tickets** £7; £5 concessions. **Credit** (advance bookings only) MC, V. **Map** p64 A2.
Phone for details of private tours and literary lunches and suppers.

Mercat Walking Tours

Mercat House, Niddry Street South, EH1 (557 6464/www.mercattours.com). Bus 23, 27, 28, 28A, 35, 41, 42, 45. **Open** Information 9am-6pm daily. **Tours** Mary King's Close (advance booking essential; tour times vary) 11.30am-9.30pm daily. Hidden Underground Vaults May-Sept hourly 11am-4pm daily; Oct-Apr noon, 4pm

daily. Ghosts & Ghouls 7pm, 8pm daily. Ghost Hunter Trail Apr-Oct 9.30pm, 10.30pm daily; Nov-Mar 9.30pm daily. Secrets of the Royal Mile 11am daily. **Meeting point** Mercat Cross, St Giles', High Street. **Tickets** Mary King's Close £5. Hidden Underground Vaults £6. Ghosts & Ghouls £7.50. Ghost Hunter Trail £6. Secrets of the Royal Mile £6. **Credit** MC, V. **Map** p64 B1.

Witchery Tours

352 Castlehill, Royal Mile, EH1 (225 6745/ www.witcherytours.com). Bus 23, 27, 28, 28A, 35, 41, 42, 45. **Open** Information 10am-9pm daily. **Tours** (advance booking only; phone for times) Ghost & Gore Tour May-Sept usually 7pm, 7.30pm daily. Murder & Mystery Tour usually 7pm, 7.30pm daily. **Meeting point** Outside Witchery Restaurant, Castlehill. **Tickets** Ghost & Gore Tour £7; £4 concessions. Murder & Mystery Tour £7. **Credit** AmEx, MC, V. **Map** p64 A1.
Scream and giggle your way around town.

Sightseeing

Feeding love). Infirmary Street, opposite, leads up to the Old High School (1777), Old Surgeon's Hall (1697), and the Victorian premises that once housed the Royal Infirmary where Joseph Lister discovered the benefits of antiseptic surgery. At the end of Infirmary Street on Nicolson Street is **New Surgeon's Hall**, built in 1832.

As the Cowgate funnels under South Bridge, with the tenements soaring up on either side, it is hard to conjure a sense of the openness of the area in the 16th century when it was where the nobility and chief men of the city lived. There is a large relief model of the Old Town on the ground floor of the Museum of Edinburgh (*see p75*), which gives a good indication of what it was like at the time. By the middle of the 19th century, the Cowgate had become one of the most densely populated parts of the city, and the physical reality of its location below the Bridges was accentuated by the poverty of its inhabitants. Although it is no longer a wasted ravine of dilapidated architecture, regeneration here has mostly been geared to the glory of hedonistic excess and alcohol consumption. At night the area has taken over from Lothian Road as the place for students and local youth to wander drunkenly around, and it is now closed to through traffic after 10pm.

Beyond the towering backs of the new court buildings, the Cowgate passes under George IV Bridge. Immediately on the left is the **Magdalen Chapel** (*see below*). Dwarfed by surrounding tenements, it is supposedly where the first General Assembly of the Church of Scotland was held in 1578. In the bloody days of the late 17th century the chapel served as a mortuary for those executed Covenanters whose bodies were buried round the corner, in Greyfriars Kirkyard.

Magdalen Chapel

41 Cowgate, EH1 (220 1450). Bus 2, 23, 27, 28, 41, 42, 45. **Open** 9.30am-4pm Mon-Fri. **Admission** free. **Map** p64 B2.

Built between 1541 and 1547, with the steeple added in 1626, the Chapel is the headquarters of the Scottish Reformation Society, but is still open to visitors. Of note is the only surviving pre-Reformation stained glass in Scotland: four fading rounds that were inserted in 1553 and are, frankly, a bit of a disappointment. More interesting are the 'brods' (receipts for gifts of money or goods to the chapel) dating from the 16th to the 19th centuries that wrap round the walls like a frieze, and the Deacon's Chair (1708).

Greyfriars & Chambers Street

At the end of the Cowgate, Candlemaker Row leads back up the hill towards Greyfriars and George IV Bridge. The real mystery of **Greyfriars Kirk** (*see p79*) has nothing to do with its ghostly grey friars, its poltergeists assaulting tourists or the estimated 80,000 corpses that were squeezed into its kirkyard. The central conundrum is the unparalleled interest generated by a certain shaggy hound who turned up his toes in 1872. Bobby was the loyal mutt who lived by his late master's grave for 14 years until his own death and became an object of affection for many Edinburgh citizens. His statue is on the corner of Candlemaker Row and George IV Bridge. The misleading notice in the kirkyard says Bobby 'was buried nearby' his master; in fact, when Bobby died, the minister at the time waited until cover of darkness to plant the pooch in the only unconsecrated plot left. The minister had a better handle on the great scheme of things than many visitors since.

Greyfriars Kirkyard has played a pivotal role in the history of Scotland. It is where the National Covenant was signed in 1638 and where the bodies of executed Covenanters were buried alongside common criminals. They, and survivors of the Battle of Bothwell Brig (1679; *see p13*), were kept in the south-west corner of the yard in the Covenanters' Prison under desperate conditions for five months. The Martyrs' Monument, with its chilling inscription, 'Halt passenger, take heed of what you do see, This tomb doth shew for what some men did die', is their memorial and can be found in the north-east part of the yard. Wandering around the kirkyard when there's a haar (sea mist) causes a palpable time-slip effect, but even on a sunny day there are hardly any modern buildings in sight to break the historical spell. The 17th-century **George**

The People's Story. *See p76.*

One's *pied-à-terre* in the Scottish Capital – the **Palace of Holyrood House**. *See p74.*

Heriot's School (*see p81*) and a portion of the **Flodden Wall** add to the atmosphere.

Opposite Greyfriars, the plain but graceful lines of the new **Museum of Scotland** (*see below*) mask a warren of winding corridors that open up on to spectacular drops and huge spaces. The roof and turret restaurant give fantastic views of Arthur's Seat and the Castle. Next door, along Chambers Street, is the **Royal Museum** (*see below*), which was designed by Captain Francis Fowke along conventional, Victorian lines and completed in 1888. Although they are distinct entities, the two museums are linked inside. Across from the imposing steps of the Royal Museum is the Matthew Architecture Gallery (closed to the public).

Younger than the universities of St Andrews or Glasgow, **Edinburgh University** dates from 1582. **Old College**, now its central focus, occupies the original site, backing on to Chambers Street. It was built by Robert Adam, who started the work in 1789, and William Playfair, who finished it after the interruption of the Napoleonic Wars. Rowand Anderson added the landmark dome in 1883.

Entrance to the main courtyard is either through the small entrance of the **Talbot Rice Gallery** (*see p80*), up West College Street, or through the monumental arch on Nicolson Street. Certain areas of Old College are accessible to the public, notably the **Playfair Library** (where guided tours in the Easter and summer vacations at 1pm show off one of the city's finest classical interiors) and the old **Upper Museum** (now part of the Talbot Rice Gallery). The Upper Museum features a table from Napoleon's lodgings on St Helena with a cigar burn made, allegedly, by the Corsican snowbird himself. For details of how to join these tours contact the **University of Edinburgh Centre** (*see p81*).

Greyfriars Kirk

2 Greyfriars Place, Candlemaker Row, EH1 (visitor information 226 5429/www.greyfriarskirk.com). Bus 2, 23, 27, 28, 41, 42, 45. **Open** *Apr-Oct* 10.30am-4.30pm Mon-Fri; 10.30am-2.30pm Sat. *Nov-Mar* 1.30-3.30pm Thur or by appointment. **Admission** free. **Map** p309 F6.
Greyfriars Kirk pulls off the trick of being simple but not austere. Formerly the site of a Franciscan friary, it dates from 1620 but was severely damaged, then rebuilt, after a fire in 1845. The small visitors' exhibition on the church's 400-year history contains a display about the National Covenant, but most people go to see the original portrait of Greyfriars Bobby (John MacLeod, 1887).

Museum of Scotland & Royal Museum

Chambers Street, EH1 (225 7534/www.nms.ac.uk). Bus 2, 23, 27, 28, 41, 42, 45/Nicolson Street–North Bridg buses. **Open** 10am-5pm Mon, Wed-Sat; 10am-8pm Tue; noon-5pm Sun. **Admission** free. **Credit** *Shop* MC, V. **Map** p309 F6.
These two museums, distinct in tone but joined together, house three cafés and a well-stocked shop and together form a perfect wet-weather attraction. The **Museum of Scotland**, designed by Benson and Forsyth in 1998, houses all the Scottish artefacts owned by National Museums of Scotland, many of which were previously on display in the Portrait Gallery. The displays wind up from the basement, where Scotland's geological beginnings are shown,

Feeding love

Music, known for being both the food of love and the brandy of the damned, is rather difficult to represent historically. The University of Edinburgh, however, has done its best with two internationally significant collections of historical musical instruments. On the Cowgate, in St Cecilia's Hall (suitably named after the patron saint of musicians), is the **Russell Collection of Early Keyboard Instruments**, which amounts to 51 instruments: harpsichords, spinets and virginals (which produce a note by plucking the strings) and clavichords and early pianos (in which the strings are struck). This is a living museum for restoration, the study of keyboard organology and performance practice. The instruments date from the mid-16th century and many are beautifully painted works of artistic, as well as technical, merit. The elliptical and serenely decorated St Cecilia's Hall (1763, Robert Mylne) is Scotland's oldest purpose-built concert hall and is still in use – once a year for concerts using instruments from the collection.

Further south, in the dark recesses of the Reid Concert Hall, is **Edinburgh University's Collection of Historic Musical Instruments**. The 1,000-strong collection serves to illustrate the evolution of instruments since the 16th century. While most of the items are kept locked away in glass cases, the museum also contains a sound laboratory, which makes good use of modern technology to give a hands-on illustration of exactly how sound waves are created and to investigate the way they are influenced by the shapes brisof different instruments.

Plucking at the strings: **St Celia's Hall**.

Edinburgh University Collection of Historic Musical Instruments

Reid Concert Hall, Bristo Square, EH8 (650 2423/www.music.ed.ac.uk/euchmi). Bus 2, 23, 27, 28, 41, 42, 45. **Open** *Sept-July* 3-5pm Wed; 10am-1pm Sat. *Aug* 10am-1pm Mon-Fri. **Admission** free. **Map** p309 F6.

Russell Collection of Early Keyboard Instruments

St Cecilia's Hall, Cowgate, EH1 (650 2805/ www.music.ed.ac.uk/russell). Bus 30, 35/ Nicolson Street–North Bridge buses. **Open** *Sept-July* 2-5pm Wed, Sat (except public & university holidays). *Aug* 10.30am-12.30pm Mon-Sat. **Admission** £3; £2 concessions. **No credit cards**. Map p64 C2.

to the top floors which are dedicated to the 20th century. The policy of covering only those eras for which there are artefacts means there are some breaks in continuity and some rather strange omissions, notably those Scottish leaders who were defeated by the English. There is a huge amount to see, however, displayed in such a way as to provide a genuine understanding of its historical context. Free daily tours are held at 2.15pm and 3.15pm.

The **Royal Museum** boasts lofty Victorian galleries and a beautiful atrium. All the favourites of the Victorian museum-maker's art are here with much more besides: geology, anthropology, fossils, taxonomy, costumes, Chinese art and industry are all well represented and displayed. Some areas, such as the glass cases full of stuffed animals, are of the traditional improve-your-mind Victorian variety, but other exhibits, including the interactive shark display, are innovative and good for children. The museum's temporary exhibitions and frequent lectures are usually excellent, and there are free tours of the museum at 2.30pm every weekday except Thursday, and at 3.30pm on Sunday.

Talbot Rice Gallery

Old College, South Bridge, EH8 (650 2211/www. trg.ed.ac.uk). Nicolson Street–North Bridge buses. **Open** 10am-5pm Tue-Sat. **Admission** free. **Map** p310 G6.

Situated just off William Playfair's stately, grand Old Quad is the relatively recent addition of the Talbot Rice Gallery. Opened in 1975, the gallery is named after the Watson Gordon Professor of Fine Art, David Talbot Rice, famed for his writings on Islamic art. Although it houses the University's Torrie Collection, consisting of Dutch and Italian Old Masters, the greatest part of this vast and lofty space is given over to temporary exhibitions, ranging from solo shows by established Scottish artists to group shows by recent graduates.

University of Edinburgh Centre

7-11 Nicolson Street, EH8 (650 2252/www.ed.ac.uk). Nicolson Street–North Bridge buses. **Open** 9.15am-5pm Mon-Fri.
The shop-front for all things related to Edinburgh University, including tours of the Old College.

Heriot's & the Vennel

South from Greyfriars, along Forrest Road towards the Meadows (*see p106*), **Lauriston Place** marks the edge of the Old Town. To the east, and directly across from the end of Bristo Place, is the rather pompous **McEwan Hall** (1897), which was gifted to the university by local brewing magnate Sir William McEwan and is used for ceremonial occasions. Behind it is the **Reid Concert Hall**, which hosts classical concerts (*see p209*) and houses the **Edinburgh University Collection of Historic Musical Instruments** (*see p80* **Feeding love**).

George Heriot's School (*see below*), off Lauriston Place, was not originally inside the perimeter of the Flodden Wall and only became part of the Old Town with the building of the **Telfer Wall** (named after its mason, John Tailefer) in the 1630s. Opposite the school are the rather over-romantic buildings of the **Royal Infirmary**, designed by David Bryce, with help from Florence Nightingale, in 1870. In 2002 the Infirmary was in the process of moving to a new site, south-east of Edinburgh at Little France; the old site has been sold for redevelopment.

Turning north up Heriot Place leads to the **Vennel**, a steep flight of steps down to the Grassmarket. The best preserved portion of the **Flodden Wall** is here, including its only remaining bastion, which was built from rubble collected from Bruntsfield Links.

George Heriot's School

Lauriston Place, EH3 (229 7263). Bus 23, 27, 28, 45. **Open** *June-mid Aug* phone for details. Closed Sept-May. **Admission** free. **Map** p309 F6.
School prefects give historical tours of this fine 17th-century building. Heriot, a goldsmith and jeweller to James VI & I, was known as the Jinglin' Geordie. His original legacy was for the education of 'puir, fatherless bairns' but the school was used in its early days as a military hospital for Cromwell's troops.

Grassmarket

There has been a market in the Grassmarket since at least 1477 – a 1977 plaque on a rock here commemorates the 500th anniversary of the date when the area first received its charter from James III. Along **King's Stables Road** at the north-west corner of the Grassmarket, gardens provided the raw material for a vegetable market from the 12th century, while the Grassmarket itself held livestock sales. When England's Edward III occupied the Castle in the 1330s, King's Stables Road also became the site of a medieval tournament ground. This practice was shortlived; David II put a stop to it when Scotland regained the Castle in the mid-14th century (*see pp8-9*).

But the Grassmarket also has a darker history as a regular venue for executions. Among the victims were many Covenanters, who are remembered in the small walled memorial at its east end. The most famous execution to take place here, however, was the Porteous lynching in 1736, given literary form in Sir Walter Scott's *The Heart of Midlothian*. John Porteous was an unpopular captain of the town guard, who on 14 April 1736, was in charge of the hanging of two smugglers in the Grassmarket. Sensing trouble, he sealed off the area with guardsmen so that the execution could take place. The mob reacted by throwing stones and Porteous ordered his men to open fire: three in the crowd were killed and a dozen wounded. Porteous was tried for murder and found guilty. He was to be hanged on 20 July, but a royal warrant from Queen Caroline reprieved him. Not for long, though. An angry mob broke into the Old Tolbooth on the Royal Mile on 19 July, dragged Porteous down to the Grassmarket and hanged him. He was buried in Greyfriars Churchyard; there's still an entrance called **Porteous Pend** at the south-west corner of the Grassmarket, next to Mary Mallinson Antiques.

The north side of the Grassmarket is now dominated by a row of pubs and restaurants. Among them is the **White Hart Inn** where Robert Burns supposedly wrote 'Ae Fond Kiss'. It is also where the protagonist in Iain Banks' *Complicity* gets some hints about the whereabouts of a dismembered body. At the west end of the row are the new **Granny's Green Steps**, which lead up to Johnston Terrace and a possible walk around the base of Castle Rock, climbing back through the gate on the Castle Esplanade. More direct routes back are straight up **Castle Wynd** at the centre of the row, or up the **West Bow** (confusingly at the east end of the row) and Victoria Street on to George IV Bridge.

Sightseeing

New Town

Edinburgh can boast one of the original new towns, a planned development designed to replace cramped, dilapidated and worn-out buildings.

The Castle keeps watch over **Princes Street Gardens**. *See p83.*

When the upstanding burghers of 18th-century Edinburgh sat in their stinky, cramped, over-crowded, sky-scraping tenements, they could look out across the water of Nor' Loch to the pleasant pasture known as the 'long dikes' that ran along the rise of ground going down to the Forth.

This land provided a dream of escape, and in 1752 the dream was given voice by the Provost of the day, George Drummond, when a pamphlet was published proposing that the 'royalties' of the city – the land gifted from the crown – be increased to include this land to the north. Over the next 80 years, this greenfield site was turned into the elegantly curving streets and classical grey stone buildings we know today.

The New Town originally referred solely to the development of Princes, George and Queen Streets under a plan drawn up by James Craig in 1766. Today the name is used to describe the succession of developments running north from Princes Street that were built in the late 18th and early 19th centuries. As a gracious,

upmarket residential alternative to the cramped Old Town, the New Town was consciously out to impress. If its wide streets, grassy squares and classical style of architecture contrast sharply with the mood and look of the Old Town today, the difference was even greater when it was first built.

Shops and offices now occupy the original New Town, but further north the quiet, residential streets have changed little over the centuries. Edinburgh's New Town is regarded as one of the best examples of romantic classical architecture in the world and its well-ordered streets and circuses are a delight to wander around.

Princes Street

Princes Street is where the people of Edinburgh shop. It marks the grand dividing line between the Old and New Towns. Shops and department stores, on the north side of the street only, look south across Princes Street Gardens, with the drama of Edinburgh Castle, the jagged skyline of the Old Town and the brooding presence of Salisbury Crags, Arthur's Seat and Calton Hill delivering a stunning vista.

Princes Street Gardens, originally the site of Nor' Loch, occupy the ravine that runs below the Castle, between the ridge of the Old Town and Princes Street. Craig's original plans had them as gardens with a central canal. As early as 1769 private builders were planning construction on the south side of Princes Street, at the east end next to North Bridge, but fortunately for posterity, 14 owners of buildings along Princes Street – including David Hume – protested against the development. They presented an interdict to the council to halt all work on the south side, citing Craig's plan and the 'free air, and an agreeable prospect' that had enticed them from the Old Town in the first place. The council, however, wanted to allow the construction of buildings on the south side as long as they were no higher than the level of Princes Street, as exists today at Princes Mall by Waverley Bridge. The battle raged in the courts and went as far as the House of Lords, until being finally settled by an Act of Parliament in 1816, preserving the south side gardens as a pleasure ground, in perpetuity.

Today the Princes Street Gardens are well-clipped, rolling swathes of grass, crossed with bench-lined paths. In clement weather, they are an ideal place to rest or stroll. Crossing the bridges in the west garden leads to an interesting walk around the base of Castle Rock and a path that runs from behind the bandstand up to the Castle Esplanade (*see p61*).

At the extreme west end of Princes Street Gardens is the Episcopalian church of **St John's** (*see p84*). Consecrated in 1818, it is reckoned to hold one of the finest collections of stained glass in Scotland; the café below the church is a quiet oasis from the bustling street. Behind is the Presbyterian **St Cuthbert's** (*see below*), in a large, tree-crowded graveyard where many famous people are interred.

Statues of numerous famous city residents edge the gardens. At the west end is Sir James Young Simpson, the Victorian pioneer of the use of chloroform in childbirth who was frequently found self-anaesthetised on the floor of his lab. Allegedly. He stands opposite the coolly classical 1930s building that houses Fraser's department store at No.145 (*see p161*), the first of Princes Street's architecturally inconsistent parade of shops. (The broadcaster Moray McLaren famously lambasted the street as 'one of the most chaotically tasteless streets in the United Kingdom'.)

The street's original 1780s façade has long since deteriorated into an unendearing mishmash of overdressed department-store

Victoriana with minimalist 20th-century additions, interspersed with decaying shop fronts. However, many of the shops have second- or third-storey cafés or restaurants with excellent views of the Castle and Old Town. Waterstone's (*see p165*), Boots (*see p175*) and Jenners (*see p161*) are all good places to take the weight off shopping-weary legs.

Many town planners and style purists view Princes Street as Edinburgh's architectural Achilles' heel and there has been a succession of proposals to implement stylish homogeneity. In 1938 the idea was to rebuild in glass and steel. In 1958, a series of high-level pedestrian walkways linking each building was proposed. 1998's plan was for a shopping mall below street level, with entries from the Gardens. The idea reached the public inquiry stage of the planning process and has simmered away ever since, with only the **Playfair Project** at the Royal Scottish Academy (*see p84*) coming to fruition, though mutterings of extending the project continue. Plans to cut back traffic have, however, already had a positive effect with private cars banned from travelling east along the street.

St Cuthbert's

5 Lothian Road, EH1 (229 1142/www.st-cuthberts. net). Princes Street buses. **Open** *June-Sept* 10am-4pm Mon-Sat. *Mid Mar-May* 12.30-2pm Mon-Fri. Closed Oct-mid Mar. **Map** p304 A2.

Legend has it that a church was built here soon after the death of St Cuthbert, a Northumbrian who beat the drum for early Christianity and died in 687. According to the record books, however, the first church on the site was built in the 12th century when David I granted land for the purpose on the edge of the Nor' Loch. The church has a colourful history: it was caught up in various sieges of Edinburgh Castle, occupied by Cromwell's troops in 1650, then by Bonnie Prince Charlie's in 1745. Not surprisingly, the building has gone through many incarnations. The current one only dates back to 1894, although the steeple was built in 1789. The graveyard provides a shady retreat in the heart of the city and shelters a number of notable inhabitants, including artist Alexander Nasmyth (who painted the famous portrait of Robert Burns), the logarithm inventor John Napier and the city's original drugs writer, Thomas de Quincey. He penned *Confessions of an English Opium Eater* in 1822, beating Irvine Welsh to the punch by around 170 years. Some of the graveyard's 19th-century inhabitants didn't stay below ground for long – their corpses were the target of 'resurrectionists' or grave robbers. The lookout tower on the corner of Lothian Road and King's Stables Road is a reminder of those times. Inside, St Cuthbert's has a large frieze behind the apse, based on Leonardo da Vinci's *Last Supper*. Other assorted artwork and one of the church's stained-glass windows were commissioned from Tiffany's in New York. Very un-Presbyterian.

St John's Episcopal Church

*3 Lothian Road (229 7565/www.stjohns-edinburgh.
org.uk). Princes Street buses.* **Open** 9am-5pm daily.
Admission free. **Map** p304 A2.

This great Episcopalian theme park, with assorted
shops and a café in the basement, was started just
ahead of the Act of Parliament forbidding further
building south of Princes Street in 1816 and consecrated in 1818. Its stained glass is said to be
the finest collection under one roof in the whole of
Scotland, although its relentless, 19th-century
worthiness and sheer Victorian vulgarity can be
overwhelming. The window best suited to contemporary tastes is in the chapel (built in 1935). It is a
muted blue and purple affair showing Christ
praying by the Sea of Galilee. There is a memorial
to John Stuart Forbes who was killed at the battle of
Little Big Horn (Custer's last stand), on the church's
north wall, while the burial ground contains memorials to Sir Henry Raeburn and Sir Walter Scott's
mother, Margaret Rutherford, among others.

The Mound

On the west side of the junction between The
Mound and Princes Street a statue of the wig-
maker turned poet, Allan Ramsay, stands over
a floral clock dating from 1903. But the area
is dominated by the twin Doric temples of the
Royal Scottish Academy (*see p85*), facing
Princes Street, and the **National Gallery of
Scotland** (*see below*) behind it. These were
designed by William Playfair, the 19th-century
architect behind many of Edinburgh's classical
revival buildings. The plainer and more refined
National Gallery was built 20 years after the
rather more embellished Royal Scottish
Academy, which is topped by sphinxes and
an incongruous statue of the young Queen
Victoria. Originally the statue was displayed
at street level, but it is said that Victoria was
displeased by her chubby appearance, and
demanded its roof-top elevation to avoid
close scrutiny by her subjects.

During the Festival, the flat, quiet, cobbled
expanse known simply as 'the bottom of the
Mound' becomes a hive of activity: clothes
stalls, performance artists and musicians jostle
for space and attract huge crowds. At the time
of writing, however, the area is a building site,
in the midst of being transformed into the bold
new **Playfair Project**. This is the National
Galleries of Scotland's grand plan to upgrade
the whole area. The Royal Scottish Academy
is being refurbished to make it suitable for the
best touring art exhibitions (due for completion
in time for the Monet at Vétheuil exhibition
in summer 2003). At the same time, the area
between the RSA and the National Gallery is
being hollowed out, to create a link between the
two buildings with new underground exhibition

and lecture areas, a permanent café and other
visitor facilities. This second phase of the
development is due for completion in 2005.

National Gallery of Scotland

*The Mound, EH2 (624 6200/www.nationalgalleries.
org). Princes Street buses.* **Open** 10am-5pm Mon-Sat;
noon-5pm Sun. Extended hours during the Festival
(phone for details). **Admission** free; £1-£5 charge
for special exhibitions. **Credit** *Shop* AmEx, MC, V.
Map p304 C2.

The National Gallery is one of the city's landmark
classical revival buildings, built by William Playfair
in 1848. Originally housing both the Royal Scottish
Academy (*see above*) and the National Gallery, it
became the latter's exclusive home in 1911.
Sumptuously decorated in stately home style, the
succession of galleries are bedecked with a rich collection of paintings, sculpture and furniture. From
early Florentine and Renaissance art – including
Raphael's *Bridgewater Madonna*, Hugo van der
Goes' *Trinity Panel* and a *Madonna and Child* by
Botticelli – the collection courses through the cen-
turies. Poussin's *Seven Sacraments* is a high point,
as are Rubens' *The Feast of Herod* and Joshua
Reynolds' *The Ladies Waldegrave*. French art is well
represented by Watteau, Chardin and those key
players of impressionism, Monet and Pissarro.
A lower gallery, built in the 1970s, is given over to
Scottish art and luminaries such as Wilkie and
Raeburn, painter of the so-called 'Skating Minister'

Assembly Hall & New College. *See p88.*

(otherwise known as *Rev Walker Skating on Duddingston Loch*). The vicar is one of the gallery's big cultural exports and is found on everything from fridge magnets to chocolates (both of which are conveniently on sale in the gallery shop). A temporary café is set up in the gallery grounds from mid-July to September.

Royal Scottish Academy

The Mound, EH2 (558 7097). Princes Street buses. Closed until Summer 2003. **Map** p304 C2.

The Royal Scottish Academy grandly lords it over Princes Street. Built originally to house the Society of Antiquaries and the Royal Society, the robustly neoclassical building was designed by William Playfair in the 1830s. Converted in 1911 into the headquarters of the Royal Scottish Academy, the building will fill the role of a large-scale temporary exhibition space when the full-scale improvements are finished in 2003.

East end of Princes Street

Jenners (*see p161*), the world's oldest privately owned department store, commands a corner position on Princes Street and St Andrew Street. Founded in 1838 by two Leith drapers, it was extravagantly rebuilt in 1893 after a fire destroyed the original building. An estimated 25,000 people crowded the streets for the unveiling of its elaborately carved, statue-encrusted frontage, which was inspired by the façade of Oxford's Bodleian Library. Across St Andrew Street stands Scotland's first steel-framed store, built in 1906, and today housing Burton's. It is ornately topped by a group of gilded figures perched on a small belvedere and wrestling with an open-work sphere.

Gothic excess reaches great heights in the **Scott Monument** (*see p86*), a memorial to Sir Walter Scott, the prolific 19th-century author and promoter of Scotland's romantic past. Dubbed the city's 'medieval space rocket', it was originally to have been sited in the less public residential enclave of Charlotte Square, but instead the statue dominates the skyline on the corner of Waverley Bridge (named after Scott's *Waverley* novels) and Princes Street. John Ruskin, the 19th-century art critic known for his cutting ripostes, likened it to a misplaced church spire. There are great views from the top. The white Carrara marble statue by Sir John Steell that sits in the middle of the monument appropriately shows Scott – an advocate of Scottish national dress – wearing a rustic shepherd's plaid, with his dog, Maida, at his feet. To the left of the Scott Monument, and somewhat overshadowed by its excessive extravagance, is a diminutive statue of the Scots-born Victorian missionary and explorer, David Livingstone.

Princes Street ends with the **Balmoral Hotel** (*see p41*), a huge late-Victorian edifice. Its clock usually runs three minutes fast to hurry passengers to Waverley Station just down the steps beneath it – except over Hogmanay when it announces the new year to the thousands who throng Princes Street below. Facing the hotel and North Bridge is the regal **General Register House** (*see p86*), which was built in 1774 by Robert Adam (the key member of the famous Adam dynasty of architects), and still houses the National Archives of Scotland. The best impression of the Register House – perhaps, the most perfect example of classical restraint in Edinburgh – is gained from across the road in front of the GPO building. In front of Register House, the statue of the Duke of Wellington, hero of the Battle of Waterloo, gallops towards North Bridge.

Looking east along Waterloo Place is a fine view of Calton Hill (*see p96*), crowned by the National Monument and the Nelson Monument. Round the corner to the left, on Leith Street, there is a small explosion of 1960s architectural brutalism in the form of the **St James Shopping Centre** (*see p163*), built on the site of an 18th-century square. On the other side of Register House, West Register Street leads past New Register House (housing the **General Register Office**; *see below*) through to St Andrew's Square and George Street and, conveniently, passes the **Café Royal** (*see p151*). This is not just a good pub for a spot of refreshment but is also an extravagantly dressed late 19th-century building. The spectacular central bar is offset by a succession of tiled murals picturing Scottish inventors including Michael Faraday and James Watt.

General Register House

2 Princes Street, EH1 (535 1314/www.nas.gov.uk). Princes Street buses. **Open** 9am-4.30pm Mon-Fri. **Admission** free. **Map** p304 D1.

Designed by Robert Adam and planned while North Bridge was still being built, General Register House was first opened in 1789, when part of the building was completed, but was not finished until the 1820s under Robert Reid. It is home to the National Archives of Scotland and is the oldest purpose-built archive repository still in use in Europe, holding public records of government, churches, the law and businesses; searching the archives for historical research purposes is free. The NAS has over 60km (35 miles) of shelving in its three sites in Edinburgh, which include West Register House (*see p89*), where plans are kept. Facsimiles of nationally important documents such as the Declaration of Arbroath and the Articles of Union of 1707 are displayed in the foyer. Readers tickets are issued on personal application and require proof of identity.

The making of the New Town

The wide and grand George Street forms the backbone of Edinburgh's original New Town – the first of the series of developments planned to provide extra and more gracious living space to those who could afford it. In the first half of the 18th century, it was realised that Edinburgh was getting too cramped and, in 1752, a long and wordy pamphlet was published setting out proposals to enlarge the town to the north and south. The proposals were largely down to the work of George Drummond, the Lord Provost, and were – for the most part – put into effect over the next 80 years.

The first stage was the building of North Bridge, which started in 1765. The following year, an architectural competition was held to find a plan for the New Town. It was won by 21-year-old James Craig's simple and sensible solution. The layout of three parallel roads – Princes, George and Queen streets – ended by two squares, replaced Craig's earlier design of radial roads, which was inspired by the Union Jack – a symbol that was a bit too highly charged for the Scots after the 1707 Act of Union. Craig, however, was obviously keen for royal approval. He dedicated his final plan to George III, who in turn had an influence on the names of the streets. George Street is named after the monarch and Princes Street after his sons. The story goes that the original name of St Giles was dropped as it reminded the King of a sleazy quarter of London. The architectural plans are on view in the **Museum of Edinburgh** (*see p75*) on the Canongate in the Old Town.

Although the slope of the hill down from George Street seems smooth now, a considerable amount of landforming went into the construction of the New Town streets. Between 1781 and 1830, as the New Town expanded, it is reckoned that over two million cartloads of earth were removed and taken to create the Mound. You can get a good sense of the formidable construction work at the spot where the end of India Street looms over North West Circus Place. A proper junction would have made too much of a gradient, and the raised end of India Street shows just how much the roads were raised above ground level to give the houses basements and to flatten out the land.

General Register Office

New Register House, 3 West Register Street, EH1 (334 0380/www.gro-scotland.gov.uk). Princes Street buses. **Open** 9am-4.30pm Mon-Fri. **Admission** £17 day pass; £10 part-day pass (after 1pm); £65 week pass. **Credit** MC, V. **Map** p304 D1.

The purpose-built General Register Office for Scotland contains records of all births, marriages and deaths in Scotland since 1855, census records up to 1901, and 3,500 old parish registers from between 1553 and 1854. Designed by Robert Mathieson, who also designed the old GPO building across the road, it is modelled on the General Register House next door (*see p85*) and was completed in 1863. A pass is needed to view the records and, as there are only 100 search places, it is advisable to book ahead.

Scott Monument

East Princes Street Gardens, EH2 (529 4068/ www.cac.org.uk). Princes Street buses. **Open** *Mar-May* 10am-6pm daily. *June-Sept* 9am-8pm Mon-Sat; 10am-6pm Sun. *Oct* 9am-6pm Mon-Sat; 10am-6pm Sun. *Nov-Feb* 9am-4pm daily. **Admission** £2.50. **No credit cards**. **Map** p304 C2.

This over-elaborate and ornate counterpoint to the austerity of most of Edinburgh's architecture is a fitting memorial to Sir Walter Scott, who orchestrated George IV's celebrated tartanising visit to Edinburgh in 1822. Designed by the self-taught architect George Meikle Kemp, the monument manages to incorporate statuettes of 84 of Scott's characters and was completed in 1846, 14 years after Scott's death. Kemp himself drowned in the Union canal under mysterious circumstances in 1844. The views from this 61m (200ft) city-centre landmark are superb, but the final flight of steps up to the very pinnacle are a tight squeeze and can be claustrophobic.

St Andrew Square

Named after Scotland's patron saint, St Andrew Square sits at the eastern end of George Street, home to Edinburgh's smartest shops. Right at the centre of the square is the **Melville Monument**, a 40-metre (135-foot) Doric column inspired by Rome's Trajan Column and topped by a statue of Henry Dundas, first Earl of Melville, a notorious 18th-century political wheeler dealer.

The square has long been the financial heart of Edinburgh. The Royal Bank of Scotland has its headquarters in a former mansion on its east side. The mansion was built in 1772 for Sir Laurence Dundas on the site that, in Craig's plan, was reserved for St Andrew's Church, and is set back from the square, with a private lawn – a rare sight in the New Town. It is a mark of Sir Laurence's political muscle that he was able to overrule the council's planning orders. The bank is still a working branch and the sumptuously decorated iron dome of the Telling Room (1860) is open during banking hours. Next door, the Bank of Scotland is housed in an outlandishly loud pseudo palazzo with rooftop statues built in 1851. The banking hall is once again very fine and is also open during banking hours.

In the north-east corner of the square is the new development of the bus station and Harvey Nichols (*see p159*). To the north of the square, an explosion of Gothic-cum-medieval architecture is delivered by the **Scottish National Portrait Gallery** (*see below*), at the east end of Queen Street. A confident, late-19th-century building dotted with pinnacles and sculptures of intellectual heroes from down the ages, its red sandstone façade is best seen in the late evening summer sun. It does not, however, fit in with the classical constraint of much of the New Town. The huge foyer, decorated with murals recounting Scotland's history, is definitely worth a look. It seems fitting that Sir Henry Raeburn, portrait artist to Edinburgh's Enlightenment luminaries, lived over the way at 32 York Place. Raeburn owned large parts of what is now Stockbridge and was responsible for much of the building there.

The east end of George Street begins with the 1940s green and black former **Guardian Royal Exchange** office. It is Scandinavian in tone, with a vast front door elaborately carved and flanked by columns and bronze figures. Just past it is the **Dome** (*see p152*), which was once a bank but, like many other former financial institutions that once lined George Street, has been transformed into a vast drinking den. Epitomising the grandiose excess of Edinburgh's 19th-century banks, its richly decorated domed interior is worth seeing. It may even have prompted John Ruskin's 1853 critical onslaught on the city's liberal use of classical columns: 'Your decorations are just as monotonous as your simplicities.'

Opposite the Dome is **St Andrew's Church**, built in 1787, and originally intended for the plot of land appropriated by Dundas. Although the exterior of the church is dwarfed by its surrounding buildings, the cool interior is no minor achievement in classical grace. It was at St Andrew's that the Assembly of the Church of Scotland was convened in May 1843, during which 472 ministers marched out of the church, down Dundas Street to the Tanfield Hall to establish the Free Church of Scotland in what was known as 'the Disruption' (*see p18*).

Reflections on **Charlotte Square**. *See p88.*

Scottish National Portrait Gallery

1 Queen Street, EH2 (624 6200/www.national galleries.org). Bus 4, 8, 10, 12, 15, 16, 17, 26. **Open** 10am-5pm Mon Sat; noon-5pm Sun. Extended hours during Festival (phone for details). **Admission** free; £1-£5 for special loan exhibitions. **Credit** *Shop* AmEx, MC, V. **Map** p306 F4.

Housed in an elaborately pinnacled Gothic revival edifice, the Portrait Gallery is an essential visit for those wanting to get to grips with Scotland's heritage or check out its more contemporary heroes and heroines. The foyer is decorated with stunning murals of important moments in Scottish history, while paintings of kings and queens, including Mary, Queen of Scots and Bonny Prince Charlie, give a brilliant visual guide to the rise and fall of the Scottish monarchy. The upper galleries are filled with portraits of statuesque, tartan-dressed lairds and ladies. A further gallery is devoted to 20th-century achievers in concurrence with the gallery's policy of actively purchasing and commissioning portraits of celebrated living Scots. Portraits include designer Jean Muir, dancer Moira Shearer, writer Irvine Welsh and actor Sean Connery. A downstairs gallery hosts small temporary shows of work by contemporary artists, while one upstairs gallery is becoming increasingly strong on contemporary photography shows – both Magnum photographers and the Kobal Photographic Portrait Award have featured in the past. The shop is well stocked and the Queen Street Café's home baking is recommended (*see p141*).

Sightseeing

George Street

A flamboyant-looking statue of George IV, erected to mark his visit to Edinburgh in 1822, stands at George Street's junction with Hanover Street. This is a good spot to take in the view.

To the north, down Hanover Street past the Royal Botanic Garden and over the Firth of Forth, lies Fife. To the south, you get a full sense of the neo-classical vigour of the Royal Scottish Academy and, beyond, a view of the **Assembly Hall & New College** on the crest of the Mound. The Assembly Hall & New College was built on a direct axis with Tolbooth Church (now The Hub information centre for Edinburgh International Festival; see p64), which stands behind at the top of the Lawnmarket. In fact, from George Street, it appears that the Assembly Hall & New College have borrowed the church's imposing spire. This architectural pun was no accident on the part of the designer, William Playfair, and would have been well understood by his contemporaries: Tolbooth Church was started in 1842 as the Assembly Hall for the Church of Scotland but, following the Disruption of 1843, became the Assembly Hall for the Established Church. In designing the Assembly Hall & New College for the newly formed Free Church and orienting them so carefully on the Mound, Playfair obviously felt a little ecclesiastical humour would not go amiss.

Further west along George Street are the **Assembly Rooms**. Built by public subscription in 1787, the rooms became a favoured haunt of Edinburgh's Regency partying set. It was here that Sir Walter Scott 'came out' as author of the Waverley novels in 1827 and Charles Dickens was among many famous literary figures to have delighted audiences here. During the Festival, the building is transformed into one of the Fringe's largest venues.

This stretch of George Street was once a popular quarter for Edinburgh's literary types. The poet Shelley and his first wife Harriet Westbrook honeymooned at 84 George Street, above today's Victoria Wine shop, and Scott lived around the corner at 39 North Castle Street. No.45 George Street was the headquarters of the influential literary journal, *Blackwood's Magazine*, which counted Henry James and Oscar Wilde among its contributors. More recently, **Milne's** bar (*see p153*), on the corner of Hanover and Rose Streets, was a popular 1960s hangout for a generation of Scottish writers such as Norman MacCaig and Sorley MacLean. Their photographs and words still hang on the wall of the basement bar.

Bank of Scotland. *See p87*.

Charlotte Square

Concluding George Street on the west side is Charlotte Square. Named after George III's wife, Queen Charlotte, it was designed by Robert Adam in 1791 and is now one of Edinburgh's classiest residential enclaves. Adam conceived and designed the frontages and the façades – discreetly ornamented with sphinxes and pediments – to create a coherent whole, but each house was designed and built separately.

The head office of the **National Trust for Scotland** (*see p89*) is at Nos.26-31, on the south side of the square, and is open to the public. It has a small art gallery, a shop and a café. The north side of the square has the best-preserved façade, with the Trust's **Georgian House**, at No.7 (*see p89*), offering the chance to see how the interior of a domestic house would have looked when the square was built. No.6 is the official residence of Scotland's first minister. A monument to Prince Albert, husband of Queen Victoria, sits in the central grassy area overlooked by **West Register House** (*see p89*), a grandly domed and porticoed affair originally built as St George's Church. The square has been home to numerous illustrious residents, the most notable being Alexander Graham Bell, the inventor of the telephone, who was born in 1847 at 16 South Charlotte Street.

Just off Charlotte Square is **Young Street**. One of an ordered network of narrow streets that run along either side of George Street, it reveals more about Craig's New Town plan. Tucked away from the grander streets, this is where the less financially fortunate lived. It is also a favoured haunt of one Inspector John Rebus, who drinks at the Oxford Bar (*see p153*) in Ian Rankin's best-selling detective novels.

To the north of Young Street, parallel to George Street, are **Queen Street** and **Queen Street Gardens**. These gardens, like the many others that punctuate the New Town, were created as stretches of disciplined ruralness for the residents of the grand squares and terraces to enjoy and remain accessible only to residents. Further along Queen Street, at No.8, is a townhouse built by Robert Adam and Thomas Hamilton's **Royal College of Physicians**.

Georgian House

7 Charlotte Square, EH2 (226 3318/www.nts.org.uk). Princes Street buses. **Open** *Apr-Oct* 10am-6pm daily. *Nov, Dec, mid Jan-Mar* 11am-4pm daily. Closed 2wks Jan. **Admission** £5; £3.75 concessions. **Credit** *Shop* MC, V. **Map** p304 A1.

The National Trust for Scotland has refurbished this prestigious, Robert Adam-designed residence to recreate the sumptuous glory it enjoyed when rich businessman John Lamont lived here in the early 19th century. The rooms, from drawing room to kitchen, contain period furnishings, right down to the newspapers. There's a guide in each room to relate anecdotes about lifestyle and furnishings, and everything can be looked at right up close – so long as you don't touch.

National Trust for Scotland

Head office: 26-31 Charlotte Square, EH2 (243 9300/restaurant reservations 243 9399/ www.nts.org.uk). Princes Street buses. **Open** *Gallery* 10am-5pm Mon-Sat; noon-5pm Sun. *Shop & coffee house* 10am-6pm Mon-Sat; noon-5pm Sun. *Restaurant* 6-11pm daily. **Admission** free. **Credit** *Shop* MC, V. **Map** p304 A1.

The National Trust for Scotland has spent £13.6 million restoring these four townhouses to their original state and making them suitable as modern offices. The public rooms, which are entered at No.28, allow visitors to see many of the original features, such as plasterwork and wallpaper. Three galleries upstairs give the NTS the opportunity to show off some of its art collection, including important works by 20th-century Scottish artists, which are on loan to the Trust and are displayed in the grand drawing room, featuring some impressive Regency furnishings. There are pointers to the Trust's other properties and considerable land-holdings around Scotland as well as information on the conversion itself. The ground-floor coffee house is a stylish place to pause during the day, while the restaurant at No.27 is proving popular at night.

West Register House

Charlotte Square, EH2 (535 1314). Princes Street buses. **Open** 9am-4.30pm Mon-Fri. **Admission** free. **Map** p304 A1.

The West Search Room of the National Archive of Scotland contains maps and plans, records of government departments and microfilm records. There is a small permanent exhibition of maps and plans that manages to show, albeit rather dryly, how the geography of Scotland has been shaped by man over the last few hundred years.

Dundas Street & environs

A gridiron of grandly ordered streets continues north from Queen Street down the hill to the Water of Leith. The streets are lined with solid, well-proportioned sandstone residences turned slate grey with age. The area around **Dundas Street** is considered to be the heart of today's New Town, although it was constructed after the first 18th-century development.

It is one of six further developments built in the early 19th century as speculative ventures on the part of the landowners cashing in on Edinburgh's need for upmarket dwellings. Scottish property laws allowed landowners to stipulate architectural style, so the New Town's cohesive classical formality is played out with little interruption. Resolutely residential and exclusive, these new areas did not wish to attract outsiders or Old Town hoi polloi. Churches aside, there were originally no public buildings, squares or markets: only in recent decades have shops and restaurants opened along the main roads. Dundas Street itself also contains a number of private art galleries. There is still a classy air to the area, but it is now home to a wider social mix. The best way to explore this part of the New Town is simply to follow your feet; it is nearly impossible to get lost.

Look out for stone-carved inscriptions of famous inhabitants on the front of their former residences. Robert Louis Stevenson lived just below Queen Street Gardens at 17 Heriot Row. It is said that as a sickly child these gardens provided inspiration for his novel *Treasure Island*. Later, as a young bohemian in his signature black velvet jacket, he bypassed the elegance of the New Town and headed uphill to the Old Town and its more rough-and-ready drinking haunts or downhill to Leith Walk.

Cutting across Dundas Street is **Great King Street**. Built in 1804, it is a brilliant embodiment of the classical New Town look. Fanlights, windows and even chimney stacks are symmetrically arranged to give maximum impact to the architectural grandeur. Another famous New Town resident, JM Barrie, author of *Peter Pan*, lodged as a student at No.3.

Gothic excess: **Scott Monument**. *See p85.*

Just beyond lies **Drummond Place**, named after George Drummond, who was six times Lord Provost and driving force behind the construction of the first New Town. Built in a horseshoe shape, with a central garden and cobbled roads, it sums up the New Town's ethos for urban living: smart tenement buildings were consciously designed to look like upmarket houses, with ample front doors and high ceilings, overlooking a spacious oasis of greenery. Doubtless finding pleasure in all this was Compton Mackenzie, the author of *Whisky Galore*, who lived at No.31 Drummond Place.

The **Moray Estate** is one of the grandest of the New Town's residential quarters. It lies to the west of Howe Street and is best approached from Heriot Row. Built on land belonging to the Earl of Moray in 1822, this development is formed by a succession of linked crescents. The architectural climax comes in Moray Place, an overbearing, 12-sided circus, punctuated by sturdy columns set into the façade. This represents New Town classical formality at its proudest.

Western New Town

Beyond Charlotte Square, the New Town continues its thrust towards the west and Haymarket, with neo-classical architecture continuing into the Westend. However, the area starts with the great, red-stone edifice of the **Hilton Caledonian Hotel** (*see p43*). The building was frowned upon by natives when it appeared in 1903 as something more suited to vulgarian Glasgow. It was originally a railway hotel; the adjacent station closed in 1965, though the frieze over the former station entrance survives in the foyer by the hotel bistro.

Caught between West Maitland Street and Queensferry Street, the **Westend** would be an architectural jewel in the crown of most cities, but in Edinburgh seems rather dull – almost a corporationjunct – when compared to the dramatic excess of the rest of the New Town. However, this area is pleasant to wander around, and fits neatly into the physical landscape as it meets the gorge of the Water of Leith to the north. The small shops and hostelries in William Street and Stafford Street show what the whole New Town could have been like if such a vulgar idea as consumerism had been accepted by the original planners. The only street of any real distinction is Melville Street, which ends in the area's only construction of note: the episcopal cathedral of **St Mary's** (*see below*), entered from Palmerston Place. The main building was completed in 1879 on land gifted for the purpose by the sisters Barbara and Mary Walker, but the triple spires, which form an integral part of Edinburgh's skyline, were not finished until World War I. Next door, the cathedral Choir School contains murals by Phoebe Anne Traquair. The school is not normally open to the public, although it does hold occasional concerts and exhibitions during the Festival.

St Mary's Episcopal Cathedral

Palmerston Place, EH12 (225 6293/www.cathedral. net). Bus 3, 3A, 12, 25, 25A. **Open** 9am-6pm Mon-Fri; 9am-5pm Sat, Sun. **Map** p308 B6.

Monumental from the outside, St Mary's continues the theme inside with an interior like a great vaulted box. As fits such a relatively young cathedral, the building and furnishings borrow wildly from different styles and times. There is a chapel dedicated to King Charles, who created the diocese of Edinburgh in 1633, which contains some interesting copies of artefacts. Unusually, the lectern is not an eagle, but a pelican. The choir, which was the first in Britain to use girl trebles, practises in the adjacent Choir School and sings at all the daily services. The four manual organ, a Father Willis, was enlarged in 1931 and last refurbished in 1995. Both choir and organ are involved in regular concerts (*see p210*).

Stockbridge

Bridging the gap between the classy New Town and the scenic Water of Leith.

Dean Terrace and the **Water of Leith**: rural idyll in the city.

Tucked neatly into the hill below the New Town, Stockbridge is a bohemian adjunct that connects the regimented streets above to the meandering curves of the Water of Leith. Despite the name, until 1785 there was only a wooden pedestrian bridge across the Water of Leith here, while carts and stock were required to pay a toll to cross a dangerous ford.

Dean Village, upriver from the bridge, was the centre of the small-scale industry of mills and tanneries that lined the banks of the Water of Leith in the 18th century. Downriver, the **Royal Botanic Garden** moved to its current location in Inverleith in 1823.

Being downhill from the New Town had its disadvantages: the river soon became a general sewer and rubbish tip. However, such a valuable amenity could not remain that way and the Water of Leith has now been cleaned up and the path along its banks, known as the **Water of Leith Walkway**, extended from Edinburgh's southern edge right down to the Forth. Stockbridge itself retains an air of separateness from the rest of the city, with turn-of-the-century tenemented streets, genteel terraces and occasional villas that are architecturally more interesting than those in other, monotonously conformist, suburbs of Edinburgh.

From St Stephen Street to the Botanics

In the late 1960s and early 1970s cheap rented accommodation turned Stockbridge into a bohemian student heartland. Re-gentrification blunted the groovy edge during the economic boom of the 1990s, but second-hand shops still line Stockbridge's main shopping area of **Deanhaugh Street** and **Raeburn Place**. **St Stephen Street**, just across the bridge on the edge of the New Town, was once home to Nico (of Velvet Underground fame) and had a wealth of junk-cum-antique shops, only a few of which remain. On the corner of St Stephen Street is the **Bailie** (225 4673), a cosy drinking hole that has several photographs showing Stockbridge in its earlier days.

Further along are Regency-style shops and a marooned old gateway that is the last vestige of Stockbridge's meat and vegetable market. The market was built in 1826 after a public campaign led by one Captain Carnegie, and was a coup for local shoppers as town officials had hoped that Stockbridge, like neighbouring New Town, would aspire to residential classiness and strive to be a market-free zone. Thankfully, it is not.

Sightseeing

Along **India Place**, on the corner with Gloucester Street, is **Duncan's Land**, built in the late 1790s and one of the area's oldest buildings. It is now a restaurant. The stone for Duncan's Land, including the carved lintel inscribed with the phrase 'Fear Only God 1650', was recovered from buildings in the Lawnmarket that were demolished to open up the Mound . It was the birthplace, in 1796, of David Roberts, the painter of Middle Eastern souks and Pharaonic temples, known for his penchant for dressing up as a sheik. Opposite Duncan's Land, a mass of modern flats stands on the site of a series of streets demolished in the name of slum tenement clearance in the 1960s and 1970s.

The present bridge was built in 1900 and crosses the Water of Leith at Kerr Street and Deanhaugh Street. Along Hamilton Place, past the Theatre Workshop (*see p228*) and Saxe-Coburg Street, is the low-slung, neoclassical **Edinburgh Academy** on Henderson Row. Built in 1824, it was the fittingly austere location for the filming of *The Prime of Miss Jean Brodie*. Down Saxe-Coburg Street itself lies the quaint 1820s square, **Saxe-Coburg Place**.

Not all building in 19th-century Edinburgh was as classically regimented as the New Town. **The Colonies**, which lie on the north side of Glenogle Road, between Saxe-Coburg Place and the Water of Leith, are the first of a series of artisan dwellings that were built by the Edinburgh Co-operative Building Company from the 1860s onwards. They defy Edinburgh's usual preference for tenements. Eleven narrow streets (named after members

St Bernard's Crescent. *See p94.*

and supporters of the co-operative) are lined with two-storey stone terraces. Unusually, they are double sided, in that the entrance to the upper level dwelling is from external steps that run from one street, with access to the ground floor dwelling from the opposite side.

From the Stock Bridge, the **Water of Leith Walkway** makes a small break at Bridge Place at the west end of Glenogle Road. It restarts almost at the far end of Arboretum Avenue, turning down Rocheid Path to Inverleith Row. Here it breaks once again, continuing at the far end of Warriston Crescent, from where it is a pleasant walk down to Leith.

The **Royal Botanic Garden** ('Botanics'; *see p93*) with its collections of world importance

City walks Galleries and graveyards

The Water of Leith is one of Edinburgh's hidden attractions and forms the basis of some great, verdant walks. This Stockbridge stroll takes in the village of Dean, the Dean graveyard and the galleries. You'll find other suggestions for walks along the river at the Water of Leith Visitors' Centre (*see p111* **Canal dreams**) several miles upstream.

Joining the Walkway at **Saunders Street**, just by the bridge, the path enters one of its most dramatic stretches through a ravine between the New Town and the private Dean Gardens to the north-west. Along the Walkway you'll come to a neoclassical circular temple, **St Bernard's Well**. Apparently three schoolboys discovered a mineral water spring there in 1760. Cashing in on the craze for 'taking the waters', in 1788 Lord Gardenstone

commissioned architect Alexander Nasmyth to build a temple to replace an earlier wellhouse. The pump room (only occasionally opened to the public) is richly decorated in mosaics. Above, standing beneath the temple's dome, is a statue of Hygeia, the goddess of health.

Further along the Walkway, there are epic views of **Dean Bridge**, which was built in the 1820s by engineer Thomas Telford. To the north of the bridge stands **Holy Trinity Church**, built as an 1830s reproduction of the English Perpendicular style.

As the Walkway passes under Dean Bridge and rises along Miller Row to Old Dean Bridge, it enters **Dean Village**, originally called the Village of the Water of Leith. Mills first clustered here in the 15th century; the and well-kept beds is at the north end of Arboretum Avenue. At its heart is **Inverleith House** (*see below*) and the Terrace Café (*see p141*). The lawns at the front of the house give an unusual view of the castle. **Inverleith Park**, opposite the entrance to the Botanics on Arboretum Place, has a purpose-built boating pond past the memorial gardens over to the left.

Inverleith House

Royal Botanic Garden, Inverleith Row, EH3 (552 7171/www.rbge.org.uk/inverleith-house). Bus 8, 17, 23, 27. **Open** *Nov-Feb* 11am-3.30pm daily. *Mar, Apr* 11am-5pm daily. *May-Oct* 10am-5pm daily. **Admission** free. **No credit cards. Map** p305 C2.
A sturdy but stately stone mansion with brilliant views of Edinburgh's skyline, Inverleith House dates back to the late 18th century. It was converted to a gallery in 1960 and was, until 1984, home to the Scottish National Gallery of Modern Art (*see p95*). Situated slap bang in the middle of the Royal Botanic Garden (*see below*), Inverleith House enjoys a degree of splendid isolation from the city-centre art scene. Venture past the herbaceous borders to discover one of Edinburgh's finest gallery spaces, with a strong and zappy exhibitions programme. The house is now run by the Botanic Garden, which is why the shows make frequent reference to the natural world, though they are not confined to botanical paintings and displays from the Botanics' extensive archives. Callum Innes has shown here, along with Myron Stout, Agnes Martin and famed bricklayer Carl Andre. As well as showing work by international artists, Inverleith House keeps a sharp eye on local up-and-coming artists, by curating group shows of home-grown talent and hosting the Absolut Scotland Open art competition.

Royal Botanic Garden

Inverleith Row, EH3 (552 7171/www.rbge.org.uk). Bus 8, 17, 23, 27. **Open** *Nov-Feb* 10am-4pm daily. *Mar, Apr, Sept, Oct* 10am-6pm daily. *May-Aug* 10am-8pm daily. **Admission** free. **Credit** *Shop* V. **Map** p306 D2.
A gentle stroll among the greenery of the Botanic Garden will revive any traveller weary of notching up the city's sights. One of only two Royal Botanic Gardens in Britain (the other is London's Kew), Edinburgh's was founded in 1670 when botany and medicine were closely linked. Originally sited next to the Palace of Holyroodhouse, it moved to its present site (by way of two other locations) in 1823. Today, 28 hectares are home to over 2,000 specimens of trees, a rock garden, a world-famous collection of rhododendrons, a peat garden and the Pringle Chinese Collection, modelled on the mountainous environment of south-west China. The Pringle is the largest collection of Chinese plants outside China and is the fruit of the special interest taken by Scottish scientific explorers over the last 150 years. The garden's ten glasshouses include the impressive Temperate Palm House which at 21m (70ft) high is the tallest in Britain. In the middle of the garden is Inverleith House (*see above*) and the Terrace Café (*see p141*). The gift shop next to the West Gate has an interesting selection of plants for sale, and some fascinating publications about the Garden, the work carried out there and Scottish wild plants.

The Raeburn Estate

Back in Stockbridge, just off Deanhaugh Street at the top of Leslie Place, lies the **Raeburn Estate**. An early 19th-century speculative property development by the artist Sir Henry

Incorporation of Baxters (bakers) ran 11 watermills, supplying milled meal to the whole of Edinburgh. Today, Dean Village is faintly reminiscent of a Bavarian village, with gabled houses staggered along a deep gorge. It is a surprisingly quiet and secluded spot considering its proximity to the city centre. Bell's Brae (brae is Gaelic for 'upper part') runs steeply up to Dean Bridge. Formerly the main road running north out of Edinburgh, the Brae is still lined with a rich agglomeration of 17th-century stone buildings.

Opposite Old Dean Bridge is **Baxter's Tolbooth**, which was given an unappealing makeover in the 1970s. Still visible, however, is a stone carved with wheat sheaves and bakers' shovels with the inscription 'God's Providence Is Our Inheritance', which dates from 1675.

Just beyond the bridge is West Mill, now converted into flats, and **Well Court** (1884), which was built as artisan housing in an act of Victorian philanthropy by John Ritchie ▶

Royal Botanic Garden. *See p93.*

Raeburn, it seduced the moneyed classes to move down the hill. Although the whole is less triumphal in scale than the New Town, **St Bernard's Crescent** is an architectural heavyweight, with thick Grecian columns and vast front doors. Over the way is the rather more delicate **Danube Street**, with wrought-iron balconies and rooftop balustrades. Behind this show of architectural propriety, Dora Noyce ran a brothel until the 1980s. Known for serving liquid refreshment from a silver teapot, the infamous Mrs Noyce described her establishment as 'more of a YMCA with extras'.

Overlooking the Water of Leith is Dean Terrace, which rises up to Ann Street. Bijou and unassuming, **Ann Street** is today one of Edinburgh's most exclusive residential addresses. Named after Raeburn's wife, it has dolls' house-like proportions compared with the lofty heights of the New Town. There is a cottage-garden ambience to the street, with each terraced house fronted by a small garden. Many famous residents have found refuge here, including Thomas de Quincey, the 19th-century author of *The Confessions of an English Opium Eater.*

The Dean

To the west and up the hill from Ann Street is the one-time **Dean estate**. John Learmonth bought the estate with an eye to financial gain in 1825. As Edinburgh's Lord Provost, Learmonth negotiated the building of Dean Bridge to cross the Water of Leith and link the land to the city. Not entirely successful on the money-making front, thanks to a saturated mid 19th-century property market, Learmonth's development fell short of his aspirations. Later, rows of tenements with bay windows were added. They continue to stand proud along the east of Queensferry Road.

From further along Queensferry Road, look north down Learmonth Avenue for a view of what looks like a castle imported from a Disney landscape. This is **Fettes College**, a private school for boys built in the 1860s. A flamboyant coupling of the French chateau and Scots Baronial styles, it is topped by a soaring clock tower. Tony Blair was educated here, as was James Bond. According to espionage fiction, Bond was sent to Fettes after an 'incident' with a maid at his former school, Eton College. And there are those who say that Hogwart's, Harry Potter's school, is based on Fettes. Back on Queensferry Road is Stewart's **Melville College**. Another architectural flight of fancy, this is an 1848 hybrid of Renaissance and Jacobean styles marched out in a sea of leaded domes. It was built as one of Edinburgh's many so-called 'pauper palaces', funded by wealthy benefactors to school and house poor, often orphaned, children. Just around the corner, off Dean Path, is **Dean Cemetery** (*see below*

▶ ## Galleries and graveyards (continued)

Findlay, former proprietor of the *Scotsman* newspaper, whose own home overlooked the village.

Leaving the Walkway here and going up Dean Path leads to the main entrance of the **Dean Cemetery**. It was laid out in 1845 and among its famous dead are architect William Playfair, pioneering photographer David Octavius Hill and the man who inspired Conan Doyle's Sherlock Holmes, Dr Joseph Bell. The tombs are among the most magnificent and bombastic in Edinburgh, built for wealthy and powerful men who knew exactly how they wanted to be remembered. At the far end of the graveyard, down the main path leading straight away from the gatehouse, there is a gate in the wall (open

summer 9am-5pm; winter 9am-dusk; closed public holidays) leading to the back of the **Dean Gallery**. As you pass through it, note the pyramid-shaped tomb of Andrew Rutherford and the much more restrained, neoclassical tomb of William Playfair.

Once in the grounds of the gallery, ignore the little path next to the wall and instead cross the gallery car park and go up the steps in order to pass through an intriguing sculpture by the outspoken Scottish artist Ian Hamilton Finlay.

Across Belford Road is the **Scottish National Gallery of Modern Art**. The cafés in both galleries make good places to stop for a bite to eat: the Gallery of Modern Art café has access to a rear garden on sunny days.

Sightseeing

Galleries and graveyards), and on the far side, the **Dean Gallery** and the **Scottish National Gallery of Modern Art** (for both, *see below*). The grounds of both are open to the public, even if not visiting an exhibition.

The Dean Gallery was built by Thomas Hamilton in 1833 as the Dean Orphan Hospital. Usually one for the severe classical repertoire, here Hamilton loosened his architectural style and opted for showy roof-top pavilions. The Gallery of Modern Art was designed as the John Watson Institution by William Burn in the 1820s. The lawn to the front has recently been landscaped by Charles Jencks into a dramatic landform; a stepped, serpentine-shaped mound is reflected in three crescent-shaped pools of water.

Dean Gallery

Belford Road, EH4 (624 6200/www.national galleries.org). Bus 13. **Open** 10am-5pm Mon-Sat; noon-5pm Sun. **Admission** free; £1-£5 charge for special loan exhibitions. **Credit** *Shop* AmEx, MC, V. **Map** p308 A5.

Opened in 1999 as part of the National Galleries of Scotland's empire, the Dean Gallery neighbours the National Gallery of Modern Art; you can easily combine a visit to both in a day. Criticised in some quarters for the upmarket-shopping-mall feel of its ground floor and the large amount of space given over to work by Sir Eduardo Paolozzi (there is a mock-up of the sculptor's studio), the Dean does, nevertheless, hold one of Britain's strongest collections of surrealist and Dada artworks. Drawn from the collections of Roland Penrose and the celebrated collector and marmalade heiress Gabrielle Keiller, it includes work by the big boys of surrealism: Dali, Giacometti, Miró and Picasso. The Study Collection

room contains a fascinating array of text and surreal artefacts. Keen researchers can request access to the library. The upstairs galleries are given over to temporary shows by 20th-century artists and have included exhibitions by Gary Hume, Magritte and the Scottish Colourists. *See also p94* **Galleries and graveyards**.

Scottish National Gallery of Modern Art

Belford Road, EH4 (624 6200/www.national galleries.org. Bus 13. **Open** 10am-5pm Mon-Sat; noon-5pm Sun. **Admission** free; £1-£5 charge for special loan exhibitions. **Credit** *Shop* AmEx, MC, V. **Map** p308 A5.

Since 1984, Scotland's national collection of modern art has been housed in this 19th-century neoclassical edifice set in parkland, dotted with sculptures by Paolozzi, Henry Moore and Dan Graham. The gallery makes an ideal day-trip destination, particularly as its sister gallery, the Dean Gallery (*see above*), lies just over the way.

Any hints at austerity are forgotten once you step inside the airy galleries. Works from the permanent collection of 20th-century Scottish art are displayed downstairs. The collection is not so strong on art by Scotland's bright young things, but is hot on more established artists, particularly the so-called 1980s Glasgow Boys – Peter Howson, Steven Campbell, Adrian Wiszniewski and Ken Currie. Upstairs is given over to international art: big names from fauvism, surrealism and abstract expressionism such as Matisse, Magritte, Picasso and Pollock feature alongside British greats like Francis Bacon, Helen Chadwick and Damien Hirst. The permanent collection is augmented by temporary exhibits such as the Bürgi Collection of works by Paul Klee. *See also p94* **Galleries and graveyards**.

Sightseeing

If you are in a hurry, you can get to the Water of Leith Walkway on the left of **Belford Bridge**. This is also a quick way to get to the Westend and St Mary's Episcopal Cathedral (*see p90*). A more pleasant and leisurely way to return to Stockbridge is to go through the Gallery of Modern Art's car park, and take the stepped path down to the Walkway. This gives a splendid view of **Donaldson's School for the Deaf**, designed by William Playfair in the 1840s. Its ornate grandeur appealed to Queen Victoria, who suggested taking up residence here rather than at the Palace of Holyroodhouse. Turning right along the Walkway leads to Roseburn, turning left takes you under Belford Bridge, through shady nooks to Well Court and Dean Village.

Dean Gallery.

Calton Hill & Broughton

A hill on the edge of old Edinburgh is at the heart of the city's new hedonism.

You can see almost all of Edinburgh from Calton Hill, as the city sweeps down from the Pentland Hills to the Firth of Forth. Climb a few steps higher, to the top of the Nelson Monument and the view is even better: from here you get an unrivalled sense of the bulk and anarchy of the Old Town, the set formality of the New Town and the modern chaos of North Edinburgh and Leith's docks. On a clear day, the views north over the Forth to Fife, and beyond, or east down the coast towards North Berwick are also splendid.

The hill is a favoured and atmospheric spot. Though the smoking chimneys are long gone since the advent of Clean Air Acts, when a sunny summer afternoon turns chilly and a sea mist, known on the east coast of Scotland as a 'haar', sweeps up from the Forth, the view of mist-torn chimneys and tenements creates an impression of what Edinburgh was like when it was called 'Auld Reekie'. This hill is on the edge of old Edinburgh; it's where you'll find the **City Observatory**, from which 19th-century science regimented time. But it also lies in the heart of new Edinburgh and is the site of the modern **Beltane** celebrations (*see p184*), when revived pagan rituals mark time's passage.

Waterloo Place

Calton Hill is approached by most visitors from the west: along Princes Street or across North Bridge. Looking up, the succession of neoclassical monuments that crown the hill make it easy to understand why Edinburgh retains the accolade of the 'Athens of the North'. What is rather more strange is that the name came before the Greek-inspired architecture was built – from the city's inclusion in the itineraries of the grand tours of the late 18th century, and from its relationship with imperial, 'Roman' London. The classical-styled architecture followed to justify and immortalise the phrase.

Turning the corner from North Bridge into **Waterloo Place** brings the visitor face to face with the full impact of that 19th-century neoclassical architecture. Some call it balanced and perfectly proportioned; others may find it stultifying in its grey formality – small wonder that Edinburgh still retains a reputation for dour rectitude, even if it is slightly less strong

than in the past. A glimpse of what lies underneath this upright moral fibre though, is visible down to the left of **Regent Bridge**: just by the Pivo Caffé (*see p155*) is the spot where Renton ran into a car in the opening scenes of *Trainspotting*. The bridge is an impressive structure built over a 15-metre (50-foot) deep ravine.

A few yards further along, Waterloo Place bisects the **Old Calton Burying Ground**. The steps to the right lead up to the largest part of the graveyard, the last resting place of many of the main figures of the Enlightenment. The two most imposing memorials are Robert Adam's tower for the philosopher and historian David Hume and the obelisk to the political reformers of 1793-4 who were transported for having the audacity to demand the vote for the Scots. A plaque at the entrance lists some further inhabitants of note. The cemetery is worth a wander if you have time. Past the most imposing monuments, at the far left corner of the cemetery, the view from the back of the tombs gives an unusual and photogenic panorama of Edinburgh Castle, with the Venue nightclub (*see p212*) immediately below. The rather Gothic building backing on to the back corner of the graveyard is the old **Governor's House** of Calton Gaol. Designed by Archibald Elliot, it was considered to be in bad taste when it was built in 1815. The house is the first piece of turreted architecture visible from East Coast trains into Waverley Station and is often, quite vocally and amusingly to those in the know, mistaken for the Castle itself.

The Burying Ground was divided into two in 1815, when Princes Street was extended and the North Bridge built. Before then, access to Calton Hill had been via the steep road of the same name, which now runs from the end of Waterloo Place down to Leith Street. **Rock House**, set back above the road on the north side, is one of the only houses in Edinburgh to have good views both north and south and was home to a succession of photographers from the 1830s until 1945. These included David Octavius Hill, whose work, in collaboration with Robert Adamson, gave photography credibility as a modern art form. Some 5,000 of their calotype photographs form the basis for the extensive photographic collection at the Museum of Scotland (*see p79*).

The most direct route up Calton Hill from here is via the steps at the end of Waterloo Place. After the first set of steps, either go straight ahead and meander up the side of the hill or, if you have more energy, take the steep steps to the right.

Regent Road

Before the final assault on the hill, however, Regent Road, leading straight on from Waterloo Place, has a few sights to offer. The big building on the right is **St Andrew's House**, which was built on the site of Calton Gaol. A sturdy example of modernist 1930s architecture, it has a formality and presence that make it a suitable home for the civil service.

The first part of the gaol was built in 1791-5. A new prison building and the Governor's House (*see p96*) were added in 1815. Public executions used to take place on the prison roof, in full view of the crowds on Calton Hill, until 1864.

On the left of Regent Road, just before the vehicular access to Calton Hill and next door to the **Royal High School**, was the site of the permanent vigil for a Scottish Parliament. It seemed an auspicious site: the Royal High School was fully expected to house the new Scottish Parliament, since it had already been converted into a debating chamber before the failed referendum for a Scottish Assembly in 1976. However, after the 'yes-yes' vote of autumn 1997, the government said 'no-no' to

the Royal High School and chose the Holyrood site. At the top of the road there is now a permanent **memorial** to the vigil in the form of a cairn carrying a brazier basket for a beacon. The tarmac of the pavement, since replaced, had been scorched and burned by the braziers that warmed those keeping watch during the long, cold nights between 1992 and 1997. The memorial recalls the 1,980 days of the vigil and contains stones brought from the streets of Paris, from the home of Burns and from the top of Ben Nevis.

The Royal High School, designed by Thomas Hamilton and modelled on the Temple of Theseus in Athens, was completed in 1829. It is the most extensive of the neoclassical buildings of that time, with a massive Doric central block and pillared wings. Because of its monumental size, it is difficult to get a proper perspective, even when walking past on the other side of Regent Road, so it's best to notice the detail here and contemplate its grandeur from one of the closes at the lower end of the Royal Mile.

Just across the road from the Royal High School is Hamilton's **Robert Burns Memorial**, a small circular Greek temple that is completely out of tune with its purpose. The large collection of Burns memorabilia that was once displayed here can now be seen in the Writers' Museum (*see p67*).

It's worth straying this far in order to take in the view up to the Castle (*see p61*) and down to the Palace of Holyroodhouse (*see p74*), the

'You knew just what I was there for,' at the Blue Moon on **Broughton Street**. *See p99*.

dome of Our Dynamic Earth (see p74) and the Canongate Churchyard (see p73). The paths on the right lead down to Calton Road and provide a suitable shortcut to Holyrood if you're not going back up the hill. A few steps past the Burns Memorial is the entrance to the **New Calton Graveyard**, which is large but not overly fascinating.

Calton Hill

Arriving, slightly puffed, at the top of the steps, you're confronted by a large cannon. This rather magnificent beast is Portuguese in origin and provides a suitable accompaniment to many a wedding photograph, with the **Nelson Monument** (see p99) thrusting boldly in the background. All very symbolic. Nearby is a set of 12 Doric columns that form the **National Monument** to those who lost their lives in the Napoleonic Wars. It was erected in the 1820s, and although it is generally regarded with affection nowadays, it was dubbed 'Edinburgh's Disgrace' at the time. This was because the original plans to build a replica of the Parthenon were thwarted by lack of funds; public donation raised only half the £42,000 required for the project.

The building in the walled grounds is the **City Observatory** (see below **Time piece**) by William Playfair (1774), based on the Temple of the Winds in Athens. Various attempts have been made to open the observatory and its grounds as a visitor attraction, but none has so far been successful. At present, the only way to visit it is through the Astronomical Society of Edinburgh (556 4365). The Society meets on most Friday evenings and can arrange group visits throughout the year. The three-storey Gothic tower which forms the south-western corner of the walls is the original City Observatory by James Craig (1792), which was never put to the use for which it was designed, while in the opposite corner is a disused astronomical dome that has housed several aborted visitor attractions. Incorporated into the south-eastern wall of the observatory is Playfair's monument to his uncle, Professor John Playfair.

The circular building to the south-west of the observatory is another Playfair copy. It is a monument to the philosopher Dugald Steward and based on the monument to Lysicrates on the Acropolis at Athens. Looking west from here, the modern monstrosity in the foreground is the St James Centre (see p163), while down to the right is the giant Omni shopping and leisure complex. The roundabout behind it is Picardy Place.

Although the public is free to wander around and enjoy the views from most parts of Calton Hill, the **Regent Gardens** to the east are private and belong to the residents of the **Regent**, **Carlton** and **Royal Terraces**.

Time piece

Knowing the time with precision is vital to those piloting ships. On a clear day or night with a correct clock, an accurate compass, and a chart of the heavens, you can work out exactly where you are on the globe. Observatories have long been integral to safe shipping, because it is from their fixed points that the time can be set by the sun and other stars.

The City Observatory in Edinburgh was founded for this purpose in 1774 and in 1812 began serving time for merchant ships docked at Leith. Inside the observatory is the Politician's Clock – so-called because it has two faces. The first, facing into the observatory, was used to set the time. The second faced out so that ships' captains could set their timepieces, which they had to carry all the way up from Leith Docks.

In the early 19th century one Captain Wauchope, who was brought up in Niddrie, had a simple idea to save captains the journey: a ball could be placed in a spot visible from a distance and dropped at an exact time each day. The first 'time ball' was tested by the Admiralty at Portsmouth, but Edinburgh's city fathers pleaded poverty when Captain Wauchope suggested that they build one in Edinburgh. In the 1850s, however, Westminster allocated money to help establish Edinburgh's time service and the time ball was erected on top of the Nelson Monument in 1852.

To this day, at five minutes to one, the ball is raised to the cross on the white mast to be dropped at precisely 1pm – except when it is too misty or the wind is too high. One o'clock was chosen as the perfect moment, in order to give the astronomer time to finish his noon observations before the ball was dropped. Timing is now taken from Greenwich, but, originally, the ball was dropped automatically, using a battery system connected to the main clock in the observatory.

Calton Hill with New St Andrew's House in the foreground. *See p98.*

These New Town terraces are unique in that they follow the contours of the hill and not a grid pattern, and are regarded as being fine examples of New Town architecture (*see p86* **The making of the New Town**).

Nelson Monument

Calton Hill, EH7 (556 2716/www.cac.org.uk). Bus 30, 40. **Open** *Apr-Sept* 1-6pm Mon; 10am-6pm Tue-Sat. *Oct-Mar* 10am-3pm Mon-Sat. **Admission** £2.50. **No credit cards. Map** p307 G4.

The view from the top of this monument makes the entry price and the steep climb all worthwhile. (It's worth investing in the brochure to help work out what you're looking at.) The monument was designed in the shape of Nelson's telescope by Robert Burn in 1807. In 1852, a time ball was erected at the top of the monument (*see p98* **Time piece**), and in 1861 a steel wire over 1,220m (4,000ft) long was attached between the monument and the Castle to facilitate the firing of the 1pm gun that still shocks the unwary to this day. Be warned that, with 143 steps, it's quite a climb to the top, the door up there is only 42cm (17in) wide and the parapet is sturdy but not very high.

Broughton

Although not part of Calton Hill, Broughton is an easy walk from here. Near the **Greenside Church** – referred to imaginatively by Robert Louis Stevenson as 'the church on the hill' – on the north side of the hill is a gateway that will take you towards Broughton.

Picardy Place, the huge roundabout at the top of Leith Walk, was once home to a colony of Protestant French silk weavers who fled to Edinburgh from Picardy in 1685. Today it is the site of a statue of Sherlock Holmes, whose creator, Sir Arthur Conan Doyle, was born at 11 Picardy Place (now demolished). For a bit of light relief, there are also two outsize sculptures of a foot and a grasshopper by the Leith-born artist Sir Eduardo Paolozzi in front of the Roman Catholic cathedral of **St Mary's** and opposite the new **Omni** leisure complex.

Broughton Street is a bustling and lively community with plenty of good bars, cafés and restaurants for the weary. It is the centre of Edinburgh's gay community and wears its name of the Pink Triangle with pride (*see p204*). At the bottom of the street, across the roundabout, is **Mansfield Church**, with walls covered in murals by Phoebe Traquair. The church has been bought by the Mansfield Traquair Trust and, while the whole building is being turned into offices, the murals are being restored for public display. Continuing down the hill, **Bellevue Crescent** on the left provides one of the more elegant and least triumphal of New Town façades. Further down, there is a path off Broughton Road (next to the Tesco superstore), which leads through the **Warriston Cemetery** and, along the **Water of Leith walkway**, on to Leith. At the very bottom of the hill is **Canonmills**, with the Botanic Garden beyond (*see p92*).

Arthur's Seat & Duddingston

A pocket of rugged Scottish scenery in the heart of the capital.

Craning for a view of **Arthur's Seat** from Calton Hill.

Arthur's Seat

No other city in Europe has such a mass of splendidly rugged countryside at its heart as Edinburgh has in the extinct volcano, Arthur's Seat. It might have remained dormant for the last 350 million years or so and been submerged under the sea for much of that time, but as it looms sternly over the city, the lava flows that have shaped the local geography are still clearly visible. Conan Doyle thought the hill so distinctive and universally recognisable that he referred to it in his dinosaur epic, *The Lost World*, to conjure up an appropriately primordial image in his readers' minds.

Kings, queens, poets, authors, painters and plenty of ordinary residents have found tranquillity and inspiration on Arthur's Seat. Hundreds of paths crisscross the park and it is easy to get the feeling of being deep in the countryside (*see p103* **Climbing the Seat**).

The face Arthur's Seat presents to the Old Town is the dark, forbidding curve of **Salisbury Crags**. A path, the **Radical Road**, runs directly below the rock face. Like so much else in Edinburgh, the road was Sir Walter Scott's idea, a scheme to keep former soldiers occupied after they had finished their military service. Along the Radical Road in the southernmost quarry is a rock face known as **Hutton's Section**, which 18th-century scientist James Hutton used to demonstrate his theory that Salisbury Crags were formed by molten lava, and which helped in his invention of the modern discipline of geology. Hutton's memory and discoveries are honoured in the multimedia visitor attraction **Our Dynamic Earth** (*see p74*), aptly sited a stone's throw from the north end of the Radical Road.

There is a tendency to think that the hill's name is some sort of reference to King Arthur, but this is far from likely. From the earliest times it was simply referred to as the Crag; one of the earliest recorded names for the area is Craggenemark, which means 'dead man's rock'. In all likelihood, the name is a corruption of Archer's Seat; it has been suggested that it comes from the Gaelic Ard-na-Said, meaning the Height of Arrows.

Whatever its etymology, the area has been in use since prehistoric times; there are mounds and hollows on the eastern slopes, indicating where people once lived. Since the Bronze Age and right up to medieval times, terraces were carved into the side of the hill for farming. These are known as 'runrigs' in Scotland, and are distinctly visible on the east side of the hill from Dunsapie Loch and towards the top of Crow Hill. Above Salisbury Crags there are the remains of Iron-Age ramparts that were part of a stockade-type fort some time in the period 500-100 BC.

By the 12th century, the area was jointly owned by the Scottish royal family and the Church. One holy day in 1128 King David I, who was staying in Edinburgh Castle, went hunting on Arthur's Seat and was attacked by a large stag. In a dream that night he is said to have been told to found an Abbey; he did, and called it Holyrood (*see p8*). He also gave his lands on Arthur's Seat to the Abbey in whose ownership they remained until the Reformation, when the whole park came into the hands of the Crown.

Holyrood Park, which encompasses the whole of Arthur's Seat, was first enclosed by James V, who had a wall built around it in 1540. Queen Victoria and Prince Albert enjoyed staying at Holyrood and it was under Albert's plans to landscape and improve the park that **Queen's Drive** (then Victoria Drive) was built in 1856. The park's two lochs – St Margaret's Loch down by Holyrood and Dunsapie Loch up by Dunsapie Hill – were also created at this time. By all accounts Prince Albert's improvements to Holyrood Park were sorely needed, as Edinburgh's open sewers ran into the bogs at the end of the Radical Road.

Although there are few signs of any habitation in Holyrood Park now, it has been home to many people since the first prehistoric farmers. Notably, in the 16th century it became a sanctuary for debtors: if they could get their heads over the boundary, then they were safe. The first time the sanctuary was used in this way was in the 1530s; the last in 1880. The debtors lived in cottages to the south and east of Holyrood Palace and included many high flyers such as Thomas de Quincey, who wrote several books from his lodgings in the park, and King Charles X of France who spent two years in Holyrood Palace itself.

Turning left at the Holyrood Palace entrance to the park, Queen's Drive passes **St Margaret's Loch**, with the ruined **St Anthony's Chapel** perched above it. Just before the loch, there is a grille set into the wall on the right. This is **St Margaret's Well**, the surround of which originally stood near Restalrig Church where, during the plague years, a spring was relied upon as a source of clean water. The surround was removed in 1860 to make way for a railway depot and used to cover the natural spring at Holyrood.

Duddingston

From the north-east end of **Dunsapie Loch** a steep path leads down into Duddingston. Alternatively, continue along Queen's Drive to the foot of the hill, where it joins Holyrood Park Road, and turn left down towards Duddingston, passing beneath the rock formations named Lion's Haunch and Samson's Ribs.

The name Duddingston is said to have come from a Gaelic word meaning 'the house on the sunny side of the hill'. The area has been settled since the 12th century, but artefacts from the late Bronze Age have also been found here. The chief occupations of the parishioners of Duddingston were farming (the soil is very fertile) and weaving a coarse flaxen material known as 'Duddingston hardings'. Salt was another mainstay.

Duddingston Village is tiny, consisting mainly of the Causeway and Old Church Road, set back off the main road of Duddingston Road West. The village and its surrounding green belt were declared a conservation area in 1975, and it remains a little slice of countryside in the midst of a big city.

Duddingston Loch has provided modern Edinburgh with one of its favourite symbols and an unofficial logo for the city: the wry painting of *Reverend Robert Walker Skating on Duddingston Loch* by Sir Henry Raeburn (1756-1823), now in the National Gallery of Scotland (*see p84*). Accounts from the 19th century describe the loch as swarming with multitudes of skaters whenever it froze. The loch is also virtually synonymous with the sport of curling. Edinburgh devotees of 'the roaring game' migrated to Duddingston in 1795 when their traditional ground at the Nor' Loch below Edinburgh Castle was drained and its replacement at Canonmills met with indifference. The club attracted many eminent citizens, and every frosty day the magistrates led a procession to the loch 'with great pomp and circumstance'. Rules formulated at Duddingston were adopted by curlers all over the country.

Sightseeing

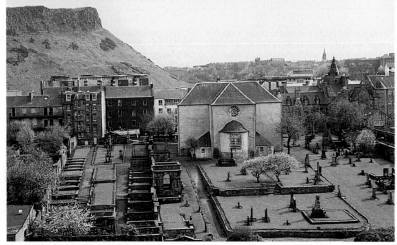

The imposing **Salisbury Crags** glower over the Old Town. *See p100.*

Frozen or not, the loch has always been a popular spot due to its sheer natural beauty. It is just over 500 metres (1,640 feet) long and less than 250 metres (820 feet) at its widest point. The lakeside outside Duddingston Village is usually crowded with ducks, geese and swans paddling around on the lookout for bread. It is a bird sanctuary too, with a heronry in the trees at the western end and bitterns in the reed beds. The best views of the loch, for ornithological purposes, are from the slopes above Queen's Drive.

The small octagonal building at the edge of the loch is **Thomson's Tower**, named after Reverend John Thomson (1778-1840), the most famous of the parish's ministers. It was Thomson who gave rise to the enduring Scots phrase 'we're a Jock Tamson's bairns', meaning that everyone shares the same humanity and none is innately better than any other. Sir Walter Scott was a friend of Thomson's and frequently visited. He wrote part of *The Heart of Midlothian* in the tower at the foot of the Manse's garden. The well-connected Reverend Thomson, a landscape painter, also played host to JMW Turner at the Manse.

Duddingston Kirk dates from 1124 and has a Norman arch separating the chancel and the nave. The north aisle was added in 1631, and many alterations have been made to the building since, such as the enlarging of the windows, which have destroyed many of the original features. However, the church carvings, especially those around the south doorway, are rough and ready but fascinating, and include the image of a fully-dressed Christ

on the cross. This particular carving has suggested to some scholars that the original church was actually the work of Saxons.

The little tower, on the left of the church gates, now called **Session House**, was originally a watchtower. At the height of 'resurrectionist' activity, the graveyard had to be guarded to prevent the bodies of the freshly buried dead being stolen and sold to anatomists for dissection.

On the right-hand side of the gates is the 'loupin-on stone', a stepped platform to help horsemen mount. An iron collar called 'the jougs' (from the word 'yoke'), in which wrongdoers were clamped, is attached to the wall behind. Common to most parishes at one time, the Duddingston jougs are now almost unique in having survived in their original place.

Across the road is the west entrance to the **Causeway**, Duddingston Village's main street. The Causeway is a narrow road, with Arthur's Seat looming above the roofs of the big houses set back from the road. Weary travellers would often stop in Duddingston to dismount and seek rest and refreshment. The **Sheep Heid Inn** (*see p155*) on the Causeway is one of the oldest public houses in Scotland and was a favourite of James VI and I. In 1580 the King presented the landlord with a ram's head, which was later stolen.

Duddingston is proud of the fact that Bonnie Prince Charlie slept here on 19 September 1745. He held a Council of War before the Battle of Prestonpans and decided to stay close to his forces rather than head back to Holyrood Palace for the night. Where he actually slept has been

City walks Climbing the Seat

The peak of **Arthur's Seat** (251 metres/823 feet), along with its lower neighbour, **Whinney Hill**, is at the centre of the 260-hectare (650-acre) Holyrood Park, now run by Historic Scotland. The hill is crossed by numerous paths and walkways and encircled by Queen's Drive, which has entrances off Holyrood Road, London Road and the top of Dalkeith Road. It can also be approached from the south-east side via Duddingston Road West.

The scene of many pleasant afternoon strolls, the park has also seen its share of tragic, accidental cliff accidents. Wear strong shoes that will not slip on the grass and take enough clothing to keep out the wind if the weather is not clement.

The easiest way to get to the top of Arthur's Seat is to take a taxi to **Dunsapie Loch** and then climb up the obvious path opposite the car park there. The walk takes you more or less straight up a grass slope, which is not overly steep, with a final stretch along a path over bare rock to the summit.

The quickest way to get to the top completely on foot is to enter the park by the **Albert Gate** next to the Commonwealth swimming pool. From the roundabout, walk along the pavement up Queen's Drive to the end of the Radical Road. Here, take the path to the right above Queen's Drive that leads straight ahead up very steep steps to the **Nether Hill** and then up to the summit.

Alternatively, go through the gap between Salisbury Crags and Arthur's Seat and follow the slightly less strenuous path to the right, known as **Piper's Walk**, which rises above Hunter's Bog. A few hundred metres along, on the right, are steep steps cut into the hill that lead up to the left of the summit and then wind around it to meet the path from Dunsapie Loch.

To find out more about the park, the **Rangers Lodge** by the gates of the Palace of Holyroodhouse has an interesting display of its history. It also publishes guides about the park and can give advice about its wildlife and uses over the years.

From the Lodge, the walk to the summit looks the most daunting, but it is in fact a less strenuous route than the walk from the Albert Gate. Turn left on to Queen's Drive and take the gently sloping path up to the right beyond the more steeply ascending start of the Radical Road. This comes out on to a path that divides at the beginning of the valley known as **Hunter's Bog**: you can take the right turn for the top of **Salisbury Crags** or continue straight ahead towards the south end of Piper's Walk. The best way to the top from here, though, is to go up the grassy incline to the left, which rises by way of slopes and paths to the top of the steps above Piper's Walk.

Once on the summit, the views are stunning on a fair day. The panorama encompasses the outer suburbs of Edinburgh in the west, Bass Rock protruding from the waves in the east, the hills of Fife in the north and the Pentland Hills in the south. The trig point names the peaks that can be seen and provides a pleasant spot from which to consider the stroll back: down the path to the right of Dunsapie Loch car park to Duddingston, where the Sheep Heid Inn (*see p155*) is conveniently placed for a restorative pint. Or three.

Historic Scotland Ranger Service
Holyrood Park Information Centre, 140 Holyrood Road, EH8 (556 1761). Bus 30. **Open** 10am-4pm Mon-Thur; 10am-3.30pm Fri. **Admission** free. **Map** p310 J5.

the subject of much conjecture – it was finally decided the white pebble-dashed cottage at the end of the Causeway was the most likely place.

Through the village away from Arthur's Seat, Duddingston Road is the location of the area's main attraction for some visitors: **Duddingston Golf Course** (*see p223*). The course celebrated its centenary in 1995. It's located in the grounds of the **Mansion House**, a neoclassical building with a Corinthian portico, which was constructed in 1768 by Sir William Chambers as a bachelor pad. The Mansion House is currently occupied

by a firm of architects and signposted by some rather unwelcoming 'private road' signs, but it's worth a glimpse through the trees. Also look out for the folly known as the **Temple**, at the 16th tee, which gave the golf club its logo.

Over the main road from the entrance leading to the clubhouse is the **Innocent Railway** walkway and cycle track. The path sadly doesn't afford any views of the **Bawsinch Nature Reserve** over the wall, or **Prestonfield Golf Course** (667 1273) on the other side, but does lead back to the Salisbury Crags end of Holyrood Park.

South Edinburgh

Scottish history permeates the city's southern streets.

Edinburgh's south side is the great swathe of the city that stretches from Lauriston Place south to Blackford Hill. To the east is St Leonard's, while the west is bounded by Lothian Road and Morningside. It contains beautiful green spaces, academic institutions, and streets and buildings where the narrative of Scottish history is apparent to even the most casual passer-by. But for all the middle-class morality of its sprawling tenements, Edinburgh's underbelly is still glittering darkly, just beneath the façade.

Lothian Road & Tollcross

The street leaving the Grassmarket on the way to Lothian Road is **West Port**, named after a gate that once stood here and former home to 19th-century murderers Burke and Hare, who sold their victims to university anatomists (*see p18* **Body matters**). At the top of West Port, at the junction of High Riggs and East Fountainbridge, is Main Point. At one time this was a key exit from Edinburgh, with roads leading to Glasgow, Stirling and Carlisle. In 1770, a rather pleasant house was built on the site. It is now surrounded by tenements and more modern buildings, but back then it took the common name given to any residence at an apex – a gusset house. This particular gusset house looks a little shabby these days and its ground floor is occupied by the Burke & Hare pub, in which gussets of a rather different sort (and a lot more besides) are revealed. The concentration of several similar establishments within a short distance, and a streak by one of the pub's artistes at the 2001 Open golf tournament, led locals to term this area the 'pubic triangle'.

For those of a less voyeuristic tendency, the area has some excellent second-hand bookshops, many of which have very good sections devoted to Edinburgh and Scotland. Going up Lady Lawson Street from West Bow, the Sculpture Court of the **Edinburgh College of Art** is through the large gates on the left-hand side. At the top of the street, on the corner with Lauriston Place, the red-brick **Lothian & Borders Firestation** (228 2401), built in 1898, is now the force's administrative headquarters. The station isn't open to the public, but fire officers will give a tour of the small collection of historic firefighting equipment to those with a special interest. Turning to the right, Lauriston Place leads down to Tollcross, while turning left takes you towards Forrest Road and Greyfriars (*see p78*).

Lothian Road itself, which dates back to the 1780s, comes alive at night with the overflow from its pubs and bars. Although many of these are far from salubrious, the area has outgrown its reputation for drunken violence as even larger and more modern drinking dens have opened on the Cowgate and at Fountainpark. The road has a long history of hedonism – it was a favourite haunt of the young Robert Louis Stevenson, escaping the bourgeois claustrophobia of his New Town home. Rather less earthy entertainment is provided at the **Usher Hall** (*see p209*), which was built in 1914 with a £100,000 gift from the brewer Andrew Usher. Edinburgh's premier concert hall, it was recently extensively refurbished with all-new heating and wiring after the ceiling developed a rather unfortunate tendency to fall down. It is situated between the **Royal Lyceum Theatre** (*see p227*), with its glass façade and opulent auditorium, and the

Star-gazing at the **Royal Lyceum Theatre**.

Traverse Theatre (*see p228*), which, with a rather more modern practicality, is housed in the purpose-built basement of the modern offices of Saltire Court. The **Traverse Café Bar** (*see p157*) is a good spot to find refreshment at any time of day.

Tollcross, scene of nefarious dealings and goings-on in early Irvine Welsh and Ian Rankin novels, has also cleaned up its appearance. The only fixes available now are cultural: in the **Cameo Cinema** (*see p198*) on Home Street and the red-stoned Edwardian baroque of the **King's Theatre** (*see p227*), just up the road. The Bank of Scotland building on Earl Grey Street – built in what could be described as late 20th-century international airport vernacular – blandly dominates its surroundings, but there is an architectural treat in the area: the **Barclay Church** at the foot of Bruntsfield Place. Built by the maverick architect FT Pilkington in 1864, the church once held a congregation of 1,200 in steeply raked banks of seats. Unfortunately, lack of cash curtailed the ornamentation on the outside, but it is still a unique and fascinating building. Although it is not generally open to the public, there is still an active Church of Scotland congregation and services are held every Sunday.

Edinburgh College of Art

Lauriston Place, EH3 (221 6032/www.eca.ac.uk). Bus 23, 27, 28, 45. **Open** *College* 10am-5pm Mon-Fri; 10am-2pm Sat. *Exhibitions* phone for details. **Admission** free. **Map** p309 E6.

The Edinburgh College of Art operates a year-round programme of exhibitions. For many, the highlights are the annual degree shows in June, when the public can eye up (and purchase) future art stars. The college puts on regular shows by artists from all over the world, taking in everything from photography to installations.

Nicolson & George Squares

The eastern part of the area, around Nicolson Street at Surgeons Hall, is where Burke and Hare took their freshly deceased victims. The troubled history of anatomy is remembered in the **Playfair Hall**, home to the Royal College of Surgeons of Edinburgh and the **Museum of Pathology & Anatomy** (*see below*). Another William Playfair design, its elegantly proportioned façade is balanced by the glass wall of the **Festival Theatre** opposite (*see p228*). Access to the Playfair Hall is limited and can only be gained via the Museum and the **Sir Jules Thorn Exhibition of the History of Surgery** on Hill Square, whose displays are not for the weak of stomach (*see below*).

Not all of the University of Edinburgh's buildings are as historically rich as the Old College (*see p81*). The arts and social science campus at **George Square** is home to a phalanx of ugly 1960s blocks. Although the library was designed by Sir Basil Spence, the campus caused quite a fuss when it was constructed as most of the 18th-century square was demolished to make room for it. The original tenements on the west side of the square give a hint of what it was like when Sir Walter Scott spent his early years there (at No.25). Just to the north and east of George Square, the empty block now used as a car park marks the old area of **Bristo**, which was also demolished to make way for university buildings. Facing Bristo Square – a favourite spot for skateboarders – are Teviot Row Student Union and the McEwan Hall. Conveniently nearby, in West Nicolson Street, is **Peartree House** (*see p157*), a 17th-century building that is now a pub with a capacious beer garden.

Museum of Pathology & Anatomy

Playfair Hall, Royal College of Surgeons of Edinburgh, 18 Nicolson Street, EH8 (527 1649/www.rcsed.ac.uk/geninfo/museums.asp). Nicolson Street–North Bridge buses. **Open** by appointment only to groups of 12-24. **Admission** phone for details. **Map** p310 G6.

Housed in Playfair's magnificent and well-preserved Royal College of Surgeons (opened in 1832), this is a working museum for the study of human disease. The collections of pathological anatomy – grouped according to the parts of the human body – are there to display diseases, abnormalities and deformities. Close perusal by the lay person with a sense of imagination is quite distressing. Public admission is by booking well in advance only and in groups of at least 12. The guide is chosen according to the knowledge of the visitors. No admission for under-15s.

Sir Jules Thorn Exhibition of the History of Surgery/Dental Museum

9 Hill Square, EH8 (527 1649/www.rcsed.ac.uk/geninfo/museums.asp). Nicolson Street–North Bridge buses. **Open** 2-4pm Mon-Fri. **Admission** free. **Map** p310 G6.

Tucked away in the square behind Surgeons Hall, this hidden treasure tells the history of surgery in the city since 1505, when the Barber Surgeons were granted a Charter. In providing the links between the growth of Edinburgh and increases in medical knowledge of its surgeons and anatomists, the exhibition manages to say a lot about both city and profession. There's quite a bit to read, but the exhibits are well displayed – if occasionally on the macabre side. The floor above the Sir Jules Thorn Exhibition is dedicated to modern surgical practice. The Dental Museum takes up an adjoining room and, although not as well laid out, provides telling insights to the history of dentistry for anyone prepared to read between the lines.

The southern suburbs

South Edinburgh is dotted with large green spaces, notably the Meadows, Blackford Hill and the Braid Hills. But before the late 18th-century population explosion that saw Edinburgh expand beyond the Old Town, the whole area south of North Meadow Walk was open country. The Meadows' Burgh Loch supplied the city's (somewhat brackish) water. At times of low rainfall, the water level dropped, turning the loch into a swamp. A piped supply was started from Comiston in 1676 and Burgh Loch was drained, eventually leaving the **Meadows** as they appear now. These days the area is basically a great big sports park, where it's easy to pick up casual games of football on Sunday afternoons.

In 1886 the Meadows was the site of the ambitious International Exhibition of Industry, which was housed in a huge temporary structure at the western end. The Exhibition left the city several permanent souvenirs. Among them are the whale jawbones at **Jawbone Walk** on Melville Drive, which were a gift from the Zetland and Fair Isle knitting stand, and the memorial pillars where Melville Drive joins Brougham Place. Down Causewayside from the east end of the Meadows is a refurbished garage that was designed in the 1930s international modern style by Sir Basil Spence. Also to the east, on the other side of South Clark Street on the way towards Arthur's Seat, lies **St Leonard's**. This largely residential area is fairly unremarkable, but it is the home to Iain Rankin's fictional detective, Inspector Rebus, who is stationed at St Leonard's Police Station.

South of the old Burgh Loch of the Meadows lay the **Burgh Muir**, or town heath, given to Edinburgh in 1128 by David I. Merchiston Castle (*see below*) lay at the western edge of this open countryside that sprawled south towards the Pentlands. But the heath's days were numbered: while the upper classes moved north out of the Old Town in the early 19th century, the middle classes moved south to build the suburbs of Bruntsfield, Marchmont, Morningside and the Grange on its grassy reaches. Ironically, in the 16th and 17th centuries (and possibly as early as the 1400s, when the plague first came to Scotland), the Burgh Muir was where the dying victims of epidemics would be banished to expire. Its other role was as a rallying ground for Scots armies. The royal standard was pitched on the **Bore Stone** (a rock with a hole in it) on Burgh Muir, then carried off at the head of the army. This last happened before the Scottish defeat at Flodden in 1513. The Bore Stone is

now displayed on a plinth on Morningside Road next to the old church at the corner of Newbattle Terrace. It was fixed there in 1852 by Sir John Stuart Forbes, who claimed he had rescued it from the indignity of lying prone in a field. Just around the corner, on Newbattle Terrace, is the **Dominion Cinema** (*see p199*). Its fine art deco interior makes it easier to forgive the rather bleak façade.

Marchmont was built between 1876 and 1914 in Scottish baronial style. The cobbled sweep of Warrander Park Road gives a general flavour, although the area now has a student ghetto atmosphere. Nearby, on Whitehouse Loan and incorporated into James Gillespie's High School, is **Bruntsfield House**: a 16th-century landmark on the old Burgh Muir.

Grange Cemetery on Beaufort Road is the city's neatest burial ground. Both Thomas Chalmers and Thomas Guthrie, who helped found the Free Kirk in 1843, are here. One imagines that neither would have approved of the fictional goings-on at St Trinian's, the louche school for girls created by cartoonist Ronald Searle and immortalised in a series of 1960s films. The series was inspired by two girls from the real St Trinian's at neighbouring Palmerston Road – a short-lived establishment at No.10 that opened in 1922, moved over to Dalkeith Road, then closed in 1946.

Craigmillar & Merchiston

Sitting cheek by jowl with one of the city's shabbiest housing schemes are the impressive remains of the 14th-century **Craigmillar Castle**. The approach from Niddrie Mains Road through the housing estates of Niddrie and Craigmillar reveals a side of Edinburgh that most visitors don't see and gives the best sense of the castle's grandness. As this road has no pavement, however, the most sensible approach is up the path from the grounds of the new Royal Infirmary of Edinburgh, just north of the bus stop.

Another act of academic vandalism was perpetrated in the 1960s at the south-western extreme of the Burgh Muir, this time by Napier College of Commerce and Technology (now Napier University). Its Colinton Road campus, situated around **Merchiston Castle**, can only be described as appalling. The 15th-century L-plan tower house once had such features as a moat and a secret passage. Early in its history it fell into the hands of the Napier family, of whom John Napier (1550-1617) – mathematician and inventor of logarithms – is the most celebrated scion. In the 1830s Merchiston Castle became a school, but a century later it fell into disuse, until Napier College took it over.

Blackford Hill itself was acquired for the
city in 1884, when George Harrison was Lord
Provost. His work is remembered in the large
red stone archway on the road up to the
observatory – it looks somewhat incongruous in
the middle of a modern suburb. The hill makes
for a good Sunday afternoon stroll or early
morning walk, somewhat less strenuous than
Arthur's Seat. A good route on to the hill is
from the pond on Cluny Gardens, but there is a
rather gentler amble to be had along its south
side, from Braid Road along the Braid Burn and
past the Hermitage of Braid. Herons have been
sighted hereabouts – it's the kind of bucolic
vale where it's easy to forget you're in a city.
Farther south still lie the Braid Hills, with
two golf courses and yet another great view
of Edinburgh and beyond (on a clear day you
can see Ben Lomond).

Heading in the other direction along Braid
Road, towards Morningside, leads to the spot
where the last public execution for highway
robbery took place in Edinburgh. In December
1814, two men mugged a man delivering a horse
to the city from the Borders. They said all they
got was four pence. The victim said he lost £5,
bread and a spleuchan (tobacco pouch). The sad
pair were strung up at the place where 66 Braid
Road now stands; all that's visible are two
recessed squares where the gibbet was fixed.
Stick around for any length of time absorbing
the atmosphere, and you'll notice the curtains
twitching: they still keep a tight grip on their
spleuchans in these parts.

Hermitage of Braid

69A Braid Road, EH19 (447 7145). Bus 11, 15.
Open 2-5pm Mon-Thur, Sat; 2-4pm Fri; noon-5pm
Sun. **Admission** free.
This late 18th-century villa in the middle of the valley (also known as the Hermitage of Braid) acts as a
countryside information centre. It's aimed mainly at
children and has a rudimentary tearoom in its basement, open on Sundays.

Royal Observatory Visitor Centre

Blackford Hill, EH9 (668 8405/www.roe.ac.uk/vc).
Bus 24, 38, 41. **Open** 10am-5pm Mon-Sat; noon-5pm
Sun. **Admission** £3.50; £2-£2.50 concessions.
Credit MC, V.
When light pollution became too strong on Calton
Hill, the Royal Observatory moved to Blackford Hill.
The city has since grown to meet the Observatory,
which gives picturesque views of Edinburgh from
the south. Although there are telescope sessions on
winter Friday evenings – weather permitting – this
is not a working observatory but rather an important telescope research centre. The extensive visitor
centre is excellent, however: basic astronomical science is clearly explained, the history of astronomy
in Edinburgh is intriguingly told and the universe
is beautifully illustrated.

George Square. *See p105.*

Craigmillar Castle

Craigmillar Castle Road, off Old Dalkeith Road,
EH16 (661 4445/www.historic-scotland.gov.uk).
Bus 2, 14, 21, 24, 32, 33, 38, 42, 49. **Open** *June-*
Sept 9.30am-6.30pm daily. *Oct-May* 9.30am-4.30pm
Mon-Wed, Sat; 9.30am-12.30pm Thur; 2-4.30pm
Sun. **Admission** £2.20; 75p-£1.60 concessions.
Credit AmEx, MC, V.
This substantial and atmospheric ruin is now
managed by Historic Scotland. An L-shaped tower
house, surrounded by a later curtain wall, it was
razed by the Earl of Hertford after the English invasion of 1544, but later refurbished. The castle
was a favourite spot for Mary, Queen of Scots, who
retreated here after the murder of her favourite,
David Rizzio, in 1566. Because of the large number
of French people in Mary's court who took up
residence in the surrounding area, the region immediately to the south of the castle became known as
'Little France'.

Blackford

Sitting on top of Blackford Hill like a twin
teacake tribute to Victorian empiricism is the
Royal Observatory. It took over the work
of the observatory on Calton Hill when light
pollution there became too great in the late
19th century. When the new building was
completed in 1895, it was well outside the city
boundary. It has a well-designed visitor centre
that allows access to the flat roof between the
domes from where there is an excellent view
of the city's northern aspect (there are a couple
of small telescopes for anyone who wants a
close-up look). Every Friday night during
the winter, weather permitting, there's a
public observing session with a six-inch
refracting telescope.

West Edinburgh

Venture off the tourist trail to explore the areas west of the centre.

Edinburgh has never been a city to look towards the west. That way, after all, Glasgow lies. So it is that west Edinburgh, the part of the city stretching from Lothian Road out towards the bypass and the airport, is an area often neglected by visitors. Much of it is residential, but there is the odd sight to see, including caged beasts, some of the earliest signs of habitation in the area and reminders of Edinburgh's economic engines, both old and new.

The Exchange

Scots have a reputation for being canny with their money, and it is not a reputation that Edinburgh is about to dispel. In the modern money market, however, the city's banks have deserted the grand telling halls of the New Town – leaving them to be turned into grown-up play pens – and built themselves rather less glorious but nonetheless monumental modern offices. As the 20th century worked its way to a moneyed close, the area around the **West Approach Road** and **Lothian Road** saw a £350-million construction extravaganza described by the city's public relations team at the time, in predictably overblown terms, as Edinburgh's most important development since the New Town.

First on the scene, in 1985 (before a formal development strategy had been hatched), was the almost Eastern European façade of the **Sheraton Grand Hotel** (*see p51*). This was followed in 1988 by a city council plan to promote the area as a new financial district known as the **Exchange**. Investment managers Baillie Gifford had Rutland Court, with its mirror-shades chic, built on the West Approach Road in 1991, but the heart of the new area was to be the emblematic **Edinburgh International Conference Centre**. Designed by Terry Farrell, this opened on Morrison Street in 1995 and resembles an ambitious upturned engine part.

Soon the big names were moving in. Scotland's largest company, **Standard Life**, opted for new headquarters on Lothian Road in 1997, while the **Clydesdale Bank** erected its Plaza on the other side of the West Approach Road. The overall effect is reminiscent of London's Broadgate but with less Gordon Gecko sociopathy. At least the Standard Life building,

by the Michael Laird Partnership, made an attempt to incorporate more creative elements, courtesy of sculptor John Maine (gates, entrance) and artist Jane Kelly (lights, railings). But beating them all for sheer verve is the **Scottish Widows** headquarters on Semple Street by Glasgow's Building Design Partnership. Completed in 1998, the main crescent block begs to house something more interesting than a pensions management company. But then, that's what generated the cash to pay for this kind of architecture in the first place.

Proof of the paucity of imagination that can afflict modern buildings can be seen by contrasting these big and brash 1990s upstarts with the late-Victorian **FT Pilkington tenements** along Fountainbridge at the corner of Grove Street. Although blackened with grime, the touch of a Gaudi-esque imagination is still unmistakable.

Fountainbridge

At the height of the 19th-century beer frenzy, Edinburgh had over 40 breweries. Now there are just two. The biggest is the **Fountain Brewery** on Fountainbridge (not open to visitors), part of Scottish & Newcastle's empire and a manufacturing centre for two million barrels of iconic fizz each year, including McEwan's Export, McEwan's Lager and Younger's Tartan Special. Its huge, purple-lit chimney looms over the whole area at night and is also responsible for the pungent smell of yeast that hangs over west Edinburgh from time to time.

Much of the brewery's output does not go far: the **Fountainpark** leisure complex is just over the road, after all. Thrown together with all the bright, modern contempt that the worst contemporary architecture has for its users, it is home to several large nightclubs and bars, a large bowling alley, a 13-screen cinema, and the **Shaping a Nation** visitor attraction (*see p109*).

At the end of Dundee Street on Angle Park Terrace is the **Athletic Arms** (337 3822): a pub which sadly no longer serves the best pint of McEwan's 80/- in town, but which is still fondly known as the Diggers on account of the workers from the nearby graveyard who used to frequent it after work. For a great pint in the area it is better to visit the **Cally**

Guarding **Lauriston Castle**. *See p111*.

The tour ends with a ten-minute flight simulator-type ride over Scotland's lochs and monuments; the simulator is used for amusement-style rides, too.

Gorgie & Dalry

Edinburgh, west of the Castle, was once a bucolic stretch of farms and small hamlets. From the 12th century, at the latest, the area in immediate proximity to the Castle was given over to market gardening. Such rural tranquillity hardly seems credible given the riot of tenements and late-20th-century developments that are crammed into the area now. But seek out some of the older buildings, and the picture of a time when life was rather slower than today gradually emerges.

Down Distillery Lane, for instance, off Dalry Road at Haymarket, there's a beautiful 18th-century mansion called **Easter Dalry House** (now an office) – Haymarket Station now stands in the house's garden. Further out along Dalry Road, on Orwell Place, is **Dalry House** – a survivor from the early 17th century. Hidden away in a residential warren, it is hard to imagine this beige-harled effort as an old Scots manor with extensive grounds. Although it is thoroughly respectable these days (it is run by Age Concern), one former owner, John Chiesley, wasn't quite so douce. He was executed for murder in 1689, then buried in the back garden.

Further out is the rather dejected area of **Gorgie** where Heart of Midlothian play their football at **Tynecastle Stadium** (*see p221*). Opposite is the child-pleasing **Gorgic City Farm** (*see p195*). At the junction of Gorgie Road and Balgreen Road, is the hidden surprise of **Saughton Park**. Here, there are beautifully kept winter gardens, centred round a public greenhouse, and a formal rose garden. This is also a good point to access the **Water of Leith Walkway** (*see p111* Canal dreams).

Even further out, just off the western end of Gorgie Road, sits the architectural mishmash of **Saughton Prison**, Edinburgh's lock-up since 1919. Its ghoulish claim to fame is that it was the site of the city's most recent execution. A total of four men have been dispatched at Saughton, proving that the 20th century was not all that more liberal than the 17th. The last to go, George Alexander Robertson, was found guilty of murder and hanged in June 1954. His body and three others lie buried inside the precincts of the jail. Still at the end of Gorgie Road, but behind the Shell petrol station, is **Stenhouse Mansion**. This three-storey block was built in 1623 and would once have stood out from the surrounding countryside along the Water of Leith. Now it is run by Historic Scotland (668 8600) as a conservation and

Sample Room (*see p157*), which sells beer from the independent **Caledonian Brewery** (*see below*), situated nearby on Slateford Road. The brewery has been going from strength to strength, winning prizes and plaudits for its beers: Caledonian 80/, Deuchers IPA and the organic Golden Promise (*see also p152* **Only here for the beer**).

Caledonian Brewery

42 Slateford Road, EH11 (brewery 337 1286/ tours 623 8066/www.caledonian-brewery.co.uk). Bus 4, 28, 35, 35A, 44/Slateford rail. **Open** tours by appointment. **Tickets** phone for details. **Credit** MC, V.

A near-disastrous fire in 1994 allowed this forward-thinking brewery, which still uses original brewing methods, to build a visitors' centre and let the public in. Nowadays the brewery is doing so well that visits can be arranged for groups of five or more by appointment only. The only exception is during the Caledonian Beer Festival, held annually over a weekend in early June, when a vast number of ales are there for the sampling.

Shaping a Nation

Fountainpark, Dundee Street, EH11 (229 0300). Bus 28, 34, 35. **Open** 2.30-9.30pm Mon; noon-7pm Tue-Thur; noon-9.30pm Fri-Sun. **Admission** £4.50; £3 concessions. **Credit** MC, V. **Map** p308 B7.

With a modern hands-on approach to Scottish history, this attraction provides amusement for those with more limited attention spans. Beside the displays about great Scottish inventors and feats of Scottish engineering, there are quizzes on all aspects of Scotland and interactive computer programmes that delve a little deeper into Scottish history.

Sightseeing

restoration centre, and is so well hidden that few locals even know it's there. The motto above the door reads, 'Blisit be God for all his giftis', a grace from the days when the master of the house, Patrick Eleis, could have looked back at the Castle, two and a half miles (four kilometres) away over open land.

Corstorphine & Cramond

North of the railway line is the much more up-market residential side of the tracks, although there are still a few sights of note. Scotland's home of rugby is the **Murrayfield Stadium** (*see p222*) off Corstorphine Road. Further out is **Edinburgh Zoo** (*see p194*), which will please younger children. (As bizarre rituals go, the daily penguin parade takes some beating.) Like most modern zoos, Edinburgh's is actively involved in conservation.

For good views, climb **Corstorphine Hill**, behind the Zoo. Best accessed via the steep Kaimes Road, the wooded hill is a favourite with mountain bikers and dog walkers. The trees hide the best views around **Corstorphine Hill Tower** on its peak, but there are good lookout points to the east of the higher reaches of the zoo. This is the point known as **Rest-and-be-thankful**, where travellers could get their first real view of Edinburgh when travelling in from the west. These early visitors would have been bemused to see and hear the animals in the Zoo's African Plains enclosure, which dominates the scene nowadays.

Still further north, towards the Firth of Forth, the road to Cramond village passes **Lauriston Castle**. Originally a 1590s tower house, the castle was built for Sir Archibald Napier, and extended during the 1820s. Overlooking the

Firth of Forth and close to the centre of Edinburgh, Lauriston is typical of the large villas which once provided rural seclusion for Edinburgh's powerful and wealthy families. The croquet lawns at the front of the house are home to the **Edinburgh Croquet Club**.

Cramond, home to the fictional Mr Lowther who Muriel Spark's Miss Jean Brodie visited on Sunday afternoons, was actually the earliest settlement in the Lothians. Waste has been found from the camps of Mesolithic people who inhabited the area in 4000 BC. The Romans arrived in about 140 AD and their remains have been excavated behind the sea-wall car park, in the Manse gardens, where there are boards giving information about the second-century bathhouse. The finds, including a remarkable white lion found in the river Almond, are displayed in the Museum of Edinburgh (*see p75*).

During the 20th century Cramond became a commuter town and summer retreat for Edinburgh residents, but before this it had been a thriving port. In the 18th century the waterpower available from the Almond proved irresistible to industrialists, who built iron mills along its banks; the village became an exporter of nails around the world. The small **Cramond Heritage Trust** museum (*see below*) offers an intriguing slant on local history and is open on the quayside during summer weekends.

Cramond Heritage Trust
The Maltings, Riverside, Cramond Village, EH4. Bus 41, 42. **Open** *June-Sept* 2pm-5pm Sat, Sun. Closed Oct-May. **Admission** free. **No credit cards**. This one-roomed museum has a different tableau illustrating one aspect of local history every year, but the central displays of Roman, church and industrial histories remain the same.

Cramond waterfront, where the Almond meets the Forth.

City walks Canal dreams

Mass transport and the ability to harness energy were at the heart of the industrial revolution. Both are obvious in west Edinburgh. The first signs are at the top of Lothian Road, on the corner with Fountainbridge, where the large corner block of **Lothian House** is built on the site of the original terminus of the Union Canal at Port Hopetoun. The reliefs on the building commemorate the canal and its uses.

The **Union Canal** was completed in 1822, linking up with the Forth & Clyde Canal to Glasgow at Camalon, near Falkirk. In to the canal terminus at Lothian Road came passengers, coal and building materials; out went merchants' goods, horse manure and more passengers. Not, it must be stressed, always in the same barge.

The current terminus is further along on the south side of Fountainbridge. It was being developed with canal-side apartments in mid 2002, but is still a good place to start an interesting meander away from the city centre. The best way on to the canal is from **Gilmore Park**, where it crosses the canal over the old lift bridge (moved from its original site on Fountainbridge). From here there is an easy amble along the canal out to **Slateford**, where an eight-arch aqueduct, finished in 1822, carries the canal across the Water of Leith alongside the railway bridge (built 26 years later). At one end of the aqueduct there are access steps that descend to the **Water of Leith Visitor Centre** (*see below*). Although flat, the towpath is not the most scenic of routes, so you may want to hop on the 28 or 35 bus from Fountainbridge, which drop off here. The Centre contains good local information and an interesting, child-friendly exhibition about wildlife on the river.

From here there is a pleasant circular walk that takes about an hour. From the aqueduct, continue along the canal until it is crossed by a bridge; follow the path under and then over the bridge, and on to an old railway line that

leads to the start of the deep, wooded gully of **Colinton Dell**. At this point the Water of Leith Walkway joins the disused railway; for a longer walk, continue straight on, up the Dell, passing waterfalls and open meadows, before following the path through a tunnel towards Balerno and Juniper Green.

Alternatively, to get quickly back to the Centre from the start of the Dell, turn left and drop back down the Walkway to cross the river at **Bog's Bridge**; once over the water turn left again. The path follows the river closely and in this shady valley you can see dippers and, if you are lucky, the occasional flash of a kingfisher. After passing a small, tumbled-down grotto on the right, the path comes out on Lanark Road, opposite the Visitor Centre.

Water of Leith Visitor Centre

24 Lanark Road, West Edinburgh, EH14 (455 7367/www.wateroflieth.edin.org). Bus 44, 44A. **Open** *Apr-Sept* 10am-4pm daily. *Oct-Mar* 10am-4pm Wed-Sun. **Admission** £1.90; £1.20-£1.40 concessions; £5 family. **No credit cards**.

Lauriston Castle

Cramond Road South, Davidsons Mains, Cramond, EH4 (336 2060/www.cac.org.uk). Bus 1, 41, 42. **Open** *House* Apr-Oct 11am-5pm Mon-Thur, Sat, Sun; Nov-Mar 2-4pm Sat, Sun. *Grounds* 9am-dusk daily. **Admission** *House* (by guided tour only) £4.50; £3 concessions. *Grounds* free. **No credit cards**.
Set in large, reasonably well kept grounds on the way to Cramond, the 16th-century fortified house

was left in trust to the nation by William Reid in 1926. He and his wife were enthusiastic antiques collectors who furnished the house throughout with their collections. William Reid also brought his furnishing expertise to bear on a wider public as proprietor of Morison & Co, one of Scotland's leading cabinetmakers at the time. The house interior can only be viewed on the 50-minute tour, which starts at 20 past the hour (during opening hours).

Sightseeing

Leith

Yuppies and restaurants have replaced fishwives and warehouses in the fiercely independent port of Leith.

The Leith town motto, 'persevere' is perfect for the port that was, for centuries, the most important in Scotland, and which has always made use of its economic importance to the capital to square up to its dominant neighbour. From the Middle Ages onwards, Leith's trading links across the North Sea to the Netherlands and also south to France, Portugal and the Mediterranean were supported by a strong shipbuilding industry. The history of Leith and Edinburgh might be inextricably linked, but the people of the port have always felt distinct from their neighbours in the city and have traditionally cast themselves as tenacious underdogs, ready to correct anyone who assumes they're from Edinburgh.

The bad feeling goes right back to 1329 when Robert the Bruce included Leith in his Charter to Edinburgh. This gave the city so much control over the harbour that the captain of a ship berthed at Leith could not unload any cargo until the correct taxes had been paid three miles (five kilometres) inland at the Edinburgh Tolbooth. In a further Charter of 1428, James I gave Edinburgh the right to exact tolls from boats entering the port. Until 1833, all of Leith's foreign trade was controlled by Edinburgh; over the years, resentment in the port became understandably bitter.

There were a few years of separation for Leith. When the first modern docks were laid out in the early 1800s they cost so much to construct that Edinburgh had to declare itself bankrupt. The docks were effectively nationalised in 1825 and, in 1833, an Act of Parliament made Leith an independent parliamentary burgh. Independence was shortlived, however. The town never managed to generate enough income to sustain itself and amalgamation became increasingly likely after World War I, despite its unpopularity among the Leith populace. Leithers voted 29,891 to 5,357 against amalgamation in a last-ditch, toothless referendum in 1919, but financial constraints were against them, and Edinburgh and Leith were merged in 1920. In 2002, the British government attempted to rename the Leith constituency for Westminster as 'North Edinburgh' – a proposal that utterly failed to acknowledge centuries-old differences between the city and the port.

Whatever the politics, it is undeniable that Edinburgh and Leith have physically merged into one another along Leith Walk, the mile-long thoroughfare that links them. **City Limits**, the pub opposite Pilrig Church at 379 Leith Walk, marks the point where Edinburgh and Leith join; the dividing line cuts through the middle of the bar. The pub was formerly known as the Boundary Bar, due to the legend – sadly apocryphal – that deeply ingrained resentment among drinkers on the Leith side of the bar prevented them from crossing to the other side of the pub at closing time to take advantage of Edinburgh's later opening hours. The pub's name change in early 2002 united city and port in a rare moment of shared condemnation.

Leith Walk

Entering Leith along Leith Walk from the city centre brings you straight to the **Kirkgate**. Historically, this was the hub of the town, but the original buildings have been torn down and replaced with a faceless shopping arcade backing on to high-rise flats. In Leith, you're never far from a town planner's bungle. Diagonally across from the Kirkgate are a supermarket and the aquatic playground **Leith Waterworld** (*see below*), which both stand on the site once occupied by Leith Central Station. Before the station was demolished, its abandoned buildings gave Irvine Welsh the name of his book *Trainspotting* – a typically sardonic euphemism for scoring heroin at the (derelict) station. The hard drugs scene of the 1980s, as featured in the novel, threatened to tar Leith's reputation permanently, but the town's continuing regeneration is helping it to shake off its image as a junkie-ridden place of permanent industrial decline. The conversion of bonded warehouses into loft space is only the latest stage of a transformation that has also seen the advent of designer bars and cafés along the shore front.

Leith Waterworld

377 Easter Road, EH6 (555 6000). Leith Walk buses. **Open** *Summer* 10am-5pm daily. *Winter* 10am-5pm Fri-Sun. **Admission** £3.20; £2.20 concessions; free under-5s. **No credit cards.** **Map** p307 J1.

The Shore basks in the sunshine of regeneration.

This leisure pool is the best in Edinburgh and great for families. Attractions include the full range of wave machines, river runs, bubble beds, water slides, flumes and a learner lagoon.

Leith Links

To the east of the Kirkgate, at the foot of Easter Road, lie the green spaces of **Leith Links**. As Leith's traditional common land, the Links have been used for everything from cattle-grazing to archery contests. The Links also have a strong claim to be the home of golf, although the game has been prohibited here since 1907. Although the golf course on the Links was second to St Andrew's in seniority in 1593, the game's first set of rules was formulated in Leith. A large memorial stone opposite Links Lane commemorates the occasion – a competition of the Honourable Company of Golfers on 7 March, 1744. The 13 rules were subsequently adopted at St Andrew's, while the Honourable Company moved away from Leith, first to Musselburgh and then to Muirfield in East Lothian, due to overcrowding.

The Links also have more tragic associations. In 1560, the English army dug in here and besieged the town. Two of the 16th-century gun emplacements, Giants Brae and Lady Fyfe's Brae, can still be seen as grassy mounds. Nowadays, the Links are mainly used for dog-walking, football games and by visiting fairs.

Down Constitution Street, towards Bernard Street and the Shore, is **South Leith Parish Church**, which was rebuilt after being destroyed by cannon fire in the 1560 siege. Continuing along Constitution Street, subtle architectural ornaments begin to reflect the maritime nature of the area: the cosy **Port O'Leith** pub (58 Constitution Street; 554 3568) has a true seafaring atmosphere, with a huge array of flags and memorabilia, left to the bar by grateful seamen. Other fine pubs include **Nobles** (with beautiful stained-glass windows) at 44A Constitution Street (554 2024).

Signs of civic prosperity are visible in buildings such as the **Leith Assembly Rooms** and, round the corner in Bernard Street, the elegant, domed **Old Leith Bank**. This is Leith's financial centre, where many of the upmarket new businesses that flooded into Leith during its regeneration in the 1980s are concentrated. For refreshment, the **Carriers Quarters** pub (42 Bernard Street; 554 4122), built in 1785 and barely changed since, is a marvellous haven, particularly on winter nights.

The Shore

The Shore, the street overlooking the Water of Leith, is where Leith's regeneration is most apparent. The area has been lovingly restored, and new but appropriate buildings have been added. Lining the stretch between the bright

The old **swing bridge** brings pedestrians into port.

and airy **Raj** Indian restaurant, located at 88-91 Henderson Street (553 3980), and **Malmaison**, a breathtakingly restored seamen's mission that is now a hotel (*see p53*), are ample opportunities for good drinking and dining. But the Shore really comes into its own on summer evenings when al fresco drinking, normally anathema to the Scots, seems perfectly natural.

The **King's Wark** pub (*see p158*) on the corner of the Shore and Bernard Street is the only surviving remnant of James I's 'wark'. This was a storage point for cargo destined for royal use. The wark came into being around 1428, when James extended the port, and was enlarged by subsequent monarchs throughout the following centuries, until, at one time, it covered several blocks.

Despite the smart new apartment blocks and business premises that now thrive in the streets between the Shore and Constitution Street, it is still possible to imagine the haphazard tangle of narrow alleys from centuries past. It is here that the port's first loft spaces opened, and were quickly snapped up by affluent professionals with bohemian aspirations. Historically, the most notable building is **Lambs House** on Water's Close, a 17th-century tenement that was restored by the National Trust and is now run as an old people's home.

On the quay side itself, rather hidden by the sculpted wrought-iron railings and young trees opposite No.30 The Shore, there is a plaque commemorating the place where George IV first set foot in Scotland with the words 'Geo IV Rex O Felicem Diem' in 1822.

Although the old swing bridge where the river enters the docks is now pedestrianised, some parts of Leith docks are still commercial concerns, so access to these areas is limited. Signs indicate which parts are out of bounds, but you can wander around the rest of the area – make the most of it before the remaining warehouses are converted into funky new shopping malls or hotels. The Tall Ships Race, which docked at Leith in 1996, gave the first real indication of the area's potential as a major event venue, as thousands of people gathered to see the ocean-going sailing vessels.

Although Leith is less threatening than Lothian Road or the Cowgate at pub closing time on a Friday or Saturday, it's nevertheless not sensible to wander around the docks at night. Strangers to Leith should exercise discretion when choosing their pubs and try to remain on the main thoroughfares later in the evening. Women on their own should certainly avoid Coburg Street and Coalhill at night, as they'll attract the attention of kerb-crawlers. For several years these streets were the centre of the Leith 'tolerance zone', a liberal scheme for managing street prostitution that was withdrawn in 2001 due to complaints from incoming residents. Attempts to create a new zone elsewhere in the city have so far come to nothing.

North Leith

Leith is divided by the Water of Leith; the area to the west of the river mouth is called North Leith and to the east is South Leith. Described by Robert Louis Stevenson as 'that dirty Water of Leith' and deserving of its grimy reputation, the river has been cleaned up over the last 25 years, although scum and rubbish still collect at the bridges. The **Water of Leith Walkway** (*see p92* **Galleries and graveyards** *and p111* **Canal dreams**) starts at the northern end of the Sandport Place Bridge and follows the riverbank right to the heart of Edinburgh. It is one of the best walks in the city.

North Leith is best approached via Great Junction Street, which is a busy thoroughfare of grocers, down-market clothing shops, funeral directors and a couple of grim indoor markets. During shopping hours, it is usually thronging with senior citizens. Many of Leith's younger residents have been rehoused in outlying housing schemes. One of the few sights off Great Junction Street is **Leith Victoria Swimming Pool** on Junction Place, which opened in 1896.

Over Junction Bridge, the corner of Ferry Road and North Junction Street is overlooked by a gable-end mural depicting the history of Leith as a jigsaw puzzle. Portrayed as the final piece of the jigsaw (and the target of some mud-slinging by local kids), is a picture of a Sikh man reaching to take the outstretched hand of the community. Most of the Sikhs in Edinburgh live in Leith, and their temple is in a converted church just back over the bridge and down Mill Lane towards the Shore. To the left of the mural are two grand but unfussy buildings, **Leith Library** and **Leith Theatre**. They both opened in 1932 and are superb examples of economical design, with the theatre's portico following the curve of the library's semicircular reading room. Straight ahead is North Junction Street, where **Leith School of Art** inhabits the oldest Norwegian seamen's church outside Norway, a small Lutheran kirk dating from 1868.

The spire of **North Leith Parish Church** on Madeira Street, its impressive classical columns tucked away off the main road, marks the area where Leith Fort once stood. In 1779, John Paul Jones sailed up to Leith on a ship donated by the French and demanded £20,000 in compensation for British atrocities in America. A sudden storm forced him to cancel his plans, but the scare prompted the building of a fort housing 100 men, who, until its completion in 1809, were permanently encamped on the Links. Only guardhouses and parts of the wall remain, and on its site are the forbidding blocks of flats that inherited the name.

Despite its seedy nocturnal arrangements, Coburg Street, which connects the Shore with Ferry Road and runs parallel with the Water of Leith, is worth passing through in the daylight. Points of interest include the Dutch-style steeple of the ruined **Old St Ninian's Church** and the old **North Leith Churchyard**. A detour into Couper Street, opposite, brings you to **EASY** (Edinburgh Architectural Salvage Yard; *see p163*), an Aladdin's cave of old fireplaces, pews, doors and other flotsam. Straight over the bridge from Bernard Street, past the grand columns of the Custom House and down Dock Place, lies the **Waterfront Wine Bar** (*see p158*). It was one of the first venues to lure solvent professionals to the area; it has since been joined by the excellent fish restaurant **Skippers** (*see p134*) and a trendy, over-designed café-bar, **Bar Sirius** (*see p157*).

Round the corner, on Commercial Quay, the developments have been far more dramatic. A row of bonded warehouses running almost the entire length of Commercial Street has been renovated into desirable apartments, upmarket shops, glass-fronted restaurants and stylish offices. Facing them, across the quayside, is an imposing piece of post-modern architecture that houses the **Scottish Executive**. Its design is

Malmaison. *See p114.*

Sightseeing

certainly uncompromising, and is not to everyone's taste, but its boldness epitomises the spirit of redevelopment that has been taking place here, where the old and new interlock with surprising ease.

On the north side of the Executive, the whole port area is being reclaimed, with plans for a huge new 'village' of flats and gardens. The first major part of the development is Terence Conran's **Ocean Terminal** (*see p161*), a vast, upmarket shopping mall in the shape of an ocean liner. Inside the mall are the Conran restaurant, Zinc (*see p135*), a three-floor Debenhams and the visitors' centre for the **Royal Yacht Britannia** (*see below*), which is moored up just outside. The redevelopment of Leith has been so spirited and decisive that it was chosen as the final resting place for the Royal Yacht, which ferried the royal family around the world for 40 years.

Royal Yacht Britannia

Ocean Terminal, Ocean Drive, EH6. (555 5566/ www.royalyachtbritannia.co.uk). Bus 11, 22, 34, 35, 36, 49. **Open** *Apr-Sept* 9.30am-4.30pm daily. *Oct-Mar* 10am-3.30pm daily. **Admission** £7.75; £5.95 OAPs; £3.75 concessions; £20 family. **Credit** AmEx, DC, MC, V. **Map** p311 Hx.

Even ardent Republicans could find a great deal of interest aboard the *Royal Yacht Britannia*, whether it's the Queen's telling passion for flowery and chintzy furniture coverings or the tiny cabin-space allocated to the admirals who captained the ship. The tradition of cleaning and polishing every item every day has continued, so that, even though the Britannia was decommissioned in 1997, setting foot on her is almost like stepping back to the 1950s. Small wonder that certain members of the royal family voiced a preference to see her scuttled rather than opened to the public. Price of admission includes self-guided audio tour. *Britannia* closes an hour and a half after the last admission times.

Newhaven

Following the shoreline west along Lindsay Road, and on past the gleaming white silos of Chancelot Mill, leads to the old fishing village of **Newhaven**. Much of the original village has been pulled down, but there are still some original fishermen's cottages in the streets near the shore. Up until the 20th century, Newhaven was a very insular community, thought to have descended from the intermarriage of locals and the shipbuilding craftsmen brought over from France, Scandinavia, Spain and Portugal by James III. Newhaven became famous for its sturdy and colourfully dressed fishwives who used to carry their creels full of fresh fish up to Edinburgh to sell every morning. The once-flourishing **Fishmarket**, built in 1896, now

uses up only a fraction of the space that it once covered; instead the long red building has become home to a branch of Harry Ramsden's fish and chip shop and the **Newhaven Heritage Museum** (*see below*). Although small, this is a vibrant community museum, renowned for its child-friendly exhibits, which include recordings of local residents recalling their working lives in the early 20th century. It is also a bit of a hangout for the older generation, who are happy to regale the interested visitor with stories.

Newhaven Heritage Museum

24 Pier Place, EH6 (551 4165/www.cac.org.uk). Bus 7, 10, 11, 16, 22, 32. **Open** noon-4.45pm daily. **Admission** free. **Map** p311 Ex.

What this one-room museum lacks in size it makes up for in vitality. It needs to as it's quite a trek from the middle of town – east of Leith on the Forth shore, next to Harry Ramsden's; the fishwives made this journey every day loaded down with their creels of fish to sell door-to-door round the city. The Newhaven living history project has done its job well and the recorded memories are vibrant and telling, although the accents might prove quite difficult to non-locals. Other exhibits are a little wordy but child friendly.

Portobello

East of Leith, along the shore of the Forth, past the docks, the sewage works and several large warehouse retail outlets lies a two-mile stretch of golden sand. This is **Portobello** beach where all Edinburgh used to go on a sunny bank holiday. Portobello, incorporated into Edinburgh in 1896, was a popular holiday destination not just for people from Edinburgh but from all over Scotland. The remnants of this trade are visible everywhere in town, from the long promenade on the front to the wealth of cafés on the High Street. In the 1970s, families were dragged there for a day at the sea – as remembered in the irony-laden local punk anthem 'Ain't no surf in Portobello' by The Valves – and today it makes a pleasant destination for a sand-kicking day trip.

Until 1979 one of the resort's biggest attractions was the lido, which was built in the 1930s and used waste energy from the local power station to heat the water. The closure of the power station in 1977 was the death knell for the lido, but there's still a decent swimming pool at **Portobello Swim Centre** (*see p225*) at the east end of the promenade. Head along the prom to indulge in some seaside amusements. There's enough harmless fun to be had to make even a dreich Scottish summer afternoon pass in a rose-tinged mist of candy floss.

Eat, Drink, Shop

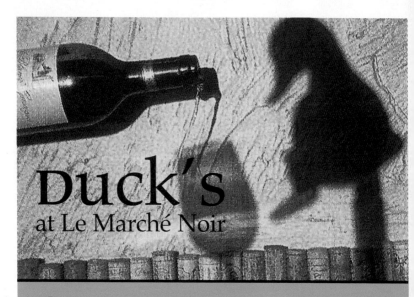

Duck's
at Le Marché Noir

Contemporary Scottish Cuisine

with international **flair**

www.ducks.co.uk
enquires@ducks.co.uk

Duck's | 2/4 Eyre Place, Edinburgh   EH3 5EP
at Le Marché Noir | Tel: (0131) 558 1608   Fax: (0131) 556 0798

Restaurants

There's choice, there's quality, but how much international-standard cuisine?

Rogue: stirring up some tasty trouble on Edinburgh's restaurant scene. *See p134.*

Edinburgh has one Michelin star. It belongs to **Restaurant Martin Wishart** in Leith (*see p135*) – a small establishment without too many tables where Mr Wishart can keep a strict eye on quality control.

So is the city a culinary backwater? Hardly. The range and choice of food in Edinburgh today is wider than it has ever been. The Michelin inspectors may not think they're quite starry enough, but Edinburgh has a whole posse of fine, established restaurants – **The Atrium** (*see p132*), **Number One** (*see p127*) and **(fitz)Henry** (*see p134*) spring to mind – that are among the very best in Scotland and offer sublime cooking.

Does the Edinburgh scene get complacent, then? Not at all. Celebrity TV chef Gary Rhodes opened Rhodes & Co in the city centre in 1999 but it shut in early 2002 – a clear demonstration of the fact that it takes more than a famous face to stay the course.

People are still giving it a go, mind; 2001 and 2002 saw some very important openings. The respected David Ramsden, who used to run (fitz)Henry, launched **Rogue** (*see p134*) to

much acclaim; James Sankey (The Atrium, blue bar café) and Tony Singh (Royal Yacht Britannia) opened **Oloroso** (*see p127*); the **North Bridge Brasserie at the Scotsman Hotel** (*see p121*) finally arrived; and **La Garrigue** (*see p120*) quietly sneaked on to the scene with its top-notch French regional dishes. Even **Yo! Sushi** (*see p125*) ventured beyond the south-east of England to open a branch in Edinburgh. To a casual observer, these openings are all evidence of a thriving restaurant culture; diners have never had it so good.

If you want a formal vegetarian dinner, you can have it. Edinburgh also has Indian, Thai, and Chinese restaurants galore. There are any number of small establishments serving decent mod-Brit nosh and good fish. Neighbourhood Italians? Easy! Tapas? No problem! But has the city got the clientele, the economic base, and the sheer desire to compete on an international level with the very best in New York, Paris and London? Are Edinburgh's best restaurants really good, or just good in Scottish terms? There's only one way for the travelling gourmet to find out: get stuck in.

Restaurants

For babelicious staff

The Apartment (see p129) has gorgeously cool waiters and waitresses to go with the cutting-edge cuisine.

For a wallet-busting blow-out

You'll require a very deep wallet to dine at either **Oloroso** (see p127) or the **Secret Garden** (see p123).

For a taste of Japan

Bonsai (see p131) brings the best of Japan to Edinburgh.

For a politically correct lunch

Susie's Wholefood Diner (see p132) is so right on it hurts.

For technical accomplishment

Restaurant Martin Wishart (see p135) stuns with its high-maintenance, exquisite dishes.

For enjoying the bonhomie of a voluble restaurateur

Silvio Praino at **Scalini** (see p125) is the host with the most.

For wonderful views

The Tower at the Museum of Scotland (see p123) has one of the best panoramas in town.

WHAT'S SCOTS?

Many Edinburgh restaurants serve food with a Scottish twist, so it's hard to know whether to describe certain places as Scottish or Modern British. In this chapter, we've saved the category 'Scottish' for more self-consciously tartan establishments (in terms of ingredients, decor or setting).

PRACTICALITIES

Few places have strict dress codes these days. As a general rule, the pricier the joint, the smarter the clientele. It's only common sense that you don't turn up to **The Pompadour** (see p125) in charity shop chic; but if you're unsure call ahead first.

It's standard practice to pay ten per cent on top of the bill for service. Some restaurants will add this automatically (while insisting that it is 'optional'; so if service wasn't up to scratch you should deduct the charge). Be wary of places that include service on the bill and still leave a space for a gratuity on your credit card slip.

Finally, during the Festival season (August to early September) many restaurants are open much later than indicated in the year-round times; these extended hours can change from year to year, so it's best to phone first to check.

Old Town

American

Mamma's

30 Grassmarket, EH1 (225 6464). Bus 2, 23, 27, 28, 41, 45. **Open** noon-11pm Mon-Thur, Sun; noon-midnight Fri, Sat. **Main courses** £5-£8. **Credit** MC, V. **Map** p309 E6.

'Traditional' American pizzas and *panzerotti* keep a surprisingly wide customer base smiling. The pizzas go up to 16 inches and as well as all the usual toppings there are more off-the-wall offerings such as haggis and cactus. A fun, loud, sometimes cramped eaterie, with cool waitresses and macho nachos – what more could you want?
Branches: 1 Howard Street, Inverleith Row, Stockbridge, EH3 (558 7177); 2 Broughton Place, Broughton, EH1 (558 8868).

Fish

Creelers

3 Hunter Square, EH1 (220 4447). Bus 35/Nicolson Street–North Bridge buses. **Open** June-Sept noon-2.30pm, 5.30-10.30pm Mon-Thur, Sun; noon-2.30pm, 5.30-11pm Fri, Sat. Oct-May noon-2.30pm, 5.30-10.30pm Mon, Wed, Thur, Sun; 5.30-10.30pm Tue; noon-2.30pm, 5.30-11pm Fri, Sat. **Main courses** £11-£17. **Credit** AmEx, DC, MC, V. **Map** p304 D3.

The couple who own this bistro and restaurant also have a branch and a smokehouse on the Isle of Arran, and the husband worked for years on trawlers off the west coast. The upshot of all this is that they are the ideal people to source the best fish and seafood. A typical dish would be fillet of cod with a black olive tapenade. Eating outside can be pleasant in the summer, if somewhat crowded during the Festival season (mind the buskers). No smoking in the restaurant before 2pm at lunchtime or 9.30pm in the evening.

French

La Garrigue

31 Jeffrey Street, EH1 (557 3032/www.lagarrigue. co.uk). Bus 30, 35/Princes Street buses. **Open** noon-2.30pm, 6.30-10.30pm Tue-Sat; noon-2.30pm Sun. **Main courses** £9.50-£17.25. **Credit** AmEx, DC, MC, V. **Map** p310 G5.

Jean-Michel Gauffre used to be executive chef at the city's Sheraton Hotel, but luckily he packed that in and opened La Garrigue (in summer 2001). The restaurant has mod-rustic decor and serves food from the Languedoc that reminds you why it's fun to eat out. Whether you choose the simple savoury tarts, the juniper and ham-stuffed rabbit leg, or tuna steak with basil dressing you will be happy. Although more hyped restaurants have arrived on the Edinburgh scene in recent times, few are more capable.

Maison Bleue

36-38 Victoria Street, EH1 (226 1900/www.maison-bleue.co.uk). Bus 2, 23, 27, 28, 41, 42, 45. **Open** noon-3pm, 5-11pm Mon-Sat; noon-3pm, 5-10pm Sun. **Main courses** £8-£12. **Credit** DC, MC, V. **Map** p304 C3.
Taking to the extreme the idea that a little bit of what you fancy can only be beneficial, Bleue's menu is composed of *bouchées*, literally mouthfuls of food – global tapas is perhaps a more helpful term. Typical examples include salmon and crab fish cakes, vegetable tempura and own-made duck confit. Sleek.

Global

The Reform

267 Canongate, EH8 (558 9992). Bus 30, 35. **Open** noon-2.30pm, 5.30-10.30pm daily. **Main courses** £8-£19.50. **Credit** AmEx, MC, V. **Map** p310 H5.
Once upon a time this was a Scottish restaurant in the heart of Edinburgh's tourist strip, but a French manager and Australian chef transformed it in 2000 into a fusion wonderland. Typical modern blonde wood decor and a cool feel provide the setting for such menu novelties as scallop and strawberry soup, or pan-fried kangaroo with berry jus. It's a refuge for tourists who have had quite enough *Braveheart* for one day, thank you.

Indian

Khushi's

16 Drummond Street, EH8 (556 8996). Nicolson Street–North Bridge buses. **Open** noon-3pm, 5-9pm Mon-Thur; noon-3pm, 5-9.30pm Fri, Sat. **Main courses** £4.50-£5.50. **No credit cards.** **Map** p310 G6.
Khushi's back-to-basics approach to curry won't find favour with those who like their dishes intensely rich or creamy and their decor decadently luxurious, but since it has been thriving for decades it must be doing something right. Cheap, cheerful, spartan and unlicensed (free corkage), it's a good spot to fill up for little money. Khushi's probably felt quite bohemian once and remains something of an Edinburgh institution, but with so many alternatives now on offer, its best days may be behind it.

Mexican

Viva Mexico

41 Cockburn Street, EH1 (226 5145/www.viva-mexico.co.uk). Bus 35/Princes Street, Nicolson Street–North Bridge buses. **Open** noon-2pm, 6-10.30pm Mon-Sat; 6.30-10pm Sun. **Main courses** £9.95-£14.95. **Credit** AmEx, DC, MC, V. **Map** p304 D3.

All the usual Mexican suspects are here: head to the downstairs dining room for a splendid collection of moustaches, courtesy of the black and white photos, and for Margaritas that are well regarded by those in the know. This restaurant has been here forever, and we love it really.

Modern British

The Dial

44-46 George IV Bridge, EH1 (225 7179). Bus 23, 27, 28, 41, 42, 45. **Open** noon-3pm, 6-11pm daily. **Main courses** £8.95-£18.95. **Credit** AmEx, DC, MC, V. **Map** p309 F6.
White walls, paper lanterns and twisting banisters ensure that the Dial's decor makes as bold a statement as its menu. Top-notch Scottish produce is given an eclectic treatment that is, at times, reassuringly familiar, and, at others, totally unexpected. The stir-fried salmon with mangetout, ginger and coriander has more than a touch of the Pacific Rim about it, while the ribeye Angus with mash and a filo parcel of own-made pâté is conspicuously 'nu-Scottish'. The Dial is in a basement, so it's easy to miss the entrance.

Howie's

10-14 Victoria Street, EH1 (225 1721/www.howies.uk.com). Bus 23, 27, 28, 41, 42, 45. **Open** noon-2.30pm, 6-10.30pm daily. **Set dinner** £15.50 2 courses; £17.95 3 courses. **Credit** AmEx, MC, V. **Map** p310 H7.
The Howie's chain seems to have stepped into the mid-price value gap left behind by the collapse of French budget stalwart Pierre Victoire. These are the kinds of places that young courting couples might use for a first dinner date or older marrieds might use for a reliable meal out. Scottish produce forms the foundations of the set menus and this is forged into the likes of fish cakes and pan-fried fillets of chicken with a Madeira and coriander jus. **Branches**: 208 Bruntsfield Place, South Edinburgh EH10 (221 1777); 4 Glanville Place, Kerr Street, Stockbridge, EH3 (225 5553); 29 Waterloo Place, Calton Hill, EH1 (556 5766); **Flaming Red** 63 Dalry Road, West Edinburgh, EH11 (313 3334).

North Bridge Brasserie at The Scotsman Hotel

20 North Bridge, EH1 (622 2900). Nicolson Street–North Bridge buses. **Open** 12.15-2.30pm, 6.15-10pm Mon-Thur; 12.15-2.30pm, 6.15-10.30pm Fri-Sun. **Main courses** £6.95-£19.95. **Credit** AmEx, DC, MC, V. **Map** p304 D2.
Housed in the former offices of the *Scotsman* newspaper, this upmarket hotel opened for business in 2001 (*see p43*). Its brasserie faces on to North Bridge in what used to be the newspaper office's entrance foyer, so there's a high ceiling, with tables upstairs around the balcony level. The menu is flexible: you could just have a vegetarian salad or a selection of sushi, or indulge yourself with half-a-dozen oysters followed by a ribeye steak. Teething troubles in the

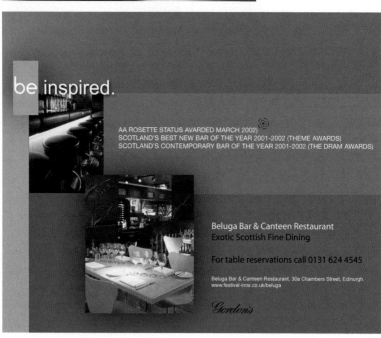

hotel's first year meant the opening of its full-on restaurant (Restaurant 399) was delayed well into 2002, but it should be up and running by the time you read this.

The Tower

Museum of Scotland, Chambers Street, EH1 (225 3003/www.tower-restaurant.com). Bus 2, 23, 27, 28, 41, 42, 45. **Open** noon-11pm daily. **Main courses** £11.95-£20. **Credit** AmEx, DC, MC, V. **Map** p309 F6.

Situated like an eagle's nest at the top of the Museum of Scotland, the Tower has incomparable views of Edinburgh (and yeah, we do mean better than Oloroso, *see p127*). By night, when the Castle is floodlit, it is almost enough to make you forget about the food. But not for long. Oysters, crabs' claws, lobster and seafood platters battle it out with tuna and green bean salads, char-grilled ribeye steaks, carpaccios of beef and a deluxe interpretation of the much-maligned prawn cocktail. The surroundings are elegant and sophisticated. No smoking.

Scottish

Dubh Prais

123B High Street, EH1 (557 5732/www.bencraig house.co.uk/dubh.html). Bus 35/Nicolson Street–North Bridge buses. **Open** noon-2pm, 6.30-10.30pm Tue-Fri; 6.30-10.30pm Sat. **Main courses** £11.90-£16.50. **Credit** AmEx, MC, V. **Map** p304 D3.

James McWilliams is the chef and owner of this basement restaurant on the Royal Mile and he reckons that he was serving Scottish cuisine before anyone else knew what it was. Well, he may be right, but more pertinently the Dubh Prais (that's 'black pot' in Gaelic, fact fans) has long provided a serious standard of food. Naturally, the raw ingredients are the best that Scotland has to offer and McWilliams allows their flavours to shine through. Despite the Royal Mile location, this is no tourist trap.

Jackson's Restaurant

209 High Street, EH1 (225 1793/www.jacksons-restaurant.co.uk). Bus 35/Nicolson Street–North Bridge buses. **Open** noon-2.30pm, 6-10.30pm daily. **Main courses** £11.95-£16.95. **Credit** AmEx, DC, MC, V. **Map** p304 D3.

Since Jackson's decor has a number of points in common with a Scottish hunting lodge, it is fitting that the fruits of hunting, shooting and fishing, as well as careful cattle-rearing, should feature so heavily on the menu. It is all done well and, while tourists are far from being the only ones to dine in the white linen surroundings, the chatter in here is a cosmopolitan mix of tongues.

The Witchery by the Castle/ The Secret Garden

352 Castlehill, EH1 (225 5613/www.thewitchery.com). Bus 23, 27, 28, 35, 41, 42, 45. **Open** noon-4pm, 5.30-11.30pm daily. **Main courses** £13-£20. **Credit** AmEx, DC, MC, V. **Map** p304 C3.

The Witchery is actually two restaurants: the Witchery by the Castle and the adjacent Secret Garden. The food is of the same quality in both dining rooms, but the latter has won a deserved reputation for its romantic setting. (It's the kind of vaguely Jacobean, candlelit space that makes Middle Englanders go all gooey.) Taken together, the two restaurants remain a top Edinburgh destination, but food-wise, price doesn't always equal quality, and skill levels in the kitchen wax and wane rather too frequently for comfort. However, the pre-/post-theatre menu at the Secret Garden is always a fine bet. And, if you do go for the full deal, you can be sure of good coffee to soften the pain of the bill.

Spanish

Igg's/Barioja

Igg's: 15 Jeffrey Street, EH1 (557 8184). Bus 30, 35/Princes Street buses. **Open** noon-2.30pm, 6-10.30pm Mon-Sat. **Main courses** £12-£19.50.
Barioja: 19 Jeffrey Street, EH1 (557 3622). **Open** 11am-11pm Mon-Sat. **Main courses** £1-£6.50.
Both: **Credit** AmEx, DC, MC, V. **Map** p310 G5.

'Plush' is a suitable term for the food at Iggy Campos' place. He sources all of his meat from the organic farm at Stobo Castle and then his chefs perform wonders with it. Next door and under the same ownership is the fun, informal and tapas-tastic Barioja.

Vegetarian

Bann UK

5 Hunter Square, EH1 (226 1112/www.urbann. co.uk). Bus 35/Nicolson Street–North Bridge buses. **Open** 11am-10pm Mon-Fri; 10am-11pm Sat, Sun. **Main courses** £8.50-£10.50. **Credit** AmEx, MC, V. **Map** p304 D3.

Handily placed for the Royal Mile, Bann UK is one of three restaurants slugging it out for the title of Edinburgh's top veggie venue. It's the most mod-designery of the three; it's open late; the food is reliably good, and there's a fine selection of Scottish beers and some organic wines too. Mushroom in filo, gruyère and leek sausages and a killer vanilla cheesecake are all reasons to book a table. Yum.

Black Bo's

57-61 Blackfriars Street, EH1 (557 6136/www.blackbos.com). Bus 35/Nicolson Street–North Bridge buses. **Open** 6-10.30pm Mon-Thur, Sun; noon-2pm, 6-10.30pm Fri, Sat. **Main courses** £9.50-£10.50. **Credit** MC, V. **Map** p310 G5.

Very much a vegetarian restaurant – as opposed to a café or diner – Bo's quietly accepts the praise that's continually heaped on it and gets on with the business in hand: producing innovative, high quality vegetarian cuisine that's impossible to pin down. The menu changes according to the whim of the chef patron; veggie bean bakes and nut loaves don't get a look in, but idiosyncratic concoctions of fruit and veg do. Adventurous to say the least.

Eat, Drink, Shop

Fish food

For the true Edinburgh fish experience, forget seared tuna and pan-fried scallops and try instead a 'fish supper' (battered fish and chips) with 'salt and sauce' from a local fish and chip shop. Sauce is unique to Edinburgh and is a viscious, brown, vinegar-based concoction that looks as though it contravenes every United Nations chemical weapons limitation resolution; however, it adds a spicy zing to a fish supper and should be tried at least once. Edinburgh natives swear by it, but visitors can find the resulting finger-licking experience a bit messy; ask for 'salt and vinegar' when you order if you want to avoid it. Adventurous eaters should also look out for haggis, black pudding and white pudding (all cooked in batter) as alternatives to the usual fish, sausage, pie or chicken.

For a proper fish supper in Edinburgh, try **L'Alba D'Oro** (5 Henderson Row; 557 2580) and **L'Aquila Bianca** (17 Raeburn Place; 332 8433) in Stockbridge; or the **Deep Sea** (2 Antigua Street; 557 0276) and **Rapido** (79 Broughton Street; 556 2041) in Broughton.

Legume

11 South College Street, EH8 (667 1597). Nicolson Street–North Bridge buses. **Open** noon-2pm, 5.30-9pm Mon-Thur, Sun; noon-2pm, 5.30-10pm Fri, Sat. **Set menu** £13.95 2 courses; £16.95 3 courses. **Credit** AmEx, DC, MC, V. **Map** p310 G6.
Legume opened in 2002 as the new kid on the block in the city's veg top three (along with Bann UK and Black Bo's). If there was such a thing as a French vegetarian restaurant, Legume might actually be it (mushroom soup, risottos, ratatouille). The proprietors have a done a decent job of jazzing up the interior of a quiet room, and if the Polish waitress is still there when you visit, you'll have a totally excellent time.

New Town

Fish

Café Royal Oyster Bar

17A West Register Street, EH1 (556 4124). Princes Street buses. **Open** noon-2pm, 7-10pm daily. **Main courses** £14-£19.50. **Credit** AmEx, DC, MC, V. **Map** p306 F4.
Adjacent to the equally ornate Café Royal Circle Bar (*see p151*), this classy and rather grand Victorian restaurant prides itself on classic fish dishes, which

it does remarkably well. Not that customers have to go the whole hog and eat a full meal: half-a-dozen oysters will give any seafood-lover a refreshing taste of the briney. This was a destination restaurant in Edinburgh before most others listed in this guide were even thought of.

The Mussel Inn

61-65 Rose Street, EH2 (225 5979/www.mussel-inn.com). Princes Street buses. **Open** noon-10pm Mon-Sat; 12.30-10pm Sun. **Main courses** £9.50-£13. **Credit** AmEx, DC, MC, V. **Map** p309 E5.
This is a kind of back to basics seafood restaurant: the shellfish come direct from the owners' farms; the food is prepared very simply; and the surroundings are colourful and perfectly comfortable but don't boast too many frills. Kilo pots of mussels are a favourite and, when accompanied by a bowl of chips and mayo, seem to make the world a better place. Rather tempting choc pud as well.

French

Café d'Odile

French Institute, 13 Randolph Crescent, EH3 (225 5685). Bus 13, 19, 29, 36, 37, 41, 42. **Open** noon-2pm Tue-Sat. **Set menu** £6.65 2 courses; £7.35 3 courses. **No credit cards**. **Map** p308 C3.
Some French restaurants are about as Gallic as *le chewing gum*; Odile's, set in the basement of the ever-active French Institute, is the real deal, even if it isn't licensed (corkage charge). Odile works her home cooking around what was available that morning and tends to follow the season's produce: everything will be ultra fresh, but a strawberry tart ain't going to feature in January. In fine weather, the outside tables provide a pleasant view of the large sweep of trees beyond the garden. It's popular with ladies who lunch – others should follow their lead.

Café Saint-Honoré

34 North West Thistle Street Lane, EH2 (226 2211/ www.icscotland.co.uk/cafe-sthonore). Bus 13, 19A, 24, 28. **Open** *Sept-July* noon-2.15pm, 5-10pm Mon-Fri; 6-10pm Sat. *Aug* also 6-10pm Sun. **Main courses** £13.50-£17.60. **Credit** AmEx, DC, MC, V. **Map** p304 B1.
Burnished mirrors, a checked floor and lots of wood panelling make this hard-to-find restaurant a dead ringer for a classic French bistro. The food is less obviously Gallic but certainly not to be sniffed at. In fact, this is where many of Edinburgh's other restaurant managers and chefs come on their nights off. Early diners can take advantage of the reduced-price offers available weekdays from 5pm to 7pm. No smoking in the main dining area.

Duck's at Le Marché Noir

2-4 Eyre Place, EH3 (558 1608/www.ducks.co.uk). Bus 23, 27, 36. **Open** noon-2.30pm, 6.30-10pm Mon-Thur; noon-2.30pm, 6.30-10.30pm Fri, Sat; 6.30-9.30pm Sun. **Main courses** £14-£20. **Credit** AmEx, DC, MC, V. **Map** p306 E3.

A well-established French/Scottish restaurant run by the unique Malcolm Duck, this New Town restaurant has one of the best wine lists in the city. The food is serious, with dishes like herb crumbed salmon and scallop boudin with creamed leeks and tarragon beurre blanc taking considerable effort and expertise to create. Wine-tasting dinners are a regular feature.

French

The Pompadour Restaurant

Caledonian Hilton Hotel, Princes Street, EH1 (222 8777). Princes Street buses. **Open** 12.30-2.30pm, 7-10pm Tue-Fri; 7-10pm Sat. **Main courses** £15.95-£23. **Credit** AmEx, DC, MC, V. **Map** p304 A2.

This restaurant dates from the 1920s, apparently, and has all the trappings of an old-fashioned, top-drawer dining experience: a tinkling pianist, gliding staff, extravagant desserts and lemons wrapped in muslin so you can squeeze them over the asparagus. It's French in the most chi-chi of ways. Everyone should do it once, but take a credit card with lots of slack.

Italian

Cosmo

58A North Castle Street, EH2 (226 6743). Princes Street buses. **Open** 12.30-2.15pm, 7-10.45pm Mon-Fri; 7-10.45pm Sat. **Main courses** £14.50-£21.50. **Credit** AmEx, MC, V. **Map** p304 A1.

Appealing to the more mature and better-heeled customer, Cosmo is an Edinburgh institution, albeit one that doesn't like to shout about its status. A million miles away from the usual pizza and pasta joints, Cosmo is all about classic Italian cooking, with an emphasis on fish. Trainers and a T-shirt are definite sartorial no-nos.

Pizza Express

32 Queensferry Street, EH2 (225 8863). Bus 13, 19, 29, 36, 37, 41, 42. **Open** 11.30am-midnight daily. **Main courses** £4.80-£7.60. **Credit** AmEx, DC, MC, V. **Map** p308 C5.

This is the no brainer choice. You're visiting Edinburgh; you're tired; it's been a long day schlepping around the sights, and you just want something familiar, hassle free, and dependable. And here it is. The Stockbridge branch is the most interesting, with tables overlooking the river; the city centre branches are more eat 'n' go.
Branches: 23 North Bridge, Old Town, EH1 (557 6411); 1 Deanhaugh Street, Stockbridge, EH4 (332 7229).

Scalini

10 Melville Place, Queensferry Street, EH3 (220 2999/ www.scaliniristorante.com). Bus 13, 19, 29, 36, 37, 41, 42. **Open** noon-2.30pm, 6-10pm Mon-Sat. **Main courses** £7.20-£15.50. **Credit** AmEx, DC, MC, V. **Map** p308 C5.

Scalini is an intimate, basement restaurant that tends to keep things simple (and effective) rather than use over-complicated, fussy ideas. Silvio Praino is the

Old-school glamour: **Pompadour**. *See p125.*

exuberant owner; should you visit, you will almost certainly make his acquaintance. There's a cool wine list and no smoking.

Japanese

Yo! Sushi

66 Rose Street, EH2 (220 6040/www.yosushi.com). Princes Street buses. **Open** noon-10pm daily. **Main courses** £5.50-£16.50. **Credit** AmEx, MC, V. **Map** p304 A1.

The London sushi bar chain finally landed in Scotland in 2001 and has been a big hit – not surprising given the sheer lack of Japanese eateries north of the border. It follows the same formula as the branches in London: a conveyor belt passes the bar seats and booths with plates carrying an astonishing variety of dishes prepared by chefs in the central kitchen space. Tuna maki, salmon sashimi, and lots, lots more. Yo! Sushi on the ground floor is the eating part, while downstairs you'll find the bar and snack-stop, Yo! Below (*see p154*).

Modern British

Martin's

70 Rose Street, North Lane, between Castle Street & Frederick Street, EH2 (225 3106). Princes Street buses. **Open** noon-2pm, 7-10pm Tue-Fri; 7-10pm Sat. Closed 24 Dec-23 Jan. **Main courses** £16-£22. **Credit** AmEx, DC, MC, V. **Map** p304 B1.

Eat, Drink, Shop

The Bonham: a touch of class.

Not easy to find but worth the effort, Martin Irons' restaurant is a showcase for Scottish produce. Irons realised the value of attentive sourcing and organic ingredients years before most restaurateurs, and Edinburgh diners have been reaping the benefits ever since he opened Martin's in 1983. The restaurant has established an enviable reputation that is richly deserved. From the vegetables to the lamb and the fish, you can be sure that (as far as possible) everything is just as nature intended. No smoking except for private bookings.

Number One, The Restaurant

Balmoral Hotel, 1 Princes Street, EH1 (557 6727). Princes Street buses. **Open** noon-2pm, 7-10pm Mon-Thur; noon-2pm, 7-10.30pm Fri; 7-10.30pm Sat; 7-10pm Sun. **Main courses** £19.50-£22.50. **Credit** AmEx, DC, MC, V. **Map** p304 D2.
The flagship eaterie in what many consider to be Edinburgh's grandest hotel, Number One is a high-class restaurant perfect for very special occasions. The decor is a subtle and sumptuous exercise in oriental design, while the wine list will keep the most demanding oenophile intrigued. The restaurant's premier status is reflected in the unstinting use of luxury ingredients and in the sophisticated techniques of head chef Jeff Bland, who is also in charge of the kitchens at the more relaxed and less expensive Hadrian's at the Balmoral (557 5000).

Oloroso

33 Castle Street, EH2 (226 7614). **Open** noon-2.30pm, 7-9.30pm daily. **Main courses** £17-£26. **Credit** AmEx, DC, MC, V. **Map** p304 B1.

Its creators (Sankey and Singh) have great credentials; its design values are flawless; it's got great views, a roof terrace, a lounge bar, and altogether the whole Oloroso experience is fun, fun, fun. Up to a point. This place certainly oozes 21st-century chic, but it remains to be seen whether it can live up to the sky-high expectations it has generated. A rethink some months down the line? We shall see... *See also p153.*

The Restaurant at the Bonham

Bonham Hotel, 35 Drumsheugh Gardens, EH3 (623 9319). Bus 13, 19, 29, 36, 37, 41, 42. **Open** noon-2.30pm, 6-10.30pm Mon-Fri; noon-3pm, 6.30-10.30pm Sat; noon-3pm, 6-10.30pm Sun. **Main courses** £11.50-£18. **Credit** AmEx, DC, MC, V. **Map** p308 C5.
The Bonham is one of those hotels that keeps turning up in style guides and its restaurant fits the mould perfectly: a high-ceilinged room, with lots of wood panelling, quality art works and little contemporary flourishes in the fixtures and fittings. Food-wise, you're looking at the likes of roast squab pigeon followed by prosciutto-wrapped chicken supreme with spiced barley risotto and lime leaves sauce. Utterly excellent for lunch on a sunny day when light streams in through the windows.

Scottish

Haldanes

39A Albany Street, EH3 (556 8407/www.haldanes restaurant.com). Bus 8, 13, 17. **Open** noon-1.30pm, 6-9.30pm Mon-Fri; 6-9.30pm Sat, Sun (lunchtimes by reservation only). **Main courses** £15.50-£21.50. **Credit** AmEx, DC, MC, V. **Map** p306 F4.
George Kelso is the chef-patron at this well-appointed and highly rated basement restaurant in the New Town. Scottish produce is very much to the fore (Haldanes is a member of the Scotch Beef Club) and Kelso is a keen proponent of preparing as much from scratch as possible. Haldanes has deliberately aimed for a country house feel and this is helped by customers being able to retire to the lounge or study for after-dinner drinks and coffee.

Keepers

13B Dundas Street, EH3 (556 5707/www.keepers. sagehost.co.uk). Bus 23, 27. **Open** noon-2pm, 6-10pm Tue-Fri; 6-10pm Sat. **Main courses** £12.95-£15.95. **Credit** AmEx, MC, V. **Map** p306 E4.
Deep in the New Town, this basement restaurant consists of interconnected, candle-lit cellars that are ideal for that gaze-into-each-other's-eyes occasion. The Scottish staples of beef, game and salmon are all treated with a steady panache, but for a real treat, the chef excels at dishes like saddle of rabbit with a vermouth and truffle sauce.

Winter Glen

3A Dundas Street, EH3 (477 7060). Bus 23, 27. **Open** noon-2pm, 6.30pm-late Mon-Sat. **Main courses** £10.50-£13. **Credit** AmEx, MC, V. **Map** p306 E4.

Eat, Drink, Shop

Scottish icons Haggis

Haggis is minced lung, heart and liver from a sheep, mixed with oatmeal and pepper and cooked in a sheep's stomach. Since ancient times all kinds of peoples have eaten bits of animal in a wrap of skin, stomach or intestine. Yet the world regards haggis as Scottish thanks to Robert Burns, whose 'Address to a Haggis' fixed the dish as a national comestible. It was written in 1786 on Burns' first visit to Edinburgh when, even 80 years after the Act of Union, the authorities were still trying desperately to replace the vestigial traces of Scottish culture with more English pronunciation and ways. Burns was never one to like pretence or pretentiousness so this was his splenetic, patriotic, democratic response.

Eaten since at least the 13th century in Scotland, sales of haggis rocket for 25 January when Scots around the world, celebrate Burns' birthday. A recitation of the 'Address' (it's perfect for declaiming at high volume) is accompanied by haggis and copious amounts of whisky.

A vegetarian version of the haggis was invented in 1984 for the launch of the Scottish Poetry Library – unlike Scotland's bard, many modern poetry lovers are of a vegetarian persuasion. You can buy an own-made traditional or a vege haggis at Macsweens of Edinburgh (see p174). Or try it in an Edinburgh restaurant – most of the Scottish eateries in this chapter should be able to oblige.

Eat, Drink, Shop

Another of New Town's basement establishments, Winter Glen distinguishes itself by winning countless awards. The menu changes regularly, but you can expect marinated seafood and Scottish smoked salmon, or breast of chicken stuffed with woodland mushrooms served with a carrot and cumin sauce.

Spanish

Tapas Olé
10 Eyre Place, EH3 (556 2754). Bus 13, 23, 27, 36. **Open** noon-10pm daily. **Main courses** £2.50-£6.50. **Credit** MC, V. **Map** p306 E3.
Neither branch of Tapas Olé holds back on the party spirit, although the original branch on Eyre Place has a basement dining area in which to corral the more raucous parties. Best enjoyed with friends and a few bottles of wine, Tapas Olé provides a relaxed and chatty atmosphere in which to fill up with hot tapas. It is also cheaper to get to than Andalucía.
Branch: 4 Forrest Road, Old Town, EH3 (225 7069).

Thai

Siam Erawan
48 Howe Street, EH3 (226 3675). Bus 13, 19A, 24, 28. **Open** noon-2.30pm, 6-11pm Mon-Sat; 6-10.30pm Sun. **Main courses** £8.50-£11.50. **Credit** MC, V. **Map** p306 D4.
A polite venue in the heart of the New Town, Siam Erawan specialises in yum dishes, in which the meat and seafood are cooked very quickly in a spice and stock combination to give them a unique hot and sour flavour. For something unusual try the curried roast duck with grapes, sweet basil and toasted spices.
Branch: **Erawan Express** 176 Rose Street, New Town, EH2 (220 0059); **Erawan Oriental** 14 South St Andrew Street, New Town, EH2 (556 4242).

Vegetarian

Henderson's Salad Table & Wine Bar
94 Hanover Street, EH2 (225 2131). Bus 23, 27. **Open** 8am-10.30pm Mon-Sat. **Main courses** £4.75. **Credit** AmEx, MC, V. **Map** p304 C1.
Founded in the 1960s, Henderson's has lasted the course well. The original basement eaterie is still going strong and around the corner there is Henderson's Bistro, which is a touch more comfortable. To enjoy Henderson's at its best, take a friend along for the evening, head for the salad table and wine bar, buy a shedload of salads and bread and some organic wine, then go down into the 'jazz cellar' where you could find some melancholy gents playing acoustic guitar.
Branch: **Henderson's Bistro** 25 Thistle Street, New Town, EH2 (225 2605).

Stockbridge

American

Bell's Diner
7 St Stephen Street, EH3 (225 8116). Bus 19A, 24, 28. **Open** 6-10.30pm Mon-Fri, Sun; noon-10.30pm Sat. **Main courses** £6.50-£12.50. **Credit** MC, V. **Map** p306 D3.
Burgers and steaks form the bulk of the menu at this tiny Stockbridge restaurant. Bell's has been around for more years than most people care to remember and few have tired of it yet. People tend to rediscover it from time to time and delight in the simplicity of decent burgerdom. The beef and chicken varieties come in various sizes, and no less attention is paid to the veggie burger.

Chinese

Loon Fung
*2 Warriston Place, Inverleith Row, EH3 (556 1781).
Bus 8, 17, 23, 27.* **Open** noon-11.30pm Mon-Thur;
noon-1am Fri; 2pm-1am Sat; 2pm-midnight Sun. **Main
courses** £7-£18. **Credit** AmEx, MC, V. **Map** p306 F2.
Down on Canonmills and handily placed for the
Botanic Gardens, Loon Fung is one of Edinburgh's
better Cantonese restaurants. There's a great selection of dim sum, and specials include baked crab in
ginger sauce and steamed chicken with mushrooms.
Often busy when everywhere else is deserted, it's
been a stalwart of the scene for years.

Mexican

Blue Parrot Cantina
*49 St Stephen Street, EH3 (225 2941). Bus 19A, 24,
28.* **Open** 5-11pm Mon-Thur, Sun; noon-11pm Fri,
Sat. **Main courses** £7.90-£12.95. **Credit** MC, V.
Map p306 D3.
A touch more adventurous than the usual fajita
factories, this basement cantina on Stockbridge's
once boho St Stephen Street throws in the odd unexpected ingredient from time to time. Try the sautéd
whole chillies or the Mexican steak.

Calton Hill & Broughton

Chinese

China China
*10 Antigua Street, EH1 (556 9791). Playhouse
buses.* **Open** noon-11pm daily. **Buffet** £4.99-£10.99.
Credit AmEx, MC, V.
Imagine a dirt-cheap Chinese canteen with a nod to
IKEA design values and you've got China China. It
costs around a fiver at lunchtime, £8 early evening,
and a tenner for dinner, for which you get an 'all you
can eat' buffet (drink is extra). The food is fairly
standard canteen fare, with a decent choice of
Chinese dishes that won't spoil on a hotplate, followed by fresh fruit. It's all very jolly and quite often
absolutely packed out.

Spanish

The Tapas Tree
*1 Forth Street, EH1 (556 7118/www.tapastree.co.uk).
Bus 8, 17/Playhouse buses.* **Open** 11am-11pm daily.
Main courses £3-£10.50. **Credit** AmEx, DC, MC, V.
Map p307 G3.
One of a kind when it first opened, the Tapas Tree
now has competition but holds its position well.
The upstairs area is quite small and well-suited to
dining à deux, while the bigger downstairs room
lends itself to large-scale celebrations. Chorizo,
patatas bravas, chillied prawns and so on give a taste
of the Iberian experience. Despite a rapid turnover,
advance booking is advised at the weekends.

South Edinburgh

American

The Buffalo Grill
*14 Chapel Street, EH8 (667 7427/www.buffalo
grill.co.uk). Bus 41, 42.* **Open** noon-2pm, 6-10.15pm
Mon-Fri; 6-10.15pm Sat; 5-10pm Sun. **Main courses**
£7-£15. **Credit** MC, V. **Map** p310 G7.
With every kind of steak, from Cajun to carpetbags,
teriyakis to Delmonicos, and as many burger variations as you care to dream of, this is where it's at if
you want to get busy on the beef. Lots of Edinburgh
restaurants offer a steak but this is the only place
that offers them all. Although it isn't licensed
(there's no charge if you take your own bottle), the
original branch always seems fully booked, and the
Stockbridge outpost is pretty much the same way.
Branch: 1 Raeburn Place, Stockbridge,
EH4 (332 3864).

Chinese

Dragon Way
*74 South Clerk Street, EH8 (668 1328). Bus 3, 5, 7,
8, 14, 29, 31, 33, 37, 49.* **Open** noon-11.30pm daily.
Main courses £7.50-£15. **Credit** AmEx, DC, MC,
V. **Map** p310 H8.
The decor here is a riot of red and gold pagodas,
dragons and flowers, only partially eclipsed by the
indoor waterfall and fish pond. Seafood is the speciality but don't overlook the crispy duck, which is
good enough to make a grown man weep. Service
and environment-wise, it's the complete opposite of
China China (*see above*). Lovely dumplings.

Fish

Sweet Melinda's
11 Roseneath Street, EH9 (229 7953). Bus 24, 41.
Open 7-10pm Mon; noon-2pm, 7-10pm Tue-Sat.
Main courses £11.30-£14.50. **Credit** MC, V.
Map p309 F8.
One of the very few restaurants in the culinary
desert of Marchmont, Sweet Melinda's is a charming, one-roomed find that majors in seafood and
game. Among the starters, the Thai fish cakes with
sweet chilli dipping sauce are big sellers, while the
char-grilled tuna steaks with salsa verde add zest
to the mains. The lunchtime menu offers scaled-
down dishes along the same lines as the dinner
menu, for about half the price. There is always a
vegetarian option on offer.

Global

The Apartment
*7-13 Barclay Place, Bruntsfield Place, EH10 (228
6456). Bus 11, 15, 16, 17, 23, 45.* **Open** 6-11pm
Mon-Fri; noon-3pm, 6-11pm Sat, Sun. **Main courses**
£4.30-£9.90. **Credit** DC, MC, V. **Map** p309 D8.

Eat, Drink, Shop

Cafe Hub.
The kind of place you want to tell your friends about.
(But then decide to keep to yourself.)

Dinner

Exhibitions

Lunch

Drinks

Concerts

Culinary Events

Brunch

Coffee

Castlehill, Royal Mile
Edinburgh
Open daily
Reservations 0131 473 2067
www.eif.co.uk/the hub

EDINBURGH'S FESTIVAL CENTRE
Main sponsor ✳ BANK OF SCOTLAND

A seriously funky space that pulls off its minimalist styling well. The Apartment has nicked some of the best ideas from around the world and pulled them together neatly. The North African marinated spicy lamb balls with merguez and basil, wrapped in melted goat's cheese, are just one example of the kitchen's inventiveness. You'll end up eating a bunch of things on a skewer, but you'll like it. Fresh as it is, the Apartment attracts an older crowd as well as the capital's trend-setters because it's slap bang in the middle of an urban middle class area. A branch is due to open on George IV Bridge in summer 2002.

Nicolson's

6A Nicolson Street, EH8 (557 4567). Nicolson Street–North Bridge buses. **Open** noon-3pm, 5pm-late daily. **Main courses** £10. **Credit** AmEx, MC, V. **Map** p310 G7.

An airy first-floor space with a vaguely art deco feel, this is possibly the only place in the capital to sell the South American spirit *pisco*. As far as the food is concerned, Nicolson's menu runs from dishes such as *gado gado* to scallop and herb salad with fresh coconut and lime. The minute steaks are good too, for the less adventurous. Although it should not be considered the main draw, the Martini selection also bears closer investigation.

Indian

Ann Purna

45 St Patrick Square, EH8 (662 1807). Bus 3, 5, 7, 8, 14, 29, 31, 33, 37, 49. **Open** noon-2pm, 5.30-11pm Mon-Fri; 5.30-11pm Sun. **Main courses** £5-£7.50. **Credit** MC, V. **Map** p310 G7.

This is a family-run vegetarian eaterie with Gujarati overtones, near the university. The food is good value, the staff are friendly, and it's a delightful little place to pass an hour or two.

Kalpna

2-3 St Patrick Square, EH8 (667 9890). Bus 3, 5, 7, 8, 14, 29, 31, 33, 37, 49. **Open** noon-2pm, 5.30-11pm Mon-Sat; 5.30-11pm Sun. **Main courses** £4.50-£7.50. **Credit** MC, V. **Map** p310 G7.

A familiar and long-standing friend to Edinburgh's lovers of Indian vegetarian food, the Kalpna offers a bargain buffet lunch and hosts the evergreen regional buffet every Wednesday night. Chow down on the likes of mild but filling *khumb masala* (mushrooms cooked in coconut milk with tomatoes, coriander, onions and garlic). No smoking.

Kebab Mahal

7 Nicolson Square, EH8 (622 7228). Bus 2/North Bridge buses. **Open** noon-midnight Mon-Thur, Sun; noon-2am Fri, Sat. **Main courses** £4.50-£6.75. **Credit** AmEx, DC, MC, V. **Map** p310 G6.

A late-night munchie pick-up point for many a tired and emotional reveller, the Kebab Mahal also has basic sit-in facilities. It's not the lap of luxury by any stretch of the imagination, but the cheap, quick and

Funky fusion at **The Apartment**. *See p129.*

pretty decent curries and kebabs all do their job well. No alcohol (most of the student punters have had quite enough already).

Suruchi

14A Nicolson Street, EH8 (556 6583). Nicolson Street–North Bridge buses. **Open** noon-2pm, 5.30-11.30pm daily. **Main courses** £6.95-£9.95. **Credit** DC, MC, V. **Map** p310 G6.

Handily situated across from the Festival Theatre, Suruchi offers an interesting alternative to the standard curry house menu. Proprietor Herman Rodrigues is a bit of a scholar of Indian cooking and is often over there digging up new recipes and spices, while priding himself in sourcing Scottish ingredients. Cultural evenings of Indian music and dance feature from time to time. The premises of the thali restaurant in Leith were once a Swiss restaurant with decor straight out of the power-dressing 1980s – bizarre surroundings, but good thalis.
Branch: Suruchi Thali Restaurant
121 Constitution Street, Leith, EH8 (554 3268).

Japanese

Bonsai

46 West Richmond Street, EH8 (668 3847/ www.bonsaibarbistro.co.uk). Bus 2/Nicolson Street–North Bridge buses. **Open** noon-late daily. **Main courses** £2-£5. **Credit** MC, V. **Map** p310 G6.

A Scottish chef plus a Japanese maître d' equals a sweet bistro with a range of simple Japanese dishes slanted to a Western palate (avocado and red pepper *makizushi* for instance) – no gooey fermented things on this menu. Friendly, small, informal, it's as cute as a kilted Pokémon.

Eat, Drink, Shop

Modern British

The Atrium
10 Cambridge Street, EH1 (228 8882/www.atrium restaurant.co.uk). Bus 1, 10, 11, 15, 16, 17, 24, 34. **Open** noon-2pm, 6-10pm Mon-Fri; 6-10pm Sat. **Main courses** £14.50-£22. **Credit** AmEx, DC, MC, V. **Map** p309 D6.
Andrew Radford's entrepreneurial skill in the culinary field has been a boon for Edinburgh since the 1990s. The Atrium is the mainstay of operations, although the more informal blue bar café upstairs is pretty damn good too. The Atrium has innovative modern British cuisine that uses carefully sourced Scottish ingredients. Attention to detail is paramount and although the decor is unconventional, it won't put the frighteners on older couples and businessmen, who form a large proportion of the restaurant's regular clientele. One of Edinburgh's best restaurants of any description.

Blonde
75 St Leonard's Street, EH8 (668 2917). Bus 2, 21. **Open** 6-10pm Mon; noon-2.30pm, 6-10pm Tue-Sun. **Main courses** £7.95-£9.95. **Credit** AmEx, DC, MC, V. **Map** p310 H7.
Formerly a branch of Howie's (*see p121*), this is one of a number of small, cared-for Edinburgh restaurants where you'll find good cooking in a relaxed environment. Scottish ingredients with a contemporary twist are reliably executed by the competent kitchen, so that you can get on with your conversation without worrying about your order. If this was your neighbourhood snack shack, you'd be very happy. By the way, the name comes from the blonde wood interior, rather than the staff's hair colour.

The Marque
19-21 Causewayside, EH9 (466 6660). Bus 3, 5, 7, 8, 29, 31, 37, 42, 49. **Open** 11.45am-2pm, 5.45-10pm Tue-Thur; 11.45am-2pm, 5.45-11pm Fri; 12.30-2pm, 5.45-11pm Sat; 12.30-2pm, 5.45-10pm Sun. **Main courses** £11.50-£16.50. **Credit** MC, V. **Map** p310 H8.
Aiming towards the top of Edinburgh's restaurant jungle, this fine restaurant is getting it right with its eclectic modern British menu. Without unnecessary fad or faff, the Marque looks a bit further afield for many of its influences, so you may find spices from the Far East pepping up your breast of Bresse chicken, while the cheese selection comes with great chutneys and pickles, and there are good-value pre- and post-theatre menus. Tempting as it is, stealing the beautiful cutlery is frowned upon.
Branch: Marque Central 30B Grindlay Street, South Edinburgh, EH3 (229 9859).

Stac Polly
8-10 Grindlay Street, EH3 (229 5405/www.stacpolly. co.uk). Bus 1, 10, 11, 15, 16, 17, 24, 34. **Open** noon-2pm, 6-10.30pm Mon-Fri; 6-10.30pm Sat; 6-10pm Sun. **Main courses** £14.95-£17.95. **Credit** AmEx, MC, V. **Map** p309 D6.

Named after a mountain in the far north of Scotland, the two Stac Pollys are decked out in the natural colour scheme of the scenery around Ullapool (without the rain and the midges, of course). The haggis and filo pastry starter has an invincible reputation, but main courses like saddle of venison on black pudding risotto are worthy successors.
Branch: 29-33 Dublin Street, New Town, EH3 (556 2231).

Thai

Ayutthaya
14B Nicolson Street, EH8 (556 9351). Nicolson Street–North Bridge buses. **Open** noon-2.30pm, 5.30-11pm daily. **Main courses** £7-£8. **Credit** AmEx, DC, MC, V. **Map** p310 G6.
The venue may be small but the menu is extensive: old favourites like tom yum soup, satays and green curries are much in evidence but it's also worth exploring a little off the beaten track. The *gai yang* – a whole grilled chicken marinated in honey and spices, served with a sweet chilli sauce – is delicious.
Branch: **Sukhothai** 23 Brougham Place, Tollcross, South Edinburgh, EH3 (229 1537).

Thai Orchid
44 Grindlay Street, EH3 (228 4438). Bus 1, 10, 11, 15, 16, 17, 24, 34. **Open** noon-2.30pm, 5.30-10.30pm Mon-Fri; 5.30-10.30pm Sat, Sun. **Main courses** £7.50-£10.50. **Credit** AmEx, DC, MC, V. **Map** p304 A3.
Handy for all kinds of arts venues (The Filmhouse, Usher Hall, Traverse Theatre, Lyceum Theatre), this family-run eaterie has beavered away for some years, building its reputation. It's not spectacular or trendy, but after a meal here you'll go away happy.

Vegetarian

Susie's Wholefood Diner
51-53 West Nicolson Street, EH8 (667 8729). Bus 2, 41, 42/Nicolson Street–North Bridge buses. **Open** *Sept-July* 10am-8pm Mon; 10am-9pm Tue-Sat; noon-9pm Sun. *Aug* phone for details. **Main courses** £4.20-£5.50. **No credit cards**. **Map** p310 G6.
A firm fixture on the lunch circuit for many of the students at nearby Edinburgh University, Susie's is a laid-back, self-service diner that runs the full gamut of veggie delights from falafel and soups to chillies, curries and bakes. You'll eat well here, as long as the overweening atmosphere of smugness doesn't put you off your food.

West Edinburgh

Caribbean

Caribbean Connection
3 Grove Street, EH3 (228 1345). Bus 1, 2, 28, 34, 35. **Open** 7-9.30pm Wed-Sat. **Main courses** £10. **Credit** MC, V. **Map** p308 C6.

Run by a cheery couple who have spent many a year in the Caribbean, this great little joint looks like a roadside shack – all wooden planks and Jamaican bric-a-brac. The food is spicy and sweet; special mention must go to the wet jerk rub – barbecued chicken or pork marinated with herbs and spices. The restaurant is unlicensed, but there's no corkage charge if you bring your own bottle. Booking is as essential as the Bob Marley soundtrack.

Chinese

Oriental Dining Centre

8 Morrison Street, EH3 (221 1288). Bus 1, 2, 10, 11, 15, 16, 17, 24, 34, 35. **Open** *Rainbow Arch* noon-midnight daily. *Noodle Shack* 5.30pm-1.30am daily. *Cellar Bar* noon-3am daily. **Main courses** *Rainbow Arch* £6.50-£7; *Noodle Shack* £5.* **Credit** AmEx, MC, V. **Map** p309 D6.

There are two different outlets under the umbrella of the Oriental Dining Centre. Rapid bowls of steaming udon noodles provide a quick refuelling stop at the upstairs **Noodle Shack**, while the ground-floor **Rainbow Arch** offers the full banquet-till-you-burst option. Henry's Cellar Bar and jazz venue is also here (*see p214*).

Make the **Caribbean Connection**. *See p132.*

Indian

Indian Cavalry Club

3 Atholl Place, off West Maitland Street, EH3 (228 2974). Bus 3, 4, 12, 21, 25, 26, 31, 33, 44. **Open** 11am-2pm, 5.30-11.30pm daily. **Main courses** £8-£9. **Credit** AmEx, DC, MC, V. **Map** p308 C6.

You'll either like the faux colonialist Raj atmosphere or you'll hate it. Either way, once you've got over the mock military uniforms of the waiters, you'll notice that the food's not half bad and the decor is not quite as mad as at some other Indian restaurants. Allegedly, even the waiters lighten up eventually.

Italian

Piatto Verde

7 Dundee Terrace, EH11 (228 2588). Bus 1, 28, 34, 35. **Open** 5-11pm Mon-Thur, Sun; 5pm-midnight Fri, Sat. **Main courses** £6.50-£11. **Credit** MC, V. **Map** p308 A8.

A rustic little down-home Italian in the western tenements, where you might end up sharing the big table on busy evenings with other pilgrims who are here for the fun rather than the finesse. There are vegetarian choices on the menu, specials on the blackboard, comfort risottos and desserts.

Santini

Sheraton Grand Hotel, Lothian Road, EH1 (221 7788). Bus 1, 10, 11, 15, 16, 17, 22, 24, 34. **Open** 12.30-2pm, 6.30-10.30pm Mon-Fri; 6.30-10.30pm Sat. **Main courses** *Bistro* £5-£7. *Restaurant* £19-£20. **Credit** AmEx, DC, MC, V. **Map** p309 D6.

In the heart of the financial district, somewhere in the mod-bland architectural wasteland between the Sheraton Hotel and the Edinburgh International Conference Centre sits Santini. Given the number of 'traditional' Italian restaurants in the city (rubber mozzarella and tasteless tomato salad), this sleek and chic eaterie is quite a departure. Mr Santini also has restaurants in London and Milan.

Japanese

Yumi

2 West Coates, EH12 (337 2173/www.yumi restaurant.btinternet.co.uk). Bus 12, 26, 31. **Open** 6.30-10.30pm Mon-Sat. **Set menu** £25-£40. **Credit** DC, MC, V. **Map** p308 A6.

If you've ever harboured fantasies of being in one of Ian Fleming's Bond novels then Yumi might just be the place for you. It has an exoticism that probably went down a bundle in the novelist's time but seems a bit out of touch these days. The restaurant's quite pricey and rather formal with set meals and a sub-urban atmosphere, and it is certainly not the kind of place where you mix 'n' match dishes then throw back a few Bacardi Breezers. Japan-watchers will probably feel that Yo! Sushi (*see p125*) is a more accurate representation of contemporary Nippon. Reservations are essential.

Eat, Drink, Shop

Zinc: Conran style in Edinburgh. *See p135.*

Modern British

Rogue

Scottish Widows Building, 67 Morrison Street (228 2700). Bus 1, 2, 28, 34, 35. **Open** noon-3pm, 6-11pm Mon-Sat. **Main courses** £5-£22. **Credit** AmEx, MC, V. **Map** p308 B6.

Dave Ramsden used to run the estimable (fitz)Henry on a quiet backstreet in Leith but had his eye on bigger and better things in the city centre. In summer 2001 he pulled Rogue from the hat – that year's most significant restaurant opening. It manages to be both bold and discreet – bold once you get in, discreet because it can take a while to find. Rogue has the sort of spacious decor that makes you believe you're in London, and a happily informal menu of metropolitan standard. It's location in the heart of Edinburgh's financial district determines the type of lunch custom; evenings attract a different clientele. A definite hit.

Leith

Fish

Fishers

1 The Shore, EH6 (554 5666/www.fishersbistro. co.uk). Bus 1, 16, 22, 35, 36. **Open** noon-4pm, 6-10.30pm Mon-Sat; 12.30-10.30pm Sun. **Main courses** £10.95-£14.95. **Credit** AmEx, DC, MC, V. **Map** p311 Jy.

This is a long-established favourite with a loyal clientele, so it's surprising that it took the owners until 2001 to open a larger branch in the city centre. The fish is good, with culinary flourishes that add real interest; the nautical theme decor shouldn't make you seasick; and the cheeseboard is certainly worth a dabble.

Branch: Fishers in the City 58 Thistle Street, New Town, EH2 (225 5109).

The Shore

3-4 The Shore, EH6 (553 5080). Bus 1, 16, 22, 35, 36. **Open** *Bar* 11am-midnight Mon-Sat; 12.30-11pm Sun. *Restaurant* noon-2.30pm, 6.30-10pm Mon-Sat; 12.30-3pm, 6.30-10pm Sun. **Main courses** £12-£16. **Credit** AmEx, MC, V. **Map** p311 Jy.

Everyone in Edinburgh has a personal favourite from the several fish restaurants in Leith. They're all pretty damn good, but the Shore may well be the most relaxed. Guests can eat in the restaurant proper or in the more smoky environs of the bar, where regular folk and music sessions add another element to the experience. The fish dishes can be more than a little adventurous.

Skippers

1A Dock Place, EH6 (554 1018/www.skippers.co.uk). Bus 1, 16, 22, 35, 36. **Open** 12.30-2pm, 7-10pm Mon-Sat; 12.30-2.30pm, 7-10pm Sun. **Main courses** £12.95-£20. **Credit** AmEx, DC, MC, V. **Map** p311 Jy.

Skippers is still here, thank goodness. The restaurant was a Leith groundbreaker when the surrounding area was still full of scrapping sailors and ladies of the night. These days, modern (sanitised) apartment housing is the order of the day, but when it comes to decently prepared fish in an unpretentious room, Skippers is still tough to beat.

French

(fitz)Henry

19 Shore Place, EH6 (555 6625/www.fitzhenrys.com). Bus 1, 16, 22, 35, 36. **Open** noon-2.30pm, 6.30-10pm Mon-Thur; 12.30-2.30pm, 6.30-10.30pm Fri; 6.30-10.30pm Sat. **Main courses** £12-£20. **Credit** AmEx, MC, V. **Map** p311 Jy.

Dynamic David Ramsden, the original driving force behind this modern French-style restaurant, upped sticks to open Rogue in 2001 (*see p134*) but the people who took over here (Alan Gordon Morrison and Valerie Faichney) haven't let standards slip. Housed in an old warehouse with designer flourishes, it offers a thoroughly modern French-biased menu: how about sardine in crepinette to start, followed by grilled tuna steak with Puy lentil salad perhaps? Don't let the quiet location fool you – (fitz)Henry has a deservedly impressive reputation.

Restaurant Martin Wishart

54 The Shore, EH6 (553 3557/www.martin-wishart.co.uk). Bus 1, 16, 22, 35, 36. **Open** 12.30-2.30pm, 7-10pm Tue-Fri; 7-10pm Sat. **Main courses** £18.50-£20. **Credit** MC, V. **Map** p311 Jy.
The best restaurant in Edinburgh? Michelin would have us believe so – it's the only one in the city with a star. Certainly the kitchen has to be the most technically accomplished. The dining room may be small and a little prim, but the food is simply awesome; classical French cooking with modern spin and innovation is Mr W's forte. Booking is advisable.

The Vintner's Rooms

The Vaults, 87 Giles Street, EH6 (554 6767/ www.thevintnersrooms.demon.co.uk). Bus 1, 7, 10, 14, 22, 32/52, 34. **Open** noon-2pm, 7-10pm Mon-Sat. **Main courses** £15-£19. **Credit** AmEx, MC, V. **Map** p311 Jy.
Perfect for a romantic night out, the Vintner's Rooms is housed in an ancient wine warehouse in Leith and is one of Edinburgh's better restaurants. Soft candle lighting, the best Scottish produce and cooking with a French undercurrent are the main selling points. There are dining tables in the bar if you want to eat in an airier environment, but they can't match the intimate atmosphere of the restaurant. No smoking.

Indian

Britannia Spice

150 Commercial Street, EH6 (555 2255/www. britanniaspice.com). Bus 1, 16, 22, 35, 36. **Open** 12.15-2.15pm, 5-11.45pm daily. **Main courses** £7.95-£15.50. **Credit** AmEx, DC, MC, V. **Map** p311 Jy.
Decked out like the nearby Royal Yacht *Britannia*, this 150-cover restaurant serves up a variety of decent Thai, Sri Lankan, Nepalese and Bangladeshi dishes. The nautical theme of the decor is quite fun if you're in the mood (hello sailor), and the food is ship-shape too.

Italian

Ristorante Tinelli

139 Easter Road, EH7 (652 1932). Bus 1, 35. **Open** noon-2.30pm, 6.30-11pm Tue-Sat. **Main courses** £7.50-£14.50. **Credit** AmEx, DC, MC, V. **Map** p307 J3.
Not the most fashionable end of town and not the city's most promising exterior either, but Tinelli's has done good business over the years thanks to the Lombardy cooking and the eponymous owner's hospitality. Many of Edinburgh's married couples have fond memories of Ristorante Tinelli and wedding anniversaries are not an uncommon excuse

for dinner here. Otherwise, it's a neighbourhood restaurant par excellence and quite handy for the Hibernian FC football stadium.

Mexican

Salsa Hut

3a Albert Street, EH7 (554 4344). Bus 7, 10, 12, 14, 16, 22, 25. **Open** 6-10pm Tue-Sun. **Main courses** £7.50-£7.90. **No credit cards. Map** p307 H2.
Mad neighbourhood cantina with an authentic, hand-knitted feel and plenty of chutzpah. Imagine muddy rave dance tent meets tortilla chips 'n' dips in one of Leith's scabbier tenements and you'll begin to get the idea. Salsa Hut seems to be run by slightly spacey young women who all have DJ boyfriends. It offers all the Mex staples, adequately handled, and actually makes for a pleasant alternative destination for this neck of the woods. You can even bring your own booze, hurrah.

Modern British

The Rock Restaurant

78 Commercial Street, EH6 (555 2225). Bus 1, 16, 22, 35, 36. **Open** 6-10pm Tue-Fri; 6-10pm Sat, Sun. **Main courses** £15.95-£33.95. **Credit** AmEx, DC, MC, V. **Map** p311 Jy.
The Rock has a clean, minimalist look that is matched by incredible concentration in the open-plan kitchen. This combination makes it the most sophisticated place on Commercial Street's restaurant row. Typical starters are chillied squid and balsamic dressed potatoes or seared sea bass on hiniman sauce, while main courses include the likes of oven roasted duck breast glazed with orange shiraz sauce. The natural habitat of expense account execs, the Rock has just started offering early evening deals that put it more firmly within the reach of everybody else. Book a lunch table for four or more and staff will arrange transport within Leith and the New Town.

Zinc Bar & Grill

Ocean Terminal, Ocean Drive, Victoria Dock, EH6 (553 8070). Bus 11, 22, 34, 35, 36, 49. **Open** noon-11pm Mon-Thur; noon-midnight Fri-Sun. **Main courses** £8.50-£15. **Credit** AmEx, DC, MC, V. **Map** p311 Jx.
Autumn 2001 and a Sir Terence Conran-designed shopping arcade descended on Edinburgh's waterfront. The Conran restaurant on the first-floor 'food terrace' caused a fair degree of excitement in the city – a mark of Edinburgh graduating to a higher plane of consumption and economic health perhaps. Sky-high expectations perhaps made it inevitable that reviews of the restaurant during winter 2001-2002 were decidedly mixed. In truth, the food is perfectly passable (the usual mod Brit panoply of veggie pasta, fish-on-something, steaks, and more) but rather unexciting. Zinc is, however, Edinburgh's finest restaurant in a shopping centre. No one has yet decided if this is a good thing.

Eat, Drink, Shop

Cafés

Enjoy everything from skinny mochas to traditional tea and scones.

Laundry and lattes at the **Lost Sock Diner**. *See p143.*

Should every Starbucks in Edinburgh be taken out into the deepest part of the North Sea and consigned to a watery grave, with cinnamon topping? There are café owners all over the city who might say so, glad to be rid of the competition. By spring 2002 there were an incredible 13 branches of **Starbucks** in the Scottish capital including five on Princes Street and George Street alone. In addition, several other chains have arrived in Edinburgh in recent years (Costa, Pret à Manger, **Coffee Republic**) leaving less and less space for more individual home-grown establishments, or so one would have thought.

But the good news is that relatively few cafés have been squeezed out – so far – by the rising wave of skinny lattes and sunrise muffins. That's because the chains and the more individual places offer very different things. Each Starbucks will give you exactly the same coffee and cake every time if you want. But for traditional tea and scones you go to **Clarinda's** or **Chatterbox** instead. Edinburgh also offers venues where you could get a nasty cut from the waiter's chiselled cheekbones (**Blue Moon**) or accent (**Glass & Thompson**).

The dividing line between having a coffee, a snack, and a formal slap-up feed is as vague as ever in Edinburgh's restaurants, cafés, and bars. ('Pecan slice and an espresso, or a glass of red and some mushroom ravioli, or six pints of lager and a packet of crisps?') So what constitutes a café? We've used a pretty wide set of criteria and included different kinds of places where the eating is informal and a full meal is either not available or not compulsory.

Old Town

Bean Scene

67 Holyrood Road, EH8 (557 6549/www.beanscene. co.uk). Buses 30, 35. **Open** 8am-10pm Mon-Sat; 10am-10pm Sun. **Credit** MC, V. **Map** p310 H5.

A Scottish chain (hurrah) with mod-groovy branches in Edinburgh and Glasgow, and more in the pipeline, serving the typical coffee, sandwiches and pastries combo. The people who run this outlet, near the new parliament building, are dedicated to making it work. It's a nice place to hang out and has regular live music of the jazz/acoustic variety.
Branch: 99 Nicolson Street, South Edinburgh, EH8 (667 8159).

Eat, Drink, Shop

The best Cafés

Blue Moon Café
Gay comfort zone. *See p141.*

California Coffee Co
The best coffee in town. *See p144.*

Favorit
Funky and open late. *See p138.*

Glass & Thompson
New Town class. *See p 139.*

Kaffe Politik
Brilliant breakfasts. *See p144.*

Pâtisserie Florentin
Coolest cakes. *See p139.*

Plaisir du Chocolat
Need we translate? *See p139.*

Stromboli
Pie heaven. *See p145.*

Valvona & Crolla
Legendary. *See p143.*

The Bookstop Café
4 Teviot Place, EH1 (226 6929). Bus 23, 27, 28, 45.
Open 9am-6pm Mon-Fri; 10am-6pm Sat. **Credit** DC,
MC, V. **Map** p309 F6.
A small, independently run bookshop and café that
these days is much more about coffee than books
(there are only a few bookshelves left). The hiss of
the Gaggia and the occasional bing bing whrrr of a
modem – there's internet access here too – are the
only things to disturb the muffin-munching, coffee-
quaffing clientele. Thoughtfully sited next to one of
Edinburgh University's main drags, the Bookstop
Café seems to have found its niche among the city's
sizeable student population.

Café Hub
Castlehill, EH1 (473 2067/www.eif.co.uk/thehub).
Bus 23, 27, 28, 35, 41, 42, 45. **Open** 9.30am-10pm
daily. *Festival* 9.30am-midnight daily. **Credit** AmEx,
MC, V. **Map** p304 C3.
An integral part of The Hub (*see p64*), Edinburgh's
Festival Centre, this bright yellow café manages to
be all things to all people. From early-bird breakfasts to civilised nightcaps and accomplished dinners, the menu offers a balanced selection of open
sandwiches, saucy salads, baked dishes and juicy
steaks. Alternatively, if you just need a relaxed cup
of coffee or a restorative pot of tea then Café Hub
offers welcome and tasty relief. There's a café terrace too, which is a thoroughly pleasant spot, if the
weather's OK.

The Cafeteria
*Fruitmarket Gallery, 45 Market Street, EH1 (226
1843/www.fruitmarket.co.uk/cafe.html). Princes
Street buses.* **Open** 11am-5pm Mon-Sat; noon-5pm
Sun. **Credit** DC, MC, V. **Map** p304 D2.
Big baguette melts are the order of the day in the
café of the Fruitmarket, possibly Edinburgh's
hippest art gallery (*see p71*). Fresh danishes keep
the mid-morning grazers happy and there's always
a selection of gateaux for the more leisurely afternoon browser. But it's at lunchtime that you'll witness the real action, with staff aiming to refuel
customers with pasta and melts in under an hour.
No smoking.

Clarinda's
69 Canongate, EH8 (557 1888). Bus 30, 35.
Open 9am-4.45pm Mon-Sat; 10am-4.45pm Sun.
No credit cards. Map p310 G5.
Not one to change merely for the sake of change,
Clarinda's seems to have always been a feature
on the oft-volatile Royal Mile catering scene.
Homebaking is the name of the game here and this
place is sure to find approval in the hearts of those
who appreciate the beauty of a well-turned-out bun.

The Elephant House
*21 George IV Bridge, EH1 (220 5355/www.elephant-
house.co.uk).* **Open** 8am-
11pm Mon-Fri; 9.30am-11pm Sat, Sun. **Credit** MC, V.
Map p304 C3.
A popular and spacious café, packed with all sorts
of figurines of, yes, elephants. In term time, it's busy
with students bunking off from the nearby National
Library and idling over a cup of coffee and perhaps
a piece of cake. The back room has a fair Old Town
view. No smoking in the front room.

Elephant's Sufficiency
*170 High Street, EH1 (220 0666/elephants
sufficiency@bigfoot.com). Bus 23, 27, 28, 35,
41, 42, 45/Nicolson Street–North Bridge buses.*
Open *Winter* 8am-5pm Mon-Fri; 9am-5pm Sat, Sun.
Summer 8am-11.30pm Mon-Sat; 8am-10.30pm Sun.
No credit cards. Map p310 G5.
Very usefully located on the Royal Mile, this little
café with a fab name is a good place to sit outside in
the summer and watch the passing fauna. Lawyers
and MSPs from the nearby courts and parliament
(until it moves to Holyrood) are among the customers getting stuck into the usual soups and sandwiches. As far as possible, only Scottish ingredients
are used in the cooking.

Favorit
*19-20 Teviot Place, EH1 (220 6880/www.favorit
edinburgh.co.uk). Bus 23, 27, 28, 45.* **Open** 8am-
3am daily. **Credit** AmEx, DC, MC, V. **Map** p309 F6.
With its long opening hours, Favorit provides
everything from breakfast for workers in a hurry to
nightcaps for clapped-out clubbers. The sandwiches
have an American slant, with pastrami and gruyère
on rye being typical. Favorit also acts as a deli and
gadget shop, so if you drop in for a smoothie, don't

be too surprised if you walk out with a new espresso machine. The decor is as cool as the concept. **Branch**: 30-32 Leven Street, Tollcross, South Edinburgh, EH3 (221 1800).

The Forest

9 West Port, Grassmarket, EH1 (221 0237/www. theforest.org.uk). Bus 2. **Open** noon-11pm daily. **Credit** MC, V. **Map** p304 B3.

The Forest is a 'community volunteer run event and information space artist collective' kind of place near the art college that hosts evening discussions, movies and workshops. Sinky sofas, tasty tortillas, healthy salads, ethereal young women, earnest young men.

Lianachan

15 Blackfriars Street, EH1 (556 6922). Bus 35/ Nicolson Street–North Bridge buses. **Open** 10am-7pm Mon-Fri; 10am-5.30pm Sat; noon-5pm Sun. **No credit cards**. **Map** p310 G5.

With a name that means 'wee meadow' in Gaelic, it is perhaps no surprise that this café is strong on organic teas and fresh fruit juices. There is also the odd Greek item on the menu. It's a laid-back kind of place, with New Age and '60s music and works by local artists on the walls. Teenie goths and skatepunks sometimes come here when they're not hanging out in nearby Cockburn Street.

Lower Aisle Restaurant

St Giles' Cathedral, High Street, EH1 (225 5147). Bus 23, 27, 28, 35, 41, 42, 45/Nicolson Street–North Bridge buses. **Open** 8am-4.30pm Mon-Fri; 10am-2pm Sun. *Festival* 8am-4.30pm Mon-Sat; 10am-2pm Sun. **No credit cards**. **Map** p304 D3.

Set in the vaults of St Giles' Cathedral, the Lower Aisle isn't exactly the place for a party, but it is handy for a simple and filling lunch while you're on the tourist trail, especially if you like baked potatoes. There's history in them there walls.

Glass & Thompson: New Town's finest.

On the Mound

2-3 North Bank Street, EH1 (226 6899/www.onthe mound.com). Bus 23, 27, 28, 41, 42, 45. **Open** 8.30am-5.30pm Mon-Fri; 10am-6pm Sat. **Credit** AmEx, MC, V. **Map** p304 C2.

At the top of the Mound, this is a convenient tourist stop-off for coffee and cake or a light meal, but its speciality is music. Acoustic musicians are welcome – come with your *clarsach* or fiddle and join in a jam. Not quite as robust as pubs with music sessions, but interesting all the same.

Pâtisserie Florentin

8 St Giles Street, EH1 (225 6267). Bus 23, 27, 28, 41, 42, 45. **Open** 7am-11pm daily. **No credit cards**. **Map** p304 C3.

A bit of a refurb in 2002 spruced up this French-flavoured old place. It's a long-standing favourite among locals, and possibly the original Edinburgh home of the killer almond croissant. Famous, fantastic pâtisserie, of course, and snacky savouries too.

Plaisir du Chocolat

251-3 Canongate, EH8 (556 9524). Bus 30, 35. **Open** 10am-6pm Tue, Wed; 10am-6pm, 7.30pm-late Thur-Sat. **Credit** AmEx, DC, MC, V. **Map** p310 H8.

Opened in late summer 2000, Plaisir instantly gained a reputation as one of the best cafés in the city. It's a salon with the biggest list of teas in Christendom and artisan hot chocolate concoctions that make women weep with joy and quasi-sexual delight. Co-owner and chef Bertrand Espouy runs a good kitchen, too; the French savouries (spinach and goat's cheese tart perhaps, or a Mediterranean platter) are highly accomplished. Foodies will enjoy a very fulfilling lunch here, while hot choc junkies will simply expire with pleasure.

New Town

If these places are busy, you may want to try **Peckham's** (48 Raeburn Place, EH14; 332 8844). It's more of a deli than a café, but does have some tables for snacking.

Coffee Republic

40 Queensferry Street, EH2 (226 3870). Bus 13, 19, 29, 36, 37, 41, 42. **Open** 7.30am-5.30pm Mon-Fri; 9.30am-4.30pm Sat. **No credit cards**. **Map** p308 C5.

Small, smart, discreet, refuge-like, and despite being part of a chain, it's not Starbucks, which makes it worth visiting for sheer novelty value. Coffee, cakes and sandwiches.

Glass & Thompson

2 Dundas Street, EH3 (557 0909). Bus 23, 27. **Open** 8.30am-5.30pm Mon-Sat; 11am-4.30pm Sun. **Credit** MC, V. **Map** p306 E4.

If a café could be said to be 'very New Town' then Glass & Thompson would be it. Surrounded by fine art and antiques shops, it is conspicuously smart and chi-chi, and serves very fine delicatessen food with a definite continental flavour. The

Eat, Drink, Shop

waiting staff will probably be discussing their next exotic holiday (which you can't afford) while they sort out your order.

Grande Cru
79 Hanover Street, EH2 (226 6427). Bus 23, 27.
Open 10am-1am Mon-Wed, Sun; 10am-2am Thur-Sat. **Credit** MC, V. **Map** p306 E4/5.
The café that thinks it's a wine bar (or is that the other way round?). The place is spacious and central, with comfy seats by the window and reasonable panini and light meals for snackers.

James Thin Booksellers Café
57 George Street, EH2 (220 2943). Bus 41, 42/ Princes Street buses. **Open** 9am-5pm Mon-Sat. **Credit** MC, V. **Map** p304 B1.
James Thin Booksellers went bankrupt early in 2002, but the café concession will remain (it's not run by the shop). Local office workers have their lunch here, while a more mature clientele set down their shopping bags and take a much-needed break. A glimpse of a more traditional and polite Edinburgh.

Palm Court
Balmoral Hotel, 1 Princes Street, EH1 (556 2414). Princes Street or Nicolson Street–North Bridge buses. **Open** 10am-1am daily. *Coffee served* 10am-noon daily. *Lunch served* noon-2.30pm daily. *Afternoon tea served* 3-5pm daily. *All-day menu served* 11am-1am daily. **Credit** AmEx, DC, MC, V. **Map** p304 D2.
The Balmoral, quite possibly Edinburgh's grandest hotel, lays on a slap-up afternoon tea in its sumptuous Palm Court. There are no crusts on the sandwiches and the cake selection can lead to agonies of indecision. (Also, dig that live music.) While staff may not throw you out if you turn up in jeans and a T-shirt, you'll be the only one dressed that way.

Queen Street Café at the Scottish National Portrait Gallery
1 Queen Street, EH2 (557 2844). Bus 4, 8, 10, 11, 12, 15, 16, 17, 26, 44, 45. **Open** 10am-4.30pm Mon-Sat; noon-4.30pm Sun. **No credit cards.** **Map** p306 F4.
Although it's not quite a venerable Edinburgh institution, the National Portrait Gallery (*see p86*) nonetheless has a reassuring feeling for tradition. The café is good for a gossip and a scone, even if the pictures of stern Scottish founding fathers in the gallery can be a bit unsettling.

Starbucks
Waterstone's, 128 Princes Street, EH2 (226 3610). Princes Street buses. **Open** 8am-7pm Mon-Sat; 10.30am-6pm Sun. **Credit** AmEx, MC, V. **Map** p304 A2.
Object of ire for anti-globalisation protestors, Starbucks at least has the advantages of dependability and familiarity. And it helps that the staff in the Edinburgh branches are nice people. This particular one has the attraction of the surrounding bookshop and a fine view of Edinburgh Castle.
Branches: throughout the city.

Stockbridge

Café Newton
Dean Gallery, 72 Belford Road, EH4 (623 7132). Bus 13. **Open** 10am-4.30pm Mon-Sat; noon-4.30pm Sun. **No credit cards. Map** p308 A5.
Big bowls of soup mopped up with chunks of crusty bread sell well here, although they face stiff competition from the toasted focaccia. Food aside, the most startling feature of this smallish café is its use as an extra room of the Dean Gallery (*see p95*). Paolozzi's huge plaster of Newton in thoughtful pose dominates the room.

The Gallery Café
Scottish National Gallery of Modern Art, 74 Belford Road, EH4 (624 6309). Bus 13. **Open** 10am-4.30pm Mon-Sat; noon-4.30pm Sun. **No credit cards.** **Map** p308 A5.
The Gallery Café is perennially popular, and not just with the city's art hounds. The real value of this place becomes apparent on fine summer days when people take their snacks outside and soak up the rays in peace. For details of the gallery, *see p95*.

Maxi's
33 Raeburn Place, EH14 (343 3007). Bus 19A, 24, 28. **Open** 8.30am-6pm Mon; 8.30am-11pm Tue-Sat; 10am-6pm Sun. **Credit** AmEx, DC, MC, V. **Map** p305 C4.
Maxi's is a happy and popular caff that's been around since the late 1990s. Located in a very bourgeois neighbourhood not that far from the Royal Botanic Garden, the space is airy and light, with blonde wood and blue paint – all very 'now' but in an accessible way. Stop for a fast coffee, or sit and dawdle with a bargain bottle of malbec, a panini and a salad. Maxi's becomes more like a restaurant in the evenings.

The Terrace Café
Royal Botanic Garden, Inverleith Row, EH3 (552 0616). Bus 8, 17, 23, 27. **Open** 9.30am-6pm daily (earlier closing times Oct-Apr; phone for details). **Credit** MC, V. **Map** p305 C2.
The Botanics (*see p93*) are a popular spot for an afternoon wander and the café next to Inverleith House (*see p93*) is a handy pitstop, with light lunches of the quiche and salad variety, plus sandwiches and cakes. The real beauty is the view over the city with the castle dominating the skyline, and doncha just luurve those squirrels! No smoking, except on the terrace.

Calton Hill & Broughton

Blue Moon Café
36 Broughton Street, EH1 (556 2788). Bus 8, 17/ Playhouse buses. **Open** 10.45am-11.30pm Mon-Fri; 9am-11.30pm Sat, Sun. **Credit** MC, V. **Map** p306 F3.
At the heart of Edinburgh's pink triangle, this gay-run but straight-friendly café-bar is a popular meeting and eating place, especially at weekends,

Eat, Drink, Shop

Cafés

Plaisir de Chocolat: chocolate nirvana and great cakes too. *See p139.*

See also p205.

when the atmosphere steps up a gear to accommodate the high spirits of the clubbing brigade. Food can be quite hearty: burgers, nachos, macaroni cheese, haggis, pasta and cooked breakfasts. There's a small room looking directly on to Broughton Street as well as a nice book and accoutrement shop in the basement. *See also p205.*

Café Libra
5A Union Street, EH1 (556 9602). Playhouse buses. **Open** 9am-4pm Mon-Fri; 10am-4pm Sat. **No credit cards. Map** p307 G3.
A small basement joint seating around 20 people, Café Libra may not boast interior design by the latest style guru but it does do the all-day breakfasts, toasties and omelettes that are the mark of a real and lovingly run caff.

Embo
29 Haddington Place, Leith Walk, EH7 (652 3880). Bus 7, 10, 12, 14, 16, 22, 25, 49. **Open** 7.30am-3.30pm Mon-Fri; 9am-4.30pm Sat. **No credit cards. Map** p307 G3.
The only gripe about this café is its short opening hours. If you catch it when it's open, perch yourself on a stool, watch the world go by on Leith Walk, and tuck into a panini with one of a zillion fillings. A small, friendly and cared-for spot.

Lost Sock Diner
11 East London Street, EH7 (557 6097). Bus 8, 13, 17. **Open** 9am-4pm Mon; 9am-10.30pm Tue-Fri; 10am-11pm Sat; 11am-5pm Sun. **No credit cards. Map** p306 F3.

Adjacent to a launderette (hence the name), this is a funky little neighbourhood diner that dishes up burgers, nachos, cooked breakfasts, sandwiches and the like. In the evening, dishes such as poached salmon are added to the menu. It attracts a youthful crowd (the bank of TVs showing MTV may have something to do with it), and is often mobbed for weekend brunch.

Mediterraneo
73 Broughton Street, EH1 (557 6900). Bus 8, 17/ Playhouse buses. **Open** 7.30am-6pm Mon-Thur; 7.30am-10pm Fri, Sat; 9.30am-4.30pm Sun. **Credit** MC, V. **Map** p306 F3.
Not only does it do a thriving lunchtime trade in takeaway baguettes, but family-run Mediterraneo also has a pleasant sit-down area. Most of the food displays the owners' Italian roots; the staff here can do things with grapes and a piccante sausage that your tastebuds wouldn't dare dream about.

Valvona & Crolla
19 Elm Row, EH7 (556 6066/www.valvonacrolla. com). Bus 7, 10, 12, 14, 16, 22, 25, 49. **Open** 8am-6pm Mon-Sat.
This family-run bistro is in the rear of the famed deli (*see p171*). The temptation to loosen your purse strings before you've even got to the dining area is immense, yet firm resolution will be rewarded – the virtues of great Italian cooking are shown to their best advantage here, so getting a table at lunchtimes and at the weekend isn't easy. Informal, friendly and, for many, the best café/bistro in town. No smoking.

South Edinburgh

Black Medicine Co
*2 Nicolson Street, EH8 (622 7209). Nicolson Street–
North Bridge buses.* **Open** 8am-8pm Mon-Sat; 9am-
8pm Sun. **Credit** MC, V. **Map** 310 G6.
The black medicine in question is coffee, which is
served up in several varieties at this rather rugged-
looking café. The walls are rough stone and the furniture is chunky and wooden, giving the place a bit
of an outdoorsy feel. It's comfy enough, though, and
the large windows are excellent for talent-spotting.

Café Grande
*184 Bruntsfield Place, EH10 (228 1188). Bus 11,
15, 16, 17, 23, 45.* **Open** 9am-11pm Mon-Wed; 9am-
midnight Thur-Sat; 10am-10pm Sun. **Credit** MC, V.
Map p309 D8.
A cosy establishment with warm red tones, this
place has something of a dual personality. By day,
it's a two-roomed café selling cakes, pastries, burgers and breakfasts. At night, the menu switches to
more substantial fare, with dishes such as seafood
risotto and steaks. A family affair.

California Coffee Co
*St Patrick Square, EH8 (667 2366). Bus 3, 5, 7, 8,
14, 29, 31, 33, 37.* **Open** 7am-9pm Mon-Fri; 10am-
9pm Sat, Sun. **No credit cards**. **Map** p310 G7.
Dr Who got it wrong. Turning a former police box
into a time-travelling Tardis is a waste of resources
when it could be turned into an al fresco coffee booth
instead. The coffee-makers can rustle up your java
juice any which way at California Coffee. Great for
warming your hands on a bitter summer morning.
Branches: throughout the city.

Chatterbox Tea Room
*1 East Preston Street, EH8 (667 9406). Bus 3, 5, 7,
8, 14, 29, 31, 33, 37, 49.* **Open** 8.30am-5pm Mon-
Fri; 9am-5pm Sat; 11am-5pm Sun. **No credit cards**.
Map p310 H8.
Millennia have come and gone, Scotland has gained
its own parliament, but Chatterbox remains. This
small traditional – dare one say frilly? – tearoom has
a strong core of regular locals as well as visitors
from the nearby Commonwealth swimming pool
and student residences.

Elephants & Bagels
*37 Marshall Street, Nicolson Square, EH8 (668
4404/www.elephant-house.co.uk). Nicolson Street–
North Bridge buses.* **Open** 8.30am-5pm Mon-Fri;
10am-5pm Sat, Sun. **Credit** MC, V. **Map** p310 G6.
The baby sister operation to the Elephant House, the
E&B doesn't sell many pachyderms but it's big on
the bagel side of the equation. Popular with students,
who often take away their goodies for impromptu
picnics in George Square during the summer.

The Engine Shed
19 St Leonard's Lane, EH8 (662 0040). Bus 2, 21.
Open 10.30am-3.30pm Mon-Thur; 10.30am-2.30pm
Fri; 10am-4pm Sat. **No credit cards**. **Map** p310 H7.

Tasty toasties at **Kaffe Politik**.

Somewhat off the main drag but handy for a hike
up Arthur's Seat, the Engine Shed is a vegetarian
café that also serves vegan meals, with fresh bread
that is baked on the premises. It's staffed by adults
with learning difficulties (under supervision) so is
worth supporting on all kinds of levels.

Festival Theatre Café
*13-29 Nicolson Street, EH8 (662 1112). Bus 2/
Nicolson Street–North Bridge buses.* **Open** 10am-
6pm daily; later on performance nights. **No credit
cards**. **Map** p310 G6.
There are two ways to look at the Festival Theatre
Café. Depending on your point of view, the huge
glass plate windows that front the theatre (*see p268*)
allow you a prime view of passersby or they make
you feel as if you're stuck in a goldfish bowl. Not
possessed of the best-kept wine list in town, but popular with local workers for lunch. No smoking.

ITS Organic
*15 Bread Street, EH3 (228 9444/www.its-organic.
com). Bus 1, 2, 10, 11, 15, 16, 17, 22, 24, 34,
35.* **Open** 7.30am-4pm Mon-Fri; 10am-4pm Sat.
No credit cards. **Map** p309 D6.
More of a takeaway really, but there are a few tables
for anyone who wants to work their way through a
pile of organic porridge in the morning, or some
hearty soups at lunch. Depite the disturbing absence
of an apostrophe in the name, it's a great idea that's
well executed: choose randomly from the menu and
you can still feel healthy.
Branch: 7 William Street, New Town, EH3
(226 2444).

Kaffe Politik
*146-148 Marchmont Road, EH9 (446 9873). Bus
24, 41.* **Open** 10am-10pm daily. **No credit cards**.
Map p309 F8.
Prior to this place popping up a few years back,
Marchmont was very badly served for cafés. Now it
has one of the best-looking caffs in the city. Black
and white photos of assorted politicos cover one wall
and gaze balefully over the assorted students and
locals as they sup smoothies, dither over speciality

teas and munch on the wonderful home-baked goodies. The scrambled eggs with Swiss cheese and chives on toast is absolute cholesterol hell – as well as breakfast heaven.

Luca's

16 Morningside Road, EH10 (446 0233/www.s-luca. co.uk). Bus 11, 15, 16, 17, 23, 45. **Open** 9am-10pm daily. **Credit** DC, MC, V.

Famed for the ice-cream at its Musselburgh café, this branch near Holy Corner (loads of churches) also offers a range of club sandwiches, panini melts and pizzas. But who needs sensible food when there are nut sundaes and Caribbean longboats to be enjoyed? **Branches**: 28-32 High Street, Musselburgh (665 2237); 2 Niddrie Mains Road, Craigmillar (661 3827).

McFeely's Bookstore Café

30 Buccleuch Street, EH8 (662 8570). Bus 41, 42. **Open** 10am-5pm Mon-Sat. **Credit** MC, V.

The second-hand bookshop opened in 1998 and a basement café followed in 2001. It is right in the middle of university-land; term time sees the tables hogged by low-spending students averaging a latte an hour. At other times, passing bibliophiles and tourists appreciate the light menu and secure hidey-hole atmosphere.

Metropole

29-33 Newington Road, EH9 (668 4999). Bus 3, 5, 7, 8, 29, 31, 37, 49. **Open** 9am-10pm daily. **No credit cards**. **Map** p310 H8.

Deep in the heart of studentland, this converted bank lends an air of faded grandeur to the simple act of sipping a cappuccino. The Metropole is a firm believer in the idea that variety is the spice of life; the adventurous customer could come in here every day for a month and still not sample all the speciality teas and coffees. No smoking.

Ndebele

57 Home Street, Tollcross, EH3 (221 1141/www. ndebele.co.uk). Bus 10, 11, 15, 16, 17, 23, 27, 45. **Open** 10am-10pm daily. **Credit** AmEx, MC, V. **Map** p309 D7.

Instantly popular from the moment it opened its doors a few years back, this African-themed café is genuinely different from anything else you'll find in Edinburgh. Where else could you get speciality South African sausages called *boerewors*?

Stromboli

20 Bruntsfield Place, EH10 (229 7247). Bus 11, 15, 16, 17, 23, 45. **Open** 8.30am-7.30pm Mon-Thur; 8.30am-5pm Fri, Sat. **Credit** AmEx, MC, V.

Known as the Breadwinner bakery once upon a time, this establishment has happily reinvented itself as a café and takeaway. There are trendy looking liquid-filled tables and an abstract expressionist painting of the eponymous volcano to keep you amused while you tuck into utterly fabulous pies (puff pastry filled with assorted stir-fries), as well as all kinds of baked-on-the-premises savouries, pleasant pâtisserie, soups and salads.

Two Thin Laddies

103 High Riggs, EH3 (229 0653). Bus 10, 11, 15, 16, 17, 23, 24, 27, 45. **Open** 8am-5pm Mon-Sat; 10am-5pm Sun. **No credit cards**.

This friendly café at the heart of Tollcross opens early for those seeking breakfast en route to work (unlike some of the café-bars with breakfast menus). Bright and wholesome with a menu that also features bakes, salads and legendary macaroni cheese. **Branch**: 6 Grassmarket, South Edinburgh, EH1 (476 2721).

West Edinburgh

Cornerstone Café

St John's Church, corner of Princes Street & Lothian Road, EH2 (229 0212). Princes Street buses. **Open** 9.30am-4pm Mon-Sat; extended hours during Festival. **No credit cards**. **Map** p304 A2.

A popular lunchtime haunt of weary shoppers and office workers, the Cornerstone Café is housed in the vaults of St John's and serves up reasonable salads, baked spuds and the like. In the summer, people seem to like sitting on the terrace outside by the gravestones and peering into the adjacent cemetery. No smoking (well, look what it does to you).

Filmhouse Bar

88 Lothian Road, EH3 (228 6382). Bus 1, 10, 11, 15, 16, 17, 22, 24. **Open** 10am-11.30pm Mon-Fri; 10am-12.30am Sat, Sun. **Food served** 10am-10pm daily. **Credit** AmEx, MC, V. **Map** p304 A3.

Not the place to spend an entire evening, but the Filmhouse is a hassle-free and convivial place to meet before a movie. Tuck into all sorts of grub including burgers, cakes, vegetarian and vegan dishes. It was refurbished in 2001, so catch it while it's still relatively bright and shiny.

Leith

Daniel's Bistro

88 Commercial Street, EH6 (553 5933). Bus 1, 16, 22, 35, 36. **Open** 10am-10pm daily. **Credit** MC, V. **Map** p311 Jy.

One of the better places among the row of restaurants on the quayside opposite the Scottish Office, Daniel's deals in authentic food from Alsace. Hearty raclettes, confits of duck and choucroûtes take pride of place on the menu. The setting is light, bright and modern, and there's a no-smoking conservatory. More of a restaurant at lunch and in the evening, but it's certainly OK to stop in for a coffee.

Malmaison

1 Tower Place, Leith, EH6 (468 5001). Bus 1, 16, 22, 35, 36. **Open** 7-10am, noon-2.30pm, 6-10.45pm Mon-Fri; 8-10.30am, noon-2.30pm, 6-10.45pm Sat, Sun. **Credit** AmEx, DC, MC, V. **Map** p311 Jx.

Although Malmaison – one of Edinburgh's funkier hotels (*see p53*) – has a decent restaurant, it's hard to beat sitting outside on the waterfront on a sunny day with a cappuccino and pastry from the café-bar.

Pubs & Bars

Hops, grapes and plenty of malts.

Edinburgh's drinking scene has been thriving for centuries: Robert Burns wrote about it; Robert Louis Stevenson wallowed in it; and, even today, in a list of Scotland's top ten pubs at least half would be in Edinburgh.

Older pubs with big island bars and decorative ceilings still exist, but there is also an increasing number of new 'style' bars with sleek steel and smooth wood interiors, where drinkers can enjoy anything from a bottle of Merlot to a pint of organic Edinburgh beer. Local company Montpeliers is responsible for bars like **Indigo Yard**, **Rick's** and the latest venture **Opal Lounge** (*see p217*), which combines bar, restaurant and club. These determinedly fashionable meeting spots place almost as much emphasis on eating as drinking, and though they aren't cheap, they have proved hugely popular with Edinburgh's young (and not-so-young) professionals.

WHERE TO GO

Some of the areas best known for pubs, such as Rose Street, the Grassmarket and the Westend, continue to draw in huge numbers, particularly at the weekends. However, these streets trade on their reputation as popular drinking spots and on the sheer quantity of pubs they offer, rather than necessarily providing a quality imbibing experience.

George Street and neighbouring streets have undergone a regeneration in recent years, with new bars and restaurants in among the upmarket clothes shops. Some of these ventures – inevitably – are branches of chains such as Wetherspoon's and All Bar One, but even these high-street stalwarts have succeeded in raising the bar stakes in the New Town by satisfying local office workers, and leading the way in the renovation and reuse of former bank buildings.

OPENING HOURS AND LICENSING

It's often said that you can get a drink in Edinburgh at any time of the day or night. However, while the drinking hours are a lot more relaxed than in England and most other parts of Scotland, the 24-hour drinking binge is more myth than reality. It's true there are pubs, near the docks in Leith and the goods yards at Haymarket, for example, that still open at 5am or 6am, but this is definitely the exception rather than the rule. Usually, pubs open at 11am and shut at 11pm or midnight, with some city centre pubs staying open until 1am. Establishments

with a music licence can stay open until 3am, and during the Festival and Fringe, opening hours are often extended, some to as late as 5am.

Old Town

Bam Bou
66-67 South Bridge, EH1 (556 0200). Nicolson Street–North Bridge buses. **Open** 11am-1am daily. **Food served** noon-7pm Mon-Sat; noon-4pm Sun. **Credit** MC, V. **Map** p304 D3.
A corner pub with a vaguely oriental theme. The first-floor bar has big windows but a rather corridor-like feel, while downstairs is loud and busy, with DJs spinning their stuff at weekends. There's a good value 'eat as much as you want' Sunday breakfast.

Bannermans
212 Cowgate, EH1 (556 3254). Nicolson Street–North Bridge buses. **Open** noon-1am Mon-Sat; 12.30pm-1am Sun. **Food served** noon-10pm Mon-Sat; 12.30-10pm Sun. **Credit** AmEx, DC, MC, V. **Map** p309 F6.
Once renowned for its beer and long wooden benches, Bannermans is now barely distinguishable from the other imbiberies on Cowgate. Some underground appeal is retained by stone walls and arches, but the effect is spoiled by flashy TVs showing cartoons. A Playstation is available for finger-twitching game freaks during the day and there's a room at the back with a pool table and a big screen.

Bar Kohl
54 George IV Bridge, EH1 (225 6936). Bus 23, 27, 28, 41, 42, 45. **Open** noon-1am Mon-Sat. **Food served** noon-2.30pm Mon-Sat. **Credit** MC, V. **Map** p304 C3.
Bar Kohl offers loud dance music, a regular clientele and a vast range of different flavours and brands of vodka. It's shut for a couple of weeks around January every year for the annual vodka-buying trip, so you can be sure you're getting the real deal. Expansion into the premises next door will give loyal vodka fans a bit of welcome drinking space.

Beehive Inn
18-20 Grassmarket, EH1 (225 7171). Bus 2, 23, 27, 28, 41, 42. **Open** 11am-1am Mon-Fri; 10.30am-1am Sat; 11.30am-1am Sun. **Food served** noon-10pm daily. **Credit** AmEx, DC, MC, V. **Map** p304 C3.
This is one of the better of the overrated pubs on Grassmarket, although it isn't cheap. Its best asset is the beer garden. During the summer drinkers tend to spill into the street, but it's far preferable to sit behind the pub, looking up at the Castle and the modern DanceBase building.

High spirits at the **Bow Bar**.

Beluga

30A Chambers Street, EH1 (624 4545). Nicolson Street–North Bridge buses. **Open** 10am-1am daily. **Food served** 10am-9pm daily. **Credit** AmEx, MC, V. **Map** p309 E7.

This downstairs bar and restaurant is located on the site of Edinburgh's old dental hospital. Decked out in steel, dark wood and black vinyl, the bar has high tables and low-slung seats, perfect for lounging. There's a long drinks menu and a variety of DJs on most nights. It's a good spot for relaxing on Sunday, but it's crowded on Friday and Saturday nights.

Biblos

1A Chambers Street, EH1 (226 7177). Nicolson Street–North Bridge buses. **Open** 8am-11pm daily. **Food served** 8am-9pm daily. **Credit** AmEx, MC, V. **Map** p309 F6.

Biblos was once a bookshop but has been converted into a bar with huge glass windows on to the street. Table service is erratic but the food is worth the wait. Breakfasts are served from 8am. There's a long cocktail list and good coffee.

Black Bo's

57-61 Blackfriars Street, EH1 (557 6136). Nicolson Street–North Bridge buses. **Open** 4pm-1am daily. **Credit** MC, V. **Map** p310 G5.

A mainstay in the life of any self-respecting bohemian, Bo's is – more often than not – where it's at. The place is tiny and by about 10pm it's usually packed and enveloped in a thick fug of blue smoke. DJs play unobtrusive selections of Latin, house and hip hop and the emphasis is on convivial, half cut banter.

Bow Bar

80 West Bow, EH1 (226 7667). Bus 23, 27, 28, 41, 42, 45. **Open** noon-11.30pm Mon-Sat; 12.30-11pm Sun. **No credit cards. Map** p304 C3.

A small pub with brewery mirrors and big windows. It's best known for its wide selection of malt whiskies but the guest ales are well kept too. No music here, but it can still be noisy due to the lively chatter of the regulars, including MSPs and workers from the Parliament.

Top five Style bars

Beluga
Laid-back afternoons and lively nights. *See above.*

Oloroso
New bar with stunning views. *See p153.*

Rick's
Martini-drinkers' heaven. *See p153.*

Traverse Café Bar
Drink, eat, talk – and see some theatre. *See p157.*

Yo! Below
Massage and sushi to complement your beer. *See p154.*

City Café
19 Blair Street, EH1 (220 0125). Nicolson Street–North Bridge buses. **Open** 11am-1am daily. **Food served** 11am-11pm daily. **Credit** AmEx, DC, MC, V. **Map** p304 D3.

This chrome-edged, diner-like space, with booths and pool tables at the back and bar tables at the front, packs in the punters. There are sweeties on the menu and the downstairs DJ bar is open on Friday and Saturday nights.

The Doric Tavern
15-16 Market Street, EH1 (225 1084). Bus 23, 27, 28, 41, 42, 45. **Open** noon-1am Mon-Sat; 12.30pm-1am Sun. **Food served** noon-4pm daily; snacks 5-11.30pm daily. **Credit** AmEx, MC, V. **Map** p304 C2.

This first-floor wine bar has a well-known restaurant, but the bar food is good too. Snacks such as houmous and pitta bread, or cheese and oatcakes help stave off hunger while you work your way through the long wine list.

EH1
197 High Street, EH1 (220 5277). Nicolson Street–North Bridge buses. **Open** 9am-1am daily. **Food served** 9am-7pm daily. **Credit** AmEx, DC, MC, V. **Map** p304 D3.

A modern bar with minimalist neutral decor and wooden twists, EH1 is perched at the top of Cockburn Street. It's a popular eaterie in the daytime with tables outside during the summer months, but becomes a proper bar in the evening, with a good selection of wines.

Frankenstein
26 George IV Bridge, EH1 (622 1818). Bus 23, 27, 28, 41, 42, 45. **Open** 10am-1am daily. **Food served** 10am-9pm daily; snacks 10am-11pm daily. **Credit** AmEx, MC, V. **Map** p304 C3.

Ignore the claims about it being established in 1818 – this four-floor pub opened in 1999 in a dramatically refurbished former Pentecostal church. The top floors overlook a ground-floor bar where pictures and models of Frankenstein's monster reinforce the Gothic theme, while the basement has lots of nooks and crannies for creatures of the night to hide out in. It gets very busy here with hordes of eager drinkers often queuing outside to get in.

Greyfriars Bobby
34 Candlemaker Row, EH1 (225 8328). Bus 2, 23, 27, 28, 41, 42, 45. **Open** 11am-1am Mon-Sat; 12.30pm-1am Sun. **Food served** noon-6pm daily. **Credit** MC, V. **Map** p309 F6.

Scottish icons Whisky

Blended whisky can be found anywhere in the world, and there is a huge export market, especially to the US and Japan. But Scotland is the place to come to sample the widest variety of single malts. Whereas a blend is made from mixing several different whiskies of varying age and quality, a single malt is the product of one distillery and has a more distinctive, individual and complex taste. Malts are usually divided into regions, each of which has its own characteristics: **Laphroaig** has a typical peaty Islay flavour; **Talisker**, made in Skye, is a Highland malt and tastes smoky; Speyside malts like **Balvenie** are smoother. The nearest distillery to Edinburgh is **Glenkinchie** in Pencaitland.

You'll find single malts from distilleries all over Scotland in Edinburgh's pubs, including some from distilleries no longer in operation. Blended whisky is readily available too, but with such an array of single malts to choose from you probably won't need it. In Edinburgh the dedicated whisky drinker will be able to find a different malt for every day of the year.

While some prefer their whisky neat, many say that you can't properly appreciate the taste of a malt without adding some water. A jug will be provided by the bar staff, or sometimes there's a tap on the bar, so drinkers can add the water themselves. How much is up to individual taste: add a little at a time until you're happy; don't drown the whisky – somewhere between half as much water as whisky, or as much water again will often be about right. Adding anything other than water will deaden the taste of the whisky and horrify the sensibilities of the publican, so if you like ice, coke or lemonade with your dram, stick to the cheaper blends.

To sample fine single malts in a convivial environment, try the following hostelries:

Bennet's
Best whisky gantry in the city. *See p156.*

The Blue Blazer
Wide range of whisky in amiable surroundings. *See p156.*

Bow Bar
Traditional bar for discerning drinkers. *See p147.*

Cloisters
Comfortable pub with impressive selection. *See p156.*

Kays Bar
Cosy bar for late-night drams. *See p153.*

Located just behind the statue of its namesake, this pub is a pleasant enough place, serving cheap student meals.

Iguana Café & Bar

41 Lothian Street, EH1 (220 4288). Nicolson Street–North Bridge buses. **Open** 9am-1am Mon-Thur, Sun; 9am-3am Fri, Sat. **Food served** 9am-10pm daily. **Credit** AmEx, MC, V. **Map** p309 F6.
This bar has a bleak outlook, facing the concrete façade of the student union and a busy road, but the interior is better, with modern decor of wood and twisted metal. The list of cocktails is long and accompanied by some decent food, with table service. Regular DJs turn up the heat inside and there are seats outside in the summer.

The Jolly Judge

7 James Court, 493 Lawnmarket, EH1 (225 2669). Bus 23, 27, 28, 35, 41. **Open** noon-midnight Mon, Thur-Sat; noon-11pm Tue, Wed, Sun. **Food served** noon-2pm daily. **No credit cards. Map** p304 C3.
A real fire and other touches give this small pub the feel of an old tavern. Busy with tourists, locals and MSPs, it's a great place to stop off while trekking down the Royal Mile, but can get really busy at New Year. Tables in the courtyard in fine weather.

The Last Drop

74 Grassmarket, EH1 (225 4851). Bus 2, 23, 27, 28, 35, 41, 42, 45. **Open** 11am-1am Mon-Sat; 12.30pm-1am Sun. **Food served** noon-7.30pm daily. **Credit** AmEx, MC, V. **Map** p304 B3.
The name is not a reminder to the publican to change the barrel, but a reference to the pub's location opposite the former site of the city gallows – you can buy T-shirts to prove it. It's cosy inside, and always busy with students and tourists.

Logie Baird's

Bank Hotel, 1 South Bridge, EH1 (556 9940). Nicolson Street–North Bridge buses. **Open** 9am-1am daily. **Food served** 9am-8.45pm daily. **Credit** AmEx, DC, MC, V. **Map** p304 D3.
The bar of the Bank Hotel (*see p39*) has seats by the bar or in the back room, but the best spots are found above the bar, via a spiral staircase. TVs and a big screen suggest this is a good place for watching sport, but they're all located in awkward places, and the sound is often turned down.

Malt Shovel Inn

11-15 Cockburn Street, EH1 (225 6843). Nicolson Street–North Bridge buses. **Open** 11am-midnight Mon-Thur; 11am-1am Fri, Sat; 12.30pm-midnight Sun. **Food served** 11am-8pm Mon-Thur; 11am-6pm Fri, Sat; 12.30-5pm Sun. **Credit** MC, V. **Map** p304 D2.
Its location, near to Waverley Station, makes the Malt Shovel Inn an ideal meeting place between the Old and New Towns. The three interlinked rooms beyond the bar are usually busy (but not packed) with customers enjoying beers, wines and the usual bottled drinks.

Maxie's Bistro & Wine Bar

5b Johnston Terrace, EH1 (226 7770). Bus 23, 27, 28, 35, 41, 42, 45. **Open** 11am-11pm daily. **Food served** 11am-11pm daily. **Credit** AmEx, MC, V. **Map** p304 B3.
Recently moved from its former Southside home, Maxie's is now tucked away round the corner from the Castle and is more bistro than wine bar. That said, there's a good selection of wine by the glass or the bottle, and you'll still find some low tables near the bar, surrounded by sumptuous red seating and lots of cushions. The roof terrace at the back looks down Victoria Street and into the Grassmarket.

McGuffie's Bar

15 Market Street, EH1 (225 5243). Bus 23, 27, 28, 41, 42, 45. **Open** 11am-1am Mon-Thur; 10am-1am Fri, Sat. **Food served** 11am-6pm Mon-Thur; 10am-6pm Fri, Sat. **Credit** (over £5) MC, V. **Map** p304 C2.
This is a basic and friendly pub downstairs from the Doric, and in fact shares the ladies' loos upstairs. Pies and snacks are available during the day.

Mitre

133 High Street, EH1 (524 0071). Bus 2, 23, 27, 28, 35, 41, 42, 45. **Open** noon-11pm Mon-Wed; noon-midnight Thur; noon-1am Fri, Sat; 12.30-11pm Sun. **Food served** 12.30-6pm daily. **Credit** AmEx, MC, V. **Map** p304 D3.

A handy hangout on the tourist trail, this Royal Mile pub has tall windows that are opened in the summer to give a clear view of the High Street. A big screen shows big-match sport.

Negociants

45 Lothian Street, EH1 (225 6313). Nicolson Street–North Bridge buses. **Open** 9am-3am Mon-Sat; 10am-3am Sun. **Food served** 9am-10pm daily; snacks until late daily. **Credit** MC, V. **Map** p309 F6.
It's table service only in this late-opening student bar, where pricy Belgian beers and wine are offered by somnambulant serving staff. You won't get in unless there's a spare table.

Nicol Edward's

29-35 Niddry Street, EH1 (556 8642). Nicolson Street–North Bridge buses. **Open** 4pm-3am daily. **No credit cards**. **Map** p304 D3.
A new pub with a rabbit warren of rooms including three bars, a chill-out area and a very popular entertainment room. This place was clearly designed with students in mind; it would not be surprising to find them hanging out here for several days at a time.

Oxygen

3-5 Infirmary Street, EH1 (557 9997). Nicolson Street–North Bridge buses. **Open** 10am-1am Mon-Sat; noon-1am Sun. **Food served** noon-9pm daily. **Credit** AmEx, MC, V. **Map** p310 G6.
When it opened, this bar's gimmick was selling canisters of pure oxygen along with the usual wine, bottled beers and cocktails. Unfortunately, when it came to a choice between oxygen and cigarettes, the bar's smoking patrons won and the redundant name became an ironic comment on the bar's fug-filled interior. DJs from Wednesday to Saturday.

Royal Oak

1 Infirmary Street, EH1 (557 2976). Nicolson Street–North Bridge buses. **Open** 9am-2am Mon-Sat; 12.30pm-2am Sun. **No credit cards**. **Map** p310 G6.
This legendary pub has a poky ground floor bar, with the basement only open later and at weekends. Entertainment consists of regular folk music sessions plus heated debates from some of the more vocal customers. The Oak tends to become very crowded after 1am when neighbouring pubs shut.

Sandy Bell's

25 Forrest Road, EH1 (225 2751). Bus 35/Nicolson Street–North Bridge buses. **Open** 11am-12.30am Mon-Sat; noon-11pm Sun. **No credit cards**.
Map p309 F6.
The violins above the bar give a clue to the importance of music in this well-known and very popular Edinburgh pub. Folk sessions take place within its narrow confines every evening.

Siglo

184-186 Cowgate, EH1 (240 2850). Bus 23, 27, 28, 41. **Open** noon-1am daily. **Food served** noon-2.30pm, 6-9pm Mon-Fri; noon-9pm Sat, Sun. **Credit** (food orders only) AmEx, DC, MC, V. **Map** p304 D3.

Café Royal Circle Bar. *See p151.*

This is a lively two-storey bar with a Spanish theme and a good location on the former site of the Green Tree. Pop in on your way to a club and you'll find the upstairs DJ getting the drinkers on their feet.

The Three Sisters

139 Cowgate, EH1 (622 6801). Bus 23, 27, 28, 41, 42, 45. **Open** 9am-1am daily. **Food served** noon-9pm daily. **Credit** AmEx, MC, V. **Map** p304 D3.
An absolutely cavernous, dark pub with a beer yard at the front. When it's busy, there's no hope of finding friends here among the drunken throng – even if they've managed to work their way through the long queues on the street outside. The intimate booths near the front door are the best feature.

Wash

11-13 North Bank Street, EH1 (225 6193). Bus 23, 27, 28, 35, 41, 42, 45. **Open** noon-1am daily.
Food served noon-7pm Mon-Wed, Sun; noon-9pm Thur-Sat. **Credit** MC, V. **Map** p304 C3.
The pub at the top of the Mound combines a '70s look with a sophisticated laid-back style and a decent cocktail and wine list. The upper floor has comfy couches, but the whole place often feels a bit abandoned, even when there are other drinkers in.

Whistle Binkie's

6 Niddry Street, EH1 (557 5114). Nicolson Street–North Bridge buses. **Open** 6pm-3am daily. **Credit** MC, V. **Map** p304 D3.

The scene of many Edinburgh late-night drinking sessions, this basement bar offers nightly live music and long opening hours for those 2am emergencies. The narrow back rooms are where late-night friendships are made – friendships you would probably rather forget about in the morning.

The World's End
4 High Street, EH1 (556 3628). Bus 35/Nicolson Street–North Bridge buses. **Open** 11am-1am Mon-Fri; 10am-1am Sat, Sun. **Food served** noon-9pm Mon-Fri; 10am-9pm Sat, Sun. **Credit** MC, V. **Map** p304 D3.
Marking the old boundary of the city of Edinburgh rather than the imminent apocalypse, this stone-walled lively pub is well-placed for weary tourists to rest. It's popular with locals too, who tend to hang about around the bar.

New Town

The Abbotsford
3 Rose Street, EH2 (225 5276). Princes Street buses. **Open** 11am-11pm Mon-Sat. **Food served** noon-3pm Mon-Sat. **Credit** MC, V. **Map** p304 C1.
A very attractive old pub with an island bar and long tables. Good beer, knowledgeable bar staff and a pleasant atmosphere make this a perfect spot for whiling away an afternoon, or for enjoying a night-cap after dinner.

All Bar One
29 George Street, EH2 (226 9971). Bus 13, 19, 28, 40/Princes Street buses. **Open** 11.30am-midnight Mon-Thur; 11.30am-1am Fri, Sat; 12.30-11pm Sun. **Food served** 11.30am-10pm Mon-Sat; 12.30-9.30pm Sun. **Credit** AmEx, MC, V. **Map** p304 C1.

Pub etiquette

It is usual in Edinburgh to go to the bar for your drinks; table service is available in some establishments, but these may charge you extra for the privilege. In most places, bar service is far quicker, anyway.

If the bar is busy, you may have to wait to be served, but the best bar staff will know who's next. Don't be tempted to try to expedite matters by shouting out or waving money; you'll just annoy the staff. If you are about to be served but you know someone else was waiting before you, it is considered good bar etiquette to point that person out to the person serving.

Tipping bar staff is permitted, but is definitely not expected. If you do want to reward good or friendly service, just say 'and one for yourself' at the end of the order, and the staff will add the cost of an extra drink on to your bill.

An archetypal example of a former bank becoming 'a trendy wine bar' – or in this case a modern chain pub with a long list of wines and delusions of grandeur. It can get very noisy in the main bar, but arrive early at lunchtime or in the evening and you'll be able to grab a seat in the more pleasant rooms at the front. The food isn't cheap but it's usually tasty, and the menu changes regularly.
Branch: Exchange Plaza, Lothian Road, South Edinburgh, EH3 (221 7951).

Bar 38
126-128 George Street, EH2 (220 6180). Bus 13, 19, 28, 40, 41, 42, Princes Street buses. **Open/food served** 11am-1am Mon-Sat; 11am-midnight Sun. **Credit** AmEx, DC, MC, V. **Map** p304 A1.
Wall sculptures and attractive coloured lighting provide interest for the eye at this popular after-work place. Nibbles to share include whole baked camembert or tortilla chips with dips, and there are delicious non-alcoholic cocktails too. The unisex toilets made headlines when the Edinburgh branch opened.

Bert's Bar
29-31 William Street, EH3 (225 5748). Bus 3, 4, 12, 21, 25, 26, 31, 33. **Open** 11am-11pm Mon-Wed; 11am-midnight Thur-Sat. **Food served** noon-2pm Mon-Sat; snacks 11am-close Mon-Sat. **Credit** AmEx, DC, MC, V. **Map** p308 C5.
A small chain of pub-themed pubs – yes, really. What this means in practice is a welcoming atmosphere, old-fashioned decor and good beer. Both the West End and Stockbridge branches serve excellent pies with a range of fillings. Rugby is popular, and there's big-screen sport in Stockbridge.
Branch: 2-4 Raeburn Place, Stockbridge, EH4 (332 6345).

Café Royal Circle Bar
19 West Register Street, EH2 (556 1884). Princes Street buses. **Open** 11am-11pm Mon-Wed, Sun; 11am-midnight Thur; 11am-1am Fri, Sat. **Food served** 11am-7pm daily. **Credit** AmEx, DC, MC, V. **Map** p304 D1.
The big island bar dominates this attractive pub where the walls are decorated with 19th-century Royal Doulton tiles featuring famous figures. It can get very busy in here, especially in the early evening after work, when the big booth seating is at a premium and the noise level rises. Bar snacks, including oysters, are available during the day, and the Oyster Bar next door serves more elaborate meals. The Bistro Bar round the corner and upstairs has good decor but little charm.

The Cambridge
20 Young Street, EH2 (225 4266). Bus 13, 19, 30, 41, 42. **Open** 11am-11pm Mon-Thur; 11am-midnight Fri; 6pm-midnight Sat. **Food served** 12.30-3pm, 5-8.30pm Mon, Wed; 12.30-3pm Tue, Thur-Sat. **Credit** MC, V. **Map** p304 A1.
Popular with office workers, this pub can get noisy on Friday nights, but at other times it's a tranquil, friendly place for a drink or lunch.

Eat, Drink, Shop

Clarks Bar

*142 Dundas Street, EH3 (556 1067). Bus 23,
27.* **Open** 11am-11pm Mon-Wed; 11am-11.30pm
Thur-Sat; 12.30-11pm Sun. **No credit cards.**
Map p306 E3.

A traditionally male-dominated New Town bar,
Clarks is renowned for the quality of its beer. Office
workers on their way home nip in for a pint, and to
admire themselves in the narrow, mirrored tables.

The Cumberland Bar

*1-3 Cumberland Street, EH3 (558 3134). Bus 23,
27.* **Open** 11am-11.30pm Mon-Wed; 11am-12.30am
Thur-Sat; 12.30-11pm Sun. **Food served** noon-
2.30pm daily. **Credit** MC, V. **Map** p306 E3.

A row of tall beer founts welcomes drinkers to this
elegant wooden pub. There's a very good range of

beers and whisky, and a small and quiet beer
garden to the side. It's known as the haunt of
Edinburgh's legal profession.

The Dome

*14 George Street, EH2 (624 8624). Bus 13, 19, 28,
40, 41, 42/Princes Street buses.* **Open** *Main bar*
11.30am-1am Mon-Sat; 12.30pm-1am Sun. *Frazer's
Bar* 10am-late Thur-Sat. **Food served** noon-late
daily. **Credit** AmEx, DC, MC, V. **Map** p304 C1.

Underneath the vaulted cupola of this grandiose
former bank building is a large central bar surrounded by carefully placed seating and plants.
Food is served throughout the day, but it doesn't
come cheap. Frazer's Bar, at the front of the same
building, is decorated in luxurious art deco style,
with wood-panelled walls.

Only here for the beer

Gone are the days when pubs offered only
two beer pumps and four bottles of spirits;
today, anything from heather ale to absinthe
is available in Edinburgh. Although many
Scots stick to drinking lager, whether Scottish
brands like McEwan's and Tennent's or the
huge range of imported draught or bottled
labels, the city's strength lies in its high
number of real ale pubs.

Edinburgh has traditionally been an
important brewing city, able to exploit the
high-quality barley grown in the Scottish
lowlands. In the boom period around 1900
there were over 30 breweries in the city.
There were still over a dozen at the start of
the 1960s, but by the end of that decade
nearly all had been bought up and closed
down by bigger companies. At one point it
looked as though the UK-wide firm Scottish
& Newcastle would be the only brewery left
in Edinburgh, but a management buyout
at the nearby **Caledonian Brewery** in 1987
ensured that this independent also survived.

Award-winning Caledonian beer is widely
available throughout the city and beyond.
The brewery still uses original 19th-century
equipment for brewing, which can be seen
on the brewery tours (*see p109*). Look out
for the rounded Caledonian 80/-, the lighter
Deuchars IPA and the organic Golden
Promise, which lives up to its name.

Other smaller, independent breweries
have been opened in Edinburgh in recent
years, only to close again soon afterwards.
Small-time enthusiasts struggle to get their
beers distributed, because so many pubs
and bars are owned or tied into deals with
large, corporate breweries. Apart from

Caledonian, **Fisherrow** in Musselburgh is
currently the only independent brewery in
operation in the vicinity.

Scottish beer is generally richer, heavier
and more malty than English beer, as it uses
fewer hops. It is often referred to in terms
of shillings (written as /-), usually prefaced
by 70 or 80. The reasons for this peculiar
practice are unclear, but one theory suggests
that shillings originally denoted the cost of
the barrel of beer. The number of shillings
certainly gives an indication of the strength
of the brew, with 80/- stronger than 70/- or
60/-. Seventy shilling beer is often referred
to as 'heavy', while 80/- is known as 'export',
a throwback to the time when it was brewed
to be sent out to the soldiers in India.

The following list is our selection of the
best places in Edinburgh to sample real ale.

The Abbotsford

Friendly city centre pub with island bar.
See p151.

Bert's Bar

Successful modern recreation of an old-
fashioned pub. *See p151.*

Caley Sample Rooms

Best place to taste beer from the nearby
Caledonian brewery. *See p157.*

The Cumberland

Tall beer founts dispensing an impressive
range of beers. *See above.*

Guildford Arms

Real ale from all over Britain, including some
of the smaller breweries. *See p153.*

Grape

*The Capital Building, 13 St Andrew Square, EH2
(557 4522). Princes Street buses.* **Open** 11am-
midnight Mon-Thur; 11am-1am Fri, Sat; 11am-11pm
Sun. **Food served** noon-close daily. **Credit** AmEx,
DC, MC, V. **Map** p304 D1.
This spacious L-shaped bar is organised into different seating areas with comfy couches, bar stools,
carpet and armchairs. As the name promises, there's
a wide selection of wine available, but other drinks
tend to be expensive. Grape is a good place for a daytime chat and a coffee, but watch out for the stairs
after a few drinks. Very busy on Friday nights.

Guildford Arms

*1-5 West Register Street, EH2 (556 4312). Princes
Street buses.* **Open** 11am-11pm Mon-Thur; 11am-
midnight Fri, Sat; 12.30-11pm Sun. **Food served**
noon-2.30pm daily. **Credit** MC, V. **Map** p304 D1.
The old Guildford Arms at the east end of Princes
Street serves a wide range of real ales, plus filled
rolls during the day and popular but pricey
lunches. Check out the circular snug at the back.

Indigo Yard

*7 Charlotte Lane, EH2 (220 5603). Bus 19, 29, 30,
36.* **Open** 8.30am-1am daily. **Food served** 8.30am-
10pm daily. **Credit** AmEx, MC, V. **Map** p308 C5.
Popular with besuited after-work drinkers and off-
duty footballers, this is a striking bar converted from
an old courtyard. The tables at the back are an excellent spot for a meal, and although the drinks can be
expensive, ordering at the bar will avoid a charge for
table service. Despite being directly in front of Pizza
Express, the tables outside belong to Indigo Yard.

Kays Bar

*39 Jamaica Street, EH3 (225 1858). Bus 13, 19A,
24, 28, 28A.* **Open** noon-1am daily. **No credit
cards.** **Map** p306 D4.
Hidden away in the back of the New Town, Kays is
popular with local businessmen, but don't let that
put you off. Instead, snuggle up by the real fire in
the busy front room to sample some of the regular
guest ales, or hide out in the cosy back room with a
good malt whisky.

The Kenilworth

*152-154 Rose Street, EH2 (226 1773). Princes Street
buses.* **Open** 11am-11pm Mon-Thur; 11am-1am Fri,
Sat; 12.30-11pm Sun. **Food served** noon-8pm daily.
Credit AmEx, DC, MC, V. **Map** p304 B1.
It may be slightly seedy-looking nowadays, but this
pub, named after Sir Walter Scott's novel, is a listed
building and has more character than many of its
neighbours on Rose Street. It's a traditional place,
with wall tiles, high stained-glass windows, a big
island bar and a family room at the back.

Milne's

*35 Hanover Street, EH2 (225 6738). Bus 23, 27, 28,
41, 42, 45.* **Open** 11am-1am Mon-Sat; 12.30pm-1am
Sun. **Food served** 11am-10pm Mon-Sat; 12.30-10pm
Sun. **Credit** AmEx, DC, MC, V. **Map** p304 C1.

This big pub on the corner of Hanover and Rose
Streets was once the haunt of local writers such as
Hugh MacDiarmid, though it's far less distinguished
now. There are several different areas, including a
basement with a real fire and Gothic booths. The
first floor room looks out on to Rose Street.

Oloroso

*33 Castle Street, EH2 (226 7614). Princes Street
buses.* **Open** noon-1am daily. **Credit** AmEx, MC, V.
Map p304 B1.
Look out for the very discreet entrance on Castle
Street, and then take the lift to this new third floor
bar and restaurant with amazing views over
Edinburgh. There are tables by the bar and huge
couches at the windows where you can soak up
the panorama and the good cocktails. Expensive
appearance – food and drink to match. *See also p127.*

The Oxford Bar

*8 Young Street, EH2 (539 7119/www.oxfordbar.
com). Bus 13, 19, 29, 37, 41, 42.* **Open** 11am-1am
Mon-Sat. **No credit cards.** **Map** p304 A1.
A small and basic pub that's famous for being the
haunt of writer Ian Rankin and his creation
Inspector Rebus. Sometimes it's hard to get in due
to the number of people crowding around the bar,
but there's usually space in the side room with its
open fire. If the Oxford is your sort of pub, you'll
probably end up staying all evening.

Rick's

*55a Frederick Street, EH2 (622 7800). Bus 13, 19,
28, 30/Princes Street buses.* **Open** 7am-1am daily.
Food served 7am-11pm daily. **Credit** AmEx, MC,
V. **Map** p304 B1.
Part of Edinburgh's Montpeliers mini-chain, Rick's
has got the steel-and-wood look just right, which
means it's very popular, especially with footballers
and a slightly older crowd. The great cocktail list
changes regularly and includes a fine range of
Martinis. Laid-back during the day; livelier at night.

Ryan's Bar

*2-4 Hope Street, EH2 (226 6669). Princes Street
buses.* **Open** 10.30am-1am Mon-Sat; noon-midnight
Sun. **Food served** 10.30am-10pm Mon-Sat; noon-
10pm Sun. **Credit** AmEx, MC, V. **Map** p304 A1.
This is a busy, noisy 'party' pub – a typical Westend
establishment, with a dress code of no trainers or
jeans at the weekends. You can jig along to DJs in
the main bar or be entertained by pianists in the
cellar bar. The café opens at 7.30am during the week
for breakfasts served at your table.

Standing Order

*62-66 George Street, EH2 (225 4460). Bus 13, 19,
28, 40, 41, 42/Princes Street buses.* **Open** 11am-1am
daily. **Food served** 11am-11pm daily. **Credit**
AmEx, MC, V. **Map** p304 B1.
It's still possible to see the safe from the time when
this large building was a bank. These days it's a
spacious Wetherspoon's pub with no-smoking
rooms, no music and no children. Service can be

slow, but the Standing Order does have frequent drinks offers, including very cheap beer, which may make it worth the wait.
Branch: **The Foot of the Walk** 183 Constitution Street, Leith, EH8 (553 0120).

Wally Dug

32 Northumberland Street, EH3 (556 3271). Bus 23, 27. **Open** 11am-midnight Mon-Wed; 11am-1am Thur-Sat. **Credit** MC, V. **Map** p306 A4.
Tucked away in a small basement in the New Town, the Wally Dug combines good beer with excellent service. Not surprisingly, it can get pretty busy but there are often seats in the small rooms at the back.

Whighams Wine Cellars

13 Hope Street, Charlotte Square, EH2 (225 9717). Princes Street buses. **Open** noon-midnight Mon-Thur; noon-1am Fri, Sat. **Food served** noon-10pm Mon-Thur; noon-9pm Fri, Sat. **Credit** AmEx, MC, V. **Map** p304 A1.
A series of small wine cellars lit by dozens of candles creates an intimate, cosy atmosphere that's ideal for drinks à deux. The long wine list is supplemented by specials chalked up on the blackboards. Seafood is the speciality and is served all day.

Yo! Below

66 Rose Street, EH2 (220 6040). Princes Street buses. **Open** noon-midnight Mon-Thur, Sun; noon-1am Fri, Sat. **Food served** noon-10pm Mon-Thur, Sun; noon-11pm Fri, Sat. **Credit** AmEx, MC, V. **Map** p304 A1.
Located beneath Yo! Sushi (*see p125*), Yo! Below is a huge room with low tables and big mattress seats. Drinkers pour their own beer from the tap on each table (keep an eye on the meter), while karaoke-singing serving staff circle with nibbles and other drinks. If that's not enough to keep you amused, there are DJs, tarot-card readers and masseurs.

Stockbridge

The Antiquary

72-78 St Stephen Street, EH3 (225 2858). Bus 23, 27. **Open** 11.30am-12.30am Mon-Sat; 11am-12.30am Sun. **Food served** 11.30am-2.30pm Mon-Sat; 11am-2.30pm Sun. **Credit** MC, V. **Map** p306 D3.
A long basement pub that is split into two sections by the bar, the Antiquary can feel cold when empty but warms up considerably when there are a few drinkers in. The old stone walls and other original features are rather upstaged by such modern additions as large flat-screen TVs. Big Sunday breakfasts.

Hector's

47-49 Deanhaugh Street, EH4 (343 1735). Bus 19A, 24, 28. **Open** 11am-midnight Mon-Wed, Sun; 11am-1am Thur-Sat. **Food served** 6-9.30pm Mon-Thur; noon-3pm Fri-Sun. **Credit** AmEx, MC, V. **Map** p305 C3.
A modern counterpart to Bert's (*see p151*) on the opposite corner, Hector's has smooth, neutral walls and a long, well-chosen wine list. It's good for cosy chats by candlelight, or for nestling by the fire.

Calton Hill & Broughton Street

The Barony Bar

81-83 Broughton Street, EH1 (557 0546). Bus 8/Playhouse buses. **Open** 11am-midnight Mon-Thur; 11am-1am Fri, Sat; 12.30-11.30pm Sun. **Food served** 11am-10pm Mon-Sat; 12.30-10pm Sun. **Credit** MC, V. **Map** p306 F3.
A small wooden pub with character, the Barony is popular with a mixed crowd, and attracts a slightly older clientele than some of its Broughton Street neighbours. It gets crowded at weekends and finding a seat is unlikely; those who are sitting down probably won't be leaving in a hurry.

The Basement

10A-12A Broughton Street, EH1 (557 0097). Bus 8/Playhouse buses. **Open** noon-1am daily. **Food served** noon-10.30pm daily. **Credit** AmEx, MC, V. **Map** p306 F3.
When Broughton Street first became hip, much of its kudos came courtesy of the Basement. It's a dark place with tables made from bits of old machinery, giving it a pseudo-industrial feel. The bar staff wear Hawaiian shirts that are as loud as the music.

Cask & Barrel

115 Broughton Street, EH1 (556 3132). Bus 8/Playhouse buses. **Open** 11am-12.30am Mon-Wed, Sun; 11am-1am Thur-Sat; 12.30pm-12.30am Sun. **Food served** noon-2pm daily; snacks noon-late daily. **Credit** MC, V. **Map** p306 F3.
A roomy corner pub with a lively, friendly atmosphere, the Cask is popular with beer drinkers and Hibs fans. A great place to sink a few pints.

Peartree House: perfect for sunny, summer days. *See p157.*

Mezz

49-51 London Street, EH1 (556 9808). Bus 8, 13, 17. **Open** 11am-1am Mon-Sat; 12.30pm-1am Sun. **Food served** noon-8pm daily. **Credit** MC, V. **Map** p306 F3.

The latest addition to the Broughton Street area bar scene, the former Bellevue has been completely refurbished and is now almost unrecognisable. The new bar takes its name from the mezzanine level, and although it is nothing out of the ordinary, its light, bright interior offers a pleasant alternative to some of the darker imbiberies along this stretch, and is proving justly popular.

The Outhouse

12A Broughton Street Lane, EH1 (557 6668). Playhouse buses. **Open** 11am-1am daily. **Food served** noon-4pm daily. **Credit** MC, V. **Map** p307 G3.

Drinkers wandering down Broughton Street could easily miss this bar tucked away down a lane. The Outhouse is fairly small and gets really crowded, but the punters go back again and again, especially when the popular beer garden is open during the summer months.

Phoenix

46 Broughton Street, EH1 (557 0234). Bus 8/ Playhouse buses. **Open** 8am-1am Mon-Sat; 12.30pm-1am Sun. **Credit** MC, V. **Map** p306 F3.

The Phoenix is a very popular pub despite (or perhaps because of) its lack of sophistication and its bog-standard decor. Late night drinkers – whether locals or students – gather here in droves. The cellar bar is open at weekends.

Pivo Caffé

2-6 Calton Road, EH8 (557 2925). Bus 30, 40. **Open** 4pm-1am daily. **Credit** MC, V. **Map** p307 G4.

Pivo's Czech theme is obvious throughout, from the photos of Prague on the walls, a Czech video on a loop, and of course all that Czech beer behind the bar. Even those who don't usually drink lager will enjoy sampling the range of draught and bottled beer. This is a popular pre-club venue, with DJs spinning tunes at the weekend.

PopRokit

2 Picardy Place, EH1 (556 4272). Playhouse buses. **Open** 11am-1am daily. **Food served** noon-7pm daily. **No credit cards. Map** p307 G4.

A busy pre-club bar. Hang out in the ground-floor bar area where the glass windows look out to Picardy Place or head downstairs to the big basement, where DJs, funky lighting and coloured walls keep the party atmosphere alive.

Arthur's Seat

Sheep Heid Inn

43-5 The Causeway, EH15 (656 6951). Bus 4, 44, 45. **Open** 11am-11pm Mon-Wed; 11am-midnight Thur-Sat; 12.30-11pm Sun. **Food served** 11am-8.30pm Mon-Sat; 12.30-8.30pm Sun. **Credit** MC, V.

This famous old pub is all the incentive you need to walk across Arthur's Seat. Situated in a cobbled street in Duddingston Village, it's a cosy place to spend a cold evening, warming yourself with beer. There's a beer garden for finer weather and a skittle alley in case you get bored.

South Edinburgh

Bennet's

8 Leven Street, EH3 (229 5143). Bus 11, 15, 16, 17, 23, 45. **Open** 11am-12.30am Mon-Sat; 11am-11.30pm Sun. **Credit** MC, V. **Map** p309 D7.
Next door to the King's Theatre, Bennet's is excellent for watching thespians and theatre-goers at play. Survey the huge whisky gantry while sitting at the map-covered tables, sample the decent beer, or indulge in a post-performance G and T, dahling.

The Blue Blazer

2 Spittal Street, EH3 (229 5030). Bus 2, 35. **Open** 11am-1am daily. **No credit cards.** **Map** p309 D6.
The Blue Blazer's high windows ensure that no one can see in from the street. Once inside this two-roomed corner bar, drinkers are well away from the busy Tollcross pubs and can relax with atmospheric lighting, good beer and a wide range of malts.

Cameo Bar

38 Home Street, EH3 (228 4141). Bus 11, 15, 16, 17, 23. **Open** 5.30-11pm Mon-Thur; 1-11.30pm Fri, Sun; 1pm-1am Sat. **No credit cards.** **Map** p309 D7.
This bar is a tiny room in a fine Edinburgh cinema (*see p198*). Drinks can be taken into the film at certain times. Not to be confused with the Cameo Bar in Leith (*see p158*).

The Canny Man's

237 Morningside Road, EH10 (447 1484). Bus 11, 15, 16, 18. **Open** noon-11pm Mon-Wed; noon-midnight Thur, Sat; noon-1am Fri; 12.30-11.30pm Sun. **Food served** noon-3pm, 6.30-9pm Mon-Fri; noon-3pm Sat; 12.30-3pm Sun. **No credit cards.**
This Morningside establishment has a reputation for rather unpredictable service – encouraging regulars-only at certain times and refusing some drinkers altogether. But don't be put off, because the chances are you'll receive a friendly welcome in an extremely unusual environment. There's everything from musical instruments to model ships hanging from the ceiling and lining the walls here.

Cloisters

26 Brougham Street, EH3 (221 9997). Bus 11, 15, 16, 17, 23, 45. **Open** 11am-midnight Mon-Thur; 11am-12.30am Fri, Sat; noon-midnight Sun. **Food served** noon-3pm Mon-Fri; noon-4pm Sat, Sun. **No credit cards.** **Map** p309 D7.
An old parsonage has been converted to create a comfortable pub with a strong reputation for beer and whisky. The whisky gantry was made from wood reclaimed from a disused church. Regulars include staff from the nearby Infirmary (until its move) and students.

Hogshead

30-32 Bread Street, EH3 (221 0575). Bus 2, 35. **Open** 11am-1am daily. **Food served** noon-9pm Mon-Fri; noon-8pm Sat, Sun. **Credit** AmEx, MC, V. **Map** p304 A3.

Traverse Café Bar. *See p157.*

Part of the Hogshead chain, this pub continues the tried and tested formula of offering a range of beers and cheap food. It is reasonably spacious, but once the crowds of students pour in, getting to the bar becomes a distant dream. This branch is welcoming, with big couches and bright walls; the basement branch near Princes Street is more barn-like.
Branch: 22 Castle Street, New Town, EH2 (226 1224).

The Human Be-in

2-8 West Crosscauseway, EH8 (662 8860). Nicolson Street–North Bridge buses. **Open** 11am-midnight Mon-Fri; noon-1am Sat, Sun. **Food served** 11am-9pm daily; snacks until close daily. **Credit** AmEx, MC, V. **Map** p310 G7.
The cube seats and benches at this surprisingly roomy slate-and-wood-effect bar aren't as comfortable as they are tasteful, so head for the booth seating at the back. There's laid-back table service during the day, and DJs appear most nights. An ideal hideout for students who are avoiding the library.

Meadow Bar

42-44 Buccleuch Street, EH8 (667 6907). Bus 41, 42. **Open** 11.30am-1am daily. **No credit cards.** **Map** p310 G7.
The Moo Bar, as this is known, is in student country but is also popular with other young folk. Metal sculptures on the walls show snakes and cows' heads. There are cheap drinks offers during the day.

Monboddo

34 Bread Street, EH3 (221 5555). Bus 2, 35. **Open** 10am-midnight Mon-Wed; 10am-1am Thur-Sat; noon-midnight Sun. **Credit** AmEx, DC, MC, V. **Map** p309 D6.
This modern bar in the Point Hotel attracts after-work and weekend drinkers who settle down in front of the big glass windows to unwind. A long wine and champagne list, and daily happy hour offers.

Montpeliers

159-161 Bruntsfield Place, EH10 (229 3115). Bus 11, 15, 16, 17, 23, 45. **Open** 9am-1am daily. **Food served** 9am-10pm daily. **Credit** AmEx, DC, MC, V. **Map** p309 D8.

Popular with a diverse crowd in Bruntsfield and beyond, Monty's always seems busy. At night it's dark but atmospheric and has a more traditional feel than Rick's (*see p153*) and the other modern style bars owned by the Montpeliers company.

Peartree House

36 West Nicolson Street, EH8 (667 7533). Nicolson Street–North Bridge buses. **Open** 11am-midnight Mon-Thur; 11am-1am Fri, Sat; 12.30pm-12.30am Sun. **Food served** noon-2.30pm Mon-Fri. **No credit cards. Map** p310 G7.

Inside, Peartree House is dark and not particularly attractive, but interiors don't matter when the sun shines and the rows of benches in the extensive beer garden fill up. It's very near the main university buildings so there's a strong student presence.

Traverse Café Bar

10 Cambridge Street, EH1 (228 5383). Bus 1, 10, 11, 15, 16, 17, 22, 24. **Open** 10am-1am Mon-Sat. **Food served** noon-8.30pm Mon-Sat; tapas noon-late Mon-Sat. **Credit** MC, V. **Map** p304 A3.

This roomy, dark and extremely popular theatre bar is downstairs from the booking office and next to the theatres. There are always special offers on whisky and bottled beer, and the cheap and delicious bar snacks are available until late six days a week. It's ideal post-theatre, pre-club or just for meeting people whenever.

West Edinburgh

Caledonian Ale House

1-3 Haymarket Terrace, EH12 (337 1006). Bus 2, 3, 4, 21, 25. **Open** 11am-12.30am Mon-Sat; noon-12.30am Sun. **Food served** 11am-5pm Mon-Sat; noon-5pm Sun. **Credit** DC, MC, V. **Map** p308 B6.

Right next to Haymarket Station, the Caledonian Ale House creates a conducive atmosphere with candles on the tables, decent beer on tap and some good wine. There's a bistro upstairs and meals are served in the bar during the day.

Caley Sample Room

58 Angle Park Terrace, EH11 (337 7204). Bus 4, 28, 35. **Open** 11.30am-midnight Mon-Thur; 11.30am-1am Fri, Sat; 12.30pm-midnight Sun. **Food served** 11.30am-9pm Mon-Sat; 12.30-9pm Sun. **Credit** MC, V. **Map** p308 A8.

Close to the Caledonian Brewery, the Caley Sample Room always has plenty of local beers on offer. It's a large open room with benches in the middle and smaller tables under the window; if the seats are full, there's always a barrel to perch your drink on. It's a good spot for TV football, and also handy after a visit to Murrayfield or Tynecastle. Hot pub food is available daily.

Cramond Inn

30 Cramond Glebe Road, EH4 (336 2035). Bus 41, 42. **Open** 11am-11pm Mon-Thur, Sun; 11am-midnight Fri, Sat. **Food served** 11am-2.30pm, 6-9.30pm Mon-Fri; noon-9.30pm Sat; 12.30-9.30pm Sun. **Credit** MC, V.

Tucked away in Cramond, a conservation village on the coast about five miles from the city centre, this pub is quite cramped inside, with nooks and crannies to get holed up in. It gets very busy on summer Sundays when Edinburgh folk go for a walk along the River Almond. The food is popular, and there's parking nearby.

Cuba Norte

192 Morrison Street, EH3 (221 1430). Bus 2. **Open/food served** noon-midnight Mon-Wed; noon-1am Thur-Sat; 4pm-midnight Sun. **Credit** AmEx, MC, V. **Map** p308 C6.

This Cuban bar on the quickest route between Lothian Road and Haymarket can get very busy at weekends, and is popular with groups who come to eat tapas and drink cocktails. Once the rum has worked its magic, there's a dancefloor downstairs for a spot of salsa.

Golden Rule

28-30 Yeaman Place, EH11 (622 7112). Bus 28, 34, 35. **Open** 11am-11.30pm Mon-Sat; 11am-midnight Fri; 12.30-11pm Sun. **No credit cards. Map** p308 B8.

Divided into a traditional top bar and a more modern downstairs bar, the Golden Rule serves a good range of drinks, from wines and excellent guest ales to Belgian fruit beers and lagers. Snacks are on offer all day. It gets very busy after football matches at nearby Tynecastle, and is handy for Fountainpark's clubs and multiplex cinema.

Murrayfield Hotel

18 Corstorphine Road, EH12 (337 1844). Bus 12, 26, 31, 100. **Open** 11am-11pm Mon-Thur, Sat, Sun; 11am-midnight Fri. **Food served** noon-9.30pm daily. **Credit** (for food orders only) AmEx, MC, V.

The large bar and beer garden at this hotel get very busy indeed when there's a rugby international – not surprising considering it's right opposite Murrayfield Stadium. On quieter days, families are made welcome and the filling bar food is served all day. A good stopping off place on the way to the Zoo.

Leith & Newhaven

Bar Sirius

7-10 Dock Place, EH6 (555 3344). Bus 1, 6, 22, 35, 36, 49. **Open** 11.30am-11pm Mon-Wed; 11.30am-1am Thur-Sat; noon-11pm Sun. **Food served** noon-9pm Mon-Thur, Sat, Sun; noon-4pm Fri. **Credit** MC, V. **Map** p311 Jy.

This brightly coloured bar is spacious and relaxed: ideal, in fact, for lounging around in. The food is excellent value, with brunch available at weekends. There's also a Hangover Cure breakfast, which adds a Bloody Mary to the fry-up.

On the first floor of the new Ocean Terminal shopping centre, the Ocean Bar has splendid views across the water. The terrace and balconies are done out in slatted wood, reminiscent of a ship; inside, coloured booths and bar stools add to the bright and breezy atmosphere. The drinks menu is long.

Old Chain Pier

32 Trinity Crescent, EH5 (552 1233). Bus 10, 11, 16, 32. **Open** 11am-11pm Mon-Wed; 11am-midnight Thur-Sat; 12.30-11pm Sun. **Food served** noon-4.30pm, 6-9pm daily. **Credit** MC, V.
Run by well-known Edinburgh publican Drew Nicol, this pub on the front at Newhaven has beautiful views over the water. There are huge portions of good food and regular guest ales. Definitely worth the walk or bus trip from the city centre.

The Pond

2 Bath Road, EH6 (467 3825). Bus 12, 16, 35, 36. **Open** 4pm-1am Mon-Wed; 2pm-1am Thur-Sat; 1pm-1am Sun. **No credit cards**.
This bar is worth the little walk along Salamander Street. It's full of groovy, kitschy items, such as autographed photos of soap stars, film posters and a moving picture of a waterfall. And, yes, there is a pond – next to the car park in the back yard.

Enjoy liquid delights at **The Pond**.

Cameo Bar

23 Commercial Street, EH6 (554 9999). Bus 1, 6, 22, 35, 36, 49. **Open** noon-10pm daily. **Food served** noon-10pm daily. **Credit** MC, V. **Map** p311 Jy.
An increasingly popular bar with comfortable velvet booths, the Cameo has a big screen in the busy back room, and a comfortable front room that's eminently suited to a few pints and the Sunday papers. The pub food is tasty and there's a restaurant right next door.

iso-bar

7 Bernard Street, EH6 (467 8904). Bus 1, 6, 22, 35, 36, 49. **Open** 10.30am-1am daily. **Food served** 10.30am-5pm daily. **Credit** MC. V. **Map** p311 Jy.
One of the latest Leith bars to be reinvented for the younger crowd, the iso-bar is long, narrow and dark, but the laid-back ambience and friendly bar staff dispel the gloom. The wooden booths and tables are functional but attractive, and the window seat is great for a spot of people-watching.

King's Wark

36 The Shore, EH6 (554 9260). Bus 1, 6, 22, 35, 36, 49. **Open/food served** noon-11pm Mon-Thur; noon-midnight Fri, Sat; 11am-11pm Sun. **Credit** MC, V. **Map** p311 Jy.
This corner pub is one of the oldest in the area. It's a pleasant, wood-panelled spot with an extensive menu; the kind of place to pop into for a few glasses of wine when you're out for the evening.

Ocean Bar

Ocean Terminal, Ocean Drive, EH6 (553 8073). Bus 1, 6, 22, 35, 36, 49. **Open** noon-midnight Mon-Thur, Sun; noon-1am Fri, Sat. **Credit** AmEx, MC, V. **Map** p311 Hx.

Starbank Inn

64 Laverockbank Road, EH5 (552 4141). Bus 10, 11, 16, 32. **Open** 11am-11pm Mon-Thur; 11am-midnight Fri, Sat; 12.30-11pm Sun. **Food served** noon-2.30pm, 6pm-late Mon-Fri; all day Sat, Sun. **Credit** MC, V. **Map** p311 Ex.
Just a few yards from the Old Chain Pier, the Starbank sits slightly higher up and has great sea views. It's bright and airy, with a conservatory at the back, and offers wines and guest ales. The food is popular; snacks include buckets of prawns.

Timberbush

28 Bernard Street, EH6 (476 8080). Bus 1, 6, 22, 35, 36, 49. **Open/food served** 8am-1am daily. **Credit** MC, V. **Map** p311 Jy.
This roomy café-bar has big tables at which you can munch on light meals such as soups and paninis, or just relax with a coffee. In fact, Timberbush doesn't feel like a bar at all… except for the area upstairs, that is, which has big couches and is a great spot from which to peer down at the world.

The Waterfront Wine Bar

1C Dock Place, EH6 (554 7427). Bus 1, 6, 22, 35, 36, 49. **Open** noon-11pm Mon-Thur; noon-midnight Fri, Sat; 12.30-11pm Sun. **Food served** noon-9pm Mon-Sat; 12.30-9pm Sun. **Credit** AmEx, MC, V. **Map** p311 Jy.
A paddle steamer waiting room in a former life, the Waterfront is now a cosy bistro and bar. Nautical charts and other unidentifiable maritime objects are tastefully scattered about for a touch of sea-going charm. The food at the Waterfront is very good and the vine-covered conservatory by the water is the best place to eat it.

Eat, Drink, Shop

Shops & Services

Edinburgh's shopping reputation may be based on tartan, whisky and haggis, but these days the city has far more to offer the discerning consumer.

Shopping in Edinburgh is set to change dramatically in August 2002 with the arrival of **Harvey Nichols** on St Andrew Square. Even before the store's scheduled opening, such a major and upmarket player in the retail market has had a knock-on effect. It has given some grounds to Edinburgh's boast that it is gradually catching up with Glasgow, Scotland's undisputed shopping capital – and caused existing retailers to sharpen their images and brighten up their sales floors in anticipation of some serious shopping wars.

The problem for Edinburgh has been its failure to create the sort of city-centre malls and shopping enclaves that modern shoppers demand. Only in 2002 were the tired old **St James Centre** (*see p162*) and **Princes Mall** (*see p161*) joined by **Ocean Terminal** in Leith (*see p161*).

Edinburgh could offer a world class shopping experience. **Princes Street** should be, without doubt, one of *the* streets to shop in, with its magnificent view up to the castle across verdant gardens. Instead, only the 19th-century department store **Jenners** (*see p161*) links to the city's retail past – when Princes Street was dominated by grand, family-run institutions. Today high-street chains and bargain outlets dominate the street; designer fashion outlets are located on George Street, which is the place to make serious dents in the credit card.

Where the Scottish capital does make its presence felt is in the small, specialist shops that dominate areas like Thistle Street Lane in the New Town and Victoria Street, Cockburn Street and St Mary's Street in the Old Town. Even the Royal Mile's purveyors of tartan kitsch have their own charm, while the more seriously minded shops selling whisky (*see p172*) and hiring out kilts (*see p170* **The kilt**) make this stretch the place to head for some proper tourist souvenirs. More lasting memories of Scotland are to be bought in the excellent antiques shops that cluster dustily in areas like the West Bow and Grassmarket in the Old Town, the West Port and along Causewayside in South Edinburgh and, with rather more ostentatious formality, in Dundas Street in the New Town. *See also p163* **Antiques and collectibles**.

The village atmosphere of many of the city's neighbourhoods also encourages the welcome continuation of shopping habits that can seem old-fashioned and even a little quaint to the modern-day shopper. Neighbourhoods like **Morningside**, **Tollcross** or **Stockbridge** are fairly self-contained, with residents still doing their daily shopping at local chemists, grocers, butchers and fishmongers.

OPENING HOURS

These days, many shops have longer and more flexible opening hours. Usual hours are still 9am until 6pm Monday to Saturday, but lots of places stay open late on Thursday, and, despite the opposition of the major churches, are also open on Sunday. The opening times we list below are year-round, but be aware that branches may keep slightly different hours and that many shops stay open longer during the Festival and before Christmas.

One stop shopping

Department stores

Most of the major UK department stores including **Debenhams**, **Fraser's** (part of House of Fraser), **Marks & Spencer** and **Bhs** can be found on Princes Street, but **Jenners** towers above the rest, with a mock-classical façade and several floors of luxury goods. For everyday quality products, **John Lewis** is the local favourite. Branches of many major department stores can also be found at the **Gyle Centre** (*see p161*) and the newly built **Ocean Terminal** (*see p161*).

Bhs

64 Princes Street, New Town, EH2 (226 2621/ www.bhs.co.uk). Princes Street buses. **Open** 9am-5.30pm Mon-Wed; 9am-8pm Thur; 9am-6pm Fri, Sat; 11am-5pm Sun. **Credit** AmEx, MC, V. **Map** p304 C2. Basic, everyday fashion and household goods that won't break the bank.
Branch: Ocean Terminal, Leith, EH6 (555 3284).

Debenhams

109-112 Princes Street, New Town, EH2 (225 1320/www.debenhams.com). Princes Street buses. **Open** 9.30am-6pm Mon-Wed, Fri; 9.30am-8pm Thur; 9am-6pm Sat; 11am-5pm Sun (hours may vary). **Credit** AmEx, DC, MC, V. **Map** p304 B2.

Debenhams has hired fashion and interior designers to improve its brand in recent years.
Branch: Ocean Terminal, Leith, EH6 (553 8100).

Fraser's

145 Princes Street, New Town, EH2 (225 2472/ www.houseoffraser.co.uk). Princes Street buses.
Open 9am-5.30pm Mon-Wed, Fri; 9am-7.30pm Thur; 9am-6pm Sat; 11am-5pm Sun (hours may vary according to season). **Credit** AmEx, MC, V.
Map p304 A2.
Part of the House of Fraser chain of reliable stores.

Jenners

48 Princes Street, New Town, EH2 (225 2442/ www.jenners.com). Princes Street buses. **Open** 9am-5.30pm Mon, Wed; 9.30am-5.30pm Thur; 9am-7.30pm Thur; 9am-6pm Fri, Sat; noon-5pm Sun (hours may vary according to season; phone for details).
Credit AmEx, DC, MC, V. **Map** p304 C2.
The world's oldest independent department store, known as the Harrods of Scotland, opened its doors in 1895. Six stately floors brim over with merchandise, including international designer wear, a huge toy department and a food hall specialising in Scottish and international delicacies. With add-ons including a hairdresser's, beauty salon and photographic studio, it's almost a self-contained village. A sight as well as a shop.

John Lewis

69 St James Centre, New Town, EH1 (556 9121/ www.johnlewis.com). Princes Street or Nicolson Street–North Bridge buses. **Open** *Jan-Nov* 9am-5.30pm Mon-Wed, Fri; 9.30am-7.30pm Thur; 9am-6pm Sat. *Dec* hours vary; phone for details.
Credit MC, V. **Map** p306 G4.
Still never knowingly undersold, John Lewis stocks everything from blank tapes to kitchen equipment, fashion accessories, millinery and furniture.

Marks & Spencer

54 Princes Street, New Town, EH2 (225 2301/ www.marks-and-spencer.co.uk). Princes Street buses.
Open 9am-6pm (clothes & homewares), 9am-7pm (food) Mon-Wed, Fri; 9am-8am Thur; 8.30am-6pm Sat; 11am-5pm Sun. **Credit** AmEx, MC, V.
Map p304 C2.
Menswear, childrenswear, homewares and food; for womenswear visit 91 Princes Street.
Branches: 21 Gyle Avenue, EH12 (317 1333); 91 Princes Street, New Town, EH2 (225 2301).

Shopping centres

Cameron Toll

6 Lady Road, South Edinburgh, EH16 (666 2777/ www.camerontoll.co.uk). Bus 3, 8, 33, 80. **Open** 7.30am-10pm Mon-Sat; 8am-7pm Sun. **Credit** varies.
A large shopping complex about 15 minutes' bus journey south of the city centre dominated by Sainsbury's, with around 50 other high-street outlets dealing in gifts, household accessories, travel, beauty supplies and fashion.

Fort Kinnaird Retail Park

Newcraighall Road, South Edinburgh, EH15 (www.fortkinnaird.com). Bus 14, 40. **Open** times vary. **Credit** varies.
Located 20 minutes' bus ride from the city centre, Fort Kinnaird is the new umbrella brand name for a retail park consisting of the Fort and an exciting new 117,500-square-foot development of 21 units. Boasting a superb location on the outskirts of Edinburgh, directly alongside the A1 and with excellent public transport links, Fort Kinnaird delivers the kind of environment now demanded by the current retail fashion market. Well-known outlets already in place include Marks & Spencer, Gap, H&M, Borders, the Link, JD Sports, Pizza Hut, Next, Boots, Racing Green, New Look, Laura Ashley and Dorothy Perkins.

Gyle Centre

South Gyle Broadway, West Edinburgh, EH12 (539 8828/www.gyleshopping.com). Bus 22.
Open 8am-10pm Mon-Fri; 8am-8pm Sat; 9am-8pm Sun. **Credit** varies.
Chain stores such as Marks & Spencer, Boots and Sainsbury's are laid out along with smaller fashion and gift shops in an attractive and surprisingly intimate mall. The Centre is a 20-minute bus journey on the main west road out of the city, on the way to the airport.

Ocean Terminal

Ocean Drive, Leith, EH6 (555 8888/www.ocean terminal.com). Bus 11, 22, 34, 35, 36, 49, C3.
Open 10am-8pm Mon-Fri; 9am-7pm Sat; 11am-6pm Sun. **Credit** varies. **Map** p311 Hx.
Ocean Terminal is the latest stage in the continuing transformation of Leith from former industrial wasteland to a thriving commercial centre. There are dozens of shops in addition to a cinema, several bars and restaurants and the Royal Yacht *Britannia* visitor centre (*see p116*). High-street names such as Bhs and Debenhams dominate the shopping selection, but the centre itself is also worth visiting for the lovely views from its cruise-ship style balconies over the Forth.

Princes Mall

Princes Street (east end), New Town, EH1 (557 3759/www.princesmall-edinburgh.co.uk). Princes Street or Nicolson Street–North Bridge buses. **Open** *Jan-July, Sept-Nov* 8.30am-6pm Mon-Wed, Fri, Sat; 8.30am-7pm Thur; 11am-5pm Sun. *Aug, Dec* extended hours; phone for details. **Credit** varies.
Map p304 D2.
On the site of an old fruit and veg market, this mall's crude concrete exterior encroaches vulgarly on to the glorious vista from the east end of Princes Street. Inside are three bland and airy floors of shopaholics' delight. Outlets selling designer gear, CDs and bargain books sit alongside one-off shops specialising in Scottish gifts, upmarket jewellery and educational science toys.The ground floor is dominated by cafés and fast-food outlets, providing sustenance for hungry shoppers.

Eat, Drink, Shop

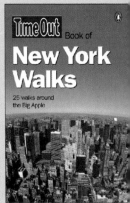

Antiques and collectibles

In a city dominated by old buildings, it's no surprise that there are plenty of places to find antiques and retro collectibles. In fact there's at least one outlet in every area of the city packed with such goodies.

Causewayside, which runs south from the west end of the Meadows in Sciennes, South Edinburgh (map p310 H8) is a particularly good spot, with around a dozen antique shops lining the first few blocks of the road. Most specialise in pre-1950s furniture but there are plenty of curios for collectors among the crockery and other ornaments. The wry sign above the Antiques Fine Art Gallery says it all: 'Connoisseurs to the Impecunious Gentry'.

Remember also to check out **Greenside Car Boot Sale** on a Sunday morning (see p176), and the city's charity shops (look them up in the Yellow Pages), particularly in **Newington**, **Morningside** and on the lower half of **Leith Walk**. Charities have become canny to the worth of some of their donations, and have upped their prices accordingly, but bargains can still be hunted down, from a mint set of Royal Doulton China for £195 to authentic 1960s jewellery for pennies.

Architectural Salvage Yard

Unit 6, Couper Street, Leith, EH6 (554 7077/ www.easy-arch-salv.co.uk). Bus 1, 16, 22, 32, 34, 35, 36. **Open** 9am-5pm Mon-Sat. **Credit** MC, V. **Map** p311 Hy.
A treasure chest of artefacts from a bygone era, tucked away in a huge Leith warehouse. Church pews, Victorian baths and sundials are among the salvaged goods. The gangways connecting the different floors make it feel like you're in the cargo hold of an old sailing ship.

Bacchus Antiques

95 West Bow, Old Town, EH1 (225 6183). Bus 2, 3, 27, 28, 41, 42. **Open** 11am-5pm Mon-Sat. **Credit** MC, V. **Map** p304 C3.
Specialising in memorabilia related to golf, Bacchus also sells small silver ornaments and jewellery.

Retro Interiors

36 St Mary's Street, Old Town, EH1 (558 9090). Bus 35/Nicolson Street–North Bridge buses. **Open** 10.30am-5.30pm Tue-Sat. **No credit cards. Map** p310 G5.
Retro Interiors is undoubtedly the best place for high-quality authentic furnishings from the 1950s to the 1970s. Fans of exotica, kitsch and op-art decor will be in seventh heaven here. Furniture, pictures, glassware, lights, ornaments and oddities fill two floors of this attractively laid-out shop; almost all of the stock is in mint condition, and not necessarily priced as high as you'd think.

St James Centre

Leith Street, New Town, EH1 (557 0050/www. thestjames.com). Princes Street or Playhouse buses. **Open** 7.30am-6.30pm Mon-Wed, Fri, Sat; 7.30am-8.30pm Thur; noon-5pm Sun. **Credit** varies. **Map** p307 G4.
It might look like a concrete grey fortress but the St James Centre is undoubtedly handy, situated as it is near Waverley Station at the east end of Princes Street, between the Old and New Towns. There are two entrances to the mall: one on Leith Street and one over the bridge from Calton Hill. At the heart of the centre is a branch of John Lewis, but there are dozens of other shops, including outlets dealing in everthing from electrical goods, fashion and sports equipment to gifts, stationery

and chocolate treats. Snack food outlets and a seating area upstairs at the Leith Street entrance provide a welcome rest-stop.

Auctioneers

Christies, Scotland

5 Wemyss Place, New Town, EH3 (225 4756/ www.christies.com). Bus 19, 29, 29A, 37, 37A, 41, 42. **Open** 9am-1pm, 2-5pm Mon-Fri. **No credit cards. Map** p306 D4.
For the times and dates of auctions for antiques and paintings, check out the listings posted in the window. This famous auction house is geared towards serious collectors, but amateurs will find something to interest them too.

Eat, Drink, Shop

Amsterdam · Barcelona · Berlin · Boston · Brussels · Budapest
Buenos Aires · Chicago · Copenhagen · Dublin · Edinburgh · Florence
Havana · Hong Kong · Istanbul · Las Vegas · Lisbon · London
Los Angeles · Madrid · Miami · Milan · Moscow · Naples
New Orleans · New York · Paris · Prague · Rome · San Francisco
South of France · Sydney · Tokyo · Venice · Vienna · Washington, DC

The **Time Out City Guides** spectrum

Available from all good bookshops and at www.timeout.com/shop

www.timeout.com   www.penguin.com

Books

At Festival time, the annual **Book Festival** (*see p187*) takes over Charlotte Square in the New Town and you can meet the author of your purchase. During the rest of the year **Waterstone's** has regular Meet the Author events, advertised in the shop window and in Edinburgh's listings magazine, *The List*. A nominal fee is charged for some events, but this is often redeemable against purchase of the book that's being publicised. Others are free. Book early, as even free events are ticketed.

Bauermeister Booksellers

19 George IV Bridge, Old Town, EH1 (226 5561/ www.bauermeister.co.uk). Bus 23, 27, 41, 42. **Open** 9am-8pm Mon-Fri; 9am-5.30pm Sat; noon-5pm Sun. **Credit** AmEx, MC, V. **Map** p304 C3.

Tourist guidebooks, maps, magazines, plus educational and cut-price fiction titles dominate the two floors of this respectable mainstream bookshop.

Beyond Words

42-44 Cockburn Street, Old Town, EH1 (226 6636/ www.beyondwords.co.uk). Nicolson Street–North Bridge buses. **Open** 10am-6pm Tue-Sat; noon-5pm Mon, Sun. **Credit** MC, V. **Map** p304 D3.

A small, tranquil shop devoted to photography, with titles covering topics from art and design to celebrity portraits. Also useful for finding more offbeat visual mementos of Scotland. Discreet pine bench seating around the shelves invites casual browsing.

Body & Soul Bookshop

52 Hamilton Place, Stockbridge, EH3 (226 3066/ www.bodyandsoulbooks.com). Bus 35, 35A. **Open** 11am-5.30pm Mon-Sat. **Credit** AmEx, MC, V. **Map** p306 D3.

This is a relaxed, scented and pleasant shop selling a broad range of books, magazines, CDs and gifts related to alternative health, New Age spirituality and gay and lesbian lifestyles. Body & Soul also publishes *Being*, Scotland's leading mind, body and spirit magazine.

The Cook's Bookshop

118 West Bow, Old Town, EH1(226 4445/ www.cooks-book-shop.co.uk). Bus 23, 27, 41, 42. **Open** 10.30am-5.30pm Mon-Sat. **Credit** AmEx, MC, V. **Map** p304 C3.

Clarissa Dickson-Wright's snug nook of a bookshop is filled with new and second-hand cookery titles covering almost everything imaginable that's edible. Many are connected to her hugely successful *Two Fat Ladies* television cookery programme. A cosy, ramshackle layout and old-fashioned fireplaces add to the shop's home kitchen feel.

Deadhead Comics

27 Candlemaker Row, Old Town, EH1 (226 2774/ www.deadheadcomics.com). Bus 23, 27, 41, 42. **Open** 10am-6pm Mon-Sat; 12.30-5.30pm Sun. **Credit** MC, V. **Map** p309 F6.

Fans of mainstream *Marvel* and DC superhero titles will find just what they want here. Deadhead also stocks independent and small-press publications and fantasy role-playing cards and figures.

McNaughtans

3A Haddington Place, Leith Walk, Broughton, EH7 (556 5897/mcnbooks@globalnet.co.uk). Playhouse buses. **Open** 9.30am-5.30pm Tue-Sat. **Credit** MC, V. **Map** p307 G3.

Tucked away at lower-ground level, this gloomy-looking bookshop hides a haven of high-quality second-hand literary treasures. Browsers welcome.

Tills Bookshop

1 Hope Park Crescent (Buccleuch Street), South Edinburgh, EH8 (667 0895). Nicolson Street–North Bridge buses. **Open** noon-7.30pm Mon-Fri; 11am-6pm Sat; noon-5.30pm Sun. **Credit** MC, V. **Map** p310 G7.

This small, bright shop on the edge of the Meadows has been a favourite hangout for students and beatniks of all ages for years, and the cult film posters in the windows are just one clue to its appeal. A high-quality range of reasonably priced second-hand university textbooks is fleshed out with collectable and pulp fiction, plus non-fiction books, TV annuals and those original '50s, '60s and '70s posters.

Waterstone's

128 Princes Street, New Town, EH2 (226 2666/ www.waterstones.co.uk). Princes Street buses. **Open** 8.30am-8pm Mon-Sat; 10.30am-7pm Sun. **Credit** AmEx, DC, MC, V. **Map** p304 A2.

Three attractive, spacious floors of titles are separated into specialist areas, each kept up to date by helpful and knowledgeable staff. This branch is also home to a Seattle Coffee Company café, which has fine views of Princes Street Gardens and the Castle. **Branches**: 13-14 Princes Street, New Town, EH1 (556 3034); 83 George Street, New Town, EH2 (225 3436).

West Port Books

145 West Port, South Edinburgh, EH1 (229 4431/ www.portbooks.freeserve.co.uk). Bus 1, 2, 10, 11, 16, 17, 35. **Open** 10.30am-5.30pm Mon, Thur, Fri; noon-5.30pm Tue, Wed, Sat. **Credit** MC, V. **Map** p309 E6.

A fantastically labyrinthine second-hand bookshop near the Grassmarket, laid out in a warren of rooms on two floors, and overflowing with second-hand and remaindered books, classical records and sheet music. Especially good for art books.

Word Power

43 West Nicolson Street, South Edinburgh, EH8 (662 9112/www.word-power.co.uk). Nicolson Street–North Bridge buses. **Open** *Jan-Nov* 10am-6pm Mon-Fri; 10.30am-6pm Sat. *Dec* also noon-4pm Sun. **Credit** AmEx, DC, MC, V. **Map** p310 G6.

The only radical bookshop in Edinburgh is a vibrant centre for the capital's alternative writing scene. Holds an extensive stock of women's, gay and alternative books, magazines and fanzines packed into a small but bright space. The owner hosts the annual Radical Book Fair in mid May (*see p185*).

Eat, Drink, Shop

Retro chic at **Herman Brown**. *See p168.*

Electronics & computing

Dixons

120 Princes Street, EH2 (226 3711/www.dixons. co.uk) Princes Street buses. **Open** 9am-5.45pm Mon, Tue, Fri; 9.30am-5.45pm Wed; 9am-7pm Thur; 9am-6pm Sat; 11.30am-5.50pm Sun. **Credit** AmEx, DC, MC, V. **Map** p304 B2.

No-nonsense electronic goods chain with an extensive choice of all the basic goods, from CD, Video and DVD players to computers, televisions and cameras, all at reasonably affordable prices. Also stocks a good range of accessories.
Branch: 66 St James Centre, EH1 (556 1200).

Scotsys Applecentre

95-97 Nicolson Street, South Edinburgh, EH8 (0845 606 2641/www.scotsys.co.uk). Nicolson Street–North Bridge buses. **Open** 10am-5.30pm Mon-Sat. **Credit** AmEx, MC, V. **Map** p310 G6.

This is the place for all things Apple Macintosh, from new computers to softwear, support, supplies and peripherals.

Fashion

For details of where to hire kilts, accessories or full Highland dress, *see p170* **The kilt**.

Big Ideas
96 West Bow, Grassmarket, Old Town, EH1 (226 2532/www.bigideasforladies.co.uk). Bus 2, 23, 27, 28, 42, 45. **Open** 10am-5.30pm Mon-Sat. **Credit** AmEx, MC, V. **Map** p304 C3.
A stock of upmarket continental labels provides a refreshingly bright and eye-catching range of day- and eveningwear for women of size 16 and upwards. Don't miss the permanent sale rails in the branch down the road, which also has a further range of casualwear.
Branch: 116 West Bow, Grassmarket, Old Town, EH1 (226 2532).

Corniche
2 Jeffrey Street, Old Town, EH1 (556 3707). Bus 35/Nicolson Street–North Bridge buses. **Open** *Jan-July, Sept-Nov* 10am-5.30pm Mon-Sat. *Aug, Dec* also noon-4pm Sun. **Credit** AmEx, MC, V. **Map** p310 G5.
The quietly hip ethnic decor of this spacious Old Town outlet complements the discerning range of women's designer wear by the likes of Vivienne Westwood, Jean-Paul Gaultier and Alexander McQueen. Keep an eye out for the regular end-of-line specials. The other branch stocks menswear.
Branch: 4 Jeffrey Street, Old Town, EH1 (557 8333).

Crombie Retail Ltd
63 George Street, New Town, EH2 (226 1612/www.crombie.co.uk). Bus 28, 40, 41, 42/Princes Street buses. **Open** 9.30am-6pm Mon-Wed, Fri; 9.30am-7pm Thur; 9am-6pm Sat; noon-5pm Sun. **Credit** AmEx, DC, MC, V. **Map** p304 C1.
Renowned worldwide for almost 200 years for the Crombie coat – beloved of American presidents, teddy boys and East End gangsters – the oak-panelled elegance of this gentlemen's outfitters sums up the classic, genteel side of the city. A classic Crombie, either single or double-breasted, will set you back £499.

Cruise
14 St Mary's Street, Old Town, EH1 (556 2532). Bus 35/Nicolson Street–North Bridge buses. **Open** 10am-6pm Mon-Wed, Fri; 10am-7pm Thur; 9am-6pm Sat; noon-5pm Sun. **Credit** AmEx, DC, MC, V. **Map** p310 G5.
With designers such as Stone Island, Armani, Dolce & Gabbana and Hugo Boss – and prices to match – it's no wonder that this well-established outlet is a fashion favourite with both Edinburgh's well-heeled clubbers and its upmarket hipsters. Would-be fashion victims will love the minimalist, whitewashed surroundings not to mention the luxurious and exclusive pampering service.
Branch: 94 George Street, New Town, EH1 (226 3524).

Cult Clothing
7-9 North Bridge, Old Town, EH1 (556 5003). Nicolson Street–North Bridge buses. **Open** 9.30am-6pm Mon-Wed, Fri, Sat; 10am-7pm Thur; noon-5pm Sun. **Credit** AmEx, DC, MC, V. **Map** p304 D2.
Possibly the hippest of Edinburgh's clubwear shops, and certainly the loudest, with a thumping instore soundtrack to match the trendy Custard Shop, Addict and Carhartt gear. Prices, however, are affordable.

Jigsaw
49 George Street, New Town, EH2 (225 4501/www.jigsaw-online.com). Bus 28, 40, 41, 42/Princes Street buses. **Open** 10am-6pm Mon-Wed, Fri; 10am-7.30pm Thur; 9am-6pm Sat; noon-5pm Sun. **Credit** AmEx, MC, V. **Map** p304 B1.
This chain's style of hip, sexy but wearable clothes (for the over-25s) remains perennially popular.

Karen Millen
53 George Street, New Town, EH2 (220 1589/www.karenmillen.com). Bus 28, 40, 41, 42/Princes Street buses. **Open** 10am-6pm Mon-Wed, Fri, Sat; 10am-7pm Thur; noon-5pm Sun. **Credit** AmEx, DC, MC, V. **Map** p304 B1.
Gorgeous dresses, jumpers and coats from the London-based chain, in clean, lean surroundings.

Momentum Surf Shop
22 Bruntsfield Place, South Edinburgh, EH10 (229 6665/momentum@surfzone.co.uk). Bus 10, 11, 15, 16, 17, 23. **Open** *Jan-July, Sept-Nov* 10am-6pm Mon-Sat. *Aug, Dec* also 10am-6pm Sun. **Credit** MC, V. **Map** p309 D8.
Well-priced, high-quality skateboarding and surf-wear for fashion-conscious sporty types.

Pie in the Sky
21 Cockburn Street, Old Town, EH1 (220 1477/pieintheskyltd@hotmail.com). Bus 35/Nicolson Street–North Bridge buses. **Open** 9.30am-6pm Mon-Wed, Fri, Sat; 9.30am-7pm Thur; noon-5pm Sun. **Credit** AmEx, MC, V. **Map** p304 D3.
This well-established student haunt close to Waverley Station specialises in cheap tie-dye and rainbow clothes, hats, bags, jewellery and incense.

TK Maxx
Meadowbank Retail Park, London Road, EH7 (661 6611/www.tkmaxx.co.uk). Bus 4, 5, 15, 40, 44, 45. **Open** 10am-8pm Mon-Fri; 9am-6pm Sat; 11am-5pm Sun. **Credit** AmEx, MC, V.
A massive warehouse of end-of-line bargain-priced stock from names such as Prada, Red Or Dead and Levi's. Men's, women's and children's clothing, plus accessories, household goods and luggage make this a popular one-stop shop for families. Be prepared to rake through rails and endure long queues, particularly at weekends.

Whistles
97 George Street, New Town, EH2 (226 4398). Bus 28, 40, 41, 42/Princes Street buses. **Open** 10am-6pm Mon-Wed, Fri; 10am-7.30pm Thur; 9am-6pm Sat; noon-5pm Sun. **Credit** AmEx, DC, MC, V.

Eat, Drink, Shop

Whistles' own range of fashionable, highly wearable and moderately expensive clothes sits well beside other designer labels in this branch of the London boutique chain.

Children

New & Junior Profile
88-92 Raeburn Place, Stockbridge, EH4 (332 7928). Bus 24, 28, 36. **Open** 9am-5.30pm Mon-Sat. **Credit** MC, V. **Map** p305 C3.
Pretty and practical clothes in bright colours and folksy designs for babies at mid-range prices, plus children's toys and furniture.

Shoos
8 Teviot Place, Old Town, EH1 (220 4626). Bus 2, 23, 27, 28, 41, 42, 45. **Open** 9.30am-5pm Mon-Fri; 9am-5.30pm Sat. **Credit** MC, V. **Map** p309 F6.
Shoos is a small shop that specialises in Start-Rite footwear for tiny feet.

Fetish

Leather & Lace
8 Drummond Street, Old Town, EH8 (557 9413). Nicolson–North Bridge buses. **Open** 10am-9pm Mon-Sat; noon-9pm Sun. **Credit** DC, MC, V. **Map** p310 G6.
Home to a wide range of magazines, toys and equipment for those with an ever-active imagination to match their ever-active bedroom lives. If the knotty problem of restraint comes up, the friendly staff can point you in the right direction. There's a big video section.

Whiplash Trash
53 Cockburn Street, Old Town, EH1 (226 1005). Bus 35/Nicolson–North Bridge buses. **Open** 10.30am-5.30pm Mon-Wed, Fri, Sat; 10.30am-6pm Thur. **No credit cards. Map** p304 D3.
Good range of PVC, leather and rubber gear.

Jewellery

Hamilton & Inches
87 George Street, New Town, EH2 (225 4898/www. hamiltonandinches.com). Bus 28, 40, 41, 42/Princes Street buses. **Open** 9.30am-5.30pm Mon-Fri; 9.30am-5pm Sat. **Credit** AmEx, DC, MC, V. **Map** p304 B1.
The reputation of this upmarket jeweller's, which opened in 1866, has been sealed in the past few years with the patronage of none other than Tiffany of New York. The late-Georgian interior, with its gilded columns and ornate plasterwork, is just as awe-inspiring as the glittering gems themselves.

Scottish Gems
24 High Street, Old Town, EH1 (557 5731/www. scottish-gems.co.uk). Bus 35/Nicolson–North Bridge buses. **Open** *June-Aug* 10am-6pm Mon-Sat; 11am-4pm Sun. *Sept-May* 10am-5.30pm Mon-Sat. **Credit** AmEx, DC, MC, V. **Map** p310 G5.

Modern Scottish jewellery, including well-crafted Celtic wedding rings from £20 up to over £300. **Branch**: 162 Morningside Road, South Edinburgh, EH10 (447 5579).

Scottish

For kilt tailoring and kilt hire *see p170* **Scottish icons: The kilt**.

Edinburgh Woollen Mill
453 Lawnmarket, Old Town, EH1 (225 1525). Bus 23, 27, 28, 35, 41, 42, 45. **Open** *Jan-Apr* 9.30am-5.30pm Mon-Sat; 11am-5pm Sun. *May-Dec* 9am-7pm Mon-Fri; 9am-6pm Sat; 11am-5pm Sun. **Credit** AmEx, MC, V. **Map** p304 C3.
A well-established, traditional woollenwear outlet, with branches scattered around the city, the Edinburgh Woollen Mill sells a range of good-quality traditional clothes, shawls, rugs and scarves, all at affordable prices.
Branches: Romanes & Patterson 62 Princes Street, New Town, EH2 (225 4966); 139 Princes Street, New Town, EH2 (226 3840).

Second-hand

15 The Grassmarket
15 Grassmarket, Old Town, EH1 (226 3087/www. vintagelinens.co.uk). Bus 2, 23, 27, 28, 35, 41, 42, 45. **Open** *Sept-July* noon-6pm Mon-Fri; 10.30am-5.30pm Sat. *Aug* noon-8pm Mon-Sat; 2-6pm Sun. **No credit cards. Map** p309 E6.
This small cavern-like shop in the heart of the Old Town offers period lace, linen and velvet curtains as well as clothing. Check out the pre-1950s men's suits, the tweed jackets and an impressive selection of trilby hats.

Flip of Hollywood
59-61 South Bridge, Old Town, EH1 (556 4966). Nicolson Street–North Bridge buses. **Open** *Sept-July* 9.30am-5.30pm Mon-Wed; 9.30am-6pm Thur-Sat. *Aug* also noon-5pm Sun. **Credit** MC, V. **Map** p310 G6.
This branch of the national chain of American clothing shops has seen better days. It's now geared more towards modern skate, surf and student wear, but is still worth checking out for the extensive range of well-priced second-hand jeans, cords, cowboy shirts, jackets and coats.

Herman Brown
151 West Port, South Edinburgh, EH1 (228 2589). Bus 2, 28. **Open** noon-6pm Mon-Sat. **Credit** AmEx, MC, V. **Map** p309 E6.
This classy retro shop stocks well-made second-hand and vintage clothes. Prices start from around £6 for tops and less than £15 for dresses, while authentic vintage items cost more. Herman Brown's eye-catching range of quirky jewellery and a good selection of bags and accessories should complete that perfect outfit.

WM Armstrong & Son

83 Grassmarket, Old Town, EH1 (220 5557/ www.armstrongsvintage.co.uk). Bus 2, 23, 27, 28, 35, 41, 42, 45. **Open** 10am-5.30pm Mon-Thur; 10am-6pm Fri, Sat; noon-6pm Sun. **Credit** MC, V. **Map** p304 C3.

The oldest second-hand shop in the capital was originally set up as a gentlemen's outfitter in 1840, but is now the city's leading retrowear chain, despite the emphasis on quantity rather than quality. New stock arrives daily and prices start from £15 for evening dresses, £10 for jeans, £15 for a leather jacket and £20 for cashmere sweaters; it also stocks kiltwear. The biggest selection is in the main Grassmarket branch, the Clerk Street branch is big on evening wear, while the Rusty Zip outlet has many half-price bargains and also offers occasional one-day sales.
Branches: 64-66 Clerk Street, South Edinburgh, EH8 (667 3056); **Rusty Zip** 14 Teviot Place, Old Town, EH1 (226 4634).

Shoes

Barnets Shoes

7 High Street, Old Town, EH1 (556 3577). Bus 35/Nicolson Street–North Bridge buses. **Open** 9am-5.15pm Mon-Fri; 9am-6pm Sat; 11am-5pm Sun. **Credit** AmEx, MC, V. **Map** p310 G5.

Small and low-key, this is an unassuming purveyor of high-quality workwear and outdoor shoes and boots at budget prices.

Carina Shoes

25 Jeffrey Street, Old Town, EH1 (558 3344). Bus 24, 35, 35A. **Open** 9.30am-5.30pm Mon-Sat. **Credit** AmEx, MC, V. **Map** p310 G5.

This intimate yet spacious shop provides a suitably plush backdrop to a range of high-class continental footwear. If you find the prices too steep, wait for the sales, when you can find real bargains among the quality brands.

Jones Bootmaker

32 George Street, New Town, EH2 (220 1029/www.jonesbootmaker.com). Bus 28, 40, 41/Princes Street buses. **Open** 9am-5.30pm Mon-Wed, Fri, Sat; 9am-7pm Thur; noon-5pm Sun. **Credit** AmEx, MC, V.

An upmarket shop, with shoes for men and women. Women's shoes include a bridal range, while Reggae, Hip and Hop are the monikers for a range of soft-leathered and thick-laced men's shoes.
Branch: Unit 6, Princes Mall, EH1 (557 0295).

Schuh

6 Frederick Street, New Town, EH2 (220 0290/ www.schuh.co.uk). Bus 13, 19A, 24, 28. **Open** 9am-6pm Mon-Wed; 9am-8pm Thur; 9am-6pm Fri, Sat; 11am-6pm Sun. **Credit** AmEx, MC, V. **Map** p304 B1.

This large central outlet of the popular Scottish chain has a fantastic range of trendy own-make and brand-name shoes, boots and trainers, including

Royal Mile Whiskies. *See p172.*

many outrageous styles. This is the place to find cheaper versions of the latest styles, or those thigh-high, spike-heeled PVC boots. Look out for the price-slashing winter and summer sales.
Branch: 32 North Bridge, Old Town, EH2 (225 6552); Ocean Terminal, Leith, EH6 (555 3766).

Florists

Clare Florist

Jenners, 48 Princes Street, New Town, EH2 (225 7145/www.clareflorist.co.uk). Princes Street buses. **Open** 9am-5.30pm Mon-Wed, Fri, Sat; 9am-7pm Thur; noon-5pm Sun. **Credit** AmEx, MC, V. **Map** p304 C2.

All the branches of this city-wide chain offer a good selection of classic blooms.
Branches: 18-20 Easter Road, Leith, EH7 (659 6596); 4 Hutchison Terrace, South Edinburgh, EH14 (538 5799).

Narcissus

63 Broughton Street, Broughton, EH1 (478 7447/ enquiries@narcissusflowers.co.uk). Bus 8, 13, 17. **Open** 9am-6pm Mon-Sat; 1-5pm Sun. **Credit** AmEx, DC, MC, V. **Map** p306 F3.

Narcissus is a small, low-key shop that sells a select range of simple but exotic blooms and plants, including impressively tall cacti. It also offers a full range of services, including international and national deliveries.

Scottish icons The kilt

No major shopping visit to Scotland is complete without getting kitted out in the national Highland dress. OK, so it was all invented by Walter Scott to impress George IV when he came to visit Edinburgh in 1822 (*see p14* **The tartaniser**), but this 19th-century interpretation of an 18th-century adaptation of traditional work clothes is actually the bee's knees. Frankly, if you're a bloke, you're better off wearing a kilt at a wedding than looking like a geek in top hat and tails – whether in the home counties or the Highlands. And as the Tartan Army of Scottish football supporters can attest, even when worn with casual clothes there's no harm in raising the question of what exactly is worn *under* the kilt. Just don't do as Robbie Williams did and accessorise with white trainers – they are a serious sartorial no-no. Samuel L Jackson was rather more suave when he became the latest celebrity to make a splash in a kilt and, of course, there's always the chance to ape Mel Gibson's *Braveheart* look – St Andrew's flag make-up optional.

Putting together the full outfit – kilt (or tartan trousers known as trews), sporran (a small pouch worn around the waist), knee-high woollen cream kilt socks, 'ghillie' brogues, jacket, shirt, kilt tie (or bow tie) and kilt pin – is best done by a professional outfitter. Many is the red face at a wedding brought about by wearing the wrong kind of shirt. Then there are the various styles of jacket, from 17th-century Jacobean to classic Prince Charlie and modern updated casual kiltwear. Getting your Highland dress 'just so' is a sartorial minefield; allow the experts to advise you on the right style for the occasion.

Of course there's also the tricky business of finding an appropriate tartan. A lack of Scottish blood in the veins shouldn't put you off. There are several tartans that anyone can wear, whether they have a clan or district tartan in their heritage or not: the Black Watch, the Hunting Stewart, the Caledonia and the Jacobite. There are even tartans created for Scottish football clubs. Some outlets have the facilities to create a completely new tartan and in the **Old Town Weaving Company** (*see p61*) you can see the cloth being made. It's not all menswear either: women can pick up kilted skirts (including minis), tartan sashes and white jabot (ruffled) shirts in the same outlets.

Clusters of highland outfitters throng the Royal Mile (not for nothing is it known as the Tartan Mile), making it easy to shop around for the best deal, with further well-respected firms in Grassmarket, Haymarket, Bruntsfield and Leith. And if the full expense of being measured up for a personally tailored outfit is a bit hard on the wallet, there's always the option to hire.

Also, don't forget the plentiful souvenir shops around the Royal Mile, which offer additional and perhaps blasphemous opportunities to accessorise or even customise your outfit with an 'authentic' *Sgian Dubh* (sheathed knife), or an 'I'm a wee monster' Nessie T-shirt.

Geoffrey (Tailor) Highland Crafts

57-59 High Street, EH1, Old Town (557 0256/ www.geoffreykilts.co.uk). Bus 35/Nicolson Street–North Bridge buses. **Open** 9am-5.30pm Mon-Wed, Fri, Sat; 9am-7pm Thur; 10am-5pm Sun. **Credit** AmEx, DC, MC, V.

Food & drink

Finding groceries or a basic bite to eat in the centre of Edinburgh, particularly in the New Town, can be awfully difficult, even for the city's residents.

Marks & Spencer food hall (*see p161*) provides the expected quality, **Jenners'** food hall (*see p161*) goes way upmarket and the **Sainsbury's** on Charlotte Square is handy for New Town office workers. **Tesco Metro** on Nicolson Street (No.94; 456 2400) and **Scotmid** in Tollcross (Leven Street; 229 7656) are also very convenient for a quick snack. For freshly

produced and largely organic food and drink, don't miss the **Farmers' market** held twice a month at Castle Terrace (*see p176*).

Delicatessens

Margiotta

77 Warrender Park Road, South Edinburgh, EH9 (229 8228). Bus 24. **Open** 7.30am-10pm Mon-Sat; 8am-10pm Sun. **Credit** MC, V. **Map** p309 F8. Although prices are generally considerably higher than you'd pay elsewhere, this well-stocked deli is very handy for those moments when you just have to have some red pesto and everywhere else is shut. **Branches**: throughout the city.

Sales, hire and tailoring of full or individual dress items, and home to Howie Nicholsby's 21st Century range of kilts (including features such as combat pockets and styles including plain and ever-trendy black). Also offers casual affordable kilts from £160, including ones in polyester viscose, for those allergic to wool. The branch is in the Old Town Weaving Company (see p61).
Branch: 555 Castlehill, Old Town, EH1 (557 0256).

Highland Laddie
6 Hutchison Terrace, South Edinburgh, EH14 (455 7505). Bus 4, 28, 35/Slateford rail. **Open** 9.30am-5pm Mon-Sat. **Credit** AmEx, MC, V.
Tartan hire for men and children with good, old-fashioned service and attention to detail. Expect to pay around £53 for a full adult outfit – including jacket, waistcoat and shoes – while a miniaturised version for kids costs from £32 to £42. The hire period runs from Thursday to Sunday.
Branch: Highlander 30-32 Haymarket Terrace, South Edinburgh, EH3 (313 2863).

Kinloch Anderson
Commercial Street/Dock Street, Leith, EH6 (555 1390/www.kinlochanderson.com). Bus 1, 16, 22, 35, 36. **Open** 9am-5.30pm Mon-Sat. **Credit** AmEx, DC, MC, V. **Map** p311 Jy.
Outfitters to the Royal Family, Kinloch Anderson is as highbrow an establishment as that connection suggests. High-quality fabrics, tailoring, service and a reputation going back to 1868, together with a canny business sense, have turned the brand into

a worldwide name. With innovations such as the Breacan, an off-the-peg kilt for casual wear at £160, it's easy to see why.

McCalls of the Royal Mile
11 High Street, Old Town, EH1 (557 3979/ freephone 0800 056 3056/www.mccalls. co.uk). Bus 35/Nicolson Street–North Bridge buses. **Open** 9am-5.30pm Mon-Wed, Fri; 9.30am-7.30pm Thur; 9am-5pm Sat; noon-4pm Sun. **Credit** AmEx, MC, V. **Map** p310 G5.
McCalls hires out Highland dress for men and boys, and has a toybox available to keep the latter amused in the shop. There's a set price of £32.50 for everything bar the socks and insurance.

Nicolson Highlandwear
189 Canongate, Old Town, EH8 (556 4763). Bus 30, 35. **Open** 9am-5.30pm Mon-Sat; noon-4pm Sun. **Credit** AmEx, DC, MC, V. **Map** p65 D1.
Tailored outfits, accessories plus an impressive selection of shoes for hire or sale, together with a specialist computerised tartan design service.

Hugh MacPherson (Scotland) Ltd
17 West Maitland Street, New Town, EH12 (225 4008). Bus 3, 4, 12, 21, 25, 26, 31. **Open** 9am-6pm Mon-Fri; 9am-1.30pm Sat. **Credit** AmEx, DC, MC, V. **Map** p308 C6.
Kiltmakers for men, women and children, with hire and sale of outfits available. MacPherson also provides outfits for pipe bands and country dancing. Weekend hire rates for adult outfits start at £45 (not including shirt), with children's outfits from £33, plus a deposit of £30.

Peckhams
155-159 Bruntsfield Place, South Edinburgh, EH10 (229 7054/www.peckhams.co.uk). Bus 10, 11, 15, 16, 17, 23. **Open** 8am-midnight Mon-Sat; 9am-midnight Sun. **Credit** MC, V. **Map** p309 D8.
This huge grocer's shop, located to the south-west of the city centre, has shelves stretching right up to the ceiling, all of which are full of tempting luxuries. Peckhams is a good one-stop shop for all manner of exotic sweet and savoury delicacies and drinks. What's more, it's also licensed to sell alcohol until midnight.
Branches: 48 Raeburn Place, Stockbridge, EH4 (332 8844); Unit 12, Waverley Rail Station, New Town, EH1 (557 9050).

Valvona & Crolla
19 Elm Row, Broughton, EH7 (556 6066/www. valvonacrolla.com). Playhouse buses. **Open** *Jan-July, Sept-Nov* 8am-6.30pm Mon-Sat. *Aug, Dec* also Sun, times vary. **Credit** AmEx, MC, V. **Map** p306 G3.
Run by the families of Valvona and Crolla since the 1930s, this long narrow Italian food shop is famed for the mouthwatering range of Mediterranean edibles that cram the shelves. In recent years it has risen to the challenge of the big supermarkets by going upmarket, concentrating on speciality goods while keeping prices at a reasonable level. Fresh mozzarella and plump Sicilian tomatoes are imported overnight from Italy, and the exotic range of spirits and liqueurs now includes the demon absinthe.

Eat your heart out, Willy Wonka: **Casey's Confectioner's**. *See p173.*

The addition of a small, much-frequented café tucked away at the back, has only enhanced this deli's reputation. *See p143.*

Drink

Better Beverage Company

204 Morrison Street, New Town, EH3 (476 2600). Bus 2, 11, 28, 34, 35. **Open** 11am-5pm Mon-Sat. **No credit cards. Map** p308 C6.
The friendly staff at this intimate outlet could turn anyone into a coffee lover; the quality range of beans will satisfy even the most discerning connoisseur.

Oddbins

223 High Street, Old Town, EH1 (220 3516/www. oddbins.com). Bus 35/Nicolson Street–North Bridge buses. **Open** 11am-9pm Mon-Thur; 9am-10pm Fri; 10am-10pm Sat; 12.30-8pm Sun. **Credit** AmEx, MC, V. **Map** p304 D3.
Best of the chain drinks retailers, Oddbins stocks a huge range of beers, wines and liqueurs. Edinburgh branches also have more whiskies than any of their English cousins, including the occasional cask-strength single malt. The sandwich boards outside give details of tastings.
Branches: throughout the city.

Peter Green & Co

37A-B Warrender Park Road, South Edinburgh, EH9 (229 5925/www.petergreenwines.com). Bus 24. **Open** 10am-6.30pm Tue-Thur, Sat; 10am-7.30pm Fri. **Credit** MC, V. **Map** p309 E8.
Green's has a diverse selection of wines and over 100 whiskies. Tastings take place on most Fridays from 4.30pm to 7.30pm.

Royal Mile Whiskies

379 High Street, Old Town, EH1 (225 3383/www. royalmilewhiskies.co.uk). Bus 35/Nicolson Street– North Bridge buses. **Open** Sept-July 10am-6pm Mon-Sat; 12.30-6pm Sun. *Aug* 10am-8pm Mon-Sat; 12.30-8pm Sun. **Credit** AmEx, MC, V. **Map** p304 C3.
A traditional façade shields a classic range of whiskies, with over 300 varieties available. The free tastings on Saturday afternoons during peak season should whet the appetite.

Scotch Malt Whisky Society

The Vaults, 87 Giles Street, Leith, EH6 (554 3451/www.smws.com). Bus 23, 27, 28, 35, 41, 42. **Open** 10am-5pm Mon-Wed; 10am-11pm Thur-Sat; 11am-10pm Sun. **Credit** AmEx, MC, V. **Map** p311 Jy.
Unique malt whiskies, bottled direct from single casks are available to members only. If you're a bit of a whisky buff, skip the commercial malts, phone for a tasting programme and join the society. The resulting pleasure more than compensates for the membership fee of £75 for the first year (which includes a bottle of whisky with full tasting notes) and £25 per year thereafter.

Scotch Whisky Heritage Centre

354 Castlehill, Old Town, EH1 (220 0441/www. whisky-heritage.co.uk). Bus 23, 27, 28, 35, 41, 42. **Open** 10am-6pm daily (licensed from 12.30pm on Sundays). **Credit** AmEx, DC, MC, V. **Map** p304 C3.
Try before you buy from the broad range of commercial whiskies at the Centre's friendly bar and gift shop. Both the shop and the bar are open to all, whether or not you've taken part in the Centre's tour (*see also p63*).

Ethnic

Lupe Pinto's Deli
24 Leven Street, South Edinburgh, EH3 (228 6241/
www.lupepintos.com). Bus 11, 15, 16, 17, 23. **Open**
10am-6pm Mon-Wed, Fri, Sat; 10am-7pm Thur;
12.30-5.30pm Sun. **Credit** MC, V. **Map** p309 D7.
Every inch of available space in this small shop is
crammed with Mexican, Spanish and Caribbean
products. If you want authentic salsa or a string of
chillies, you'll find them here. And if they're not here,
you can be sure the dedicated staff will try to order
them. The shop also has a national mail order service and is due to open a branch in Glasgow (313
Great Western Road; 0141 334 5444).

Pats Chung Ying Chinese Supermarket
199-201 Leith Walk, Leith, EH6 (554 0358).
Bus 7, 10, 12, 14, 16, 22. **Open** 10am-6pm daily.
Credit MC, V. **Map** p307 H2.
For Chinese food fans: frozen, fresh and packaged
goods in a vast, modern shop.

Fruit & veg

Argyle Place
Marchmont, South Edinburgh, EH9 (no phone).
Bus 24, 41. **Open** hours vary. **Credit** varies.
Map p309 F8.
A busy strip of fruit and veg shops on the south side
of the city, where locals go for cheap produce.

Health food & vegetarian

Holland & Barrett
18 Nicolson Street, South Edinburgh, EH8
(667 6002/www.hollandandbarrett.com). Nicolson
Street–North Bridge buses. **Open** 9am-5.30pm
Mon-Sat. **Credit** MC, V. **Map** p310 G6.
Basic vegetarian and vegan supplies, health sup-
plements and healthy snacks.

Nature's Gate
83 Clerk Street, South Edinburgh, EH8 (668 2067).
Nicolson Street–North Bridge buses. **Open** 10am-
7pm Mon, Wed-Fri; 10am-6pm Tue, Sat; noon-5pm
Sun. **Credit** MC, V. **Map** p310 G7.
A surprisingly wide range of vegetarian and vegan
foods, both pre-packed and fresh, fill this small,
wooden-shelved shop. There's also an impressive
selection of organic wines and beers.

Real Foods
37 Broughton Street, Broughton, EH1 (557 1911/
www.realfoods.co.uk). Bus 8, 13, 17. **Open** 9am-7pm
Mon-Wed, Fri; 9am-8.30pm Thur; 9am-6.30pm Sat;
10am-6pm Sun. **Credit** MC, V. **Map** p306 F3.
A veritable one-stop supermarket for the vegetarian,
vegan and organic enthusiast, even if the prices are
not always low.
Branch: 8 Brougham Place, South Edinburgh,
EH3 (228 1201).

Late-night grocers

Alldays
91-93 Nicolson Street, South Edinburgh, EH8
(667 7481). Nicolson Street–North Bridge buses.
Open 24hrs daily. **Credit** MC, V. **Map** p310 G6.
Late-night munchies can be satisfied here with a
wide range of food and drink mainstays and treats.
Branches: throughout the city.

Costcutter
125 Lothian Road, South Edinburgh, EH3 (622
7191/www.costcutter.co.uk). Bus 1, 10, 11, 15, 16,
17, 22, 24. **Open** 24hrs daily. **Credit** MC, V.
Map p304 A3.
A basic range of grocery and household supplies.
Branches: throughout the city.

Sainsbury's
185 Craigleith Road, Blackhall, EH4 (332 0704/
www.sainsburys.co.uk). Bus 24, 38, 41, 42. **Open**
7am-midnight Mon-Fri; 7am-10pm Sat; 8am-8pm
Sun. **Credit** AmEx, MC, V.
This branch of Sainsbury's supermarket, by the
junction of Queensferry Road west beyond
Stockbridge, has an extensive range of quality produce and household supplies. Other facilities include
a coffee shop, three ATMs, Supasnaps, Sketchley
dry cleaners, free parking and assistance for people
with mobility difficulties.
Branches: Sainsbury's Central 9-10 St Andrew's
Square, New Town, EH2 (225 8400); Moray Park,
London Road, Abbeyhill, EH7 (656 9377);
Savacentre Cameron Toll, South Edinburgh,
EH16 (666 5200).

Specialist

Caseys Confectioners
52 St Mary's Street, Old Town, EH1 (556 6082).
Bus 35/Nicolson Street–North Bridge buses.
Open 9am-5.30pm Mon-Fri; 9.30am-5.30pm Sat.
No credit cards. Map p310 G5.
Only the prices have changed in this old-fashioned
sweet shop since it first opened in 1954. It still has
a picture-postcard, art deco exterior, while the interior is packed with row upon row of colourfully filled
jars of mouthwatering sweets, all of which are hand-
made on the premises.
Branch: 28 East Norton Place, Abbeyhill,
EH7 (no phone).

Crombies of Edinburgh
97-101 Broughton Street, Broughton, EH1
(557 0111/www.sausages.co.uk). Bus 8, 13, 17.
Open 8am-6pm Mon-Fri; 8am-5pm Sat. **Credit**
MC, V. **Map** p306 F3.
Top-quality meats from local farms are sold here,
but it's the extensive and inventive range of pies and
sausages that get the queues stretching out of the
door. Try one of Crombies' venison, wild boar and
apple sausage in your Sunday fry-up and you'll soon
know why.

Eat, Drink, Shop

The Fudge House

*197 Canongate, Old Town, EH1 (556 4172/www.
fudgehouse.co.uk). Bus 30, 35.* **Open** 10am-6pm
Mon-Sat; noon-5pm Sun. **Credit** AmEx, MC, V.
Map p310 H5.

Blocks of fudge are sold by weight in 24 delicious
flavours, including Highland cream, pecan and
chocolate swirl, and Italian nougat. It's difficult not
to be tempted by the smell as you walk past – the
fudge is made on the premises, and there are demon-
strations and tastings throughout the day.

Iain Mellis Cheesemonger

*30A Victoria Street, Old Town, EH1 (226 6215/
www.ijmellischeesemonger.com). Bus 23, 27, 28, 41,
42.* **Open** 10am-6pm Mon-Fri; 9.30am-6pm Sat;
11am-4pm Sun. **Credit** MC, V. **Map** p304 C3.

Only the most olfactorily challenged of passers-by
could miss the pungent odour from this small,
galley-shaped cheesemonger, situated just a step
away from the Royal Mile. Organic food and vegetables are also sold. Try a slice of gubbeen.
Branches: 6 Bakers Place, Stockbridge, EH3 (225
6566); 205 Bruntsfield Place, South Edinburgh, EH10
(447 8889).

MacSweens of Edinburgh

*Dryden Road, Loanhead, EH20 (440 2555/www.
macsween.co.uk). Bus 37.* **Open** 8.30am-5pm Mon-
Fri. **Credit** MC, V.

So dedicated are the MacSweens to their haggis that
every single batch is tasted by one of the family.
Vegetarian haggis is also available. MacSweens'
haggis is also stocked in Peckhams (*see p171*) and
Jenners (*see p161*).

Mr Boni's

*4 Lochrin Buildings, Tollcross, South Edinburgh,
EH3 (229 5319/www.mrbonis-icecream.co.uk). Bus
11, 15, 16, 17, 23, 45.* **Open** 12.30-10pm Mon-Fri;
10.30am-10pm Sat; 12.30-9pm Sun. **Credit** MC, V.
Map p309 D7.

This family-run ice-cream institution opened 75
years ago and Mr Boni, the grandson of the founder,
is still dreaming up new recipes to add to the rota of
300 imaginative flavours. Every single one is made
from fresh, natural ingredients. Pooh Bear Crunch
is a bestseller.

Health & beauty

Beauty products & cosmetics

Jo Malone

*93 George Street, New Town, EH2 (478 8555/
www.jomalone.co.uk). Bus 28, 40, 41/Princes Street
buses.* **Open** 10am-6pm Mon-Wed, Fri, Sat; 10am-
7pm Thur. **Credit** AmEx, MC, V.

Highly coveted (and expensive) toiletries and per-
fumes. Fragrances are gorgeous and the skin care
range (including the delectable orange and geranium
night cream) should not be overlooked.

Lush

*44 Princes Street, New Town, EH2 (557 3177/www.
lush.co.uk). Princes Street buses.* **Open** 9.30am-6pm
Mon-Wed, Fri, Sat; 9.30am-7pm Thur; noon-5pm Sun.
Credit AmEx, MC, V. **Map** p304 D1.

Fresh ingredients are the name of the game here.
Decked out to look more like a deli than a cosmetics
store, Lush sells its soaps in wedges, sliced at the
counter like lumps of cheese.

Neal's Yard Remedies

*46A George Street, New Town, EH2 (226 3223/
www.nealsyardremedies.com). Bus 28, 40, 41/Princes
Street buses.* **Open** 10am-6pm Mon-Wed, Fri, Sat;
10am-7pm Thur; times vary Sun (phone for details).
Credit MC, V. **Map** p304 C1.

These fab-smelling alternative lotions and potions
showcase the benefits of various herbs and oils.
Book in at the treatment room if you'd prefer someone else to pamper you. This branch is closing in
September 2002, but a new shop is due to open at
102 Hanover Street, EH2 and the same phone number will be in operation.

Space NK

*97-103 George Street, New Town, EH2 (225 6371/
www.spacenk.co.uk). Bus 28, 40, 41/Princes Street
buses.* **Open** 10am-6pm Mon-Wed, Fri; 10am-7.30pm
Thur; 9am-6pm Sat; noon-5pm Sun. **Credit** AmEx,
MC, V. **Map** p304 B1.

Upmarket purveyor of smelly stuff. The staff are
perfectly turned out, the decor is minimalist and the
pongs are dearer than vintage champagne. Don't
you just love it?

Hairdressers

Cheynes

*46 George Street, New Town, EH2 (220 0777/
www.cheynes.com). Bus 28, 40, 41/Princes Street
buses.* **Open** 9am-5.15pm Mon-Wed, Fri; 9am-
7.30pm Thur; 9am-4.30pm Sat. **Credit** MC, V.
Map p304 C1.

Popular Edinburgh chain of hairdressers for men
and women, well-known for quality hair cuts, perms
and colouring. Prices start from £21.50 for a wash
and cut. Appointments necessary.
Branches: 57 South Bridge, Old Town, EH1 (556
0108); 45A York Place, New Town, EH1 (558 1010);
77 Lothian Road, South Edinburgh, EH3 (228 9977);
3 Drumsheugh Place, Queensferry Street, New Town,
EH3 (225 2234).

Patersons SA

*129 Lothian Road, South Edinburgh, EH3 (228
5252). Bus 10, 11, 15, 16, 17, 22, 24.* **Open** 9am-
6pm Mon-Wed, Fri; 10.30am-7.30pm Thur; 9am-
4.30pm Sat. **Credit** AmEx, MC, V. **Map** p304 A3.

Bright, comfortable and gay-friendly hairdresser's.
It has become so popular that it had to open up
another branch in the New Town. Prices range from
£15 to £30 for a wash and cut.
Branches: 60 George Street, New Town, EH2
(226 3121); 134 High Street, Dalkeith (660 5733).

Say cheese! **Iain Mellis Cheesemongers**. *See p174.*

Woods the Barbers

*12 Drummond Street, South Edinburgh, EH8
(556 6716). Nicolson Street–North Bridge buses.*
Open 8.30am-5pm Mon, Tue, Thur, Fri; 9am-1pm
Wed; 8.30am-4pm Sat. **No credit cards.**
Map p310 G6.
A classic barber that's great for a quick cut. Prices
start at a reasonable £5 for a short back and sides.

Pharmacies

Boots

*101-103 Princes Street, New Town, EH2 (225 8331/
www.wellbeing.com). Princes Street buses.* **Open**
9am-6pm Mon-Wed, Fri, Sat; 9am-7.30pm Thur;
noon-5pm Sun. **Credit** MC, V. **Map** p304 B2.
This is Edinburgh's largest branch of the reliable
health, toiletries and cosmetics supplies favourite.
Branches: throughout the city.

Napiers Dispensary

*1 Teviot Place, Old Town, EH1 (225 5542/www.
napiers.net). Bus 2, 23, 27, 28, 41, 42.* **Open** 10am-
6pm Mon; 9am-6pm Tue-Fri; 9am-5.30pm Sat; 12.30-
4.30pm Sun. **Credit** MC, V. **Map** p309 F6.
An historic dispensary dating back to 1860. Today
it is a medical herbalist's, stocking homeopathic
medicines, organic and ecological cosmetics and toiletries, plus essential oils, vitamins, herbal teas and
Bach flower remedies. The clinic next door offers
alternative body treatments, including acupuncture,
homeopathia, psychotherapy and osteopathy.
Branches: **Napiers Clinic** 18 Bristo Place,
Old Town, EH1 (225 5542); 35 Hamilton Place,
Stockbridge, EH3 (315 2130).

Treatments & therapies

The Edinburgh Floatarium

*29 North West Circus Place, New Town, EH3 (225
3350/www.edinburghfloatarium.co.uk). Bus 13, 19A,
24, 28.* **Open** 9am-8pm Mon-Fri; 9am-6pm Sat;
9.30am-4pm Sun. **Credit** MC, V. **Map** p306 D4.
The sea salt floats are the main attraction here –
bliss out in a flotation tank for just £25 – but there's
also beauty and health treatments and a shop selling New Age books, crystals and gifts.

The Whole Works

*Jacksons Close, 209 Royal Mile, Old Town, EH1
(225 8092/www.wholeworks.co.uk). Bus 35/Nicolson
Street–North Bridge buses.* **Open** 9am-8pm Mon-Fri;
9am-5pm Sat. **No credit cards. Map** p64 C1.
Acupuncture, aromatherapy, dreamwork, chiro-
practice, reiki and shiatsu are just some of the
treatments on offer at this alternative therapy centre.

Household

For cooking equipment and other household
goodies, also try **Studio One** (*see p181*).

Habitat

*32 Shandwick Place, New Town, EH2 (225 9151/
www.habitat.net). Bus 3, 4, 12, 21, 25, 26, 31, 33,
44.* **Open** 9am-5.30pm Mon-Wed, Fri; 9am-7pm
Thur; 9am-6pm Sat; 11.30am-5.30pm Sun. **Credit**
AmEx, DC, MC, V. **Map** p308 C5.
Popular household chain store with affordable,
attractive furnishings and furniture on three laid-
back, roomy floors at the west end of Princes Street.

Eat, Drink, Shop

Avalanche: indie mecca. *See p177.*

Halibut & Herring
89 Westbow, Old Town, EH1 (226 7472). Bus 23, 27, 28, 35, 41, 42. **Open** 10am-6pm Mon-Sat; 11am-5pm Sun. **Credit** MC, V. **Map** p304 C3.
Clockwork diving submarines, op-art see-through shower curtains and a colourful range of soaps and ceramics made in a workshop in Musselburgh have established this small chain of shops as a firm local favourite for quirky bathroom treats.
Branches: 31 Raeburn Place, Stockbridge, EH4 (332 5687); 108 Bruntsfield Place, South Edinburgh, EH10 (229 2669).

IKEA
Straiton Road, Loanhead, South Edinburgh, EH20 (448 0500/www.ikea.co.uk). Bus 37. **Open** 10am-10pm Mon-Fri; 10am-7pm Sat; 10am-6pm Sun. **Credit** MC, V.
The long-awaited Scottish branch of the phenomenally successful Swedish chain has proved to be just as popular as all the others. Sleek, modern furnishings for every part of the home are laid out on two massive floors, but be prepared for the no-frills, do-it-yourself service and long queues that go with the exceptionally low prices.

Inhouse
28 Howe Street, New Town, EH3 (225 2888/www.inhousenet.co.uk). Bus 18, 19A, 24, 28. **Open** *Sept-July* 9.30am-6pm Mon-Wed, Fri; 10am-7pm Thur; 9.30am-5.30pm Sat. *Aug* also noon-5pm Sun. **Credit** MC, V. **Map** p306 D4.

Two floors of designer names such as Alessi, plus high-street brands, with delightful trinkets to catch the eye at every turn. Upstairs is mainly larger furniture; downstairs is the real Santa's grotto, ideal for practical but unusual household furnishings and accessories.

James Gray & Son
89 George Street, New Town, EH2 (225 7381). Bus 28, 40, 41/Princes Street buses. **Open** 9am-5.30pm Mon-Sat. *Dec* also 11am-5pm Sun. **Credit** AmEx, MC, V. **Map** p304 B1.
Traditional city-centre ironmonger's and hardware shop with an extensive range of quality goods for the home and garden, although not exactly the cheapest around.

Lakeland
52 George Street, New Town, EH2 (220 3947/www.lakeland.co.uk). Bus 28, 40, 41/Princes Street buses. **Open** 9am-5.30pm Mon-Sat. **Credit** MC, V. **Map** p304 B1.
Two floors housing every kitchen accessory you could ever need, plus many more eccentric inventions you never even knew existed.

Laundry & repairs

Canonmills Launderette
7-8 Huntly Street, Brandon Terrace, New Town, EH3 (556 3199). Bus 23, 27, 36. **Open** 8am-8pm Mon-Fri; 8am-5pm Sat; 9pm-5pm Sun. **Credit** MC, V. **Map** p306 G2.
Same-day dry-cleaning service for items that arrive before noon. Prices range from £4.25 to £6.50 per item, while a wash costs £3.

Kleen Cleaners
10 St Mary's Street, Old Town, EH1 (556 4337). Bus 35/Nicolson Street–North Bridge buses. **Open** 8.30am-6pm Mon-Fri; 10am-1pm Sat. **No credit cards. Map** p310 G5.
Dry cleaning, plus speedy repairs and alterations.

Markets

Farmers' market
Castle Terrace, South Edinburgh, EH1 (no phone). Bus 23, 27, 28, 35, 41, 42. **Open** 9am-2pm 1st & 3rd Sat of the month. **Credit** varies. **Map** p304 A2/3.
The markets attract over 40 specialist producers, most of whom sell produce they have grown themselves. There's plenty of meat, with an emphasis on organic produce, plus fish (and lobster in season), free-range eggs (including quail and duck eggs), cheeses and seasonal vegetables and fruit. Some home producers also take part in the market, providing liqueurs, bread and chutneys.

Greenside Place Car Boot Sale
Level 2 in car park off Leith Street, Broughton, EH1 (no phone). Playhouse or Princes Street buses. **Open** 10am-2pm Sun. **No credit cards. Map** p307 G4.

With room for up to 200 stalls, this car boot sale, run by a mixture of professional traders and ordinary folk clearing out their attics, is a mecca for bargain hunters. The kind of place you might just find an antique vase worth thousands among the bric-a-brac, antiques and junk on offer for £1. Haggling is acceptable, although by no means always expected. The car boot sale is not dangerous, but, as in any other crowded place, keep your valuables close at hand.

Ingliston Market

Off Glasgow Road (A8), West Edinburgh, past Edinburgh Airport (no phone). Scottish Citylink service 900/902 to Glasgow. **Open** 10am-4pm Sun. **Credit** varies.

Around 100 traders sell mostly clothes, household and electrical goods and hippie paraphernalia in an outdoor field. There's a car boot sale alongside with anything from 20 to 200 cars (depending on the weather). If you want a cheap fleece, novelty clock or lighter, then this place will offer the best prices. Just make sure you check the quality first.

New Street Indoor Sunday Market

Waverley Car Park, New Street, Old Town, EH8 (no phone). Bus 30, 35. **Open** 10am-4pm Sun. **No credit cards**. **Map** p310 G5.

There are usually more traders than cars at this general market, unless Greenside (*see p176*) is full (around Christmas), when the spillover to New Street can make Sunday morning bargain hunting something of a marathon.

Mobile phones

Carphone Warehouse

25 Princes Street, New Town, EH2 (08707 204 026/www.carphonewarehouse.com). Princes Street buses. **Open** 9am-6pm Mon-Wed, Fri, Sat; 9am-7pm Thur; 11am-5pm Sun. **Credit** AmEx, DC, MC, V. **Map** p304 D2.

Carphone Warehouse offers a vast, well-priced selection of mobile phones and pagers. **Branches**: throughout the city.

Music

CDs & records

Avalanche

17 West Nicolson Street, South Edinburgh, EH8 (668 2374/www.avalancherecords.co.uk). Nicolson Street–North Bridge buses. **Open** 9.30am-6pm Mon-Sat; noon-6pm Sun. **Credit** MC, V. **Map** p310 G6.

The original branch of Kevin Buckle's record shop opened here in 1983 and is now a Scottish indie institution and a respected mini-chain, with an eclectic budget range of new and second-hand vinyl and CDs across its branches. Especially good for more obscure finds.

Branches: 28 Lady Lawson Street, South Edinburgh, EH3 (668 2374); 63 Cockburn Street, Old Town, EH1 (225 3939); 2-3 Teviot Place, EH8 (226 7666).

Backbeat

31 East Crosscauseway, South Edinburgh, EH8 (668 2666/freewheelrecords@hotmail.com). Nicolson Street–North Bridge buses. **Open** 10am-5.30pm Mon-Sat; 12.30-6.30pm Sun. **Credit** AmEx, DC, MC, V. **Map** p310 G7.

Collectors of rare vinyl and obscure CD re-issues will feel they've stumbled into aural heaven here. Frequent trips abroad by the owner ensure that there is always a huge selection of quality jazz, soul, blues, rock and pop – with 1960s and '70s sounds a speciality. Prices are pretty reasonable.

FOPP

55 Cockburn Street, Old Town, EH1 (220 0133/www.fopp.co.uk). Bus 35/Nicolson Street–North Bridge buses. **Open** 9.30am-7pm Mon-Sat; 11am-6pm Sun. **Credit** AmEx, DC, MC, V. **Map** p304 D3.

Scotland's largest independent record and CD retailer regularly sells chart releases at prices which are markedly less than the big high-street chains. This sleekly designed, modern shop is a regular stop-off for indie and dance fans, but also excellent for jazz, soul, ska and world music sounds, with two floors of stock and an apparently never-ending series of sales and special offers guaranteeing a bargain.

HMV

129-130 Princes Street, New Town, EH2 (225 7008/www.hmv.co.uk). Princes Street buses. **Open** 9am-6pm Mon-Wed, Fri, Sat; 9am-8pm Thur; 11am-6pm Sun. **Credit** AmEx, DC, MC, V. **Map** p304 A2.

A mammoth music shop, with CDs, books, T-shirts and DVDs – and now more vinyl than ever before, especially in the dance and hip hop section.
Branch: 43-44 St James Centre, New Town, EH1 (556 1236).

McAlister Matheson Music

1 Grindlay Street, South Edinburgh, EH3 (228 3827/www.mmmusic.co.uk). Bus 2, 10, 11, 15, 16, 17, 22, 24. **Open** 9.30am-7pm Mon-Wed; 9.30am-7.30pm Thur, Fri; 9am-5.30pm Sat; 1-5pm Sun. **Credit** AmEx, DC, MC, V. **Map** p308 D6.

A quiet haven for classical music and opera CDs just round the corner from the Usher Hall and down the hill from the Hub. Helpful staff and the fact that the stock reflects what's coming up in local performances and during the Festival make this a must visit. Also stocks a range of Scottish music and runs an efficient mail order service.

Ripping Music & Tickets

91 South Bridge, Old Town, EH1 (226 7010/www.rippingrecords.com). Nicolson Street–North Bridge buses. **Open** 9.30am-6.30pm Mon-Wed, Fri; 9am-7pm Thur; 9am-6pm Sat; noon-5.30pm Sun. **Credit** MC, V. **Map** p304 D3.

Rock, pop, dance and indie CDs are all here, but Ripping Tickets is best known as the place to buy advance tickets (booking fee, 50p per ticket) for rock and pop gigs in Edinburgh, Glasgow and sometimes beyond. Browse the window display to see what's coming up.

Uber-Disko

36 Cockburn Street, Old Town, EH1 (226 2134).
Bus 35/Nicolson Street–North Bridge buses.
Open 10am-6pm Mon-Sat; noon-5pm Sun.
Credit AmEx, MC, V. **Map** p304 D3.
Small, sparse and sometimes intimidating, Uber-Disko is nonetheless a well-respected name for house and techno sounds .

Underground Solushn

9 Cockburn Street, Old Town, EH1 (226 2242/
www.undergroundsolushn.com). Bus 30,35. **Open**
10am-6pm Mon-Wed, Sat; 10am-7pm Thur, Fri; 1-5pm Sun. **Credit** AmEx, MC, V. **Map** p304 D3.
Unbeatable for vinyl dance imports, with a huge choice of house, garage, techno and jungle sounds. The staff are happy to answer your questions, play requests and give insider tips for a top night of clubbing in the city.

Virgin Megastore

124-125 Princes Street, New Town, EH2 (220
2230/edinburgh.virgin@virgin.net). Princes Street
buses. **Open** 9am-6pm Mon-Wed, Fri, Sat; 9am-8pm
Thur; 11am-6pm Sun. **Credit** AmEx, MC, V.
Map p304 A2.

Three floors of CDs, videos, DVDs and computer games slap bang in the centre of town. It's the largest, most expensive selection in the city. Virgin also sells tickets for rock and pop gigs.

Instruments & sheet music

Bagpipes Galore

82 Canongate, Old Town, EH8 (556 4073/
www.bagpipe.co.uk). Bus 30, 35. **Open** *Sept-May*
9.30am-5.30pm Mon-Sat. *June-Aug* 9.30am-5.30pm
Mon-Sat; 10am-4pm Sun. **Credit** AmEx, MC, V.
Map p310 G5.
A huge range of new and second-hand pipes, ranging from plain models for £570 up to lavish ivory bagpipes. The starter tutor kit is good value, with a chanter, book and CD for £28. Those who feel a bit more adventurous can try the practice pipes at £97. Accessories include reeds and pipe bags.

Mev Taylor's

212 Morrison Street, West Edinburgh, EH3 (229
7454/www.mevtaylors.co.uk). Bus 1, 2, 28, 34, 35.
Open 9.30am-5.30pm Mon-Sat. **Credit** AmEx, MC,
V. **Map** p308 C6.
As well as being Scotland's saxophone centre, this well-known shop has a large range of fiddles and ceilidh-size accordions, plus folk sheet music.

Rae MacIntosh

6 Queensferry Street, New Town, EH2 (225 1171).
Bus 19, 29, 36, 41, 42. **Open** 9am-5.30pm Mon-Fri;
9am-5pm Sat. **Credit** AmEx, MC, V. **Map** p308 C5.
Well-priced chanters, bodhráns and penny whistles line the walls of this invitingly cosy shop. The main attraction, however, is the large stock of sheet music, spanning sounds from obscure reels to the work of modern folk heroes such as Aly Bain. The approachable staff will be happy to help you find a certain piece, even if you can only hum a few bars of it.

Varsity Music

8A-10A Nicolson Street, South Edinburgh,
EH8 (0800 614151/www.varsitymusic.co.uk).
Nicolson Street–North Bridge buses. **Open** 9am-5.30pm Mon-Sat. **Credit** AmEx, DC, MC, V.
Map p310 G6.
Well-priced instruments, from pianos and guitars to maracas and accordions, plus a solid range of music books. This is also the best place in Edinburgh to buy a new stylus for your decks.

Newspapers & magazines

International Newsagents

351 High Street, Old Town, EH1 (225 4827). Bus
35/Nicolson Street–North Bridge buses. **Open** *Sept-July* 6am-6.30pm Mon-Fri; 7am-6.30pm Sat; 7.30am-6pm Sun. *Aug* 6am-midnight Mon-Fri; 6am-1am Sat, Sun. **Credit** MC, V. **Map** p304 C3.
French, Spanish, German and American daily newspapers, in addition to an extensive range of European magazines.

Plaid: 'Helmets are in, you know'. *See p180.*

New Age delicacies at **Helios Fountain**. *See p181.*

Opticians

Dollond & Aitchison
*65 St James Centre, New Town, EH1 (558 1149/
www.dolland.co.uk). Princes Street or Nicolson
Street–North Bridge buses.* **Open** 9am-6pm Mon-
Wed, Fri, Sat; 9am-8pm Thur. **Credit** AmEx, MC, V.
Map p307 G4.
Wide range of quality frames and same-day repairs.
Eye tests also available by appointment.
Branches: 56 Newington Road, South Edinburgh,
EH9 (667 6442); 61 London Road, Greenside, EH7
(652 0806); Cameron Toll, South Edinburgh, EH16
(664 2545).

Vision Express
*Units 12-14, St James Centre, New Town, EH1 (556
5656/www.visionexpress.co.uk). Princes Street or
Nicolson Street–North Bridge buses.* **Open** 9am-
5.30pm Mon-Wed, Fri, Sat; 9am-7pm Thur; noon-5pm
Sun. **Credit** AmEx, MC, V. **Map** p307 G4.
Huge selection of spectacles, most ready within an
hour. Prices from £48 for single-vision lenses.
Branch: Gyle Centre, West Edinburgh,
EH12 (339 0176).

Photo-processing

There are numerous branches of photo-
processing shops such as SupaSnaps around
the city, but pharmacies (*see p175*) are usually
cheaper and offer all the same services,
including one-hour processing (note, though,
that this service normally carries a premium).

Jessops
*27 Shandwick Place, New Town, EH2 (229 9854/
www.jessops.co.uk). Bus 3, 4, 12, 21, 25, 26, 31, 33.*
Open 9am-5.30pm Mon-Sat; noon-4pm Sun. **Credit**
AmEx, MC, V. **Map** p308 C5.
More than a film developing service, this national
chain sells most of the quality brands of cameras
and own-brand accessories, as well as stocking
home-developing equipment and a small selection
of second-hand cameras. The knowledgeable staff
can advise on most photographic queries.
Branch: Unit 35D, Fort Kinnaird, South Edinburgh,
EH15 (657 9260).

Souvenirs

The **Royal Mile** is the place to head for
souvenirs, whether you're after quality or
kitsch (and there's plenty of the latter – a 'see-
you-Jimmy' bonnet perhaps?). **Princes Street**
also has plenty of gift shops selling tartan
teatowels and other touristy items, but overall
you'll find better bargains, not to mention more
tasteless gifts, on the Royal Mile. In the summer
months the shops at the top of the Mile stay
open late – basically until they've run out of
tourists to serve.

If you're looking for a more serious,
quintessentially Scottish souvenir, try one of
the shops listed elsewhere in this chapter: for
kilt tailoring, *see p170* **Scottish icons: The
kilt**; for whisky, *see p172*. Other gifts ideas are
listed under **Stationery & gifts**, *see p180*.

Plaid
328 Lawnmarket, Old Town, EH1 (225 4152).
Bus 23, 27, 28, 35, 41, 42. **Open** 9am-8pm daily.
Credit AmEx, DC, MC, V. **Map** p304 C3.
If you can make it in tartan, you'll find it here.

Royal Mile Sepia
*116 Canongate, Old Town, EH8 (557 8945/royal
milesepia@talk21.com). Bus 30, 35.* **Open** 10am-
6pm daily. **Credit** AmEx, MC, V. **Map** p310 G2.
Great for the 'been there, done that, taken the picture'
tourist. Don 18th-century Highland costumes, have
your picture taken and collect a dozen prints.

The Scotland Shop
*18-20 High Street, Old Town, EH1 (557 2030). Bus
35/Nicolson Street–North Bridge buses.* **Open** 10am-
6pm Mon-Sat; 11am-6pm Sun. **Credit** AmEx, MC. V.
Map p310 G5.
Fearsome Braveheart-styled swords, cutlasses and
equally scary tartan porcelain dolls bedeck the window of the Scotland Shop. But the neat interior also
contains a wide range of reasonably priced and
rather more low-key Scottish paraphernalia.

The Tartan Gift Shop
*54 High Street, Old Town, EH1 (558 3187). Bus 35/
Nicolson Street–North Bridge buses.* **Open** 9am-5pm
Mon-Sat; 11am-4.30pm Sun. **Credit** MC, V.
Map p310 G5.
A small, traditional shop aimed mainly at men, with
a large stock of kiltwear accessories, golf balls,
engraved hip flasks and ornamental knives. Also
good for cheaper, quality tartan rugs and tartan
household accessories.

Whigmaleeries Ltd
*334 Lawnmarket, Old Town, EH1 (225 4152). Bus
23, 27, 28, 35, 41, 42.* **Open** 10am-7pm daily.
Credit AmEx, DC, MC, V. **Map** p304 C3.
Reproduction weapons, jewellery and a family history research service in elegant surroundings.

White Dove
*140 High Street, Old Town, EH1 (220 1566/
www.white-dove.co.uk). Bus 35/Nicolson Street–North
Bridge buses.* **Open** 9.30am-6pm daily. **Credit**
AmEx, MC, V. **Map** p304 D2.
A fine range of tacky novelties in the back (past the
wizard and troll fantasy figures). *The* place to come
for the obligatory whisky-flavoured condoms.

Sport & outdoor

Blacks Outdoor Leisure
*13-14 Elm Row, Broughton, EH7 (556 3491/
www.blacks.co.uk). Bus 7, 12, 17.* **Open** 9am-5.30pm
Mon-Sat; noon-4pm Sun. **Credit** AmEx, MC, V.
Map p306 G3.
Quality rucksacks, clothes and equipment for hik-
ers, skiers and ramblers, housed over two floors.
The tent department is especially good.
Branch: 24 Frederick Street, New Town,
EH2 (225 8686).

Millets
*12 Frederick Street, New Town, EH2 (220 1551/
www.millets.co.uk). Bus 19, 24, 28, 29, 30, 37.*
Open 9am-5.30pm Mon-Wed, Fri, Sat; 9am-6.30pm
Thur; 11.30am-5pm Sun. **Credit** AmEx, MC, V.
Map p304 B1.
City centre outlet with a near-unbeatable range of
budget-priced outdoor basics, from waterproof jackets to tents and rucksacks.

Tiso
*123-125 Rose Street, New Town, EH2 (225 9486/
www.tiso.co.uk). Princes Street buses.* **Open** 9.30am-
5.30pm Mon, Wed, Fri, Sat; 10am-5.30pm Tue;
9.30am-7.30pm Thur; noon-5pm Sun. **Credit** AmEx,
MC, V. **Map** p304 B1.
Pretty much *the* department store for the outdoor
type: the four floors of Tiso are packed with all manner of sports and survival equipment, clothes and
accessories. It's popular outlet for pros and begin-
ners, with knowledgeable staff who'll find you what
you really need.
Branch: 41 Commercial Street, Leith,
EH6 (554 0804).

Stationery & gifts

Aitken Dott & Son/Miller Graphics
*36 North Bridge, Old Town, EH1 (225 1006/www.
millers-graphics.co.uk). Nicolson Street–North Bridge
buses.* **Open** 9am-5.30pm Mon-Sat. **Credit** AmEx,
MC, V. **Map** p304 D2.
A centrally located professional stationery suppli-
ers split into two parts. The basement specialises
in paper and card of all shades, sizes and weights,
as well as printing and photocopying facilities.
Upstairs is a wide selection of paints, pens, gift cards
and stationery.

Crystal Clear
*52 Cockburn Street, Old Town, EH1 (226 7888).
Bus 7, 8, 21, 31, 80.* **Open** 10am-6pm Mon-Wed,
Fri, Sat; 10am-7pm Thur; noon-5pm Sun. **Credit** MC,
V. **Map** p304 D3.
Crystal Clear is a tiny but atmospheric Old Town
shop packed with self-help, spiritual and occult
books, plus crystals, Buddhist singing bowls, wind
chimes and relaxation tapes. Owner Thom
McCarthy is often around to offer friendly and
knowledgeable advice.
Branches: **Wildwood Books** 16 High Street, Old
Town, EH1 (557 4888); **Golden** 109 High Street,
Old Town, EH1 (624 3777).

Digger
*35 West Nicolson Street, South Edinburgh, EH8
(668 1802). Bus 35/Nicolson Street–North Bridge
buses.* **Open** 9am-6pm Mon-Fri; 10am-6pm Sat.
Credit AmEx, MC, V. **Map** p310 G6.
A small, colourful shop brimming over with well-
priced crafts including the likes of wind chimes,
wooden Indian carvings and mirrors, Digger also
stocks plenty of amusing and pretty pocket-money
gift ideas.

He's friendly really: **Bill's Tattoo Studio**.

Squeeze through the inevitable hordes of teenagers flipping through the posters to find a great range of postcards, featuring everything from the Simpsons to saucy 3D winking ladies.

Studio One
10-16 Stafford Street, New Town, EH3 (226 5812). Bus 3, 4, 12, 21, 25, 26, 31, 33. **Open** 9.30am-6pm Mon-Wed, Fri; 9.30am-7pm Thur; 9.30am-5.30pm Sat; noon-5pm Sun. **Credit** MC, V. **Map** p308 C5.
Studio One is a popular basement shop filled with ethnic and trendy gifts and household furnishings. The children's nook is good for pocket-money curiosities and novelties, while the Morningside Road branch has a good range of quality kitchen utensils and crockery.
Branch: Studio One Cookshop 71 Morningside Road, South Edinburgh, EH10 (447 0452).

Tattoos & body piercing

Bill's Tattoo Studio
73 Elm Row, Broughton, EH7 (556 5954). Playhouse buses. **Open** 8.30am-5pm Mon, Tue, Thur, Fri; 7.30am-5pm Sat. **No credit cards. Map** p306 G3.
This is a traditional tattoo and piercing parlour. Bill might appear a bit abrasive at first, but relax: he won't let you walk out with anything you'll regret later. Prices start from £20 for a basic tattoo.

Tribe Body Manipulations
47 West Nicolson Street, South Edinburgh, EH6 (622 7220/www.tattoos.tribe.co.uk). Nicolson Street–North Bridge buses. **Open** noon-6pm Tue-Sat. **No credit cards. Map** p310 G5.
Alternative tattoos and piercing of any body parts you care to think of are available in this small, friendly shop that also stocks a wide range of original body jewellery. Tattoos cost from £20 and appointments are necessary.

Toys & games

Aha Ha Ha
99 West Bow, Old Town, EH1 (220 5252). Bus 23, 27, 28, 41, 42, 45. **Open** *Jan-July, Sept-Nov* 10am-6pm Mon-Sat. *Aug, Dec* also noon-4pm Sun. **Credit** AmEx, MC, V. **Map** p304 C3.
The oversized Groucho moustache and glasses over the front door are only the tip of the chuckles to be found in this cheap and infinitely cheerful shop. Jokes, novelties, disguises and trashy wigs fill the jolly interior.

Balloon & Party Shop
3 Viewforth Gardens, off Bruntsfield Place, South Edinburgh, EH10 (229 9686/www.balloonandparty. co.uk). Bus 11, 16, 17, 23. **Open** 10am-6pm Mon-Fri; 10am-5.30pm Sat. **Credit** MC, V. **Map** p309 D8.
An unassuming little shop selling banners and all manner of balloons and accessories to make your party go with a swing or even a bang. A decoration service is also available.

Eden
37-39 Cockburn Street, Old Town, EH1 (220 3372). Bus 35/Nicolson Street–North Bridge buses. **Open** 9.30am-6pm Mon-Wed, Fri, Sat; 9.30am-7pm Thur; noon-5pm Sun. **Credit** AmEx, MC, V. **Map** p304 D3.
Ethnic wooden crafts and textiles, plus brightly coloured oddities such as inflatable chairs and furry personal organisers.

George Waterston & Sons
35 George Street, New Town, EH2 (225 5690). Bus 28, 40, 41/Princes Street buses. **Open** *Jan-Nov* 9am-5.30pm Mon-Wed, Fri, Sat; 9am-6.30pm Thur. *Dec* also noon-5pm Sun. **Credit** MC, V. **Map** p304 B1.
This central veteran stationer's, established in 1752, sells a wide range of gift cards, writing and office supplies in its split-level shop. Also has excellent facilities for printing personalised stationery.

Helios Fountain
7 Grassmarket, Old Town, EH1 (229 7884/www. helios-fountain.co.uk). Bus 2, 23, 27, 28, 41, 42. **Open** 10am-6pm Mon-Sat; noon-5pm Sun. **Credit** AmEx, MC, V. **Map** p304 B3.
You'll find Celtic jewellery, crafts, trinkets and a huge selection of beads for necklaces or bracelets on one side of the shop; vegetarian, vegan and New Age books on the other. Plus – it goes without saying – a suitably old-fashioned hippie, alternative lifestyle ambience.

Kick Ass
34 Cockburn Street, Old Town, EH1 (622 7318/ www.kickassposters.co.uk). Bus 35/Nicolson Street– North Bridge buses. **Open** 9.30am-6pm Mon-Wed, Fri, Sat; 9.30am-7pm Thur; noon-5pm Sun. **Credit** AmEx, MC, V. **Map** p304 D3.

Eat, Drink, Shop

Masks and 'taches: **Aha Ha Ha**. See p181.

Early Learning Centre

67-79 Shandwick Place, West Edinburgh, EH2 (228 3244/www.elc.co.uk). Bus 11, 15, 16, 17, 23, 45. **Open** 9am-5.30pm Mon-Sat; noon-4pm Sun. **Credit** AmEx, MC, V. **Map** p308 C5.

The Early Learning Centre has established a nation-wide reputation as the place to find safe, educational and well-priced toys, games and playsets for tots, toddlers and pre-pubescents. There's even a play area where kids (and their parents) can test out their purchases. It's particularly good for children's art equipment.

Branches: 61 St James Centre, New Town, EH1 (558 1330); Gyle Shopping Centre, South Gyle Broadway, West Edinburgh, EH12 (538 7172).

Games Workshop

136 High Street, Old Town, EH1 (220 6540/www. games-workshop.com). Bus 35/Nicolson Street–North Bridge buses. **Open** *Jan-July, Sept-Nov* 10am-6pm Mon, Fri-Sun; 10am-8pm Tue-Thur. *Aug* 10am-8pm Mon-Fri; 10am-6pm Sat, Sun. *Dec* 9am-6pm Mon, Fri-Sun; 9am-8pm Tue-Thur. **Credit** MC, V. **Map** p304 D3 .

War-gaming figures and accessories, plus regular workshops and battle enactments.

Monkey Business

167 Morrison Street, West Edinburgh, EH3 (228 6636). Bus 1, 2, 28, 34, 35. **Open** 9.30am-5.30pm Mon-Fri; 9.30am-5pm Sat. **Credit** MC, V. **Map** p308 C6 .

Bouncy castles available for hire (£45 and £140 per day), with free delivery, set-up and collection. There's also fancy dress hire, plus fireworks and a smaller selection of jokes, novelties, wigs and masks.

Wonderland

97 Lothian Road, South Edinburgh, EH3 (229 6428/ www.wonderlandmodels.com). Bus 11, 15, 16, 17, 24, 34. **Open** *Jan-Oct* 9.30am-6pm Mon-Fri; 9am-6pm Sat. *Nov, Dec* also noon-5pm Sun. **Credit** AmEx, MC, V. **Map** p304 A3.

A breathtaking range of model cars, trains and planes, plus horror, sci-fi and cult favourite action figures.

Travel

Haggis Backpackers

60 High Street, Old Town, EH1 (557 9393/www. radicaltravel.com). Bus 35/Nicolson Street–North Bridge buses. **Open** 8am-6pm Mon-Sat; extended hours during summer, phone for details. **Credit** MC, V. **Map** p310 G5.

Interesting, off-beat and laid-back tour operator run by travellers for travellers.

STA Travel

27 Forrest Road, Old Town, EH1 (226 7747/www. statravel.co.uk). Bus 23, 27, 28, 41, 42. **Open** 9.30am-6pm Mon-Wed; 9.30am-7pm Thur; 10am-5.30pm Fri; 11am-5pm Sat. **Credit** MC, V.

This agency caters mainly for younger travellers. **Branch**: 72 Nicolson Street, South Edinburgh, EH8 (667 9390).

Video hire

Alphabet Video

22 Marchmont Road, South Edinburgh, EH9 (229 5136/www.alphabetvideo.co.uk). Bus 24, 41. **Open** 2-10pm daily. **No credit cards**. **Map** p309 F8.

Renowned source of mainstream, independent, classic and cult films. To become a video club member (£5 charge), take along two pieces of ID with your name and address. Hire costs from £1 for a two-day rental. If the film you want is not listed among the 4,000 titles in stock, Mark Alphabet will try to search it out for you. Beautiful tropical fish add to the pleasure of browsing in this idiosyncratic shop.

Arts & Entertainment

By Season

If it's August, it must be the Festival. But Edinburgh has other seasonal delights.

Just as the weather in Edinburgh is at its most extreme during winter and summer, so cultural and festive activity in the city tends to reach a climax during these two seasons. With the frost and darkness of winter come the light and festivity of **Capital Christmas** and Edinburgh's **Hogmanay**, while in summer the long days and generally agreeable temperatures make favourable conditions for the frenzy and buzz of the **Festival**. These seasonal events also bring the biggest number of tourists to into the city – in August Edinburgh fills to capacity and (almost) beyond. Spring and autumn are traditionally quieter periods and probably the best time to experience the true essence of Edinburgh without the hullabaloo of its major event attractions.

For those events marked 'tbc', the exact date was yet to be confirmed as this guide went to press; always phone to check these first. For details of Edinburgh's most important annual events look online at www.edinburghfestivals. co.uk. Tickets for most festivals are available from The Hub (348 Castlehill, Old Town, EH1 2NE (473 2000).

Spring

Edinburgh International Science Festival

Information: 220 1882/box office 473 2070/ www.sciencefestival.co.uk). **Open** *information* 9am-5pm Mon-Fri. **Tickets** (available from The Hub; *see above*) prices vary; phone for details. **Dates** 4-15 April 2003; 2004 dates tbc.

The Science Festival, founded in 1987, is a bold and successful attempt to maintain a focus on the sciences by providing lectures and events that make science and technology accessible, interesting and fun. Without dumbing down, the Festival has become adept at putting a controversial and topical slant on scientific subjects, with around 200 public events held in over 20 venues around Edinburgh. Events attract not only maximum media exposure, but also scientific heavyweights from around the world. The Science Festival is split into two halves: a popular science programme demonstrates how science has been beneficial to the lay person, often with a localised perspective, while the family programme has interactive children's events held in four venues, each catering to a different age range, and with a different scientific focus.

Light my fire: **Beltane Fire Festival**.

Beltane Fire Festival

Calton Hill, EH7 (information 228 5353). Bus 30, 40. **Times** 10pm-dawn. **Admission** free. **Map** p307 G4. **Date** 30 Apr.

One of the four major quarters of the Celtic year, Beltane is a millennia-old druid tradition marking the transition from winter to spring and heralding a prosperous and fertile new year. The modern ritual was reinvented in 1988 by Angus Farquhar of radical art activists nva. Since then, and under the guidance of the Beltane Fire Society, the event has grown into a mass of fire, drumming and painted bodies acting out all manner of fertility and seasonal rites, watched by an audience of around 15,000. The centrepiece of the night is the ritual procession of the May Queen, followed by the death and rebirth of the Green Man and the lighting of a huge bonfire. The celebrations are slightly different every year, with recent events witnessing the involvement of international fire and street theatre companies. Take a flask of whisky to toast the May Queen, and follow the Society's advice to wear what you dare.

Edinburgh Independent Radical Book Fair

Assembly Rooms, George Street, New Town. Princes Street buses. Information: Word Power Bookshop, 43 West Nicolson Street, South Edinburgh, EH8 (662 9112/books@word-power.co.uk). **Admission** charged for some events; phone for details. **Date** mid-May. **Map** p309 E5.

This event, held over a long weekend, usually takes place in the Assembly Rooms on George Street and is organised by Word Power bookshop (*see p165*). The book fair consists of readings, book launches and panel discussions and focuses on the promotion of books from small, independent and radical publishing houses.

Scottish International Children's Theatre Festival

Various city-centre theatres (information 225 8050/box office 228 1404/www.imaginate.org.uk). **Open** *Information* 9am-5pm Mon-Fri. *Box office* 10am-6pm Mon-Fri. **Tickets** prices vary; phone for details. **Credit** MC, V. **Date** last wk in May.

For one week some of the best children's theatre companies perform in a variety of venues across the city. Indigenous talent is always on display alongside respected international companies, often performing newly written productions and adaptations. At its best, this is powerfully evocative stuff, and since most productions have only a lower age limit, it's something big kids will also enjoy. A word of warning, though: tickets sell fast and there are very few public performances, so it's best to reserve your tickets as soon as the brochure is published at the beginning of April.

Summer

Meadows Festival

The Meadows, South Edinburgh, EH3. Bus 24, 41, 42. **Admission** free. **Map** p309 E/F7, p310 G7. **Date** 1st wknd in June.

More a local event than a full-blown festival, this weekend-long event transforms the Meadows into a bustling hive of activity. The much hackneyed 'something for everyone' phrase best applies to this eclectic assortment of live music, family entertainment, stalls and fairground rides.

Pride Scotland

Information: 1D4, Templeton Buildings, Templeton Street, Glasgow G40 1DA (0141 556 4340/www.pridescotland.org). **Date** mid June.

Founded to celebrate the pride in the lifestyles of lesbian, gay, bisexual and transgendered people, Pride Scotland – like Pride events throughout the world – is really an excuse for a whacking great knees up. It is usually held over a weekend in mid to late June, and its location alternates between Glasgow and Edinburgh; it will be held in the Meadows, South Edinburgh (maps p309 F7, p310 G7) in 2003 and at Glasgow Green in Glasgow in 2002 and 2004.

T in the Park

Balado Airfield, near Kinross, Perthshire (information 0870 169 6879/TicketMaster 0870 169 0100/www.tinthepark.com). **Tickets** (also available from The Hub) prices vary; see the website for details. **Credit** AmEx, MC, V. **Dates** 13, 14 July 2002; 2003 & 2004 dates tbc.

Having outgrown its Strathclyde Park origins, Scotland's biggest outdoor music festival moved to a disused airfield in rural Perthshire in 1997. Since then it has attracted luminaries from the British and international music scene, as well as around 50,000 eager music fans each day. Confirmed acts for 2002 include Oasis, Primal Scream, Groove Armada and Green Day, and pop fans can usually expect a token act from the Kylie/Robbie stable. The festival is as famous for its atrocious weather as for its music, so leave the good gear (in all senses of the word) at home and invest in wellies, a cagoule and a tipple courtesy of sponsors Tennents.

The Festival

The biggest misnomer of the Festival is the name itself. 'The Festival' is, in fact, a collection of six different festivals and events, each with its own distinct feel and organisation, but all held in Edinburgh during August. It's difficult to keep track of what's happening where, which event is in which programme, what to see and what to steer clear of, but a brief outline of the six major Festivals should help. *See also p186* **Surviving the Festival.**

Jazz & Blues Festival

Information 467 5200/tickets 668 2019/www.jazzmusic.co.uk. **Open** *Information* 9am-5.30pm Mon-Fri or daily during the Festival. *Ticket line* 10am-6pm daily. **Tickets** prices vary; phone for details. **Credit** MC, V. **Dates** 26 July-4 Aug 2002; 25th July-3rd Aug 2003; 2004 dates tbc.

Presenting 'the best of jazz to the biggest audience', the Festival covers most of its remit with the free Jazz on a Summer's Day in Princes Street Gardens and Mardi Grass in the Grassmarket. It also manages to cover the full range of jazz forms, in venues from the Playhouse to pubs and cabaret bars.

Edinburgh Military Tattoo

Castle Esplanade, Old Town, EH1 (information & tickets 225 1188/www.edintattoo.co.uk). **Bus 23, 27, 28, 35, 41, 42, 45.** **Open** *Information* Sept-July 10am-4.30pm Mon-Fri; Aug 10am-9pm Mon-Fri; 10am-10.30pm Sat; 10am-4.30pm Sun. **Tickets** £9-£25; £2.50 supplement for 10.30pm Sat. **Credit** AmEx, MC, V. **Map** p309 E5. **Dates** 2-24 Aug 2002; 1-23 Aug 2003; 6-28 Aug 2004.

First performed in 1950 as the army's contribution to the Festival, the Tattoo has become its single most popular event, with 200,000 tickets sold every year. By show-time, there is rarely an empty seat on the temporary stands that line the Castle Esplanade. Umbrellas are a definite no-no, so come dressed for

Surviving the Festival

Edinburgh's population trebles in August. That means there are one million people out there ready to jump that queue or nab that last ticket. You've got to have your wits about you at all times; ready to pounce at the right moment. Never forget this sentiment: in true Darwinian style, only the fittest will survive.

PLANNING AND PROGRAMMES

Even the festival organisers themselves are probably confused when it comes to making sense of the umpteen programmes. But never fear, help is at hand in the form of an indispensable website ready to take you by the hand and lead you through the quagmire. At **www.edinburghfestivals.co.uk** you can access each individual Festival website. From there, you can scrutinise programmes or order your own copies. It's advisable to order only the brochures for the genres you're most interested in: heavy metal fans will get little satisfaction from the International Festival and the wasted expense could have been spent on precious tickets. Instead, make brief notes of the highlights of the different festivals and add those to your wish list.

Once the must-have hard copies arrive, equip yourself with a highlighter pen, the tipple of your choice and peruse them thoroughly. At this stage select only the shows that you consider completely unmissable. Deliberations on secondary choices can be made once you get to Edinburgh.

Tickets for the International Festival, the Tattoo and anything involving a celebrity will undoubtedly go first, so if that's your bag, snap them up at least one month in advance. The hottest tickets of every year's Festival are for the firework concert in Princes Street Gardens on the last Saturday of the Festival. These tickets are for the best seats of all, in the gardens themselves, and are mostly only available by postal application (contact the Hub on 473 2001), although a few are held back until the week before the display. The views are good, however, from all over town and it's worthwhile prolonging your stay to witness the waterfall of fire crashing down the sides of the castle and experience the ground shaking as the big mortars thrust their pyrotechnic loads into the sky.

TICKETS AND ITINERARY

Now comes the part that's second only in the fun stakes to the Festival itself: booking tickets and planning your itinerary. Bookings

inclement weather. Although it is a militaristic display, the Tattoo is also a pageant of colour that uses its hundreds of performers, fireworks and the Castle backdrop to stunning effect. The Queen is expected to attend a performance to celebrate her Jubilee year in 2002.

The Fringe

Information, programmes & tickets: The Fringe Office, 180 High Street, Old Town, EH1 1QS (226 5257/www.edfringe.com). Bus 35/Nicolson Street–North Bridge buses. **Open** *Postal & internet bookings from early June. Box office mid June-end Aug 10am-7pm daily.* **Tickets** *prices vary; consult the Fringe programme for details.* **Credit** MC, V. **Map** p309 F5. **Dates** 4-26 Aug 2002; 3-25 Aug 2003; 2004 dates tbc.

At the very first International Festival, in 1947, eight uninvited companies held performances. However, the term 'Fringe' was not used until the following year, when Robert Kemp wrote in the *Evening News* of 14 August that 'Round the fringe of official Festival drama there seems to be more private enterprise than ever before'. By the end of the 1950s, performers were describing themselves as being 'on the Fringe'. From day one, the Fringe has been self-selecting. All a performer or company

needs is a venue and enough money to buy a listing in the Fringe programme. With money and space as the only quality control mechanisms, the truly avant-garde rubs shoulders with the steadfastly traditional; the really appalling with the most professional; the never-will-be hopefuls along with the Gielguds of the next generation. The Fringe certainly lives up to its reputation as the greatest arts festival in the world. In 2001, there were 1,555 productions staged by 683 companies. Theatre and comedy make up the majority of the performances, but music, visual art and children's events have grown in prominence in recent years. T on the Fringe (a fringe of the Fringe) makes up a large proportion of the popular music remit. In 1998, the Fringe decoupled itself from the EIF and now starts one week earlier.

Edinburgh International Festival

Tickets & information: The Hub, 348 Castlehill, Old Town, EH1 2NE (473 2001/www.eif.co.uk). Bus 23, 27, 28, 35, 41, 42, 45. **Open** *Box office early Apr-late July 10am-5pm Mon-Sat; late July-31 July 9am-7.30pm Mon-Sat; 10am-7.30pm Sun.* **Tickets** *prices vary; see website for details.* **Credit** AmEx, MC, V. **Dates** 11-31 Aug 2002; 10-30 Aug 2003; 15 Aug-4 Sept 2004.

booking ahead for both these festivals, as they are renowned for being places where authors and directors get to meet their public.

What you plan to see and do will depend entirely on the duration and timing of your stay. For fans of the more popularist Fringe, another insider's tip is to stay early. Two-for-one ticket offers are a godsend for the financially stretched and venues never fill up fully during the first weekend of the Fringe, so you'll enjoy a more personal experience. While you're in Edinburgh, watch out for ticket touts loitering around bigger venues and the Royal Mile with reams of complimentary tickets. The standard of these shows isn't likely to be as high as you might like, but at least your money will go further; what's more, the higher quality shows you have chosen yourself will seem so much better in comparison.

Those with the stamina to stay for the duration can afford the liberty of being more selective in their choices. Nevertheless, avoid the temptation of being too prescriptive, too early – it may only last one month, but a safe bet at the Festival is rarer than a Glaswegian. Rest assured, the top recommendations don't emerge until at least the second week of the Festival, if not later.

can be made by telephone or post, and most festivals now have a facility to book online. Spend astutely, though; out-of-town lodgings and peanut butter sandwiches do not a happy Festival-goer make. When planning your itinerary, a top tip is to base it around the Book and Film Festival events, which are mostly one-offs. You might even consider

▶

The first, although not, now, the biggest, of the six festivals is the Edinburgh International Festival. It was founded in the midst of post-war austerity in 1947, following the concerted efforts of the Lord Provost John Falconer, Harry Wood of the British Council and Rudolph Bing, who became its first director. The aim was then, and still is now, to 'provide the world with a centre where, year after year, all that is best in music, drama and the visual arts can be seen and heard in ideal surroundings'. Festival performances take place in most of the larger venues around Edinburgh, and they are generally by theatre, music and dance companies of the highest calibre. The programme is published in April (phone the above number to order a copy). The Ticket Centre at the Hub sells tickets for most of Edinburgh's festivals.

Edinburgh International Film Festival

Information & tickets: Filmhouse, 88 Lothian Road, EH3 (information 229 2550/administration 228 4051/www.edfilmfest.org.uk). Bus 1, 10, 15, 16, 17, 22, 24, 34. **Tickets** *(also available from The Hub; see p184)* £7; £4.50 concessions. **Credit** MC, V. **Map** p309 D6. **Dates** 14-25 Aug 2002; 13-24 Aug 2003; 2004 dates tbc.

When the folk at the Edinburgh Film Guild got wind of the plans for the International Festival they were incensed. A modern festival that did not celebrate film, the quintessential artistic medium of the 20th century? The Guild, with its founder Norman Wilson and the *Scotsman*'s film critic Forsyth Hardy at the controls, staged the first Edinburgh International Festival of Documentary Films in 1947. Since then its tight documentary remit has been broadened and although it is no longer 'the only film festival worth a damn', as John Huston said in 1972, the two weeks of screenings are the place to see and be seen in the international film industry. The festival is a hotbed of premières from the finest young British filmmaking talent, an important showcase for new British and continental films before general release, and a forum for a Hollywood blockbuster or three to hold their European openings.

Edinburgh International Book Festival

Charlotte Square Gardens, New Town, EH2 (information 228 5444/www.edbookfest.co.uk). Bus 13, 19, 29, 30, 41/Princes Street buses. **Open** 9.30am-late daily. **Tickets** prices vary; phone for details. **Credit** MC, V. **Map** p309 D5. **Dates** 10-26 Aug 2002; 9-25 Aug 2003; 2004 dates tbc.

► # Surviving the Festival (continued)

Having programmed a good proportion of your days in Edinburgh, check your budget, taking into account pre-booked tickets, travel expenses, accommodation costs and spending money. This is a fairly obvious necessary evil, but one which will enhance your enjoyment of the Festival in the long run. Packing is another unpleasant task, but when bearing in mind the unpredictable weather, coupled with the sweltering hot temperatures of most venues, it's wise to bring a little of everything.

AT THE FESTIVAL

Immediately on arrival make two purchases: the *Scotsman* and the *List*. The former carries a good selection of up-to-the-minute reviews, the latter gives a good general overview of the Festival through previews and reviews.

There are two extreme types of Festival-goer: the itinerary-bound believer in firm plans and the laid-back follower of the coolest vibe. An itinerary allows you to remain focused and optimise your show-going potential. Veer towards this approach if time is limited or the number of shows you see is important. However, if you're in town for more than a weekend or the hipness factor of the shows you see means a lot to you, hang around in

the bar after a show to find out the best tips. This approach can send you off to some unexpectedly groovy treats. Probably the best option is to combine both approaches.

Although your first day in Edinburgh will leave you buzzing with cultural input and ready to drop after running from show to show, by the second day, you will be an old hand. Your opinion will be sought by new arrivals and you'll be able to compare your opinions with those in the papers. However eager a Festival darling you are, remember to take it easy. You're here for enjoyment, it shouldn't be a chore.

VENUES

Fringe-goers should avoid the temptation to concentrate on the big three venues, namely the **Gilded Balloon** (*see p219*), the **Pleasance** (*see p213*) and the **Assembly Rooms** (*see p213*). Although their separate programme makes for easy reading, it's a dangerous and limiting trap that leaves the rest of the Fringe starved of an audience – and audiences bereft of some very fine performances.

It should be every Fringe-goer's duty, nay, desire, to see at least one idiosyncratic show in an obscure venue. The kudos of having seen *Macbeth* performed in Scots at a tiny, temporary venue is far greater than dozing through half an hour of duff stand-up. Open-air venues, or those which last only for the

The Book Festival occupies a tented village in the centre of Charlotte Square. Notable for the number of authors it attracts and its lack of publishing trade professionals, it continues to grow, drawing new audiences, particularly for its strong programme of children's events.

Edinburgh Mela
Pilrig Park, Leith (information 557 1400/www. edinburgh-mela.co.uk). Bus 11, 13, 36. **Admission** free. **Map** p307 G1. **Dates** 31 Aug-1 Sept.
The term 'Mela' comes from the Sanskrit word 'gathering' and describes festivals on the Indian sub-continent. Although its roots are Asian, the Edinburgh Mela is designed for everyone to enjoy, and has become Scotland's biggest multicultural event. Forty thousand people descended on Pilrig Park in 2001 to celebrate the city's diversity through music, family entertainment and a host of competitions and shows.

Autumn

Doors Open Day
Information: Cockburn Association, Trunk's Close, 55 High Street, Old Town, EH1 (557 1856/www. cockburnassociation.org.uk/open). **Admission** free. **Dates** 28 Sept 2002; 2003 date tbc.

On one day a year (usually the last Saturday in September) the Cockburn Association persuades the owners of many of Edinburgh's finest private buildings to join a Europe-wide movement and open their doors to the public. The buildings range from disused sewerage plants to stately homes, and participants change from year to year.

Hallowe'en: Samhain
From Castle Esplanade to Parliament Square, High Street, Old Town, EH1 (information 228 5353). **Date** 31 Oct.
As Beltane heralds the start of summer, so Samhain marks the end, with celebrations that coincide with Hallowe'en and are second only in scale to Beltane. Members of Beltane Fire Society again take to the streets with much frenzied dancing, fire and beating of drums. A procession moves from Castle Esplanade, down the Royal Mile to Parliament Square where the summer court, led by the Green Man, is banished to the magical realm for winter.

Bonfire Night
Date 5 Nov.
Modern Scots have a certain ambivalence towards Guy Fawkes – the fact that his gunpowder plot of 1605 was against Scotland's James IV is somehow

duration of the Festival, are a treat. In recent years the **Spiegeltent** and the **Big Top** on the Meadows have played host to superb, slightly alternative productions.

There are also venues that everyone should visit at least once. The bustling marquee of **Charlotte Square**, home to the Book Festival; the sophisticated cool of the **Filmhouse** (*see p199*); the quaint intimacy of the **Stand Comedy Club** (*see p219*); and the grand elegance of the **Festival Theatre** (*see p268*) all add an individual dynamic to the festivals. Similarly, **Fringe Sunday**, located on the Meadows, is unmissable. Acts from fire-eaters to mime artists and musicians converge on the grassy expanse and perform for free. **T on the Fringe** is a fairly recent addition to the Fringe programme. It boasts a varied selection of top bands playing in the two main venues of the **Liquid Room** (*see p212*) and the **Corn Exchange** (*see p211*).

GETTING AROUND

Getting around Edinburgh, especially to the out-of-town venues, is easy. The city is so compact that Shank's pony is the most popular form of transport. Bus services are generally reliable, although congestion on main thoroughfares can absorb precious show-seeing time. Plan extra time for your journey whatever your preferred mode of transport; welcome distractions in the form of street theatre and lazy, grassy sunspots are never far around the corner.

NIGHTLIFE

As night falls on Edinburgh, the biting mist rises from the East, signalling time to make the most of the Festival's famed nightlife. Extended opening hours in August mean you can party hard into the night. The buzzing courtyard next to the **Pleasance** is a good place to start; the Festival's other social centre, the **Traverse Bar** (*see p157*) is where the true thespians set out from, while hard-core hedonists naturally take in both. Most venues offer shows well into the wee small hours, and everyone should witness the infamous bear-pit of **Late 'n' Live** at least once a Festival.

Club runners try to attract the Festival crowd but, in the transitory world of dance music, only the most mainstream can get their DJs booked far enough ahead to get into the Fringe brochure. Check out the flyers in bars and pubs for an idea of what is going on.

As with the whole of the Festival, keeping your ear to the ground and your feet ready to go where the vibe is most productive will ensure the most positive natural selection. Moreover, it's the only way to stay atop of the Festival chain and leave without serious scars.

It's **Hogmanay!** *See p190.*

masked by the fact that it was also against the English Parliament. However, Edinburgh is unlike other Scottish cities and although its New Year and Festival fireworks displays are legendary, Bonfire Night doesn't register quite as highly on the celebration scale. The biggest event is council-run and takes place at Meadowbank Stadium (*see p224*; tickets approximately £4).

Winter

Capital Christmas

www.edinburghscapitalchristmas.org.
What started out as a few events to brighten up the month of December has grown into a full-blown festival, complete with its very own programme. Capital Christmas is the result of a collaboration between Unique Events and the City of Edinburgh Council, and is a mix of live entertainment, family attractions and other events. The programme is published in October, but usually includes Winter Wonderland – the largest outdoor skating rink in Britain, complete with fairground rides and a mini-market; the Edinburgh Wheel – a large Ferris wheel, adjacent to the Scott Monument; and the German Market, on a site next to the National Gallery. The theme of bringing light into the darkness is highlighted by two major events: typically a large-scale international street theatre performance and the Grand Fantastical Parade along Princes Street.

Edinburgh's Hogmanay

Information & passes: Hogmanay Box Office, The Hub, Castlehill, Edinburgh EH1 1BW (www.edinburghshogmanay.org). **Date** 29 Dec-1 Jan.
Scotland is the home of Hogmanay and Edinburgh has a reputation as the best place to celebrate. For the uninitiated, Hogmanay is New Year's Eve; the night when people throughout Scotland traditionally take to the streets, kiss everyone in sight as the bells ring out at midnight, and afterwards go 'first footing' with a lump of coal, a bun and a drop of the hard stuff.

Edinburgh became so notorious for its good-natured celebrations that in 1993 the City of Edinburgh Council instigated an official three-day festival. Borrowing wisely and widely from Scottish tradition, Edinburgh's Hogmanay, now a four-day extravaganza, features the infamous street party, live music in the gardens, ceilidh dancing in George Street, marching bands, processions, street theatre and several events for the more foolhardy and energetic on Ne'er Day itself. Besides the official celebrations, every local place of revelry is ringing with clubs, ceilidhs, live acts, dancing and merry-making until the wee small hours. Most pubs are licensed to 3am and nightclubs till 5am.

Crushing almost caused a tragedy in 1996 and in 1997 it was decided to limit the numbers in the town centre and restrict access from 6pm on New Year's Eve to those with passes. However, crowd safety concerns have not dampened the party atmosphere: with just 100,000 street party passes on offer,

anyone lucky enough to get one will undoubtedly witness something special. Passes are offered on a ballot basis and applications are normally opened to the public in October. Members of the First Foot Club (around £15 annual fee) are eligible for a pass, as are those purchasing tickets for one of the major concerts. Those without tickets can still see the Seven Hills Fireworks – three minutes of pyrotechnics detonated from each of the city's seven volcanic hills, best viewed from North Bridge or the Meadows.

Turner Watercolours

National Gallery of Scotland, The Mound, New Town, EH2 (624 6200/www.natgalscot.ac.uk). Bus 23, 27, 28, 41, 42, 45. **Open** 10am-5pm Mon-Sat; noon-5pm Sun. **Admission** free. **Map** p309 E5. **Date** 1-31 Jan.
Over 40 Turner watercolours were bequeathed to the National Gallery of Scotland in 1900 by Henry Vaughan, who stipulated that they should only be exhibited in January when the light is at its weakest and least destructive. They are exhibited at the National Gallery of Scotland (*see p84*), along with Turner's illustrations of Thomas Campbell's poems.

Burns Night

Date 25 Jan.
It is the custom of Scots the world over to foregather on 25 January, consume the sacred foods – haggis, neeps (turnips) and tatties (potatoes) – sup of the sacred whisky and recite the sacred texts. For this night is the birthday of Robert 'Rabbie' Burns, Scotland's Bard. Burns Suppers happen in private homes across the city and among members of Burns associations. There are also public gatherings at restaurants and hotels around the town. Theatres and bookshops play host to readings of Burns' work, although these tend to be more sober affairs. It's best to get invited to someone's home, otherwise things can appear over-formal or unbearably laced with tartan kitsch. If a native invitation is not forthcoming, grab a haggis supper each from the nearest chip shop, pass round the whisky (one bottle per person should just about do it) and read from a book of Burns' poems until the drink has loosened tongues. Some of them are extremely bawdy, although 'Tam o' Shanter' is a great story and the 'Address to a Haggis' a true celebration of the working man.

Turner watercolours: on show in January.

Children

Parks, puppets, penguins, and plenty of fun.

Edinburgh is a great city to visit with kids; it's easy to walk round, has loads of green spaces and plenty to do in all weathers. While the locals are famously reserved with adults, they can be surprisingly chatty with the 'weans'. Most of the attractions that appeal to children are instantly visible as soon as you hit the centre of town: the castle looms above the shops, and Arthur's Seat, the huge local volcano, is conveniently perched at the end of the High Street. Increasing pedestrianisation means that the parts of town where children can meander about safely are expanding, and if short legs get tired, a big black taxi is a convenient alternative. Fares are reasonable; there are seats for five passengers, all with seatbelts; and pushchairs don't need to be folded. On standard buses five- to 15-year-olds pay 50p and under-fives go free, and although the open-top guided tour buses are more expensive, they allow you to get on and off all day for the price of a single ticket (*see p57*).

An invaluable guidebook is *Edinburgh for Under Fives*, available from most local bookshops (£5.95). The Edinburgh Tourist Board will send out information on current children's events and staff can provide detailed information about suitable accommodation for families over the phone.

Events & entertainment

Many of Edinburgh's annual events (*see chapter **By Season***) include activities for kids. The **Netherbow Arts Centre** (*see p227*) often stages plays and storytelling sessions for children and runs the Easter Puppet and Animation Festival. Most other theatres have some sort of pantomime or children's show at Christmas. There is always an excellent reinterpretation of a classic fairy or folk story aimed at five- to ten-year-olds at the **Royal Lyceum** (*see p227*). The **Theatre Workshop** (*see p228*) produces an alternative show for the over-fives, while the offering at the **Traverse Theatre** (*see p228*) usually includes a singalong for small children. And for traditional panto – complete with dancing girls, a cross-dressing dame and plenty of glitzy glitter – the **King's Theatre** (*see p227*) always comes up trumps. The **Odeon** cinema (*see p199*) runs a Saturday morning club for children, the Movie Mob. The

soulless **UGC** complex at Fountain Park (*see p199*) has films for kids, ten-pin bowling and the Turboventure (a motion-simulator ride where the seats move in synchronisation with what's happening on the double-sized cinema screen). The newest and comfiest cinema is the **Ster Century** (*see p199*), with ludicrously cheap kids' films at weekends. Also worth checking out is the **City Art Centre** (*see p71*), which hosts the sort of blockbuster exhibitions that will attract children; it also has a café with high chairs.

Exploring the city

Old Town, Arthur's Seat & south Edinburgh

There's plenty to keep the most boisterous kids occupied at **Edinburgh Castle**. You can hire a bulky Walkman-style audio tour, but kids are unlikely to take much notice of it and most prefer to explore for themselves. Allow a couple of hours, and get there in good time for the one o'clock gun salute; this is fired daily (except on Sunday) – with a satisfyingly big bang and a puff of smoke – by a stiffly marching artillery man. The castle is still an army HQ so there are plenty of real soldiers about, which contributes to the atmosphere. In addition, small fry will find lots of open rocky spaces to scramble around on, some scary precipices to peer over and very exciting dungeon bits to explore. The rather staid military museums are probably less appealing, but don't miss the little cemetery for military dogs. The teeny church often has weddings at weekends and the spacious café has dull but child-friendly food.

The Royal Mile itself is riddled with alleyways and courtyards that are perfect for exploring – quite a few lead to open spaces that are good for a run-about or a picnic. **Dunbar's Close** (137 Canongate) conceals a replica of a 17th-century garden, and is a particularly peaceful spot.

Worth considering for older kids on a sunny day is the **Camera Obscura** (*see p61*), which has some freaky holograms and good telescopes, while the **Brass Rubbing Centre** (*see p72*) is a useful rainy day standby. The **Museum of Childhood** (*see p72*) is frustratingly full

Arts & Entertainment

Looking out for the English from **Edinburgh Castle**. *See p191.*

of marvellous toys that kids can't touch, but as compensation there's a dolls' house, buttons to push, attractive replica wooden toys to play with, and a particularly well-stocked shop. The **People's Story** (*see p76*) – a museum on Edinburgh life, is entertaining for children, with lots of life-size figures of people at work, plus noises and even smells.

The fabulous **Our Dynamic Earth** (*see p74*), with its sensory attractions, is a big hit with most children: icebergs to touch; earthquakes to feel; rainforests to walk through. Look out for the Bone Zone soft play area, complete with brilliant ball-ejecting volcanoes.

You don't need to buy a ticket to use Our Dynamic Earth's simple café, which is the only convenient place to fuel up before you make your assault on **Arthur's Seat** (*see p100*), just a short walk away. On your way to the hill, call in on the Park Rangers (based in a lodge at 140 Holyrood Road; open 10am-4pm Mon-Fri); they will give you maps and suggest suitable walks. If the office is closed, there are maps and information in the window. There's a choice of routes up the hill: to the right is the steep cliff-face path known as the Radical Road, which is only suitable for older children who are more competent at walking; to the left is the flat main road to St Mary's Loch, with its swans and ducks; or you can go roughly straight ahead, which takes you up some gentle slopes. From here, the climb to the top of Arthur's Seat is quite straightforward, but it is a long haul with a bit of a scramble at the end. If it's likely to prove too much for little legs, get a taxi up to Dunsapie Loch, climb the last bit of hill and then walk down instead.

South of the Royal Mile, the beautiful **Royal Museum** and its new modern extension, the **Museum of Scotland** (for both, *see p79*), are perfect for wet days and entry is free. There's loads of space, massive stuffed animals, indoor goldfish ponds, plenty of buttons to push (with

interesting results), a roof terrace, glass lifts and lockers to stash pushchairs and coats. The cafés are dull and overpriced, but the children's Discovery Centre (in the Museum of Scotland) is terrific; it's sometimes booked for school parties, so phone ahead to check. And every weekend afternoon there are Quickies for Kids, free ten-minute themed tours on anything from ancient Egyptians to elephant's tusks.

South along Forrest Road and Middle Meadow Walk lie the **Meadows**, a big grassy space with three playgrounds: one at each end, with a toddler park in the middle. Funfairs are held here from time to time. It's a great place to let off steam but watch out for dog mess and speeding students on bikes.

New Town, Calton Hill, Stockbridge & west Edinburgh

For kids the unique attraction of **Princes Street** is that it only has shops on one side; the other side is a rolling grassy park with steep windy paths leading up to the castle. Not only is there lots of open space, plenty of ice-cream vans and a playground at the West End, but it also has a railway line running through the middle; if you wave like mad from the bridge behind the Ross Bandstand you get a hoot in return from passing train drivers. In the westernmost corner of the gardens are a snack bar, toilets and often a delightful Edwardian merry-go-round.

Looking east along Princes Street you catch tempting glimpses of **Calton Hill** (*see p98*) topped by a row of Grecian columns. A flight of steps from Waterloo Place will get you to the top of the hill in no time for splendid views of the city and beyond. Calton Hill makes an excellent alternative to Arthur's Seat if you are short of time or energy. There are a couple of visitor attractions at the top, monuments and lots of rather grubby grass.

To the north of the New Town is the **Royal Botanic Garden** (*see p92*) – a godsend for lively kids and their parents. Not only does it have acres of greenery, no cars and absolutely no dog mess, but there are also loads of friendly squirrels and ducks to feed, glasshouses with huge goldfish, a pricey café with high chairs, an outdoor eating area and nappy-changing facilities. The Exhibition Hall, behind the Glasshouse Experience, has some good hands-on exhibits. There's also a playground opposite the West Gate, behind the hedges in Inverleith Park.

In Dean Village to the south, the **Scottish National Gallery of Modern Art** and the new **Dean Gallery** (for both, *see p94*) sit across the road from each other. The art in the Dean Gallery, a former orphanage, will probably appeal to youngsters most as it includes Paolozzi's massive metal giant and a replica of his chaotic studio. But it is worth crossing the road to the Scottish National Gallery of Modern Art to admire the transformation of its open lawns into a sensational 'landform sculpture' by Charles Jencks, creating a series of interlocking slopes curving round shallow ponds. The café here is bigger and less formal than the one at the Dean Gallery and has outside tables.

A steep path from the rear of the Gallery of Modern Art takes you to the **Water of Leith Walkway**, a ribbon of riverside paths that meander through the city to the docks. A good itinerary is to take one of the free hourly gallery buses from the Mound to the Scottish National Gallery of Modern Art, then follow the river downstream through pretty Dean Village, ending up in Stockbridge. St Stephen Street has lots of little eateries but the real burgers at **Bell's Diner** (*see p128*) usually prove popular all round. Maps and information can be obtained from the **Water of Leith Visitors' Centre** (*see p111* **Canal dreams**), where there are also interactive exhibits allowing children to examine the river and its plant and animal life in detail.

Leith

The Shore area in Leith is developing at a furious rate and now includes the **Royal Yacht Britannia** (*see p116*) and the **Ocean Terminal shopping mall** (*see p161*), with its standard shops, Billy Bubbles adventure play centre, and Ster Century Cinema (*see p199*). To the west in Newhaven, there is a pretty harbour and the charming **Newhaven Heritage Museum** (*see p116*), where kids get to dress up as fishermen and fishwives. Just beyond the museum is Charlie Chalk's adventure play area in the Brewsters Pub (*see p196*). Across the road from the harbour a bleak-looking church has been hollowed out to create the extraordinary **Alien Rock** climbing centre (*see p225*).

Out of town

A half-hour train ride from Waverley Station brings you to the small East Lothian town of **North Berwick**, with its harbour, summer boat trips to the Bass Rock, ice-cream shops, fabulous new Sea Bird Centre (*see p195*), rockpools and a shallow sea-water paddling pool on the sandy beach. *See also p254.*

Gullane, an hour's drive or bus ride east of the city, has a good clean beach with toilets. Eight miles (13 kilometres) south-east of town is **Dalkeith Country Park** (*see p258*), which has an adventure playground with elevated walkways for over-fours, a café, woodland paths and spooky Victorian riverside tunnels.

The seabirds and ancient monastic ruins of **Inchcolm Island and Abbey** (*see p260*), together with the ferry boat trip to get there, are a sure-fire hit with kids. Take the *Maid of the Forth* boat from South Queensferry, which also stops at **Deep Sea World** (*see p194*).

The most exciting castles close to the capital are **Linlithgow Palace** (*see p260*) and **Tantallon Castle** (*see p254*). Both have dizzying drops, so hang on to the kids.

Active kids

With mountains and sea on the doorstep, there are myriad opportunities for outdoor activities around Edinburgh. And if you have to stay in town, there are still ways for your children to use up that surplus energy – indoors and outdoors. In addition to the places listed below, former church converted to a climbing centre **Alien Rock** (*see p225*) holds children's classes at weekends, and **Murrayfield Ice Rink** (*see p224*) is a favourite among junior skaters. Ski enthusiasts can have private lessons or join a weekend class at Europe's longest artificial ski slope, at **Midlothian Ski Centre** (*see p225*).

Paolozzi's giant at the Dean Gallery.

Arts & Entertainment

Gorgeous **Gorgie City Farm**. See p195.

Laserquest

56B Dalry Road, West Edinburgh, EH11 (221 0000/
www.laserquest.co.uk). Bus 3, 21, 22, 33, 44. **Open**
11am-11pm Mon-Sat; 11am-7pm Sun. **Admission**
£4 per game. **No credit cards. Map** p308 A/B7.
You can zap them with laser fire and they can
zap you back, and you all go home in one piece.

Leith Waterworld

377 Easter Road, EH6 (555 6000). Leith Walk
buses. **Open** *Summer* 10am-5pm daily. *Winter*
10am-5pm Fri-Sun. **Admission** £3.20; £2.20
concessions; free under-5s. **No credit cards.**
Map p307 J1.
Edinburgh's best swimming pool for kids includes
a gently sloping beach for toddlers, a wave machine,
flumes, river rapids and bubble beds. Plus generously sized changing rooms.

Port Edgar Marina & Sailing School

South Queensferry, EH30 (331 3330/www.port
edgar.com). Bus 43. **Open** *Marina* Apr-Sept 9am-
7.30pm daily. Oct-Mar 9am-4.30pm daily. *Sailing*
school times vary; phone for details. **Admission**
prices vary; phone for details. **Credit** MC, V.
Your kids can learn to sail, canoe, kayak, bike ride
and orienteer just 20 minutes' drive from the centre
of Edinburgh. Courses are suitable for children aged
eight and over, and held mainly during the summer
holidays, in July and August.

Winter Wonderland

Princes Street Gardens, New Town, EH2. Princes
Street buses. **Map** p304.
A fabulous outdoor skating rink gets rigged up here
each December.

Animal encounters

Bird of Prey Centre

Dobbies Garden World, Lasswade, Midlothian, EH18
(654 1720/www.birdsofprey.org.uk). Bus 3. **Open**
Mar-Oct 11am-5pm daily. *Nov-Feb* 11am-4pm Sat,
Sun. **Admission** £3; £1.25 children, concessions;
free under-3s. **Credit** MC, V.

The Bird of Prey Centre is home to over 30 different
species including eagles, falcons and owls. There are
extensive exhibits on the characteristics and hunting habits of the birds, plus the chance to see them
in action at the daily flying displays, held at 1.30pm
and 3.30pm throughout spring and summer.

Butterfly & Insect World

Dobbies Garden World, Lasswade, Midlothian,
EH18 (663 4932/www.edinburgh-butterfly-
world.co.uk). Bus 3. **Open** *Summer* 9.30am-5.30pm
daily. Closed winter. **Admission** £4.35; £3.35
children, concessions; free under-3s. **Credit** MC, V.
Butterflies are hatching all year round in this tropical greenhouse paradise, also housed at Dobbies
Garden World. And, for the brave, there are more
scary creatures too: the jovial keepers lead beastie-
handling sessions at noon and 3pm daily involving
snakes, tarantulas, and very brave children.

Deep Sea World

North Queensferry, Fife, KY11 (01383 411 411/
www.deepseaworld.com). North Queensferry rail
then 10min walk. **Open** *Mar-Oct* 10am-6pm daily.
Nov-Feb 11am-5pm Mon-Fri; 10am-6pm Sat, Sun.
Admission £6.50; £5 concessions; £4.25 children.
Credit MC, V.
This award-winning fishy paradise takes you under
the sea. There are aquariums with lots of educational information, a feely fish pool where you can
get 'hands-on' experience of the fish, plus films, educational lectures and a café. You can even feed the
sharks, or watch the divers do it (every half hour).

Edinburgh Zoo

Corstorphine Road, West Edinburgh, EH12 (334
9171/www.edinburghzoo.org.uk). Bus 12, 26, 31.
Open *Apr-Sept* 9am-6pm daily. *Oct, Mar* 9am-5pm
daily. *Nov-Feb* 9am-4.30pm daily. **Admission**
£7; £4-£5 concessions; £4 4-14s; free under-3s.
Credit MC, V.
Edinburgh Zoo has loads of animals, including all
the favourites (pandas, hippos, snakes), but its principal claim to fame is its army of penguins, the
largest number assembled in captivity anywhere.

The penguin parade, held at 2pm every day between March and October, is undoubtedly one of the city's most bizarre sights. There's also an education centre at the Zoo, which runs popular touchy-feely sessions, where staff tell you about the animals and let you handle them (usually rabbits, snakes, chinchillas and so on).

Gorgie City Farm

Gorgie Road, South Edinburgh, EH11 (337 4202). Bus 1, 2, 3, 21, 25, 33, 34 , 38. **Open** *Mar-Oct* 9.30am-4.30pm daily. *Nov-Feb* 9.30am-4pm daily. **Admission** free.

This lovely informal spot is only ten minutes by bus from Princes Street, and has all the farmyard faves, plus a rabbit's cuddle corner, a playground and a good café with high chairs.

Scottish Seabird Centre

The Harbour, North Berwick, EH39 4SS (01620 890 202/www.seabird.org). North Berwick rail then 10min walk. **Open** *Apr-Sept* 10am-6pm daily. *Oct-Mar* 10am-4pm Mon-Fri; 10am-5.30pm Sat, Sun. **Admission** £4.95; £3.50 children, concessions. **Credit** MC, V.

A stunningly successful and beautiful new museum perched on the edge of the sea, surrounded by sandy beaches and rockpools full of hermit crabs. There's masses to do: kids can zoom in on nesting birds with live action video cameras, watch them through telescopes, or see short films indoors. Excellent loos and a nice café.

Indoor play centres

Clambers at the Royal Commonwealth Pool

21 Dalkeith Road, South Edinburgh, EH16 (667 7211). Bus 2, 14, 21, 33. **Open** *Children aged 3-8* 10am-6pm Mon-Fri; 10am-4.15pm Sat, Sun. *Accompanied under-3s* 10am-2pm Mon-Fri during term time only. **Admission** £1.60 per 45min session. **No credit cards. Map** p310 J8.

A large, safe enclosed play area with soft play, a climbing wall and a fairly grim café.

Charlie Chalks & the Fun Factory

Brewsters, Newhaven Quay, Newhaven, Leith, EH10 (555 1570). Bus 7, 10, 11, 16, 32. **Open** 10am-9pm Mon, Wed, Fri; 11am-9pm Tue, Thur, Sat. **Admission** £1.60 per 45min session. **Credit** MC, V. **Map** p311 Ex.

A large and exciting indoor play area attached to a pub/restaurant, with a safe section for toddlers. Near the Newhaven Heritage Museum (*see p116*).

The Jelly Club

Unit 10B, Peffermill Industrial Estate, South Edinburgh, EH16 (652 0212/www.jellyclub.co.uk). Bus 21. **Open** 9.30am-6.30pm daily. **Admission** £2.45-£4.10 per 2hr session. **Credit** MC, V.

A vast indoor play centre for children aged 12 and under, though it's a bit too wild for toddlers. Soft play, abseiling, pedal cars, chutes, ball pools, and a café.

Top ten Green spaces

Arthur's Seat
Wander along the paths amid the rugged scenery of the local volcanic plug. *See p100.*

Blackford Hill & Hermitage of Braid
Whether you stay by the relatively civilised Blackford pond or take a hike over the hill you will soon feel miles away from the city in this nature reserve. *See p107.*

Calton Hill
You can see for ever from the top of this hill just off the end of Princes Street. *See p98.*

Cramond village
A cute waterside village where the Almond meets the Forth, with riverside walks, swans, pubs and a rowing-boat ferry. *See p110.*

Dunbar's Close Garden
Hidden away at 137 Canongate is a secret 17th-century garden. *See p73.*

Greyfriars Kirkyard
Historically significant and famously spooky, but the biggest attraction for kids is the statue of the little dog, Greyfriars Bobby, just outside the entrance. *See p78.*

Modern Art Gallery/Dean Gallery
These two galleries, one opposite the other, are surrounded by acres of lawns, currently being transformed by some stunning garden design. *See p95.*

Princes Street Gardens
There's a play park at the West End, opposite Gap. *See p83.*

Royal Botanic Garden
Acres of lush greenery, squirrels and glasshouses. *See p93.*

Water of Leith Walkway
It's only a teeny river but it has carved a delightful green corridor through the city. *See p92* **Galleries and graveyards** *and* p111 **Canal dreams**.

Arts & Entertainment

Little Marco's at Marco's Leisure Centre

55 Grove Street, West Edinburgh, EH3 (228 2141).
Bus 1, 22, 28, 34, 35. **Open** 10am-5pm daily.
Admission (per 1.5hr session) £3; £2 children
with special needs. **Credit** MC, V. **Map** p308 C7.
A soft play area best suited to the over-fives
(maximum age ten). Children must be supervised.

Eating out

Pubs

Pubs that serve full meals are allowed to admit
children until 8pm, at the bar staff's discretion.
There are also several inns around the city
fringes where play sheds have been tacked on to
the pub. The food can be uninspiring, but most
can be relied on to provide chips and pizza, so
the kids love them. Among the better ones are:
Charlie Chalks at Brewsters (*see p195*); the
Cramond Inn (Glebe Road, Cramond Village,
EH4; 336 2035); **Ratho Park Hotel** (101
Dalmahoy Road, Kirknewton; 333 1242).

Fun & games

Better food is available at **Umberto's**
(2 Bonnington Road Lane, Leith, EH6; 554
1314), where booth tables form a train, no one
minds the kids running around and there's an
outdoor playground. Kids can make their own
pizzas at **Guiliano's** on the Shore in Leith (554
5272) and at **Est Est Est** (135 George Street,
EH2, New Town; 225 2555). At café-style **China
China** (556 7252), on Leith Walk at Antigua
Place, you can help yourself to a vast array of
Chinese dishes and keep going back for more.
Under-fives eat free, under-12s for half-price.

Good food

More sophisticated places that will satisfy
an adult palate but also welcome children
include: the **blue bar café** at the Atrium
(*see p132*), with blonde wood and fun glass
lifts; the sophisticated and spacious French-
style **Malmaison Brasserie** in the Leith
hotel of the same name (*see p53*); and
Valvona & Crolla (*see p143*), a classy
Italian café guaranteed to make a fuss of
the nippers (but service can be slow).

Central eats

The Royal Mile is no longer the culinary desert
it once was. On the High Street, **Di Placido's**
Italian deli (Nos.36-38; 557 2286) has great
sarnies to take away, plus a few tables on the
streets outside. Nearby, at No.43, is the new

Swiss Chalet at the Netherbow Arts Centre
(556 2647). Serving both meals and snacks,
it rates very high in the child-friendly stakes,
with an outdoor courtyard, high chairs and
a nappy-changing area. Further up the High
Street, at No.235, is the **Filling Station** (226
2488), a large American-style diner, also with
high chairs and a nappy-changing area. Just
off the centre of the High Street on Cockburn
Street at No.63A is the **Southern Cross Café**
(622 0622), which looks like a café but serves
really tasty adult food plus child-friendly
pastas and things with chips.

If it's pizza the kids are hankering after,
head for North Bridge towards the middle
of the Royal Mile, where you'll find **Pizza
Express** at No.23 (557 6411) and **Pizza Hut**
on the other side (No.46; 226 3038). Both have
branches across Edinburgh.

Sunday lunch

For a bargain Sunday lunch head for the
rather bland **Holiday Inn** (107 Queensferry
Road, Blackhall, EH4; 332 2442). The food
is surprisingly good, under-12s eat free, and
there's a well-equipped outdoor play park.
If you're after something more posh, try the
very swish **Hadrian's** (557 5000), in the
Balmoral Hotel (*see p41*). Every Sunday
between 12.20pm and 3pm a dizzying variety
of buffet choices is served, omelettes are cooked
in front of you and a jazz band entertains.

Practicalities for parents

Babysitting/childminding

The top hotels provide their own babysitting
and/or childminding facilities. Otherwise, the
following organisations can provide babysitters
or someone to take the children out for the day.

Butterfly Personnel

*7 Earlston Place, London Road, Calton Hill,
EH7 (659 5065).* **Open** *Office* 8am-6pm Mon-Fri.
No credit cards.

Edinburgh Crèche Co-op

297 Easter Road, Leith, EH6 (553 2116).
Open *Office* 9am-4pm Mon-Fri. **No credit cards.**

Equipment hire

Baby Baby Equipment Hire

*45 Glendevon Place, West Edinburgh, EH12
(337 7016).* **Open** no specific office hours; please
phone at reasonable times. **No credit cards.**
If you've left an essential item at home, Baby Baby
will deliver pushchairs, cots, backpacks, kids' car
seats and more.

Film

The many faces of Edinburgh on film, and a guide to the city's cinemas.

Trainspotting. A shot in the arm for Edinburgh's cinematic profile.

Sean Connery, perhaps the world's most famous Scot, and a son of Edinburgh, is unequivocal about the city's filmic qualities: 'I've filmed in most of the world's great cities, which makes coming home all the better. To me, Edinburgh seems to have been built as a film set.' And despite the city's modest size, it has been fairly well-represented on the silver screen over the years. Sure, there have been the predictable tourist-oriented short films, and even the Disney-tastic excesses of *Greyfriars Bobby* (1961) – which tells the story of the unavoidable wee Highland terrier who stayed near the grave of his master in Greyfriars Churchyard for 14 years. But the city, and its inhabitants, have also been dealt with in terms other than the sentimental or the scenic.

There is a small group of Edinburgh movies in which, as David Bruce points out in his book *Scotland the Movie*, the character of the city is integral to the feel of the film. In the *Battle of the Sexes* (1959) the depiction of the city as 'cold, hidebound, reactionary and harbouring homicidal tendencies' is used by Peter Sellers to great comic effect, with ominous undercurrents. This perceived aspect of Edinburgh's character is also portrayed in *The Prime of Miss Jean Brodie* (1968), adapted from

the novel by Muriel Spark, which won Maggie Smith the Oscar for Best Actress in 1969.

The darker side of city life has been addressed on celluloid by directors spurning the picturesque tourist end of town in favour of the down-at-heel outer estates. *Conquest of the South Pole* (1989) caught the depression of unemployment in a peculiarly fascinating light when it portrayed a group of unemployed lads in Leith re-enacting Amundsen's Polar journey. Similarly, *Shallow Grave* (1994), the first film from the *Trainspotting* production team, reflected the zeitgeist of the early 1990s when yuppie greed seemed capable of anything.

The grim but surreal heroin epic *Trainspotting* (1996) was the international smash that put Edinburgh squarely on the cinematic map. (Although the interiors were shot in Glasgow, the location work was done in Edinburgh.) It was swiftly followed by *Mary Reilly* (1996), a reworking of the Jekyll and Hyde story, for which Julia Roberts and John Malkovich spent a few days filming in Edinburgh. Unfortunately *The Acid House* (1999), author Irvine Welsh's follow-up to *Trainspotting*, in no way emulated the success of its predecessor.

Battle of the Sexes portrays a hidebound and reactionary Edinburgh.

There remains a healthy interest in adaptations of works by Edinburgh-based authors. Jonny Lee Miller played the lead in *Complicity* (2000), a big-screen version of Iain Banks's best-selling tale of gruesome murders in and around Edinburgh; while *Women Talking Dirty* (2001) – an adaptation of Isla Dewar's novel portraying the unlikely friendship between an oddball single mother and a shy cartoonist – was marred by Helena Bonham Carter's dubious attempt at a Scottish accent, but made Edinburgh look beautiful.

Meanwhile, Ewan McGregor returned to his native Scotland in early 2002 to film an adaptation of Scottish beat writer Alex Trocchi's *Young Adam* on the canals between Edinburgh and Glasgow. And when it's not busy playing itself, Edinburgh has doubled for numerous other locales: as Christminster (a fictional version of Oxford), for example, in *Jude* (1996), Michael Winterbottom's adaptation of Thomas Hardy's novel, *Jude the Obscure*.

The **Edinburgh International Film Festival** (*see p187*) is an important showcase for new European films. Nevertheless, the Scottish film industry itself has its industrial and practical bases in Glasgow. Glasgow is also home to Scottish Screen, a government-funded organisation that helps companies use Scotland as a base. And while there has been talk recently of a film studio opening on the outskirts of Edinburgh in a scheme championed by Sean Connery, it looks more likely it will go to Glasgow instead.

PRACTICAL INFORMATION

Film programmes change on Fridays. Full listings are carried in *The List* magazine, with the *Edinburgh Evening News* and the *Scotsman*

running limited listings. Films are classified as: (U) – for universal viewing; (PG) – parental guidance advised for young children; (12), (15) and (18) – no entry for those aged under 12, 15 and 18 respectively.

Most of the city's cinemas have disabled access and toilets, but it's always best to phone to check first.

Cinemas

With four multiplexes, two old-style picture houses and two dedicated arthouse cinemas, Edinburgh enjoys greater film access than most cities. There should be even greater choice after August 2002, when two other venues are scheduled to be up and running. The **ABC Film Centre** (120 Lothian Road) opened its doors in 1938 as the Regal, and boasted the city's largest screen until it was closed down for redevelopment in 2001. However, the good news is that it is to reopen as a four-screen cinema complex. The other opening is yet another multiplex, a 12-screen Warner Village site at the Omni Centre on Greenside Place.

The profusion of multiplexes in the city hasn't done much to increase viewing choice, as they tend to run practically identical mainstream fare. This is something of a concern to discerning cinema goers, who witnessed the recent closure of the Lumiere, an arthouse located within the Royal Museum that has now gone dark indefinitely.

The Cameo

38 Home Street, South Edinburgh, EH3 (recorded information 228 2800/box office 228 4141/www .cameocinema.co.uk). Bus 10, 11, 15, 16, 17. **Tickets** £3.50 Mon; £5.20 Tue-Sun; £3.50 concessions. **Credit** MC, V. **Map** p309 D7.

A comfy, cheerful and friendly independent cinema, run from London but showing the imaginative end of the cinematic spectrum. If you want endorsement it's Quentin Tarantino's favourite Scottish cinema and the venue at which he premiered *Reservoir Dogs*. Screen One's airline seats are comfortably spacious and the top-quality sound is cranked right up for the late-night screenings of modern cult movies. On the other hand, if lazing in front of a film on Sunday afternoon's your thing the Cameo runs a double bill each week. Screens Two and Three are bijou to the point of being miniscule, but the sightlines are good enough. Before 11pm, drinks from the bar may be taken into the auditorium.

The Dominion

18 Newbattle Terrace, Morningside, South Edinburgh, EH10 (box office 447 4771/recorded information 447 2660). Bus 11, 15, 16, 17, 18, 23. **Tickets** £3.70-£5.90; concessionary prices available all day Mon & before 6pm Tue-Sun. **Credit** MC, V.

Cinema-going as it used to be. This independent picture palace is still run by the Cameron family for whom it was built in 1938. The Camerons have a hands-on approach and like to make sure their customers are always satisfied. The building is classic art deco, although it's now divided into four screens. The screening policy is in keeping with the douce location in Morningside and oriented towards family entertainment, although commercial realities mean that the odd 18-rated film is not precluded. Screen One's Pullman seats are probably the comfiest in town. Hot snacks are available before 6pm in the basement café bar, which stays open until the end of the last film; drinks may taken into the auditorium.

Filmhouse

88 Lothian Road, South Edinburgh, EH3 (228 2688). Bus 1, 2, 10, 11, 15, 16, 22, 35. **Tickets** £3.50-£5.50; £2-£4 concessions. **Credit** MC, V. **Map** p304 A3.

This is the British Film Institute's representative cinema in Edinburgh, which means top-quality movies from around the world, the big current arthouse releases and regular screenings for classic movies – although these tend to have short runs. Screen One's sound system is state of the art and powerful, in contrast to the system in tiny Screen Three, which just about manages to drown out the noise of the projector. The Filmhouse is the centre for the Edinburgh International Film Festival and has a relentless round of themed mini-festivals throughout the year including French, Italian, Spanish, Greek, Czech, gay and documentary events. The bar is laid-back and convivial (*see p145*), and runs an extremely popular and very challenging film quiz on the second Sunday of each month.

Odeon

7 Clerk Street, South Edinburgh, EH8 (667 0971/ recorded information & credit card bookings 0870 505 0007). Nicolson Street–North Bridge buses. **Tickets** £3.20-£5.20; £3.20 concessions; £1.50 kids' show Sat am. **Credit** AmEx, DC, MC, V. **Map** p310 G7.

This centrally located member of the Odeon chain has five screens. It shows big commercial movies, with shows for kids on Saturday mornings and grown-up late-nighters on Fridays and Saturdays. Screen One is huge, although some of the smaller screens are a little scrappy. A café-bar is open in the evenings and drinks can be taken into the film.

Odeon Wester Hailes

Westside Plaza, 120 Wester Hailes Road, Wester Hailes, West Edinburgh, EH14 (453 1569/recorded information & credit card bookings 0870 505 0007). Bus 3, 18, 28, 32, 33. **Tickets** £3-£5.30; £3.20 concessions. **Credit** AmEx, MC, V.

This modern, eight-screen multiplex is located to the west of the city centre. A licensed bar is open every evening and refreshments are also served in an ice-cream bar: coffee, soft drinks, ice-cream, snacks and sweets should cater for most tastes.

Ster Century

Ocean Terminal, Ocean Drive, Leith, EH6 (553 0700). Bus 11, 22, 34, 35, 36, 49. **Tickets** £4.50-£5.50; £3-£3.50 concessions; £14 family. **Credit** MC, V.

Another of Edinburgh's brand-new multiplexes, this one is located out of town, down at the docks at Ocean Terminal at Leith. Don't let the surrounding shopping complex put you off; there are superb views of the Firth from the bar and grill opposite the cinema. The Ster Century is well-appointed, with state-of-the-art sound and vision. Mainstream films dominate the programme, with kids' matinees on weekday mornings.

UCI

Kinnaird Park, Newcraighall Road, Newcraighall, South Edinburgh, EH15 (669 0777/recorded information & credit card bookings 0870 010 2030). Bus 14, 32, 40. **Tickets** £4.25-£5.25; £3.65-£3.95 concessions. **Credit** AmEx, MC, V.

Modern 12-screener multiplex in the Kinnaird Shopping Park about 20 minutes out of Edinburgh. It lacks the atmosphere of the older cinemas and shows almost solely mainstream films, but has decent equipment and a good selection of sweets for munchies during the films.

UGC

Fountain Park, 130-133 Dundee Street, West Edinburgh, EH11 (228 8788/recorded information & credit card bookings 0870 902 0417). Bus 28, 34, 35. **Tickets** £2.50-£5.20; £3-£3.20 concessions. **Credit** AmEx, MC, V.

Located in Sean Connery's old stomping ground of Fountainbridge, the UGC is Edinburgh's first multiplex to be situated close to the city centre (it's a five-minute walk from Lothian Road). It boasts 13 screens, including the three-storey-high, crystal-sharp Iwerks screen, which comes into its own for mountaineering and undersea shorts. Although the cinemas are comfy, and there's ample leg-room, the UGC scores no higher in ambience than the average supermarket. It has a café-bar and the usual food stalls.

Arts & Entertainment

Galleries

Instead of trading on its auspicious past, Edinburgh's art scene is finally looking to the future.

In art, as in much of its cultural life, Edinburgh has suffered from a tendency to rest on its historical laurels. With its magnificent (once radical) architecture and an enviable history of groundbreaking art and pioneering photography in the 18th and 19th centuries, it has been easy for the city to fall into the trap of becoming an elegant museum to its Enlightenment past.

The city has a host of public venues and, to the continuing chagrin of Glasgow, still houses the Scottish national collections (these are listed

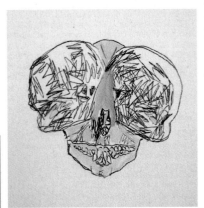

Sally Osborn at **doggerfisher**. See p202.

within the relevant Sightseeing chapters starting on p59). Each one of these institutions is becoming more clued up to the modern business of art, with a noticeable growth in marketing, merchandising and blockbuster shows. The **National Gallery of Scotland** (*see p84*), in particular, has been undergoing an overhaul, with a wholesale redevelopment of its premises on The Mound.

While you shouldn't miss out on any of these historical treats you should also be aware that the city has a vibrant visual culture, an art college that has been dragging itself slowly but surely into the 21st century and a growing number of public spaces and commercial art galleries that support contemporary art. Of the former, the stunning **Inverleith House** (*see p93*) and the **Fruitmarket Gallery** (*see p71*) are your best bets for quality shows featuring international names.

In the commercial sector ambitious galleries like the **Ingleby** and **doggerfisher** are bringing upmarket gloss and streetwise savvy to a scene made more lively by Edinburgh's recent financial boom. Corporate buyers are on the move: when Deutsche Bank opened a new Scottish HQ in Edinburgh in 2001, the company bought and displayed the work of hot Scottish artists like Christine Borland and Callum Innes.

If you prefer decorative arts, traditional landscapes or quality Scottish historical works, head for Dundas Street, where long-established outfits such as **Bourne Fine Art** trade.

One of the most curious anomalies of recent years is that the Edinburgh Festival doesn't include visual art in its official programming. Nevertheless, galleries in both the public and private sectors always save their best and most ambitious exhibitions for the summer months. During August and September you can find out some of what's on by checking the rear section of the annual Fringe programme. Throughout the year you'll also find listings in the Scottish newspapers, *Galleries* magazine or the *List* magazine.

Bellevue Gallery

4 Bellevue Crescent, Broughton, EH3 (558 8368/ www.bellevuegallery.co.uk). Bus 8, 13, 17. **Open** noon-6pm Wed-Sat or by appointment. **Credit** MC, V. **Map** p306 F3.

Talent spotting

Since the late 1980s the Scottish art scene has been in extraordinary health, shaking off its parochial image and embracing internationalism. The reputation of the Glasgow School of Art for producing acknowledged stars like Douglas Gordon and Christine Borland has tended to overshadow the rest of the country; that city, after all, is now considered to be the best place outside London for emerging artists to set up base. However, Glasgow's preeminence shouldn't obscure the growing dynamism of Edinburgh's artists, the creative flow that exists between the two cities and the emergence of nearby Dundee as a hotbed of activity with an excellent art school and a venue (Dundee Contemporary Arts) of international stature.

While Edinburgh's public venues, places like the Stills Gallery (*see p72*), have done much to support new artists in recent years, the Collective Gallery (*see p71*), an artist-run space in Cockburn Street, wins the prize for consistently nurturing and developing new talent. Moreover, Edinburgh College of Art, once a rather woolly institution, has given itself a shakedown and has many new dynamic staff members, particularly in sculpture and research. There's certainly no such thing as a generic Edinburgh artist; the diversity of the scene is encouraged by the growing presence of international students at the College and by projects like ProtoAcademy, an artist-led offshoot that encourages the exchange of ideas and artists across Europe.

The most prominent of Edinburgh's current stars is abstract painter **Callum Innes** who some years ago resisted the pressure to move to London or New York, keeping his base in the city of his birth. His work can be seen in the Scottish National Gallery of Modern Art (*see p95*) or in shows at the Ingleby Gallery (*see p203*), while his international status has been recently boosted by an exhibition touring major American museums.

Edinburgh artists with growing reputations include **Chad McCail** who has a long-term involvement with the Collective Gallery, and whose billboard-style paintings reveal him to be a genuine idealist and a unique voice on the British scene. Other artists to emerge from the Collective include **Kate Gray** and **Paul Carter**.

Another leading figure on the scene is **Wendy McMurdo** whose uncanny digital images have explored the secret lives of children, while prominent painters include **Moyna Flannigan**, whose odd composite portraits drawn from memory (as featured here) demonstrate a spontaneity and a smart handling of paint, and **Donald Urquhart**, who has reinvented the landscape tradition by a cool analysis of place. Snapping at their heels is a whole host of younger talents: keep your eyes open and look out in listings publications for artist-led events and activities.

Just beyond bohemian Broughton Street the neighbourhood opens out into a rather lovely New Town crescent where you'll find this pleasant sunny space on the ground floor of a terraced house. Having recently changed hands, the relaunched Bellevue Gallery shows middlebrow decorative and fine art that's easy on the eye. Recent graduates mingle with more mature names in painting, photography and applied arts.

Bourne Fine Art

6 Dundas Street, New Town, EH3 (557 4050). Bus 23, 27. **Open** *10am-6pm Mon-Fri; 11am-2pm Sat.* **No credit cards. Map** *p306 E3.*
Dundas Street, one of the New Town's busiest thoroughfares, is home to many of Edinburgh's upmarket commercial galleries. One of the grandest is Bourne Fine Art, with its distinctive bow window façade. The gallery specialises in traditional Scottish landscapes and portraiture dating from the 1700s onwards. You'll find paintings from a range of historical luminaries from across the centuries, including figures like Sir David Wilkie and Sir William MacTaggart, as well as work by hugely popular Scottish colourists such as Francis Cadell. More recently the gallery has shown work by well-established living artists.

doggerfisher

11 Gayfield Square, Broughton, EH1 (558 7110/ www.doggerfisher.com). Playhouse buses. **Open** *11am-6pm Thur-Sat or by appointment.* **Credit** *AmEx, MC, V.* **Map** *p307 G3.*

In a converted tyre garage on the edge of a quiet square is doggerfisher's impressive white cube premises. This young gallery is a leading Scottish venue for contemporary art and has already made a splash on the international art circuit. In a city dominated by tradition, this energetic outfit is a rare private space that puts its money into supporting the exciting emerging artists who have transformed Scotland's international reputation over the last decade. Don't miss it.

Edinburgh Printmakers

23 Union Street, Broughton, EH1 (557 2479/www. edinburgh-printmakers.co.uk). Playhouse buses. **Open** *10am-6pm Tue-Sat.* **Credit** *MC, V.* **Map** *p307 G3.*
There is a strong printmaking tradition in Scotland, and Edinburgh Printmakers, founded in 1967, is probably the country's leading gallery dedicated to contemporary prints. As well as a rolling exhibition programme, which is international in outlook and often quite ambitious at Festival time, the gallery shows work in other media, including jewellery. But as the open view over the working print room suggests, the venue is best known for its long-standing active collaboration with leading artists. For the purchaser, this means an excellent opportunity to buy affordable prints from contemporary artists like Graham Fagen and Moyna Flannigan.

Eye Two Gallery

66 Cumberland Street, New Town, EH3 (558 9872). Buses 13, 23, 27. **Open** *10am-6pm Mon-Fri; 10am-4pm Sat.* **No credit cards. Map** *p306 E3.*

Leon Morrocco at **Open Eye Gallery**. *See p203.*

Galleries

A more recent offshoot of the Open Eye Gallery (*see below*) but with a quite different feel and an upmarket, international outlook. Eye Two specialises in prints: a visit might turn up anything from a post-impressionist lithograph to a pop art silkscreen. Its changing exhibitions are particularly strong on Brits like Patrick Caulfield and sometimes also feature an America heavyweight such as Robert Rauschenberg. The prices here are often better than those in comparable London institutions, so well worth a look for the collector.

Ingleby Gallery
6 Carlton Terrace, Calton Hill, EH7 (556 4441/ www.inglebygallery.com). Buses 30, 35, 40. **Open** 10am-5pm Tue-Sat or by appointment. **No credit cards. Map** p307 J4.

This classy gallery is housed in one of Sir William Playfair's grand townhouses looking out on to the Palace of Holyroodhouse and Arthur's Seat. It's chic, discreet and has an increasingly loyal clientele both at home and on the art fair circuit. Doubling up as a family home, it holds regular private views, including Saturday morning events for 'middle youth' whose lifestyle is more kids, coffee and croissants than champagne. That said, the Ingleby is one of the city's most ambitious operations, with a world-class roster of artists including Howard Hodgkin, Ian Hamilton Finlay and Callum Innes. This is the place to come for upmarket abstract painting, classy ceramics and work by established British photographers like Thomas Joshua Cooper and Susan Derges.

The Leith Gallery
65 The Shore, Leith, EH6 (553 5255/www.the-leith-gallery.co.uk). Buses 1, 16, 22, 35, 36, 49. **Open** 11am-5pm Tue-Fri; 11am-4pm Sat. **Credit** AmEx, MC, V. **Map** p305 Jy.

The Leith Gallery is a successful commercial gallery specialising in contemporary Scottish art, and enjoys an enviable location on The Shore overlooking Leith Harbour. There are no aspirations towards championing the avant-garde so expect to find predominantly landscapes and beach scenes from a diverse range of Scotland-based artists. Look out for its shows of recent graduates, which can be lively.

Merz
87 Broughton Street, Broughton, EH1 (558 8778/ www.merzart.com). Bus 8/Playhouse buses. **Open** 11am-5pm Tue-Sat. **Credit** MC, V. **Map** p306 F3.

This shop front gallery on a bright corner spot of busy Broughton Street is the baby of Callum Buchanan, former owner of the Bellevue. Friendly, packed and eclectic, this gallery has everything from small bronzes of sheep to a funky Brit Art print. This is the kind of place where you might just unearth an unexpected treasure.

Open Eye Gallery
75-9 Cumberland Street, New Town, EH3 (557 1020/www.openeyegallery.co.uk). Buses 13, 23, 27. **Open** 10am-6pm Mon-Fri; 10am-4pm Sat. **No credit cards. Map** p306 E3.

John Bellany at **Open Eye Gallery**.

With over 21 years in the business, Open Eye is a vibrant, friendly gallery on a quiet New Town Street. Husband and wife team Tom and Pam Wilson have built up a reputation for supporting Scottish artists, so you'll find established figures like John Bellany and Leon Morrocco rubbing shoulders with younger painters and applied artists. While the paintings and sculpture tend to avoid the cutting edge, the jewellery and ceramics are often a sure step away from high street conventionality.

Patriothall/WASPS Gallery
Patriothall Studios, off 48 Hamilton Place, Stockbridge, EH3 (225 1289). Buses 24, 28, 36. **Open** noon-6pm daily. **No credit cards. Map** p306 D3.

WASPS provides studio space across Scotland for predominantly young and emerging artists and all its premises provide a fertile hunting ground for the talent spotter. This informal space, off the beaten track in a Stockbridge courtyard, usually features work by some of the 60 or so artists working in the building; its a great place to see and buy new work.

Time Out Edinburgh Guide **203**

Gay & Lesbian

It's no San Francisco here, but the gay community likes to be scene and heard.

Edinburgh's gay calendar is dominated by a number of high-profile annual events. During the Edinburgh Festival and Hogmanay festivities, gay venues are open throughout the day and are mobbed into the wee small hours. The Lesbian & Gay Switchboard's phenomenally popular fundraising ceilidhs on Valentine's Day and Hallowe'en draw hordes of pink punters to the Assembly Rooms, while the Gay Pride event in June, held alternately in Glasgow and Edinburgh, is a chance for the GLBT communities in both cities to take to the streets in celebration (*see p185*). Beyond these seasonal offerings, Edinburgh's gay bars and clubs cater for most tastes: from dark 'n' dirty men-only bars to cheesily camp clubs, lesbian dance nights and relaxed mixed cafés.

It's not all happy hours and hedonism, though. Sure, the city has plenty of up-for-it clubbers, cruisers and carousers and plenty of clubs, bars and nightspots to cater for them, but there is also a large number of gay people here who live a very conventional, bourgeois and off-scene existence: big Georgian flat in the New Town, long-term partner, high-paid professional job and a cultured but relatively conservative social life. This suggests either that sexuality is no longer an issue in Edinburgh (or, at least, not a subject for discussion), or that the city tends to attract gay people for whom full-on scene socialising is not a priority. Gay life there certainly is, but this city is no San Francisco.

Among the visible and thriving gay community, however, the mood remains confident and optimistic, however. The bars, cafés, clubs and shops around Broughton Street, Picardy Place and the top of Leith Walk have developed a gay-friendly reputation to such an extent that the area is known locally – with a certain amount of irony – as the 'pink triangle'. It's not so much a gay hot spot as a place where same-sex couples can walk hand in hand without raising too many eyebrows.

What's more, since the repeal of Section 28 (a law that tried to prevent any teaching about homosexuality in schools) and the creation of a new Scottish parliament that gives a genuine voice to minorities, there has been a strong sense on Edinburgh's gay scene that active campaigning and community action can really lead to change. There has been empirical evidence of this, too: gay activism had a high-profile success in 2000 when it persuaded the Bank of Scotland to abandon a proposed commercial partnership with anti-gay TV evangelist Pat Robertson.

Examples of active gay groups in the city include the Stonewall Youth Group, a police liaison team and a gay parents' group (for all, *see chapter* **Resources A-Z: Gay & lesbian**).

INFORMATION

The **Lesbian & Gay Centre** in Broughton (60 Broughton Street; 478 7069) is a hub of community activity. Hang out at the centre's **Nexus Café** (*see p206*), or at the neighbouring **Blue Moon Café** (*see p205*), and you'll soon find out what's going on. Alternatively, you can find details of events from the **Gay Switchboard** or **Lesbian Line** (for both, *see chapter* **Resources A-Z: Gay & lesbian**), and from the free magazines *Scotsgay*, or *The List*.

Arts & entertainment

The **Fringe** (*see p186*) usually stages a fair number of gay- and lesbian-interest productions as part of its programming, while at other times of the year, the **Traverse Theatre** (*see p228*) sometimes features new gay writing. Also, check out **Oot on Tuesday** – a gay stand-up night at the Stand Comedy Club, and the **Filmhouse** (*see p199*) or the **Cameo** (*see p198*) cinemas for gay- and lesbian-interest films.

OOT on Tuesday

The Stand, 5 York Place, New Town, EH1 (558 7272/www.thestand.co.uk). Bus 4, 8, 10, 11, 12, 15, 16, 17, 26. **Open** 9pm 2nd Tue of mth. **Admission** £5; £4 concessions. **Credit** MC, V. **Map** p304 F4.
This intimate basement venue hosts monthly gay stand-up comedy from the best entertainers around, compered by Edinburgh's very own Craig Hill.

Bars

CC Blooms

23-4 Greenside Place, Leith Walk, Broughton, EH1 (556 9331). Playhouse buses. **Open** 11pm-3am (bar from 7pm) daily. **Admission** free. **No credit cards. Map** p307 G3.
Ever-popular hot and sweaty, cheesily camp mixed bar and club that can feel like a sauna on summer weekends. Downstairs it's all naked torsos and

pumping tunes. If you're looking to pick up a friend for the night, you'll probably need to look no further than CC Blooms.

The Claremont

133-5 East Claremont Street, Broughton, EH7 (556 5662/www.scifipub99.freeserve.co.uk). Bus 8, 13, 17. **Open** 11am-1am daily. **Credit** MC, V. **Map** p306 F2.
This gay-run bar hosts men-only nights on the first and third Saturdays of the month, attracting the leather, denim, skinhead, uniform and bear crowds. Food available. Other nights are mixed.

Frenchies

87-9 Rose Street Lane North, New Town, EH2 (225 7651). Princes Street buses. **Open** 1pm-1am daily. **No credit cards. Map** p309 D5.
This small bar (it's a bit like a sitting room) attracts an eclectic mix of gay men, TVs and trans-sexuals. Weekends are very busy, with Sunday afternoon karaoke a big hit. Happy hour is from 6pm to 8pm daily.

Habana

22 Greenside Place, Leith Walk, Broughton, EH1 (558 1270). Playhouse buses. **Open** noon-1am Mon-Sat; 12.30pm-1am Sun. **Credit** MC, V. **Map** p307 G3.
Next to the Playhouse Theatre, this small, neon-lit bar, complete with tiled floor, has a bit of an Ibizan vibe. It's a great pre-club meeting place, and in summer the tables spill on to Leith Walk.

Laughing Duck

24 Howe Street, New Town, EH3 (220 2376). Bus 13, 19A, 24, 28. **Open** noon-midnight Mon-Thur, Sun; noon-1am Fri, Sat. **Credit** AmEx, DC, MC, V. **Map** p306 D3.
A gay institution in the 1980s, the Laughing Duck went straight for 15 years, but now it's back and better than ever. It's a spacious, comfy bar with a whole mix of seating – from couches and booths to benches – and a chatty, unpretentious clientele of slightly older men and their admirers. The downstairs function room is used for open mic, goth and quiz nights. Food available.

New Town Bar

26B Dublin Street, New Town, EH3 (538 7775). Bus 4, 8, 10, 11, 15, 16, 17, 20. **Open** noon-1am Mon-Thur, Sun; noon-2am Fri, Sat. **Credit** MC, V. **Map** p306 F4.
A popular cruise bar just down from the Portrait Gallery that attracts gay men of all types, sizes and ages. The upstairs bar is busy, with a friendly ambience. The anything-goes downstairs club opens late in the evening at weekends.

Planet Out

6 Baxter's Place, Broughton, EH1 (524 0061). Playhouse buses. **Open** 4pm-1am Mon-Fri; 3pm-1am Sat, Sun. **Credit** MC, V. **Map** p307 G3.
Perhaps the friendliest bar in the whole city, Planet Out has a real community feel and attracts a mixture of gay men and women who are generally up for a good time and ready to chat. There are events

Hot cheese to go at **CC Blooms**. *See p204.*

such as quizzes, karaoke nights and theme nights throughout the week; phone to check what's on during your visit.

Stag & Turret

1-7 Montrose Terrace, Calton Hill, EH7 (661 6443). Bus 30, 40. **Open** noon-1am daily. **No credit cards. Map** p307 J3.
Although it's near the Calton Hill cruising ground and popular with men, this ground-floor bar is one for the ladies too. There's karaoke on Friday nights and a women's darts team.

Cafés

Blue Moon Café & Out of the Blue

1 Barony Street, Broughton, EH1 (556 2788/shop 478 7048). Bus 8, 13, 17. **Open** *Café* 11am-11pm daily. *Shop* noon-7pm Mon-Fri; noon-6pm Sat, Sun. **Credit** MC, V. **Map** p306 F3.
The hub of Edinburgh's gay scene, this establised, friendly café stretches over three rooms. There's good food and the potential for great chats, and if you need to find out what's happening in gay Edinburgh you need only ask the waiters. The cosy room at the back has a coal fire and work by local artists on the walls, while downstairs is the **Out of the Blue** shop, which stocks a comprehensive selection of books, mags, toys, underwear and videos. The staff are helpful.

Karaoke and quizzes are all part of socialising at the bubbly **Planet Out**. *See p205.*

Nexus
LGB Centre, 60 Broughton Street, Broughton, EH7 (478 7069). Bus 8, 13, 17. **Open** 11am-11pm daily. **Credit** MC, V. **Map** p306 F3.
At the back of the Lesbian & Gay Centre (*see p204*) is this intimate café bar with big windows overlooking a garden. An interesting selection of food and snacks is available and there's internet access in the corner. A range of community groups meet here.

Clubs

The best clubs have a mixed door policy, allowing gay, lesbian and straight clubbers to all get together in a heady frenzy. There are no exclusively gay venues in the city, but many Edinburgh clubs hold gay nights on specific nights of the week, such as **Joy** at Ego or **Tackno** at Club Mercado. Flyers giving discounted entry are available in selected bars, some of which – **CC Blooms**, for example (*see p204*) – hold club nights of their own. Check the bar reviews for details. For further details of the venues listed here, *see chapter* **Nightlife**.

Angel Delight
The Venue, 15-17 Calton Road, Calton Hill, EH8 (557 3073). Bus 30, 35, 40. **Open** 10pm-3am every 4th Fri of mth. **Admission** £6; £5 concessions. **No credit cards**. **Map** p310 G/H5.

Angel Delight is Edinburgh's sole women-only club night and runs monthly on a Friday. A percentage of the profits go to charity.

Eye Candy
Club Mercado, 36-39 Market Street, Old Town, EH1 (226 4224/www.clubmercado.com). Bus 23, 27, 28, 41, 42/Nicolson Street–North Bridge buses. **Open** 11pm-3am Sat fortnightly. **Admission** £10; £8 concessions; £6 in fancy dress. **No credit cards**. **Map** p309 F5.
Every other Saturday, resident DJs Nejat Barton, Graeme Popstar and Neil Crookston entertain the crowds with their glam music and style.

Joy
Ego, Picardy Place, Broughton, EH1 (478 7434). Playhouse buses. **Open** 10.30pm-3am Sat fortnightly. **Admission** £8-£10. **No credit cards**. **Map** p307 C4.
Joy is one of Edinburgh's most famous and busiest gay club nights, offering hands-in-the-air house, chart and party sounds every second Saturday. The top-notch DJs include Maggie and Alan, Trendy Wendy and Sally Finlay.

Luvely
The Liquid Room, 9C Victoria Street, Old Town, EH1 (225 2564/www.liquidroom.com). Bus 23, 27, 28, 41, 42, 45. **Open** 10.30pm-3am 1st Sat of mth. **Admission** £12; £10 concessions. **No credit cards**. **Map** p304 C3.

Arts & Entertainment

A two-room clubbing extravaganza with DJs Jared, GP, Tommy K and Newton & Stone playing everything from house to chart and party tunes. Runs once a month on a Saturday.

Mingin

Studio 24 (upstairs), Calton Road, Calton Hill, EH8 (558 3758). Bus 24, 25, 35, 35A. **Open** 10.30pm-3am Sat fortnightly. **Admission** £6. **No credit cards. Map** p310 H5.
Brian Dempster and Alan Joy play hard house and dark, sexy trance at this gay-friendly club.

Tackno

Club Mercado, 36-39 Market Street, Old Town, EH1 (226 4224/www.club-mercado.com). Bus 23, 27, 28, 41, 42/Nicolson Street–North Bridge buses. **Open** 10.30pm-3am last Sun of mth. **Admission** £6; £5 concessions. **No credit cards. Map** p314 D2.
DJ Trendy Wendy whips this packed club into a frenzy with her mix of dance and pop sounds. Oh, and did we mention the fancy dress themes, the tacky music and the camp lip-sync acts?

Taste

The Honeycomb, 15-17 Niddry Street, Old Town, EH1 (556 2442). Nicolson Street–North Bridge buses. **Open** 11pm-3am Sun. **Admission** £8; £6 concessions. **No credit cards. Map** p310 G5.
Start the evening at pre-club Taste in the Gilded Balloon on Cowgate (226 6550), then head to this lively and up-for-it club under the auspices of DJs Fisher & Price. While they play a mix of garage and house music, things get slightly funkier in the back room.

Up!

The Venue, 15-17 Calton Road, Calton Hill, EH8 (557 3073). Bus 30, 35, 40. **Open** 10.30pm-3am Sat monthly. **Admission** £9; £7 concessions. **No credit cards. Map** p310 G/H5.
A mixed monthly club night hosted by DJ Nic Cavendish and guests, who spin trance-style sets.

Work

Ego, Picardy Place, Broughton, EH1 (478 7434). Playhouse buses. **Open** 10.30pm-3am Thur monthly. **Admission** £8; £6 concessions. **No credit cards. Map** p307 G4.
Monthly club night where resident DJs Pete Owen and Rob Hunter play a mix of party and house to a mixed crowd.

Cruising

Calton Hill (*see p98*), at the end of Princes Street, has a fabulous view and attracts contingents of gay sun-worshippers during the summer months. By night it's popular for close encounters of a sexual kind. Be careful, though – it's dangerous, and the nearby piece of land between London Road and Royal Terrace is even scarier. **Warriston Cemetery**, just north of Stockbridge (map p306 E1), on the other hand, is a long-standing cruising ground that has a reputation for being reasonably safe.

Saunas

No.18

18 Albert Place, Leith Walk, Broughton, EH7 (553 3222/www.no18sauna.co.uk). Bus 7, 10, 12, 14, 16, 22, 25, 49. **Open** noon-10pm daily. **Admission** £9; £7 concessions. **No credit cards. Map** p307 H2.
Discreetly situated off Leith Walk, No.18 spreads out over two floors. There's a reception, TV lounge/café, cabins and lockers on the ground floor; in the basement is a jacuzzi, sauna, video lounge, steam room and dark room. It attracts an eclectic mix of men and feels relatively clean.

Townhouse Sauna & Gym

53 East Claremont Street, Broughton, EH1 (556 6116). Bus 8, 13, 17. **Open** noon-11pm Mon-Wed, Sun; noon-midnight Fri, Sat. **Admission** £9; £6 concessions. **No credit cards. Map** p306 F3.
On four floors, this elegant townhouse has the sauna in the basement, with a dark area and massage parlour on the top floor. In between there are smoking and non-smoking lounges. It's busy and clean, with helpful staff.

A quiet afternoon at **Nexus.** See *p206.*

Music

Edinburgh has a thriving classical scene, but now other genres are catching up.

Classical & Opera

Edinburgh's classical music diary is packed to the gills during the International Festival (*see p185*), particularly now that late-night concerts have been added to the programme. But those looking for entertainment during the remaining 11 months of the year won't be disappointed either.

Classical music

Scotland's two main orchestras are regular visitors to the capital, with the **Royal Scottish National Orchestra** a regular at the Usher Hall and the **Scottish Chamber Orchestra** enjoying a loyal following at the Queen's Hall. Between them they keep Edinburgh's discerning concert-goers busy for much of the year, although the main season falls between October and May, when both play on average one concert a week.

The RSNO's Pops in March is always full of popular goodies, while the Proms series in June plugs the gap between the Season and the Festival in August. The orchestra's website, www.rsno.org.uk, is both up to date and informative, detailing its many innovative tributes to great composers (the recent Shostakovich series was a huge success). As its name suggests, the Scottish Chamber Orchestra is slightly smaller in scale, allowing it to pepper its season with more intimate chamber gigs. It manages some superb programming, running the gamut from the 18th to the 21st century, as well as performing the Festival's magnificent 'Last Night' concert in Princes Street Gardens. Check out www.sco.org.uk for more details.

Performing far less frequently, but no less impressively, the **BT Scottish Ensemble** and **BBC Scottish Symphony Orchestra** average around five trips to Edinburgh each season, playing a lot of unusual works and world premieres. Quality programming also comes courtesy of the **Edinburgh Quartet**, **Hebrides Ensemble**, **Dunedin Consort Sinfonia**, **Meadows Chamber Orchestra**, **Paragon Ensemble** and vocal groups **Capella Nova** and the **Scottish Chamber Choir** – all of which perform regularly during the autumn/winter season. In addition, a

Reid Concert Hall: free lunchtime concerts and historic musical instruments. *See p209.*

plethora of English and international orchestras visit the city throughout the year. Although Edinburgh isn't exactly overrun with concert halls, it certainly makes the most of what it's got. The newly refurbished **Usher Hall**, which reopened in December 2001 after a major refit, seats just under 3,000 and if further work goes ahead as planned should become a world class venue by 2005. The **Queen's Hall** may not have the most comfortable seats in Edinburgh, but this converted church is still one of the city's most popular music venues. These two venues aside, it falls on Edinburgh's ecclesiastical establishments to provide homes for musical talent. **Greyfriars Kirk**, **St Mary's Cathedral**, **Canongate Kirk** and **St Giles' Cathedral** are all popular with the choral and organ fraternities.

Queen's Hall

Clerk Street, South Edinburgh, EH8 (box office 668 2019/administration 668 3456/www. queenshalledinburgh.co.uk). Nicolson Street–North Bridge buses. **Open** *Box office* 10am-5.30pm Mon-Sat or until 15mins before performance on concert evenings. **Tickets** £2-£25. **Credit** AmEx, DC, MC, V. **Map** p310 G7.

Intimate yet spacious, this former church has seating on two levels; the stalls and balcony both have good vantage points, although there is the odd restricted view. The old wooden pews can be a tad uncomfortable for longer concerts (and seats are taken out completely for rock gigs). The Scottish Chamber Orchestra performs almost all its concerts here, as do the BT Scottish Ensemble and many fine visiting musicians. The Queen's Hall has played host to artists as diverse as Philip Glass, Julian Lloyd Webber, Sophie Ellis Bextor and local school choirs.

Reid Concert Hall

Faculty of Music, University of Edinburgh, Bristo Square, Old Town, EH8 (concert secretary 650 2423/www.ed.ac.uk/music). Bus 2, 41, 42/Nicolson Street–North Bridge buses. **Open** *Office* 9am-5pm Mon-Fri. *Concerts* 1.10pm Tue, Fri. **Map** p310 G6.

The University of Edinburgh Faculty of Music is a hotbed of young talent that is well worth tapping into. On most Tuesdays and Fridays during term time you can wander into the Reid Concert Hall and enjoy a free lunchtime concert at 1.10pm. You never know what you'll get – an organ recital, soprano and piano duo or even a visit from the Edinburgh Quartet – the only guarantee is that the performance will always be of a high standard. The students also programme evenings at Greyfriars Kirk, Canongate Kirk and Old St Paul's on Jeffrey Street; these are performed by their many musical societies: the Symphony Orchestra, Savoy Opera Group, Chamber Orchestra, Renaissance Singers… the list goes on. Reid Hall also houses the Edinburgh University's unique collection of historic musical instruments (*see p80* **Feeding love**).

Usher Hall

Lothian Road, South Edinburgh, EH1 (box office 228 1155/administration 228 8616/www. usherhall.co.uk). Bus 1, 10, 11, 15, 16, 17, 24, 34. **Open** *Box office* 9am-8pm Mon-Fri; 9am-5.30pm Sat or until 8pm on performance days. **Tickets** prices vary. **Credit** AmEx, MC, V. **Map** p304 A3.

Closed for part of 2001 while it underwent a £9 million refit, the Usher Hall is now back in business. The Edinburgh home of the Royal Scottish National Orchestra and also a major Festival venue, this impressive theatre with 2,700-seater auditorium welcomes an eclectic bunch through its doors. Everyone from children's entertainers the Happy Gang to country old-timer Willie Nelson has played here, but the excellent acoustics and extensive chorus seating make it best suited to classical performances. An appeal is currently in progress to fund further improvements over the next three years.

Churches

Edinburgh has many wonderful old churches and two cathedrals, some of which are used as concert venues, particularly during the Fringe. Year round, the following places of worship double up as musical havens for Edinburgh's numerous orchestras and choirs.

Canongate Kirk

153 Canongate, Old Town, EH8 (Queen's Hall 668 2019). Bus 30, 35. **Open** *Concerts & recitals* phone for details. **Tickets** (available from Queen's Hall) prices vary; phone for details. **Map** p310 H5.

Situated on the Royal Mile, the Kirk was built in 1688. The Canongate parish includes the Palace of Holyroodhouse, which means that it's the local place of worship for the Queen when she's in town. During the rest of the year, it provides a good home for choral groups and chamber orchestras.

Greyfriars Tolbooth & Highland Kirk

2 Greyfriars Place, Candlemaker Row, Old Town, EH1 (225 1900/tickets from Queen's Hall 668 2019/www.greyfriarskirk.com). Bus 2, 23, 27, 28, 41, 42, 45. **Open** *Concerts & recitals* phone for details. **Tickets** (available from Queen's Hall) £4-£6. **Credit** AmEx, MC, V. **Map** p309 F6.

This lovely old church is a great place to visit, whether to take in a concert or simply to stroll through the graveyard. The musical programme features roughly four concerts a month, ranging from the wonderful BBC Scottish Symphony Orchestra to local school choirs. A quarterly leaflet details all forthcoming concerts, plus information on services and lectures.

St Giles' Cathedral

Parliament Square, Old Town, EH1 (visitors' centre 225 9442). Bus 23, 27, 28, 35, 41, 42, 45/Nicolson Street–North Bridge buses. **Open** *Concerts & recitals* phone for details. **Tickets** prices vary; phone for details. **Map** p304 D3.

Arts & Entertainment

Founded in the 1100s, this impressive cathedral has been the scene of executions, riots and celebrations. These days you're more likely to find a visiting US choir raising the roof with their heavenly voices or a guest musician playing the cathedral's acclaimed Rieger organ. A free concert takes place at 6pm most Sundays.

St Mary's Episcopal Cathedral

Palmerston Place, New Town, EH12 (225 6293/ www.cathedral.net). Bus 3, 4, 12, 13, 21, 25, 26, 33. **Open** *Services with music* Sung Eucharist 10.30am Sun. Evensong 5.30pm Mon-Fri; 3.30pm Sun. *Concerts & recitals* phone for details. **Tickets** (concerts & recitals) prices vary; phone for details. **Map** p308 B6.

Regular recitals on the Father Willis organ at 4.30pm each Sunday are just one of the musical highlights at this magnificent cathedral. The Choir of St Mary's sings regularly here, and during the summer (and in particular during the Fringe) visiting choirs perform.

Stockbridge Parish Church

Saxe Coburg Street, Stockbridge, EH3 (332 0122/ tickets from Queen's Hall 668 2019). Bus 19A, 24, 28, 36. **Open** *Concerts & recitals* phone for details. **Tickets** (available from Queen's Hall) £2-£5. **Credit** AmEx, MC, V. **Map** p306 D3.

There are no regular music events at this charming church, but it's very popular for one-off concerts organised by local chamber groups and choirs.

Opera

Although nowhere near as extensive as the city's classical music calendar, Edinburgh's operatic schedule is still fairly busy. The national company, **Scottish Opera**, has its base in Glasgow, but all its productions tour to both Edinburgh and Aberdeen. The wonderful **Festival Theatre** is Scottish Opera's base in the capital; it performs an average of eight works a year here – popular repertoire pieces such as *Cosi fan tutte* and *Madame Butterfly* and the odd new work. Most exciting is the current Ring Cycle series: the first two parts of Wagner's epic were staged in 2000 and 2001, with *Siegfried* to follow in August 2002. The whole Cycle, including *Götterdämmerung*, will be performed in 2003. Scottish Opera's website (www.scottishopera.org.uk) features archive information and details of current productions. The annual visit from the talented opera students of Glasgow's Royal Scottish Academy of Music and Drama to the Festival Theatre is another highlight to look out for.

The **Edinburgh Playhouse** (*see p227*) has started hosting large-scale works such as *La Traviata* and *Aida*, brought to the city by international companies. Although not always of the highest standard, the shows are reliably spectacular and usually entertaining. Gentle operettas of the Gilbert and Sullivan variety are regularly staged at the **King's Theatre** (*see p227*). And finally, the Festival puts on operas at both the Festival Theatre and the King's Theatre.

Edinburgh Festival Theatre

13-29 Nicolson Street, South Edinburgh, EH8 (box office 529 6000/administration 662 1112/ www.eft.co.uk). Nicolson Street–North Bridge buses. **Open** *Box office* 10am-8pm Mon-Sat (until 6pm when no performance); 4pm-curtain Sun (performance days only). *Telephone booking* 11am-8pm Mon-Sat (until 6pm when no performance); 4pm-curtain Sun (performance days only). **Tickets** £5.50-£55. **Credit** AmEx, DC, MC, V. **Map** p310 G6.

A theatrical venue has stood on this Nicolson Street site since 1830, albeit in different guises. Its present incarnation opened to the public in 1994, maintaining the original 1920s proscenium structure inside but coated in sleek glass panels outside. This mix of old and new is also reflected in the programming, with innovative modern dance one week followed by century-old opera the next. A large orchestra pit and fine acoustics make this the ideal venue for Scottish Opera, as well as proving popular with rock, jazz and folk musicians. And the vast stage attracts major dance companies such as Scottish Ballet, Nederlands Dans Theatre and Ballet Rambert (*see p228*). There is seating on three levels, and ticket prices cater for all budgets (the dress circle has wonderful views but can be prohibitively expensive for opera or ballet).

Rock, Folk & Jazz

Rock, pop & dance

Edinburgh is often seen as Glasgow's poorer cousin as far as rock and pop music is concerned. Apart from a few, sporadic but notable exceptions – the Bay City Rollers, the Proclaimers and adopted son Finlay Quaye spring to mind – the city has largely failed to produce its share of musical success stories. However, as local fans are quick to point out, while Glasgow has bred international superstar acts like Texas and Travis, Edinburgh has been quietly producing its own crop of local musicians, producers, remixers and DJs, who release material on small, independent labels. These labels do much to nurture a homegrown music scene, and innovative spirit abounds in a range of musical fields.

The indie rock scene has been hit hard by the closure of live music dives the Attic and the Cas Rock in 2000. Although somewhat seedy, these spaces cherished up-and-coming bands; today, with rents soaring across the city, gig-goers are

increasingly pushed towards more commercial
and less intimate venues. Despite this, the scene
continues to flourish, with established guitar
groups such as Huckleberry, Annie Christian
and Idlewild still working the circuit. The latter,
now signed to Parlophone, look set to break
through to the big league with their thoughtful
indie rock escapades. Among a steady slew
of new hopefuls are Fugazi-style rock outfit
Degrassi and Ballboy, a moody combo who
have released a number of outspoken and
intelligent records including the *I Hate Scotland*
EP. Both bands are signed to enterprising
Edinburgh-based label, SL Records.

Ska is currently enjoying an energetic revival
in the city thanks to club nights such as Dr
No's at the Bongo Club and the Ska Club at the
Venue, which provide a platform for local bands
Bombskare and Latin-charged ska act, Big
Hand. Indeed, a great number of Edinburgh's
gigs take place within the club scene, with
nights at the somewhat raw, bohemian hotspot
the **Bongo Club** (14 New Street, Old Town,
EH8; 556 5204/558 7604/www.outoftheblue.
org.uk) frequently featuring live indie rock,
funk, soul, ragga and hip hop acts as well as
DJs. This 320-capacity leftfield live music
and club space is expected to close by the
end of 2002 to make way for yet another hotel
complex, leaving a gaping hole in the city's live
music scene. But the vocal and motivated bunch
behind the Bongo are looking for a new home,
so don't expect them to go away just because
their building is being demolished.

Hip hop has long enjoyed a ferocious
following in the city, nurtured by local labels
Yush and Oh-Eye Records. Yush pools the
talents of local and international artists and
incorporates diverse styles including breakbeat
and ragga, while Oh-Eye concentrates on
Edinburgh's exceedingly talented DJs and MCs,
including Scottish DMC Champion Ritchie
Ruftone, and the Scotland Yard crew. Proof
postive that Edinburgh is a fertile breeding
ground for the hip hop stars of tomorrow was
shown by local lad Neall Dailly, aka DJ Plus
One, who won the World DMC Champion title
in 2001 at the tender age of 20.

House music fans, meanwhile, are not left out
in the cold. Spurred on by the success of their
club nights, real deal house enthusiast Gareth
Sommerville (Ultragroove) and down-tempo
to chunky house veteran George T (Tribal
Funktion) are currently producing tracks
for their own labels as well as international
imprints. Deep house DJ/producer Aquabassino
has already gone on to achieve global success,
signing to Laurent Garnier's F Communications
label to release his debut album. Drum 'n' bass
does well under the auspices of the Bass Trap

Liquid Room. *See p212.*

label and Messrs G-Mac and DJ Kid. If dance
music is your thing, head to record shack
Underground Solus'shn (*see p178*). Most of the
dance music producers mentioned work there.

Venues

La Belle Angele
*11 Hastie's Close, Cowgate, Old Town, EH1
(225 7536/www.la-belle-angele.co.uk). Bus 23, 27,
28, 41, 42, 45/Nicolson Street–North Bridge buses.*
Open times vary; phone for details. **Admission**
£5-£10. **No credit cards. Map** p304 F6.
This L-shaped live music and club space has been
gradually upgraded over the past two years with
state-of-art sound and lighting rigs. As a consequence,
promotion company Cosmos, which previously based
its operations at the Venue (*see p212*), has now moved
the majority of its live music shows here: everything
from local acts to big name tours.

Café Royal
*17 West Register Street, Old Town, EH1 (557 4792).
Princes Street or Nicolson Street–North Bridge buses.*
Open noon-1am daily. **Admission** free. **Credit**
AmEx, DC, MC, V. **Map** p304 D1.
The upstairs, 280-capacity function room of this old
world bar is used for live gigs. Unfortunately, with
no in-house stage and PA systems, it can be a costly
experience for promoters to stage full-scale events
here, so shows are mainly of an acoustic variety.

Corn Exchange
*10 Newmarket Road, off Chesser Avenue, West
Edinburgh, EH14 (477 3500/www.ece.uk.com). Bus
4, 28, 35, 44.* **Open** times vary; phone for details.
Admission £8-£20. **Credit** AmEx, MC, V.
A converted slaughterhouse is Edinburgh's attempt
to create its own equivalent of Glasgow's hallowed
Barrowland Ballroom. With a capacity of 2,500 and
a lot of money spent to ensure its acoustic qualities,
it can, given a sizeable crowd, be an atmospheric
place to see a band. Gigs have been sporadic since
its opening in 2000, however.

Arts & Entertainment

Breaking the sound barrier

The charts have been left pretty much undented by Edinburgh talent in the 30 years since the overwhelming triumph of tartan that was the Bay City Rollers. Edinburgh acts continually find it hard to break through on a national, never mind an international, scale, and all too often, bands and musicians are forced to leave the city in the hope of making it big elsewhere. Edinburgh has no 'scene' like the Glasgow sound that thrived in the '80s and '90s, and little or no music business to support the talent it produces; major national record companies seem uninterested in seeking out talent in a city with no obvious musical identity.

But if commercial success has proved elusive, this lack has not dampened the enthusiasm and innovation of the city's numerous musicians. From influential early '80s bands such as Josef K, to Davey Henderson's Fire Engines and Nectarine No.9, to new indie band Ballboy, current music press favourites Boards of Canada, and dance artists like Huggy (Burger Queen) and Aquabassino, the city of Edinburgh has consistently produced music of a quality to rival that of its contemporaries on the west coast.

What's more, it seems as though Edinburgh audiences are finally being rewarded for their loyalty with a higher musical profile. Although the city's many small clubs offer a stimulating programme of local bands and up-and-coming acts, the lack of decent-sized venues means it has been hard to attract bigger names to the capital. With the opening of the 3,000-capacity **Corn Exchange** (*see p211*) however, things appear to be moving in the right direction. Bands that previously bypassed Edinburgh on their way to Glasgow's famous Barrowland Ballroom are now adding the city to their tour schedules – including prodigal daughter Shirley Manson who returned with her band Garbage in 2002 – and this in turn seems to be whetting the appetite and increasing demand for live music elsewhere.

Contemporary music now plays a part in the annual Edinburgh festival, with both **T on the Fringe** (an indoor version of the T in the Park music festival) and **Planet Pop** (www. planetpop.co.uk) proving successful, with eclectic bills of rock, pop and dance. Live concerts are firmly established as part of Edinburgh's Hogmanay celebrations. And establishment stalwarts like the Edinburgh Playhouse (*see p267*), the Usher Hall (*see p209*) and even Edinburgh Castle are realising that it pays to make room occasionally among the touring musicals, classical programmes and military extravaganzas for the odd rock and pop experience.

Arts & Entertainment

Liquid Room

9C Victoria Street, Old Town, EH1 (225 2564). Bus 23, 27, 28, 41, 42, 45. **Open** times vary; phone for details. **Admission** £5-£11.50. **No credit cards**. **Map** p304 C3.

Now used regularly by the better local bands and some illustrious out-of-towners, the Liquid Room has a reputation that continues to rise along with the scale of the bands it attracts. The upstairs bar and gallery give a great view of the stage.

The Venue

17-21 Calton Road, Calton Hill, EH8 (557 3073). Bus 30, 40. **Open** times vary; phone for details. **Admission** £4-£9. **No credit cards**. **Map** p310 G5.

A veritable institution on Scotland's live music circuit, the Venue was slowly being run into the ground until new management moved in at the end of 2001. Sound systems have since been overhauled and lighting rigs upgraded, but the main floor of this three-level space still provides the classic rock dive atmosphere on which smaller touring bands thrive. Local, triple-band nights are still a programme staple.

Folk & roots

Spurred on by devolution, the opening of the new Scottish Parliament and consequent concerns over cultural identity, Scotland's folk scene is flourishing like never before. Edinburgh is undoubtedly the epicentre of this remarkable flowering, and is now home to more folk-related music groups than anywhere else in the UK.

The city's large folk contingent is made up of Edinburgh-born musicians, emigré Highlanders and Hebrideans, enthusiasts from Fife and the north-east, a sprinkling of Orcadians and Shetlanders and a good number of English and Irish exports. Folkies flock to the capital in part because it's a nice place to live, boasting more than its fair share of late-night drinking dens in which to enjoy a fiddle session. But also because it provides an opportunity for them to bring their own distinct traditions to the scene's musical melting pot. Traditional forms of folk music played on bagpipes, bodhrans and accordions are mixed in with roots flavours from across the globe to create an 'ethnic' vibe that's as rich as it is diverse.

Just as the folk scene embraces world music influences, so it breaks down musical boundaries by inviting all manner of rock, jazz and dance influences to contribute to the mix. Cross-over acts like Shooglenifty, Martyn Bennett, the Tartan Amoebas and Croft No.5 introduce a dance-based dimension, while up-and-coming groups like the Battlefield Band, Back Of The Moon and Fine Friday bring youthful vitality to traditional forms, thus dispelling the myth that folk music is all about bearded men wearing Arran sweaters. If you're looking to sample some of the city's adventures in folk music, the Edinburgh Folk Club at the **Pleasance** offers a solid and reasonably diverse diet of traditional and contemporary sounds, as does the **Blind Poet**. **Whistle Binkies** makes generous concessions to folk within its eclectic agendas and (for as long as it remains) the **Bongo Club** is a great place to check out cross-over acts. Bigger venues such as the main hall of the **Hub**, the **Edinburgh Festival Theatre** (*see p228*), the **Queen's Hall** and the **Assembly Rooms** (54 George Street, New Town; 220 4349) all stage occasional gigs by Celtic and world-music acts. The Assembly Rooms is also home to a highly popular monthly series of ceilidhs, held throughout the spring and autumn.

To gain an intimate appreciation of more traditional forms of folk, the informal pub session is hard to beat. While these are difficult to track down, the 'wee folk club' on Sundays in the basement of the **Royal Oak** on Infirmary Street and the nightly sessions at **Sandy Bell's** on Forrest Road (for both, *see p150*) are cosy and worth seeking out. The evening gigs at the **Central Bar** in Leith (7 Leith Walk, EH6; 467 3925); the Wednesday night sessions at the **Shore Bar** on the Shore, Leith (553 5080); and the evening sessions, Thursday to Sunday at the **Hebrides** on Market Street in the Old Town (No.17; 220 4213) are also good bets.

Venues

For details of the **Bongo Club**, *see p211*; for the **Queen's Hall**, *see p214*.

The Blind Poet
34 West Nicolson Street, South Edinburgh, EH8 (667 0876). Nicolson Street–North Bridge buses. **Open** 11am-1am Mon-Fri; noon-1am Sat; 6pm-1am Sun. **Open** *Gigs* 10pm Mon-Wed. **Admission** free. **No credit cards. Map** p310 G6.
A small but attractive pub to the south of the city centre, the Blind Poet offers music in the form of folk and traditional residencies.

The Hub
348 Castlehill, Old Town, EH1 (473 2000/www. eif.co.uk/thehub). Bus 23, 27, 28, 35, 41, 42, 45. **Open** *Ticket office* 10am-5pm Mon-Fri. *Concerts* times vary; phone for details. **Tickets** prices vary; phone for details. **Credit** AmEx, DC, MC, V. **Map** p304 C3.
The main auditorium of the Hub, with its bold Mediterranean colour scheme, is a good-looking venue for a variety of concerts, from classical to folk and jazz. However, musical events are infrequent and the acoustics of the room, which used to be the Assembly Hall for the Church of Scotland, are rather too echoing for any great clarity of sound.

The Pleasance
60 The Pleasance, South Edinburgh, EH8 (650 2349/www.albafolk.freeserve.co.uk/folkclubs/efc). Nicolson Street–North Bridge buses. **Admission** £6; £5 members; £4 members. *Membership* £7. **No credit cards. Map** p310 G6.
Home of the Edinburgh Folk Club, which holds sessions here every Wednesday in the Cabaret Bar, except during the Festival, when the Pleasance is taken over by the Fringe.

Whistle Binkies
6 Niddry Street, Old Town, EH1 (557 5114/www. whistlebinkies.com) Nicolson Street–North Bridge buses. **Open** 6pm-3am daily. *Gigs* 9pm, midnight daily. **Admission** free Mon-Thur, Sun & before midnight Fri, Sat; £1 after midnight Fri, Sat. **Credit** MC, V. **Map** p304 D3.
This pub is popular with the rootsy and traditional fraternity, usually featuring sessions (9pm) followed by late-night bands.

Jazz

Despite its comparatively small population, Edinburgh has nurtured a respectable roster of important jazz musicians over the years. Iconoclastic clarinetist Sandy Brown and the Royal High Gang were among those to establish international reputations in the late 1950s while, in more recent years, saxophonist Tommy Smith has been celebrated as one of the most important jazz musicians Scotland has produced. However, although Edinburgh's provision for jazz is better than that of some other, larger metropolises, artists are often tempted to leave the city to make their names and some money elsewhere.

One artist who has followed this pattern s acclaimed local jazz and blues singer Nikki King, who tried her luck in London after years working the Edinburgh circuit. Her effort was swiftly rewarded with the Perrier Young Jazz Vocalist of the Year award in 2001.

The current scene ranges from Dixieland in pubs to international jazz at the **Queen's Hall** and at **Henry's Jazz Cellar**. Promoters

A subterranean trumpet solo at **Henry's Jazz Cellar**.

Assembly Direct took over the reins at Henry's two years ago, dropping the previous bent towards jazz/hip hop fusion in favour of a more traditional musical outlook. Nevertheless, Henry's does still feature acts like the Dave Milligan Trio, who combine old standards with funkier fare. Meanwhile, the recently opened **Beat Jazz Basement**, on the former site of jazz pub Cellar No.1, has taken up where Henry's left off, bringing DJs and live acts together for improvised jam sessions.

The history of jazz is celebrated by the **Scottish National Jazz Orchestra** (01555 860599/www.snjo.co.uk) in a variety of big band sessions held throughout the year. Since its formation in 1996, the band and its celebrated director Tommy Smith have been a creative presence on the Scottish jazz scene, staging retrospective concert series that pay tribute to the likes of Basie, Ellington, Schneider and Wheeler.

The end of July or the beginning of August ushers in the **Bank of Scotland Edinburgh Jazz and Blues Festival** (*see p185*). Staged over ten days, the festival includes concert hall, theatre, club, and open-air events, with all kinds of jazz from local and international artists. The principal concerts are held at the **Queen's Hall** and the **Hub** (*see p213*), where artists as diverse as Greg Osby, Tommy Smith, Courtney Pine, Charlie Mariano and Sheila Jordan have all performed in recent years. The **Leith Jazz Festival** (www.jazz-in-scotland.co.uk) is a much more modest event in musical terms, but is a convivial weekend (usually early in June) when the pubs and restaurants around the Shore move into raucous swing mode.

Venues

The Beat Jazz Basement

1A Chambers Street, Old Town, EH1 (467 2539/ jazz@freakmarketing.com). Nicolson Street–North Bridge buses. **Open** 8pm-3am daily. **Admission** free before 11pm, £2 after 11pm Mon, Tue, Sun; free before 10pm, £3 after 10pm Wed, Thur; £3-£4 Fri; £5-£7 Sat. **No credit cards. Map** p310 G6.

A well-established jazz pub recently relaunched to become Edinburgh's leading contemporary jazz venue. Jazz-funk fusion, swing showcases and vocal jazz and blues dominate the weekday programme, while weekends have a diverse, dance-based outlook with improvised live jams fusing jazz with hip hop and house. A text message information service with details of the evening's gig is available by texting 'jazz' to the following number: 07718 933866.

Henry's Jazz Cellar

8 Morrison Street, West Edinburgh, EH3 (538 7385). Bus 2, 28, 34. **Open** 8pm-3am daily. *Music* Wed-Sun. **Admission** £5-£8. **No credit cards. Map** p308 C6.

Assembly Direct, which previously staged events at the Assembly Rooms, now schedule the programme at this late-night venue. A fairly intimate subterranean space, Henry's attracts an enthusiastic audience for the European and American acts that play here.

Queen's Hall

Clerk Street, South Edinburgh, EH8 (box office 668 2019/administration 668 3456/ www.queens halledinburgh.co.uk). Nicolson Street–North Bridge buses. **Open** *Box office* 10am-5.30pm Mon-Sat or until 15mins after start of last performance; 1hr before performance Sun. **Admission** £2-£25. **Credit** AmEx, MC, V. **Map** p310 G7.

This converted Georgian church has played host to some big names in every sphere of music. The atmosphere is intimate and the acoustics good, but the wooden pews are a bit hard. *See also p209.*

Arts & Entertainment

Nightlife

With bars, clubs and comedy venues aplenty, there's no excuse not to drink, dance and laugh your way around town.

As a nation, Scotland's not shy of sex, drugs and rock 'n' roll. The Scots drink hard, party hard and hard enough – or hard enough at least to bankroll their pleasure-seeking tendencies. In Edinburgh, the national hedonism is concealed somewhat by the city's austere exterior but, as the capital's catchphrase 'fur coat and nae knickers' implies, a seething underbelly of debauchery lies primed and pulsing, ready for those seeking a spot of nocturnal naughtiness.

Unlike in much of the rest of the UK, where after-hours adventuring begins at 8pm prompt to capitalise on peak drinking hours, Scotland's late licensing allows for a more leisurely start to an evening out on the tiles. The majority of Edinburgh's city centre bars are licensed until 1am, which means there's no rush to get out before 9pm. A few bars are open until 3am at which hour the club venues also call time.

Pre-club bars

At worst, style-bar culture can seem smug and self-satisfied, dominated by trendy twenty-somethings posing in the latest labels. At best however, it represents a happy meeting ground between pub and club; a place that stays open until 1am, sports a pair of decks in the corner and hires someone to use them rather than just sticking on the latest mix CD.

The great granddaddy of Edinburgh's pre-club scene is the **City Café** (*see p148*), an old haunt of author Irvine Welsh and a popular springboard to nearby Cowgate club venues **La Belle Angele** and **The Honeycomb**. **EH1** (*see p148*), **Iguana** (*see p149*) and oriental-style bar **Bam Bou** (*see p146*) act as similar drinking dens cum filter funnels for the clubs.

In the north of the city, style-conscious **Pop-Rokit** (*see p155*) warms up weekend outings to next door club venue, **Ego**, while dancefloor devotees frequenting **The Venue** and **Studio 24** on Calton Road opt for Czech style bar **Pivo** (*see p155*) as their watering hole of choice.

Then there are those pre-club spaces where you're likely to stay all night: at **Wash** (*see p150*) stunning views of the city are set to a retro cool soundtrack of the best in '60s and '70s funk and soul, while at **Black Bo's** (*see p147*) the atmosphere of down-at-heel sophistication will add spice to your night on the town.

Clubs

It may not boast the sheer scale nor the sophistication of Glasgow, but the capital's club scene is eclectic and thriving.

Techno boffins were served considerably well for over ten years by legendary night Pure. It shut up shop in 2000 but still stages one-off specials bringing back big-shot acts like Andrew Weatherall, Richie Hawtin, Luke Slater and Green Velvet, who made their names at Pure in the 1990s. The techno mantle has now been taken up by the likes of **Pillbox** and **Dogma** (formerly Lost) and if it's hard bag you're after, **Studio 24** is the best venue at which to enjoy it.

The **drum 'n' bass** scene was, until recently, dominated by stalwart night **Manga** (at La Belle Angele), but 2001 and early 2002 saw an explosion of nascent jungle nights capitalising on the popularity of drum 'n' bass among the city's students. Similarly, **hip hop** has long enjoyed a ferocious following in the capital, with DMC turntablists Plus One and Richie Ruftone earning their stripes on the wheels of steel at nights like Seen and Scratch. The latter continues to run at **La Belle Angele**, where it combines the talents of resident DJs with US legends such as Masta Ace, Cash Money and DJ Rectangle.

Fans of **house**, the overwhelmingly prevalent style of dance music, can take their pick from real deal fare at established night **Ultragroove** at La Belle Angele; progressive, tribal tunes at **Atomic Baby**; and tracks of a more commercial bent at Club Mercado nights **Eye Candy** and **Blast**.

Those seeking specialist beats, meanwhile, can rest assured that everything from easy-listening (**Vegas**) and dub reggae (**Messenger Sound System**) to '60s garage punk (**The Go-Go**) and ska (**Dr No's**, **The Ska Club**) happily co-exist with more commercial nights on the capital's club circuit.

SAVE OUR CLUBS

Since the Scottish Parliament arrived in the city there has been a dramatic increase in city centre rents, a trend that has put underground clubbing under threat. The closure of venues Café Graffiti, Wilkie House and Noa in the past two years, and the impending closure of bohemian hotspot the **Bongo Club** (14 New Street, Old Town, EH8; office 556 5204/bar 558 7604/www.outoftheblue.org.uk) is cause for concern among Edinburgh's clubbers. The Bongo Club, part of a multimedia arts space above an old bus station, hits a truly underground vibe. Its music is eclectic (including the likes of dub reggae and ska); the accent is away from house music towards diverse beats and breaks. Redevelopment is scheduled for the end of 2002, but all may not be lost; the vocal and energetic group behind the Bongo are looking for a new venue.

INFORMATION AND PRICES

The ever-evolving nature of the nightlife scene means that venues and club nights change from one week to the next. The ones we have listed below are established nights that look set to stay the course. However, while you're in town, it's also a good idea to pick up a copy of entertainment guide *The List*, which provides the most reliable listings available. Flyers stacked up in style bars and record shops also help point out and promote one-off events. **Underground Solu'shn** (*see p178*) is always a good place to hang out if you want the inside track on Edinburgh's club scene – the staff are friendly and know their stuff.

Club admission prices vary wildly (from £2 to £20), with most venues charging little, if at all, during the week. The higher prices are for non-members even on Fridays and Saturdays. Expect to pay even more during the Festival, when clubs extend their opening hours to 5am.

The Beat Jazz Basement

1A Chambers Street, Old Town, EH1 (467 2539/jazz@freakmarketing.com). Nicolson Street–North Bridge buses. **Open** free before 11pm, £2 after 11pm Mon, Tue, Sun; free before 10pm, £2-£3 after 10pm Wed, Thur; free before 10pm, £3-£4 after 10pm Fri; £5-£7 Sat. **No credit cards. Map** p310 G6.

This subterranean jazz joint is open seven nights a week and supplies a broad spectrum that ranges from jazz-funk through swing to vocal jazz and blues. Club culture is most in evidence at the weekend improvised jam sessions, which fuse live instrumentation with decks and effects. *See also p214.*

La Belle Angele

11 Hastie's Close, Cowgate, Old Town, EH1 (225 7536/www.la-belle-angele.co.uk). Nicolson Street–North Bridge buses. **Open** times vary; phone for details. **Admission** £5-£10. **No credit cards. Map** p304 D3.

Despite its unassuming guise – a former art gallery, tucked away in a little square at the end of a dark, secluded close – La Belle Angele has long been celebrated as the epicentre of the city's underground

club scene. Facilities at the club are constantly being upgraded and recently the venue has boasted its strongest roster in a ten-year history, including hip hop night Scratch, drum 'n' bass monthly Manga and the real deal house extravaganza, Ultragroove. *See also p211.*

The Citrus

40-42 Grindlay Street, South Edinburgh, EH3 (622 7086/www.citrus-club.co.uk). Bus 1, 10, 11, 15, 16, 17, 22, 24, 34, 35. **Open** 11pm-3am Thur, Sat; 10.30pm-3am Fri. **Admission** £2-£5. **No credit cards. Map** p304 A3.

Small, indie and retro-oriented club that does well from its student clientele.

Club Mercado

36-39 Market Street, Old Town, EH1 (226 4224/www.clubmercado.com). Bus 23, 27, 28, 41, 42, 45/Nicolson Street–North Bridge buses. **Open** 4.30pm-3am Fri; 10.30pm-3am Sat. **Admission** £5-£10. **No credit cards. Map** p304 D2.

A venue where the emphasis is on sheer fun, with an unashamed tendency to celebrate the commercial and the kitsch, especially at the marvellous Tackno on the last Sunday of the month. As its name suggests, TFI Friday is an end-of-the-week after-work office party fest: be warned.

Ego

14 Picardy Place, Broughton, EH1 (478 7434). Playhouse buses. **Open** 11pm-3am Tue; 10pm-3am Fri-Sun. **Admission** £2-£8. **No credit cards. Map** p307 G4.

Once a dancehall, then a casino, Ego retains its faded grandeur of its former identities with long red velvet curtains, antique chandeliers and dramatic wall murals dominating the decor of the high-ceilinged space. These camp surroundings would not be suited to every club night, but easy-listening night Vegas and gay house night Joy flourish here. Downstairs, the Cocteau Lounge is sometimes used as a chill-out zone for the main event or hosts separate events such as '60s night The Go Go.

The Honeycomb

15-17 Niddry Street, EH1 (556 2442). Nicolson Street–North Bridge buses. **Open** 10pm-3am Thur-Sun. **Admission** free-£10. **No credit cards. Map** p310 G5.

Opened on the former site of clubbing hell-hole the Vaults in March 2001, the Honeycomb has cleaned up Edinburgh nightlife and given the dressed-up contingency a new lease of life in the process. Innovative interior design combines with a superior selection of underground club nights including the established tech-trance session Sublime and the up-and-coming drum 'n' bass monthly Behave?.

Liquid Room

9C Victoria Street, Old Town, EH1 (225 2564). Bus 2, 23, 27, 28, 41, 42, 45. **Open** times vary; phone for details. **Admission** £5-£11.50. **No credit cards. Map** p309 F6.

Lovely, lively **Liquid Room**.
See p216.

three-tier extravaganza. Following a management change, facilities have been upgraded and the roster of club nights overhauled. Legendary sessions such as techno night Pure and jackin' house shindig Tribal Funktion operated from here during the Venue's heyday in the mid-1990s; this underground vibe is currently kept alive by tech-trance showcase Concept and progressive house night Majestica. *See also p212.*

The Wee Red Bar

Edinburgh College Of Art, Lauriston Place, EH3 (229 1442). Bus 23, 27, 28, 45. **Open** *Club nights* 11am-3pm Fri, Sat. **Admission** £4. **No credit cards. Map** p309 E6.

The Art School's gang hut plays host to one-off club and live music specials, plus regular weekend shindigs. Of these, Saturday session the Egg provides a reliable mix of indie, rock and dancefloor soul. You have to be a student (anywhere) or a guest of a student to get in.

Aimed at students during the week and famed for its Friday indie crossover club Evol, this former crypt has flourished under conscientious management to become one of the city's leading live music and club venues. Recent developments include a new back room space and notable additions to the regular line-up: hedonistic house night Luvely, Scottish superclub Colours and Sunday staple, Taste. *See also p212.*

Opal Lounge

51A George Street, New Town, EH2 (226 2275). Bus 28, 40, 41, 42/Princes Street buses. **Open** noon-3am daily. **Admission** free. **Credit** AmEx, MC, V. **Map** p304 B1.

Is it a bar? Is it a restaurant? Is it a club? Not quite any of these, but trying to be them all, this chic, many-roomed basement operates a smart dress code in the evening, when charty dance music predominates. The food, served until 10pm, is oriental in nature, well prepared and not too pricey.

Studio 24

24 Calton Road, Calton Hill, EH8 (558 3758). Bus 24, 25, 35, 35A. **Open** 11pm-3am Wed; 10pm-3am Thur; 10.30pm-3am Fri, Sat. **Admission** £1-£7. **No credit cards. Map** p310 H5.

A back-to-basics club venue par excellence, Studio 24 is a two-tier space comprising a concrete-floored barn downstairs and a slightly more intimate upstairs arena. Hard techno, goth and rock nights dominate the programme, so dress down and get to grips with some raw club culture. Not to be missed.

The Venue

17-21 Calton Road, Calton Hill, EH8 (557 3073). Bus 30, 35. **Open** times vary; phone for details. **Admission** £4-£9. **No credit cards. Map** p310 G/H5.

The Venue is a three-floor live music and club venue, where each floor can host a different independent event or the whole space can be taken over for a

Discos

Edinburgh's wildlife is at its most colourful in the West End, on the Grassmarket, Lothian Road, the Cowgate, and in the newly opened Fountainpark, all of which positively throng with revellers on Friday and Saturday nights. Bare-legged girls with high heels, even higher hemlines and WonderBra busts teeter out of pubs and queue nonchalantly for clubs. The lads, sporting chinos, checked shirts and too much aftershave, stagger and pose manfully in their wake. These are the lands of the discotheque, where the meat-market mentality never went away. A night out starts with a group of pals getting tanked up on as much alcohol as they are able, as cheaply as possible, then boogying down to some chart and party sounds before getting up close and personal with a member of the opposite sex.

Mega pubs with dancefloors such as the **Three Sisters** (*see p150*) or the bars on the Grassmarket are where such shenanigans normally start out and – given the alcohol intake – frequently end.

The Ark

3 Semple Street, West Edinburgh, EH3 (229 7733). Bus 1, 2, 28, 34, 35. **Open** phone for details. **Admission** phone for details. **Credit** phone for details. **Map** p309 D7.

A mix of students and office workers from the West End frequent this one-room club space (650 capacity) to take advantage of the cheap drinks, chart and party playlist and one of the liveliest atmospheres in town.

The Cavendish

3 West Tollcross, South Edinburgh, EH3 (228 3252). Bus 10, 11, 15, 16, 17. **Open** 10pm-3am Wed, Fri, Sat; 11pm-3am Sun. **Admission** £3-£7. **Credit** (entry only) MC, V. **Map** p309 D7.

Arts & Entertainment

School Disco at **Revolution**: perfect for reliving those playground fantasies.

This was once a roller disco, with a springy floor, so it's rather fitting that the management now restricts the music to 1960s and '70s nostalgia sounds. In the main area downstairs (respectably dressed over-25s only) there is seating for those who'd rather drink and talk, but the best hangout is the upstairs Mambo Club, a long-running reggae, funk and soul night held on Fridays and Saturdays. The Cavendish should reopen in autumn 2002 after the refurbishment is complete.

Eros/Elite
Fountainpark, 65 Dundee Street, West Edinburgh, EH11 (228 1661/www.nightclub.co.uk). Bus 28, 34, 35. **Admission** £2-£5 before midnight; £4-£7 after midnight. **Credit** MC, V. **Map** p308 B8.
While the retail business park clubbing experience may not be to everyone's liking, there's no denying that the huge 2,100 capacity venue (split into Eros for the young horny types and Elite for the more discerning over-25s) pulls in the punters good and proper. So popular is it, in fact, that there are organised coaches to bring in eager party people from all over Scotland. Scary.

Gaia
28 King's Stables Road, South Edinburgh, EH1 (229 7986). Bus 2, 35. **Open** 10pm-3am Tue-Thur; 9pm-3am Fri-Sun. **Admission** £2-£4. **No credit cards**. **Map** p309 E6.
Gaia gets packed with students, who make the most of the regular cheap drinks promo nights to dance very drunkenly to a mix of indie pop, house, Latin and breakbeats. The highlight here is Tuesday's Shagtag, a pulling session based on a complex numerical flirting system.

Po Na Na
43B Frederick Street, New Town, EH2 (226 2224/ www.ponana.co.uk). Bus 19, 24, 28, 29, 30, 37. **Open** 10pm-3am daily. **Admission** £4 after 11pm, £5 after midnight Fri, Sat; free Mon-Thur, Sun. **Credit** AmEx, MC, V. **Map** p304 B1.

The Edinburgh branch of the nationwide souk-style bar-cum-club chain tends to be frequented by wealthy students and well-dressed workies. DJs play disco, funk and house tracks until 3am daily.

Revolution
31 Lothian Road, West Edinburgh, EH1 (229 7670). Bus 1, 10, 11, 15, 16, 17, 22, 24, 34. **Open** 10.30pm-3am Mon, Thur-Sat. **Admission** £4-£7. **No credit cards**. **Map** p309 D6.
A £2.5-million facelift might have left this massive venue an impressively grand interior, including four bars and a swooping lighting rig, but the clientele and their behaviour haven't changed much from its former incarnation as Century 2000: white stilettos, testosterone overload and fights in the girls' loos are not uncommon. Lots of drinks promos and a steady stream of chart and party anthems.

Subway West End
23 Lothian Road, West Edinburgh, EH1 (229 9197/ www.subwaywestend.co.uk). Bus 1, 10, 11, 15, 16, 17, 22, 24, 34. **Open** 7pm-3am Mon-Thur, Sun; 4pm-3am Fri; 6pm-3am Sat. **Admission** £1-£4. **No credit cards**. **Map** p309 D6.
Owned by Luminar, the UK's largest independent nightclub conglomerate, this large one-room space is mobbed throughout the week by frisky students and well-oiled West End workies keen to soak up the lively atmosphere at the themed party nights.

Comedy

A fine Australian stand-up once described Edinburgh as a summer camp for comedians. Granted, the weather often belies that positive description, but for the month of August at least, if you're involved in the laughter business, the **Fringe** (*see p186*) is the place to be. Television contracts and comedy awards – including the illustrious Perrier – are thrashed out in a flurry of flyers, parties and round-the-clock laughter. Make no mistake though, behind the hilarity comedy is a serious business; that one month can dictate comedians' fortunes, at least until the following August.

Apart from those four hectic weeks each year, live comedy in Edinburgh remained a bit of a damp squib until 1998, when Tommy Sheppard founded Scottish comedy's nesting ground, the **Stand**. The New Town basement venue has nurtured a keen comedy audience and now operates seven nights a week, with a varied programme that features a mix of home-grown talent and luminaries from the international circuit. Such is the demand for tickets that it's often standing room only for the five-act weekend showcase. Big-name headliners might include Ross Noble, Daniel Kitson or Adam Hills, supplemented by resident compères and local support acts: watch out for local rising stars Craig Hill, Frankie Boyle, Allan Miller and Des Clarke.

The future of Scottish comedy almost certainly lies in the hands of the Stand. Its highly successful comedy workshops are a breeding ground for new talent; many fledgling comedians find their feet at the weekly newcomers' Red Raw night and several have gone on to greater things: Stand graduate Miles Jupp won the So You Think You're Funny competition in 2001.

Since the Stand dropped its much-maligned restrictive booking policy, comedy in Edinburgh is gradually showing signs of expansion. Rumour has it that a branch of Jongleurs will open at an entertainment complex just yards from the Stand. In the meantime, local promoter and comedian **Reg Anderson** organises a variety of pub gig ventures, and Fringe mecca Gilded Balloon is a venue for touring comedians and the increasingly popular performance poetry nights from the **Big Word** camp. Garth Cruikshank and Eddie McCabe, Perrier Newcomer winners in 2001, turn out their bizarre shambolic escapades at weekly comedy quiz **Hang The VJ** and at cult cabaret **Snatch Club**, while a host of more sporadic comedy nights caters for the overflow audiences. In addition to this indigenous activity, the TV-boosted big guns of the UK-wide comedy scene periodically pass through on tour, playing the Queen's Hall (see p209), the Traverse (see p228) or the Festival Theatre (see p228). Full details of comedy events are given in The List and online at www.scottishcomedy.com.

Big Word Performance Poetry

Gilded Balloon, 233 Cowgate, Old Town, EH1 (226 6550). Bus 23, 27, 28, 41, 42, 45/Nicolson Street–North Bridge buses. **Performances** 9pm every 2nd Thur. **Admission** £4; £3 concessions. **Map** p304 D3.

Not strictly comedy, but laughter is high on the agenda at these fortnightly performances. Hosted by Jem Rolls and Anita Govan, and featuring serious poets as well as well-versed stand-ups, the Big Word venture has expanded to Glasgow, Dundee, Aberdeen and now London. The Poetry Slam at La Belle Angele, held every three months, is a must-see.

Hang the VJ & Snatch Club

Hang the VJ: Three Sisters, 139 Cowgate, Old Town, EH1 (622 6800). Bus 23, 27, 28, 41, 42, 45/Nicolson Street–North Bridge buses. **Quiz** 9pm Mon. **Admission** free. **Map** p304 D3. *Snatch Club: Liquid Room, 9C Victoria Street, Old Town, EH1 (225 2564). Bus 23, 27, 28, 41, 42, 45.* **Open** 10pm-3am Thur. **Admission** £3.50; £2.50 concessions. **Map** p304 C3.

The antithesis of straight stand-up in every possible sense. Garth Cruikshank and Eddie McCabe (in character as Harry Ainsworth and Dave Strong) have long purveyed a chaotic double act to the delight of their cult following. A Perrier Newcomer Award in 2001 raised their profile considerably, but they continue to ply offbeat absurdity at their weekly comedy quiz, Hang the VJ, and club night, the Snatch Club.

Reg Anderson's Comedy Cellar/Tavern

Cellar: Fin MacCool's, 161 Lothian Road, EH3 (622 7109). Bus 1, 10, 11, 15, 16, 17, 22, 24, 34. **Comedy** 9pm Thur. **Admission** £2. **Map** p309 D6. *Tavern: Nichol Edward's, Niddry Street, EH1 (556 8642). Nicolson Street–North Bridge buses.* **Comedy** 9.30pm Wed. **Admission** £3. **Map** p310 G5.

Sunderland-born comedian Reg Anderson is almost as famous for showcasing other stand-ups as he is for his own brand of magic, music and mirth. Thursday nights in the Fin MacCool's basement are quite an institution, and have been supplemented by his latest venture at Nichol Edwards. Expect new and established Scottish comedians with a slightly edgy feel.

The Stand

5 York Place, New Town, EH2 (enquiries 558 7373/ box office 558 7272/www.thestand.co.uk). Bus 8, 12, 16, 17, 25, 25A. **Comedy** Red Raw 8.30-10.30pm Mon. **Theme nights** (Gay, Connoisseur & Benefit Shows) 9-11pm Tue. *A Kick Up the Tabloids/Auld Reekie's Oxters/Walk Out* 9-11pm Wed. **Comedy** acts 9-11pm Thur; 9-11.15pm Fri; 9-11.30pm Sat. *Six on Sunday* (short acts) 8.30-10pm Sun. **Admission** £1 Mon; £5-£6 Tue; £4-£6 Wed; £5 Thur; £6, £5 concessions Fri; £7 Sat; £3 Sun. **Credit** MC, V. **Map** p306 F4.

By day the Stand is a seriously chilled café bar; battered sofas, intimate spaces and a simple menu create its laid-back vibe. By night the basement venue is transformed into a comedy haven comprising two performance spaces: the snug studio, with its trademark Loony Toons backdrop, is used for weekday shows. The main cabaret bar is used for the weekend showcases; it seats around 160, plus standing room.

Sport & Fitness

Where the football rivalry is friendly and golf is a sport for all.

You only have to look out across the Meadows on a sunny afternoon to see evidence of Edinburgh's sporting passions: it's a patchwork of sport, with cricket, rugby, football, tennis, golf, softball, hockey, running, walking, cycling all being played and enjoyed independently and, failing a sudden downpour, successfully.

In terms of organised participative sports, clubs tend to be organised and publicised from the city's major leisure venues. **Meadowbank Sports Centre** and the **Royal Commonwealth Pool** are two of the larger council-run centres. **Edinburgh Leisure** (650 1001) can provide details of activities and venues, while **SportScotland** (317 7200/www.sport scotland.org.uk) holds a database of governing bodies in Scotland.

Rugby is the most avidly followed spectator sport in Edinburgh, and **Murrayfield Stadium** hosts around eight of Scotland's major international home matches every year. Pro-team **Edinburgh Rugby**, now playing at Meadowbank Stadium, are a burgeoning force.

Edinburgh is a football-loving city too. City clubs **Heart of Midlothian** and **Hibernian** enjoy a healthy rivalry, but their performance pales before Glasgow giants Celtic and Rangers.

In the summer months, the golfing calendar takes over, with important competitions at **Muirfield** and **St Andrews**.

Spectator sports

American football

The arrival of the **Scottish Claymores** in 1995 – fully professional and with a strong NFL presence – established the sport in Edinburgh. Under the guidance of new coach Gene Dalquist, the team is gradually earning a solid reputation among its European counterparts. The Claymores play in the NFL Europe league between April and June. Home games are played at both **Hampden Park** in Glasgow and **Murrayfield Stadium** (*see p222*) in Edinburgh.

Scottish Claymores

Information: 205 St Vincent Street, Glasgow, G2 (0141 222 3800/ticket hotline 0500 353535/www. claymores.co.uk). **Open** *Apr-June* 9am-6pm Mon-Fri. *July-Mar* 9am-5pm Mon-Fri. **Tickets** from £12; from £4 concessions. **Credit** AmEx, MC, V.

Basketball

The recently founded **Edinburgh Rocks** is the only Scottish franchise in the UK-wide BBL Championship. Home games are played most Sunday afternoons during the September to April season, from 5pm, at The Quarry, the self-styled basketball court at **Meadowbank Sports Centre** (*see p224*).

Cricket

The presence of a national side is helping to develop the game's popularity in Scotland. The season runs from mid-April to September and in season 2003, Scotland will be competing with English and Welsh teams in Division Two of the Norwich Union League. The **Scottish Cricket Ltd** (313 7420/www.scu.org.uk) is a useful contact if you want to find out more.

Cycling

The City of Edinburgh racing team is Britain's crack track outfit, based at the velodrome at the **Meadowbank Sports Centre** (*see p224*). Highlights of the local track calendar include the **East of Scotland Grand Prix** (end of June) and the **Festival meeting** (mid-August). The velodrome is home to the **Scottish Cyclists' Union** (652 0187/www.scuweb.com), which can advise on all the cycling sports.

Football

If football was a party, Edinburgh would be hanging with the wallflowers. That's not to say football isn't popular, it's just that professional rivals **Heart of Midlothian** (Hearts) and **Hibernian** (Hibs) don't always match their fervent support with on-the-pitch skill. But there again, there isn't as much money swilling around Edinburgh as in Glasgow, where the titans of the Scottish Premier League: Celtic and Rangers (collectively known as the Old Firm), soak up the lion's share of the trophies. Nor do Edinburgh's supporters go for the violent rivalry of the Old Firm's: Edinburgh derby matches are bitterly fought on the field and vociferously supported from the terraces, but are essentially good-humoured affairs. Financial insecurity in Scottish football has done no

All eyes on the ball at **Hibernian FC**.

favours to either Hibs or Hearts, but by contrast **Livingston FC** has bucked the trend. Formed from failing Edinburgh side Meadowbank Thistle in 1995, the club has risen from the doldrums of the lower divisions to win a place in the UEFA Cup in 2002.

Heart of Midlothian FC

Tynecastle Stadium, Gorgie Road, West Edinburgh, EH11 (200 7200/shop 200 7211/tickets 200 7201/www.heartsfc.co.uk). Bus 1, 2, 3, 21, 25, 33, 34, 38. **Open** *Shop* 9.30am-5.30pm Mon-Fri; 9.30am-3pm matchdays. **Tickets** £12-£19; £6-£10 concessions. **Credit** AmEx, MC, V.

If you haven't bought tickets by phone, you can usually get them on match days from the ticket cash sales booths in McLeod Street (not from the turnstiles). Once inside the stadium, the Wheatfield Stand is a good place to watch the game.

Hibernian FC

Easter Road Stadium, 12 Albion Place, Leith, EH7 (661 2159/shop 656 7078/ticket hotline 0870 840 1875/www.hibernianfc.co.uk). Bus 1, 4, 5, 15, 19, 25, 35. **Open** *Shop* 9am-5pm Mon-Fri; 9.30am-3pm, 4.45pm-5.15pm matchdays. *Ticket office* 9am-5pm Mon-Fri; 9.30am-1pm Sat. *Ticket hotline* 24hrs daily. **Tickets** £17-£25; £10 concessions. **Credit** AmEx, MC, V. **Map** p307 J2.

Tickets can be bought over the phone, or at the ticket office until an hour before kick-off on match days; after that, pay at the turnstiles. Top spots in the stadium are the West and Famous Five stands.

Livingston FC

West Lothian Courier Stadium, Alderstone Road, Livingston, EH54 (01506 417000/www.livingstonfc.co.uk). **Open** 9am-5pm Mon-Fri; 10.30am-3pm matchdays. **Tickets** £17-£19; £10 concessions. **Credit** AmEx, MC, V.

Golf

Scotland is home to some famous golf courses, including **St Andrews** (*see p224*), the home of the Royal & Ancient (01334 460 001/www.randa. org) – the game's governing body and organiser of the British Open – and **Muirfield** (*see p224*), venue for the 2002 British Open in July.

Horse racing

The sport of kings takes place at five courses in Scotland, with around 80 days of racing a year.

Ayr

2 Whitletts Road, Ayr, KA8 (01292 264179/www.ayr-racecourse.co.uk). **Tickets** (by telephone booking only) £7-£14. **Credit** MC, V.

Scotland's largest course hosts 25 meetings a year. The biggest events are the Scottish Grand National (April) and the Ayr Gold Cup (September).

Hamilton Park

Bothwell Road, Hamilton, ML3 (01698 283806/www.hamilton-park.co.uk). **Tickets** £10-£15; free under-16s. **Credit** MC, V.

Scotland's most urban course hosts about 17 meetings from April/May to September, many in the evening, and is known as the 'Royal Ascot of the north'. The Saints and Sinners (June) meeting is the race of choice. Advice: dress to thrill.

Kelso

18-20 Glendale Roadd, Wooler, Northumberland NE71 (01668 281611/www.kelso-races.co.uk). **Tickets** £7-£15. **Credit** MC, V.

Around 13 meetings a year between September and May. The biggest events are the Novices Hurdle and the Scottish Borders National, both held in March.

A taste for adventure

The wilds of Scotland have plenty to offer adrenalin addicts. The sight of snowy mountains or fast-flowing rapids can have a strange effect, making even the usually sane want to try something dangerous. Luckily there are plenty of professionals to show you how it's done.

Aviemore

www.aviemore.co.uk.
Aviemore is the biggest winter sports centre in the UK.

C-N-Do Scotland

01786 445703/www.cndoscotland.com.
Climbing and rock scrambling specialists offering guided scrambles and climbs throughout the Scottish mainland, including Ben Nevis, Glencoe and the Cairngorms.

Monster Activities

01809 501340/www.monsteractivities.com.
Water, land and snow sports and activities in the Highlands of Scotland. There's skiing at the Nevis ski range, kayaking on Loch Oich, along with whitewater rafting, abseiling, walking, mountain biking and even tomahawk throwing. Accommodation can be arranged.

Nae Limits

01250 876310/www.nae-limits.com.
Nae Limits specialises in what it cheerfully refers to as 'adrenalin sports'. These include whitewater rafting, canyoning, cliff jumping, gorge crossing and freefall abseiling. Most activities take place in the wild terrain of Perthshire (clients are advised to stay nearby). There's skiing in winter too.

Musselburgh

Linkfield Road, Musselburgh, EH21 (665 2859/www. musselburgh-racecourse.co.uk). **Tickets** £10-£15; £5 concessions; free under-16s. **Credit** MC, V.
Scotland's oldest racecourse hosts 22 meetings per year, some in the evening, which are well attended. The Pinkie Bar was opened in 1997 by the legendary jockey Lester Piggot. Watch out for the Scottish Sprint Cup in June.

Perth

Scone Palace Park, Perth, PH2 (01738 551597/ www.perth-races.co.uk). **Admission** £4-£15. **No credit cards**.
Frequently voted the 'best small racecourse in the north', Perth hosts around ten meetings a year. Enjoy the garden party atmosphere and maybe catch a pre-meet game of polo. The biggest event of the year is the Perth Festival Meeting in April.

Rugby union

Edinburgh differs from other parts of Scotland because its club scene is so closely linked to a group of prestigious, fee-paying schools. The days when only former pupils could play for the likes of Edinburgh Accies, Heriot's, Stewart's-Melville and Watsonians are long gone, but the school-based rivalries remain.

Edinburgh's pro-team, **Edinburgh Rugby** (formerly Reivers), are now based at Meadowbank Stadium (*see p224*). Their season runs from September to April; the team have yet to fulfil their potential. Scotland's national team is based at **Murrayfield**. The **Six Nations Championship** (February to April)

and the **Autumn Test** matches (November) are a huge draw. The **BT Cellnet Cup Final** is played at Murrayfield in April.

Murrayfield Stadium

7 Roseburn Street, West Edinburgh, EH12 (SRU 346 5000/shop 346 5044/www.sru.org.uk). Bus 12, 22, 26, 31. **Open** *Office* 9am-5pm Mon-Fri & matchdays. **Tickets** from TicketMaster (0870 900 9933). **Credit** *Shop* MC, V.
Murrayfield is now fully seated. Stadium tours are run 10am-3pm Monday to Thursday. Details can be obtained from the marketing department of the SRU (Scottish Rugby Union).

Active sports

Curling

Olympic gold in 2002 brought a lot of attention, and even a little glamour, to curling. You can also get your broom out at **Murrayfield Ice Rink** (*see p224*).

Gogar Park

Gogar Station Road, West Edinburgh, EH12 (0131 339 1254/www.gocurling.co.uk/enquiries@gocurling. co.uk). Bus 100. **Open** 10am-11.45pm Mon-Fri; 10am-10pm Sat; 11am-9pm Sun. **Admission** *Peak (5.45-9.45pm Mon-Fri; all Sat, Sun)* £8.25; £4 children. *Off-peak (10am-5.30pm, 9.45-11.45pm Mon-Fri)* £7.75; £4 children. **Credit** MC, V.
A purpose-built curling rink. Phone or email to book an hour-and-a-half session. You'll be supplied with curling stones and brushes (charged at £1 per session). Prices are based on eight people using a sheet of ice. Coaching is available.

Arts & Entertainment

Cycling

The velodrome at Meadowbank Sports Centre (*see p224*) is home to the **Scottish Cyclists' Union** (652 0187/www.scuweb.com), which can advise on all the cycling sports. Non-competitive family cycling events include the **Edinburgh Cyclefest** (mid June) and the **Pedal For Scotland** Glasgow to Edinburgh cycle (mid September). **Spokes** (313 2114/ www.spokes.org.uk) and **Edinburgh Bicycle Cooperative** (228 1368/www.edinburgh bicycle.com) are both useful contacts for non-competitive cycling.

Golf

Scotland is the home of golf – some of the world's finest links courses are along the coast in East Lothian, including **Muirhead** – and there are around 70 courses within an hour's drive of Edinburgh. Golf is very much a people's game in Scotland. While there are a few snooty clubs, the majority welcome visitors with open arms. But don't turn up to a course and expect to play straight away because demand often outstrips supply – make sure you book in advance.

The Edinburgh & Lothians Tourist Board offers a discount pass for the single-minded golfer hoping to cram in as many rounds at as many courses as possible. A seven-day pass costs £5, and gives an average discount of £3-£5 per course; phone for details on 473 3800 or check out the website at www.edinburgh.org.

Braid Hills

Braid Hills Approach Road, South Edinburgh, EH10 (447 6666). Bus 11, 15, 16, 17. **Open** dawn-dusk daily. **Green fee** (per round) £13-£15. **Club hire** £11.25; £10 deposit. **Credit** MC, V.
Not one but two municipal courses. Situated against the backdrop of the Pentland Hills to the south and the Firth of Forth to the north, Braid One is among the finest courses in south-east Scotland, with challenging holes and a superb view.

Duddingston

Duddingston Road West, Arthur's Seat, EH15 (661 1005/www.duddingston-golf-club.com). Bus 4, 44, 45. **Open** dawn-dusk daily. **Green fee** (per round) £35. **Club hire** phone for details. **Credit** MC, V.
A demanding, tree-lined course set in undulating parkland towards the south-east of Arthur's Seat. Within walking distance of the city centre.

Lothianburn

Biggar Road, Hillend, South Edinburgh, EH10 (pro shop 445 2288). Bus 4. **Open** dawn-dusk daily. **Green fee** (per round) £16.50 Mon-Fri; £22.50 Sat, Sun. **Club hire** £10 per set. **Credit** AmEx, MC, V.
A hillside course perched around 900ft (270m) above sea level, again affording great views of the city. One of the cheaper private courses.

Muirfield

The Honourable Company of Edinburgh Golfers, Muirfield, Gullane, EH31 (01620 842123). **Open** (to visitors) dawn-dusk Tue, Thur. **Green fee** (per round) £90. **No credit cards**.
One of the premier golf courses in Europe, Muirfield is the venue for the 2002 British Open. Book at least six months in advance (one year for summer) to play. Maximum handicap of 18 (men), or 24 (women).

Rugby's big in Edinburgh, and **Murrayfield Stadium** is where it happens. *See p222.*

Alien Rock. See p225.

Murrayfield

43 Murrayfield Road, EH12 (337 3479). Bus 12, 22, 26, 31. **Open** (to visitors) 8am-4.30pm Mon-Fri. **Green fee** (per round) £30. **Club hire** £14. **Credit** *Shop* MC, V.

The sixth hole is the best for views of the city. Closed to unaccompanied visitors at weekends, with limited access on weekdays.

Musselburgh Old Links

Balcarres Road, Musselburgh, EH21 (665 5438). Bus 15. **Open** dawn-dusk daily. **Green fee** (per round) £8; £4.50 concessions. **Club hire** £12.50. **Credit** MC. V.

Historic nine holes in the middle of the racecourse, rumoured to be the world's oldest golf club. You can travel back in time by hiring a set of hickory clubs and guttie balls for £22.50.

St Andrews

West Sands Road, St Andrews, Fife, KY16 (01334 466666/www.standrews.org.uk). **Open** dawn-dusk daily. **Green fee** (per round) varies according to course & time of year; consult the website for details. **Club hire** £20-£30. **Credit** MC, V.

Europe's biggest golf complex, with six courses. There are also two non-members clubhouses and a driving range. Starting times on 18-hole courses should be reserved at least one month in advance, except for Saturday play, which can only be booked up to 24 hours in advance. There is no booking for the Balgove course. For the Old course, the minimum handicap required is 24 (men) and 36 (women).

Gyms & fitness centres

There are also extensive gym and fitness facilities at the **Royal Commonwealth Pool** (*see p225*) and at the **Craiglockhart Tennis & Sports Centre** (*see p225*).

Meadowbank Sports Centre & Stadium

139 London Road, Abbeyhill, EH7 (661 5351). Bus 4, 5, 15, 19, 26, 34, 44. **Open** 9am-10.30pm daily. **Rates** vary according to activity & time of day; phone for details. **Credit** MC, V.

Opened for the Commonwealth Games in 1970, this Edinburgh Leisure-run centre has facilities for athletics, badminton, squash, basketball and football, as well as a velodrome. And there are classes for children, adults and the over-50s in everything from archery to martial arts. The 13,000-seater stadium is the new home of Edinburgh Rugby and also hosts a variety of international events.

Next Generation

55 Newhaven Place, Newhaven Harbour, Leith, EH6 (554 5000/www.nextgenerationclubs.co.uk). Bus 7, 10, 11, 16, 32. **Open** (members & their guests only) 6.30am-11.30pm daily. **Rates** *Membership* phone for details; temporary membership available by arrangement. **Credit** AmEx, MC, V. **Map** p311 Ex.

Facilities for squash, badminton, basketball, beach volleyball and tennis, as well as a gym, celsius spa, mini climbing wall, and indoor and outdoor swimming pools. Crèche and restaurants on site.

One Spa

Sheraton Grand Hotel, 1 Festival Square, Lothian Road, EH3 (221 7777/www.one-spa.com). Bus 10, 11, 16, 17. **Open** 6.30am-10pm Mon-Fri; 7am-9pm Sat, Sun. **Rates** £35 half-day package; £60 full-day package. Membership also available. **Credit** AmEx, DC, MC, V. **Map** p309 D6.

Built in 2001, One Spa is the largest city centre spa in Europe. Aside from the gym and typical treatments, the top-floor ozone-infused pool and its outdoor hydrotherapy area is a distinctive feature. Hotel guests have free use of most facilities; spa treatments cost extra.

Pleasance Sports Centre

46 Pleasance, South Edinburgh, EH8 (650 2585/ recmail@ed.ac.uk). Bus 2, 21, 30. **Open** 8.30am-9.50pm Mon-Fri; 8.50am-5.50pm Sat; 9.50am-5.50pm Sun. Closed to unaccompanied guests during term time. **Rates** (non-members) £4 per session; £2 concessions. Membership also available. **Credit** MC, V. **Map** p310 G6.

A facility is attached to the University of Edinburgh; during term time it is open only to members and their guests; during vacations it's open to all.

Ice-skating

Murrayfield Ice Rink

Riversdale Crescent, West Edinburgh, EH12 (337 6933). Bus 12, 26, 31. **Open** 2.30-4.30pm, 7-9pm Mon, Tue, Thur; 2.30-4.30pm, 5-7pm, 7.30-10pm Wed; 2.30-4.30pm, 5-7pm, 7.30-9.30pm Fri; 10am-noon, 2.30-4pm, 4.30-7pm, 7.30-10.30pm Sat; 10-11.30am, 2.30-4.30pm Sun. **Admission** (includes skate hire) £2-£4.50. **No credit cards**.

As well as being home to the Edinburgh Capitals ice hockey team, this rink is used for public skating sessions and curling. The evening session on Wednesdays and Saturdays attracts a young crowd for disco skating.

Rock climbing

Meadowbank Sports Centre (*see p224*) has a climbing wall constructed mainly of brick.

Alien Rock

8 Pier Place, Newhaven, Leith, EH6 (552 7211). Bus 10, 11, 16, 32. **Open** *Summer* noon-10pm Mon-Fri; 10am-7pm Sat, Sun. *Winter* noon-11pm Mon-Thur; noon-10pm Fri; 10am-9pm Sat, Sun. **Admission** *Peak* (after 4pm Mon-Fri; before 5pm Sat, Sun) £5.50; £3-£4.50 concessions. *Off-peak* (before 4pm Mon-Fri; after 5pm Sat, Sun) £4; £3 concessions. **Credit** MC, V. **Map** p311 Ex.

A 10m wall with 50 ropes located in a former church. All the necessary equipment can be hired, including footwear. A two-hour introductory course for novices costs £25, including equipment hire. The Alien Rock 2 extension has a 300sq m wall.

National Rock Climbing Centre of Scotland

Ratho Quarry, West Edinburgh, EH28 (no phone/ www.nrcc.co.uk). **Open** from late 2002.

Once completed, this £7 million project in a disused quarry will be the biggest outdoor pursuits training centre of its kind in Europe, with 2,500m (8,200ft) of indoor surfaces, 5,000m (16,400ft) of outdoor surfaces and a specialist gym for adventure sports. Restaurant, lecture facilities, tuition, guiding service and accommodation also available.

Skiing

Midlothian Ski Centre

Biggar Road, Hillend, EH10 (445 4433). Bus 4. **Open** *Apr-July* 9.30am-9pm Mon-Sat; 9.30am-5pm Sun. *Aug-Mar* 9.30am-9pm Mon-Sat; 9.30am-7pm Sun. **Rates** *Main slope* £7.10 1st hr plus £2.90 per extra hr; £4.70 concessions plus £1.90 per extra hr. *Nursery slopes* £4.40 1st hr plus £2.15 per extra hr; £2.80 concessions plus £1.50 per extra hr. **Credit** MC, V.

Situated to the south of Edinburgh, the Midlothian Ski Centre has the longest artificial ski slope in Europe, at 400m (1,150ft). Prices include the hire of boots, skis and poles and use of the chairlift. There's an additional charge for snowboards or specialist skis.

Snooker

The Angle Club

3 Jordan Lane, Morningside, South Edinburgh, EH10 (447 8814). Bus 5, 11, 15, 16, 18, 23. **Open** 11am-midnight Mon-Thur, Sun; 11am-1am Fri, Sat. **Rates** *Snooker* £4.30 per hr. *Pool* £6 per hr. **Credit** MC, V.

Ten snooker tables, seven pool tables and a bar/café.

Marco's Snooker Halls

55 Grove Street, West Edinburgh, EH3 (228 2141). Bus 1, 22, 28, 34, 35. **Open** 8am-11pm Mon-Wed, Sun; 8am-1pm Thur-Sat. **Rates** *Snooker* £2-£4 per hr. *Pool* £2.25-£4.50 per hr. Phone for details of other facilities. **Credit** MC, V. **Map** p308 C7.

Facilities include 15 snooker and 18 pool tables as well as a bar/café. Also gyms, sunbeds, squash courts and classes.

Swimming

The city's most exciting pool for kids is **Leith Waterworld** (*see p194*), with a wave machine, rapids and other delights. It was closed at the time of writing, but due to reopen in June 2002.

Glenogle Swim Centre

Glenogle Road, Stockbridge, EH3 (343 6376). Bus 19A, 23, 24, 27, 28, 36. **Open** 8am-7.40pm Mon-Fri; 10am-3.40pm Sat; 9am-3.40pm Sun. **Admission** £2.20; £1.20 concessions. **No credit cards.** **Map** p305 C3.

Those of a less inhibited nature might enjoy the Edinburgh Naturist Swimming Club, held every Friday night.

Portobello Swim Centre

57 The Promenade, off Bellfield Street, Portobello, EH15 (669 6888). Bus 2, 15, 19, 26, 42. **Open** *Pool* 7am-9pm Mon, Tue, Thur; 7am-6pm Wed; 7am-7.45pm Fri; 9am-3.40pm Sat, Sun. *Turkish baths* 3-9pm Mon (women only); 9am-9pm Tue, Thur (men only); 9am-9pm Wed (women only); 9am-9pm Fri (mixed); 9am-4pm Sat, Sun (mixed). **Admission** *Pool* £1.80-£2.20; £1.20 concessions. *Turkish baths* (over-16s only) £5.60. **Credit** MC, V.

Recently renovated traditional Victorian pool best known for its authentic Turkish and Russian baths. It also features two swimming pools, a gym, a multi-purpose dance studio, a crèche and a café.

Royal Commonwealth Pool

21 Dalkeith Road, South Edinburgh, EH16 (667 7211). Bus 2, 14, 21, 33. **Open** 6am-9.30pm Mon-Fri; 6am-4.30pm Sat; 10am-4.30pm Sun. **Admission** *Pool* £2.50 9am-4pm Mon-Fri; £3.10 before 9am, after 4pm Mon-Fri & all day Sat, Sun. Phone for details of other facilities. **Credit** MC, V. **Map** p310 J8.

Olympic-size swimming and diving pools, plus extensive gym facilities and fitness classes.

Tennis

Craiglockhart Tennis & Sports Centre

177 Colinton Road, South Edinburgh, EH14 (444 1969/443 0101). Bus 10, 10A, 27, 45. **Open** 9am-11pm Mon-Fri; 9am-10.30pm Sat, Sun. **Rates** phone for details. **Credit** MC, V.

The tennis centre has six indoor and eight outdoor courts. The sports centre has a fitness room, badminton and squash courts and a crèche. It also runs step and aerobics classes.

Theatre & Dance

August is the hottest month for drama, but there's plenty of theatre year-round.

The best new Scottish playwriting is to be found at the **Traverse Theatre**. *See p228.*

(see p227)

Theatre

During the Festival, theatrical venues seem to spring up out of nowhere. Previously innocuous buildings suddenly display huge banners and all manner of drama takes place inside. Throughout the rest of the year things are much more predictable, with Edinburgh's nine main theatres well programmed, and largely well attended. Generally speaking, most are within a 15-minute walk of Princes Street, so fitting in a pre-theatre dinner at a city centre restaurant is easy. It's pretty easy to choose a venue too; each theatre tends to focus on a certain style of production, so you're likely to have a fair idea of what you're letting yourself in for.

The largest theatre in town is the 3,000-capacity **Edinburgh Playhouse** (*see p227*), situated at the top of Leith Walk. Here you'll find the latest touring productions from London's West End, including big budget musicals such as *Chicago, Grease, Riverdance* and *Miss Saigon*. The **Edinburgh Festival Theatre** (*see p228*) and **King's Theatre** (*see p227*) are both council-run and between them cover a vast remit, with opera, dance, music and comedy at the former, and a mix of quality touring theatre, local am-dram musicals and a lavish Christmas panto at the latter.

Take a short walk up Lothian Road from Princes Street and you'll find three venues clustered together; the **Royal Lyceum Theatre** (*see p227*), **Traverse Theatre** (*see p228*) and the **Usher Hall** (*see p209*). While the last one is dedicated solely to music, the first two often stage some of the best drama you'll see in Scotland. The Lyceum puts on around eight shows a year, performed by the in-house company, with each production running for approximately one month. The eclectic programming features everything from Chekhov, Shakespeare and Arthur Miller to a charming Christmas show and the odd musical. Around the corner at the Traverse, new writing is the name of the game, with many of Scotland's freshest young playwrights, including David Harrower, David Greig and Zinnie Harris to name but three, cutting their teeth there. It's also home to one of the most popular bars in Edinburgh (*see p157*).

Arts & Entertainment

Slightly further afield, the **Brunton Theatre** in Musselburgh (*see below*) stages an interesting mix of new theatre, dance, comedy and work by local musical groups. Amateur dramatics of varying quality can be found at the **Church Hill Theatre** in Morningside (*see below*) and at the **Netherbow Arts Centre** on the Royal Mile (*see below*), while work by students of Queen Margaret University College is performed at the **Gateway Theatre** (*see below*).

It goes without saying that all these venues are well utilised during the Edinburgh Festival, in particular the King's, Lyceum and Traverse where you'll find work of a very high calibre.

BUYING TICKETS

Tickets for many major venues can be booked through the **Ticketline** network (0870 748 9000; 10am-8pm Mon-Sat; 11am-6pm Sun). **Showstoppers** (558 9800) sells tickets for the Church Hill Theatre, while **Ticketmaster** (0870 606 3424) sells for the Edinburgh Playhouse. In other cases contact the individual box offices listed under the relevant venues.

Venues

Following the demise of the Bedlam Theatre in mid-2002, a replacement venue for Edinburgh University productions has still to be found. For details of the **Edinburgh Festival Theatre**, *see p210 and p228*.

Brunton Theatre

Bridge Street, Musselburgh, EH21 (665 2240). Bus 15, 26, 44. **Open** *Box office* 10am-8pm Mon-Sat (10am-6pm when no performance). **Tickets** £5-£10.50. **Credit** MC, V.
A 20-minute bus or car journey from Edinburgh city centre, the Brunton plays a crucial role in East Lothian's cultural life. Touring theatre and dance companies rub shoulders with traditional Scottish variety acts and am-dram musicals, as well as the odd stand-up comedian.

Church Hill Theatre

Morningside Road, South Edinburgh, EH10 (447 7597). Bus 11, 15, 16, 17, 23. **Open** *Box office* only on performance days. **Tickets** (available from individual companies or Showstoppers) £3-£10. **No credit cards**.
Well-loved and well-used, this former church plays host to countless amateur dramatics companies throughout the year, including regular shows from the highly regarded Edinburgh People's Theatre.

Edinburgh Playhouse

18-22 Greenside Place, Calton Hill, EH1 (0870 606 3424/www.ticketmaster.co.uk). Playhouse buses. **Open** *Box office* 10am-8pm Mon-Sat (until 6pm on non-performance days). *Telephone bookings* 24hrs daily. **Tickets** £7.50-£35. **Credit** AmEx, MC, V. **Map** p307 G4.

A vast stage and 3,000-seat capacity make this the ideal Scottish venue for major West End shows. Expect blockbuster musicals, lavish opera and the odd rock star (Bryan Adams, Bruce Springsteen and Bob Dylan have all played here).

Gateway Theatre

Elm Row, Leith Walk, Broughton, EH7 (317 3939). Playhouse buses. **Open** *Box office* (during term time) noon-2pm Mon-Fri & 45mins before performance. *Telephone bookings* 10am-4pm Mon-Fri. **Tickets** £4-£8. **Credit** AmEx, MC, V. **Map** p307 G3.
Home to Queen Margaret University College's drama school, the Gateway stages several student productions each year, as well as hosting exciting international drama and dance during the Festival Fringe. Box office hours are extended during the Festival in August.

King's Theatre

2 Leven Street, Tollcross, South Edinburgh, EH3 (529 6000/www.eft.co.uk). Bus 10, 11, 15, 16, 17. **Open** *Box office* 1hr before performance. *Telephone bookings* 11am-8pm Mon-Sat (until 6pm when no performance); 4-8pm Sun (performance days only). **Tickets** (also available from the Edinburgh Festival Theatre) £4-£16. **Credit** AmEx, DC, MC, V. **Map** p309 D7.
Built in 1905, this lovely old Edwardian theatre stages a quality programme of popular theatre from touring companies such as the Royal National Theatre. Oscar Wilde and Tom Stoppard comedies, Agatha Christie whodunits, Harold Pinter classics and amateur musicals are all on the menu, plus a lavish Christmas panto each year.

Netherbow Arts Centre

43-45 High Street, Old Town, EH1 (556 9579). Bus 23, 27, 28, 35, 41, 42, 45/Nicolson Street–North Bridge buses. **Open** *Box office* 10am-4.30pm Mon-Sat. **Tickets** £6. **Credit** MC, V. **Map** p304 D3.
Attached to the John Knox House (*see p72*), the Netherbow Arts Centre is at its busiest during the Scottish Storytelling Festival, the Puppet and Animation Festival and the Fringe. For the rest of the year it's home to a range of adult and children's theatre performed by local companies. There's also a pleasant café here, with a sunny courtyard that's perfect for alfresco lunching.

Royal Lyceum

Grindlay Street, South Edinburgh, EH3 (248 4848/ www.lyceum.org.uk). Bus 1, 10, 11, 15, 16, 17, 22, 24, 34. **Open** *Box office* 10am-6pm Mon-Sat. **Tickets** £1-£17.50. **Credit** AmEx, MC, V. **Map** p304 D4.
A new artistic director will take up residence at the Lyceum in autumn 2002, so future programming may change. For the moment, the in-house theatre company produces a fairly consistent line-up of quality drama, ranging from Shakespearean comedies and Scots translations of Molière to new writing and musicals.

Arts & Entertainment

The **Edinburgh Festival Theatre.**

Theatre Workshop

*34 Hamilton Place, Stockbridge, EH3 (226 5425).
Bus 23, 27.* **Open** *Box office* 9.30am-5.30pm Mon-
Fri. **Tickets** £7. **Credit** MC, V. **Map** p306 D3.
This small, friendly theatre down in Stockbridge
may not be the most prolific, but artistic director
Robert Rae has assembled a talented integrated
company of disabled and able-bodied actors. They
produce two to three shows a year, as well as a
community play each spring and an innovative
Christmas show.

Traverse Theatre

*10 Cambridge Street, Old Town, EH1 (228 1404/
www.traverse.co.uk). Bus 1, 10, 11, 15, 16, 17, 22,
24, 34.* **Open** *Box office* 10am-6pm Mon; 10am-8pm
Tue-Sat (until 6pm when no performance); 4-8pm
(performance days only). **Tickets** £4-£9. **Credit**
MC, V. **Map** p304 A3.
Two performance spaces, a trendy bar and a busy
café make this legendary theatre one of the most
popular venues in Edinburgh. As well as hosting
some of the finest Fringe theatre during August,
you can expect to find new writing, modern dance
and stand-up comedy here all year. And in June the
Traverse hosts the Children's International Theatre
Festival. The in-house company regularly produces
interesting works by contemporary Scottish and
international playwrights, with the programme
fleshed out further by visiting theatre companies
from Scotland and beyond.

Dance

Since re-opening in 1994, the **Edinburgh
Festival Theatre** has established itself as
a major international venue for dance, with a
large, well-sprung stage. Consequently, some
of the world's finest companies ply their wares
here, with Rambert, Nederlands Dans Theater,
Mark Morris Dance Group and Kirov Ballet all
recent visitors. It's also the Edinburgh base for
Scottish Ballet, which performs four shows
a year here. In spring 2002 the ballet company
was in a state of flux – about to appoint a new
artistic director and shift the emphasis from
classical ballet to modern dance – so future
programming is up in the air, but should be
interesting. Watch this space.

Scotland's other dance companies – **Scottish
Dance Theatre**, the **Ensemble Group** and
X-Factor among them – divide their time
between the Festival Theatre, the Traverse
(*see above*) and the Brunton (*see p227*). By far
the most exciting development on Edinburgh's
dance scene, however, is the opening of the
wonderful new **Dance Base**, a haven for
professional and amateur dancers alike.

Venues

Dance Base

*Grassmarket, Old Town, EH1 (225 5525/
www.dancebase.co.uk). Bus 2, 23, 27, 28, 41, 42, 45.*
Open *Administration & bookings* 10am-5pm Mon-
Fri; 10am-1pm Sat. **Tickets** phone for details.
Credit phone for details. **Map** p304 B3.
The latest jewel in Edinburgh's dance crown, this
impressive new centre houses four dance studios
and runs an extensive programme of classes and
workshops for all levels. Plans to stage regular performances should come to fruition soon, with Dance
Base already establishing itself as a popular Fringe
venue. The building's worth visiting for the interior
architecture alone.

Edinburgh Festival Theatre

*13-29 Nicolson Street, South Edinburgh, EH8
(box office 529 6000/administration 662 1112/
www.eft.co.uk). Nicolson Street–North Bridge
buses.* **Open** *Box office* 10am-8pm Mon-Sat
(until 6pm when no performance); 4pm-curtain
Sun (performance days only). *Telephone booking*
11am-8pm Mon-Sat (until 6pm when no
performance); 4pm-curtain Sun (performance
days only). **Tickets** £5.50-£55. **Credit** AmEx,
DC, MC, V. **Map** p310 G6.
Dance fans are well-served at the Festival Theatre,
with big name companies paying regular visits to
the well-equipped venue. The annual 'Dance Turns'
series every October and November is always a
treat, with major talents such as Rambert on the
bill. For details of the theatre's classical music
programming, *see p210*.

Trips Out of Town

Features

Map

Getting Started

Use Edinburgh as the perfect starting point from which to explore Scotland's manifold attractions.

Having made it to Edinburgh, it would be a shame to leave without glimpsing something of the rest of Scotland. There are many fine places within easy striking distance of the capital in **Lothian**, **Fife** and the **Borders**, and, if you've got a bit more time, it is possible to get right out into the wilds with comparative ease. Then, of course, there is **Glasgow**, Scotland's largest city and Edinburgh's rival, which is only 50 minutes away from the capital by train. It's easy to reach for shopping or sightseeing, and has an enviable cultural and nightlife scene.

In the following chapters, we concentrate on destinations that are close enough to the capital to make sense for a day trip. But we've also included some basic tourist and travel information for visitors venturing further afield to the Highlands, Islands or Trossachs (*see p270* **Going further**). If you don't want to strike out alone, there are plenty of organised trips and group tours to destinations all around Scotland, varying from guided coach tours to group backpacking and hill-walking trips (*see p264* **Trips and tours**). Finally, intrepid visitors should bear in mind that Scotland's Highlands offer the perfect terrain for a number of adventure and winter sports; for details of these, *see p222* **A taste for adventure**.

PLANNING A TRIP

The **Edinburgh & Lothians Tourist Board** on Princes Street (*see p289*) can provide information on travel, sightseeing and accommodation throughout Scotland. It's also worth investing in a good map. Ordnance Survey (OS) has the whole of Great Britain mapped in intimate detail. The two series that are likely to prove of greatest use are the Landranger (scale 1:50,000) and the Pathfinder (scale 1:25,000). Ordnance Survey maps can be bought in the **Stationery Office** (71 Lothian Road, South Edinburgh, EH3, 228 4181).

GETTING AROUND

Public transport to the more rural regions of Scotland can sometimes be a problem, so hiring your own car is often the best option. (For details of hire firms, *see p275*). Having said that, the rail system is fairly efficient and provides a network of trains to most of the larger towns. **Scotrail** (information 08457 484950/tickets 08457 550033/08456 015929/

www.scotrail.co.uk) also has some flexible travel passes that allow you to roam all over the place using trains, buses and ferries. These include the **Freedom of Scotland Travelpass** (£89 for four days' travel over eight days or £119 for eight days' travel over 15 days). If you just want to cover the Highlands then get an eight-day **Highland Rover** pass (£59 for four days' travel, including ferries to and bus travel on Mull and Skye) and discover some stupendous country that isn't accessible by car. For further details of rail travel to and from Edinburgh including information on **Waverley Station**, *see p272*.

Bus travel is another possibility, although bear in mind that services in more remote areas may be as infrequent as twice a week. Buses from Edinburgh usually depart from **St Andrew Square Bus Station** (*see p272*), closed for refurbishment until 2003. In the mean time, long-distance bus services and those to Glasgow and Fife leave from the south side of St Andrew Square. Local services and those to the Lothians leave from Waterloo Place.

PRECAUTIONS

Scotland's mountain scenery is one of the country's greatest assets but is also potentially dangerous for hillwalkers and climbers who do not observe these basic safety precautions.
● Don't overestimate your ability and fitness.
● Always tell someone where you are going and what time you plan to get back.
● Take a map, a compass and a torch.
● Wear suitable footwear and always take waterproofs with you.
● Carry a water bottle and emergency rations.
● The weather can change very quickly; if it looks like turning bad, get off the mountain.

If you're travelling to the Highlands, you should also be prepared for midges: tiny flying insects with a voracious appetite for fresh human blood. Midges breed on boggy ground, prefer still days and are at their worst between late May and early August. Their bites make you itch, and a cloud of them are enough to drive you mad. No one has yet found a repellent for them that works; however, they are deterred by citronella and herb oils such as thyme or bog myrtle. They also prefer dark- to light-coloured clothing and detest smoke.

Glasgow

Scotland's largest city is big on entertainment, shopping, nightlife and culture.

One thing that Glasgow could never be accused of is standing still in the face of change; it could even give Kylie and Madonna a run for their money in the reinvention stakes. Over the last decade or so Glasgow has turned around its well-worn image of harshness, metamorphosing into the 'Friendly City' and its very latest incarnation – the 'City of Love' (because St Valentine's relics are held in a Gorbals church, in case you were wondering). In fact, just when you think you might have Glasgow taped, it has a knack of surprising you with yet another new twist in its ever-changing profile. This profile has probably never been higher than it is at present.

As one of the first cities in the world to experience the booming growth of the Industrial Revolution, Glasgow earned a reputation in the 18th and 19th centuries as the second city of the British Empire. In the 20th century it was also one of the first European cities to feel the dramatic effects of post-industrial decline. Yet it has also set the agenda for the post-industrial world by embracing knowledge- and service-based industries such as tourism, media and culture – and by throwing in a huge dollop of self-promotion for good measure. This heady concoction has resulted in Glasgow enjoying tenures as European City of Culture and UK City of Architecture and Design – not to mention being designated the unofficial but undisputed title of style capital of Scotland.

Image is all important in this, Scotland's largest city; the place is bursting at the seams with designer retailers like Versace and Armani, as well as superlative retro-clothing shops and local clubwear designers. Glaswegians wear their labels with pride and they don't care who knows it. And when it comes to hanging out in full designer regalia, there's no shortage of style bars, restaurants and clubs designed by hipper-than-thou local artists and designers with the local McGlitterati in mind.

It's probably no surprise that as one of Britain's most happening urban centres outside London, Glasgow is something of a music mecca too. Kurt Cobain made no secret of his love for Glasgow indie bands such as the Vaselines, even going so far as to cover one of their songs on *Nirvana Unplugged*. Add to this the current crop of local bands such as Mogwai, Belle and Sebastian and the Mull Historical Society, and

it's clear that this city is still indie nirvana. And, of course, Glasgow is also home sweet home to Travis, Texas and Oscar-winning musician Craig Armstrong, composer of Baz Luhrman's *Moulin Rouge*. Glasgow's musical creativity is

The best Sights

Art Gallery & Museum, Kelvingrove
Wonderful over-the-top Victorian museum housing a world-class permanent collection of fine art, including Rembrandts, Van Goghs, and of course Mackintoshes. *See p240.*

Burrell Collection
One of the country's finest private collections on show in one of the country's most gorgeous purpose-built museums. *See p238.*

Glasgow School of Art
Charles Rennie Mackintosh's architectural masterpiece and an icon of modern 20th-century design. *See p236.*

Glasgow Science Centre
Leading-edge architecture, fun exhibits and the best views over the city. *See p233.*

Holmwood House
Glaswegian Alexander 'Greek' Thomson's finest and most elaborate villa, often described as a precursor to Frank Lloyd Wright's famous prairie houses. *See p238.*

The Lighthouse
Mackintosh's *Glasgow Herald* building is now Scotland's 'Centre for Architecture, Design & the City', with a special permanent exhibition on the great man and his work. *See p236.*

The People's Palace/Winter Gardens
Home to one of Glasgow's most cherished exhibitions, covering all aspects of Glaswegian life. Essential for social history fans. *See p237.*

Trips Out of Town

HOTELGALLERY
RESTAURANTBAR

65 BEDROOMS
2 RESTAURANTS
2 BARS
PRIVATE DINING

MEETING ROOMS

CONFERENCES
FUNCTIONS

HAIR & BEAUTY

probably boosted by the fact that the city boasts cutting-edge venues such as Nice'n'Sleazy and King Tut's, which tirelessly carry on supporting the new wave of rising stars.

If Glasgow's position at the vanguard of cool is beyond dispute, there are nevertheless a few chinks in its stylish armour. For a start, the Glaswegian penchant for cholesterolly challenged square sausage rolls washed down with Irn Bru is just one of the reasons that areas of the city have among the poorest heart disease records in Europe. And there are the sectarian divisions, which come disconcertingly to the fore when football rivals Rangers and Celtic meet in 'Old Firm' clashes.

Then there's the rivalry with its east coast neighbour. For although Edinburgh lies a mere 50 miles (80 kilometres) from Glasgow, for many, that modest distance is enough to place Scotland's two main cities poles apart. Rather than celebrate their differences and co-exist peacefully, Glasgow and Edinburgh traditionally 'enjoy' the splenetic relationship of warring neighbours. Denizens of Edinburgh refer to 'Weegie soap-dodgers' (thanks to Irvine Welsh's *Trainspotting* prose); Glaswegians trumpet their city's friendly reputation – in contrast to Edinburgh's alleged aloof coldness. And so the sweeping generalisations persist.

Although it boasts as rich a history and culture as its rival, Glasgow is not as ensnared by its own heritage as the tourist-pleasing Edinburgh. Glaswegian pride tends to be focused on the city's social, political and industrial histories, and convictions run deep for many of its still staunchly socialist population. That's not to say that there's anything po-faced about its unique and varied charms. Far from it, as the gutsy architecture, lively displays at the People's Palace Museum and boozy craic in the Scotia Bar will testify. No siree, the home of the 'soap dodger' is as vibrant as they come.

Sightseeing

The waterfront

'I'm gonna move on up to the waterfront' crooned Glaswegian Jim Kerr, way back in the heady '80s when his band Simple Minds were kings of rock. Kerr's vision seems to have been mightily prophetic, because Glasgow is indeed movin' on up to the waterfront. Huge developments have recently been taking place on the Clyde, and it's now a good starting point for exploring the city. Down by the river, on the north side, the **Clyde Walkway** provides a pleasant stroll underneath the numerous city-centre bridges.

Beginning at the west end of Glasgow Green, head westwards along the Broomielaw, home of Glasgow's burgeoning financial district, and it'll be pretty impossible to miss one of the city's high tech landmarks, Foster and Partners' **Clyde Auditorium** (*see p248*), or 'Armadillo' as it's now affectionately known. The groovy, aluminium form of the Armadillo has recently been eclipsed, however, by the spectacular sight of the new **Glasgow Science Centre**, across the Clyde at Pacific Quay. Within the centre, the titanium-clad IMAX cinema and Science Mall are not only seriously hip examples of leading-edge design but are also great fun to visit. And the Centre's Glasgow Tower is the place for views that are either breathtaking or stomach-churning, depending on your disposition.

The Science Mall's glass front overlooking the river is a perfect location for a bit of boatspotting: there's a view of the **Tall Ship at Glasgow Harbour**, the *SV Glenlee*, one of the few Clydebuilt sailing ships still in existence; in summer you may see the **Waverley**, the world's only sea-going paddle steamer, on one of her cruises 'doon the watter' to the Isle of Bute and other west coast locations. Then there's the Clyde Waterbus, which ferries shoppers to the new behemoth shopping centre at Braehead, or to **Clydebuilt**, part of the Scottish Maritime Museum, also located at Braehead.

Clydebuilt/Scottish Maritime Museum

The Scottish Maritime Museum at Braehead, King's Inch Road, G51 (0141 886 1013/www.scottish maritimemuseum.org). Bus 23, 25, 55. **Open** 10am-6pm Mon-Sat; 11am-5pm Sun. **Admission** £3.50; £1.75 concessions. **No credit cards.**

One of the Scottish Maritime Museum's three sites, Clydebuilt tells the intertwined story of Glasgow and the Clyde through three hundred years of history – from trading to shipbuilding. Interactive exhibits make it fun for kids as well as maritime buffs, especially if you take the Clyde Waterbus from the city centre to get there (*see p252*).

Glasgow Science Centre

50 Pacific Quay, G51 (0141 420 5000/www.gsc. org.uk). Exhibition Centre rail. **Open** *Science Mall* Nov-Mar noon-6pm Mon-Fri, Sun; 10am-6pm Sat; Apr-Oct 10am-6pm daily. *IMAX & Tower* Nov-Mar noon-6pm Mon-Thur, Sun; noon-8pm Fri, Sat; Apr-Oct 10am-6pm Mon-Thur, Sun; 10am-8pm Fri, Sat. **Admission** *Science Mall* £6.50; £4.50 concessions. *IMAX* £5.50; £4 concessions. *Tower* £5.50; £4 concessions. *Double ticket* (2 attractions) £9.50; £7 concessions. *Triple ticket* (3 attractions) £14; £10 concessions. **Credit** MC, V.

The GSC Science Mall, with its plethora of interactive exhibits, demonstration theatres and planetarium, is a big hit with children and science fans. The fully rotating Glasgow Tower is an attraction for

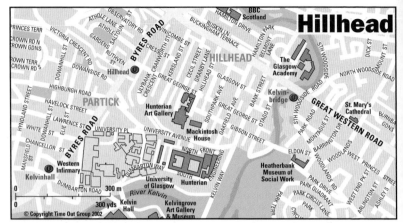

anyone wanting an unrivalled and unforgettable view of the city. The Science Centre also houses an IMAX cinema with Scotland's biggest screen.

The Tall Ship at Glasgow Harbour

100 Stobcross Road, G3 (0141 339 0631/www. thetallship.com). Exhibition Centre rail. **Open** *Mar-Nov* 10am-5pm daily. *Dec-Feb* 11am-4pm daily. **Admission** £4.50; £3.25 concessions. **Credit** MC, V. **Map** p314 A2.

An opportunity to explore the tall ship *SV Glenlee*, one of only five Clydebuilt sailing ships remaining afloat. Launched in 1896, she stands as an impressive reminder of the Clyde's shipbuilding legacy. *Glenlee* once served as a long-haul cargo vessel; today visitors can learn about life aboard from an interactive and audio exhibition.

Waverley Paddle Steamer

Waverley Excursions, Waverley Terminal, G3 (0141 243 2224/www.waverleyexcursions.co.uk). Anderston rail. **Sailings** *July, Aug* 9.30am Mon; 10am Fri, Sat; 11am Sun. No sailings Sept-June. **Admission** varies. **Credit** MC, V.

Built in Glasgow in 1947, the Waverley paddle steamer is one of the city's best-loved summer attractions. The simple charm of a trip down the water is a perfect antidote to Glasgow's shopping, pubbing and clubbing onslaught.

City centre

The wealth and prosperity generated by the trading and commercial prowess of this second city of the British Empire helped transform the current city centre from a semi-rural suburb of the old medieval city into one of the most elegant urban centres in the country. It's small but perfectly formed; laid out in a grid pattern, not unlike that of that other great second city, Chicago. It is also, in common with Chicago,

a definitively 19th-century city, albeit a characteristically Victorian one. The River Clyde, historically the main artery along which the city's wealth flowed, leads to the physical and symbolic heart of the city, in the shape of **George Square**, a former swamp that now hosts a plethora of events such as live music at Hogmanay. The magnificent **City Chambers** to the east of the square, which were opened by Queen Victoria in 1888, are the most potent representation of Glasgow's former 'second city' status.

Spreading away from the south-east of George Square is the **Merchant City**, formerly the centre for Glasgow's sugar and tobacco traders. The sugar and tobacco business brought prosperity to the city in the early 19th century, but as Glasgow's trading prowess declined in the late 19th and 20th centuries the Merchant City's pre-eminence also waned and the area suffered. The boom years of the 1980s, however, heralded the beginning of the area's renaissance – and the continuing proliferation of trendy bars, bistros and boutiques.

The main thoroughfare of **Ingram Street** connects the Merchant City to the city centre proper and culminates in **Royal Exchange Square**. The **Gallery of Modern Art** (GOMA, *see p236*) is at the heart of Royal Exchange Square and punctuates the end of the Merchant City experience.

Candleriggs, or Merchant City East, as its more upwardly mobile denizens would describe it, is home to the city's more understated and charming live venues, such as the **Old Fruitmarket** (*see p248*) and **Café Gandolfi** (*see p241*), a Glasgow institution with a wooden interior designed by Tim Stead. To the south lies **Trongate**, marked by the Tolbooth Steeple, at the intersection of five roads, including **Argyle Street**. The clock steeple belongs to the newly and handsomely refurbished **Tron Theatre** (*see p249*) to the east. Just off the main Argyle Street shopping drag is the **Argyle Arcade**, an attractive and airy Victorian glass-roofed thoroughfare, lined with jewellers' shops, which links on to **Buchanan Street**, the discerning shopper's paradise.

To the south of Argyle Street, **Chisholm Street** and **Parnie Street** are worth more than a passing glance, not only for the unorthodox but eye-catching marriage of red and blond sandstone tenements, but for the quirkiest shops in the city: tattoos, comics, signed footballs and tropical fish are just some of the eccentric goodies on offer around here. The adjoining **King Street** is a centre for art galleries and collectives of a conceptual persuasion. These include the **Transmission Gallery** (No.28, 0141 552 4813/www.transmissiongallery.org), Art Exposure on nearby Parnie Street (No.19, 0141 552 7779/www.artexposuregallery.com), Glasgow Print Studio (No.22, 0141 552 0704/ www.gpsart.co.uk) and Street Level Gallery (No.26, 0141 552 2151/www.sl-photoworks. demon.co.uk). With a number of studios above the galleries themselves, this is one of the more bohemian and buzzing parts of the city centre. King Street swerves and culminates in King's Court, a great venue for the serious second-hand and vintage clothes shopper. **Paddy's Market**, an elaborate junk-fest, lies just over the road; if it's soda streams and Richard Clayderman LPs you're after, then this is the place for you.

Along the gentle curve of the railway line towards the Clyde are three of Glasgow's most established and well-loved drinking dens. The Stockwell Triangle – consisting of the **Victoria Bar**, the **Clutha Vaults** and the 250-year-old **Scotia Bar** (for all, *see p242*) all around Stockwell Street – is a hub for folk music.

The pedestrianised **Buchanan Street** is an area of more upmarket shops. Just off the main drag, on Mitchell Lane, is the first public building designed by Charles Rennie Mackintosh (*see p239* **Mackintosh**), built in 1895 to house the *Glasgow Herald*. It is now, after a spectacular makeover, home to the **Lighthouse**, Scotland's Centre for Architecture, Design & the City (*see p236*). At the very north of the street, past the Buchanan Galleries, is the **Royal Concert Hall**, one of Glasgow's least impressive monoliths.

Sauchiehall Street is legendary – the mere mention of it can bring a tear to the eye of an expat Glaswegian. Highlights include the **Willow Tearoom** (1904), the only remaining tearoom designed by Charles Rennie Mackintosh; it was commissioned by the formidable Kate Cranston, a pioneer of the genteel tearoom society that was so prevalent in Glasgow in the late 19th century. The new **Centre for**

The appliance of science: an exhibit at **Glasgow Science Centre**. *See p233.*

Contemporary Arts (*see below*), housed in a building by that other Glasgow great, Alexander 'Greek' Thomson, is one of the country's most cutting-edge and stylish venues for contemporary art and performance. The eight-storey **Baird Hall of Residence**, further west along Sauchiehall Street, is one of the most audacious art deco monuments in Scotland – its 1930s high-tech bravado displays a kind of Flash Gordon fantasy theatricality.

A sharp incline to the north of Sauchiehall Street leads up to **Garnethill**, a mainly residential area that is not only the centre of Glasgow's Chinese community but also contains Garnethill Synagogue, the oldest Jewish place of worship in the city. The **Glasgow School of Art** (*see below*), Mackintosh's masterpiece, balances on this perilously steep hill. A view south takes in the exotic spire of St Vincent Street Church designed by Alexander Thomson.

Centre for Contemporary Arts

350 Sauchiehall Street, G2 (0141 352 4900/www. cca-glasgow.com). Cowcaddens tube. **Open** 11am-11pm Mon-Thur; 11am-midnight Fri, Sat; 11am-6pm Sun. **Admission** free; ticket prices vary. **Credit** MC, V. **Map** p314 A2.
Recently opened after a major facelift, this is one of the most handsome and important arenas for contemporary art and performance in the country. There's a cool, minimalist restaurant in the interior courtyard, and a groovy bar upstairs.

Gallery of Modern Art

Queen Street, G1 (0141 229 1996). Buchanan St tube/Queen St rail. **Open** 10am-5pm Mon-Thur, Sat; 11am-5pm Fri, Sun. **Admission** free. **Map** p314 D3.
Glasgow architect David Hamilton was responsible for the portico addition to the Cunninghame Mansion (1778), now home to a lively, eclectic and controversial modern art collection. The two-tier café has terrific views of the city's skyline and good-value fare.

Glasgow School of Art

167 Renfrew Street, G3 (0141 353 4500/www.gsa. ac.uk). Cowcaddens tube/Charing Cross rail. **Open** *Tours* July, Aug 11am, 2pm Mon-Fri; 10.30am, 11.30am, 1pm Sat, Sun; Sept-June 11am, 2pm Mon-Fri; 10.30am, 11.30am Sat. *Shop* 10am-5pm Mon-Fri; 10am-1pm Sat. **Admission** *Tours* £5; £4 concessions; free under-10s. **Credit** AmEx, MC, V. **Map** p314 C2.
Charles Rennie Mackintosh's masterpiece and an icon of 20th-century design. The must-see views of this must-see building are the façades of the northhand west wings, and particularly the library beyond. The interior is only open to the public on guided tours but is well worth taking the trouble to view. *See also p239* **Mackintosh**.

The Lighthouse

11 Mitchell Lane, G1 (0141 221 6362/www.thelight house.co.uk). St Enoch or Buchanan St tube/Central Station rail. **Open** 10.30am-5pm Mon, Wed-Sat;

Bar at the **Centre for Contemporary Arts**.

11am-5pm Tue; noon-5pm Sun. **Admission** £1; free concessions. *Mackintosh Interpretation Centre* £2.50; £2 concessions. **Credit** MC, V. **Map** p315 D3.
Charles Rennie Mackintosh's *Glasgow Herald* building has metamorphosed into the snappily named Lighthouse, Scotland's Centre for Architecture, Design & the City. With a constantly evolving programme of exhibitions and events, this is a lively addition to Glasgow's cultural scene. It includes the Mackintosh Interpretation Centre, a state-of-the-art facility that provides an understanding of Charles Rennie's art, architecture and design, as well as giving an orientation to the main Mackintosh sites around the city.

Old Town & East End

East of the shopping thoroughfares and chic bars and restaurants of the Merchant City beats the city's historic heart; Glasgow Cross fans eastwards from the intersection of Trongate, Gallowgate, High Street and Saltmarket. Sights include the People's Palace and the Cathedral.

This area was the old centre of the city before the 19th-century surge westwards, and, although it lacks the vibrancy of the Merchant City, it has rich pickings for anyone with an interest in Glaswegian history. The city was effectively founded at the point where the Molendinar Burn flowed into the Clyde, now the site of the High Court. The McLennan Arch, which faces the court, marks the entrance to the city's most famous public space, **Glasgow Green**. This stretch of parkland, which is currently undergoing an extensive facelift, is Europe's oldest public park, and it supports over 800 years of memories and experiences. It doubled as both fairground and hanging place, although these days it's more famous for hosting the annual Bonfire Night fireworks display, Glasgow Fair Festival and the annual Summer Gig on the Green. The **People's Palace** and the **Winter Gardens** (for both, *see below*) are the main permanent attractions on the Green.

Renaissance Venice makes a striking appearance opposite the People's Palace, in the guise of one of the city's most quirky buildings, **Templeton's Carpet Factory** (1889). Designed by William Leiper, and based on the Doges' Palace, the building is one of the finest examples of decorative brickwork in existence, and a rare find in Glasgow, an essentially stone city. Just off the Green where it borders on Greendyke Street is the **Homes for the Future** development, one of the cornerstone projects of Glasgow's year as the UK City of Architecture and Design. This ambitious housing development has managed to reclaim the lost urban spaces north of the Green with some of the most attractively modern and cutting-edge architecture to be found in the country.

To the north of the Green lies the handsome **St Andrew's in the Square** (*see p247*), a former church that now hosts traditional Scottish music events and also houses a restaurant/bar. Further north still are the twin thoroughfares of **Gallowgate** and **London Road**. These two streets form the boundary of Glasgow's famous weekend market, the **Barras**, which is worthy of a whole Sunday morning bargain-hunting expedition in itself. A stroll here after dark, however, is not recommended. The biggest and most popular of Glasgow's ballrooms, the famous **Barrowland** (*see p247*), adjoins the market. Unveiled on Christmas Eve 1934, it subsequently had its huge neon sign taken down during World War II when it was realised that German planes were using it for navigation. Its current fame rests on its status as a rock concert venue. Just look for that unmissable sign.

Snaking up the High Street, north of the Gallowgate, is a cluster of attractions including **Glasgow Cathedral**, the **Provand's Lordship**, the **Necropolis** and the **St Mungo Museum of Religious Life & Art**. Sadly, but vitally, they are all that remains of the heart of the medieval city.

Glasgow Cathedral
Castle Street, G4 (0141 552 6891/0988/ www.glasgowcathedral.org.uk). High Street rail. **Open** *Apr-Sept* 9.30am-6pm Mon-Sat; 2-5pm Sun. *Oct-Mar* 9.30am-4pm Mon-Sat; 2-4pm Sun. **Admission** free. **Map** p315 F2.
Glasgow's patron saint, St Mungo, whose tomb can be found in the crypt, founded Glasgow Cathedral in 543 on the site of a burial ground consecrated by St Ninian. Parts of the current building date from the 12th century, making it one of Scotland's oldest medieval churches.

Necropolis
Glasgow Necropolis Cemetery, 50 Cathedral Square, G4 (0141 552 3145). High Street rail. **Open** 24hrs daily. **Admission** free. **Map** p315 F2.
The first non-denominational 'hygienic' graveyard in Scotland was inspired by the famed Père Lachaise cemetery in Paris. It was intended to provide the industrialists and merchants of the 19th century city with a dignified resting place.

The People's Palace/ Winter Gardens
Glasgow Green, G4 (0141 554 0223/ www.glasgow.gov.uk). Bridgeton rail. **Open** 10am-5pm Mon-Sat; 11am-5pm Sun. **Admission** free. **Map** p315 F4.
The red sandstone People's Palace, which was built in 1898, originally served as a municipal and cultural centre for the city's working class. It now houses one of Glasgow's most cherished exhibitions, covering all aspects of Glaswegian life, and particularly the city's social and industrial history. The adjoining Winter Gardens is one of the most elegant Victorian glasshouses in Scotland.

Provand's Lordship
3 Castle Street, G4 (0141 552 8819). High Street rail. **Open** 10am-5pm Mon-Thur, Sat; 11am-5pm Fri, Sun. **Admission** free. **Map** p315 F2.
Glasgow's only medieval house was built in 1471. Mary Queen of Scots is believed to have slept here on one of her many jaunts around Scotland.

St Mungo Museum of Religious Life & Art
2 Castle Street, G4 (0141 553 2557). High Street rail. **Open** 10am-5pm Mon-Thur, Sat; 11am-5pm Fri, Sun. **Admission** free. **Map** p315 F2.
The main reason to visit this museum is to see Dali's awesome *Christ of St John of the Cross*. St Mungo's takes no part in Glasgow's undesirable sectarian predilections; it's a multi-faith museum with its own Zen garden for some instant karma.

South Side

The West End may be the city's bohemian hub, but the South Side, with its rich ethnic diversity, is probably the city's most cosmopolitan area. Most of the South Side is residential, encompassing many different and disparate districts, from affluent Newton Mearns to the rather less affluent housing estates, such as Castlemilk.

Just over the Clyde from the city centre, the **Gorbals**, previously one of the most notorious areas in the city, is fast becoming one of its most desirable addresses, thanks to a visionary regeneration programme. The area also boasts one of the best theatres in Britain. The **Citizens' Theatre** (*see p248*) was founded in 1943 by James Bridie as a theatre for the people, and it is justly world famous for its risk-taking and cutting-edge productions – Glasgow's theatre-goers are equally impressed by its low ticket prices. The **Tramway** (*see p249*), one of the city's swankiest contemporary art and performance venues, is also close by.

Some of the best examples of Alexander 'Greek' Thomson's architecture can also be found on the South Side. The **Caledonia Road Church** (1856) on Cathcart Road in the Gorbals was inspired by the Acropolis. A fire in 1965 destroyed the painted interior, leaving only the portico and tower intact. It's still worth a visit, though. Also check out **Langside**, a double villa in Mansionhouse Road built in 1856, and **Holmwood House** in Netherlee (*see below*), built shortly afterwards and regarded as Thomson's finest villa. The Thomson-designed terraces of Regent Park, in the district of Strathbungo to the west of Queen's Park, have been designated a conservation area since the 1970s. Both Thomson and Mackintosh lived here.

Another South Side landmark worth more than a passing glance is Mackintosh's **Scotland Street School Museum**. The South Side is dramatically punctuated by Glasgow's largest parks; in fact, the city as a whole boasts more parks per head of population than anywhere else in Europe. These include **Bellahouston**, where you'll find **House for an Art Lover**, a modern construction based on plans submitted by Mackintosh for an architectural competition in 1901. In **Pollok Park**, Glasgow's largest park – at 146 hectares – and probably its most beautiful, you'll find the main South Side attractions: **Pollok House** and the **Burrell Collection**.

No round-up of sites south of the city would be complete without mention of the National Stadium at Hampden Park, home to Scotland's national football team. The

Scottish Football Museum is a recent addition to the stadium, with a permanent display on Scottish football's finest moments and a programme of temporary exhibitions.

Burrell Collection

Pollok Park, 2060 Pollokshaws Road, G43 (0141 287 2550). Pollokshaws West rail, then 10min walk. **Open** 10am-5pm Mon-Thur, Sat; 11am-5pm Fri, Sun. **Admission** free.

Sir William Burrell gave his prodigious collection of art and artefacts to the city of Glasgow in 1944. One of the jewels in Glasgow's cultural crown, the collection encompasses treasures from ancient Egypt, Greece and Rome, and ceramics from various Chinese dynasties, as well as European decorative arts including rare tapestries and stained glass. It also boasts one of the finest collections of impressionist and post-impressionist paintings and drawings in the world. Try to come on a sunny day, when the reflected light in the interior glass-roofed courtyard is breathtaking.

Holmwood House

61-3 Netherlee Road, G44 (0141 637 2129/www. nts.org.uk). Cathcart rail. **Open** *Apr-Oct* noon-5pm daily; access may be restricted at peak times. Groups must pre-book. **Admission** £3.50; £2.60 concessions. **No credit cards**.

Alexander Thomson's finest and most elaborate villa. Visitors can see the progress being made on the conservation and restoration of the architect's richly ornamental classical interior.

House for an Art Lover

Bellahouston Park, 10 Dumbreck Road, G41 (0141 353 4770/www.houseforanartlover.co.uk). Dumbreck rail. **Open** *Apr-Sept* 10am-4pm Mon-Thur, Sun; 10am-3pm Sat. *Oct-Mar* 10am-4pm Sat, Sun; times may vary, phone to check **Admission** £3.50; £2.50 concessions. **Credit** AmEx, MC, V.

Built according to the plans Mackintosh submitted to a German architectural competition in 1901, the house has been recently completed to mixed reactions.

Pollok House

Pollok Park, 2060 Pollokshaws Road, G43 (0141 616 6410/www.nts.org.uk). Pollokshaws West rail, then 10min walk. **Open** 10am-5pm daily. **Admission** £5; £3.75 concessions; free children. **Credit** MC, V.

This magnificent 18th-century mansion houses the Stirling Maxwell collection of Spanish and European paintings, including some beautiful works by Goya. In addition, there's one of the country's finest collections of works by William Blake.

Scotland Street School Museum

225 Scotland Street, G5 (0141 287 0500/www. glasgow.gov.uk). Shields Road tube. **Open** 10am-5pm Mon-Thur, Sat; 11am-5pm Fri, Sun. **Admission** free. **Map** p314 B4.

A real Mackintosh treat, this majestic school building is now a newly refurbished museum offering an insight into Glaswegian schooling in the first half of the 20th century.

Mackintosh

The legacy of Charles Rennie Mackintosh looms large over the city of Glasgow. City-centre bins, benches and just about every other street accessory designed for or after 1990 is an ersatz variation on a Mackintosh stylistic theme, affectionately known to locals as 'Mockintosh'. Mockintosh mania aside, the city is the best – some would say only – place to experience the work of one of the most original and dynamic architects and designers of the late 19th and early 20th centuries.

Mackintosh's greatest public buildings can be seen in and around Glasgow; some of the most important are reviewed on pp235-241. The **Martyrs' Public School** (1896), just north of the Cathedral, is an example of his early architectural style. In the city centre is the **Daily Record Building** (1901), one of the hidden treasures of the area, combining curvilinear, art nouveau forms with geometric patterns set into glazed brick. It can only be viewed from Renfield and St Vincent Lanes. The **Scotland Street School Museum** (see p238) is best seen at night to appreciate the full illuminated impact of its glass, Scots baronial-type turrets.

Although Mackintosh is most often associated with the **Willow Tearoom** (see p235), his *pièce de résistance* is undoubtedly the **Glasgow School of Art** (see p236).

And then there's the house he designed, but never saw built: the **House for an Art Lover** (see p238).

Mackintosh's other masterpiece is **Hill House** (West Upper Colquhoun Street, 01436 673900/www.nts.org.uk; open Apr-Oct 1.30-5pm daily but phone to check), which involves a trip to Helensburgh, 45 minutes by train from Glasgow (trains leave from Queen Street Station every half hour). Walter Blackie, director of the well-known Glasgow publishers, commissioned not only the house and garden but much of the furniture and all of the interior fittings and decoration. Today the rooms seem as modern as they must have been in 1904 when the Blackie family moved in.

For a thorough exploration of Mackintosh's life and work, begin with the **Lighthouse** (see p236), in the old *Glasgow Herald* building in the city centre. The location is apt – the Herald was Mackintosh's first public commission. The Lighthouse's Mackintosh Interpretation Centre guides visitors through the great man's achievements, influences and legacy, using interactive displays and detailed studies of key buildings – placed in social, cultural and physical context. From here there is also access to the Mackintosh tower, part of the original design, which affords views over the city that take in some of his most important buildings.

Great Western Terrace.

Scottish Football Museum

National Stadium, Hampden Park, Somerville Drive, G42 (0141 616 6100/ www.scottishfa.co.uk). King Park or Mount Florida rail. **Open** 10am-5pm Mon-Sat; 11am-5pm Sun. **Admission** *Museum* £5; £2.50 concessions. *Stadium tours* £2.50; £1.25 concessions. **Credit** MC, V.

OK, so Scottish football may not be up there with the world's greatest these days, but if names like Kenny Dalglish, Dennis Law, Bill Shankly, Jock Stein and the Lisbon Lions make your heart beat faster, you'll enjoy a visit here.

West End

The huge dome and imposing façade of the **Mitchell Library**, Europe's largest reference library, unofficially divides the West End from the city centre. The West End, it has to be said, has a character all of its own. A dual personality has evolved through its role as the soft play area for the city's huge student population and as the happy hunting ground for the bourgeois and bohemian, or bourgeois bohemian (as probably best describes the quintessential Westender). All this adds up, as you might imagine, to a cornucopia of bars, coffee shops, delis and health food emporiums – and a lot more besides.

One of the main arteries serving the West End is the seemingly never-ending **Great Western Road**, built in 1836 after relentless pressure from Glasgow's middle classes, who wanted a route out of the overcrowded, industry-polluted city centre. Now the road itself contributes to that pollution. To the south are domestic terraced buildings from the same period, which are among the city's most splendid architectural features. Highlights are **Park Circus** (1857-63) and **Park Terrace** (1855). Further west, flanking Great Western Road, **Great Western Terrace** (1867) is the definitive Glasgow terrace designed by Alexander 'Greek' Thomson.

The **Botanic Gardens** is the place to be seen during Glasgow's short summer. But **Byres Road**, just beyond the Gardens' main gates, is the real heart of the West End, both in terms of shopping and as the locus of Studentsville. Radiating from this main thoroughfare can be found the charming little lanes, including **Dowanside** and **Cresswell**, which are a must-visit for second-hand and vintage clothes and unusual gifts. **Ashton Lane** is home to arguably the comfiest cinema in the city, the **Grosvenor** (*see p245*), as well as a host of cafés and bars, which range from the cheap and cheerful to the seriously swanky.

The **University of Glasgow** dominates this area, and indeed the whole of the West End skyline, with its overwhelming Gothic revival presence. The bizarre concrete façade of the Mackintosh House at the **Hunterian Art Gallery & Museum**, next door, forms a strange but tantalising juxtaposition. To the east of the University is the 34-hectare Kelvingrove Park. First laid out as pleasure grounds in the 1850s, on a hot day it becomes instantly packed, but on the other 364 days of the year, it's an oasis of calm. The striking red sandstone confection that is the **Art Gallery & Museum, Kelvingrove** was built to hold the 1901 International Exhibition and dominates the southern end of the park. The nearby **Museum of Transport** on Argyle Street completes the West End Museum Mile.

Art Gallery & Museum, Kelvingrove

Kelvingrove, G3 (0141 287 2700/www.clyde-valley.com/glasgow/kelvingr.htm). Kelvinhall tube/Partick rail. **Open** 10am-5pm Mon-Thur, Sat; 11am-5pm Fri, Sun. **Admission** free. **Map** p234.

One of the highlights of the gallery and museum is its world-class permanent collection of fine art, including 17th-century Dutch paintings, impressionist works, and Scottish art and artefacts. Among them are works by the Glasgow Boys (a loosely connected group of painters working in the late 19th century) and Mackintosh.

Botanic Gardens & Kibble Palace

730 Great Western Road, G12 (0141 334 2422/www.glasgow.gov.uk). Hillhead tube. **Open** *Palace* Apr-Oct 10am-4.45pm daily; Nov-Mar 10am-4.15pm daily. *Gardens* 7am-dusk daily. **Admission** free. **Map** p234.

The gardens are dominated by the huge dome of Kibble Palace, a beautiful feat of Victorian engineering. An extensive restoration project is currently under way.

Hunterian Museum & Art Gallery

University of Glasgow, Hillhead Street, G12 (0141 330 5431/www.hunterian.gla.ac.uk). Hillhead tube. **Open** 9.30am-5pm Mon-Sat. *Mackintosh House* 9.30am-12.30pm, 1.30-5pm Mon-Sat. **Admission** free. **Map** p234.

Scotland's largest print collection, including the finest works on paper by Mackintosh are housed in the Hunterian Art Gallery. The gallery leads on to the Mackintosh House, and includes a recreation of the architect's home in Southpark Avenue, where he lived from 1906 to 1914. Built in 1807, the Hunterian is Scotland's oldest public museum, and among its archaeological treasures are several dinosaurs – as befits the Scottish Centre for Dinosaur Research.

Mitchell Library

North Street, G3 (0141 287 2999/www.glasgow.gov.uk). Charing Cross rail. **Open** 9am-8pm Mon-Thur; 9am-5pm Fri, Sat. **Map** p314 B2.

With over one million books and documents, this is the largest reference library in Europe.

Museum of Transport

1 Bunhouse Road, Kelvinhall, G3 (0141 287 2720). Kelvinhall tube/Partick rail. **Open** 10am-5pm Mon-Thur, Sat; 11am-5pm Fri, Sun. **Admission** free. **Map** p234.

This is one of Britain's better transport museums. It includes the Clyde Room, which celebrates – as well as mourns – Glasgow's lost shipbuilding industry.

Where to eat & drink

Not surprisingly, given its size, Glasgow has a wide choice of restaurants, pubs and bars. We list a range of main course prices for restaurants.

City centre

Café Gandolfi

64 Albion Street, G1 (0141 552 6813). Argyle St or High St rail. **Open** 9am-11.30pm Mon-Sat; noon-11.30pm Sun. **Main courses** £6-£13. **Credit** AmEx, MC, V. **Map** p315 E3.

Well-established port of call in the Merchant City, with a devoted following. Tim Stead's rich natural wood interior is a good excuse to pop into this café and restaurant for coffee and cake, lunch with a Mediterranean bent, or a robust dinner majoring in Scottish produce.

Le Chardon d'Or

176 West Regent Street, G2 (0141 248 3801). **Open** noon-2.30pm, 6-10.30pm Mon-Fri; 6-10.30pm Sat. **Main courses** £14.50-£19.50. **Credit** AmEx, MC, V. **Map** p314 C2.

Classic French food with an individual flourish, from Brian Maule, former head chef at the Michelin-starred Le Gavroche. Scottish produce is used where possible; flavours are wonderful.

Corinthian

191 Ingram Street, G1 (0141 552 1101/www.corinthian.uk.com). Buchanan St tube. *Restaurant* noon-2.30pm, 6-10pm Mon-Fri; 6-10pm Sat. *Main bar* 11am-3am Mon-Sat; noon-3am Sun. *Piano bar* 9pm-3am Mon-Fri; 5pm-3am Sat, Sun. *Cocktail bar* 5pm-3am Fri, Sat. **Main courses** £10-£16. **Lunch & pre-theatre menu** 2 courses £9.75; 3 courses £12.50. **Credit** AmEx, MC, V. **Map** p315 E3.

Housed in what was described by the *Guardian* as 'Glasgow's finest Grade-A listed building', the Corinthian comprises a piano bar, cocktail bar and the most opulent main bar in the city of Glasgow. The restaurant serves a good range of Modern European food.

Fratelli Sarti

121 Bath Street, G2 (0141 204 0440). Buchanan St tube. **Open** 8am-10.30pm Mon-Sat (licence until 1am); noon-10.30pm Sun. **Main courses** £5.95-£12.50. **Credit** AmEx, DC, MC, V. **Map** p315 D2.

This charming family-run restaurant proudly lives up to its '100% authentic Italian' motto. It straddles the restaurant/bistro/ deli dividing lines, and is often busy, especially at weekends – so book in advance. **Branches**: 133 Wellington Street, G2 (enquiries 0141 248 2228/bookings 0141 204 0440); **Il Gran Caffe** 42 Renfield Street, G2 (0141 572 7000).

Groucho St Jude's

190 Bath Street, G2 (0141 352 8800/www.grouchosaintjudes.com). Buchanan St tube. **Open** *Restaurant* noon-3pm, 6-10.30pm Mon-Thur; 6-11pm Fri; 6-11pm Sat; 6-10.30pm Sun. *Bar* noon-midnight Mon-Sat; 6pm-midnight Sun. **Main courses** £10.50-£18.50. **Credit** AmEx, DC, MC, V. **Map** p314 C2.

Something of a McGlitterati hangout, Glasgow's Groucho oozes cool retro chic. It also serves a spot-on contemporary European menu, and the bar offers a mean cocktail.

The Horseshoe

17 Drury Street, G2 (0141 229 5711). Buchanan Street tube. **Open** 11am-midnight Mon-Sat; 12.30pm-midnight Sun. **Main courses** £2.80-£3.20. **Lunch menu** (Mon-Sat) 3 courses £2.95. **No credit cards. Map** p315 D3.

In a city of drinking institutions, this is the one to end them all. It boasts the longest continuous bar in the UK – as the *Guinness Book of Records* attests. More important is the friendly atmosphere of its traditional surroundings. Famed also for its ridiculously cheap three-course lunches.

Lowdown

158A Bath Street, G2 (0141 331 4061). Buchanan St tube. **Open** 11.30am-1am Mon-Thur, Sun; 11.30am-3am Fri, Sat. **Main courses** £5.50-£6. **Tapas** 3 dishes £10; 6 dishes £19.50. **Credit** AmEx, MC, V. **Map** p314 C2.

The current big flavour on the Glasgow bar scene, this vast and coolly spartan basement space seems to have struck the right balance between the über-hip style factor and the essential elements of a well-stocked bar with excellent-value bar food (three tapas for a tenner), not to mention top service. The punters come in their droves, so arrive early for a seat.

The Rogano

11 Exchange Place, Buchanan Street, G1 (0141 248 4055/www.rogano.co.uk). Buchanan St tube/Queen St rail. **Open** *Restaurant* noon-2.30pm, 6.30-10.30pm daily. *Café* noon-11pm Mon-Thur, Sun; noon-midnight Fri, Sat. **Main courses** *Restaurant* £17.50-£33.50. *Café* £7.95-£11.95. **Credit** AmEx, DC, MC, V. **Map** p315 D3.

A fabulous example of art deco style – it's worth visiting for the interior alone. The restaurant's menu is traditional, with fish a forte. Downstairs, Café Rogano has a slightly more modern menu.

The Scotia

112 Stockwell Street, G1 (0141 552 8681). St Enoch tube/Argyle Street rail. **Open** 11am-midnight Mon-Sat; 12.30pm-midnight Sun. **Main courses** £1.95-£3.95. **No credit cards. Map** p315 D3.

This traditional pub, situated close to the river, claims, like a zillion others, to be Glasgow's oldest public house. It is the busiest and most famous of the three bars that make up the so-called Stockwell Triangle – the other two are the **Victoria Bar** (159 Bridgegate; 0141 552 6040) and the **Clutha Vaults** (167 Stockwell Street; 0141 552 7520). Vibrant live music sessions can be found at all three, and the Victoria Bar even plays host to a troupe of Morris dancers on Wednesday evenings.

Old Town & East End

The Inn on the Green

23 Greenhead Street, G40 (0141 554 0165/ www.theinnonthegreen.co.uk). Bridgeton rail. **Open** noon-2.30pm, 6pm-late Mon-Fri; 6pm-late Sat, Sun. **Main courses** £11.75-£16.75. **Credit** AmEx, MC, V.

Situated on the fairly isolated eastern fringe of Glasgow Green, the Inn manages to combine a laid-back piano bar vibe with food that is best summarised as robust, sturdy Scottish fare. The unlikely mix attracts plenty of punters – so it seems jazz and haggis can make happy bedfellows after all. The Inn also has good accommodation (B&B £75 double).

Café Source

1 St Andrew's Square, off Saltmarket, G1 (0141 548 6020/www.cafesource.co.uk). St Enoch tube/High St rail. **Open** 11am-11pm Mon, Tue; 11am-midnight Wed-Sat; 12.30pm-11pm Sun. **Main courses** £3.95-£7.95. **Credit** MC, V.

Downstairs from the wonderful St Andrew's church hall, this cosy basement bar has a folksy feel. The menu – hearty and Scottish – also reflects this. However, the bar's contemporary style makes sure the place doesn't tip into 'hoots mon' twee territory.

South side

Heraghty's

708 Pollokshaws Road, G41 (0141 423 0380). Pollokshields East rail. **Open** 11am-11pm Mon-Thur; 11am-midnight Fri, Sat; 12.30-11pm Sun. **No credit cards.**

This authentic Irish bar is the place to watch a Celtic match or listen to some genuine Irish blarney, rather than the city centre's manufactured theme bars.

1901

1534 Pollokshaws Road, G43 (0141 632 0161). Shawlands rail. **Open** *Bistro* noon-9.30pm Mon-Sat; 12.30-9.30pm Sun. *Bar* noon-11pm Mon-Thur; noon-midnight Fri, Sat; 12.30-11pm Sun. **Main courses** £6.95-£15.90. **Early evening menu** 2 courses £9.95. **Credit** MC, V.

A recent addition to the South Side scene, this bar/bistro has already established a loyal fan base due in most part to its relaxed vibe and no nonsense Mediterranean nosh. Live jazz on Sundays.

West End

Amyrillis: One Devonshire Gardens

1 Devonshire Gardens, G12 (0141 337 3434). Bus 11, 20, 51, 66. **Open** noon-2pm, 6.45-10.15pm Mon-Fri, Sun; 6.45-10.15pm Sat. **Set menu** 3 courses £35; 6 courses £45. **Credit** AmEx, MC, V.

Gordon Ramsay, Michelin-starred culinary and megastar, is behind this spectacular gastronomic experience in one of Scotland's most exclusive hotels (*see p251*). This is as good as it gets, but be prepared to book well in advance.

Mother India

28 Westminster Terrace, Sauchiehall Street, G3 (0141 221 1663). Kelvinhall tube then 10min walk. **Open** 5-10.30pm Mon, Tue; noon-2pm, 5.30-10.30pm Wed, Thur; noon-2pm, 5.30-11pm Fri; 5-11pm Sat, Sun. **Main courses** £5.75-£11.50. **Corkage** 95p. **Credit** AmEx, MC, V. **Map** p314 A2.

Excellent authentic Indian home cooking, served in relaxed, comfortable, no-fuss surroundings make Mother India one of Glasgow's most popular Indian restaurants. Plenty of choice for vegetarians. Bring your own bottle.

Stravaigin

28-30 Gibson Street, G12 (0141 334 2665/ www.stravaigin.com). Kelvinbridge tube. **Open** *Café-bar* 11am-11pm Mon-Thur; 11am-midnight Fri, Sat; 12.30-11pm Sun. *Restaurant* 5-11pm Tue-Thur; noon-2.30pm, 5-11pm Fri-Sun. **Main courses** *Café-bar* £5.45-£12.95. *Restaurant* £16.95; 2 courses £21.95; 3 courses £26.95. **Credit** AmEx, DC, MC, V. **Map** p234.

Stravaigin has won awards for its honest Scottish produce, served with an exotic twist. The bar menu is also excellent.

The Ubiquitous Chip

12 Ashton Lane, G12 (0141 334 5007/ www.ubiquitouschip.co.uk). Hillhead tube. **Open** *Restaurant* noon-2.30pm, 5.30-11pm Mon-Sat; 12.30-2.30pm, 6.30-11pm Sun. *Brasserie* noon-11pm Mon-Sat; 12.30-11pm Sun. **Main courses** £7.25-£15.45. **Dinner menu** 3 courses £34.95. **Credit** AmEx, DC, MC, V. **Map** p234.

Housed in a converted mews stable, the Ubiquitous Chip is a Glasgow institution – and deservedly so. The constantly evolving menu makes use of seasonal Scottish produce. The bar, and new 'wee bar', attract an older crowd than other imbiberies on Ashton Lane, and achieve that rare feat of being civilised and boisterous at the same time. The excellent wine and malt whisky selection is another reason to visit.

The best Restaurants

Amyrillis: One Devonshire Gardens

Media star and *chef du jour* Gordon Ramsay brings his celestial culinary vision back to Scotland. We are not worthy. *See p242.*

Café Gandolfi

Charming Merchant City institution with a large and devoted following. Good food and good looks. *See p240.*

Mother India

Probably the best Indian home cooking in a city renowned for its outstanding Indian restaurants. *See p242.*

Stravaigin

Justifiably famous for its honest Scottish cuisine with a twist. Excellent bar menu too. *See above.*

Uisge Beatha

232 Woodlands Road, G3 (0141 564 1596). Kelvinbridge tube. **Open** 11am-midnight Mon-Sat; 12.30pm-midnight Sun. **Main courses** £4.95-£6.75. **Credit** AmEx, MC, V. **Map** p234/p314 A1.

An over-the-top kitsch Scottish bar that looks like a Highland hunting lodge. The Uisge Beatha (meaning 'water of life' – whisky) incorporates tartan, stuffed stags' heads and log fires into its decor, and amazingly, it just about gets away with it. The varied clientele is testament to its enduring popularity.

University Café

87 Byres Road, G11 (0141 339 5217). Hillhead or Kelvinbridge tube. **Open** 9am-10pm Mon, Wed-Fri; 9am-10.30pm Sat; 10am-10pm Sun. **Main courses** £1.60-£4.50. **No credit cards. Map** p234.

The University Café is famous for both its fabulous 1950s-style decor and its hearty food. Ice-cream is a speciality; it has won innumerable awards.

Shops

Glaswegians take shopping seriously. And retailers take Glasgow pretty seriously: the city is the second biggest retail centre in the UK, and attracts upmarket names like Gianni Versace, who located his first British store here (in the **Italian Centre**, *see p245*).

Cruise

180 Ingram Street, City centre, G1 (0141 572 3232). Buchanan Street tube/Queen Street rail. **Open** 10am-6pm Mon-Wed, Fri; 10am-7pm Thur; 9.30am-6pm Sat; noon-5pm Sun. **Credit** AmEx, DC, MC, V. **Map** p315 E3.

Glasgow's preoccupation with clothes borders on the obsessive, and Cruise has something of a monolithic presence in the city's fashion consciousness. Here you can buy the best range of men's and women's designer gear in the city from the largest independent retailer in Europe.

Branch: Cruise Jeans, 223 Ingram Street, City centre G1 (0141 229 0000).

Dr Jives

111-113 Candleriggs, City centre, G1 (0141 552 5451/www.drjives.com). Buchanan Street tube/Queen Street rail. **Open** 10am-6pm Mon-Sat; 1-5pm Sun. **Credit** AmEx, DC, MC, V. **Map** p315 E3.

This trendy Merchant City shoppers' favourite stocks exclusive brands for men and women such as Vintage Levi's and YMC, and is Glasgow's only Stussy outlet. Quirkier labels such as Hysteric Glamour, a mixed bag of gadgets, accessories and footwear make it an essential one-stop for the city's bright young things.

House of Fraser

21-45 Buchanan Street, City centre, G1 (0141 221 3880/www.houseoffraser.co.uk). St Enoch tube. **Open** 9.30am-6pm Mon-Wed, Fri; 9.30am-8pm Thur; 9am-6pm Sat; noon-5.30pm Sun. **Credit** AmEx, DC, MC, V. **Map** p315 D3

Trips Out of Town

Symbol of Glasgow shopping: the peacock at **Princes Square**. *See p245.*

Classic and classy department store with a sumptuous emporium feel and a traditional emphasis on beauty and luxury.

Inhouse

24-26 Wilson Street, City centre, G1 (0141 552 5902/www.inhousenet.co.uk). Buchanan Street tube/Queen Street rail. **Open** 10am-6pm Mon-Wed, Fri; 10am-7pm Thur; 9.30am-5.30pm Sat. **Credit** MC, V. **Map** p315 E3.

Handily located in super-trendy Merchant City, this place will hit the spot if it's a Philippe Starck lemon squeezer or an Alessi kettle that you're after. There are also some gulpingly expensive contemporary furniture classics.

Missing

9-11 Wellington Street, City centre, G2 (0141 248 1661/www.missing.co.uk). Central Station rail. **Open** 9.30am-6pm Mon-Sat; 11am-6pm Sun. **Credit** MC, V. **Map** p314 C3.

Indie vinyl and CD heaven. Missing always has a broad and excellent range of second-hand and new releases in stock, making it music central for Glasgow scenesters and musos. In addition, both city centre and West End shops double as handy ticket outlets for CPL and DFC promotions, the companies that deal with many Barrowland, King Tut's and Garage gigs.
Branch: 685 Great Western Road, West End, G11 (0141 334 7966).

Mr Ben Vintage Clothing

Unit 6, King's Court, King Street, City centre, G1 (0141 553 1936). St Enoch tube. **Open** 10.30am-5.30pm daily. **No credit cards**. **Map** p315 E3.

An absolute must for young retro cool dudes, this Glasgow stalwart has an ace selection of second-hand and vintage clothing. Famous for its unassailable collection of '70s Y-fronts.

Gallery III

25 King Street, City centre, G1 (0141 552 1394/ www.gpsart.co.uk). St Enoch tube. **Open** 10am-5.30pm Tue-Sat. **Credit** AmEx, DC, MC, V. **Map** p315 E3.

As the retail outlet for the Glasgow Print Studio, this is the place to go for exclusive prints by the cream of Scottish artistic talent, from John Byrne to Elizabeth Blackadder. New graphic art by emerging artists is also well represented.

Starry Starry Night

19-21 Dowanside Lane (off Byres Road), West End, G12 (0141 337 1837). Hillhead tube. **Open** 10am-5.30pm Mon-Sat. **Map** p234.

One of the quaintest wee retro and vintage clothes shops in the city. It's hidden away down an easily missable lane just off Byres Road, so keep your eyes peeled.

23rd Precinct

23 Bath Street, City centre, G2 (0141 332 4806/www.23rdprecinct.co.uk). Buchanan St tube. **Open** 10am-6pm Mon-Sat; noon-5pm Sun. **Credit** AmEx, DC, MC, V. **Map** p315 D2.

Glasgow's thriving club scene is well facilitated by vinyl hub 23rd Precinct. Knowledgeable dance specialists run this retail outfit, which also has its own music publishing company and is home to specialist dance label Limbo. Most of the staff DJ around town, so this is a good place for information on the local club scene.

Shopping centres & arcades

Buchanan Galleries Shopping Centre
220 Buchanan Street, City centre, G1 (0141 333 9898/www.buchanangalleries.co.uk). Buchanan St tube/Queen Street rail. **Open** 9am-6pm Mon-Wed, Fri, Sat; 9am-8pm Thur; 11am-5pm Sun. **Credit** varies. **Map** p315 D2.
In a city of shopping centres, the Buchanan Galleries tops them all. Although it's a bit of a monstrous carbuncle, it nevertheless offers everything you could possibly want at both ends of the shopping scale.

Decourcy's Arcade
Cresswell Lane, off Cresswell Street, West End, G12 (0141 334 6673 ground floor/0141 334 6959 top floor). Hillhead tube. **Open** 10am-5.30pm Mon-Sat; noon-5pm Sun. **Credit** varies. **Map** p234.
Bit of a boho hangout, this one. Decourcy's recently made the Independent's list of the top 25 reasons to visit Glasgow.

Italian Centre
7 John Street, City centre G1 (0141 552 6368). Buchanan St tube/Queen Street rail. **Open** 8am-6pm Mon-Sat. **Credit** varies. Map p315 E3.
This compact hub of boutiques and café-bars at the northern end of Merchant City exerts a magnetic power upon the city's more colourfully clad denizens.

Princes Square
48 Buchanan Street, City centre, G1 (0141 221 0324/www.princes-square.com). St Enoch tube. **Open** Shops 9.30am-6pm Mon-Wed, Fri; 9.30am-8pm Thur; 9am-6pm Sat; noon-5pm Sun. Bars & restaurants 10am-midnight Mon-Sat; 11.30am-5pm Sun. **Credit** varies. **Map** p315 D3.
The vigorous regeneration of Glagow's city centre began with the building of this shopping centre, which houses mainly upmarket outlets.

Arts & entertainment

Glaswegians are not known for holding back when it comes to a party. And if it's sport or culture you're after, there's plenty of that too.

TICKETS AND INFORMATION
For listings information, peruse the fortnightly List or the Glasgow Evening Times. Glasgow City Council's website (**www.glasgow.gov.uk**) has a relatively useful events page divided into sections for theatre, music, sport, visual arts, family and festivals. The **Ticket Centre** is also a useful source of information.

Ticket Centre
Candleriggs, City centre, G1 (0141 287 5511). **Open** Phoneline 10am-8pm Mon-Sat. **Credit** AmEx, MC, V. **Map** p315 E3.
Sells tickets for venues and events over the phone, for a booking fee.

Film

There are a number of city-centre cinemas in Glasgow, ranging from mainstream to arthouse. Here's where to go for your celluloid fix.

Glasgow Film Theatre
12 Rose Street, City centre, G3 (0141 332 8128/www.gft.org.uk). Cowcaddens tube. **Open** Box office noon-9pm Mon-Sat; Sun depends on performance. **Tickets** £3.90-£4.90; £2.50-£3.50 concessions. **Credit** AmEx, MC, V. **Map** p314 C2.
This is the place to see independent, arthouse and foreign releases. It was formerly the Cosmo cinema and has recently been refurbished to revisit its art deco origins. Café Cosmo in the foyer is a cosy spot to refuel before or after a film.

The Grosvenor
Ashton Lane, West End, G12 (0141 339 4298/www.grosvenorcinema.co.uk). Hillhead tube. **Open** Box office 1-7pm daily. **Tickets** £4; £2-£3 concessions. **Credit** MC, V. **Map** p234.
A West End institution, this small, two-screen cinema programmes a strong mix of mainstream and arthouse movies.

IMAX Theatre
56 Renfield Street, City centre, G2 (information & credit card bookings 0870 505 0007/www.odeon.co.uk). Buchanan St tube/Queen St rail. **Open** Phoneline 9am-9pm daily. **Tickets** £4.50; £2.50-£3.50 concessions. **Credit** AmEx, DC, MC, V. **Map** p315 D2.
A new, but already famous, titanium-clad, egg-shaped landmark of a cinema that makes for a space-age film-going experience.

Odeon City Centre Cinema
56 Renfield Street, City centre, G2 (information & credit card bookings 0870 505 0007/www.odeon.co.uk). Buchanan St tube/Queen St rail. **Open** Phoneline 9am-9pm daily. **Tickets** £4.50; £2.50-£3.50 concessions. **Credit** AmEx, DC, MC, V. **Map** p315 D2.
The last remaining traditional city-centre cinema in Glasgow. The films are mainstream and it gets packed at weekends, but with six screens to choose from you're likely to find something to suit.

UGC Renfrew Street
145-159 West Nile Street, City Centre, G1 (information & credit card bookings 0870 907 0789). Buchanan St tube/Queen St rail. **Open** Phoneline 10am-7pm Mon-Thur; 10am-9pm Fri-Sun. **Tickets** £4.50; £2.50-£3.50 concessions. **Credit** AmEx, DC, MC, V. **Map** p315 D2.
This new behemoth of a cinema (Europe's tallest) now dominates the city skyline, and has already enjoyed the ignominious honour of being voted one of the ugliest buildings in Scotland. For the die-hard cinema-goer, however, it does have what seems like a squillion screens (well, 18 actually), as well as a handily central location.

Gay Glasgow

Stylish, cool, yet warm-hearted – it stands to reason that Glasgow is the centre of Scottish gay life. Here are some of the highlights.

Gay Glasgow is centred around the Merchant City. There are bars galore here, and they're in close enough proximity to make an evening's pub crawl a viable proposition. Young lesbian and gay party-goers should try **Delmonica's** with theme nights, quizzes, sing-a-longs and dancing on the tables. The recently opened **Revolver Bar**, underground and opposite the Italian Centre, has a fantastic (and free) juke box, and attracts a more mature, butch crowd and their admirers. The **Waterloo** is the city's oldest gay bar. It's cheeky and working-class, with unpretentious and well-lived punters. Meanwhile, the **Polo Lounge**, full of antiques and chaise longues, has a luxurious atmosphere. There's a club downstairs at weekends, open from 11pm.

Bennets is the city's most popular gay club; a new top floor has been added to accommodate the crowds. A women-only night, Girls on Top, takes place here on the first Friday of the month.

The **Glasgow LGBT Centre** is a hive of activity, with an incredibly cheap café and a **Clone Zone** shop. Stonewall Scotland has offices here, as does a poets' and writers' group and the Bi-G-Les youth group.

Glasgay (information 0141 334 7126), Britain's largest lesbian and gay arts festival, takes over the city annually for nine days from late October to early November. As well as high-profile shows, movies and music, Glasgay has a thorough community outreach programme. **Scottish Pride** parades through the city in June with a march, floats and celebrations (Edinburgh and Glasgow alternate as hosts; information from the LGBT Centre; *see below*). There are cultural events throughout the year at gay-friendly venues like the **Glasgow Film Theatre** (*see p246*), which shows movies of gay and lesbian interest, and the **Tron Theatre** (*see p249*), with its eclectic programming and trendy bar. The **Stand** features monthly gay stand-up comedy, and the **Citizens' Theatre** (*see p248*), in the heart of the Gorbals, presents visually striking drama, often imbued with a gay sensibility.

If the great outdoors means more to you than a nature walk, then **Kelvingrove Park** (West End) and **Queen's Park** (South Side) are the places to cruise. They're busy day and night, but be careful out there, as gay-bashings and robberies sometimes occur.

Bennets

90 Glassford Street, City centre, G1 (0141 552 5761/www.bennets.co.uk). Buchanan St tube. **Open** 11pm-3.30am Wed-Sun. **Admission** £3-£6; £2-£5 concessions. **No credit cards. Map** p303 E3.

Delmonica's

68 Virginia Street, City centre, G1 (0141 552 4803). Buchanan St tube. **Open** noon-midnight daily. **Credit** MC, V. **Map** p303 E3.

Football

The Old Firm rivalry between Celtic and Rangers is as legendary as the sectarianism of their supporters: Celtic's are traditionally Catholic, whereas Rangers' are Protestant; Celtic play at Celtic Park, Rangers at Ibrox. The national team play at the recently refurbished Hampden Stadium, which also hosts major sporting events including the 2002 European Champion's League Cup Final.

Celtic Park

95 Kerrydale Street, G40 (ticket line 0141 551 8653/ www.celticfc.co.uk). Bellgrove rail. **Open** *Museum & tours* from 10am daily, depending on matches; phone for details. *Shop* 9am-5pm Mon-Wed, Fri, Sun; 9am-7pm Thur; 9am-1pm Sat. **Tickets** £21-£24; £12-£14 concessions. **Credit** AmEx, MC, V.
The state-of-the-art stadium also features a museum and the Celtic Superstore.

Hampden – Scotland's National Stadium

Somerville Drive, G42 (information 0141 620 4000/ www.scottishfa.co.uk). King Park or Mount Florida rail. **Open** for matches or by guided tour only; phone for details. **Tickets** *Stadium tours* £2.50; £1.25 concessions. **Credit** MC, V.
Match tickets are not sold at the stadium. For details of guided tours around the ground, contact the Scottish Football Museum (*see p240*).

Ibrox

Edmiston Drive, G51 (ticket hotline 0870 600 1993/ www.rangers.co.uk). Ibrox tube. **Open** *Shop* 10am-5.30pm Mon-Fri; 9am-6pm Sat; 11am-5pm Sun. *Stadium tours* Mon, Fri, Sun; phone for details. **Tickets** £17-£22; £10-£13 concessions. **Credit** MC, V.
As well as the Ibrox Superstore there are tours of the stadium on Mondays, Fridays and Sundays. Call for details.

The Glasgow LGBT Centre
*11 Dixon Street, off Howard Street,
City centre, G1 (0141 221 7203/
www.gglc.org.uk). St Enoch tube.* **Open**
11am-midnight daily. **Map** p303 D3.

Polo Lounge
*84 Wilson Street, City centre, G1
(0141 553 1221/www.pololounge.
co.uk). Buchanan St tube/Queen St
rail.* **Open** 5pm-1am Mon-Thur; 5pm-3am
Fri-Sun. **Admission** free Mon-Thur; £5
after 11pm Fri-Sun. **Credit** MC, V.
Map p303 E3.

Revolver Bar
*6A John Street, City centre, G1 (0141 553
2456/www.revolverdotbar.com). Buchanan
St tube/Queen St rail.* **Open** 11am-
midnight Mon-Sat; 12.30pm-midnight Sun.
Credit MC, V. **Map** p303 E3.

The Stand
*333 Woodlands Road, West End, G3
(0870 600 6055/www.thestand.co.uk).
Kelvinbridge tube.* **Open** phone for details.
Admission £3-£7; £2-£5 concessions.
Credit MC, V. **Map** p234.

The Waterloo
*306 Argyle Street, City centre, G2 (0141
229 5891). St Enoch tube/Central Station
rail.* **Open** noon-midnight Mon-Sat;
12.30pm-midnight Sun. **No credit cards**.
Map p302 A1.

Music: classical

If you want to buy tickets by phone for
City Hall, you must use the Ticket Centre
(*see p245*). Tickets are sold at the venues
on performance nights only.

City Halls
*Candleriggs, City centre, G1 (0141 287 5024/www.
glasgow.gov.uk). Buchanan St tube.* **Tickets** prices
vary. **Credit** AmEx, MC, V. **Map** p315 E3.
Although superseded by the Royal Concert Hall, the
City Hall is still used by the Scottish Chamber
Orchestra, and is a popular and charming venue.

Royal Concert Hall
*2 Sauchiehall Street, City centre, G2 (0141 353
8000/www.grch.com). Buchanan St tube/Queen St
rail.* **Open** *Box office* 10am-6pm Mon-Sat; concert
days also 1-6pm Sun. *Phoneline* 9am-9pm daily.
Tickets £8-£25. **Credit** MC, V. **Map** p315 D2.

One of Glasgow's least attractive monoliths, the
Royal Concert Hall is home to the Royal Scottish
National Orchestra and, for the last three weeks of
January, to the Celtic Connections festival. Started
in 1994, Celtic Connections has grown to become one
of the world's biggest and most prestigious roots
festivals, with a music policy encompassing old,
new, traditional and modern forms.

Royal Scottish Academy of Music & Drama
*Royal Scottish Academy of Music & Drama, 100
Renfrew Street, City centre, G2 (0141 332 4101/
box office 0141 332 5057/ www.rsamd.ac.uk).
Cowcaddens tube.* **Open** *Box office* 9am-8.30pm
Mon-Fri; 9am-4.30pm Sat; noon-4.30pm Sun.
Tickets prices vary. **Credit** MC, V. **Map** p315 D2.
Recitals, masterclasses and guest soloists feature
regularly at the concert hall of the Royal Scottish
Academy of Music and Drama.

St Andrew's In the Square
*1 St Andrew's Square, Off Saltmarket, City centre,
G1 (0141 548 6020/ www.cafesource.co.uk). St
Enoch tube/High St rail.* **Open** *Box office* 11am-
11pm Mon, Tue; 11am-midnight Wed-Sat; 12.30-
11pm Sun. **Tickets** prices vary. **Credit** MC, V.
Map p315 E4.
One of Glasgow's newest music venues is housed in
one of the city's oldest churches. This wonderful
space focuses on Scottish music: trad, folk and
ceilidhs a go go.

Music: rock, pop, roots & country

If you want to buy tickets by phone for **City
Hall** or **Barrowland**, you must use the Ticket
Centre (*see p245*). Tickets are sold at the venues
on performance nights only. The **Royal
Concert Hall** (*see above*) hosts the Celtic
Connections roots festival.

Barrowland
*244 Gallowgate, East End, G4 (0141 552 4601/
www.glasgow-barrowland.com). Argyle St rail.* **Open**
Box office performance days only, times vary; phone
for details. **Tickets** £10-£30. **No credit cards**.
Map p315 F3.
Scotland's top music venue. Once a ballroom, the
celebrated Barrowland now hosts big-name, but
nonetheless still hip and happening, rock and dance
acts. It might be a bit of a dive, but there's nowhere
quite like it and the atmosphere is electric.

The Garage
*490 Sauchiehall Street, City centre, G2 (0141 332
1120/www.cplweb.com). Charing Cross rail.* **Open**
11pm-3am Mon-Fri, Sun; 10.30pm-3am Sat. **Tickets**
£2-£6. **No credit cards**. **Map** p314 C2.
The place to see live bands before they make the leap
to the Barrowland. On club nights the Garage is a
bit of an alternative student union, and the cheap
drinks policy means that it's a popular late-night
watering hole too.

The Armadillo:
Clyde Auditorium.

Grand Ole Opry

2-4 Govan Road, South Side, G51 (0141 429 5396).
Shields Road tube. **Open** *6.30pm-12.30am Fri-Sun.*
Admission £3-£4. **No credit cards. Map** p314 A4.
A Glaswegian institution nestling south of the river.
Country fans of all ages don their gingham and
denim and gather every weekend in this tacky hall,
decorated in confederate memorabilia, to imbibe
cheap liquor, line-dance to the live band, witness the
fake shoot-out and, in a surreal twist, play bingo.
Not for the faint-hearted.

King Tut's Wah Wah Hut

*272A St Vincent Street, City centre, G2 (0141 221
5279/www.kingtuts.co.uk). Central Station rail.*
Open noon-midnight Mon-Sat. **Tickets** £3.50-£10.
Credit MC, V. **Map** p314 C2.
With a capacity of only 350, this is a small venue,
but a hot-spot on the indie touring circuit.

The Old Fruitmarket

Albion Street, City Centre, G1 (0141 287 5511).
Buchanan St tube/Queen St rail. **Open** *Phoneline*
10am-8pm Mon-Sat. **Tickets** prices vary. **Credit**
AmEx, MC, V. **Map** p315 E3.
A much-loved Merchant City venue that hosts a
whole plethora of music events, from the Jazz
Festival to country festivals, as well as acts from the
roots, folk and world music of Celtic Connections
(hosted by the Royal Concert Hall, *see p247*).

Scottish Exhibition & Conference Centre and Clyde Auditorium

*Finniestoun Quay, G3 (0141 248 3000/box office
08700 404 000/www.secc.co.uk). Exhibition Centre
rail.* **Open** *Box office* 10am-6pm Mon-Sat. *Phoneline*
9am-9pm daily. **Tickets** prices vary. **Credit** MC, V.
Map off p314 A3.
A soulless aircraft hangar of an arena is the main
venue for the biggest touring bands and stars
who come to Scotland, while the 3,000-seater Clyde
Auditorium, or 'Armadillo', provides a more intimate
atmosphere sought by more mature performers.

Theatre

Citizens' Theatre

*119 Gorbals Street, South Side, G5 (0141 429 0022/
www.citz.co.uk). Bridge Street tube.* **Open** *Box office*
10am-6pm Mon-Sat. Tickets £10; £3 concessions;
prices vary for visiting productions. **Credit** MC, V.
Map p315 D4.
Risk-taking and lively productions of new theatre
are the hallmarks at the 'Citz': even the Edinburgh
critics like it. The 600-seat main theatre concentrates
on British and foreign work, while the Circle and
Stalls studios (120 and 60 seats respectively) cram
the audience right up next to the actors for
sometimes brilliant, sometimes awful, but always
interesting, new or obscure plays.

Trips Out of Town

Cottier Theatre

93 Hyndland Street, West End, G12 (0141 357 4000/www.thecottier.com). Kelvinhall tube. **Open** *Box office* before performances only; tickets available from other outlets. **Tickets** prices vary. **Credit** varies. **Map** p234.

An unusual venue, this boldly converted church shows a mix of cabaret, comedy and small-scale touring shows. It can be draughty, but the beer garden is a rarity in Glasgow.

King's Theatre

294 Bath Street, City centre, G2 (0141 248 5153/ box office 0141 287 5511/www.kings-glasgow.co.uk). Charing Cross rail. **Open** *Box office* 10am-6pm Mon-Sat. *Phoneline* 10am-8pm Mon-Sat. **Tickets** prices vary. **Credit** AmEx, MC, V. **Map** p314 C2.

The King's Theatre is Glasgow's home of musicals, where local amateur shows alternate with large-scale touring productions.

Pavilion Theatre

121 Renfield Street, City centre, G2 (0141 332 1846/www.paviliontheatre.co.uk). Cowcaddens tube. **Open** *Box office* 10am-8pm Mon-Sat. **Tickets** £6.50-£14. **Credit** AmEx, MC, V. **Map** p315 D2.

If you're looking for the Krankies, end-of-the-pier nostalgia and big-name traditional comics, then the Pavilion is the place to come. If you're looking for serious acting, try elsewhere.

Theatre Royal

282 Hope Street, City centre, G2 (0141 332 9000/ www.theatreroyalglasgow.com). Cowcaddens tube. **Open** *Box office* 10am-6pm Mon-Sat. **Tickets** £3.50-£55. **Credit** AmEx, MC, V. **Map** p315 D2.

Home of Scottish Opera and Scottish Ballet, this place is culture central, especially when larger touring productions by the likes of the Royal Shakespeare Company are in town.

Tramway

25 Albert Drive, Pollokshaws, G41 (0141 422 2023/ www.tramway.org). Pollokshaws East rail. **Open** *Box office* 2-8pm Tue-Sat. *Phoneline* 9am-8pm Tue-Sat. **Tickets** prices vary. **Credit** MC, V.

One of the sexiest spaces in the country if it's cutting-edge art, theatre and performance that you're looking for. With appearances from the likes of Robert Lepage and the Wooster Group, it's heavyweight as well as hip.

Tron Theatre

63 Trongate, City centre, G1 (0141 552 4267/ www.tron.co.uk). St Enoch tube. **Open** *Box office* 10am-6pm Mon-Sat. **Tickets** £3.50-£11; £5-£6 concessions. **Credit** MC, V. **Map** p315 E3.

This recently refurbished gem of a theatre puts on a good mix of smaller touring productions along with its own shows. Whether or not you're seeing a performance, both the restaurant and bar here are highly recommended.

Trips Out of Town

Nightlife

As the capital of cool, Glasgow has everything from designer-oriented superclubs to truly underground venues. And with the likes of **King Tut's** and the **Barrowland**, it knocks Edinburgh into a booming bass-bin when it comes to live gigs. At the time of writing, the much-loved 13th Note club (260 Clyde Street, 0141 243 2177) – where most of Glasgow's hip bands started out – had gone into liquidation; plans were afoot to try to save it.

Clubs

The Arches

253 Argyle Street, City centre, G1 (09010 220 300/ www.thearches.co.uk). St Enoch tube/Central Station rail. **Open** 10pm-3am Fri; 11pm-4am Sat. *Box office* 9am-8pm Mon-Sat; noon-6pm Sun. **Admission** varies. **Credit** MC, V. **Map** p315 D3.
Housed in renovated railway arches beneath Central Station, the state-of-the-art Arches is one of the city's top clubbing destinations, famous for hosting techno nights such as Colours, Mishmash and especially Pressure. The funk and rare groove of the Funk Room are utterly brilliant.

The Cathouse

15 Union Street, City centre, G1 (0141 248 6606/ www.cplweb.com). Central station rail. **Open** 10.30pm-3am Thur-Sun. **Admission** prices vary. **No credit cards. Map** p315 D3.
City Centre mecca for grunge merchants and serious rockers. There tends to be a fair amount of dyed black hair and matching eyeliner among the clientele, but even so, it doesn't take itself too seriously.

Glasgow School of Art

167 Renfrew Street, City centre, G1 (0141 353 4531). Cowcaddens tube/Charing Cross rail. **Open** *Club nights* 11pm-3am Thur-Sat. **Admission** prices vary. **No credit cards. Map** p314 C2.
The place to go for weird and wonderful aural adventures. It's the trendiest of Glasgow's student union venues, and there's a varied music policy, encompassing everything from the '60s rock and soul of Divine, to the electro of My Machines and Juice. Good value: two floors; one entry price.

MAS

29 Royal Exchange Square, City centre, G1 (0141 221 7080/www.masclubbing.com). Buchanan St tube/Queen St rail. **Open** 11pm-3am daily. **Admission** £1-£10; £2-£5 concessions. **Credit** V. **Map** p315 D3.
The Sunday club, Optimo, is renowned for being musically daring – it's mainly electro but rocky oldies ranging from the Stooges to the Specials to Mudhoney are often thrown in, and all are gratefully received by a dance-crazy and loyal crowd. Stylish with a New York vibe, the club has also attracted more left-of-centre DJs like Jarvis Cocker.

Soundhaus

47 Hydepark Street, Anderston, G3 (0141 221 4659). Bus 205. **Open** 11pm-5am Fri, Sat; also occasional band nights Thur. **Admission** £6-£8. **No credit cards. Map** p314 B3.
This is *the* hot house, funk, soul, disco club ticket of the moment, and one of the only clubs in the city that can honestly call itself underground.

Pre-club bars

Bar 10

10 Mitchell Lane, City centre, G1 (0141 572 1448/ www.bar10.co.uk). St Enoch tube then 5min walk. **Open** 10am-midnight daily. **Credit** MC, V. **Map** p315 D3.
The grandaddy of the Glasgow style bars, Bar 10 has ruled the roost since the heady days of the 1980s and has worn remarkably well. It's still one of the best-looking bars in the city, designed by Ben Kelly, at a time when he was fresh from his success at the now legendary Manchester Hacienda. Bar food is available.

Nice'n'Sleazy

421 Sauchiehall Street, City centre, G2 (0141 333 0900). Charing Cross rail. **Open** 11.30am-11.45pm Mon-Sat; 12.30-11.45pm Sun. **No credit cards. Map** p314 C2.
Sleazys is the perfect find for those looking for a young and funky hangout that is without the pretensions of the style-bar set. It's a great place to find out about the local band scene – many wannabe popstars either drink in the bar or play in the scarlet dive venue downstairs.

Where to stay

City centre

ArtHouse Hotel

129 Bath Street, G2 2SZ (0141 221 6789/fax 0141 221 6777/www.arthousehotel.com). Buchanan St tube/Central Station rail. **Rates** £100-£140 double. **Credit** AmEx, DC, MC, V. **Map** p314 C2.
Hip hotel/restaurant/bar where the beautiful people come to stay and play.

Brunswick Merchant City Hotel

106-108 Brunswick Street, G1 1TF (0141 552 0001/fax 0141 552 1551/www.scotland2000. com/brunswick). Buchanan St tube/Queen St rail. **Rates** £65-£95 double. **Credit** AmEx, DC, MC, V. **Map** p315 E3.
State-of-the-art landmark hotel in the Merchant City. Highly recommended.

Glasgow Hilton

1 William Street, G3 8HT (0141 204 5555/fax 0141 204 5004/www.hilton.com). Charing Cross tube/rail. **Rates** £170-£210 double. **Credit** AmEx, DC, MC, V. **Map** p314 C2.
Rates reflect the Hilton name.

Malmaison

*278 West George Street, G2 4LL (0141 572
1000/fax 0141 572 1002/ www.malmaison.com).
Buchanan St tube.* **Rates** £120-£155 double. **Credit**
AmEx, DC, MC, V. **Map** p314 C2.
A very stylish converted church with a high quo-
tient of celebrity guests – Keanu Reeves and Ewan
McGregor have checked in here in the past.

Merchant Lodge

*52 Virginia Street, G1 1TY (0141 552 2424/fax 0141
552 4747/www.hotelsglasgow.com). Buchanan St
tube/Queen St rail.* **Rates** £55 double. **Credit** MC, V.
Map p315 E3.
Although very basic, this is a little charmer of a
hotel, based in an 18th-century building in the
Merchant City area.

Quality Central Hotel

*99 Gordon Street, G1 3SF (0141 221 9680/fax 0141
226 3948/ www.choicehotelseurope.com). Central
Station rail.* **Rates** £105 double. **Credit** AmEx, DC,
MC, V. **Map** p315 D3.
A product of Glasgow's halcyon era as the second
city of the British Empire, this 200-plus-room hotel
rises proudly above Central Station and is popular
with overseas visitors.

Old Town & East End

The **Inn on the Green** is another worthwhile
option. *See p242.*

Cathedral House Hotel

*28-32 Cathedral Square, G4 0XA (0141 552 3519/
fax 0141 552 2444). High Street rail.* **Rates** £69
double. **Credit** AmEx, MC, V. **Map** p315 F2.
This chic and minimalist hotel began its life in 1877
as a halfway house for a local prison, before being
transformed into the diocese headquarters of the
Catholic Church. The split-level café bar downstairs
is a popular lunching spot for local professionals.

South Side

Sherbrooke Castle Hotel

*11 Sherbrooke Avenue, Pollokshields, G41 4PG
(0141 427 4227/fax 0141 427 5685/www.
sherbrooke.co.uk). Dumbreck rail/59 bus.* **Rates**
£85-£150 double. **Credit** AmEx, DC, MC, V.
One of the most impressive-looking hotels in the
city – from its hilltop position it's almost like a
Caledonian Addams Family mansion. One for the
more theatrically inclined.

West End

One Devonshire Gardens

*1 Devonshire Gardens, G12 0UX (0141 339 2001/
fax 0141 337 1663/www.one-devonshire-
gardens.com). Bus 11, 20, 51, 66.* **Rates**
£165-£450 double (weekend rates on request).
Credit AmEx, DC, MC, V.

Glasgow's most exclusive hotel, with a restaurant
to match (*see p242*). It's pure unadulterated luxury
and worth every penny.

Hostels, flats & seasonal lets

Euro Hostel Glasgow

*318 Clyde Street, G1 4NR (0141 222 2828/fax
0141 222 2829/www.euro-hostels.co.uk). St Enoch
tube/Central Station rail.* **Rates** £13.75-£25 double.
Credit MC, V. **Map** p315 D3.
Overlooking the River Clyde, this unremarkable city
centre tower block offers pretty unbeatable budget
accommodation. All rooms are en suite.

Glasgow Youth Hostel (SYHA)

*7-8 Park Terrace, West End, G3 6BY (0141 332
3004/fax 0141 332 5007/ www.syha.org.uk). Bus 11,
44, 59, then 5min walk.* **Rates** (per person per night)
£10.50-£12.50; £9-£10.50 concessions. **Credit** MC, V.
Map p234.
A Georgian townhouse that was formerly a hotel,
which accounts for the en-suite-as-standard facilities. It's now a popular hostel with five to eight beds
in most rooms. The standard SYHA rate includes
continental breakfast. Meals for groups can be
booked in advance. Note that non-SYHA members
pay an extra £1, and that rates increase by £1 during
July and August.

University of Glasgow

*3 The Square, University Avenue, West End,
G12 8QQ (0141 330 5385/fax 0141 334
5465/www.gla.ac.uk/vacationaccommodation).
Hillhead tube then 5min walk.* **Open** *Office*
9am-5pm Mon-Fri. **Rates** *Self catering* from £14.
B&B from £22.50; phone for details. **Credit** MC, V.
Map p234.
The University has a wide range of very affordable
student accommodation to let, generally available
during the holidays.

University of Strathclyde

*50 Richmond Street, G1 1XP (0141 553 4148/
fax 0141 553 4149/ www.rescat.strath.ac.uk).
Bus 6, 8, 41.* **Open** *Office* 9am-5pm Mon-Fri.
Rates vary; phone for details. **Credit** MC, V.
Map p315 E2.
Most accommodation is available to rent during student holidays. The jewel in the crown is Baird Hall,
a wonderful art deco masterpiece that was formerly the Beresford Hotel and dramatically dominates
the west end of Sauchiehall Street.

West End Apartments

*401 North Woodside Road, West End, G20
6NN (0141 342 4060/fax 0141 334 8159/
www.glasgowhotelsandapartments.co.uk).
Kelvinbridge tube.* **Open** *Office* 9am-5pm Mon-Fri.
Rates £280-£490 per wk; daily rates on request.
No credit cards. Map p234.
Four apartments housed in an elegant, sandstone
building in Kelvinbridge, ideally located just off the
Great Western Road.

Communications

Post offices

There are post offices throughout the city, the majority operating within usual shop hours. To get information about your nearest one, call the helpline on 0345 223 344 (9am-6pm Mon-Fri; 8.30am-4pm Sat). There's a late-opening post office outside the Safeway supermarket at Anniesland near the city centre (900 Crow Road, G13; 0141 954 8661; open 8am-10pm Mon-Sat, 9am-8pm Sun).

Telephones

The area telephone code for Glasgow and its environs is 0141.

Health

Glasgow Dental NHS Trust

378 Sauchiehall Street, G2 (0141 211 9600). Sauchiehall Street buses. **Open** *Emergency clinic* 9-11am, 2-3pm Mon-Fri. **Map** p314 C2.

Glasgow Royal Infirmary NHS Trust

84 Castle Street, G4 (0141 211 4000). High Street rail then 2, 2A, 37 bus. **Open** *Accident & emergency* 24hrs daily. **Map** p315 F2.

Western Infirmary NHS Trust

Dumbarton Road, G11 (0141 211 2000). Kelvinhall tube. **Open** *Accident & emergency* 24hrs daily. **Map** p234.

Getting there

From the airport

Glasgow Airport (0141 887 1111) is 8 miles (14km) south-west of the city, at Junction 28 of the M8. Buses leave the airport for the city every 15mins during the day, and about every 30mins after 6pm and on Sun. The 25min journey costs £3. A taxi will take about 20min and cost about £16.

By car

Despite its all-ensnaring motorway system, Glasgow is actually easy to access by car. The M8 from Edinburgh delivers you into the heart of the city. Take Exit 15 for the East End and Old Town, 16 for Garnethill, 18 for the West End, 19 for the City centre and 20 for the South Side.

By bus or coach

Long-distance buses arrive at and depart from Buchanan Street Bus Station (0141 333 3780) at Killermont Street. There are buses to and from Edinburgh every half hr and from London every hr.

By train

Glasgow has two mainline train stations. Queen Street Station (West George Street) serves Edinburgh (trains every 15mins) and the north of Scotland. Central Station (Gordon Street) serves the West Coast

and south to England. The stations are centrally located and within walking distance of each other. For all rail enquiries call the national number, 08457 484950.

Getting around

Central Glasgow is easy to negotiate on foot, but you'll need to use public transport or hire a car if you're going further afield. Nearly all the listings in this chapter refer only to the underground or train network for reasons of space. However, the frequent bus service that runs throughout the city is well signposted at the regular bus stops. Glasgow is also served by a fleet of capacious black taxis. They're cheap, but inconveniently disappear just as the clubs turn out at 3am. As for trains, besides the inter-city services, there is a good network of low-level trains serving Glasgow's suburbs, which is run by Scotrail. The underground system, affectionately known as the Clockwork Orange, is a single, circular line that loops between the centre and the West End. To enjoy another view of Glasgow, or to travel to Braehead shopping centre or the Scottish Maritime Museum (*see p233*), hop on the waterbus at Central Station bridge.

Clyde Waterbus

07711 250 969/www.clydewaterbusservices.co.uk. **Ferry services** 10am-6.15pm Mon-Fri; 10.30-5.15pm Sat; 11am-5.45pm Sun. **Tickets** £2; £1.50 concessions. **No credit cards.**

Europcar/BCR

Terminal Building, Glasgow Airport, Inchinnan Road, Paisley, PA3 (0141 887 0414/www. europcar.co.uk). **Open** 7am-10.30pm daily. **Credit** AmEx, DC, MC, V.
Rentals (subject to change) start from £57 per day or £189 per week.

Traveline Scotland

0870 608 2608. **Open** 8am-8pm daily.
Travel information for buses and trains.

Tourist information

Greater Glasgow & Clyde Valley Tourist Information Centre

11 George Square, City centre, G2 (0141 204 4400/ fax 0141 221 3524/www.seeglasgow.com). Buchanan St tube. **Open** *Oct-Mar* 9am-6pm Mon-Sat. *Apr, May* 9am-6pm Mon-Sat; 10am-6pm Sun. *June, Sept* 9am-7pm Mon-Sat; 10am-6pm Sun. *July, Aug* 9am-8pm Mon-Sat; 10am-6pm Sun. **Credit** MC, V. **Map** p315 E2.
The Tourist Information Centre will take credit card bookings for accommodation throughout the city (£2, plus 10% deposit). It also answers general enquiries about sightseeing and local events, and supplies details of special rates in its brochure.

Around Edinburgh

Abbeys and castles for the history buffs, sand and sea for the beach bums, and acres of beautiful countryside for everyone else.

East Lothian

The weather in East Lothian tends to be brighter and drier than Edinburgh. Maybe the flat landscape bordered by the Firth of Forth and the Lammermuir Hills just makes the sky seem wider and bluer but it certainly gets more sunshine.

It is easy to get out of the capital into East Lothian, as the A1, the main road to England, sweeps through it. However, the well signposted coastal trail beginning in Musselburgh is more rewarding. Trains stop at Musselburgh, Prestonpans, Longniddry, Drem and North Berwick and the bus network can take you almost anywhere.

Traprain Law, an ancient volcanic plug, dominates the flat lowlands of East Lothian. It was once home to the Pictish tribe of Votadini; the name Lothian is derived from King Loth, a sixth-century Pictish ruler. Malcolm II took the territory for Scotland in 1018.

It was no easy claim. In the centuries that followed, English armies and land-greedy nobles from the south, made numerous forays into the area, leaving a trail of destruction. In 1216 King John of England burned the principal towns of Dunbar and Haddington, while castles such as Dirleton, Hailes and Tantallon became ever-sturdier defences.

Nevertheless, warring aside, the area enjoyed prosperity thanks to its rich and fertile soil, which led it to be dubbed 'the bread basket of Lothian'. The royal burgh of Haddington flourished and the villages of Aberlady, Athelstaneford and East Linton grew up. Today these villages, along with the coastal towns of North Berwick and Dunbar, continue to thrive and hold on to their good looks.

The coast itself, with its sandy beaches of Gullane and Yellowcraig and views across to Fife, has some good walks; the Aberlady Wildife Sanctuary (*see below*) and the John Muir Country Park (*see p254*) have signposted trails.

North of the A1

Just off the A1, and almost seamlessly attached to Edinburgh, is **Musselburgh**, known since the early 14th century as the 'honest toun', a sobriquet gained when townsfolk refused to

claim the reward for recovering the body of the Earl of Moray. Its handsome Tolbooth dates from 1591. Don't miss **Inveresk Lodge**, a National Trust property located behind the main town; the lodge is private but the gardens are sublime, sloping down to the River Esk's peaceful riverside walks.

After the Musselburgh Race Course, the coast road turns off along the B1348 and passes the **Prestongrange Mining Museum**, which is a minimal but nonetheless interesting reminder of the local industry. The unglamorous villages of Cockenzie and Prestonpans follow on in quick succession. Just to the south is where Bonny Prince Charlie routed the English at the Battle of Prestonpans in 1745.

Beyond the village of Longniddry, the full picturesque roll of the East Lothian coast takes off. A mile before Aberlady is **Gosford House**. Although only the central core remains of the original building designed by Robert Adam in the 18th century, its three-storey, Italian-style 19th-century marble hall is a fabulous statement of opulence. Aberlady itself has a neat line-up of almshouses and its fine 15th-century church houses a notable 18th-century memorial to one Lady Elibank by the sculptor Canova. A mile outside the village, on the tiny back road to Drem, is the **Myreton Motor Museum**, a privately owned hotchpotch of lovingly restored vehicles, bicycles and motoring memorabilia.

The **Aberlady Wildlife Sanctuary** is reached by crossing the footbridge from the car park just east of the village of Aberlady. Its sandy mudflats and dunes are a good spot to see wading birds and are popular with birdwatchers and other naturalists. The clean beach at Gullane is a summer-time favourite with families, while golf fanatics will recognise the Muirfield course, where the Scottish Open is sometimes played.

Five miles on, standing picturesquely at the heart of the pretty village of Dirleton, is **Dirleton Castle**. The original fortress dates from the 13th century but it was substantially rebuilt and modified in the 14th century and again in the 16th. Its grounds still contain an old bowling green as well as an early 20th-century Arts and Crafts garden and a restored Victorian garden.

Trips Out of Town

Standing proud over the landscape south of North Berwick is the **Hopetoun Monument**, a slender tower built in 1824 on the Garleton Hills in memory of the fourth Earl of Hopetoun. Take a torch if you intend climbing to the top of the tower.

The village of **Athelstaneford** is nearby on the B1343. Legend has it that in 832 the leader of the Pictish army, King Angus, saw a mass of white clouds form a diagonal cross in the sky here, prior to his battle with a mighty Saxon force headed by Athelstan. Angus believed the cross to be a sign from St Andrew and vowed that he would declare Andrew patron saint of Scotland if his army was victorious. The battle was a success for Angus who duly made St Andrew patron saint; St Andrew's cross, or the saltire, became the Scottish flag and is now the oldest flag in Europe and the Commonwealth. In Athelstaneford's churchyard there is a 1965 memorial to the creation of the flag and a **Flag Heritage Centre** (01368 863239; open Apr-Oct 10am-6pm daily), housed in a 16th-century dovecote. Athelstaneford itself was built in the 18th century by one Sir David Kinloch as a model village for his estate workers.

Moving east again is the **National Museum of Flight** at East Fortune Airfield, a popular destination for family outings. Exhibits, the oldest of which is an 1896 glider, are housed in a converted hangar. A short distance further along the B1377, the attractive village of East Linton was the birthplace of the 19th-century engineer John Rennie, who designed London's Waterloo and Southwark bridges.

North Berwick is a quaintly traditional seaside town only 40 minutes away from Edinburgh by train. The minuscule station is situated on top of a hill with a ten-minute walk down into the centre. Two clean, sandy beaches with splendid rock pools flank the old harbour area, where you'll find the fascinating, high-tech **Seabird Centre**; control your own live video camera to see nesting birds a mile away. Just beyond the Seabird Centre are **Platcock Rocks**, a promontory poking out into the Forth; follow the path between the rocks for a really satisfying scramble with the waves crashing on either side. In the summer boats leave North Berwick harbour (01620 892838, book in advance) for trips to the gannet-smothered **Bass Rock**, a vast offshore lump of volcanic basalt three and a half miles out to sea that has been a prison, fortress and monastic retreat.

Towering one mile inland from the town is another steep volcanic plug called **North Berwick Law**, which is well worth scaling for the fabulous views and in order to examine the arch on the top made out of a whale's jawbone. Walk back down through the delightful wooded

glen or through the **Lodge** (not a building but a park) with an aviary, trampolines and crazy golf in summer. The small but informative **North Berwick Museum** is slightly hidden in School Road near the tourist office.

The coast between North Berwick and the attractive seaside nature reserve of **Tyninghamme Links** – stop here for a gentle walk out to St Baldred's Cradle – is dominated by **Tantallon Castle**, a formidable, mainly 14th-century, cliff-edge fortification. The castle's rose-coloured stone ramparts command splendid views of the Bass Rock. Half a mile south of Tantallon Castle on the A198 is **Seacliff** a private beach that you can access for £1. It is a truly beautiful and secluded sandy cove, sheltered from the wind; you may even spot seals near the rock pools.

The next coastal town is the robust-looking old fishing town of **Dunbar**, reputedly the sunniest place in Scotland. The town is notable for its wide high street, 17th-century stone **Town House** and its ruined castle, which stands just above the harbour. Mary, Queen of Scots stayed at the castle on a number of occasions. In 1650 the Battle of Dunbar, which saw Oliver Cromwell defeat the Covenanters, was fought to the south-east of the town.

The famous conservationist John Muir is the town's most noted son. He was born in 1838, and his family emigrated to America when he was three. Muir went on to become a naturalist and the founding father of the US national parks. At the time of writing his birthplace at 126 High Street was in the process of being renovated and made into a museum. The **John Muir Country Park** is a vast stretch of land containing salt marshes, lagoons and a long sandy beach that lies north-west of Dunbar just outside Belhaven. It is home to a wide variety of birds and wildlife. Belhaven itself was once the port for Dunbar, but the independent **Belhaven Brewery**, founded in 1719 by local monks, sets it apart. While distilleries have their 'angel's share' – spirits that evaporate during maturation – Belhaven boasts the ghosts of drunk monks. The **Volunteer Arms** in the village is the best place to sample the brewery's exceptionally smooth 80/-.

Belhaven Brewery

Brewery Lane, Dunbar (01368 862734). **Open** pre-booked guided tours only. **Admission** £3; no under-14s allowed. **No credit cards**.

Dirleton Castle & Gardens

Dirleton (01620 850330/www.historic-scotland. gov.uk). **Open** *Apr-Sept* 9.30am-6.30pm daily. *Oct-Mar* 9.30am-4.30pm Mon-Sat; 2-4.30pm Sun. **Admission** £2.80; £1-£2 concessions. **Credit** AmEx, MC, V.

The whale-bone arch at **North Berwick Law**. *See p254.*

Gosford House
*Longniddry (estate 01875 870201/house 01875
870200).* **Open** *July-early Aug* 2-5pm Wed-Sun.
Closed mid Aug-June (open from late June in 2002).
Admission £4; £1 concessions. **No credit cards.**

Inveresk Lodge
*24 Inveresk Village, Musselburgh, East Lothian,
EH21 (01721 722 502/www.nts.org.uk).* Bus 40.
Open *Apr-Oct* 10am-6pm Mon-Fri; noon-6pm Sat,
Sun. *Nov-Mar* 10am-4.30pm or dusk daily.
Admission £4; £1 concessions; free under-16s.
Credit MC, V.

John Muir House
*126 High Street, Dunbar (01368 862585/www.
eastlothian.gov.uk/museums/www.jmbt.org.uk).*
Currently closed for refurbishment; due to reopen
spring 2003.

Myreton Motor Museum
Aberlady (01875 870288). **Open** *Oct-Easter* 1-3pm
Sun or by appointment. *Easter-Sept* 11am-4pm
daily. **Admission** £4; £1 concessions.
No credit cards.

National Museum of Flight
*East Fortune Airfield, East Fortune (01620
880308/www.nms.ac.uk/flight).* **Open** 10.30am-5pm
daily. **Admission** £3; £1.50 concessions; free under-
16s. **Credit** MC, V.

North Berwick Museum
*School Road (01620 895457/www.eastlothian.
gov.uk/museums).* **Open** *Apr-Oct* 11am-5pm daily.
Closed Nov-Mar. **Admission** free.

Prestongrange Industrial
Heritage Museum
*Morison's Haven, Prestonpans, EH32; on B1348
coast road between Musselburgh & Prestonpans*
(653 2904/www.eastlothian.gov.uk/museums).
Bus 26. **Open** *Apr-Oct* 11am-4pm daily. Closed Nov-
Mar. **Admission** free.

Scottish Sea Bird Centre
*The Harbour, North Berwick, EH39 (01620 890202/
www.seabird.org).* **Open** *Summer* 10am-6pm daily.
Winter 10am-4pm Mon-Fri; 10am-5.30pm Sat, Sun.
Admission £4.95; £3.50 concessions; family £13.50.
Credit AmEx, MC, V.

Tantallon Castle
*off A198, 2 miles east of North Berwick (01620
892727/www.historic-scotland.gov.uk).* **Open** *Oct-
Mar* 9.30am-4.30pm Mon-Wed, Sat; 9.30am-12.30pm
Thur; 2-4,30pm Sun. *Apr-Sept* 9.30am-6.30pm daily.
Admission £2.80; £1-£2 concessions.

South of the A1

Although ravaged by the warring English
on a number of occasions in the Middle Ages,
the royal burgh of **Haddington** is today an
elegantly well-heeled market town, lying
13 miles east of Edinburgh on the A1. The
birthplace of Alexander II in 1198 and of John
Knox, architect of the Scottish Reformation,
in 1515, the town is spaciously ranged around
a main high street and boasts 284 listed
buildings. The 14th-century **St Mary's
Collegiate Church** is particularly impressive
and houses the tomb of Jane Welsh, the wife
of the 19th-century writer Thomas Carlyle
and an intellectual in her own right. The **Jane
Welsh Carlyle Museum** is in her childhood
home on Lodge Street.

To the east of Haddington is **Hailes Castle**.
Dating from the 13th century, it started life as
a manor house, expanding its guest facilities to

incorporate two vaulted pit prisons. A mile south of the town is **Lennoxlove House**. Its original name was Lethington Tower but was changed in 1702 to 'Lennox love to Blantyre' for Frances, Duchess of Lennox, a famous beauty who never even lived there.

Still further south of Haddington is the toy-town-like model village of **Gifford**, built by the Marquis of Tweeddale in the 18th century for his estate workers. John Witherspoon, the first moderator of the Presbyterian Church of America and the only clergyman to sign the American Declaration of Independence, was born here. An interesting eaterie is the **Goblin Ha'** (*see p257*), which is signposted by a yogic levitating goblin. It derives its name from an underground chamber at the now-ruined **Yester Castle**, which was romantically described by Sir Walter Scott in his novel *Marmion*.

The **Lammermuir Hills** are easily accessible from nearby Longyester, from where there is a track up to the Hopes Reservoir. Scoffed at by those who would never deign to climb anything less than a Munro (mountains over 914 metres/3,000 feet), the Lammermuirs,

with their good covering of heather and sheep, are nonetheless handsome. Sir Walter Scott, ever a man with an eye for a good bit of scenery, even found them inspirational. He penned the sorrowful tale *The Bride of Lammermuir*, which was later turned into an opera, *Lucia de Lammermuir*, by the Italian composer Donizetti.

East along the A6903 heading back towards Edinburgh is the **Glenkinchie Distillery**, the most southerly whisky distillery in Scotland and the source of one of United Distillers' six 'classic' malts.

Glenkinchie Distillery Visitors Centre

Glenkinchie, Pencaitland, EH34 (01875 342004/ www.malts.com). **Open** *Jan-Mar* noon-3pm Mon-Fri. *Apr, May, Nov, Dec* 10am-4pm Mon-Fri. *June-Oct* 10am-4pm Mon-Sat; noon-4pm Sun. **Admission** £4; free under-18s. **Credit** AmEx, MC, V.

Hailes Castle

1.5 miles south-west of East Linton (Historic Scotland 668 8800/www.historic-scotland.gov.uk). **Open** *Apr-Sept* 9.30am-6pm daily. **Admission** free.

The mysteries of Rosslyn Chapel

One of Scotland's most enigmatic buildings lies just a few miles south of Edinburgh, in Roslin. Rosslyn Chapel, founded in 1446 by Sir William St Clair, a prince of Orkney, is a fantastic blend of pagan, Celtic, Christian and Masonic symbolism. Stone carvings are everywhere: hardly a surface has been spared from the mason's hand. It is said that there are more representations of the Green Man (the mythical, pre-Christian figure thought to represent fertility and renewal) in the chapel than in any other building in Britain. Over 100 have been counted.

One of the chapel's intricately carved pillars has eight dragons at its base; from their mouths emerges a vine that twists itself around the whole pillar. Its design may have been inspired by Scandinavian mythology – it seems likely that it's a representation of the Norse Tree of Knowledge, which held the heavens above the earth, together with the 'dragons of time' who bit at the base of the tree. But its medieval creator probably justified it in Christian terms as representing the Tree of Life.

Legend has it that mason's apprentice who made this work of imagination and skill was struck on the head and killed by his master in a fit of jealous rage. For this reason, the pillar

is known as the Apprentice's Pillar. Elsewhere in the chapel is a stone carving of the poor apprentice's head, complete with a scar on his right temple where the senior mason struck him. Next to him is the head of the apprentice's grieving mother, while another carving is said to be of the offending master mason himself.

Myths and mysteries abound in Rosslyn Chapel: why are depictions of New World plants, such as Indian corn, to be found in carvings made nearly 50 years before Columbus 'discovered' America? (One theory runs that Prince Henry of Orkney, the grandfather of the chapel's founder, actually reached America 100 years before Columbus.) Is the chapel a copy of Solomon's Temple in Jerusalem and therefore not really a Christian site at all? And what lies beneath its floors – the Scrolls of the original Temple, the Ark of the Covenant, the true Stone of Destiny, 20 barons or Knights Templar or even the head of John the Baptist?

Rosslyn Chapel

Chapel Loan, Roslin, EH25 (440 2159/ www.rosslynchapel.org.uk). Bus 29, 29A. **Open** 10am-5pm daily. **Admission** £4; £2.20 concessions. **Credit** MC, V.

Jane Welsh Carlyle Museum

Lodge Street, Haddington (01620 823738). Bus 15.
Open *Apr-Sept* 2-5pm Wed-Sat. Closed Oct-Mar.
Admission £1.50; £1 concessions. **No credit cards.**

Lennoxlove House

*Lennoxlove, Haddington (01620 823720/www.
lennoxlove.org).* **Open** *Easter-Oct* 2-4.30pm Wed,
Thur, Sun; occasional Sat (phone to check). Closed
Nov-Easter. **Admission** £4.25; £2.50 concessions.
No credit cards.

Where to eat

Luca's in Musselburgh, north of the A1
(34 High Street, 665 2237) is home to the
best ice-cream on the east coast.

In North Berwick, the sea air is likely to
make you ravenous for chips and the best sit-
down places are the **North Berwick Fry**,
next to the Tourist Office in Quality Street,
or the splendid ice-cream-cum-chip shop,
George's Café in the High Street. Finer fare
is available at **Miller's Bistro** (Douglas Court,
17 Market Place, 01620 890437, main courses
£6.25-£13.95), or for an old-fashioned

Edwardian atmosphere, try the grand **Marine
Hotel** (Cromwell Road, EH39, 01620 892406, set
meal £22.50 three courses) with putting green,
snooker and open air swimming pool.

For more hearty fare head south to the
Goblin Ha' Hotel in Gifford (Main Street,
01620 810244, main courses £7.25-£10.25);
the inn dates back to the 18th century. The
Waterside Bistro (Waterside, Nungate, 01620
825876, main courses £15) is a popular spot for
Sunday lunch on the banks of the River Tyne.

Where to stay

In North Berwick, the **Tantallon Inn**
(4 Marine Parade, 01620 892238, closed
2wks Oct) has double rooms for £28-£32 per
person. Or try **Browns Hotel** in Haddington
(1 West Road, 01620 822254, rates £100 double).

South of the A1, the **Eaglescairnie
Mains** (01620 810491) in Gifford is a lovely
old farmhouse bed and breakfast; rates from
£25 to £30 per person.

Getting there

By bicycle

Cycling is a viable mode of travel in this area, with
signposted routes and trails (mostly along disused
railway lines) leaving Edinburgh. Cycles can also be
put on trains (they may require pre-booking) so that
you can save your legs until you get there.

By car

Take the A1 out of Edinburgh towards Haddington.
The coastal trail is signposted at regular intervals.

By train

A local train branch line runs regular services
from Edinburgh's **Haymarket station**, through
Waverley station to Musselburgh, Prestonpans,
Longniddry, Drem and North Berwick. Some
mainline London trains stop at Dunbar.

By bus

East Lothian is served by buses from **St Andrew
Square** in Edinburgh. During refurbishment of
the bus station (until 2003), buses leave from
Waterloo Place. For further information consult
the website www.lothianbuses.co.uk, and contact
First Bus (663 9233/www.firstgroup.com/first
edinburgh). Lothian Bus services 15, 26 and 44
go to Musselburgh; bus 40 goes to Inveresk
via Musselburgh; bus 15 serves Haddington.

Tourist information

Dunbar

143 High Street (01368 863353). **Open** *Oct-May*
9am-5pm Mon-Fri. *June* 9am-5pm Mon-Sat; 11am-
4pm Sun. *July* 9am-7pm Mon-Sat; 11am-6pm Sun.
Aug 9am-8pm Mon-Sat; 11am-6pm Sun. *Sept* 9am-
5pm Mon-Sat; 11am 4pm Sun.

Trips Out of Town

Musselburgh

Old Craighall, Granada Service Station, off A1 (653 6172). **Open** *Apr, May* 9am-6pm Mon-Fri. *June, Sept* 9am-6pm Mon-Sat; 10am-3pm Sun. *July* 9am-7pm Mon-Sat; 11am-6pm Sun. *Aug* 9am-8pm Mon-Sat; 11am-6pm Sun; *Oct-Mar* 9am-5pm Mon-Fri.

North Berwick

1 Quality Street (01620 892197). **Open** *Oct-Mar* 9am-5pm Mon-Sat. *Apr, May* 9am-6pm Mon-Sat. *June, Sept* 9am-6pm Mon-Sat; 11am-4pm Sun. *July* 9am-7pm Mon-Sat; 11am-6pm Sun. *Aug* 9am-8pm Mon-Sat; 11am-6pm Sun.

Midlothian

Wildlife and rural solitude are surprisingly easy to find in the vicinity of Edinburgh. The graciously curvaceous Pentland Hills cover 22,000 acres just south of city on the A702, and are particularly convenient to reach from the city. Lord Cockburn, the 19th-century conservationist, dubbed the hills 'paradise', but Oliver Cromwell was less impressed by them. In 1650 he complained about the lack of trees: he wished to hang a sergeant for stealing a cloak but could not find the necessary branch.

Today the hills form the **Pentland Hills Regional Park**. The park encompasses a golf course, the longest dry ski slope in Europe and a country park at the hills' eastern end. From here you can travel further along the A702 to reach the Iron-Age fort of **Castle Law Hill** and even more unadulterated ruralness.

It is possible to do some serious hill-walking in the Pentlands (always observe suitable safety precautions, *see p230*), but there's also the **Glencorse Reservoir** for those who don't fancy putting in much effort. A five-minute stroll up the gentle incline from the reservoir car park plunges you straight into classic Scottish countryside: rolling hills, a pretty river, plenty of sheep and the reservoir surrounded by pines. Ready and waiting for you on the return trip is the utterly inviting **Flotterstone Inn** (*see p259*), which has low beams, roaring fires and very hearty grub – perfect if you've been hill walking for oooh, 20 whole minutes.

Just beyond is **Rullion Green**, where in November 1666, 900 Covenanters were defeated by the Royalist army under General Tam Dalyell. **Carlops**, further along on the A702, with its handsome line-up of sturdy stone cottages, was once renowned as a meeting place for witches. It also briefly marked the border between Scotland and England, after the defeat of the Scots at the battle of Neville's Cross in 1346.

Rosslyn Chapel, an intensely and ornately carved demonstration of medieval religious syncretism (*see p256* **The mysteries of Rosslyn Chapel**), is six miles (ten kilometres) south of Edinburgh at Roslin. Next to the chapel is a former inn, which in its time offered refreshments to the likes of Samuel Johnson, James Boswell and William Wordsworth. The ruins of Rosslyn Castle lie in the nearby woodlands of **Roslin Glen Country Park**, accessed from the B7003 Roslin–Rosewell road. The country park hugs the steep-sided valley of the river Esk, where there are many cliffs and caves, one of which is said to be the site of Robert the Bruce's famous encounter with the spider. And, adding further to the mysteries of the area, Dolly, the first cloned sheep, was born at the nearby Roslin Institute.

Though architecturally unremarkable, **Dalkeith** has a fine **Country Park**, which is practically in the centre of the town and surrounds the 18th-century Dalkeith House, now owned by the University of Wisconsin. The park has lovely wooded walks, a good café in the stables, a spectacular adventure playground, some intriguing riverside tunnels and a bridge spanning the River Esk which was designed by Robert Adam in 1792. Although visual reminders of the area's industrial past are few, the **Scottish Mining Museum** is an attempt to keep that heritage in mind, with its purpose-built, three-storey visitor centre, featuring interactive exhibitions and a hands-on operations centre. Older ruins have proved more permanent; **Crichton Castle** near Pathhead, built in 1591 for the Earl of Bothwell, is quite spectacular with impressive surviving features.

Crichton Castle

South-west of Pathhead, off A68 (01875 320017/ www.historic-scotland.gov.uk). Bus 3, 29. **Open** *Apr-Sept* 9.30am-6.30pm daily. *Oct, Nov* phone for details. Closed Dec-Mar. **Admission** £2.75; 75p-£1.40 concessions. **No credit cards**.

Dalkieth Country Park

Dalkeith High Street (654 1666). Bus 3, 29. **Open** 10am-5.30pm daily. **Admission** £2; free under-5s, over-65s; £7 family.

Scottish Mining Museum

Lady Victoria Colliery, Newtongrange, EH22; 9 miles south of Edinburgh on the A7 (663 7519/ www.scottishminingmuseum.com). Bus 29, 29A. **Open** 10am-5pm daily. **Admission** £4; £2.20 concessions. **Credit** MC, V.

Where to eat & stay

The **Allan Ramsey Hotel** in Carlops (01968 660258) is an old inn with accommodation (rates £50 double), bar meals and a restaurant (main

The imposing, 14th-century ruins of **Tantallon Castle**. *See p254.*

courses £12). Just a few minutes' walk from Rosslyn Chapel is the **Original Hotel** in Roslin (440 2384, rates £69 double). It also has a restaurant (main courses £10-£15). **Dalkeith's County Hotel** (152 High Street, 663 3495, rates £80 double) is a luxury town-house hotel. If you're in the Pentland Hills, don't miss the food at the **Flotterstone Inn** (01968 673717, main courses £10-£15) on the A702 at Milton Bridge.

Getting there

By car
Take the A701 to Roslin or the A702 to the Pentland Hills. Dalkeith is on the A7.

By bus
Buses leave from **St Andrew Square**, Edinburgh for the Pentland Hills, Roslin and Dalkeith. For Glencourse and Flotterstone Inn ask for buses to Milton Bridge. During refurbishment of the bus station (until 2003), buses leave from **Waterloo Place**.

Tourist information

Also check **www.midlothian-online.com**.

Scottish Mining Museum
Lady Victoria Colliery, Newtongrange, EH22; 9 miles south of Edinburgh on the A7 (663 4262). Bus 29, 29A. **Open** *Easter-Sept* 10am-5pm daily. Closed Oct Easter.

West of Edinburgh

To the west of Edinburgh, the old slag heaps or 'bings' of Livingston and Bathgate are a reminder of the area's coal mining and heavy industrial past. Closer to Edinburgh, just south of the airport, the village of Ratho is home to the **Edinburgh Canal Centre**. The centre recollects the Union Canal's construction by, among many others, the notorious murderers Burke and Hare (*see p18* **Body matters**), and the waterway's heyday in the 19th century.

The best parts of West Lothian, however, are closer to the Forth. Along the A90, and just off the B924 towards South Queensferry, is the village of Dalmeny, where you'll find **St Cuthbert's**, one of the finest Norman churches in Scotland. The carvings on the south door and a gruesome line-up of gargoyles are particularly eye-catching. Overlooking the Forth is **Dalmeny House**, a Gothic revival mansion designed by William Wilkins in 1814 and home of the Earls of Rosebery. It boasts the obligatory grand interior and, somewhat incongruously, an extensive collection of Napoleon memorabilia. **South Queensferry** lies just beyond the house. Named after Queen Margaret, wife of Malcolm III, it is an excellent place from which to view the magnificent Forth Rail and Forth Road bridges. Built between 1883 and 1890 and just over one mile long, the **Forth Rail Bridge** is made from 50,000 tons

Trips Out of Town

of red steel and is still considered one of the world's great engineering achievements. The small **South Queensferry Museum** offers an interesting insight into the history of the bridges and of the village, including the annual custom of the 'Burry Man', who every July parades through the village for nine hours wearing a costume made of burrs.

The *Maid of the Forth* ferry sails from South Queensferry to **Inchcolm Abbey**. Founded in 1123, it comprises a fine clutch of monastic buildings and is spectacularly located on Inchcolm Island in the Firth of Forth. Allow a few hours for the round trip, and spend your time picnicking and seal-spotting.

West of South Queensferry is the self-consciously grandiose **Hopetoun House**. It was designed by William Bruce in 1699 for Charles Hope, the first Earl of Hopetoun, and was enlarged by William Adam in 1721. The house stands elegantly swathed in parkland overlooking the Firth of Forth.

Further west still is **Blackness Castle**, used by Zefferelli in his film version of *Hamlet*. Its stark walls have crumbled somewhat since they were built in the 1440s but the view across the Forth from the castle promontory is still spectacular. Inland, the **House of the Binns** is the ancient seat of the Dalyells and dates from the 17th century.

Four miles south, just off the M9, is the attractive royal burgh of **Linlithgow**, famed for its royal palace where Mary Queen of Scots was born in 1542. The beautiful, ruined **Linlithgow Palace** overlooks the Loch and the Peel – a grassy lochside parkland. A walk round the bird-filled loch takes about an hour and gives you a real sense of the countryside. You can hire a rowing boat from the **Forth Federation of Anglers** (01506 611753) to fish for trout.

Behind the station is the **Canal Basin**, where you'll find the **Linlithgow Canal Centre**, which includes a museum and tearoom; the towpath is perfect for easygoing walks by the water and there are weekend cruises from Easter to October.

South of Linlithgow, the history just keeps on rolling. **Cairnpapple Hill**, near Torphichen, is a burial site dating from 3000 BC, with some of Scotland's most important prehistoric remains. The hill also gives good views over the surrounding countryside. The **Torphichen Preceptory** is a 13th-century tower with transepts built by the Knights Hospitaller of the Order of St John of Jerusalem.

Just north of Linlithgow lies the once-thriving town of Bo'ness, which today looks more than a little frayed at the edges. It does, however, boast an attraction for steam fanatics in the **Bo'ness**

& Kinneil Railway, along which steam trains run the seven-mile round trip to the **Birkhill Claymines**, where there is a guided tour.

Falkirk, west of Bo'ness, has a massive new landmark in the form of the **Falkirk Wheel**, a magnificent bird-like lift which scoops boats from the Forth & Clyde Canal and pops them into the Union Canal to reconnect the waterways between Glasgow and Edinburgh. Visitors without their own boats can buy tickets for a special amphibious vehicle ride which projects a light show on the tunnel roof. The mechanical marvel can be observed from a boardwalk and from the visitor centre with its café and play area.

Inland from Grangemouth, about 25 miles from Edinburgh, is the seemingly unremarkable village of **Bonnybridge**. Remains of the Antonine Wall – the Romans' most northerly defence, intended to keep wild Highlanders out of the Empire – are visible at a number of spots here, though a generous imagination is needed to conjure up the scene. You'll also require a fair degree of credulity to come to terms with Bonnybridge's more recent claim to fame as a mecca for Unidentified Flying Objects.

In 1992 a local businessman sighted a UFO in the area; maverick councillor Billy Buchanan took up the cause and since then has siezed this opportunity to promote Bonnybridge as a centre for extra-terrestrial activity – or a 'window area', as some UFO experts call it. According to Buchanan, about 6,000 people have seen unexplained lights in the skies around Bonnybridge, including a Toblerone-shaped object reported by Andy Swan, a cable-layer for Scottish Power, in 1994.

Buchanan believes that the nation is not taking these sightings seriously. In the name of spreading the word, he has faxed Tony Blair directly and also released a single, 'The Lights of Bonnybridge', which he sang outside No.10 Downing Street. In 2001, he instigated plans to twin Bonnybridge with Roswell in New Mexico, the US city famed for the 'crash-landing' of a flying saucer in 1947. Plans for a sci-fi theme park in the area have also been suggested.

Blackness Castle

Blackness; 4 miles north of Linlithgow on the A904 (01506 834807/www.historic-scotland.gov.uk). **Open** *Apr-Sept* 9.30am-6.30pm daily (last admission 5.30pm). *Oct-Mar* 9.30am-4.30pm Mon-Wed, Sat; 9.30am-12.30pm Thur; 2-4.30pm Sun. **Admission** £2.20; 75p-£1.60 concessions. **No credit cards**.

Bo'ness & Kinneil Railway

Bo'ness (01506 822298 www.srps.org.uk/railway). **Open** *Apr, May, Sept, Oct* Sat, Sun. *July, Aug* Tue-Sun. Phone for train times and events at other times of year. **Tickets** £4.50; £2-£3 concessions; £11 family.

Cairnpapple Hill

*Nr Torphichen, off A89 (01506 634622/www.
historic-scotland.gov.uk).* **Open** *Apr-Sept* 9.30am-
6.30pm daily. *Oct, Nov* phone for details. Closed
Dec-Mar. **Admission** £1.80; 50p-£1.30 concessions.
Credit MC, V.

Dalmeny House

*South Queensferry, EH30 (331 1888/www.dalmeny.
co.uk).* **Open** *July, Aug* 2-5.30pm Mon, Tue, Sun.
Closed Sept-June. **Admission** £4; £2-£3.50
concessions. **No credit cards.**

Edinburgh Canal Centre

27 Baird Road, Ratho (333 1320). **Cruises** *June-
Aug* 2.30pm daily. *May, Sept, Oct* 2.30pm Sat, Sun.
Closed Nov-Apr. **Admission** £6; £4 concessions.
Credit AmEx, DC, MC, V.

Falkirk Wheel

*Lime Road, Tamfourhill; 1.5 miles from centre of
Falkirk (booking line 0870 050 0208/www.falkirk-
wheel.com).* **Tickets** £6.50; £3.25-£3.50 concessions;
£16 family. **Credit** AmEx, MC, V.
There is a park and ride system in operation for this
attraction with buses to collect visitors from Falkirk
Grahamston and Camelon stations.

Hopetoun House

*South Queensferry, EH30 (331 2451/www.hopetoun
house.com).* **Open** *Apr-Oct* 10am-5.30pm daily.
Closed Nov-Mar. **Admission** £5.30; £2.70-£4.70
concessions. **Credit** DC, MC, V.

House of the Binns

*Off A904, 4 miles east of Linlithgow (01506
834255/www.nts.org.uk).* **Open** *House* May-Sept
1-5pm Mon-Thur, Sat, Sun. Closed Oct-Apr. *Park*
Apr-Oct 10am-7pm daily. Nov-Mar 10am-4pm daily.
Admission *House* £5; £3.75 concessions; £13.50
family. *Park* free. **No credit cards.**

Inchcolm Abbey

*Inchcolm Island, Firth of Forth (Historic Scotland
668 8800/www.historic-scotland.gov.uk).* **Open**
Apr-Sept 9.30am-6.30pm Mon-Sat. Closed Oct-Mar.
Admission £2.80; £1-£2 concessions.
Credit AmEx, MC, V.
The island can be reached by the *Maid of Forth* ferry
from South Queensferry *(see below).*

Linlithgow Palace

*Kirkgate, Linlithgow (01506 842896/www.historic-
scotland.gov.uk).* **Open** *Apr-Sept* 9.30am-6.30pm
daily. *Oct-Mar* 9.30am-4.30pm Mon-Sat; 2-4.30pm
Sun. **Admission** £2.80; £1-£2 concessions.
Credit AmEx, MC, V.

Linlithgow Canal Centre

*Canal Basin, Manse Road, Linlithgow, EH49
(01506 671215/www.lucs.org.uk).* **Open**
Museum & cruises Easter-June, Sept, Oct 2-5pm
Sat, Sun; July, Aug 2-5pm daily. Closed Nov-Easter.
Admission *Museum* free. *St Magdalene cruise*
£6; £3 concessions; £15 family. *Victoria cruise*
£2.50; £1.50 concessions. **Credit** MC, V.

Maid of Forth

*Ferry leaves from: Hawes Pier, South Queensferry
(331 4857/www.maidoftheforth.co.uk).* **Open** *Apr-
Oct* phone for details. Closed Nov-Mar. **Admission**
Ferry & abbey £9.95; £4-£8.50 concessions;
£24 family. **Credit** AmEx, MC, V.

South Queensferry Museum

Burgh Chambers, 53 High Street (331 5545).
Open 10am-5pm Mon-Sat; noon-5pm Sun
(last admission 4.30pm). **Admission** free.

Torphichen Preceptory

*Torphichen (Historic Scotland 668 8800/
www.historic.scotland.gov.uk).* **Open** *Apr-Sept*
10am-5pm Sat; 2-5pm Sun. Closed Oct-Mar.
Admission £1.50; 75p-£1 concessions.

Where to eat

In South Queensferry, the **Hawes Inn**
(6 Newhalls Road, 331 1990) was immortalised
by Robert Louis Stevenson in *Kidnapped*, and
serves food every day (main courses £5.95-
£12.50). The **Bridge Inn** (333 1320) in Ratho,
has two canal boat dining rooms (for parties)
and a restaurant on land (main courses £6.95-
£17). The **Hopetoun House** teashop near
South Queensferry (331 4305, closed Nov-Feb)
is very well thought of by cake aficionados.
    There are plenty of pubs and restaurants
with decent food along the High Street in
Linlithgow, including **Livingston's** at No.52
(01506 846565, closed Mon, Sun, 1st 2wks Jan,
1st wk Jun, set meals £25-£30), which is very
popular for deliciously cooked Scottish beef
and fish dishes. A good quality alternative
is the **Star & Garter Hotel** at No.1 High
Street, Linlithgow (01506 846362, main
courses £7-£15).

Where to stay

Houston House in Uphall (01506 853831)
has double rooms from around £110. A cheaper
option is the **Thornton** in Edinburgh Road,
Linlithgow (01506 844693), a spacious
Victorian house with B&B rates of around
£25 per person.

Getting there

By car

Take the A902 west of Edinburgh, then the B974
for South Queensferry. Take the M9 for Linlithgow
and Falkirk.

By bus

A regular bus service departs from **St Andrew
Square**. During refurbishment of the bus station
(May 2000-2003), bus services leave from **South
St Andrew Square**.

Trips Out of Town

Crichton Castle watches over the rolling landscape of Midlothian. *See p258.*

By train

Trains regularly depart from **Waverley** and **Haymarket** stations in Edinburgh for South Queensferry, Bo'ness, Linlithgow and Falkirk. Linlithgow is on the main Glasgow–Edinburgh line, with 4 trains every hr from Edinburgh.

Tourist information

Bo'ness

Seaview car park (01506 826626). **Open** *May-Aug* 10am-5pm daily. *Sept* noon-5pm daily. Closed Oct-Apr.

Falkirk

2-4 Glebe Street (01324 620244). **Open** *Apr, May* 10am-5pm daily. *June-Aug* 9.30am-6pm Mon-Sat; noon-4pm Sun. *Sept* 9.30am-6pm Mon-Sat. *Oct-Mar* 10am-4pm Mon-Sat.

Linlithgow

Burgh Hall, The Cross (01506 844600). **Open** *Easter-Sept* 10am-5pm daily. Closed Oct-Easter.

Fife

Looking North from any high point in Edinburgh you will see Fife on the far shore of the Firth of Forth. A Pictish stronghold in the eighth and ninth centuries, it is now a last pocket of socialism proudly returning Scotland's only Communist local councillor.

It has more than its fair share of defunct coal mines and redundant miners, however it has also got some fabulous coastline and a couple of historically interesting towns.

Dunfermline was once a seat of Scottish royals, a stop-off for pilgrims travelling north to St Andrews, and a pilgrim centre in its own right. Today the town can be somewhat intimidating, fortified as it is by roundabouts and ring roads. Yet at its core is **Dunfermline Abbey**, which has one of the finest Norman naves in Scotland. It was founded in 1070 by Queen Margaret, wife of Malcolm III, who had Benedictine monks sent up from Canterbury to establish the monastic community here. Margaret's son, the pious David I, did much to extend the Abbey. The nave was begun in 1128; its zig-zag patterned piers are reminiscent of Durham Cathedral. Robert the Bruce was buried before the high altar at Dunfermline in 1329, save for his heart, which was cut out and, legend has it, buried at Melrose Abbey (*see p266*). At the eastern end of the Abbey is the ruined Chapel of St Margaret, where Queen Margaret is buried. She was canonised after her death in 1093.

Neighbouring the Abbey are the stately remains of Dunfermline Palace. Originally a guesthouse serving the monastery, it was rebuilt in the 16th century by James VI and is where Charles I was born. The nearby **Abbot**

House Heritage Centre, an interesting 15th-century building in itself, provides a good introduction to Dunfermline's history. The industrialist and benefactor Andrew Carnegie was born in Dunfermline in 1835. He made his fortune in the US and has given his name to numerous libraries and concert halls around the world. He gifted the gardens of **Pittencrieff Glen**, just next to Dunfermline Palace, to the town in 1903.

Lying west of Dunfermline is a preserved jewel of a town. **Culross** may be small but it is full of intriguing lanes and beautifully restored houses. Once an important port, the whole place is today in the guardianship of the National Trust Scotland. Located on the hill behind the town is the ruined abbey and palace of Culross.

North-east of Dunfermline, nestling beside the Lomond Hills, along with cobbled streets and weavers' cottages, is the royal burgh of Falkland. It is home to **Falkland Palace**, which was the favoured home of James V while his daughter, Mary, Queen of Scots, hunted the surrounding country. In the grounds is one of the few remaining 'real' tennis courts, dating from 1539. Further east again, the **Hill of Tarvit Mansionhouse** near Cupar has a good collection of French furniture in a house rebuilt in 1901 by the architect Sir Robert Lorimer.

On the coast at North Queensferry is **Deep Sea World**, where a huge aquarium stretches over your head full of rays and sharks. Heading north, the coast really comes into its own around Largo Bay. This stretch of coastline up to St Andrews is known as **East Neuk**, but also goes by the name 'fringe of gold' because of its wonderful sandy beaches and the rich fishing grounds offshore. Its fishing villages were once some of the wealthiest in Scotland and are lovely, with tiny colourful houses huddled round each harbour and plenty of boats still working from them. **Elie**, whose extensive golden sands are known locally as Sahara, has a water sports outfit at No.2 High Street, that offers to drag you round the harbour on inflatables and also rents boats and pedaloes. Call 01333 330962 during the day or 01333 330942 in the evening for details.

Pittenweem has a slight bohemian air and hosts an arts festival every August. The village's name means 'place of the cave', referring to **St Fillan's Cave** in Cove Wynd, which was used as a chapel by the seventh-century missionary. The saint reputedly had miraculous powers; his arm was said to emit a luminous glow enabling him to write his sermons in the gloom of the cave.

Anstruther, the next village along the coast, is home to the **Scottish Fisheries Museum**. The museum, which overlooks the harbour,

Trips Out of Town

Trips and tours

Sightseeing tours

Capital Eyes
339 4863.
Capital will take up to seven passengers for tours within Edinburgh or outside the city as far as the Trossachs or the Borders. The Walter Scott's Borders tour costs £130.

Celtic Connections
225 3330/www.thecelticconnection.co.uk.
Celtic Connections tours combine Scotland and Ireland. Prices start at £85 for a three-day one-way trip beginning in Edinburgh and ending in Dublin.

Celtic Trails
477 5419/www.celtictrails.co.uk.
Ancient sites near Edinburgh are this company's speciality. Tours revolve around early Christian sites, many of which were already in use in pre-Christian times. The Rosslyn Chapel Trail lasts half a day and costs £20.

Rabbie's Trail Burners
226 3133/www.rabbies.com.
A good company to use if you want to tour in a group but also have a decent night's sleep. A trip from Edinburgh to Skye for three days in a minibus costs £90, but there's a choice of accommodation – from budget hostels to swanky hotels – that you pay for separately.

Backpacking tours

Lively tours are guaranteed by the various backpacking outfits. Travelling in minibuses, using hostel accommodation and sometimes even providing meals, they promise to get you into the heart of Scotland very cheaply – as long as you don't mind mucking in.

Haggis Adventures
557 9393/www.haggisadventures.com
Haggis will take you from Edinburgh to destinations in the Highlands and to the Isle of Skye. The three-day Skye High tour

costs £79 and takes in Glencoe, Skye and Loch Ness. The Compass Buster lasts six days, costs from £139, and goes as far north as Carbisdale Castle in Sutherland.

MacBacpackers
558 9900/www.macbackpackers.com.
A variety of Highland tours. The seven-day Grand Tour, leaving from Edinburgh and taking in Inverness, Fort William, Oban and the Isle of Skye, costs £145.

Wild in Scotland
478 6500/www.wild-in-scotland.com.
Wild in Scotland offers a tour of Skye and the Hebrides for six days for around £200.

Hill-walking

For other options consult the website **www.walkingwild.com**, which lists dozens of hill-walking holiday companies.

Footpath Holidays
01985 840049/www.footpath-holidays.com.
Guided walking tours of the Tweed Valley and Southern Uplands, Glencoe and West Highlands and the Isle of Skye are arranged by Footpath Holidays. A bonus is that walkers stay in good (generally four-star) hotels.

Make Tracks Walking Holidays
229 6844/www.maketracks.net.
Make Tracks organises guided walks along the Southern Upland Way, the West Highland Way, St Cuthbert's Way, the Great Glen Way, the Speyside Way, the Trossachs, Tweedside Walk, or Highland Lochs. The company will transport your luggage for you.

Walkabout Scotland
661 7168/www.walkaboutscotland.com.
Walkabout arranges guided hillwalking tours from Edinburgh to the Highlands. There are day tours, weekend breaks and longer walking holidays – and you don't have to be an experienced hill walker to join in.

tells the story of the development of the fishing industry in the village and the lives of those who worked in it. **Crail**, the oldest fishing village in East Neuk, is characterised by a host of red-tiled houses with crow-stepped gable ends. Crail's churchyard is also worth pausing at, to look at its carved memorials.

The university town of **St Andrews**, looking out over the North Sea, is a proud sort of place. According to legend, the bones of the apostle Andrew were brought here by St Rule some time after the fourth century. A cathedral was built in the apostle's honour and just when St Andrew became Scotland's patron saint, the town became its ecclesiastical capital. Now it trades more on the fact that Prince William is studying at the university here. The university, founded in 1412, is the oldest in Scotland. St Andrews is also home to the **Royal & Ancient Golf Club**. Founded in 1754, it's the big chief of the golfing world and determines the rules of the game.

St Andrews' sandy beaches are a fine place for a walk, as is **Craigtoun Country Park** just two miles from the centre. It's a civilised well-laid out park with a unique Dutch Village in the centre of its boating lake.

Abbot House Heritage Centre
Maygate, Dunfermline (01383 733266). **Open** 10am-5pm daily. **Admission** £3; £2 concessions; free children. **Credit** MC, V.

Craigtoun Country Park
Mount Melville, nr St Andrews (01334 473666). **Open** *Apr-Sept* 10.45am-5.30pm daily. Closed Oct-Mar. **Admission** £3; £1-£2.50 concessions. **No credit cards**.

Deep Sea World
Battery Quarry, Fife (01383 411411/www. deepseaworld.com). **Open** 10am-6pm daily. **Admission** £6.95; £4.95-£5.50 concessions. **Credit** MC, V.

Dunfermline Abbey
St Margaret Street, Dunfermline (01383 739026/ www.historic-scotland.gov.uk). **Open** *Apr-Sept* 9.30am-6.30pm daily. *Oct-Mar* 9.30am-4.30pm Mon-Wed; Sat; 9.30am-12.30pm Thur; 2-4.30pm Sun. **Admission** £2.20; 75p-£1.60 concessions. **Credit** MC, V.

Falkland Palace
High Street, Falkland (01337 857397/www. nts.org.uk). **Open** *Mar-Oct* 10am-5.30pm Mon-Sat (last entry 5pm); 1-5pm Sun (last entry 4pm). Closed Nov-Feb. **Admission** *Palace & gardens* £7; £5.25 concessions. *Gardens only* £3; £2.25 concessions. **Credit** MC, V.

Hill of Tarvit Mansionhouse
Cupar (01334 653127/www.nts.org.uk). **Open** *House* Apr-Oct noon-5pm daily (last entry 4.45pm). Closed Nov-Mar. *Gardens & grounds* 9.30am-sunset daily. **Admission** *House, gardens & grounds* £5; £3.75 concessions; £13.50 family. *Gardens & grounds* £2. **No credit cards**.

St Fillan's Cave
Cove Wynd, Pittenweem (01333 311495). Collect key from Gingerbread House, 9 High Street. **Open** 10am-5pm daily. **Admission** £1.

Scottish Fisheries Museum
St Ayles, Harbourhead, Anstruther (01333 310628/ www.scottish-fisheries-museum.org). **Open** *Apr-Sept* 10am-5.30pm Mon-Sat; 11am-5pm Sun. *Oct-Mar* 10am-4.30pm Mon-Sat; noon-4.30pm Sun. **Admission** £3.50; £2.50 concessions; free children. **Credit** MC, V.

Where to eat

For hot and hearty lunches, **Brambles** at No.5 College Street, St Andrews, 01334 475380, main courses £6.25-£11.95) is unbeatable. Seafood lovers will enjoy **The Cellar** in Anstruther (24 East Green, 01333 310378, closed Mon, Tue in winter, set meals £28-£35 three courses) or **Anstruther Fish Bar** (42/44 Shore Street), officially the best fish and chip shop in Scotland according to the Sea Fish Industry Authority. Massive queues testify to its supremacy.

If you're visiting Dunfermline Abbey, pop next door to the **Abbot House Heritage Centre** (01383 733266), a small café offering tasty snacks, and while you're in the area, make the detour to **Scotland's Larder** (Upper Largo, 01333 360414, www.scotland-larder.co.uk, set meal £24 three courses), a special place committed to serving the finest Scottish food. It's Michelin Guide accredited, and yet it inhabits an old farm building and is not in the least stuffy or grand.

Where to stay

In Dunfermline, the **Dawaar House Hotel** (126 Grieve Street, 01383 721886) has double rooms for £70-£80. The **Inn at Lathones** (Lathones, by Largoward, 01334 840494, rates £55-£75 per person) is a 400-year-old former coaching inn; its restaurant uses local produce where possible (main courses £8.50-£35). In Falkland, the recommended **Covenanter Hotel** (The Square, 01337 857224, rates £52 double) is another comfortable former coaching inn.

Getting there

By car
Take the A90 out of Edinburgh then the M90. Turn onto the A823 for Dunfermline; or the A921 for the coastal route. For St Andrews take the A91 off the M90.

By bus
Buses depart from Edinburgh's **St Andrew Square** for Dunfermline and St Andrews. Many buses in the area are run by Stagecoach Fife (01383 621249/www.stagecoachbus.com/fife).

By train
Trains depart Edinburgh's **Waverley station** for Dunfermline, Kirkcaldy and Leuchars.

Tourist information

A good website for tourist information on the area is **www.standrews.co.uk**. There are also tourist information offices at the **Scottish Fisheries Museum** in Anstruther (*see above*) and at the Museum & Heritage Centre in **Crail** (Marketgait, 01333 450869); both are closed in winter.

Dunfermline
1 High Street (01383 720999). **Open** *Mid Sept-June* 9.30am-5pm Mon-Sat. *July-mid Sept* 9.30am-5.30pm Mon-Sat; 11am-4pm Sun.

Kirkcaldy
19 Whytecauseway (01592 267775). **Open** *Apr-June, Sept-Dec* 10am-5pm Mon-Sat. *July, Aug* 9.30am-5pm Mon-Sat. *Jan-Mar* 10am-5pm Mon-Fri.

St Andrews
70 Market Street (01334 472021). **Open** *Apr-June* 9.30am-5.30pm Mon-Sat; 11am-4pm Sun. *July, Aug* 9.30am-7pm Mon-Sat; 10.30am-5pm Sun. *Sept* 9.30am-6pm Mon-Sat; 11am-4pm Sun. *Oct-Mar* 9.30am-5pm Mon-Fri.

The Borders

Pastoral landscapes, a handsome coastline, picturesque towns and a host of abbeys make the Borders a fascinating stretch of Scotland. It might be picture-postcard pretty on the surface, yet this area also has a long history of warfare with its English neighbours. The region was under the rule of Northumbria until Malcolm II took the land for Scotland in the early 11th century. David I founded the powerful abbeys of Kelso, Melrose, Jedburgh and Dryburgh in the 12th century, which were frequently raided by the English along with many of the border towns. In addition, the activities of the Border 'Reivers', family-based groups of cattle thieves and land-grabbers, ensured that life in these parts was never lacking in action.

Peebles is the closest Borders town to Edinburgh and nestles, somewhat smugly, beside the River Tweed. Obligatory woollen shops aside, the town offers up some surprising sights for the visitor. In the **Tweeddale Museum & Art Gallery** on the High Street there are impressive plaster copies of the Parthenon Frieze (just don't call them the Elgin Marbles), together with a copy of a frieze executed by the celebrated 19th-century Danish sculptor, Bertel Thorvaldsen for the Palazzo Quirinale in Rome. If getting plastered in the colloquial sense of the word is more appealing, the **Bridge Inn** is a characterful hostelry with some interesting old photos of Peebles.

For a rejuvenating walk take the path from Hay Lodge car park in Peebles to the 14th-century **Neidpath Castle**. From here follow the River Tweed on a three or a seven-and-a-half-mile round trip through woods and over bridges and viaducts. Further west is the marvellous **Dawyck Botanic Garden**, an outpost of Edinburgh's Royal Botanic Garden.

Pretty as a picture: the **Borders**.

East of Peebles just outside Innerleithen is the truly handsome, 1,000-year-old, **Traquair House**. Acclaimed as the oldest inhabited house in Scotland and now owned by Scotland's only female laird, the house has had numerous functions over the centuries, serving as a court for William the Lion, as a hunting lodge for Scottish royalty, as a refuge for Catholic priests and as a stronghold of Jacobite sentiment. The ever-bed-hopping Mary, Queen of Scots not only stayed here in 1566 but possibly embroidered one of the house's bedspreads. Two centuries later, in 1745, the clearly optimistic fifth Earl of Traquair wished his guest, one Prince Charles Edward Stuart, a safe journey into battle and rashly promised that he would not reopen Traquair's great gates until the Stuarts had been restored to the throne. The gates have remained closed ever since, forcing today's visitors to use the 'temporary' drive. The grounds of Traquair House include an impressive maze, a croquet lawn, a number of craft workshops, housed in the old stables, and a brewery. A fair is held here in August.

Close to Traquair House is **Melrose Abbey**, the reputed resting place of Robert the Bruce's heart. Founded in 1136 by Cistercian monks from Rievaulx, Yorkshire, the Abbey was all but destroyed by the English in 1385 but remains one of the most picturesque in the Borders.

It is not surprising that the history-packed Borders should appeal to Sir Walter Scott, the tireless promoter of Scotland's past. **Abbotsford**, just outside Melrose, was his home and is an appropriately romantic Gothic-cum-Scottish baronial pile, overlooking the Tweed. It is stuffed with relics including Rob Roy's gun, Montrose's sword and Prince Charlie's *quaich* (communal whisky cup). Always one for a good view, Scott frequently praised the nearby **Eildon Hills**, the legendary burial ground of King Arthur. You can see what he saw by visiting 'Scott's View', a few miles east of Melrose. Nearby, another hero, William Wallace, is celebrated by the gargantuan **Wallace Statue**.

Selkirk is a pretty town just south of Galashiels on the A7. Scott was Sheriff of Selkirkshire from 1799 to 1832. Selkirk is also famous for its *bannock*, a rich currant loaf. There are several bakeries in town, but **Camerons** on the High Street bakes the best. At the **Fleece** pub, the Rolling Stones were purportedly refused service because their hair was too long.

Kelso, with its capacious town square and fine 1816 Court House, has a slightly Gallic air. Standing at the point where the Teviot meets the Tweed, it is indisputably attractive. **Kelso Abbey** was founded in 1128 by David I for a community of French monks from Tiron, near Chartres. Once perhaps the finest of the Border abbeys, it was virtually destroyed in 1545. Yet what remains – principally the west façade and transept – offers a staggering show of Norman and Gothic architecture. Elsewhere in town, look out for the horseshoe embedded in Roxburgh Street (outside Safeway). According to local legend, it came off Bonny Prince Charlie's horse, when he visited the town in 1745.

Pomp and many a good circumstance are brought to mind at **Floors Castle**, overlooking the Tweed. Designed by William Adam in 1721, it was flamboyantly remodelled by William Playfair in the mid-19th century. It is now Scotland's largest inhabited castle, home to the Duke of Roxburgh, and houses a wealth of treasures. The high stone wall that surrounds the grounds was built by French prisoners of war from the Battle of Waterloo.

Mellerstain House near Gordon was begun in 1725 by William Adam and completed by his son Robert. Unusually, William Adam also landscaped the grounds – note the careful alignment of the lake and the folly on the hill. The house's Italian-style terraced gardens were added in 1909.

Back to the coast and you'll come across the tiny fishing village of **St Abb's**, which has a full quota of picture-postcard prettiness. North

of the port, the cliffs rise up to St Abb's Head, where a well-trodden pathway leads to the cliff edge. The whole of the headland is a nature reserve and, during spring, home to guillemots, razorbills and puffins. A short coastal walk to the south brings you to **Coldingham Bay**, a terrific sweep of sand with fine rock pools, a bracing breeze and some of the cleanest bathing water on this coast.

Abbotsford
Melrose (01896 752043). **Open** *Mar-Oct* 9.30am-5pm Mon-Sat; 2-5pm Sun. Closed Nov-Feb. **Admission** £4; £2-3.20 concessions. **No credit cards**.

Daywyck Botanic Garden
Stobo; on B712 (01721 760254). **Open** *Mid Feb-mid Nov* 9.30am-6pm daily. *Early Feb, late Nov* 10am-4pm daily. Closed Dec, Jan. **Admission** £3; £1-£2.50 concessions; £7 family. **Credit** MC, V.

Floors Castle
Roxburgh Estates, Kelso (01573 223333). **Open** *Easter-Oct* 10am-4.30pm daily. Closed Nov-Easter. **Admission** £5.50; £3.25-£4.75 concessions. **No credit cards**.

National Wallace Monument. See p269.

Stirling Castle defended the most important strategic position in Scotland. *See p269.*

Mellerstain House

Gordon (01573 410225). **Open** *Easter, May-Sept* 12.30-5pm Mon-Fri, Sun. *Oct* 12.30-5pm Sat, Sun. Closed Nov-Apr. **Admission** *House & gardens* £5.50; £3-£5 concessions. *Gardens only* £3. **Credit** MC, V.

Melrose Abbey

Abbey Street, Melrose (01896 822562/www.historic-scotland.gov.uk). **Open** *Apr-Sept* 9.30am-6.30pm daily. *Oct-Mar* 9.30am-4.30pm Mon-Sat; 2-4.30pm Sun (last entry 30mins before closing). **Admission** £3.30; £1.20-2.50 concessions. **Credit** AmEx, MC, V.

Neidpath Castle

1 mile west of Peebles on A7229 (01721 720333). **Open** *Mid June-early Sept* 10.30am-4.30pm Mon-Sat; noon-4.30pm Sun (also open Easter & May holidays). Closed mid Sept-mid June. **Admission** £3; £1-£2.50 concessions; family £7. **No credit cards**.

Traquair House

Innerleithen (01896 830323/www.traquair.co.uk). **Open** *Easter-May, Sept-Oct* 12.30-5.30pm daily. *June-Aug* 10.30am-5.30pm daily. Closed Nov-Easter. **Admission** £5.50; £2.60-£4 concessions. **Credit** DC, MC, V.

Tweeddale Museum & Gallery

Chambers Institute, High Street, Peebles (01721 724820). **Open** *Nov-Mar* 10am-noon, 2-5pm Mon-Fri. *Apr-Oct* 10am-noon, 2-5pm Mon-Fri; 10am-1pm, 2-4pm Sat. **Admission** free. **No credit cards**.

Where to eat

A picturesque choice is the **Tibbie Shiels Inn** (St Mary's Loch, 01750 42231, closed dinner Sun, closed Mon-Wed in winter, main courses £3.50-£10), an old haunt for writers that overlooks the water. **Kailzie Gardens**, near Peebles (01721 720007, open daily) has a tea shop that serves good home baking. Also try the **Ship Hotel** (Harbour Road, Eyemouth, 01890 750224, main courses £5-£6).

Where to stay

In Peebles, the **Peebles Hydro Hotel** (01721 720602, rates £64.50-£73 per person) has great views of the town and good facilities: swimming pool, whirlpool, tennis courts, and a health and beauty salon. For B&B in an 18th-century farmhouse, contact Mrs Debby Playfair at **Morebattle Tofts**, Kelso (01573 440364, closed Nov-Mar, rates £50 double). The **George & Abbotsford Hotel** (High Street, Melrose, 01896 822308, closed Christmas and New Year) has doubles for around £69, while the four-star **Philipburn House** in Selkirk (01750 720747, closed 1st 2wks Jan) has double rooms for £110.

If you're looking for something cheaper, try the **Castle Rock Guest House**, Murrayfield, St Abbs (01890 771715, rates £27 double) or **Garth House** (7 Market Street, Coldstream, 01890 882477, rates £17.50 single).

In Duns, **Barniken House Hotel** (18 Murray Street, 01361 882466, rates £60 double) has a large garden with a nine-hole putting green. And for a stunning location, you can't beat **Coldingham Youth Hostel** (Coldingham Sands, Coldingham, 01890 771298, rates £9 adult, £7.75 child, membership fee £6), situated right on the beach.

Trips Out of Town

Getting there

By car
Take the A701, followed by the A703 to Peebles.

By train
It is almost impossible to reach the Borders by train. The nearest train station is in Berwick-upon-Tweed, from where there are connecting buses to Galashiels and other destinations.

By bus
Buses depart from **St Andrew Square**, Edinburgh. During refurbishment of the bus station (until 2003), buses leave from **South St Andrew Square**.

Tourist information

Also, try online at **www.scotborders.co.uk**.

Jedburgh
Murray's Green (01835 863435). **Open** *Oct-Mar* 9.30am-4.30pm Mon-Sat. *Apr, May* 9.30am-5pm Mon-Sat; noon-4pm Sun. *June, Sept* 9.30am-5.30pm Mon-Sat; noon-4pm Sun. *July, Aug* 9am-6pm Mon-Sat; noon-4pm Sun.

Kelso
Town House, The Square (01573 223464). **Open** *Nov-Mar* 11am-3pm Mon-Sat. *Apr, May* 10am-5pm Mon-Sat; 10am-1pm Sun. *June, Sept* 9.30am-5pm Mon-Sat; 10am-2pm Sun. *July, Aug* 9.30am-5.30pm Mon-Sat; 10am-2pm Sun. *Oct* 10am-4pm Mon-Sat; 10am-1pm Sun.

Melrose
Melrose Abbey House, Abbey Street (01896 822555). **Open** *Apr, May* 10am-5pm Mon-Sat; 10am-1pm Sun. *June* 9.30am-5pm Mon-Sat; 10am-2pm Sun. *July, Aug* 9.30am-5.30pm Mon-Sat; 10am-2pm Sun. *Sept* 9.30am-5pm Mon-Sat; 10am-2pm Sun. *Oct* 10am-4pm Mon-Sat; 10am-1pm Sun. *Nov-Mar* 11am-3pm Mon-Sat.

Peebles
23 High Street (01721 720138). **Open** *Oct-Dec* 9.30am-5pm Mon-Sat; phone for Sun opening times. *Jan-Mar* 9.30am-4pm Mon-Sat. *Apr, May* 9.30am-5pm Mon-Sat; 10am-2pm Sun. *June, Sept* 9.30am-5.30pm Mon-Sat; 10am-4pm Sun. *July, Aug* 9.30am-6pm Mon-Sat; 10am-4pm Sun.

Stirling

According to an ancient saying 'To hold Stirling is to hold Scotland'. For centuries Stirling's position just above the River Forth at the meeting of Scotland's Highlands and Lowlands made it a key strategic stronghold. Two of the most significant battles against English rule took place nearby: in 1297 William Wallace defeated the English at the Battle of Stirling Bridge and in 1314 Robert the Bruce conquered Edward II's forces at Bannockburn. (There's a **heritage centre** on the battle site.)

Castle Rock was probably first occupied in the 600s, yet today's **Stirling Castle** dates mainly from the 15th and 16th centuries and combines a robust fortress with a Royal Palace. Below it on Castle Wynd is **Argyll's Lodgings**, one of Scotland's most stunning examples of a 17th-century grand townhouse. There is a palpably French château feel to the place, particularly in the turreted courtyard. Over the way is **Mar's Wark**, the impressive stone remains of what was once a grand Renaissance-style house built by the Earl of Mar. Next door is the **Church of the Holy Rude**, which has one of the few surviving medieval timber roofs in Scotland.

Beyond Stirling Old Bridge, and about a mile north-east of the town, an oddly shaped tower dominates the skyline. It is the **National Wallace Monument** commemorating the hero of the Battle of Stirling Bridge, and the subject of the film *Braveheart*. Built in 1860, it houses Sir William Wallace memorabilia including his double-edged sword.

Argyll's Lodging
Castle Wynd (01786 450000/www.historic-scotland.gov.uk). **Open** *Summer* 9.30am-6pm daily (last admission 5.30pm). *Winter* 9.30am-5pm daily (last admission 4.30pm). **Admission** *Argyll's Lodging & Stirling Castle* £7; £1.50-£5 concessions. *Argyll's Lodging only* £3; £1.20-£2.25 concessions. **Credit** AmEx, DC, MC, V.

Bannockburn Heritage Centre
Glasgow Road, Stirling; off the A91, 2 miles south of Stirling (01786 812664/www.nts.org.uk). **Open** *Heritage centre* Mar, Nov-late Dec 10.30am-4pm daily. Apr-Oct 10am-6pm daily. Closed late Dec-Feb. **Admission** £3.50; £2.60 concessions; free under-18s; £9.50 family. **Credit** MC, V.

National Wallace Monument
Abbey Craig, off A91, 1 mile north-east of Stirling (01786 472140). **Open** *Apr, May, Oct* 10am-5pm daily. *June* 10am-6pm daily. *July, Aug* 9.30am-6.30pm daily. *Sept* 9.30am-5pm daily. *Nov-Feb* 10.30am-4pm daily. **Admission** £3.95; £2.75-£3 concessions; £10.75 family. **Credit** AmEx, MC, V.

Stirling Castle
Castle Esplanade, Stirling (01786 450000/www.historic-scotland.co.uk). **Open** (last entry 45mins before closing) *Summer* 9.30am-6pm daily. *Winter* 9.30am-5pm daily. **Admission** £7; £2-£5 concessions. **Credit** AmEx, MC, V.

Where to eat

Two recommendations in the centre of Stirling are the very reasonably priced **Barnton Bar & Bistro** (3 Barnton Street, 01786 461698, main courses £3.20-£4.95) and **Hermann's** at the Tolbooth near Stirling castle (Broad Street,

Trips Out of Town

Going further

If you have an opportunity to travel further afield and discover more of Scotland's staggering scenery, grab it. Here are some pointers to help plan trips to three of the country's most popular destinations. For details of organised tours to these and other areas, *see p264* **Trips and tours**.

The Trossachs

The Highlands converge with the Lowlands in the Trossachs, an area of lochs, rivers and hills. It takes about an hour and a half to reach the region from Edinburgh and you'll need a car to explore it thoroughly. **Loch Lomond**, to the west of the Trossachs, is Scotland's largest and most famous loch. The Trossachs' website (www.trossachs.org.uk) has lots of general information, while the Loch Lomond website (www.loch-lomond.net) has a comprehensive list of accommodation, boat hire firms and maps. There are tourist information centres in **Callander** (Rob Roy & Trossachs Visitor Centre, Ancaster Square; 01877 330342) and **Aberfoyle** (Trossachs Discovery Centre, Main Street, Aberfoyle; 01877 382352).

The Highlands & Isle of Skye

Fort William is a good point from which to explore the Highlands, with many of the major mountains and glens within striking distance: Glen Coe, Ben Nevis, Glen Nevis, the West Highland Way and Loch Ness. The Road to the Isles (more prosaically known as the

A830) takes you from Fort William on a dramatic 46-mile journey through lochs, forests and mountains to Mallaig where you can board a boat for **Skye**. A number of websites can help you plan your trip: www-road-to-the-isles.org.uk; www.ecossenet.com and www.visitscotland.com are all worth a look. There are tourist information centres at **Fort William** (Highlands of Scotland Tourist Board, Cameron Square; 01397 703781) and on **Skye** (2 Lochside, Dunvegan; 01470 521581). For more information about Fort William, see www.visit-fortwilliam.co.uk.

Isle of Mull

Mull is the easiest major island to get to because its mainland ferry port, **Oban**, is only three hours' drive or four-and-a-half hours on the train from Edinburgh. Mull has it all: castles, heathery hills, glistening sandy beaches, miniature train trips and boat excursions to Staffa and Fingal's Cave – not to mention the world's smallest theatre and its own unique cheese and whisky. The main town, **Tobermory**, not only inspired a Womble, but is a picturesque huddle of multi-coloured houses and lively pubs grouped round a harbour. Mull has a comprehensive website (www.isle.of.mull.com) that lists all kinds of accommodation, and there is a tourist information office on the island (Main Street, Tobermory; 01688 302610), aswell as one in Oban (Albany Street; 01631 563122).

01786 450 632, main courses £11.50-£16.50). Hermann's menu offers a bizarre but tasty combination of Austrian strudels and traditional Scottish dishes.

Where to stay

The **Golden Lion** (8 King Street, 01786 475351, rates £97 double) is a handsome Stirling hotel dating back to 1876. A cheaper option is the **youth hostel** on St John Street (01786 473442, rates £11.50-£12.50 adult, £10 child). It's for SYHA members only, but you can join at the hostel. Membership costs £6 and is valid at all SYHA hostels for one year.

Getting there

By car

Stirling is 40 miles north of Edinburgh on the A91.

By train

There are hourly trains from Edinburgh's **Waverley station**. The journey takes about 55mins. Stirling station is within 5mins walk of the main street.

By bus

The M9 express bus run by Citylink (08705 505050) leaves hourly from **Waterloo Place** in Edinburgh and takes 1hr. Slower buses to Stirling run by First Bus (663 9233) take 2hrs and leave twice an hr. These arrive at Stirling bus station on Goosecroft Road, close to the centre of town.

Tourist information

For more information, see **www.stirling.co.uk**.

Stirling

41 Dumbarton Road (01786 475019). **Open** *May, June, Sept, Oct* 9am-5pm daily. *July, Aug* 9am-7pm. *Nov-Apr* 10am-5pm daily.

Directory

Directory

Getting Around

Arriving & leaving

By air

Edinburgh Airport EH12 (333 1000) is about 10 miles (16km) west of the city centre, north of Glasgow Road. The airport is about 25 minutes' drive from Princes Street and services flights from continental and English airports. Cheap airlines **Go** (0870 607 6543; www.go-fly.com) and **Easyjet** (0870 600 0000; www.easyjet.com) fly to Edinburgh from airports in England and Ireland. **British Airways** (from UK 0845 773 3377; www.britishairways.com) flys to Edinburgh from Heathrow. Flights also leave Edinburgh for the north and Highlands and Islands of Scotland.

TO AND FROM THE AIRPORT

The cheapest and quickest way to travel to and from the airport is the dedicated bus service **Airlink 100** (555 6363, open 24 hours). These modern blue and white buses stop at Maybury, Corstorphine, Edinburgh Zoo, Murrayfield and the West End. Services leave the airport 4.50am-12.20am Mon-Sat, 5.30am-midnight; the service from Waverley Bridge runs 4.20am-11.46pm Mon-Sat; 5.20am-11.26pm Sat, Sun. Buses are low-floor double-deckers with ample luggage space and easy access for wheelchair users and buggies. Tickets cost £3.30 adult (£2 5s-15s) one way; £5 adult (£3 children) open return; free under-5s. The Airlink Day Saver, £4.20 adult (£2.50 child) allows one

journey to or from the airport and unlimited travel for the whole day on the Lothian Buses network (*see p273*). Ridacards (*see p273*) are also valid on Airlink 100.

Skycab Taxis (333 2220) also cover the distance quickly. The service covers every flight in and out of the airport (from approximately 5am-11pm); journey time is 20-25 minutes, rising to to 30 minutes during rush hours (7.30-9.30am and 4.30-7pm Mon-Fri). The fare is around £12-£14, depending on the time of day and the number of passengers. Most taxis in the city have one seat adapted for disabled passengers (*see also p278*).

By bus/coach

St Andrew Square Bus Station

Clyde Street, New Town, EH1. Princes Street buses. **Map** p306 F4. Coaches arriving in Edinburgh from England and Wales are run by Britain's most extensive coach network, National Express (0870 580 8080). Coaches serving the whole of Scotland are run by Scottish Citylink (0870 550 5050). The St Andrew Bus Station, in the city centre, was closed for redevelopment at the time of writing. Reopening is scheduled for late 2003. Until then buses to Glasgow and Fife and long-distance services have been relocated to the south side of St Andrew Square, while East Lothian buses are running from Waterloo Place, near the East end of Princes Street.

By train

Waverley Station

Waverley Bridge, New Town, EH1 (train information 0845 748 4950). Princes Street buses. **Map** p304 D2. Edinburgh's central railway station serves the East Coast main lines to London and Aberdeen. Scotrail services leave for destinations

throughout Scotland, including a shuttle service (every 15mins) to Glasgow and connections to the West Coast. Local services go to East and West Lothian.

Haymarket Station

Haymarket, Edinburgh, EH12 (train information 08457 484950). Bus 2, 3, 4, 12, 26, 31, 33, Airlink. **Map** p308 B6. On the main line to Glasgow. Most trains travelling north and west from Waverley stop here, as do local services to West Lothian.

Getting around

To fully appreciate the beauty, elegance, charm and contrasts of the city centre and its environs, Edinburgh is best explored on foot. Walking around the city is safe and can provide a rewarding experience, but do exercise the usual caution at night (*see p287*). Individuals with a nervous disposition should avoid the areas of the city with abundant and rowdy nightlife such as Lothian Road and the Cowgate. A useful way to orient yourself and get an overview of the major tourist sights is on one of the guided bus tours (*see p57*) or themed walking tours (*see p74* **Witches and wynds**).

Getting around the centre of Edinburgh by **bus** is reasonably fast and reliable, and passes – Daysavers and Ridacards – are available (*see p273*). **Driving** in town can be stressful and more hassle than it's worth, especially as city-centre parking can be problematic.

Taxis are numerous, if rather pricey. **Cycling**, on the other hand, is a fast and efficient way of getting around, both in the city centre and further afield as long as you don't mind a few cobbled streets and the odd hill.

The City of Edinburgh Council's **Greenways scheme**, introduced in 1997, has made public transport quicker and more efficient in the city centre. Greenways road lanes are painted green with red road markings. Buses, licensed taxis and cycles have unrestricted access to green lanes at all times, while private vehicles have restricted access during rush hours and at peak times. All the major routes into the city centre are covered by the scheme. Signs at the roadside show when and where stopping is permitted.

For information on getting around **Glasgow**, see p252. Travel information for other destinations is given in the **Around Edinburgh** chapter.

Public transport

Buses

Edinburgh has extensive bus networks that give ready access to most of the city day and night. The ubiquitous maroon and white buses (some now being displaced by harlequin red, gold and white low floor buses) are run by **Lothian Buses**, which has a seven-day 24-hour telephone enquiry line, on 555 6363. Also, check the website www. lothianbuses.co.uk. Lothian Buses' city centre **Travelshops** (see below) provide details and maps of all Lothian Buses services in Edinburgh and the Lothians.

Throughout this guide, we have listed Lothian Buses only, as they cover the majority of bus services throughout Edinburgh and into Mid and East Lothian. As parts of town are served by many different routes, we have grouped buses for three of the busiest streets or areas together in our listings.

Below are the groupings used, together with a list of bus routes that serve those streets or areas:

Princes Street buses (not all routes travel the full length of street) 1, 3, 4, 10, 11, 12, 15, 16, 17, 21, 22, 24, 25, 26, 30, 31, 33, 34, 40, 44, 44A
Nicolson Street–North Bridge buses
3, 5, 7, 8, 14, 29, 29A, 31, 33, 37, 37A, 49

Playhouse buses
1, 4, 5, 7, 8, 10, 11, 12, 14, 15, 16, 17, 19, 19A, 22, 25, 34, 44, 44A, 49

Edinburgh's other main bus company is FirstBus, which incorporates SMT, Eastern Scottish, Lowland Omnibuses and Midland Scottish. Although both Firstbus and Lothian Buses run parallel services along many routes at similar prices, day tickets are not transferable between the companies. For information on Firstbus services and routes call 663 9233. For **sightseeing tours**, see p57.

Lothian Buses Travelshops

27 Hanover Street, New Town, EH2. Bus 23, 27, 28, 41, 42, 45/Princes Street buses. **Open** 8.30am-6pm Mon-Sat; 10am-1pm, 2-5pm Sun. **Map** p304 C1.
Waverley Bridge, New Town, EH2. Princes Street buses. **Open** 8.30am-6pm Mon-Sat; 10am-1pm, 1.45-5pm Sun. **Map** p304 D2.

NIGHT BUSES

Night buses, operated by Lothian buses, run seven days a week and depart from Waverley Bridge at 12.15am, 1.15am, 2.15am, 4.15am Sun-Thur night and 12.15am, 1.15am, 2.15am, 3.15am on Fri, Sat nights. There is a flat fare of £1.60 which allows one passengers to make one transfer to another night service at Waverley Bridge, on production of a valid ticket. A free map and timetable can be picked up at Lothian Buses Travelshops.

FARES & RIDACARDS

Bus fares are based on a stage system; fares and fare stages are listed on individual service timetable leaflets and at bus stops. Bus drivers don't give change, so ensure you have the correct fare before boarding. There is no on-the-spot fine for travelling without a valid ticket or pass but action may be taken later. Prices, offers and concessions are

subject to change so contact a Lothian Buses Travelshop or phone for information.

Adult fares

Single journey tickets start from 50p (1-2 stages). Travelling 3-8 stages, which will get you across the city centre, costs 80p; 9-13 stages 90p; 14 or more stages £1. You can buy a **Daysaver** multiple journey ticket from the driver of the first bus you board (or from Travelshops). This costs £2.20 and allows unlimited travel around the Lothian Buses network for a day (not Airlink or tours). It's worth waiting till 9.30am to get an off-peak **Bargain Daysaver**, which costs £1.50 and is valid all day.

Child fares

Children under 5 travel free (up to a maximum of two children per adult passenger). The children's fare is charged for ages 5 to 15 inclusive, a flat fare of 50p per journey. A **Child Daysaver** ticket is £1.50.

Ridacard

The GoSmart! Electronic Ridacard gives unlimited travel on normal Lothian Buses services (but not tours). For adults, a 1wk Ridacard costs £10.50; 4wks £30.50. Junior Ridacards (ages 5-15 inclusive) are £6.50 for 1wk; £18 for 4wks. Buy from Lothian Buses Travelshops (see above).

Trains

Most rail services in Scotland are run by **Scotrail**. Details of services and fares are available from National Rail Enquiries (08457 484950, 24 hours daily). The information desk at Waverley Station (see p272) has timetables and details of discount travel, season tickets and international travel. As well as Waverley and Haymarket (see p272), the city has two suburban stations at South Gyle and Slateford.

Taxis

Black cabs

Most of Edinburgh's taxis are black cabs. They take up to five passengers and have facilities for travellers with disabilities. When a taxi's yellow 'For Hire' light is on, you can stop it in the street. Many taxi companies take credit cards, but check when you book or get in. After midnight taxis are scarce and in demand, and raise their rates. If you want to phone for a taxi, use the Yellow Pages; larger companies with facilities for the disabled traveller and a 24-hour service are **Capital Castle Taxis** (228 2555), **Central Radio Taxis** (229 2468), **City Cabs** (228 1211) and **Computer Cabs** (272 8000).

Private hire cars

Minicabs (saloon cars) are generally cheaper than black cabs and may be able to accommodate more passengers (some use people carriers for up to eight passengers). However, private hire cars are not permitted to use the Greenways routes. Private-hire companies with facilities for passengers with disabilities include **Bluebird Private Hire** (621 6666), and **Persevere Private Hire** (555 3377/553 7711). It's a good idea to call round first to get the best price.

Complaints or compliments about a taxicab or private hire company journey can be made to the Licensing Board, 343 High Street, Edinburgh EH1 1PW (529 4250). Make a note of the date and time of the journey and the licence number of the vehicle.

Cycling

Edinburgh is a great place to cycle around, thanks to some successful lobbying by the local cycle campaign **Spokes** (232 Dalry Road, EH11, 313 2114/www.spokes.org.uk). The city council has invested wisely in both off-road cycle paths and road-edge cycle lanes. Although it is not compulsory for motorists to observe the latter, the lanes ease the flow of cyclists during rush hours and make some

roads safer. Cyclists can travel freely along bus lanes.

Be sensible when tethering a bike in the street: the Grassmarket, Rose Street and other pub-infested areas are prone to vandalism and theft is a problem. Otherwise, the only real worries for cyclists not on mountain bikes are the cobbled streets around the New Town.

The joy of cycling in Edinburgh is that you can fly from one side of town to the other in minutes – even when roads are blocked during the Festival. A bike also makes areas outside the centre remarkably accessible. Spokes produces three cycle maps that show all the cycle routes and paths for Edinburgh, Midlothian and West Lothian (all £4.95). There are good paths out to Cramond from Roseburn, out towards East Lothian, starting at the Innocent Cycle Path in Holyrood Park, and a bike is the perfect way to explore the Water of Leith Walkway, the Union Canal towpath or the esplanade that fronts the Forth from Cramond to Portobello.

Bike hire

BikeTrax Cycle Hire

11 Lochrin Place, South Edinburgh, EH3 (228 6333/www.biketrax.co.uk). Bus 11, 15, 16, 17. **Open** *May-Oct* 9.30am-6pm Mon-Sat. *Nov-Apr* 9.30am-5.30pm Mon-Sat. **Hire** from £10 per day. **Deposit** £100 per bike. **Credit** MC, V. **Map** p309 D7.

Edinburgh Cycle Hire

29 Blackfriars Street, Old Town, EH1 (556 5560/www.cyclescotland. co.uk). Nicolson Street–North Bridge buses. **Open** *May-Oct* 9am-9pm daily. *Nov-Apr* 10am-6pm daily. **Hire** £10-£15 per day. £50-£70 per wk. **Deposit** £100 per bike. **No credit cards. Map** p310 G5.

Driving

In conjunction with the Greenways Scheme (*see p273*), the city centre has an expanding network of one-way streets and pedestrian-only

areas. This can make driving in the centre a frustrating experience. Princes Street has limited access for private vehicles (and there are proposals to ban private cars from it altogether); it is best avoided if possible. A knock-on effect of this is that the surrounding roads are becoming increasingly busy: slow-moving traffic is the norm, especially during rush hours (7.30-9.30am, 4.30-7pm Mon-Fri). In addition to overcrowded roads, circuitous one-way routes and traffic jams, there are stringent parking restrictions, so the whole driving process may leave you feeling harassed and frustrated.

The City of Edinburgh Council takes the whole issue of transport very seriously. It employs a notoriously efficient private company to keep the streets clear of illegally parked cars – so efficient that some traffic wardens even work overnight. So if you park illegally, it is highly probable that you will get a parking fine. For the purposes of on-street car parking, the city is divided up into central and peripheral zones. In the central zone you must pay for parking between 8.30am and 6pm Mon-Sat. In the peripheral zone, payment must be made between 8.30am and 5pm Mon-Sat. Payment is either by parking meter or on-street pay-and-display ticket vending machines. Outside these zones, on-street parking is free.

The fine for parking illegally is £40 (reduced to £20 if it is paid within a fortnight). Worse, if your car is causing an obstruction, it can be towed away and impounded (*see p275*). The good news is that in Scotland the clamping of vehicles has been ruled illegal; don't let that lull you into a false sense of security, however, as zealous traffic wardens patrol the city centre.

During August the Festival makes things even worse. The High Street is pedestrianised while Chambers Street and others are also used as coach parks for the Tattoo: cars left here will be impounded.

Vehicle removal

If your car has been impounded, a fee of £105 is levied for removal, plus a £12 storage fee for every day the vehicle remains uncollected. This is in addition to the £40 parking ticket. Impounded cars are taken to the Edinburgh Car Compound, which keeps a log of all impounded cars. If your car has been stolen you should report it at once to the police.

Edinburgh Car Compound
14-16 Beaverhall Road, Broughton, EH7 (557 5244). Bus 13, 36. **Open** 7am-8pm Mon-Wed; 7am-11pm Thur-Sat; 9am-11am Sun. **Credit** MC, V. **Map** p306 F2.

24-hour car parks

Greenside Car Park
Greenside Row, Broughton, EH1 (558 3518). **Map** p307 G4.

Morrison Street Car Park
West Edinburgh, EH3. **Map** p308 C6.

National Car Parks
Castle Terrace, Old Town, EH1 (229 2870). **Map** p304 A3.

National Car Parks
Potterrow, South Edinburgh, EH8 (668 4661). **Map** p310 G6.

St James Centre
Leith Street, Broughton, EH1 (556 5066). **Map** p307 G4.

Waverley Car Park
6 New Street, Old Town, EH8 (557 8526). **Map** p310 G4.

Breakdown services

If you are a member of a motoring organisation in your home country, check to see if it has a reciprocal agreement with a British organisation.

AA (Automobile Association)
Fanum House, Upper Ground Street, Basingstoke, Hampshire RG21 4EA (enquiries 0870 544 4444/ breakdown 0800 887766/ insurance 0800 444777/new membership 0800 444999). **Open** 24hrs daily. **Credit** MC, V.
You can call the AA if you break down and become a member on the spot for £123. The first year's roadside service membership starts at £42. Its information line (0870 550 0600) gives information on International Driving Permits, route maps, Roadwatch and Weatherwatch.

Environmental Transport Association
Freepost KT 4021, Weybridge, Surrey, KT13 8RS (0193 282 8882). **Open** *Office* 8am-6pm Mon-Fri; 9am-4pm Sat. *Breakdown service* 24hrs daily. **Credit** MC, V.
The green alternative, if you don't want part of your membership fee to be used for lobbying the government into building more roads, which is what happens with the AA and RAC. Basic membership is £25 per year for individuals and £30 for families.

RAC
Great Park Road, Bristol, BS99 1RB (enquiries 0870 572 2722/ breakdown 0800 828282/motor insurance 0800 678000/new membership 0800 550550/ www.rac.co.uk). **Open** *Office* 8am-9pm Mon-Fri; 8.30am-5pm Sat, 10am-4pm Sun. *Breakdown service* 24hrs daily. **Credit** AmEx, MC, V.
Membership costs from £39 to £168, plus £90 for European cover.

Car hire

To hire a car you must have at least one year's driving experience and be in possession of a current full driving licence with no serious endorsements. Most firms insist you are over 21 and book by credit card. Overseas visitors, particularly those whose national driving licence is not readily readable by English speakers, are recommended to acquire an International Driving Licence before travelling.

Prices for car hire vary considerably between companies, and may be subject to change, so it's a good idea to ring round to find the deal that suits you best. A few of the more reputable companies are given below. Be sure to check exactly what insurance is included in the price. Also ask about special deals when booking.

Arnold Clark
553 Gorgie Road, West Edinburgh, EH11 (444 1852/www.arnoldclark. co.uk). **Open** 8am-8pm Mon, Wed-Fri; 8am-6pm Tue; 8am-5pm Sat; 11am-5pm Sun. **Credit** AmEx, DC, MC, V.
A full range of vehicles is available for hire. One-way rates upon request; corporate accounts; free courtesy coach to and from Edinburgh Airport (from Bankhead Ave branch only). Cheapest rental rates are £18 per day; £44.90 weekend; £80 seven days. You must be aged between 23 and 75 to hire here. Arnold Clark do not take cash and require a deposit of £100. The Lochrin Place branch (Map p309 D7) is most convenient for central Edinburgh car hire.
Branches: 64 Craigentinny North Avenue, EH6 (553 3323); 16 Bankhead Drive, EH11 (458 1501); Lochrin Place, EH3 (228 4747).

Hertz
Edinburgh Airport, EH12 (333 1019/central reservations 0870 5996 699/www.hertz.co.uk). **Open** *Phone line* 24hrs daily. *Office* 6.30am-11pm Mon-Fri; 8am-10pm Sat; 8am-11pm Sun **Credit** AmEx, DC, MC, V.
A wide range of manual and automatic vehicles; corporate accounts; one-way rates; collection and delivery. Cheapest rental, all inclusive, is £51per day; £69 weekend; £145 seven days. It is cheaper to hire in town than at the airport. You must be 25 or over.
Branches: 10 Picardy Place, EH1 (556 8311).

National Car Rental
Edinburgh Airport (333 1922/ central reservations 0870 56006666; freephone 0800 263263/www. nationalcar.com). **Open** *Phone line* 24hrs daily. *Office* 7am-10pm Mon-Fri; 8am-10pm Sat, Sun. **Credit** AmEx, DC, MC, V.
A wide range of manual and automatic vehicles, one-way rates and a delivery and collection service. The cheapest rental, all inclusive, is £36 per day; £57.30 weekend; £164.75 seven days. To hire, you must be 21 years of age.

Directory

Resources A-Z

Age restrictions

You have to be 18 to drink in Scotland, though there are some bars and clubs that admit over-21s only. Seventeen is the legal age for driving, though most car rental companies won't hire cars to people under 21. Sixteen is the legal age of consent.

Business

Conferences & conventions

Edinburgh Convention Bureau

4 Rothesay Terrace, New Town, EH3 (473 3666/fax 473 3636/www. edinburgh.org/conference). Bus 13, 19, 29, 36, 37, 41, 42 **Open** 9am-5pm Mon-Fri. **Map** p308 B5.
Part of the business and tourism division of the Edinburgh & Lothians Tourist Board, the ECB offers advice on finding a conference venue and help with the organisation.

Edinburgh International Conference Centre

The Exchange, 150 Morrison Street, West Edinburgh, EH3 (300 3000/ www.eicc.co.uk). Bus 1, 2, 22, 28, 34. **Open** *telephone enquiries & office* 8am-6pm Mon-Fri. **Map** p308 C6.
In the modern surroundings of the city's new financial centre, the Exchange, the EICC can accommodate up to 1,200 delegates and offers in-house catering as well as business services.

Couriers & shippers

All the major international couriers are active in Edinburgh. See the Yellow Pages under couriers for further details. All companies listed below can arrange pick-up.

DHL

Unit 15/4-15/5 South Gyle Crescent, South Gyle Industrial Estate, Edinburgh, EH12 (08701 100300; www.dhl.com). **Open** *Phone line* 24hrs daily. **Credit** AmEx, DC, MC, V.

Worldwide express delivery service. Next-day deliveries can be made within the EU (not guaranteed), and the USA if booked before 2pm.

Federal Express

1/16 Spitfire House, Edinburgh Cargo Airport, EH12. (0800 123800; www.fedex.com). **Open** *phone line* 7.30am-7.30pm daily. **Credit** AmEx, MC, V.
FedEx can deliver next day by 8am (premium service) or 10.30am (standard service) to certain destinations across the USA (mainly New York and other major cities). More than 210 countries are served.

UPS

30 South Gyle Crescent, South Gyle Industrial Estate, West Edinburgh, EH12 (08457 877 877/fax 314 6820/ www.ups.com). **Open** 8am-8pm Mon-Fri; 9am-2pm Sat. **Credit** AmEx, MC, V.
UPS offers express delivery to more than 200 countries; cheaper, slower services are also available. Deliveries to some destinations can be guaranteed to arrive by 8.30am or 10.30am the next day.

Equipment hire

PC World

1-17 Glasgow Road, West Edinburgh, EH12 (334 5953/fax 334 6169/ www.pcworld.co.uk). Bus 12, 26, 32/52, 31. **Open** 9am-8pm Mon-Fri; 9am-6pm Sat; 10.30am-6pm Sun.
PC World doesn't hire out equipment itself, but has a dedicated business centre within the store – PC World Business Direct – with a stock of 12,000 lines.

Sound & Vision AV

11B South Gyle Crescent, West Edinburgh, EH12 (334 3324/ www.sound-and-vision.co.uk). Bus 2, 12, 18, 21, 22. **Open** 8.30am-5.30pm Mon-Fri.
Will hire out anything required for a presentation, including PCs, and can produce graphics. Also has the unique (in the UK) service of a van full of equipment ready to go in case of emergencies.

Import & export

Companies House

Argyle House, 37 Castle Terrace, South Edinburgh, EH1 (0870 333 3636/www.companieshouse.gov.uk). Bus 11, 15, 16, 34, 35. **Open** 9am-5pm Mon-Fri. **Map** p304 A3.

Companies House incorporates new limited companies, and to export goods you must be registered here. It also has information on Scottish companies and foreign companies registered in Scotland.

Customs & Excise

Glasgow office, 21 India Street, Glasgow G2 4PZ (0845 010 9000/ www.hmce.gov.uk). **Open** *Phone line* 8am-8pm Mon-Fri. *Office* 9am-4.30pm Mon-Fri, 9am-4.30pm Fri.
The Glasgow office deals with all Scottish import/export licences and information as well as enquiries about VAT.

Office hire & business centres

Edinburgh Office Business Centre & Conference Venue

16-26 Forth Street, Broughton, EH1 (550 3700/fax 550 3701). Bus 8, 17. **Open** 8.30am-5.30pm Mon-Thur; 8.30am-5pm Fri. **Map** p307 G3.
Over 60 office spaces, ranging from 85 to 775sq ft.

Regus

Conference House, The Exchange, 152 Morrison Street, West Edinburgh, EH3 8EB (200 6000/fax 200 6200/ www.regus.com). Bus 2, 28. **Open** 8.30am-6pm Mon-Fri. **Map** p308 C6.
Conference House contains one- to 67-person office suites, starting at £1,000 per month. A fully furnished office can be provided, with phones, PCs, secretarial support and catering. Conference space can also be hired by the day or hour. The website allows you to see round offices and book online.

Rutland Square House

12 Rutland Square, New Town, EH1 (228 2281/fax 228 3637/www. braemore.co.uk). Bus 3, 12, 25, 31, 33. **Open** 8.30am-5.30pm Mon-Fri;. **Map** p308 C6
Twelve fully furnished offices, from £400 per month. All are hired out on a three-month minimum basis.

Secretarial services

Office Angels

95 George Street, New Town, EH2 3ES (226 6112/fax 220 6850/ www.officeangels.co.uk). Bus 28, 37, 40, 41, 42/Princes Street buses. **Open** 8.30am-6pm Mon-Fri. **Map** p304 B1.

Speak Scots

Scottish is a whole language to itself and its regional variations are legendary. The Edinburgh vernacular is constantly being transformed by newcomers from all over Scotland. Here are a few pointers.

Alba – Gaelic for Scotland.

Barry – good, excellent, attractive. A general term of acclaim.

Bampot – a nutter.

Ben – the back room of the house.

Boake – to vomit.

Chum – to accompany.

Couthy – plain or homely (of a person); agreeable, snug, comfortable (of a place).

Dinnae – don't, as in 'just dinnae go there'.

Disnae – doesn't.

Dod – a small amount, a dab. Often used in conjunction with 'wee'.

Douce – kind, gentle, soothing (pejoratively – sedate).

Dreich – wet, dull, tedious, dreary – of the weather or a person. The 'ch' is pronounced as in the German composer Bach.

Eijit – a fool, idiot.

Gallus – cheeky, self-confident or daring. In Glasgow: stylish or impressive.

Get – to go with (as in the phrase 'shall I get you down the road?').

Haar – sea mist, especially from the North Sea.

Hen – a female (informal).

Ken – know, understand – also interpolated (seemingly at random) into speech.

Laldy – as in the folk music phrase 'to give it laldy' – to play vigorously.

Loch – the Scottish word for a lake. There are only two lakes that are called 'lakes' in Scotland.

Lugs – ears.

Messages – shopping, groceries.

Mingin – smelly; of poor quality or substance.

Nash – to leave precipitously (as in 'I better nash, the pub's about to close').

Oxter – armpit.

Piece – a sandwich.

Pished – drunk.

Radge – barmy, mad, a bit too extrovert for comfort.

Scran – food.

See – take, for example (as in 'see that wee jimmy, he's well radge).

See you! – 'Hey!', 'Oi you!' or 'I say, old chap!'.

Slater – woodlouse.

Stay – live (as in 'where do you stay?').

Stushie – a fight or altercation.

Teuchter – someone from the Highlands (pejorative).

Wee – small, a small quantity.

Weejie – a Glaswegian (highly derogatory).

Youze – the plural of 'you'.

Hires out office staff at all levels, although it doesn't deal with accountants and IT specialists.

Reed Employment Solutions

13 Frederick Street, New Town, EH2 2BY (226 3687/fax 247 6850/ www.reed.co.uk). Bus 28, 37, 40, 41, 42/Princes Street buses. **Open** 8am-5.30pm Mon-Fri. **Map** p304 B1.
Temporary and permanent office, secretarial, and call centre staff.

Translators & interpreters

Berlitz

26 Frederick Street, New Town, EH2 2JR (226 7198). Bus 28, 37, 40, 41, 42/Princes Street buses. **Open** 9am-5pm Mon-Fri. **Map** p304 B1.
Berlitz will translate from or into any language under the sun. Phone for company rates.

Integrated Language Services

School of Languages, Heriot-Watt University, Riccarton, EH14 4AS (451 3159). Bus 25, 34, 35, 45. **Open** 9am-5pm Mon-Fri.
All European languages and most others can be translated. ILS also supplies interpreters and all necessary interpreting equipment for conferences. Rates on request.

Useful organisations

Edinburgh Chamber of Commerce & Enterprise

27 Melville Street, West Edinburgh, EH3 (477 7000/www.ecce.org). Bus 2, 26. **Open** 9am-5pm Mon-Fri. **Map** p308 C6.
One of the fastest-growing chambers of commerce in the United Kingdom, with international trade near the top of its agenda.

Scottish Enterprise Edinburgh & Lothian

Apex House, 99 Haymarket Terrace, West Edinburgh EH12 (313 4000/ www.Scottish-enterprise.com/ endinburghandlothian). Bus 3, 3A, 21, 25. **Open** 9am-5pm Mon-Fri. **Map** p308 B6.
A government-funded economic development, training and environmental improvement agency. There is also a division, Small Business Gateway (www.sbgateway. com) specialising in helping small businesses start up.

Scottish Executive

St Andrew's House, Regent Road, Calton Hill, EH1 3DG (556 8400/ www.scotland.gov.uk). Bus 3, 7, 8, 14, 19, 19A. **Open** 8.30am-5pm Mon-Fri. **Map** p307 G4.
This is a good starting point from which to reach the relevant departments, such as Enterprise and Tourism or Economic and Industrial Affairs.

Consumer

If you pay with a credit card, you can cancel payment or get reimbursed if there is a problem. Consider travel documentation that protects you against financial loss. The local trading standards office at the **Advice Shop**, or the **Citizens Advice Bureau** (for both, *see p281*) can advise if there is a problem.

Customs

When entering the UK, non-EU citizens and anyone buying duty-free goods have the following import limits:

● 200 cigarettes or 100 cigarillos or 250 grams (8.82 ounces) of tobacco.
● 2 litres still table wine plus either 1 litre spirits or strong liqueurs (over 22% alcohol by volume) or 2 litres fortified wine (under 22% abv), sparkling wine or other liqueurs.
● 60cc/ml perfume.
● 250cc/ml toilet water.
● Other goods to the value of: £75 for EU citizens purchasing from another EU country or £145 for travellers arriving from outside the EU.

No-one under 17 is entitled to make use of the alcohol or tobacco allowances.

The import of meat, poultry, fruit, plants, flowers and protected animals is restricted or forbidden; there are no restrictions on the import or export of currency.

People over the age of 17 arriving from an EU country have been able to import unlimited goods for their own personal use, if bought tax-paid (ie not duty-free).

However, the law sets out guidance levels for what is for personal use (and it's not as much as you might expect or hope), so if you exceed them you must be able to satisfy officials that the goods are not for resale. Just remember, they've heard it all before.

HM Customs & Excise
Edinburgh Airport, EH12 (344 3196). **Open** 6am-11pm daily.

Disabled

Listed buildings are not allowed to widen their entrances or add ramps, and parts of the Old Town have very narrow pavements, making it hard for wheelchair users to get around. However, equal opportunity legislation requires new buildings to be fully accessible – step forward the **Festival Theatre** (*see p228*) and the new **Museum of Scotland** (*see p79*).

The newer black taxis can all take wheelchairs, as can some private hire cars. Lothian Buses is replacing its buses with low-floor versions, with easy access for wheelchairs . **Bus routes** using low-floor buses at the time of writing are 3, 22, 26, 29/29A, 37/37A, 44/44A, Airlink 100 (ring 555 6363 for up-to-date details).

Edinburgh City Council publishes a booklet *Transport in Edinburgh: A Guide for Disabled Peop*le. This gives information on transport accessibility and services and assistance available to people with disabilities; it also includes a list of useful contact addresses and phone numbers. The booklet is free and can be requested from Traveline on 0800 232323 (free calls) or 225 3858 (local calls).

Most theatres and cinemas are fitted with induction loops for the hard of hearing – ask when you're booking.

For more information contact the following:

Lothian Coalition of Disabled People
Norton Park, 57 Albion Road, Calton Hill, EH7 (475 2360/enquiries@ lcodp.demon.co.uk). **Open** *telephone enquiries* 9am-5pm Mon-Fri. Publishes the free *Access Guide to Edinburgh.* Phone for a copy.

Drugs

Hard and soft drugs are illegal in Scotland as they are in the rest of the UK.

Electricity

The UK electricity supply is 220-240 volt, 50-cycle AC rather than the 110-120 volt, 60-cycle AC used in the US. Plugs are standard three-point. Adaptors for US appliances can be bought at airports. TV and video are also on different frequencies to the US, so it will not be possible to play back American camcorder footage till you get home.

Embassies and consulates

For a full list of consular offices in Edinburgh consult the phone book or Yellow Pages under Consuls and/or Embassies.

American Consulate General
3 Regent Terrace, Calton Hill, EH7 (556 8315/www.usembassy. org.uk/scotland). Bus 1, 3,5, 19/19A, 25. **Open** *Phone enquiries* 8.30am-noon, 1-5pm Mon-Fri. *Personal callers* (emergencies only) 1-4pm Mon-Fri or by appointment. **Map** p307 H4.
A limited consular service; no visas or passport replacement.

Australian Consulate
37 George Street, New Town, EH2 (624 3333). Bus 28, 37, 40, 41, 42/Princes Street buses. **Open** phone for times. **Map** p304 C1.
Offers basic services where a personal appearance is required, such as the witnessing of documents.

Consulate General of the Federal Republic of Germany
16 Eglinton Crescent, New Town, EH12 (337 2323/german-consulate @ukgateway.net). Bus 12, 13, 26, 31. **Open** 9am-noon, 1-3pm Mon-Fri. **Map** p308 B6.
A comprehensive service including issuing visas.

French Consulate General
11 Randolph Crescent, New Town, EH3 (general enquiries only 225 7954/visa enquiries 220 6324/visa enquiry line 0891 600215/passports 225 3377/legal 220 0141). Bus 13, 19, 29/29A, 37/37A. **Open** *Visas* 9.30am-11.30am. *Passports/ID cards* 9.30am-1pm, by appointment 2-5pm, Mon-Fri. **Map** p308 C5.

Italian
Consulate General
*32 Melville Street, New Town, EH3
(226 3631/220 3695/fax 226 6260).
Bus 3, 4, 12, 25/25A, 41, 42.* **Open**
Phone enquiries 9.30am-5.30pm Mon-
Fri. *Personal callers* 9.30am-12.30pm
Mon-Fri. **Map** p308 L5.

Spanish Consulate
*63 North Castle Street, New Town,
EH2 (220 1843/fax 226 4568/visas
09001 600123). Bus 28, 37, 40, 41,
42/Princes Street buses.* **Open** *Phone
enquiries* 9am-3pm Mon-Fri. *Personal
callers* 9am-noon 1-3pm Mon-Fri.
Map p304 B1.

Emergencies

In the event of a serious
accident, fire or incident,
call 999 and specify whether
you require ambulance, fire
service or police. *See also*
Helplines, *p281.*

Gay & lesbian

Help & information

Lesbian Line
(557 0751). **Open** 7.30-10pm
Mon, Thur.
A helpline for lesbians.

Lothian Gay & Lesbian
Switchboard
(556 4049). **Open** 7.30-10pm daily.
Advice on sexual health and HIV/
AIDS for gay men and lesbians.

Groups &
organisations

AD
Information 556 4049.
Social group for lesbians aged 45
and over.

Edinburgh Gay
Women's Group
Information 478 7069. **Meets** 7pm
Wed at Nexus *(see p206).*
A weekly social group for women.

Gay Dads Scotland
*Information 478 7069/www.
gaydadsscotland.org.uk.* **Meets** 8pm
last Thur of mth at LGB Centre, 58A
& 60 Broughton Street, EH1.
Monthly meeting for gay fathers.

Icebreakers
Information 556 9331. **Meets** 7.30pm
every 2nd Wed, CC Blooms *(see p204).*

Group for lesbians, gay men,
bisexuals, and transgendered people
who want to meet similar.

Juice
Information 661 0982. **Meets** 2-4pm
Fri at Solas, 2-4 Abbeymount, EH7.
Gay men affected by HIV and
AIDS meet every Friday in a group
offering information, activities
and support. A similar group for
women, Isis, meets at the same
place, 1-3pm Tue.

Stonewall
Youth Project
*Information 0845 1130 005/
www.lgbtyouth.org.uk.*
Project for young lesbians, gay men,
bisexuals and transgendered people
under the age of 26.

Health

National Health Service
(NHS) treatment is free to
whose who fall into one of the
following categories:
● European Union (EU) nationals,
plus those of Iceland, Norway and
Liechtenstein.
● European Economic Area (EEA)
nationals living in an EEA state.
● Nationals/residents of countries
with which the UK has a reciprocal
agreement.
● Anyone who at time of receiving
treatment has been in the UK for the
previous 12 months.
● Anyone who has come to the UK
to take up permanent residence.
● Students on full-time recognised
courses of study from anywhere in
the world.
● Refugees and others seeking
refuge in the UK.
● Anyone formally detained by the
Immigration Authorities.
There are no NHS charges for
the following:
● Treatment in accident and
emergency departments.
● Emergency ambulance transport.
● Diagnosis and treatment of
certain communicable diseases,
including STDs.
● Family planning services.
● Compulsory psychiatric
treatment.
If you do not fit into any of the
above categories, but wish to
find out if you still qualify for
free treatment, contact:

Primary Care
Department
*Lothian Health, Stevenson House,
555 Gorgie Road, West Edinburgh,
EH11 (536 9000).*

Accident &
emergency

The 24-hour casualty
department serving Edinburgh
is currently located at:

Royal Infirmary
of Edinburgh
*Lauriston Place, South Edinburgh,
EH3 (536 4000). Bus 8, 24, 33, 45.*
Map p309 F7.
It is scheduled to move to the Royal
Infirmary's new site at Little France
on the southern outskirts of the city
in May 2003. The new Royal
Infirmary at Little France is
currently served by buses 8, 24,
32/52, 33, 38.

Chemists

Many drugs cannot be bought
over the counter. A pharmacist
will dispense medicines on
receipt of a prescription from
a doctor. An NHS prescription
costs £6.10 per item at
present. A late-opening
dispensing chemist is **Boots**
(46 Shandwick Place, New
Town, EH2; 225 6757; open
8am-9pm Mon-Fri, 8am-6pm
Sat, 10.30am-4.30pm Sun). For
other pharmacies, *see p175.*

Complementary
medicine

Edinburgh has a thriving
alternative medicine scene.
Some of the more established
and reliable outfits are listed
below – they will provide
appointments for everything
from chiropractors and
osteopaths to herbalists and
acupuncturists as well as a
few in between that you've
probably never heard of.

Napiers Dispensary
and Clinic
*18 Bristro Place, Edinburgh, EH3.
(225 5542/www.napiers.net). Bus 23,
27, 28, 41, 42, 45.* **Open** 10am-6pm
Mon; 9am-6pm Tue-Fri; 9am-5.30pm
Sat. **Map** p309 F6.
A long established herbalist that
stocks a wide range of herbs and
remedies. The dispensary also has
a clinic staffed by a variety of
alternative practitioners.

Directory

The Whole Works

Jackson's Close, 209 High Street, EH1 (225 8092/www.thewholeworks. co.uk). Nicolson Street–North Bridge buses. **Open** 9am-8pm Mon-Fri; 9am-5pm Sat. **Map** p304 D3.
Busy city centre clinic providing a wide range of different therapies.

Contraception & abortion

Abortions are free to British citizens on the National Health Service (NHS). This also applies to EU residents and foreign nationals living, working or studying in Britain. Two doctors must agree that an abortion is justified within the terms of the Abortion Act 1967, as amended, whether it is on the NHS or not. If you decide to go private, contact one of the organisations below.

Caledonia Youth (formerly the Brook Advisory Clinic)

5 Castle Terrace, South Edinburgh, EH2 (229 3596/0800 282930). Bus 1, 10, 11, 15, 16, 17, 22, 34. **Open** noon-6pm Mon-Thur; noon-3.30pm Fri; noon-2.30pm Sat. No appointment necessary. **Map** p304 A3.
Advice on contraception, sexual problems and abortion with referral to an NHS hospital or private clinic. Contraception, sexual advice and counselling for young people under 25, including pregnancy advice and emergency contraception. For visitors based outside Scotland a £15 consultation fee is payable, plus any prescription costs.

Family Planning & Well Women Services

18 Dean Terrace, Stockbridge, EH4 (332 7941). Bus 19/19A, 24, 28. **Open** *Switchboard* 8.30am-7.30pm Mon-Thur; 9.30am-4pm Fri; 9.30am-noon Sat. *General clinics* 9.30am-7.30pm Mon-Thur (by appointment). *Young people's clinic (under 25s)* 9.30am-1pm Sat. **Map** p305 C3.
Confidential advice, contraceptive provision, pregnancy tests and abortion referral. As an NHS-run clinic, covered under the European Union E11 scheme, it provides most services free, though some charges may apply to overseas visitors. Post-abortion, pre-menstrual syndrome, menopause and psychosexual counselling is also offered. Note that, except in emergencies, you must make an appointment first.

Dental services

Dental care is free only to UK citizens in certain categories. All other patients, NHS or private, must pay; certain categories of people from some countries may be eligible for reduced dental costs. For advice, and to find an NHS dentist, contact the Primary Care Department (*see p279*). Emergency dental treatment can be obtained at:

Edinburgh Dental Institute

Lauriston Building, Lauriston Place, South Edinburgh, EH3 (536 4900). Bus 23, 27 28, 45. **Open** 9am-3pm Mon-Fri. **Map** p308 E7.
Free walk-in emergency clinic.

Western General Hospital

Crewe Road South, Stockbridge, EH4 (537 1338). Bus 19/19A, 28, 29, 37/37A, 38. **Open** 7-9pm Mon-Fri; 10am-noon, 7-9pm Sat, Sun.
Walk-in emergency clinic, for tourists/Lothian residents only; NHS charges and exemptions apply.

Doctors

If you're a British citizen or working in the city, you can go to any GP for diagnosis and treatment. People who are ordinarily resident in the UK, such as overseas students, can also register with an NHS doctor. For a list of names of GPs in your area, contact the Primary Care Department (*see p279*).

If you are not eligible to see an NHS doctor, you will be charged cost price for medicines prescribed by a private doctor.

Hospitals

The Royal Infirmary is moving from the centre of the city in Lauriston Place (*see p81*) to a newly built building on the southern perimeter of the city at Little France. The new Royal Infirmary opened in January 2002 and most departments are scheduled

to move in by late 2003. Currently, it is planned that the Eye Pavilion, Dental Hospital and GUM clinic will remain in Lauriston Place, but these plans are subject to change and visitors should contact the main switchboard to check details.

The Royal Infirmary of Edinburgh

Old Dalkeith Road, Little France (536 1000). Bus 8, 24, 32/52, 33, 38.

Opticians

For dispensing opticians, *see p179*.

Princess Alexandra Eye Pavilion

Chalmers Street, South Edinburgh, EH3 (536 3755). Bus 23, 27, 28, 45. **Map** p309 E7.
The Eye Pavilion operates a free walk-in service for emergency eye complaints.

STDs/HIV/AIDS

The Genito-Urinary Medicine (GUM) clinic (*see below*) is affiliated to the Royal Infirmary of Edinburgh. It provides free, confidential advice and treatment of STDs and non-sex related problems, such as thrush (yeast infections) and cystitis (urinary tract infections). It also offers information and counselling on HIV and STDs, and can conduct a confidential blood test to determine HIV status. Government and Health Education pamphlets – *AIDS: The Facts, Safer Sex and the Condom* and *AIDS: The Test* – are available from the GUM clinic and by post from: Health Education Board for Scotland, Woodburn House, Canaan Lane, EH10.

Solas

2-4 Abbeymount, Calton Hill, EH8 (661 0982/fax 652 1780/ www.waverleycare.org). Bus 30, 35. **Open** *Drop-in & Café* 11am-8pm Tue, Thur; 11am-4pm Wed, Fri. *Phone enquiries* 9am-5pm Mon-Fri. **No credit cards**. **Map** p307 J4.

The city's HIV/AIDS information and support centre. A wide range of support is offered (including counselling, arts workshops, support for children and young people). There is also a good café.

Genito-Urinary Medicine Clinic

Lauriston Building, Lauriston Place, South Edinburgh, EH3 (men 536 2103/women 536 2104). Bus 8, 24, 33, 45. **Open** 8.30am-4.30pm Mon-Wed, Fri; 8.30am-6.30pm Thur. *Walk-in clinic* (emergencies only) 9-10am daily; otherwise by appointment. **Map** p309 E7.
Free and confidential service that offers counselling for people who are HIV positive.

Helplines & information

Advice Shop

South Bridge, Old Town EH1 (225 1255). Nicolson Street–North Bridge buses. **Open** *Phone lines* 8.30am-4.40pm Mon-Thur; 8.30am-3.50pm Fri. *Drop-in service* 9.30am-4pm Mon-Thur; 9.30am-3pm Fri.
Advice on consumer problems and welfare benefits.

Alcoholics Anonymous

(225 2727). **Open** 24hrs daily.
Confidential, round-the-clock help and advice on drinks problems.

Childline

0800 1111. **Open** 24hrs daily.
Free and confidential national helpline for children and young people in trouble or danger.

Citizens Advice Bureau

Dundas St, New Town, EH3 (557 1500/fax 557 3543/www.cas.org.uk/ www.advicegide.org.uk). Bus 23, 27. **Open** 9.30am-4.30pm Mon, Tue, Thur; 9.30am-12.30 Wed. **Map** p306 E3.
Citizens Advice Bureaux are independent, offering free advice on legal, financial and personal matters. The only city-centre branch is at the above address. Check the phone book for other branches. The Citizens Advice Scotland website has contact details for all bureaux in Scotland.

Drinkline

(0800 917 8282). **Open** 9am-11pm Mon-Fri; 6-11pm Sat, Sun.
For help with drink problems.

Edinburgh Rape & Sexual Abuse Centre

(556 9437). **Open** 5.30-7.30pm Mon; 5-7pm Tue; 6.30-8.30pm Fri.

Free, confidential rape counselling. If you phone out of hours, leave a message and someone will call you back as soon as possible.

Edinburgh Women's Aid

97-101 Morrison Street, West Edinburgh, EH3 (229 1419). Bus 2, 28. **Open** *Walk-in* 10am-3pm Mon, Wed, Fri; 2-7pm Thur; 10am-12.30pm Sat. *Phone enquiries* as office opening.
Refuge referral for women and children experiencing domestic violence. An after-hours answerphone gives numbers for immediate help.

Gamblers Anonymous

(020 7384 3040).
Open 9am-8pm daily.
Advice is offered by members of the fellowship. Referrals to meetings.

National AIDS Helpline

(0800 567123). **Open** 24hrs daily.
A free and confidential information service on AIDS and sexual health.

NHS Helpline

(0800 224488).
Open 8am-10pm daily.
A free telephone information service giving details about local NHS services, waiting times, common diseases and conditions.

The Rights Office

Southside Community Centre, Nicolson Street, South Edinburgh, EH8 (667 6339). Nicolson Street– North Bridge buses. **Open** 10am-3.30pm Mon, Wed. **Map** p310 G6.
Walk-in centre giving free, confidential advice and advocacy.

The Samaritans

(08457 909090/221 9999).
Open 24hrs daily.
The Samaritans will listen to anyone with an emotional problem.

Victim Support

(Edinburgh helpline 0845 603 9213/ national helpline 0845 303 0900/ www.victimsupport.demon.co.uk). **Open** *Edinburgh helpline* 9am-4.30pm Mon-Fri. *National helpline* 9am-3pm Mon-Fri; 9am-7pm Sat, Sun. **Map** p310 G6.
Victims of crime are put in touch with a volunteer who provides emotional and practical support, including information on legal procedures and advice on compensation. Interpreters can be arranged.

ID

ID is not widely used in the UK as a whole or in Edinburgh in particular. You will need your

passport for changing money, travellers' cheques and so on. If you're driving, carry your International Driving Licence in case you're stopped; if you're stopped and don't have it you'll need to produce it at a police station within seven days.

Insurance

You should arrange insurance to cover personal belongings before travelling to Edinburgh, as it is difficult to organise once you have arrived.

Non-UK citizens should ensure that medical insurance is included in their travel insurance. If your country has a reciprocal medical treatment arrangement with the UK you will have limited cover, but you should make sure you have the necessary documentation before you arrive. If you cannot access the information in your own country, contact the Primary Care Department in Edinburgh *(see p279).*

Internet

It's very easy to find internet access in Edinburgh. Some libraries have internet access and more is planned, but the coverage is still patchy. There are also plenty of internet cafés such as **Web13**, *see below*.

Your existing ISP may have a POP (point of presence) that will let you connect to the internet at local rates. If all you want is to access your email while in Edinburgh, you can set up the POP mail feature of Microsoft's free Hotmail (www.hotmail.com) service.

Internet access

Web13

13 Bread Street, South Edinburgh, EH3. (229 8883/www.web13.co.uk). Bus 2, 28, 35. **Open** 10am-8pm Mon; 10am-10pm Tue-Sat; noon-6pm Sun. **Map** p309 D6.
Friendly café with knowledgeable staff offering good coffee and snacks and reasonable internet access.

Directory

Left luggage

Edinburgh Airport
(344 3486). **Open** 5am-11pm daily.
Located in the check in hall, opposite
parking zone E.

St Andrew Bus Station
Automatic left luggage lockers are
located on the south side of St
Andrews Square.

Waverley Train Station
(550 2711). **Open** 24 hrs daily.
Adjacent to Platform 11.

Legal help

If a legal problem arises,
contact your embassy,
consulate or high commission
(*see p278*). You can get advice
from a **Citizens Advice
Bureau** (*see p281*), the
Rights Office (*see p281*)
or one of the organisations
listed below. Ask about Legal
Aid eligibility. For leaflets
explaining how the system
works, write to the **Scottish
Legal Aid Board**. Advice on
problmes concerning visas and
immigration can be obtained
bfrom the **Immigration
Advisory Service**.

Edinburgh & Lothians
Race Equality Council
*14 Forth St, Broughton, EH1
(556 0441). Playhouse buses.*
Open *Office* 9.30am-1pm, 2-5pm
Mon-Fri. Phone for surgery times.
Map p307 G3.

Immigration Advisory
Service
*115 Bath St, Glasgow, G2 (0141 248
2956).* **Open** 10am-4pm Mon-Fri.
Map p304 C2.

Law Society
of Scotland
*26 Drumsheugh Gardens,
New Town, EH3 (226 7411/
www.lawscot.org.uk). Bus 13, 19,
29/29A, 37/37A, 41, 42.* **Open** 9am-
5pm Mon-Fri. **Map** p308 C5.

Scottish Legal Aid
Board
*44 Drumsheugh Gardens, New
Town, EH3 (226 7061). Bus 13,
19, 29/29A, 37/37A, 41, 42.*
Open *Office* 9am-5pm Mon-Fri.
Switchboard 8.30am-5pm Mon-Fri.
Map p308 C5.

Libraries

Central Library
*George IV Bridge, Old Town, EH1
(242 8000/www.edinburgh.gov.uk/
libraries). Bus 23, 27, 28, 42, 42, 45.*
Open 10am-8pm Mon-Thur; 10am-
5pm Fri, 9am-1pm Sat. **Map** p304 C3.
The library stocks a selection of
American and European publications
and also has a large reference section
(242 8060). You have to be a Lothian
resident to join the lending library
(242 8020). The Edinburgh Room
(242 8030) and the Scottish Room
(242 8070) are dedicated to local and
Scottish material; staff will show
users how to use the library to trace
their ancestors.

National Library of
Scotland
*George IV Bridge, Old Town, EH1
(226 4531/www.nls.uk). Bus 23, 28,
41, 42, 45.* **Open** 9.30am-8.30pm
Mon, Tue, Thur, Fri; 10am-8.30pm
Wed; 9.30am-1pm Sat. **Map** p304 C3.
The National Library of Scotland is
a deposit library, entitled to a copy of
all works published in the UK and
Ireland. It receives as many as
350,000 items annually, including
books, pamphlets, periodicals, maps
and music. The Reading Rooms are
open for reference and research;
admission is by ticket to approved
applicants. There's also a varied
programme of exhibitions on
Scottish subjects.

University of
Edinburgh Main Library
*George Square, South Edinburgh,
EH8 (650 3384; www.lib.ed.ac.uk).
Bus 41, 42.* **Open** *Term-time*
8.30am-10pm Mon-Thur; 9am-5pm
Fri, Sat; noon-5pm Sun. *Holiday time*
9am-5pm Mon, Tue, Thur, Fri; 9am-
9pm Wed. **Map** p310 G7.
With a valid matriculation card or
ISIC, international students who
aren't studying at the University may
use the library for reference purposes
only. Alternatively, full membership
is available at £30 for 3 months, £55
for 6 months or £110 for 12 months
for reference only, and £60/£100/
£160 for reference and borrowing.

Lost property

Always inform the police if
you lose anything (to validate
insurance claims). A lost
passport should also be
reported to your embassy/
consulate (*see p278*). The main
lost property offices for items
left on public transport are:

Edinburgh Airport
(344 3486). **Open** 5am-11pm daily.
The lost property office is located in
the check in hall. For items lost on
the plane, contact the airline or
handling agents.

Lothian Buses
*Lost Property Office, Annandale
Street EH7 (558 8858). Bus 7, 10,
11, 14, 22, 49.* **Open** 10am-1.30pm
Mon-Fri. **Map** p307 H2.
Charges are made for collection
of items.

Taxis
*Edinburgh Police Headquarters
Fettes Avenue, Stockbridge, EH4
(311 3141). Bus 19/19A, 28,
29/29A, 37/37A, 38.* **Open** 8am-
5pm Mon-Fri. **Map** p305 A3.
All property that has been left in a
registered black cab, as well as in
the street or in shops, gets sent here.

Trains
If items have been lost in railway
stations or trains in Scotland, contact
the individual station (see the phone
book for numbers).

Media

Most of Scotland's newspapers
– and much of its TV output –
operate on a quasi-national
basis pitched somewhere
between the regional media
and London's self-styled
'national' press.
   The attitudes and
arguments on display both
reflect and illuminate the
current state of that nebulous
beast known as Scottish
identity. From the time-
honoured east/west rivalry for
the title of Scotland's national
daily broadsheet – perpetuated
in the battle between the
Scotsman, published in
Edinburgh, and the Glasgow-
based *Herald* – to the thorny
question of the tabloid *Daily
Record*'s Rangers affiliations;
from Radio Scotland's Sony
award-winning output to the
famously surreal couthiness of
the *Sunday Post* letters page,
the cultural divergences that
impelled the long campaign for
devolution continue to pervade
the Scottish media.
   The battle rages on at the
BBC as to whether Scotland

should have its own separate six o'clock news slot. Where the actuality of devolution has had a more pronounced effect is in the virtual removal of what little Scottish coverage there was in the UK-based press. Scotland's media continues to fight its own battles and England continues to ignore them.

Newspapers

The Scotsman

www.scotsman.com
Edinburgh-based broadsheet. Has gone downmarket in recent years with film star stories and trashy features, and has abandoned its traditional devolutionary bias for a markedly opposing stance. The editorial line tends towards reactionary mid-market, while the arts and features tend to have an east-coast bias.

The Herald

www.theherald.co.uk
Glasgow-based broadsheet. Has the edge in terms of news coverage (though many argue the opposite, and the balance shifts back and forth). Any Glasgow bias in its arts and features coverage complements the *Scotsman*'s east coast orientation.

Daily Record

www.record-mail.co.uk
Glasgow-based tabloid. Scotland's best-selling daily is published by the Mirror Group. Lots of froth but some good campaigning journalism.

Evening News

www.edinburghnews.com
Edinburgh's evening daily tabloid. The latest headlines from around the world are combined with a strong local Edinburgh flavour. The Saturday Pink section carries all the sports results.

Evening Times

www.eveningtimes.co.uk
Glasgow's daily evening tabloid.

Scotland on Sunday

www.scotlandonsunday.com
The *Scotsman*'s sister publication is a bit more frothy, but has good analysis of Scottish issues.

The Sunday Herald

www.sundayherald.com
Sister paper to the *Herald*, the *Sunday Herald* combines good news reporting and analysis, and award-winning environmental coverage, with intelligent arts coverage.

Sunday Mail

www.record-mail.co.uk
Sunday sister to the *Daily Record*, with which it shares strong sports coverage and a campaigning instinct.

Sunday Post

This Dundee-published Sunday treat that was once a by-word for couthy tittle-tattle and reactionary opinion has become increasingly – and blandly – like the other Sunday tabloids. At least it's still the home of the Oor Wullie comic strip.

Sunday Times

London-based pioneer of the 'supermarket' approach to Sunday newspapers. Its ever-expanding multi-section format includes a reasonable Scottish supplement, Ecosse, comprising features, reviews and listings.

Magazines

Scotland's thriving literary scene is reflected in the disproportionate number of literary magazines per head of population. But there are also style and satirical magazines, and Scotland is even lucky enough to have its own version of *Hello!*.

Caledonia

A relative newcomer on the glossy scene, Caledonia's sales figures are hotly disputed but it's managing to hang on in there. Upmarket and slightly more weighty than the competition, *Caledonia*'s still trying to find its place in the market.

Cencrastus

Subtitled 'Scottish and International Literature, Arts and Affairs', this thrice-yearly publication has moved in a more satirical direction, and is not afraid to take the odd broadswipe at the Scottish Parliament.

Chapman

www.chapman-pub.co.uk
Established for more than a quarter of a century and currently appearing four times annually, *Chapman* is a highly regarded platform for new writing (fiction and poetry) as well as reviews and general debate on contemporary Scottish culture.

Edinburgh Review

By far the oldest of Edinburgh's literary magazines, founded in 1802, the *Review* now appears twice a year and features fiction, poetry, criticism and literary/cultural argument.

Hiya!

Unfortunately tales of its early demise were greatly exaggerated. Scotland's lightweight answer to *Hello* carries on regardless to blight another day.

Product

They seek it here, they seek it there... Product's distribution isn't up to much and neither's the pseudo-literary content. Dollops of lottery money have ensured its survival – just another reminder that money isn't everything.

Scots magazine

In continuous publication since before Culloden, this is a magazine with a real history. *Scots Magazine* sells more than 50,000 copies a month, and has pretensions to being a Scottish *Readers Digest*.

Scottish Book Collector

www.scotbooksmag.demon.co.uk
Covering Scottish books in their widest interpretation, the content of this quarterly magazine ranges from interviews with writers to new writing, reviews and various publishing matters.

Scottish Field

Scottish Field has been resurrected for the horsy rural ravers.

Listings

The List

Fortnightly listings magazine for Edinburgh and Glasgow (published on Thursdays). Visitors to either city will find that a copy will provide many a valuable shortcut when planning their time. It gives details of everything from mainstream cinema releases to readings by local writers and concerts of all sizes and genres. On the whole it's both reliable and comprehensive, though it's always worth phoning ahead to double-check before setting off to an event. It switches to weekly issues during the Festival, when its time-banded sections and extensive preview coverage offer a useful – though fallible – guide through the bewildering plethora of attractions on offer.

Scotsgay

www.scotsgay.co.uk
This Edinburgh-based magazine appears monthly and is distributed free in gay venues. It covers events related to the lesbian, gay and bisexual community, and also includes comprehensive entertainment listings.

Television

On the broadcasting front, both the BBC and ITV in Scotland opt in and out of the UK-wide output. BBC Scotland and the independent Scottish Television (STV) also contribute regularly to their respective networks. Since devolution, the ongoing debate has been as to whether or not BBC Scotland should have a 6 o'clock news slot of its own – with London saying that there's not enough Scottish news to fit the slot and Scotland disagreeing vehemently. The debate continues.

BBC Scotland's TV drama has been on something of a winning streak, with both one-off and serial dramas and comedies – Rab C Nesbitt being the best-known – while also venturing successfully into the film business with the critically acclaimed *Small Faces* and *Mrs Brown*. *Chewing the Fat*, a comedy sketch series, has achieved legendary status in Scotland – its catchphrases and gestures are a part of daily discourse. Catch it if you can – but don't expect to understand either its vernacular or its warmly cynical view of being Scottish. On the factual side, the BBC's arts documentary strand, *Ex-S*, has also picked up a good many plaudits.

STV, meanwhile, has its own soap, *High Road*, and Scottish cop drama, *Taggart* as well as a diverse range of homegrown special-interest programmes such as *Moviejuice* (arts) and *Scottish Passport* (holidays). An innovative project, New Found Land, is encouraging new Scottish writing and film making talents and producing drama for both the small and the large screen.

Both stations also broadcast much of their own, Scottish-centred sports coverage – especially in the football season.

Radio

BBC Radio Scotland
92.4-94.7 FM & 810 MW

Enjoying particularly widespread popularity and respect for its mix of talk- and music-based programming, Radio Scotland's news coverage offers an illuminating alternative to the reports from London, while its arts, documentary, sports and short-story strands are all worth listening to. The nightly rotation of music shows ranges from the *Brand New Opry*'s country selection, to folk and traditional-based sounds in *Celtic Connections* and *Travelling Folk*.

Beat FM
106.1FM/www.beat106.com

Scotland's new and liveliest addition to the music scene. Beat FM bills itself as Scotland's radio revolution and plays a wide-ranging selection of dance music, with well-respected club DJs taking over on Friday and Saturday nights.

Radio Forth
97.3 FM & 1548 MW

Edinburgh-based music-oriented commercial station, which wins awards for both its frequencies. FM and MW cater for the younger and more mature ends of the mainstream/chart audience respectively. Features local and Scottish acts and is a must for travel news.

Scot FM
101.1 FM

Country-wide, fairly downmarket approach to talk radio. Its early attempts to introduce Scotland to the shock-jock formula had mixed results, to say the least.

Money

Britain's currency is the pound sterling (£). One pound equals 100 pence (p). 1p and 2p coins are copper; 5p, 10p, 20p and 50p coins are silver; the £1 coin is yellowy-gold; the £2 coin is silver with a yellowy-gold surround. There are three Scottish clearing banks, all of which issue their own paper notes: the Bank of Scotland, the Royal Bank of Scotland and the Clydesdale Bank. The colour of paper notes varies slightly between the three, but an approximation is as follows: green £1 (Scotland only; England and Wales have done away with the £1 note); blue £5; brown £10; purple/pink £20; red or green £50; and, unique to Scotland, a bold red £100. You can exchange foreign currency at banks or bureaux de change.

It's a good idea to try to use up all your Scottish banknotes before leaving the country; the further south you go, the more wary people will be of accepting it, although it is legal tender.

While the euro is legal currency in the rest of Europe, in the UK the debate goes on. The euro is not used in the UK and is accepted in only a very small number of shops.

Banks

Banks have variable opening hours, depending on the day of the week. Minimum opening hours are 9am-4pm Mon-Fri, but some are open until 5.30pm. Cashpoint machines (ATMs), usually situated outside a bank or building society (most building societies also operate as banks), give access to cash 24 hours a day. Most will also allow you to draw money on a credit card. All you need is an ATM with a major national/international network –such as Cirrus or Plus – and your PIN number (check with your credit card company before leaving home).

Banks generally offer the best exchange rates, although they can vary considerably from place to place and it pays to shop around. Commission is sometimes charged for cashing travellers' cheques in foreign currencies, but not for sterling travellers' cheques provided you cash them at a bank affiliated to the issuing bank (get a list when you buy your cheques). Commission is charged if you change cash into another currency. You will always need identification, such as a passport, when cashing travellers' cheques.

There are branches of the three Scottish clearing banks and cash machines throughout the city. There are, however, few branches of the English clearing banks. These are situated at:

Barclays Bank

1 St Andrew Square, New Town, EH2 (0845 6000180). Princes Street buses. **Open** 9.30am-4.30pm Mon, Tue, Thur, Fri; 10am-4.30pm Wed;. **Map** p304 D1.

Lloyds TSB Bank

28 Hanover Street, New Town, EH2 (0845 3003398). Bus 28, 40, 41, 42/Princes Street buses. **Open** 9am-5pm Mon, Tue, Fri; 9.30am-5pm Wed; 9am-6pm Thur; 9am-12.30pm Sat.* **Map** p304 B1.

National Westminster Bank

8 George Street, New Town, EH2 (0845 609 0000). Bus 28, 37, 40, 41, 42/Princes Street buses. **Open** 9am-5pm Mon, Tue, Thur, Fri; 9.30am-5pm Wed. **Map** p304 B1.

Bureaux de change

You will be charged for cashing travellers' cheques or buying and selling foreign currency at a bureau de change. Commission rates, which should be clearly displayed, vary.

Banks, travel companies and the major rail stations have bureaux de change, and there are many in tourist areas. Most are open standard business hours (9am-5.30pm Mon-Fri), but one that is open longer is FEXCO Ltd, situated inside the tourist office for Edinburgh & the Lothians (*see p289*).

Lost/stolen credit cards

Report lost or stolen credit cards immediately to both the police and the 24-hour services listed below. Inform your bank by phone and in writing.
American Express
Personal card 01273 696933/ corporate card 01273 689955.

Diners Club/Diners Club International
General enquiries & emergencies 0800 46 0800.
MasterCard *0800 964767.*
Visa *0800 895082.*

Money transfers

The Information Centre above the Princes Mall (formerly Waverley Shopping Centre) can advise on Western Union money transfer. Or call Western Union direct on 0800 833833. Alternatively contact your own bank to find out which British banks it is affiliated with; you can then nominate an Edinburgh branch of that bank to have the money sent to.

Opening hours

In general, business hours are 9am-5pm. Most shops are open 9am-5pm Mon-Sat and 11am-5pm on Sun. On the whole banks open at 9am and close at 5pm on weekdays. Restaurants generally open for lunch from 11am-2pm and for dinner from 6-11pm. Many restaurants are open all day and some stay open well beyond 11pm. Officially closing time for pubs is 11pm but opening times vary considerably, and pubs in the city centre are often open later. It's no exaggeration to say you'll be able to find somewhere to drink at any time of the day or night. – should you have the stamina

Police stations

The police are a good source of information about the locality and are used to helping visitors find their way around. If you have been robbed, assaulted or the victim of any crime, look under 'Police' in the phone directory for the nearest police station, or call directory enquiries (free from public payphones) on 192. There is a **police information centre** at 188 High Street, EH1 (226

6966). In an emergency, and only in an emergency, dial 999.

If you have a complaint to make about the police, be sure to take the offending officer's ID number, which should be prominently displayed on his or her epaulette. You can then register a complaint at any police station, visit a solicitor or Citizens' Advice Bureau or contact the Complaints Department, Police Headquarters, Lothian and Borders Police, Fettes Avenue, Edinburgh, EH4 1RB (311 3377; Map p305 A3).

Postal services

The UK has a fairly reliable postal service. If you have a query on any aspect of Royal Mail services contact Customer Services on 08457 740740. For business enquiries contact the Royal Mail Business Centre for Scotland on 08457 950950. You can ask for a Royal Mail Fact File and any post office leaflets to be sent to you.

Un-deliverable mail can be collected in person from the sorting office in Brunswick Road (550 8232, map p307H3).

Post office opening hours are usually 9am-5.30pm Mon-Fri; 9am-12.30pm Sat, with the exception of the **St James Post Office**. Listed below are two other main central offices. Consult the phone book for other offices within Edinburgh:

Frederick Street Post Office

40 Frederick Street, New Town, EH2 (0845 722 3344). Bus 28, 37, 40, 41, 42/Princes Street buses. **Map** p304 B1.

Hope Street Post Office

7 Hope Street, New Town, EH2 , (226 6823). Bus 28, 37, 40, 41, 42/ Princes Street buses. Map p304 A1.

St James Post Office

8-10 Kings Mall, St James Centre, New Town, EH1. Princes Street buses. **Open** 9am-5.30pm Mon; 8.30am-5.30pm Tue-Fri; 8.30am-6pm Sat. **Map** p307 G4

Directory

Stamps

You can buy stamps at post offices and at any newsagents that display the appropriate red sign. Stamps can be bought individually (at post offices only) or, in the case of first class (for next-day delivery within mainland Britain) or second class (two- to three-day delivery in mainland Britain), in books of four or ten, at post offices, supermarkets and some shops. Prices are 19p for second-class letters (inland only) and 27p for first-class inland letters and letters weighing up to20g to EU countries (February 2002). Postcards cost 34p to send abroad. Rates for other letters and parcels vary according to weight and destination.

Poste restante

If you intend to travel around Britain, friends from home can write to you care of a post office, where mail will be kept at the enquiry desk for up to one month. The envelope should be marked 'Poste Restante' in the top left-hand corner, with your name displayed above the address of the post office where you want to collect your mail. Take ID when you collect your post. The Hope Street post office (*see above*) offers this service.

Public holidays

As Gore Vidal famously said, Edinburgh has bank holidays when no-one else does; it shares some holidays with the rest of the UK, others with the rest of Scotland and has others all of its own. Which means, of course, that it's difficult to predict what will be open on any given holiday.

On public holidays and bank holidays many shops remain open, but public transport services are less frequent. On Christmas Day and New Year's Day however, most things close down.

New Year's holiday
Wed 1 Jan 2003, Thur 2 Jan 2003; Thur 1 Jan 2004, Fri 2 Jan 2004.
Spring holiday
Mon 14 April 2003; Mon 19 April 2004.
Good Friday
Fri 18 Apr 2003; Fri 9 Apr 2004.
Easter Monday
Mon 21 Apr 2003; Mon 12 Apr 2004.
May Day
Mon 5 May 2003; Mon 3 May 2004
Victoria Day (Edinburgh only)
Mon 19 May 2003; Mon 17 May 2004.
There is an extra public holiday in 2002 for The **Queen's Golden Jubilee**
Mon 3 June 2002
August bank holiday
Mon 6 Aug 2002; Mon 4 Aug 2003.
Autumn Holiday
Mon 16 Sept 2002; Mon 15 Sept 2003
Christmas Day
Wed 25 Dec 2002; Thurs 25 December 2003
Boxing Day
Thur 26 Dec 2002; Fri 26 December 2003

Religion

Baptist

Charlotte Baptist Chapel *West Rose Street, New Town, EH2 (225 4812). Bus 28, 37, 40, 41, 42/Princes Street buses.* **Open** *Office* 9am-4pm Mon-Fri. *Services* 10am (prayer meeting), 11am, 5.45pm (prayer meeting), 6.30pm, Sun; 8pm (prayer meeting) Tue. **Map** p304 A1.

Buddhist

Edinburgh's Zen Buddhist community has a **priory** at Portobello (Brighton Place, Portobello, 669 9622/www.geocities. com/pbpriory/portobello.html) with daily meditation, a resident monk and lay followers. The **Edinburgh Buddhist Centre**, 10 Viewforth, Edinburgh 10 (228 3333, www. edinburghbuddhistcentre.org.uk) is run by the Friends of the Western Buddhist Order. Other Buddhist groups in Edinburgh have no central meeting place and tend to share space with other faiths or organisations. Phone 332 7987 for information.

Catholic

St Mary's Cathedral *61 York Place, Broughton, EH1 (556 1798). Playhouse buses.* **Open** 7am-6pm Mon-Fri, Sun; 7am-7pm Sat. **Services** 12.45pm Mon-Sat. *Vigil mass* 6pm Sat; 9.30am, 11.30am 7.30pm Sun. Confessions heard 12 noon Sat. **Map** p307 G4.

Church of Scotland

St Giles' Cathedral *High Street, EH1 (225 4363). Bus 23, 27, 28, 35, 41, 42, 45.* **Open** *Easter-Sept* 9am-7pm Mon-Fri, 9am-5pm Sat; 1-5pm Sun. *Sept-Easter* 9am-5pm Mon-Sat; 1-5pm Sun. **Services** 8am, noon Mon-Fri; noon, 6pm (Holy Communion) Sat; 8am (Holy Communion), 10am (Holy Communion), 11.30am, 8pm Sun. **Map** p304 D3.

Episcopalian

Cathedral Church of St Mary *Palmerston Place, New Town, EH12 (225 6293). Bus 3, 4, 12, 25, 31, 33.* **Open** 7.15am-6pm Mon-Sat; 7.30am-6pm Sun (till 9pm in summer). **Services** 7.30am (Eucharist), 1.05pm, 5.30pm (choral evensong) Mon, Tue, Wed, Fri; 7.30am (Eucharist), 11.30am (Eucharist), 1.05pm, 5.30pm (Eucharist), Thur; 7.30am Sat; 8am (Eucharist), 10.30am (choral Eucharist), 3.30pm (choral evensong) Sun. **Map** p308 B6.

Hindu

Edinburgh Hindu Mandir & Cultural Centre *St Andrew Place (former St Andrew's Church), Leith, EH6 (667 6064/440 0084). Bus 1, 25, 32/52, 16.* **Open**/services 12-2pm, 2nd & 4th Sun of the mth. **Map** p311 Jz.

Islamic

Mosque & Islamic Centre *50 Potterow, South Edinburgh, EH8 (667 1777). Bus 41, 42.* **Open** dawn-dusk daily. **Services** phone for details. **Map** p310 G6.

Jewish

Synagogue Chambers *4 Salisbury Road, South Edinburgh, EH16 (667 3144). Bus 3, 7, 8, 29/29A, 31.* **Open**/services phone for details. **Map** p310 J8.

Methodist

Nicolson Square Methodist Church *Nicolson Square, South Edinburgh, EH8 (662 0417). Nicolson Street-North Bridge buses.* **Open** *Basement chapel & café* 8.30am-3.30pm Mon-Fri. **Services** 11am, 6.30pm Sun. **Map** p310 G6.

Quaker

Quaker Meeting House *7 Victoria Terrace, Victoria Street, Old Town, EH1 (225 4825). Bus 23, 27, 28, 41, 42, 45.* **Open** 9am-10pm daily. **Services** 12.30pm Wed; 11am Sun. **Map** p304 C3.

Sikh

Sikh Temple *7 Mill Lane, Leith, EH6 (553 7207). Bus 1, 7, 10, 14, 32/52, 34.* **Open** phone in advance. **Services** 11.30am, 3pm Sun. **Map** p311 Hy.

Safety & security

Violent crime is relatively rare on the streets of Edinburgh, but, as in any major city, it is unwise to take any risks. Thieves and pickpockets specifically target unwary tourists. Use common sense and follow these basic rules:
● Keep your wallet and purse out of sight. Don't wear a wrist wallet (they are easily snatched). Keep your handbag securely closed.
● Don't leave a handbag, briefcase, bag or coat unattended, especially in pubs, cinemas, department stores or fast food shops, on public transport, at railway stations and airports, or in crowds.
● Don't leave your bag or coat beside, under or on the back of your chair.
● Don't wear expensive jewellery or watches that can be easily snatched.
● Don't put your purse down on the table in a restaurant or on a shop counter while you scrutinise the bill.
● Don't carry a wallet in your back pocket.
● Don't flash your money or credit cards around.
● Avoid parks after dark. Late at night, try to travel in groups of three or more.

Despite the still-popular stereotype of the red-blooded Scottish male, and that of the country's macho drinking culture, Edinburgh (central-ish Edinburgh at least) is a pretty safe and civilised place. There's generally a reasonable safety-in-numbers feel on the streets throughout Edinburgh's main drag and its immediate hinterland, even into the wee small hours (the lively entertainment scene of central Edinburgh means the streets are rarely deserted).

The main areas best avoided on you own at night are the Cowgate (mad and quite threatening when the clubs and pubs spill out across the streets) and Lothian Road (a preponderance of decidedly laddish pubs and a history of violence at chucking-out time). For women in particular, the dockside and back street areas of Leith, particularly Coburg Street, one of Edinburgh's

main red-light districts – and the Meadows – are best avoided. The latter's paths look safe and brightly lit, but prove deceptively long and tree-screened once you actually set off down them; it has been the scene of several assaults. The Royal Mile, too, perhaps more unexpectedly, has seen its share of such incidents, mainly because of the cover provided by the innumerable narrow alleys, or wynds, leading off it: it's highly picturesque by day, but it can seem spookily dark and shadowy at night.

Further afield, if you go to one of the city's big peripheral housing schemes, take local advice, and get your directions firmly sorted. The geographical layout of these areas is frequently bewildering, to say the least, and the levels of social deprivation to be found in some of them present a starkly different face of Edinburgh to the economic and architectural wealth of the centre.

Smoking

Scotland is the last bastion of smoking with the highest rates for heart disease and lung cancer in Europe to show for it. Many Scots still smoke and smoking is permissible in more public places than in the rest of the UK and far more than in the US. However, it is not allowed in cinemas or theatres and many restaurants are now banning the evil weed.

Study

While it is now home to four universities (Edinburgh, Heriot Watt, Napier and Queen Margaret), somehow the University of Edinburgh is the university in Edinburgh. Founded in 1583, it is renowned worldwide and has an unbeatable reputation for medicine and scientific

research; its degrees carry hefty academic kudos. There are eight faculties, with departments scattered across town, and the Old College boasts some stunning architecture. With this impressive historical baggage, Edinburgh University also has an – arguably justifiable – reputation for having a disproportionate number of yahs (snobs of predominantly southern English origin) among the student body.

Edinburgh is also home to a number of newer colleges and former polytechnics.

Universities/colleges

Edinburgh College of Art
Lauriston Place, South Edinburgh, EH3. Bus 23, 27, 28, 45. (221 6000/www.eca.ac.uk). **Map** p309 E6. One of the most prestigious art colleges in the UK: competition for places here is stiff. Studies on offer range from film to textiles and sculpture. Plans to merge with Heriot Watt University are currently on hold but still a possibility.

Heriot-Watt University
Riccarton Campus, Currie, EH14 (449 5111/www.hw.ac.uk). Bus 25, 34, 35, 45. A vocational university specialising in business, finance, languages, science and engineering subjects.

Napier University
Craiglockhart Campus, 219 Colinton Road, South Edinburgh, EH14 (444 2266/www.napier@ac.uk). Bus 18, 23. Founded in 1964 and named after mathematical whizz-kid John Napier, this former polytechnic with a reputation for a more eclectic (and down-to-earth) student body than Edinburgh University was granted university status in 1992. Offering predominantly vocational courses, its employment record for graduates is second to none.

Queen Margaret University Campus
Clerwood Terrace, West Edinburgh, EH12 (317 3000/www.qmuc.ac.uk). Bus 26. An assortment of predominantly degree courses – you can study everything from nursing, nutrition and tourism to management, business and drama

Directory

University of Edinburgh

Old College, South Bridge, South Edinburgh, EH8 (650 1000/ www.ed.ac.uk). Nicolson Street–North Bridge buses. **Map** p310 G6. One of the UK's oldest and most reputable universities offers a staggering range of academic degree courses. There's also a good selection of part-time extramural courses run during the day and in the evening. Its international office is at 57 George Square EH8 (650 4300).

Language courses

A full list of the vast number of schools offering English language courses can be found in the Yellow Pages. The following is a small selection of some of the best and most well known establishments. Some also offer TEFL courses; phone for rates.

Berlitz

26 Frederick Street, New Town, EH2 (226 7198/www.languagecentres. com). Bus 28, 37, 40, 41, 42/Princes Street buses. **Map** p304 B1.

Edinburgh Language Centre

10B Oxford Terrace, New Town, EH4 (tel/fax 343 6596/www.elc. mcmail.com). Bus 19, 29/29A, 36, 37/37A. **Map** p305 B4.

Institute for Applied Language Studies

21 Hill Place, South Edinburgh, EH8 (650 6200/www.ials.ed.ac.uk). Bus 7, 8, 14, 29/29A, 37/37A. **Map** p310 G6.

Regent Edinburgh

29 Chester Street, New Town, EH3 (225 9888/www.regent.org.uk). Bus 13. **Map** p308 B5.

Stevenson College

Sighthill Campus, Bankhead Avenue, Sighthill, EH11 (535 4600/www. stevenson.ac.uk). Bus 3, 20, 25, 34.

Student travel

Edinburgh Travel Centre

92 South Clerk Street, South Edinburgh, EH8 (667 9488). Nicolson Street–North Bridge buses. **Open** 9am-5.30pm Mon-Fri; 10am-1pm Sat. **Map** p310 H8. **Branch:** 3 Bristo Square, South Edinburgh, EH8 (668 2221).

The telephone code for Edinburgh is 0131. If you're calling from outside the UK, dial the international code, followed by 44 (code for Britain), then the ten-digit number starting with 131 (omitting the first 0). The code for Glasgow and its environs is 0141.

International dialling codes

Australia 00 61; **Belgium** 00 32; **Canada** 00 1; **France** 00 33; **Germany** 00 49; **Ireland** 00 353; **Italy** 00 39; **Japan** 00 81; **Netherlands** 00 31; **New Zealand** 00 64; **Spain** 00 34; **USA** 00 1.

Mobile phones

Mobile phones in the UK work on either the 900 or 1800 GSM system used throughout much of Europe. If you're travelling to the UK from Europe, check whether your service provider has a reciprocal arrangement with a UK-based provider.

The situation is more complex for US travellers. If your service provider uses the GSM system, it will probably run on the 1900 band; this means you will need a tri-band phone, and your provider must have a reciprocal arrangement with a UK provider.

The simplest option may be to buy a 'pay as you go' phone (about £40-£200). There's no monthly fee and calls are charged not by billing buy by buying (widely available) cards that slot into your phone in denominations of £10 and up. Check first that the phone is capable of making and receiving international calls.

Public phones

Public payphones take coins, credit cards or prepaid phonecards (and sometimes all three). The minimum cost is 20p. British Telecom phonecards are available from post offices and many newsagents in denominations of £2, £5, £10 and £20.

Call boxes with the green Phonecard symbol take prepaid cards. A notice in the box tells you where to find the nearest stockist. A digital display shows how many units you have remaining on your card. A number of telephone centres offering cheap international calls has sprung up around town.

International Telecom Centre

52 High Street, Edinburgh, EH1 (tel/fax 558 7114/www.btinternet. com). Bus 8, 34. **Open** 9am-10pm daily. **Map** p304 D3. Offers cheap national and international calls, internet access, email and fax facilities.

Operator services

Call 100 for the operator in the following circumstances: when you have difficulty in dialling; for an early-morning alarm call; to make a credit card call; for information about the cost of a call; and for international person-to-person calls. Dial 155 if you need to reverse the charges (call collect) or if you can't dial direct. Be warned, though – this service is very expensive.

Directory enquiries

Dial 192 for any number in Britain, or 153 for international numbers. Bear in mind that phoning directory enquiries is expensive, and only two enquiries are allowed per call.

Telephone directories

There is one alphabetical phone directory for Edinburgh; it lists business and commercial numbers in the first section followed by private phone numbers and is available at post offices and libraries.

Hotels will also have a copy. The Yellow Pages directory lists businesses and services.

Telemessages & telegrams

Call 0800 190190 to phone in your message and it will be delivered by post the next day (£8.99 for up to 50 words, an additional £1 for a greetings card). There is no longer a domestic telegram service, but you can still send telegrams abroad. Call the same number.

Time

Edinburgh operates on Greenwich Mean Time. Clocks go forward for British Summer Time on the last Saturday in March and back to rejoin GMT on the last Saturday in October.

Tipping

In Britain it is accepted that you tip in taxis, minicabs, restaurants (some waiting staff are forced to rely heavily on gratuities), hairdressers', hotels and some bars (not pubs) – ten per cent is normal. Be careful to check whether service has been added automatically to your bill – some restaurants include service and then also leave the space open for a gratuity on your credit card slip.

Toilets

It's not generally acceptable to use the toilets of cafés or bars unless you're a customer or have a small and rather desperate child. However, there are a good number of public toilets and the major department stores all have toilets. Below are some of the city's public toilets.
Hunters Square *By the Tron, Old Town, EH1.* **Open** 10am-10pm daily. **Map** p304 D3.
The Mound *Princes Street, New Town, EH2.* **Open** 10am-10pm daily. Disabled access 24hrs using National Key Scheme. **Map** p304 C2.

Princes Mall *Waverley Bridge, New Town, EH1.* **Open** 10am-6pm daily. **Map** p304 D2.
West Princes St Gardens *Princes St, New Town, EH2.* **Open** 10am-10pm daily. Disabled access from Princes Street Gardens only. **Map** p304 B2.

Tourist information

Scottish Tourist Board

19 Cockspur Street (just off Trafalgar Square), London SW1 (www.visit scotland.com). **Open** *May-Sept* 9am-6pm Mon-Fri; 10am-5pm Sat (mid June to mid Sept). *Oct-Apr* 9.30am-5.30pm Mon-Fri; noon-4pm Sat.
The Edinburgh & Lothians Tourist Board operates the information centres listed below. There is also a 24hr electronic information unit at the Edinburgh and Scotland Information Centre. The tourist board website at www.edinburgh.org has further information. For more useful websites, *see p291.*

Edinburgh & Lothians Tourist Board

Above Princes Mall, 3 Princes Street New Town, EH1 (473 3800). Princes Street buses. **Open** *Nov-Mar* 9am-5pm Mon-Wed; 9am-6pm Thur-Sat, 10am-5pm Sun. *April* 9am-6pm Mon-Sat; 10am-6pm Sun; *May, June, Sept* 9am-7pm Mon-Sat; 10am-7pm Sun. *July, Aug* 9am-8pm, Sun 10am-8pm. **Map** p304 D2.

Edinburgh Airport Tourist Information Desk

Edinburgh Airport, EH12 (473 3800). **Open** *Apr-Oct* 6.30am-10pm daily. *Nov-Mar* 7.30am-9.30pm daily.

Visas & immigration

Citizens of EU countries do not require a visa to visit the UK; citizens of other countries, including the USA, Canada and New Zealand, require only a valid passport for a visit of up to six months.

To apply for a visa, and to check your visa status before you travel, you should contact the British Embassy, High Commission or Consulate in your own country. A visa allows you entry to Britain

for a maximum period of six months. For information about work permits, *see p290.*

Home Office

Immigration & Nationality Department, Block C, Whitgraft Centre, Croydon CR9 1AT (08706 067766/www.homeoffice.gov.uk/rnd/hpg.htm). **Open** *Phone enquiries* 9am-4.45pm Mon-Wed; 10am-4.45pm Thur; 9am-4.30pm Fri.
The Home Office deals with all queries about immigration matters, visas and work permits for citizens from the Commonwealth and a few other countries.

Weights & measures

As part of Europe, Scotland uses kilos and metres – but only nominally. Most goods are also weighed in pounds (lb) and measured in feet and inches.

When to go

There's not really a best time to visit Edinburgh. That depends on what you want – if it's festivals then take your pick; if it's weather don't bank on it.

Christmas and Hogmanay (that's New Year to you) have their own festivals, the International Science Festival is held in April and the city explodes into life in August with the various arts festivals. For more on festivals, *see chapter* **By Season**.

Weatherwise Edinburgh is difficult to call. Average January temperatures range between 0° and 6° centigrade. July is the warmest month, with a 10°-19° centigrade average range. Winter days can be cold and wet but are equally lightly to be sunny and crystal clear. There's no guarantee of good weather at any time, but between the months of May and October – when the days get longer and you can finally get your thermals off – Edinburgh's a great place to be.

In summer the streets throng with tourists and it can be difficult to find an inch of pavement. Unless you're coming to visit the Festival, then autumn and spring may be better times to visit.

Women

Women travelling on their own face the usual hassles, but generally Edinburgh is a safe city to visit on your own. Take the usual precautions you'd take in any big city. See p287 **Safety & security** for where best to avoid and you should be fine.

The bigger chain hotels, of which Edinburgh boasts several, tend to be well geared to the needs of lone female guests, while many of the abundant B&Bs and guest-houses offer single rooms along with the kind of welcome that has made Scottish hospitality famous.

For a relaxed solo meal, though, cafés can often be a better (and cheaper) bet for women than restaurants, with several good city-centre ones opening late into the evening. Many of Edinburgh's bars tend to retain their macho culture, and unless you fancy hearing the latest in dreadful pick-up lines may be best avoided.

Many of the city's (black) taxi firms have now signed up to a policy of giving priority to lone women, whether they're phoning up or flagging down. Bear in mind, though, that taxis are often like gold dust between midnight and 3am at weekends; book in advance or be prepared to wait or walk.

Working in Edinburgh

Finding a summer job in Edinburgh, or temporary employment if you are on a working holiday, can be a long, drawn-out process. If you can speak English and at least one other language well, and are an EU citizen or have a work permit, you should probably be able to find something in either catering, bar/restaurant or shop work.

Graduates with an English or a foreign-language degree could try teaching. Other ideas can be found in *Summer Jobs in Britain*, published by Vacation Work, 9 Park End Street, Oxford (£8.99 plus £1.50 p&p). The Central Bureau for Educational Visits & Exchanges (3-4 Bruntsfield Crescent, EH10, 447 8024/ www.britishcouncil.org) has other publications.

To find work, look in the *Scotsman*, local and national papers, and newsagents' windows. Or write to, phone or visit employers. There is often temporary and unskilled work available; look in the Yellow Pages under 'Employment Agencies'. Increasingly bars and restaurants are advertising casual work with signs in their windows – be warned though, this is sometimes an attempt to get away with not paying the minimum wage.

For office work, sign on with temp agencies. If you have shorthand, typing or wordprocessing skills, such agencies may be able to find you well-paid assignments.

Work for foreign visitors

With few exceptions, citizens of non-European Economic Area (EEA) countries need a work permit before they are legally able to work in the UK. One of the advantages of working here is the opportunity to meet people, but for any employment it is essential that you speak reasonable English. For office work you need a high standard of English and relevant skills.

Work permits

EEA citizens, residents of Gibraltar and certain categories of other overseas nationals do not require a work permit. However, others who wish to come to the UK to work must obtain a permit before setting out.

Prospective employers must apply for a permit to Customer Relations, Work Permits (UK), Immigration and Nationality Directorate, Home Office, Level 5, Moorfoot, Sheffield, S1 4PQ (0114 259 4074/www. workpermits.gov.uk).Permits are only issued for jobs that require a high level of skill and experience. The employer must be able to demonstrate that there is no resident/EEA labour available.

There is a Training & Work Experience Scheme that enables non-EEA nationals to come to the UK to undertake training for a professional or specialist qualification, or to undertake a short period of managerial level work experience. Again, this should be applied for before leaving for the UK.

Voluntary work

Voluntary work in youth hostels provides board, lodging and some pocket money. For advice on voluntary work with charities contact the Home Office (see p289).

Working holidaymakers

Citizens of Commonwealth countries, aged 17-27, may apply to come to the UK as a working holidaymaker. This allows them to take part-time work without a work permit. They must contact their nearest British Diplomatic Post to obtain the necessary entry clearance before travelling to the UK.

Further Reference

Books

Fiction

Banks, Iain *Complicity*
A visceral, body-littered thriller, with spot-on characterisation of both city and protagonists.

Butlin, Ron *Night Visits*
'Edinburgh at its grandest, coldest and hardest... as if nothing less than such a stony grip and iron inflexibility were needed to prevent unimaginable pain,' as the TLS put it.

Hird, Laura *Born Free*
Family life on a modern Edinburgh housing estate. So well observed and humorous, it hurts.

Hogg James *Confessions of a Justified Sinner*
An ironic jibe against religious bigotry in the 17th and 18th centuries set in the turmoil of Edinburgh at that time.

Johnston, Paul *Body Politic, The Bone Yard, Water of Death*
Future detective fiction set in a nightmare vision of Edinburgh as a city state with a year-round Festival, where the impoverished populace lives to serve the needs of the tourists.

Rankin, Ian *Inspector Rebus novels*
Quality genre detective fiction, Hardbitten Detective Rebus inhabits a city that is the reality for most of its inhabitants. The earlier novels are best for gritty reality and a strong sense of place.

Scott, Walter
The Heart of Midlothian
Contains, among other things, an account of the Porteous lynching of 1736.

Stevenson, Robert Louis
Edinburgh Picturesque notes
Perceptive, witty and the source of many subsequent opinions about Edinburgh.

Spark, Muriel *The Prime of Miss Jean Brodie*
Practically the official Edinburgh novel. Schoolteacher Jean Brodie makes a stand against the city's moral intransigence.

Welsh, Irvine *Trainspotting*
The first and best of Welsh's novels focuses on the culture of drugs, clubs and unemployment that more genteel Edinburgh residents do their best to ignore.

Non fiction

Bruce, George *Festival of the North*
Story of the Edinburgh International Festival, from its conception and its birth in 1947 until 1975.

Daitches, David *Edinburgh*
A highly readable and academically sound history.

Lamond & Tucek *The Malt Whisky File*
All the distilleries and nearly every malt that's sold is reviewed, with useful tasting notes.

Prebble, John *The King's Jaunt*
Everything you could want to know (and more) about George IV's agenda-setting visit of 1822.

Youngson, AJ *The Making of Classical Edinburgh*
An exhaustive account, with superb photos and plans, of the building of the New Town.

Films

Chariots of Fire
David Puttnam (1981)
Based on the true story of the 1924 Olympics where Edinburgh sportsman Eric Liddell ran for Britain, David Puttnam's film has spectacular shots of Salisbury Crags.

The Prime of Miss Jean Brodie
Ronald Neame (1969)
Oscar-winning Maggie Smith will be forever Edinburgh's best-known schoolmarm – in her prime, of course.

Shallow Grave
Danny Boyle (1994)
Darkly humorous feature about three Edinburgh yuppies who find themselves landed with a suitcase full of drug money and a dead body.

The 39 Steps
Alfred Hitchcock (1935)
Hitchcock's loose adaptation of John Buchan's novel introduced what would become one of his enduring themes: the innocent man framed by circumstantial evidence. Shots of Edinburgh are scarce but evocative.

Trainspotting
Danny Boyle (1996)
Pitch-black comedy in this portrayal of Edinburgh's heroin culture, based on Irvine Welsh's novel.

Websites

Scotland & Edinburgh

For newspaper websites, *see p283*.
http://scotch.com
The ultimate whisky lover's guide: beautifully illustrated musings on all aspects and varieties of the noble drink.
www.edinburgh.org
The Edinburgh Tourist Board's site is long on looks but short on solid info; its search facilities are unreliable.

www.edinburgh.gov.uk
Edinburgh Council's site has useful up-to-date info and maps. The links can tell you just about anything you want to know about Edinburgh.
www.historic-scotland.gov.uk
Home pages for the government body in charge of Scotland's historic monuments. There are strong databases on listed buildings, tourist attractions, literature and events.
www.nts.org.uk
The National Trust for Scotland's site provides the opening times, prices and details of all its properties.
www.visitscotland.net
Scottish Tourist Board site, with information on accommodation, restaurants, arts, events, nightlife. Online booking and useful links.

Entertainment

http://theoracle.co.uk/index.cfm
This really is the works, not particularly designer-web, but it delivers the goods – 400 restaurant listings and the most up-to-date and extensive set of listings for Edinburgh to be found on the net.
www.eae.co.uk
A 'virtual leaflet rack', with details of forthcoming arts and entertainment fixtures. Coverage is patchy: there are no cinema listings.
www.edinburgh-galleries.co.uk
This site will tell you what's on at the main Edinburgh galleries ,and take you on a virtual tour round one or two.
www.electrum.co.uk/pubs
A virtual jaunt through Edinburgh's watering holes in the company of a wasted youth, a history geek or an architecture appreciator.
www.go-edinburgh.co.uk
Full details of all Edinburgh's nine annual festivals. Links to the Fringe and Festival programmes online.

Politics & business

www.gro.gov.uk
General Register House has information on how to trace your Scottish ancestors online.
www.scotland.gov.uk
The Scottish Executive website.
www.scottish.parliament.uk
The Scottish Parliament's website is a user-friendly guide to tell you all about itself.
www.scotweb.co.uk
Primarily an online sales forum, but there's a lot more interesting stuff, too: read *Piping World* or browse Whisky Web or the Scotweb history site.

Index

Index

National Covenant *see*
Covenanters, the
National Gallery of Scotland
84
National Library of Scotland
67, **282**
National Monument 28, 98
National Museum of Flight
254, **255**
national parks & nature
reserves
Aberlady Wildlife
Sanctuary 253
Bawsinch Nature Reserve
103
Dalkeith Country Park 258
John Muir Country Park 254
Roslin Glen Country Park
258
St Abb's Head 267
Tyninghamme Links 254
National Trust for Scotland
88, **89**
Nelson Monument **99**
Netherbow Arts Centre 227
Nether Hill 103
New Calton graveyard 98
New College *see* Assembly
Hall & New College
Newhaven 116
see also Leith & Newhaven
areas
newspapers & magazines 283
buying 179
New Surgeon's Hall 78
New Town 16-17, 28-29, 56,
82-90
accommodation 41-48
cafés 139-141
with children 192
pubs & bars 151-154
restaurants 124-128
New Year's Eve (Hogmanay)
190
Nicolson Square 105
Niddry Street 72
nightlife **215-219**
during Festival 189
gay & lesbian clubs 206-207
Glasgow 250
late-night grocers 173
night buses 273
North Berwick 254, 257, 258
North Bridge 28, 61, 70
North Leith 115-116
Noyce, Dora 94

O

Oban 270
Ocean Terminal 161
office hire 276
Old Calton Burying Ground 96
Old College 79
Old Town 9, 27-30, **59-81**
accommodation 37-41
cafés 137-139
with children 191-192
Information Centre 71
pubs & bars 147-151
restaurants 120-124
opening hours 285
opera 210
opticians 179, 280
orientation 56
Our Dynamic Earth 74, **75**, 100

P

Palace of Holyroodhouse *9*,
10, 57, 74, **75**, *79*
parks & gardens, top ten 195
Dunbar's Close Garden 73
Holyrood Park 101, 103
Meadows, the 106
Princes Street Gardens
82, 83
Queen Street Gardens 89
Royal Botanic Garden *see*
Royal Botanic Garden
see also national parks &
nature reserves
Parliament, Scottish *see*
devolution & Scottish
Parliament
Parliament House 27, 68
Parliament Square 68
Peebles 266, 268, 269
Pentland Hills 258
People's Story, the 76
Perth race course 222
pharmacies & chemists 175,
279
photography museums &
galleries
Museum of Scotland 96
Scottish National Portrait
Gallery 87
Stills Gallery 72
processing 179
Picardy Place 99
Picts, the 253, 254
Piper's Walk 103
Pittenweem 263
Playfair, William 28, 29, 84,
88, 95, 98, 267
graveyard & tomb 94
Playfair Library 79
Playfair Project 83, 84
poetry
performance poetry 219
Poetry Library, Scottish
31, **76**
see also literature &
Edinburgh *and specific
poets*
police stations 285
Police Information Centre
(museum) 69-70
politics, modern 23-25
Port Edgar Marina & Sailing
School 194
Porteous Riots 17, 81
post offices & postal services
285-286
Pride Scotland festival 185
*Prime of Miss Jean Brodie,
the* see Spark, Muriel
Princes Street **82-86**
shopping 159, 161, 180
public transport **272-273**
for trips out of town 230
pubs & bars **146-158**
children-friendly 196
gay & lesbian 204-205
Glasgow 241-243
literary pub tours 74, **77**
pre-club bars 215
pub etiquette 151
real ale specialists 152
top five style bars 147
whisky specialists 148
Pugin, Augustus 29, 63, 65

Q

Queen Margaret University
Campus 287
Queensberry House 27
Queen's Drive 101, 103
Queen's Hall **209**, **214**
Queen Street 89
de Quincey, Thomas 94, 101
graveyard 83

R

Radical Book Fair 185
Radical Road 100
radio 284
Raeburn, Sir Henry 87, 93-94,
101
Raeburn Estate **93-94**
Raeburn Place 91
railways *see* trains & rail travel
Ramsay, Allan
house 61
statue of 84
Ramsay Gardens 61
Rangers Lodge, Holyrood
Park 103
Rankin, Ian 33, 106
Ratho 259, 261
Reformation, the 11-12, 73
Regent Bridge 96
Regent Gardens 98
Regent Road **97**
Regent Terrace 98
Register House *see* General
Register House
Reid Concert Hall *208*, **209**
religion, practising, diverse
286
see also churches
restaurants **119-135**
American 120, 128, 129
best for… 120
cafés **137-145**; *see also*
cafés
Caribbean 132
children-friendly 196
Chinese 129, 133
fish 120, 129, 134
fish suppers 124
French 120-121, 124, 134-135
global 121, 129-131
Indian 121, 131, 133, 135
Italian 125, 133, 135
Japanese 125, 131, 133
Mexican 121, 129, 135
modern British 121-123,
125-127, 132, 134, 135
out of town restaurants
around Edinburgh
253-270
Glasgow 241-243
Scottish 120, 123, 127-128
Spanish 123, 128, 129
Thai 128, 132
vegetarian 123-124, 128, 132
*see also p297 restaurants
index*
'resurrectionists' **18-19**, 102
Richard III of England 10
Riddles Close 67
Robert the Bruce 8, 258, 262,
266
Robert II 9
Robert Burns & Memorial *see*
Burns, Robert

Roberts, David 92
Robertson, James 33
rock climbing 224
precautions 230
tour companies 222
Rock House 96
Roman Edinburgh &
Scotland 7, 110, 260
Roslin & country park 256,
258
Rosslyn Chapel **256**, *257*, 258
Rowling, JK & Harry Potter
books 34, 94
Royal Bank of Scotland
headquarters 86
Royal Botanic Garden 91, 92,
93, *94*
Royal College of Physicians
89
Royal Fine Art Commission
76
Royal High School 28-29
Scottish Parliament vigil 97
Royal Lyceum 227
Royal Mile 8, 27, **61-77**
map 64-65
shopping 179
walking tours 74-77
Royal Museum 79, 80
Royal Observatory 107
Royal Scottish Academy 84,
85
Royal Scottish National
Orchestra 208
Royal Terrace 98
Royal Yacht Britannia 116
rugby union 20, **222**
Russell Collection of Early
Keyboard Instruments 80

S

safety & security 287
sailing, school 194
St Abb's 267
St Andrew Square **86-87**
St Andrews 264-265, 266
golf course 224
St Andrew's church 87
St Andrew's House 29, 97
St Anthony's Chapel 101
St Bernard's Crescent *92*, 94
St Bernard's Well 92
St Cuthbert's church **83**
St Giles' Cathedral 209
St James Centre 163
St John's Episcopal church 83,
84
St Leonards' 106
St Margaret's Chapel 64
St Margaret's Loch & Well
101
St Mary's Episcopal
Cathedral **90**, 210
St Patrick's church 77
St Stephen Street 91
St Trinian's 106
Salisbury Crags 101, *102*, 103
Samhain 188
Saughton Park & Prison 109
saunas, gay 207
Saunders Street 92
Saxe-Coburg Place 92
Science Festival 184
Scotch Whisky Heritage
Centre 65

Advertisers' Index

Pleas refer to the relevant pages for addresses
and telephone numbers

Place of interest and/or entertainment	▮
Railway station	▮
Park	▯
College/Hospital	▱
Neighbourhood	LEITH
Pedestrian street	▬
Tube station (Glasgow)	Ⓤ

Maps

Street Index

Edinburgh

Edinburgh by Area

INVERLEITH PL

Inverleith
House

*Sports
Ground*

*Royal Botanic
Garden*

*Inverleith
Park*

INVERLEITH ROW

Fettes
College

*Inverleith
Pond*

Edinburgh
Academy

BRANDON TERRACE

EYRE

HENDERSON ROW

COMELY BANK RD

COMELY BANK RD

RAEBURN PLACE

HAMILTON PL

DUNDAS STREET

CUMBERLAN

S T O C K B R I D G E

DEANHAUGH ST

KERR ST

N W CIRCUS PLACE

HOWE STREET

QUEEN STS W

Water of Leith

N E W   T O W N

Queen

Street

QUEENSFERRY ROAD

*Dean
Cemetery*

Queen

N CASTLE ST

S CASTLE ST

QUEEN STREET

FREDERICK
STREET

GEORGE ST

FREDERICK ST

G

*Dean
Cemetery*

DEAN BRIDGE

D E A N

Georgian
House

Asse

BELFORD ROAD

Dean
Gallery

QUEENSFERRY STREET

CHARLOTTE
SQUARE

W Register
House

Albert
Memorial

National Trust
H.Q.

Ross B
Stan

BELFORD
BRIDGE

BELFORD ROAD

DOUGLAS
GDNS

HOPE ST

*West Princes
Street Gardens*

Scottish National
Gallery of
Modern Art

Water of Leith

PALMERSTON PLACE

W E S T E N D

SHANDWICK PL

St John's

St Cuthbert's

Water of Leith Walkway

St Mary's
Cathedral

LOTHIAN

Edinburgh
Castle

Donaldson's
School

WEST MAITLAND STREET

J O H N

Traverse
Theatre

Usher Hall

Filmhouse

Royal
Lyceum
Theatre

WEST PO

E
Col

SPITTAL ST

DEWAR
PL

Edinburgh
International
Conference
Centre

ABC
Cinema

BREAD ST

WEST COATES

HAYMARKET TERR

HAY-
MARKET

MORRISON

STREET

Haymarket
Station

ROAD

EARL GREY ST

BROUGHAM

W E S T   E D I N B U R G H

FOUNTAINBRIDGE

BROUGHAM
PLACE

L A U R I S

WEST APPROACH RD

Fountainpark

Cameo
Cinema

HOME ST

LEVEN ST

T O L L C R O S S

King's
Theatre

M

DUNDEE STREET

Union Canal

BRUNTSFIELD PLACE

Bruntsfield L

*Dalry
Cemetery*

D A L R Y

B R U N T S F I E

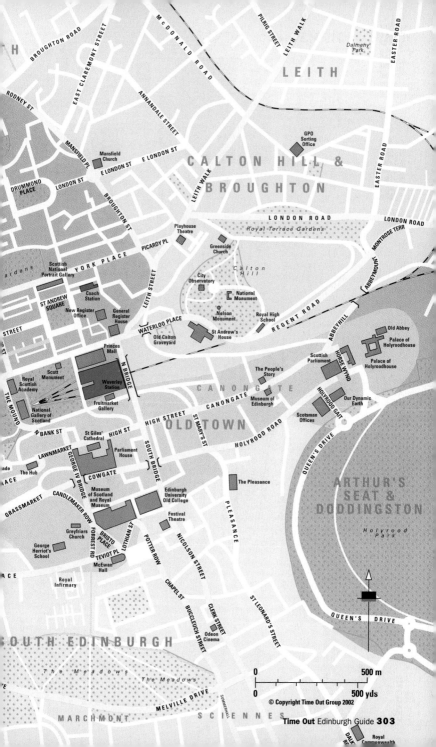

LEITH

Dalmeny Park

McDONALD ROAD

PILRIG STREET

LEITH WALK

EASTER ROAD

BROUGHTON ROAD

RODNEY ST

EAST CLAREMONT STREET

ANNANDALE STREET

GPO Sorting Office

MANSFIELD PL

Mansfield Church

E LONDON ST

E LONDON ST

CALTON HILL &

DRUMMOND PLACE

LONDON ST

BROUGHTON ST

LEITH WALK

BROUGHTON

LONDON ROAD

LONDON ROAD

Royal Terrace Gardens

MONTROSE TERR

EASTER ROAD

Playhouse Theatre

Picardy Pl

Greenside Church

Calton Hill

Gardens

Scottish National Portrait Gallery

YORK PLACE

LEITH STREET

City Observatory

National Monument

ABBEYMOUNT

ST ANDREW SQUARE

Coach Station

New Register Office

General Register House

Nelson Monument

Royal High School

REGENT ROAD

ABBEYHILL

Old Abbey

Palace of Holyroodhouse

STREET

WATERLOO PLACE

St Andrew's House

Old Calton Graveyard

Scottish Parliament

HORSE WYND

Palace of Holyroodhouse

Princes Mall

N BRIDGE

Scott Monument

Royal Scottish Academy

Waverley Station

The People's Story

HOLYROOD GAIT

Our Dynamic Earth

THE MOUND

National Gallery of Scotland

Fruitmarket Gallery

CANONGATE

CANONGATE

Museum of Edinburgh

Scotsman Offices

QUEEN'S DRIVE

BANK ST

HIGH STREET

HIGH STREET

ST MARY'S ST

OLD TOWN

HOLYROOD ROAD

ARTHUR'S SEAT & DUDDINGSTON

St Giles' Cathedral

HIGH ST

Holyrood Park

LAWNMARKET

Parliament House

GEORGE IV BRIDGE

SOUTH BRIDGE

The Hub

COWGATE

The Pleasance

CANDLEMAKER ROW

GRASSMARKET

Museum of Scotland and Royal Museum

Edinburgh University Old College

PLEASANCE

Festival Theatre

QUEEN'S DRIVE

Greyfriars Church

FORREST RD

BRISTO PLACE

LOTHIAN ST

POTTER ROW

NICOLSON STREET

George Herriot's School

TEVIOT PL

McEwan Hall

ST LEONARD'S STREET

Royal Infirmary

CHAPEL ST

CLERK STREET

BUCCLEUCH STREET

SOUTH EDINBURGH

Odeon Cinema

QUEEN'S DRIVE

The Meadows

The Meadows

MELVILLE DRIVE

SUMMERHALL

MARCHMONT

SCIENNES

0   500 m

0   500 yds

© Copyright Time Out Group 2002

DALK

Royal Commonwealth

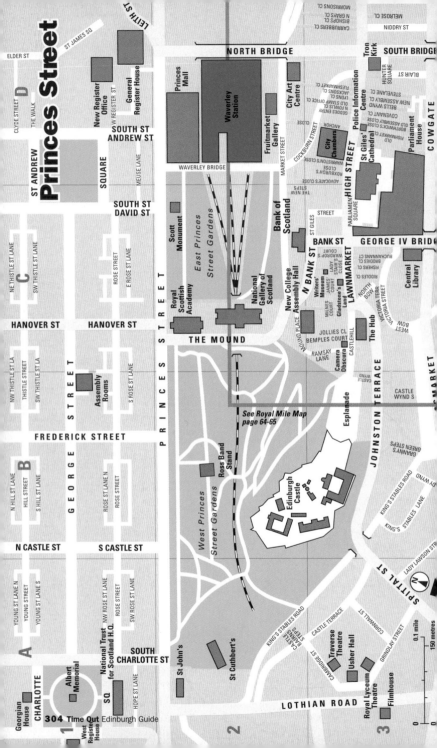

Princes Street

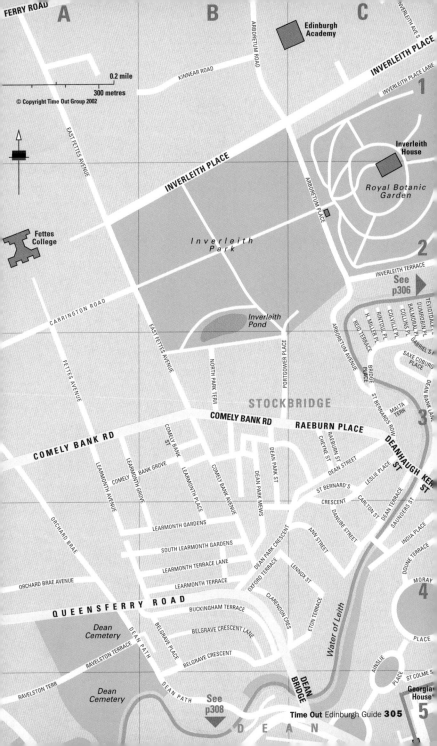

FERRY ROAD

A   B   C

Edinburgh Academy

ARBORETUM ROAD

KINNEAR ROAD

INVERLEITH AVE

INVERLEITH PLACE

INVERLEITH PLACE LANE

1

EAST FETTES AVENUE

INVERLEITH PLACE

Inverleith House

Royal Botanic Garden

Fettes College

Inverleith Park

ARBORETUM PLACE

2

See p306

INVERLEITH TERRACE

CARRINGTON ROAD

Inverleith Pond

EAST FETTES AVENUE

NORTH PARK TERR

PORTGOWER PLACE

ARBORETUM AVENUE

TEVIOTDALE
DUMBIGIN PL
BALMORAL PL
COLVILLE PL
RINTOUL PL
COLLINS PL
GABRIEL'S
H. MILLER PL

RED TERRACE
BRIDGE PLACE
ST BERNARDS ROW
MALTA TERR

SAXE COBURG PLACE

DEAN BANK LANE

STOCKBRIDGE

COMELY BANK RD

RAEBURN PLACE

DEANHAUGH ST

KER ST

3

FETTES AVENUE

COMELY BANK RD

COMELY BANK ST

COMELY BANK GROVE

LEARMONTH AVENUE

COMELY BANK GROVE

LEARMONTH PLACE

COMELY BANK AVENUE

DEAN PARK ST

DEAN PARK MEWS

CHEYNE ST
RAEBURN ST

DEAN STREET

ST BERNARD'S
CRESCENT

LESLIE PLACE

CARLTON ST

DEAN TERRACE

SAUNDERS ST

INDIA PLACE

ORCHARD BRAE

LEARMONTH GARDENS

SOUTH LEARMONTH GARDENS

LEARMONTH TERRACE LANE

LEARMONTH TERRACE

DEAN PARK CRESCENT

DANUBE STREET

ANN STREET

LENNOX ST

DOUNE TERRACE

MORAY

4

ORCHARD BRAE AVENUE

QUEENSFERRY ROAD

OXFORD TERRACE

CLARENDON CRES

ETON TERRACE

PLACE

BUCKINGHAM TERRACE

Water of Leith

Dean Cemetery

BELGRAVE CRESCENT LANE

BELGRAVE PLACE

BELGRAVE CRESCENT

AINSLIE PLACE

RAVELSTON TERRACE

DEAN PATH

ST COLME S

Dean Cemetery

RAVELSTON TERR

DEAN PATH

See p308

DEAN BRIDGE

Georgia House

5

D E A N

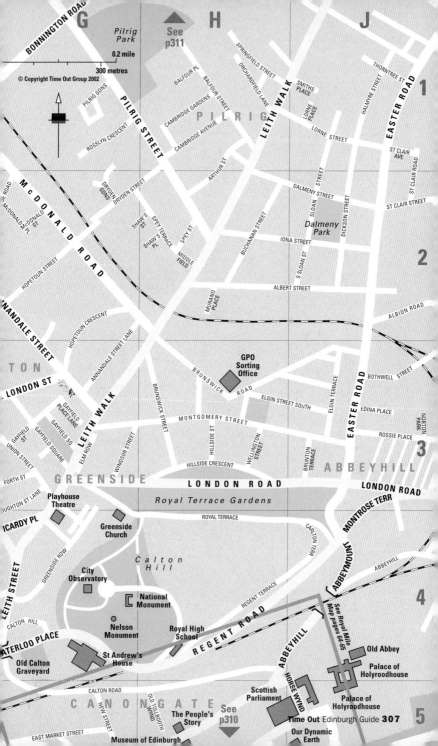

BONNINGTON ROAD

Pilrig Park

See p311

0.2 mile

300 metres

© Copyright Time Out Group 2002

PILRIG GDNS

ROSSLYN CRESCENT

PILRIG STREET

BALFOUR PL

BALFOUR STREET

CAMBRIDGE GARDENS

CAMBRIDGE AVENUE

SPRINGFIELD STREET

ORCHARDFIELD LANE

LEITH WALK

SMITHS PLACE

THORNTREE ST

HALMYRE STREET

EASTER ROAD

1

PILRIG

ARTHUR ST

DRYDEN GDNS

DRYDEN STREET

LORNE PLACE

LORNE STREET

ST CLAIR AVE

ST CLAIR ROAD

ST CLAIR STREET

McDONALD ROAD

McDONALD PL

McDONALD ST

SHAW'S ST

SHAW'S PL

SPEY ST

SPEY TERRACE

MIDDLE FIELD

BUCHANAN STREET

DALMENY STREET

SLOAN STREET

DICKSON STREET

IONA STREET

Dalmeny Park

S. SLOAN ST

ST CLAIR STREET

2

HOPETOUN STREET

ANNANDALE STREET

MURANO PLACE

ALBERT STREET

ALBION ROAD

HOPETOUN CRESCENT

ANNANDALE STREET LANE

BRUNSWICK ROAD

GPO Sorting Office

ELGIN TERRACE

BOTHWELL STREET

TON

LONDON ST

LEITH WALK

GAYFIELD PLACE LANE

GAYFIELD SQ

ELM ROW

WINDSOR STREET

BRUNSWICK STREET

MONTGOMERY STREET

HILLSIDE ST

ELGIN STREET SOUTH

WELLINGTON STREET

EDINA PLACE

ROSSIE PLACE

NORTON PARK

3

GAYFIELD ST

GAYFIELD SQUARE

UNION STREET

FORTH ST

HILLSIDE CRESCENT

BRUNTON TERRACE

ABBEYHILL

GREENSIDE

LONDON ROAD

Royal Terrace Gardens

LONDON ROAD

OUGHTON ST LANE

Playhouse Theatre

ICARDY PL

GREENSIDE ROW

Greenside Church

ROYAL TERRACE

MONTROSE TERR

ABBEYMOUNT

ABBEYHILL

Calton Hill

City Observatory

National Monument

REGENT TERRACE

CARLTON TERR

LEITH STREET

CALTON HILL

Nelson Monument

Royal High School

REGENT ROAD

See Royal Mile Map pages 64-65

ABBEYHILL

Old Abbey

Palace of Holyroodhouse

4

ATERLOO PLACE

Old Calton Graveyard

St Andrew's House

CALTON ROAD

HORSE WYND

Palace of Holyroodhouse

NEW STREET

OLD TOLLBOOTH WYND

CANONGATE

The People's Story

See p310

Scottish Parliament

Our Dynamic Earth

EAST MARKET STREET

Museum of Edinburgh

5

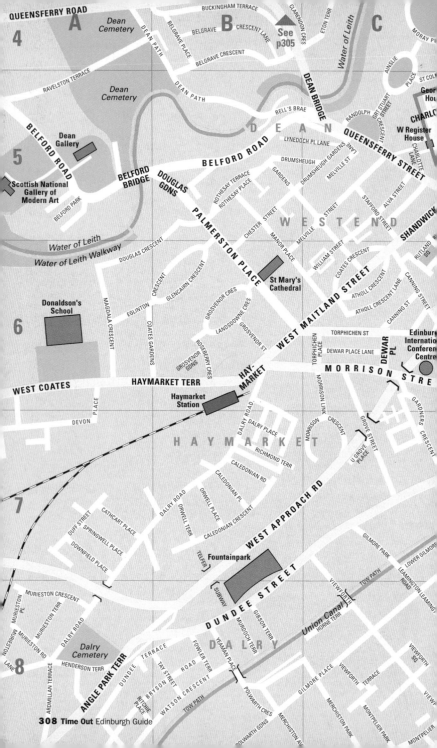

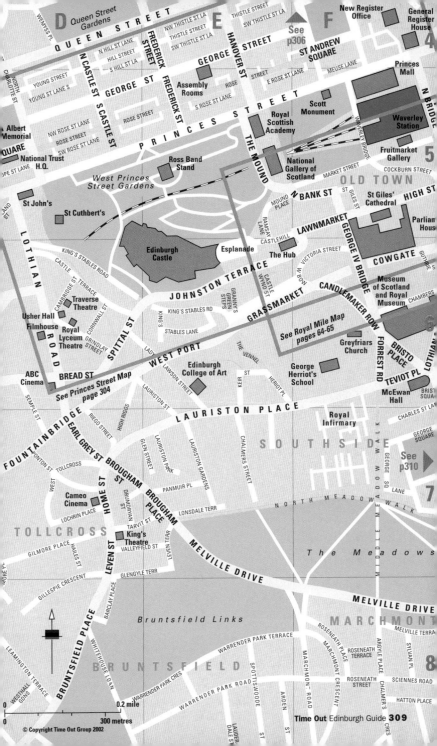

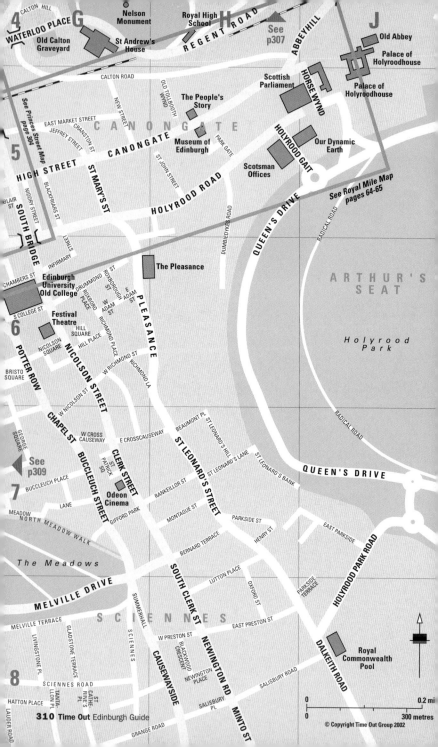

4

WATERLOO PLACE **G**
CALTON HILL
Nelson Monument
Royal High School **H**
See p307

Old Calton Graveyard
St Andrew's House
St Andrew's House
Nelson Monument
REGENT ROAD
ABBEYHILL

J
Old Abbey
Palace of Holyroodhouse

Scottish Parliament
HORSE WYND
Palace of Holyroodhouse

CALTON ROAD

OLD TOLLBOOTH WYND
The People's Story

NEW STREET
5
EAST MARKET STREET
CRANSTON ST
JEFFREY STREET
CANONGATE
Museum of Edinburgh
PARK GATE
HOLYROOD GAIT
Our Dynamic Earth

HIGH STREET
ST MARY'S ST
ST JOHN STREET

BLACKFRIARS ST
CANONGATE
Scotsman Offices

Scotsman Offices
QUEEN'S DRIVE

BLAIR ST
NIDDRY STREET
SOUTH BRIDGE
HOLYROOD ROAD

See Princes Street Map page 304

DUMBIEDYKES ROAD
RADICAL ROAD

See Royal Mile Map pages 64-65

INFIRMARY STREET
The Pleasance

CHAMBERS ST
Edinburgh University Old College

DRUMMOND ST
ROXBURGH ST
ROXBORO PLACE
W ADAM ST
ADAM ST
RICHMOND PLACE

**A R T H U R ' S
S E A T**

S COLLEGE ST
Festival Theatre
HILL SQUARE
HILL PLACE
PLEASANCE

6
NICOLSON SQUARE
W RICHMOND ST
RICHMOND LA

*Holyrood
Park*

BRISTO SQUARE
POTTER ROW
W NICOLSON ST
NICOLSON STREET

GEORGE SQUARE
CHAPEL ST
BEAUMONT PL
ST LEONARD'S HILL

RADICAL ROAD

See p309
W CROSS CAUSEWAY
E CROSSCAUSEWAY
ST LEONARD'S LANE
ST LEONARD'S BANK

7
BUCCLEUCH PLACE
BUCCLEUCH STREET
CLERK STREET
ST PATRICK SQ
RANKEILLOR ST
ST LEONARD'S STREET
QUEEN'S DRIVE

LANE
Odeon Cinema
MONTAGUE ST

MEADOW
GIFFORD PARK
PARKSIDE ST
HENRY ST
EAST PARKSIDE

NORTH MEADOW WALK
BERNARD TERRACE

The Meadows
SOUTH CLERK ST
LUTTON PLACE
PARKSIDE TERRACE

MELVILLE DRIVE
OXFORD ST
HOLYROOD PARK ROAD

MELVILLE TERRACE
S C I E N N E S
EAST PRESTON ST

GLADSTONE TERRACE
SUMMERHALL
SCIENNES
W PRESTON ST
NEWINGTON RD

LIVINGSTONE PL
BLACKWOOD CRESCENT
Royal Commonwealth Pool

8
SCIENNES ROAD
CAUSEWAYSIDE
NEWINGTON PLACE
SALISBURY ROAD
DALKEITH ROAD

HATTON PLACE
TANTALLON PL
CAST RINIE'S PL
SALISBURY PL
MINTO ST

LAUDER ROAD
GRANGE ROAD

0   0.2 mi

0   300 metres

310 Time Out Edinburgh Guide

© Copyright Time Out Group 2002

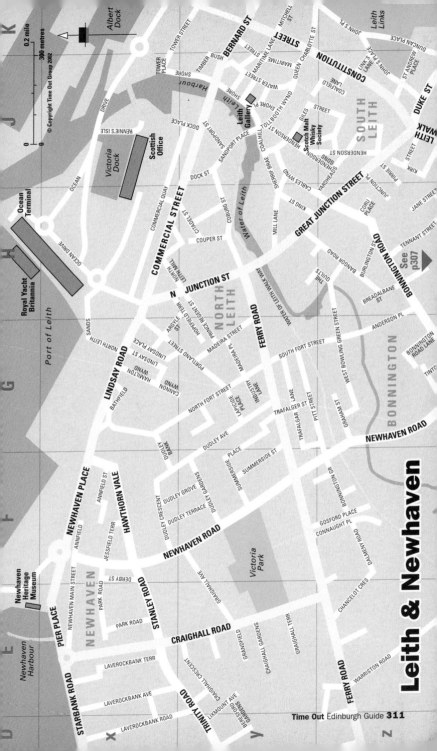

Leith & Newhaven

Albert Dock

Leith Links

BERNARD ST STREET

TOWER STREET

MITCHELL ST

JOHN S PL

DUNCAN PLACE

OCEAN PLACE

TIMBER BUSH

MARITIME LANE

MARITIME STREET

QUEEN CHARLOTTE ST

CONSTITUTION

LINK'S LANE

JOHN'S PLACE

ST ANDREW PLACE

DUKE ST

TOWER PLACE

Harbour

WATER STREET

COALFIELD LANE

SHORE PL

TOLLBOOTH WYND

Leith Gallery

GILES STREET

Scotch Malt Whisky Society

HENDERSON ST

SOUTH LEITH

LEITH WALK

STREET

KIRK ST

PIRRIE ST

Victoria Dock

DOCK PLACE

SANDPORT PLACE

RENNIE'S ISLE

Scottish Office

DRIVE

OCEAN

DOCK ST

COBURG ST

CITADEL ST

COUPER ST

CABLES WYND

SHERIFF BRAE

Water of Leith

YARDHEADS

JUNCTION PL

GREAT JUNCTION STREET

CORU PLACE

JANE STREET

COMMERCIAL STREET

COMMERCIAL QUAY

KING ST

MILL LANE

TENNANT STREET

See p307

BONNINGTON ROAD

BANGOR ROAD

BURLINGTON ST

BREADALBANE ST

N JUNCTION ST

NORTH JUNCTION ST

NORTH LEITH

FERRY ROAD

THE QUILTS

Royal Yacht Britannia

Ocean Terminal

OCEAN DRIVE

SANDS

NORTH LEITH

ARGYLE

HOPEFIELD TERR

PRINCE REGENT ST

MADEIRA PL

MADEIRA STREET

PORTLAND STREET

Port of Leith

LINDSAY ROAD

HAMILTON WYND

BATHFIELD

CANNON WYND

LINDSAY STREET

LINDSAY PLACE

NORTH FORT STREET

LAPICIDE PLACE

INDUSTRY LANE

SOUTH FORT STREET

WEST BOWLING GREEN STREET

ANDERSON PL

BONNINGTON

BONNINGTON ROAD LANE

TINTO

NEWHAVEN PLACE

ANNFIELD ST

ANNFIELD

HAWTHORN VALE

JESSFIELD TERR

DUDLEY BANK

DUDLEY AVE

DUDLEY GROVE

DUDLEY CRESCENT

DUDLEY TERRACE

DUDLEY GARDENS

SUMMERSIDE PLACE

SUMMERSIDE ST

TRAFALGAR LANE

TRAFALGAR ST

PITT STREET

GRAHAM ST

BONNINGTON GR

GOSFORD PLACE

CONNAUGHT PL

DALMENY ROAD

Newhaven Heritage Museum

PIER PLACE

NEWHAVEN

NEWHAVEN MAIN STREET

PARK ROAD

DERBY ST

PARK ROAD

STANLEY ROAD

NEWHAVEN ROAD

CRAIGHALL AVE

Victoria Park

GRANFIELD

CRAIGHALL GARDENS

CRAIGHALL TERR

CHANCELOT CRES

FERRY ROAD

Newhaven Harbour

STARBANK ROAD

LAVEROCKBANK TERR

LAVEROCKBANK AVE

LAVEROCKBANK ROAD

TRINITY ROAD

CRAIGHALL CRESCENT

CRAIGHALL ROAD

LIXMOUNT AVE

GRANDVILLE

GARDENS

WARRISTON ROAD

GRAHAM

Edinburgh Overview

To Berwick on Tweed

Gullane
Aberlady
Longniddry
Pencaitland
Glenkinchie Distillery

Cockenzie
Tranent

Inchkeith

Firth of Forth

Prestonpans
Preston Gange Mining Museum
Musselburgh Racecourse

Oxenford
Pathhead
A68

Scottish Mining Museum
Newtongrange
Gorebridge

Musselburgh

Dalkeith

A720

A7

Inchcolm

Portobello

Craigmillar Castle

CITY BYPASS

Bonnyrigg & Lasswade

Inchmickery

Cramond Island

Meadowbank

Duddingston

Holyrood Park

Leith

Newhaven

See pp305-311

EDINBURGH

Royal Observatory Visitor Centre

Loanhead

Rosslyn Chapel

Roslin

L O T H I A N

Lauriston Castle

Zoo

Murrayfield Stadium

Hillend

Midlothian Ski Centre

Penicuik

Cramond

A720

Currie

Glencourse Reservoir

L O

Inverkeithing

CITY BYPASS

Balerno

Pentland Hills

A702

North Queensferry

South Queensferry

Edinburgh Airport

Royal Highland Showground Ingliston

Ratho

Threipmuir Reservoir

A70

4 miles

Rosyth

Deep Sea World

Forth Road Bridge

M8

M9

To Glasgow

312 Time Out Edinburgh Guide

© Copyright Time Out Group 2002

6 km

0   0

Glasgow Overview

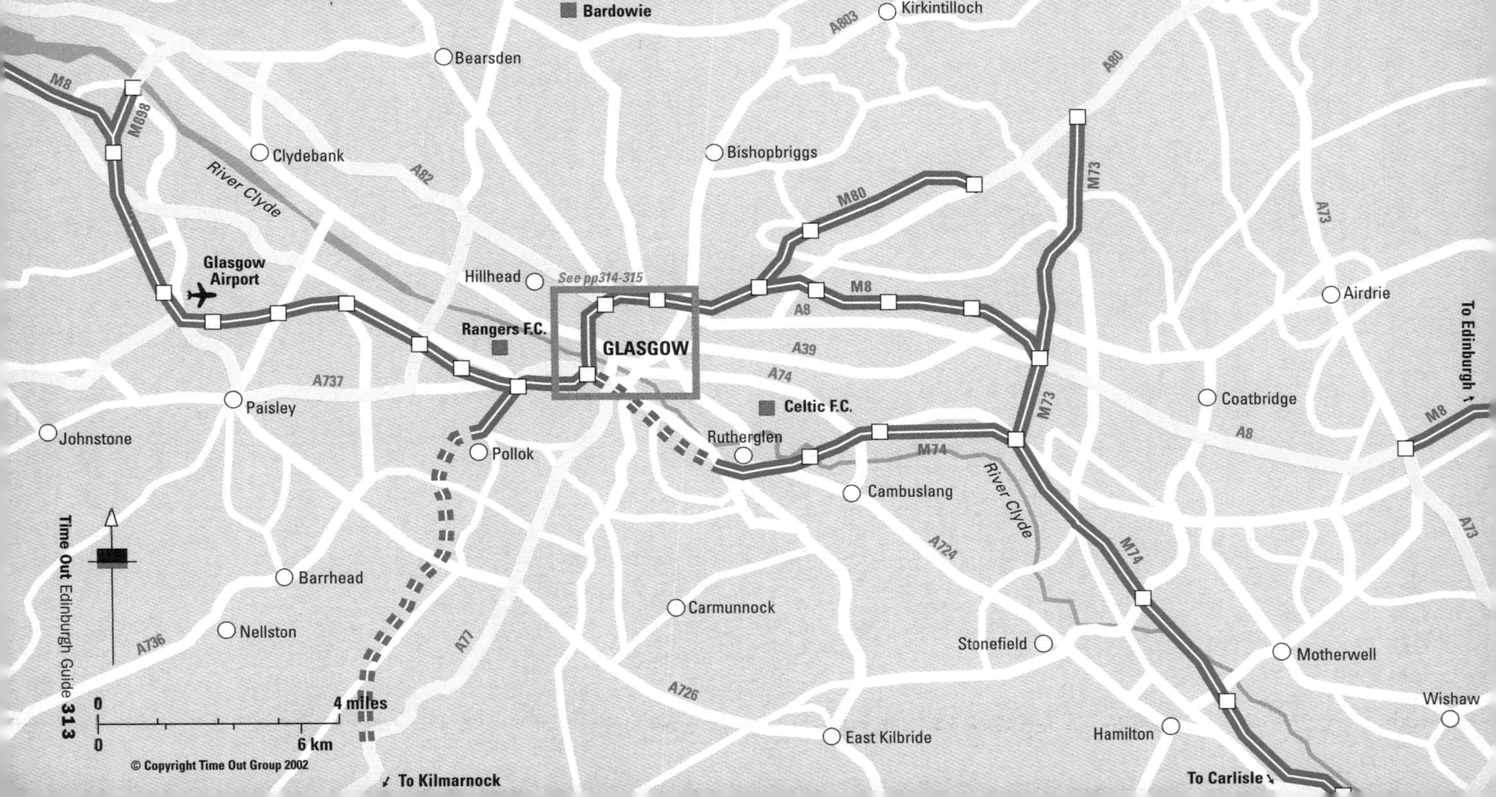

To Edinburgh

To Stirling

Cumbernauld

Airdrie

A73

A73

Coatbridge

A8

Wishaw

Motherwell

To Carlisle

M74

Hamilton

Kirkintilloch

M73

M73

River Clyde

Stonefield

A724

East Kilbride

A803

Bishopbriggs

M80

M8

A8

A39

A74

Celtic F.C.

Cambuslang

M74

Carmunnock

A726

Bardowie

Rutherglen

GLASGOW

See pp.314-315

Bearsden

Hillhead

Rangers F.C.

Pollok

A77

To Kilmarnock

A82

Clydebank

River Clyde

Glasgow Airport

A737

Paisley

Barrhead

Neilston

4 miles

6 km

Johnstone

A736

© Copyright Time Out Group 2002

M898

M8

Time Out Edinburgh Guide **313**

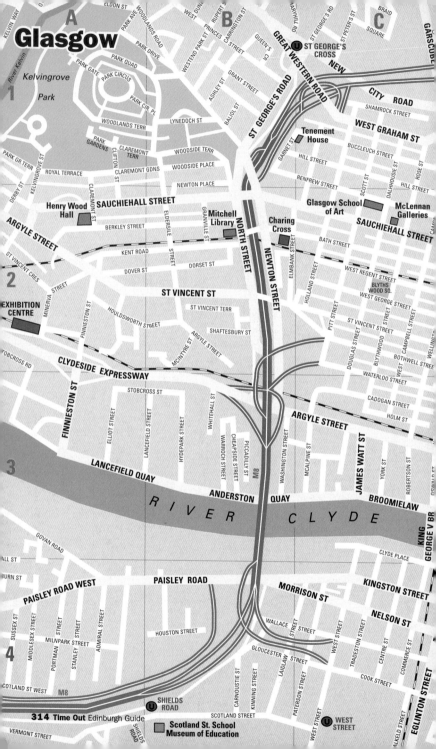

Glasgow

A   **B**   **C**

ELDON ST · WEST DUN · RUPERT ST · MARYHILL · ST GEORGE'S RD · ST PETER'S ST · BRAID SQUARE

KELVIN WAY · PARK AVE · WOODLANDS ROAD · WEST PRINCES · CARRINGTON STREET · QUEEN'S · GARSCUBE

River Kelvin

PARK DRIVE

1

Kelvingrove Park

PARK GATE · PARK QUAD · PARK CIRCUS · PARK CIR. PL · LYNEDOCH ST

PARK GARDENS · CLAREMONT TERR · WOODSIDE TERR · WOODSIDE PLACE · NEWTON PLACE

ROYAL TERRACE · CLAREMONT GDNS · CLIFTON ST

PARK GR TERR · KELVINGROVE ST · DERBY ST

CLAREMONT ST

ST GEORGE'S CROSS Ⓤ

GREAT WESTERN ROAD

NEW

CITY ROAD

SHAMROCK STREET

WEST GRAHAM ST

Tenement House

HILL STREET

GARNET ST

RENFREW STREET

BUCCLEUCH STREET

SCOTT ST

DALHOUSIE ST

ROSE ST

HILL ST

SAUCHIEHALL STREET

Henry Wood Hall

BERKLEY STREET

Mitchell Library

GRANVILLE ST · ELDERSLIE STREET

Charing Cross

Glasgow School of Art

McLennan Galleries

SAUCHIEHALL STREET

ARGYLE STREET

KENT ROAD

DORSET ST

NORTH STREET

NEWTON STREET

BATH STREET

WEST REGENT STREET

BLYTHS WOOD SQ.

ELMBANK STREET · HOLLAND STREET

ST VINCENT CRES

DOVER ST

2

EXHIBITION CENTRE

MINERVA STREET · FINNIESTON ST

ST VINCENT ST

ST VINCENT TERR

SHAFTESBURY ST

ARGYLE STREET

WEST GEORGE STREET

PITT STREET · DOUGLAS STREET · BLYTHWOOD · WEST CAMPBELL STREET · WELLING

ST VINCENT STREET

HOULDSWORTH STREET · McINTYRE ST

STOBCROSS RD

CLYDESIDE EXPRESSWAY

WATERLOO STREET

BOTHWELL STREET

FINNIESTON ST

STOBCROSS ST

WHITEHALL STREET

ARGYLE STREET

CADOGAN STREET

HOLM ST

ELLIOT STREET · LANCEFIELD STREET · HYDEPARK STREET · WARROCH STREET · CHEAPSIDE STREET · PICCADILLY ST · M8 · WASHINGTON STREET · McALPINE ST

JAMES WATT ST · YORK ST · ROBERTSON ST · OSWALD

LANCEFIELD QUAY

3

ANDERSTON QUAY

BROOMIELAW

R I V E R   C L Y D E

GOVAN ROAD

CLYDE PLACE

KING GEORGE V BR

ALL ST · BURN ST

PAISLEY ROAD WEST

PAISLEY ROAD

MORRISON ST

KINGSTON STREET

NELSON ST

SUSSEX ST · MIDDLESEX STREET · MILNPARK STREET · PORTMAN · STANLEY ST · ADMIRAL STREET

HOUSTON STREET

WALLACE STREET

WEST STREET · TRADESTON STREET · CENTRE ST · COMMERCE ST

EGLINTON STREET

4

SCOTLAND ST WEST · M8 · VERMONT STREET

GLOUCESTER STREET · LAIDLAW STREET

SHIELDS ROAD Ⓤ

SHIELDS ROAD

CARNOUSTIE STREET · KINNING STREET · PATERSON STREET · SCOTLAND STREET

WEST STREET Ⓤ

COOK STREET

FALKELD ST

Scotland St. School Museum of Education

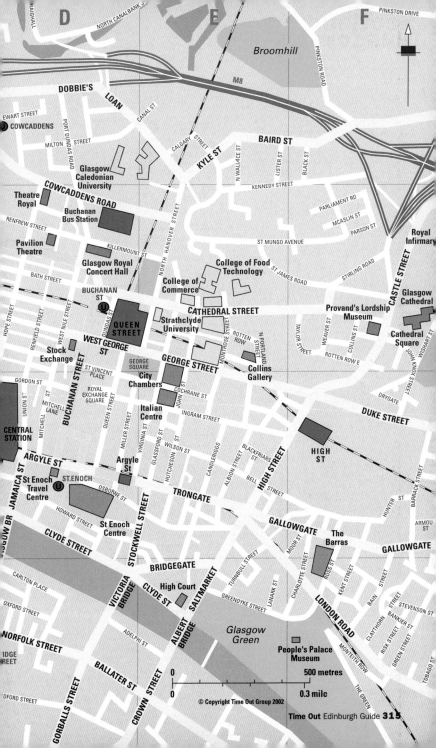

Scotland

© Copyright Time Out Group 2002